Best Practices: Excellence in Corrections

Edited by Edward E. Rhine

FOUNDED 1870

American Correctional Association
Lanham, Maryland

American Correctional Association Staff

Reginald A. Wilkinson, President
James A. Gondles, Jr., Executive Director
Gabriella M. Daley, Director, Communications and Publications
Leslie A. Maxam, Assistant Director, Communications and Publications
Alice Fins, Publications Managing Editor
Michael Kelly, Associate Editor
Sherry Wulfekuhle, Editorial Assistant
Dana M. Murray, Graphics and Production Manager
Michael Selby, Graphics and Production Associate
Jennifer Harry, Assistant Editor

Cover design by Michael Selby and Dana M. Murray. Photo by Simon Battensby/
    Tony Stone Images.

Edward E. Rhine: Best Practices Coordinating Council Chair and Project Editor, Deputy
Director, Parole, Courts, and Community Services, Department of Youth Services,
Columbus, Ohio.

Printed in the United States of America by Imperial Printing Co., St. Joseph, Michigan.

This publication may be ordered from:

American Correctional Association
4380 Forbes Boulevard
Lanham, Maryland 20706-4322
1-800-222-5646

For information on publications and videos available from ACA, contact our worldwide web
home page at: http://www.corrections.com/aca.

ISBN 1-56991-077-4

Libarary of Congress Cataloging-in-Publication Data

Best practices : excellence in corrections / edited by Edward E. Rhine.
        p. cm.
    Includes bibliographical references.
    ISBN 1-56991-077-4 (pbk.)
    1. Corrections—United States. 2. Prisons—United States.
 3. Prison administration—United States. 4. Criminals-
 -Rehabilitation—United States. I. Rhine, Edward E. II. American
 Correctional Association.
    HV9469.B47 1998
 365'.973—dc21   98-26064
                                                                CIP

Table of Contents

Foreword

Perhaps at no other point in history has the criminal justice field been at such a cross-roads as it is today. Record numbers of offenders are housed in our juvenile facilities, jails and prisons, on probation, parole or under court supervision of some type, resources are scarce, and public officials continue to espouse "get tough on crime" policies. Recent Supreme Court rulings, as well as changes in the criminal justice system in many states, have placed untold demands on the corrections profession.

And yet, despite these challenges and perhaps because of them, correctional leaders continue to strive for newer and better ways of doing their jobs. From California to Connecticut, from Alaska to Arizona, corrections professionals have devoted countless hours to developing programs and practices that work.

Throughout its 128-year history, the American Correctional Association (ACA) has been a leader in developing and promoting effective correctional programming. *Best Practices: Excellence in Corrections* is one more example of how ACA, in conjunction with hundreds of practitioners, is leading the charge for better, safer ways of incarcerating offenders, for positive change of offenders and for improved working conditions for correctional professionals.

I hope that the best practices and programs highlighted in this book will serve as a benchmark for those who wish to implement similar programs; that legislators may be encouraged to invest wisely in effective, cost-efficient and humane programming; and that the public will come to realize how corrections is working not only to make their communities safer, but also to improve their neighborhoods—through litter cleanup, building homes for the poor, increasing the literacy of other inmates, and, most importantly, by returning offenders to the community with real-world skills and goals.

The book is divided into 19 chapters, with each chapter devoted to the best practices in Adult Corrections; Adult Local Detention Facilities; Residential and Nonresidential Community Corrections; Correctional Education; Correctional Industries; Disturbance Preparedness; Employee Training; Facility Design; Health Care; Juvenile Corrections; Mental Health; Public Information; Research; Restorative Justice; Shock Incarceration; Substance Abuse Treatment; Technology and Victims.

I believe that this book will enlighten and encourage corrections staff across the nation and Canada to implement their own programs based on these models, or to expand upon these ideas in developing their own, innovative, best practices and programs.

As the Adult Corrections Committee reminds us, the security of prisons is no longer just physical security but must include effective treatment programs, work opportunities, and transitional programs to return offenders back to society with a better awareness of their role in society.

Best Practices: Excellence in Corrections is testament to the fact that not only are there programs that work, but there are many programs that work very well. If we all follow the guidance of the authors of this material, we will surely add to the body of knowledge of effective correctional programming. And that, in turn, can only be good for the corrections profession, and society as a whole.

My genuine thanks goes out to those committee members who labored long and hard to select the very best entries for inclusion in this volume; to Ed Rhine, for his editorial and academic expertise in chairing the Best Practices Coordinating Council; and to Reginald Wilkinson, my colleague and friend, for his vision and insight during the two years of his presidency. The concept of this project was borne by President Wilkinson and his vision has, indeed, become reality.

James A. Gondles, Jr.
Executive Director
American Correctional Association

Introduction

This publication, *Best Practices: Excellence in Corrections*, is an attempt to document correctional programs "that work." It is my position that nearly all federal, state, local, and private correctional agencies in America, as well as in international jurisdictions, have programs and services of which their staff can be proud. What better way is there to celebrate our successes than to communicate them to our correctional stakeholders and colleagues?

As a correctional administrator, I know firsthand how important it is to recognize the positive contributions made by our employees and agencies. Like other organizations, the Ohio Department of Rehabilitation and Correction, for example, has devised numerous ways to recognize excellence. We have employee banquets, special awards, team awards, and more.

Our agency's most recent recognition is called the "Excel Award." Excel Awards are given to institutions, departments, or offices that have developed a successful program or service. There are three criteria that awardees must meet to be eligible for this award. The program must be innovative, use quality management principles, and be benchmarkable.

This is the basic theory behind the Best Practices project, as well. We looked for programs that could be somewhat encyclopedic for correctional supervisors. That is, picking from the nineteen different categorical areas, correctional leaders will be able to locate a program that is similar to what they may be considering for their own agency. Thus, selecting programs from the Best Practices' finalists, or from the ones listed in the index, is easily done. We not only provide an abstract of each program, but list a contact person for each, as well.

When our agency is in the process of implementing a new initiative and funding is required, we often ask, "What else is out there?" If we do not know the answer, we will attempt to find out by making phone calls across the country to see if a similar program exists. Maybe, *Best Practices: Excellence in Corrections*, can eliminate some of these searches. We now have access to scores of administrators who are willing to share the secrets of their programmatic success.

Further, for the sake of the media, taxpaying citizens, and public officials, we also must be prepared to dispel misconceptions about our craft. We should not remain in the position of constantly defending our actions, but must market those programs that make a positive difference in our business and in society. This book helps to do just that.

It takes a lot of extra effort to develop and operate successful programs. The program often goes through growing pains, research is conducted, and funding must be secured. The Best Practices contained herein are symbolic of perseverance and leadership. They deserve recognition because they make a contribution to the corrections profession. Congratulations to the staffs responsible for these Best Practices entries.

In addition to the Best Practices listings, this book also contains a Foreword by ACA Executive Director, James A. Gondles, Jr. and an Afterward by Best Practices Coordinating Council Chair, Dr. Edward E. Rhine; I appreciate their support. Please make special note of the committee chairs and members who helped to select submissions to this publication. For the sake of posterity, I also have included certain relevant speeches that I made during my tenure as president.

Reginald A. Wilkinson
ACA President

Acknowledgments

There are many persons who deserve recognition both for their roles in making my term (1996-1998) as American Correctional Association president a success and for their contribution to the Best Practices project. Invariably, some notable persons or groups inadvertently will be omitted from these few paragraphs. For this, I apologize in advance.

I want to first recognize the ACA Executive Committee members for their continued leadership. These persons are completely dedicated to the ACA, its mission and its vision. Similarly, I want to thank the ACA's policy-making bodies: the Board of Governors and the Delegate Assembly. Surely, without the guidance of these two groups, progress would be less pronounced. Moreover, ACA's more than forty committees all worked tirelessly in an attempt to fulfill their constitutional and/or presidential charges. Their efforts are sincerely appreciated.

I thank the ACA past presidents for their historical and current contributions, not only to ACA, but also to the field of corrections, in general. I have mustered much of my inspiration from this august group of professionals. ACA's affiliate partners continue to make a difference throughout the United States, Canada, and beyond. Therefore, a tip of the hat to all the ACA professional affiliates, geographical, state, and dual-membership chapters for their contributions. A special mention of the Ohio Correctional and Court Services Association is appropriate. My "home" dual-membership chapter has been 1,000 percent supportive of my presidency and me. Thank you.

The Best Practices project has been a labor of love. Even if I had known how involved this initiative would have been two-years ago, I would have done it the same way. Hopefully, the contribution to correctional knowledge will be significantly enhanced through this collection of programs *that work*. The sacrifices we all made pale in comparison to the positive effect this body of work will have on our profession.

I want to thank the nineteen committees who were participants in the Best Practices project. The chairs and members of these committees are to be commended for their enthusiasm and dedication to "getting the job done." I appreciate the leadership of Dr. Edward E. Rhine for chairing the Best Practices Coordinating Council and for lending his editorial and academic abilities to this publication: one gold star for Ed. The ACA Communications and Publications staff is appreciated for their expertise and attention to detail. Director

Gabriella Daley and her staff are world-class professionals. The groups of people who probably deserve the most recognition are the administrators and program specialists who created and operate the Best Practices programs. For those agencies that have entries in this document, I offer a hearty ACA congratulations for a job well done.

James A. Gondles, Jr. and his staff, particularly, Jeffrey Washington, Debbi Seeger, and the division directors, have been especially supportive and encouraging to me for the last two years in their individual and collective roles with all of the above-mentioned projects, and more. They, at times, have served as my alter ego and conscience in regard to ACA business. At other times, they made my term fun and memorable: more gold stars.

I want to thank Ohio Governor George V. Voinovich for understanding that being president of a national organization can be time-consuming and important work. The Ohio Department of Rehabilitation and Correction staff are appreciated as well, particularly, Patricia Martin, Thomas J. Stickrath, and Tessa Unwin. Their assistance has been invaluable to me both in my capacity as director of a large correctional agency and as president of ACA.

Finally, I would like to thank my wife, LaRon, and our daughter, Brittany, for being supportive of my "extra correctional activities."

Reginald A. Wilkinson
ACA President

Adult Corrections

1

Introduction

Over the past ten years, a significant shift has occurred in correctional systems in the United States. Changes in sentencing policies, and the public's attitude toward corrections, burgeoning inmate populations, aging and outdated prison facilities, and a tougher, more violent offender, all have combined to make corrections professionals reexamine the way they do business.

Legislators and the general public are requiring a greater level of efficiency and accountability by corrections' administrators as a larger proportion of tax dollars is going to support prison facilities and programs. Correctional systems are moving toward business management practices that include greater responsiveness to constituent concerns and sensitivity to the communities that surround their correctional facilities.

At the same time that the focus of the administration of correctional facilities is changing, the management of inmate populations within those facilities is changing, as well. The security of prisons is no longer simply a function of bricks and mortar, towers, and fences. The control of the inmate population also must include effective treatment programs, work opportunities, and transitional programs designed to return the offender back to society in a structured manner. While no amount of effort can force an individual to change, opportunities for growth must be provided to those who wish to redirect their lives and return to the community with new skills and a better awareness of their role in society.

The programs included in this chapter were solicited through announcements by the American Correctional Association, the Association of State Correctional Administrators, and by word of mouth through the membership of the Adult Corrections Committee of the American Correctional Association. The initial solicitation produced fifteen submissions with an additional five coming through the extension of the submission deadline by the American Correctional Association.

A subcommittee of the Adult Corrections Committee made up of two state corrections' administrators and a national consultant ranked the submissions based on the core criteria provided by the American Correctional Association and additional criteria developed by the committee. The additional criteria focused on the ability to transfer the program to other correctional systems, the efficient use of funding, the extent of innovation, and the proven or expected effectiveness of the program.

The subcommittee then forwarded their recommendations to the full Adult Corrections Committee, which discussed each proposal and voted to include the following five submissions in this chapter. Each of these programs provides an innovative approach to the management of inmate populations and the administration of today's complex correctional systems.

The programs that follow represent efforts in five states to address the issues of prison management, from the perspectives of both correctional administration and the management of inmate behavior within facilities. Two of the programs address the overall management of prison systems, while the other three provide a glimpse into programs that target specific facets of inmate life in confinement.

Missouri—Constituent Services Office. The charge to this office is to address and resolve legitimate complaints and problems before they become the subject of grievances or litigation. The result has been a reduction of effort, time, and money that is spent devoted to responding after the fact. This program has resulted in a 73 percent reduction in grievances and complaints in twenty-nine months.

Ohio—Quality Services Through Partnership. This program brings managers and labor union representatives together to work in partnership to ensure that decisions about the management of correctional facilities are made in the most appropriate manner. Each facility has a committee that focuses on improving the quality of life for staff and inmates. Approximately 81 percent of the Department of Rehabilitation and Correction's staff have been through the program and have shown significant improvements.

Connecticut—Close Custody Phase Program. As a result of gang riots, a new program was started at Garner Correctional Institution focused on housing 450 security risk group safety threat members as long as they are affiliated with a gang. The initial phase consists of a renunciation process. The second and third phases involve intensive programming, and the final phase is designed to provide a structured process for returning the offender to the general inmate population.

Kansas—Transportation Assistance Program. This program is a cooperative effort in conjunction with a number of other criminal justice agencies that routinely transport offenders under custody. Because the participating jurisdictions work on an exchange basis, the operating costs are shared, and the security and efficiency of inmate transportation are enhanced. A total of 117 agencies in 102 counties are involved in the program.

Nebraska—Mothers' Offspring Life Development Program. This program provides an opportunity for bonding between the inmate mother and her infant, and for changing the mother's criminal behavior into that of a responsible parent and citizen. The program goes from prenatal care and parenting-skills training through regular in-house visiting with children to postrelease follow-up.

Committee chair:

Ronald J. Angelone
Director
Virginia Department of Corrections

P. O. Box 26963
Richmond, Virginia 23261-6963
(804) 674-3199

The Constituent Services Program

Introduction

Traditionally, criminal justice agencies have functioned as closed systems with limited outside interaction and only then with other law enforcement agencies. This provincial posture has resulted in weak community relations and blocked opportunities for feedback and continuous improvement. It has left many legitimate issues and concerns unresolved. It also has promoted a feeling of alienation and lack of confidence among those with whom correctional officials do business—victims, volunteers, visitors, staff, legislators, inmates, advocacy groups, and other citizens. This cultural barrier has made itself known over time in a variety of ways including increased inmate litigation, court involvement, miscommunication, internal duplication of effort, and poor public relations.

Due to the very nature of their charge to administer the court's punishments as imposed, corrections' agencies routinely face conflicting demands from those who want more, less, or different sanctions. The Missouri Department of Corrections has greatly improved the management of complaints and conflict through the creation of an Office of Constituent Services. Many dividends have been realized since the creation of this office, including: (1) substantial monetary savings to Missouri taxpayers through litigation that has been averted; (2) improved responsiveness to the unique needs of a diverse constituency; (3) a decreased workload for the judiciary due to a reduction in litigation; (4) less court involvement in departmental operations by reducing court orders and decrees; (5) improved public relations; and, (6) a reduction in the need for additional staff by decreasing duplication of effort spent responding to redundant or ongoing issues of concern.

Development and Design

In early 1993, the Missouri Department of Corrections ranked second nationally in the percentage of lawsuits filed by prisoners in comparison to other citizens in the state. Even though the department had a viable grievance procedure, which had obtained Department of Justice certification in 1992, there was an obvious need to do more. The grievance procedure's strengths were also its weaknesses. It was formal, time consuming, and did not provide immediate feedback or allow for identification of institution-specific or departmentwide problems.

In early 1994, the department established a Constituent Services Office. The office was charged with finding and resolving as quickly as possible the root causes of legitimate complaints about the department's operations. It also was charged with improving communication and understanding with its customers, and with reducing the costly duplication of staff time spent responding to inquiries and complaints routed simultaneously through a variety of offices.

Implementation

Measurable change began to occur quickly. Previously, when inmates raised concerns through the formal grievance procedure, their complaints traveled through a lengthy process of review. The remedies that were provided rarely remediated the problem. The Constituent Services Office became the department's primary mechanism for quickly identifying the underlying causes for the complaints, grievances, or lawsuits.

One particular example of problem solving stands out. Inmates held a widely shared view that the quality of medical care was poor. Drawing on statistical information from contacts made to the Office of Constituent Services, staff from the Office responded by organizing focus groups that included both inmate councils and representatives of the department's contract medical provider to discuss the concerns of the inmate population at targeted sites. During those meetings, the following issues became apparent: (1) many inmates did not practice healthy habits; (2) they had limited knowledge of community standards for service delivery; (3) they believed managed care resulted in diminished care; and, (4) they felt that every death occurring within a correctional setting was the result of poor medical care and thus avoidable.

Following these discussions, responsive educational materials were developed and distributed to the inmate population. The department also piloted a "self-declared emergency" procedure, which allowed the inmates, as necessary, to request immediate medical care, thereby avoiding a delay in treatment. A peer mortality review panel was established, as well, to review the circumstances surrounding every death and take corrective steps, when necessary. To lessen concerns, every facility's infirmary sought medical accreditation. Since then, fourteen of the fifteen clinics have been accredited, and capital improvement funds for the last clinic's repair have been requested.

These actions have resulted in better communication, education, understanding, and increased department credibility and customer satisfaction. Medical lawsuits were reduced by 72 percent, from 308 to 87 between January of 1994 through April of 1997, despite a prison population increase of 46 percent during that same period.

The Constituent Services Office also has identified a variety of questions and concerns raised by visitors about conditions of confinement, including policies and procedures governing visitation, access to mail and telephones, institutional housing, and work assignments. Previously, the department disseminated the rules to inmates and directed them to send the rules to their visitors. Not surprisingly, this did not always occur.

To proactively address the inquiries received, the Constituent Services Office developed a handbook, *For Family and Friends,* to answer the most commonly asked questions about the department's rules and regulations. The handbook is mailed directly to the visitor. Not only does it provide information to families before they visit, but staff report less time spent each day responding to routine questions formerly asked by visitors and, more importantly, less time is spent dealing with frustrated and angry visitors who unknowingly failed to follow established rules. Equally important, staff also have expressed appreciation for having this information available when training new employees or volunteers.

To more fully address the visiting operation overall, the Constituent Services Office also completed a survey of each facility's visiting room dress requirements, inmate grooming requirements, visiting restrictions imposed for misconduct, alternatives to weekend visiting room crowding, and games and activities available to the visitors' children. The results of the survey demonstrated the need to make the procedures for visitation more uniform to ensure all facilities follow shared standards that are enforced consistently. That policy is now in place. As a result of these interventions, the number complaints about visiting has been reduced significantly. Staff also report fewer confrontations with unhappy visitors.

Supporting Data

Since the Constituent Services Office was established in 1994, the Missouri Attorney General's Office reports that pending lawsuits against the department have been reduced from 1,683 in January of 1994 to 442 in April, 1997. This represents a reduction of 1,241 lawsuits or 73 percent, even though (as noted previously) the prisoner population increased 46 percent during that same period. The Attorney General's Office has conservatively estimated their average minimum cost per suit at $2,000. This does not include correction' staff time spent preparing for litigation, in trial, or in travel to court hearings. This reduction in lawsuits alone resulted in savings at a minimum of $2,482,000 in attorneys' fees for Missouri taxpayers. Nationally, the state and federal systems have placed a great deal of emphasis on averting inmate litigation when it reaches the courthouse door. The Constituent Services Office averts inmate litigation before it reaches the courthouse door.

By routing written and telephonic inquiries from a variety of internal and external sources to one place, the Constituent Services Office puts the constituent services officer in a key position to detect potential problems early, ensure they are corrected, and, in so doing, reduce costly litigation. Between January 1, 1994, when the office opened, through calendar year 1996, the Constituent Services Office responded to 1,351 inquiries received by the Governor's Office; 2,728 inquiries from state representatives and senators; 4,532 from inmate family members and friends; 4,458 from inmates; 266 from other state agencies; 267 from inmate advocate agencies; and 121 from other sources. A total of 13,723 inquiries that were received by the department were addressed expediently and courteously, and better services were provided to both customers and stakeholders.

By quick identification and correction of bottlenecks or "disconnections" within the department's operation, staff productivity, performance, and the perception of those most affected have been improved, simultaneously. Those making contact have expressed greater satisfaction that the issue has been addressed. In addition, the department has avoided duplicated complaints or litigation and the attendant negative publicity. All parties benefit through this informal mediation process.

The Constituent Services Office has reduced duplication of staff input and eliminated the need to hire additional full-time staff. For example, a one-month review revealed that out of 494 contacts to that office, 32 percent were duplicate requests sent "buckshot" by inmates to various internal and external sources. Because the letters or calls to the Governor's staff, legislators, departmental staff, inmates and their families all were routed through the Constituent Services Office, each complaint was investigated one time by one person who responded one way to each inquiry. The quickness and consistency of the reply cut costs. Preliminary calculations reveal that reduction in duplication of staff effort through the use of the Constituent Services Office decreased by one half the need for additional staff last year alone.

Conclusion

It is difficult for the department of corrections to satisfy the public all of the time because it is charged with carrying out sentences imposed by the courts and prescribed by statute, often contrary to public opinion or families' wishes. Still, the governor's office has stated: "We consider this (Constituent Services) a model for other agencies. Corrections responds to Missouri constituents more effectively than other state agencies." The governor has said, "I am encouraged by the results this office has achieved in the reduction of avoidable inmate litigation and its ability to make state government accessible to concerned citizens." A state senator testified, "The Constituent Services section of the Department of Corrections is an outstanding prototype of how state bureaucracy should interface with state elected officials. Other state departments would be well advised to replicate this office."

The Institute of Government and Public Affairs recently has completed a study for the Bureau of Justice through a grant from the American Bar Association with positive findings. That report should be forthcoming this summer. The Missouri Department of Corrections also received finalist recognition in 1996 from the Innovations in American Government program sponsored by the Ford Foundation and the John Fitzgerald Kennedy School of Government at Harvard University. The program was selected again in 1997 as a finalist for this prestigious award. As a result of this recognition, the Constituent Services Office currently is meeting with the National Institute of Justice and the Innovations in American Government to further promote this program. For its cost effectiveness, the *Corrections Cost Control and Revenue Report* featured an article on the value of a viable constituent services program in the April 1997 issue. The program also has been nominated by its peers for the Missouri Governor's Award for Quality and Productivity; that nomination is pending.

Every corrections department at the state and local level would benefit from such an office as would other public sector agencies, which serve the community. The creation of this office has served the Missouri Department of Corrections well by saving the state's citizenry many tax dollars that now can be used for other purposes and by greatly improving the department's image with those with whom it has regular contact. This program can be replicated easily and, if implemented carefully, can produce timely, efficient, and cost-effective results.

Author:

Dora B. Schriro
Director
Missouri Department of Corrections
Jefferson City, Missouri

Author/Contact:

Lisa Jones
Constituent Services Coordinator
Missouri Department of Corrections

P. O. Box 236
2729 Plaza Drive
Jefferson City, Missouri 65102-0236
(573) 526-6530

Quality Services Through Partnership

Introduction

Quality Services through Partnership, also known as QStP, is a process for continuously improving the services provided by state government. It is based on the principles of partnership, a focus on the customer, continuous learning, and teamwork. Because of the Quality Services through Partnership, management and unions work together as full partners.

Quality Services through Partnership began in Ohio in 1991 through a public/private partnership between the Xerox Corporation and the state. In February 1993, Governor George V. Voinovich and the union leadership met at the Xerox headquarters to receive training. This led to the commitment to develop Ohio's quality improvement plan in full partnership. The state and the unions have agreed to keep Quality Services through Partnership separate from the collective bargaining process. The Ohio Department of Rehabilitation and Correction became involved in the process in 1992 through the initial training provided to the director and the executive staff.

Development and Design

Total Quality Management (TQM), the basis for Quality Services through Partnership, is not a new concept. William E. Deming is recognized as the father of TQM. Mr. Deming's success in revolutionizing the Japanese economy after World War II is well known. During the early postwar era, products made in Japan were considered very poor quality. Using various quality tools, Mr. Deming taught the workers to redesign and control the production processes. Subsequently, the manufacturing industry came to accept TQM as a viable management strategy. However, many believed that TQM could work in service industries. Thus, Quality Services through Partnership became a major management initiative in Ohio.

Quality Services through Partnership enables management and unions to come together in a unique manner. Together, they work to ensure that Quality Services through Partnership is done right the first time. The partnership means that the unions have equal representation on a Quality Services through Partnership steering committee, the group that provides direction for implementation. It also means that union representatives are involved in selecting instructors and team facilitators, identifying processes for improvement, and guiding the overall effort as members of the steering committee. Employee involvement is a priority. Everyone is involved in the process.

Implementation

The Ohio Department of Rehabilitation and Correction has a Quality Services through Partnership steering committee composed of an equal number of labor and management members. This group guides and supports the Quality Services through Partnership process at the department level. Each prison, parole regional office, and other sites has a Quality Services through Partnership committee responsible for implementation at the local level. This decentralized approach enables areas to select their own facilitators, identify specific improvement projects, and tailor the change process, as needed.

Quality Services through Partnership is not a program that will be here today and gone tomorrow. It is a long-term undertaking that starts with awareness and commitment and continues until the quest for improvement becomes a daily routine in every area of the department. The quality process assists the department in accomplishing its vision and mission.

According to Mr. Deming, management has two sets of problems: "those of today and those of tomorrow." In 1992, there were a number of issues facing corrections, and it would have been easy to become mired in the problems of "today." At the outset, many staff were skeptical of the idea of becoming involved in something new when the critical issues of crowding and population escalation needed to be addressed. Fortunately, there were people of vision who saw TQM/Quality Services through Partnership as a method to address those issues. Quality Services through Partnership has a sustaining hypothesis: "If workplace problems exist or a process requires improvement, it is best to rely on the experts—those who do the work—for answers." Education became the number one priority for the empowerment of employees.

The department aggressively has pursued training for all employees in Quality Services through Partnership. Using course materials adapted from the Xerox Corporations' TQM training classes, a three-day class is offered at nonwork site locations. This provides participants with an opportunity to acquire basic knowledge about the tools of quality. To date, 81 percent (or 11,250) of all employees have completed the basic training. A summary of the course's curriculum is provided next.

DAY ONE

Interactive Skills

Continuous Improvement Process

DAY TWO

Problem Solving Process

Case Study

DAY THREE

Geezenstacks (an interactive exercise)

Ready, Set, Go (the theory of process-improvement teams)

The training accomplishes several goals, including the following: (1) providing trainees with a familiarization of the basic tools of quality, (2) offering trainees a feeling of accomplishment, (3) showing staff diversity in instructor roles, and (4) enhancing camaraderie among different levels of staff.

The department also offers additional classes to build on the fundamentals of this introduction. These classes include instruction in:

- Understanding the tools and techniques of team facilitation

- Instructor training for Quality Services through Partnership classes

- Team training

- Managing agreement

- Making effective presentations

- Understanding the steering committee's role

- Conducting effective meetings

- Making empowerment a reality for yourself and others

Upon completion of the education component, staff began to apply their knowledge. Work teams were formed to address the myriad issues facing various divisions of the department. One such team was formed through the Division of Parole and Community Services. Too much time was being spent manually collecting and reporting monthly data on caseload demands and the number of investigations completed by the Adult Parole Authority. Users of the information felt it was unreliable, incomplete, inconsistently reported, and too old to be used when disseminated.

Conclusion

Now, thanks to the team's newly developed computer program, data are entered locally. Monthly reports are generated at the field office level instead of the central office, ensuring quick access to needed numbers. Best of all, the program captures the exact data users want and includes a checking mechanism to minimize data errors. As a result, the data error rate has fallen from 2 percent (the equivalent to 300 case files) to 0 errors. In addition, managers at the local level now receive the monthly report in one week—instead of the seven weeks it took with the manual system. Finally, the time to compile reports has dropped from five days to one. The department has found that Quality Services through Partnership can be incorporated in a service industry, like corrections.

Contact:

Tessa Unwin
Public Affairs Liaison
Ohio Department of Rehabilitation and Correction

1050 Freeway Drive North
Columbus, Ohio, 43229
(614) 752-1157

Close Custody Phase Program

Introduction

In April 1993, Garner Correctional Institution, a Level-4 high-security facility for males, was rocked by a riot. This incident and other similar incidents throughout the Connecticut Department of Corrections in 1992-1993 represented unchallenged gang violence culminating in an inmate homicide at the Carl Robinson Correctional Institution. The infiltration of gangs into Connecticut's prisons was swift and spread quickly as violence and coercion pushed hundreds of inmates into professing allegiance to a gang.

In the fall of 1993, the department of corrections acknowledged that gangs were out of control in its prisons and that action must be taken immediately. Drawing on intelligence gathered through the department's security division, inmates identified as gang leaders were removed from their assigned institution and transferred to the Garner Correctional Institution and assigned to a quasi-segregated status, known as "close custody." The initial 50 and subsequent 400 inmates assigned this status were to be permanently segregated from the general population as long as they remained affiliated with a gang. The inmates were designated as security risk group safety threat members. The gangs they were associated with were labeled security risk groups.

Development and Design

In January 1994, the commissioner of corrections directed that a program be developed and implemented to allow security risk group safety threat members an avenue for reintegration back into the general prison population. The warden at the Garner Correctional Institution created a task force with representatives from diverse departments including counseling, custody, mental health, education, and addiction services. Out of this melding of professional expertise came the Close Custody Phase program. It was developed to provide inmates with an avenue for renouncing their gang affiliations while participating in mandatory alternative programming. As a result of the program, inmates could be successfully reintegrated into the general correctional population.

Implementation

The Close Custody Phase program is divided into four phases. Phase I is the most restrictive. Inmates are locked down twenty-three hours a day, and allowed only one hour out of their cell. In this phase, inmates acknowledge their gang affiliation and are housed with members of the same or nonrival gangs. They are allowed three showers, three monitored phone calls, and two noncontact visits per week. They must remain in this phase for a minimum of ninety days before they are considered for progression to Phase II.

After the ninety-day period, each inmate is reviewed by the Close Custody Review Committee comprised of close custody line staff, the unit manager, and the program manager. Inmates who have remained free of disciplinary problems for a minimum of ninety days and have indicated a desire to renounce their gang affiliation are favorably considered for assignment to the next phase.

Aggravating and mitigating factors are considered in the review process, including informal unit behavior and intelligence information showing continued gang activity. Such documented behavior or intelligence may defer favorable recommendation until the issues are resolved. Prior to progressing to Phase II, the inmates are required to sign a "letter of intent," indicating their desire and willingness to renounce their gang affiliation. They also are expected to sign an "acknowledgment of expectations," a statement that they accept and understand the expectations of the Close Custody Phase program.

In Phase II, gang affiliations no longer are acknowledged, and inmates are expected to set aside their differences in a mutually nonthreatening environment. They are assigned to squads consisting of twelve inmates of differing affiliations, with no predominance of any one particular gang. Inmates will do everything together as a squad including eating, recreating, working, and participating in programming. The squad concept helps to solidify the trust component of the program that requires inmates to work together in mutual cooperation towards a common goal. Gang affiliation is viewed and treated as an addiction.

Phase II requires sixty days of mandatory participation by inmates in programming. Such programming includes: gang awareness, behavior management, words and their meanings, nonviolent living, anger management, and conflict resolution. Upon completion of this phase, inmates progress to Phase III. The latter lasts for ninety days and represents a continuation of earlier programming. It also adds criminal thinking, social skills training, adventure-based counseling, and an education component. During Phases II and III, each inmate must participate in all programming.

Program Enforcement

The failure to participate carries tangible consequences. A demerit system ensures that inmates who are noncompliant or who fail to participate in the program are held accountable. Inmates receiving three demerits in any one phase are sent back to Phase I. Likewise, any formal disciplinary infraction will result in a return to Phase I.

The demerit system also is used during the Phase I component of the program as a tool to document poor informal inmate behavior, which does not meet the criteria as set forth in the Code of Penal Discipline. The demerit system in this phase provides crucial documented information, which aids the close custody review committee in making appropriate and informed recommendations. During the progression through Phases II and III, inmates are afforded additional privileges such as eating their meals in the chow hall and receiving contact visitation. This is an affirmation of their successful program progression and preparation for their return to the general population.

Inmates assigned to Phase I for twelve months or more and who fail to successfully participate or refuse to participate in the program are reviewed for assignment to administrative segregation at the Northern Maximum Security Institution. Upon completion of Northern's behavioral management program, they are returned to close custody at Garner Correctional Institution and placed back into Phase I. They still must complete the Close Custody Phase program before returning to the general population.

Upon successful completion of Phases II and III, each inmate attends a completion ceremony and is transferred out of close custody into a general population unit. Phase IV represents the tracking and monitoring component of the program. For 180 days, inmates who have completed the program are monitored for possible reinvolvement in gangs, and provided with supportive counseling groups. After the end of this period, they are expected to complete their incarceration on their own recognizance using the coping skills they learned in the program.

Supporting Data

To date, 385 inmates have successfully completed the Close Custody Phase program. Of those inmates, two have failed and have been returned to the Garner Correctional Institution as security risk group safety threat members. Even more, inmate violence in the department effectively has been eliminated. There have been no incidents involving gangs since the implementation of the Close Custody Phase program and other departmental incentives developed in concert with this initiative.

The Close Custody program is recognized nationally as evidenced by the visits of many other state correctional departments and the Federal Bureau of Prisons. In fact, a number of states and the Federal Bureau of Prisons are in the process of implementing modified versions of the Close Custody Phase program in their efforts to manage gang problems.

The Close Custody Phase program recently was honored with the Innovation award of the Council of State Governments. During that event, the warden of Garner Correctional Institution and his staff were approached by a representative from the John F. Kennedy School of Government at Harvard University who invited them to submit an application for their "Innovations in American Government 1997 Awards Program." They were selected in the top 100 entrants and subsequently were invited to submit their program for the 1998 award.

Conclusion

The Close Custody Phase program has proven that the issue of security risk groups can be managed and the associated violence reduced or eliminated through a high level of programmatic structure and regimentation. This goal has been realized in the department. The associated knowledge and expertise assimilated at the Garner Correctional Institution provides a network for the dissemination of relevant substantive information to other correctional departments on a national level.

Author:

Jonathan V. Hall
Major
Bridgeport Correctional Center
Bridgeport, Connecticut

Contact:

Remi Acosta
Warden
Garner Correctional Institution

P. O. Box 5500
Newtown, Connecticut 06470
(203) 270-2809

Transportation Assistance Program

Introduction

The transportation of offenders between local jails, state correctional facilities, and other agencies having jurisdiction is a time-consuming and expensive responsibility for virtually all criminal justice agencies. Agency transportation needs are driven by a variety of issues including population management requirements, the medical necessities of offenders, court-mandated appearances, and the demands of postincarceration service providers. Prisoner movement is such a frequent activity that often two or more criminal justice agencies require prisoner-transportation services during the same time frame to the same or nearly the same destinations.

The Kansas Department of Corrections operates eight correctional facilities located across the state. During fiscal year 1995, corrections officers assigned to the department's transportation unit moved more than 11,000 inmates and traveled more than 350,000 miles. To enable the department to move inmates quickly and efficiently, the department established a cooperative prisoner transportation system in conjunction with a number of other criminal justice agencies. Cooperative transportation services now are provided to and received from other agencies on an exchange basis, with no additional funds being expended. The benefits from cooperative prisoner transportation include a decrease in overall operating costs, a reduction in the number of work hours spent transporting inmates, an improvement in security of transportation services, and the establishment of a basis for other cooperative efforts.

Development and Design

In October 1993, representatives from the department of corrections met with representatives of sheriffs' departments from Douglas, Saline, Sedgwick, Shawnee, and Wyandotte counties to organize a system for sharing resources to reduce transportation costs. The result of these meetings was a Transportation Assistance Program (TAP) designed to conserve resources by reducing the duplication of services in the transportation of jail prisoners and prison inmates. Since that time, the program has grown to 117 member agencies including sheriffs' departments in 102 counties in Kansas, the U.S. Marshal's Service, and state corrections departments in Colorado, Minnesota, and Washington.

The Transportation Assistance Program was designed to provide cooperating agencies with access to the prisoner transportation services of other agencies. Each participating agency advises the Kansas Department of Corrections' transportation coordinator of their needs for moving prisoners on a regular basis. The transportation coordinator keeps track of trips in progress by the various agencies. The transportation coordinator also establishes schedules for department of corrections' trips that maximize the use of available resources, while ensuring that participating agencies retain supervision and jurisdiction over their employees and resources. All cooperative moves are planned and arranged with a "win-win" outcome for the cooperating agencies. The hallmark of the design of the Transportation Assistance Program is its simplicity. The primary elements of the Transportation Assistance Program are basic to any sound management program and include good communication, a positive attitude toward success, and a commitment to providing effective and cost-efficient law enforcement services.

Implementation

The initial implementation of the Transportation Assistance Program operations focused on the transportation unit within the Kansas Department of Corrections. Since 1989, the department has operated a centralized transportation unit for the transportation of inmates between state correctional facilities and for the return of parole violators within the boundaries of the state. With the implementation of the Transportation Assistance Program, local jurisdictions were given access to available seats on department of corrections' transportation vehicles for the movement of prisoners to the custody of the department.

Over time, this access was expanded to include transportation for court appearances, population management, and other movement needs. In conjunction with this development, cooperating agencies began providing the department of corrections with access to available seats in their transportation vehicles for movement of inmates for population management, return to court, parole violator return, interstate corrections compact movement, and other movement needs.

Supporting Data

The transportation of an offender from western Kansas to Topeka or Lansing may take as long as twelve hours driving time to accomplish a delivery process that takes a matter of minutes. The return trip is essentially downtime, with the law enforcement officer unable to perform any other community protection duties. To reduce this drain on officer work hours, one county established a contract with a private prisoner transportation company. However, the cost for this service has been as high as $300 per trip, with expenditures of up to $15,000 in one week. The use of cooperative transportation agreements can reduce the need for this type of expense.

Numerous examples of improved efficiency in operations have been reported by many of the participating agencies. One sheriff reported that between January and August 1994, outside agencies provided 21,814 miles of prisoner transportation, nearly 68 percent of the total 32,031 miles required of that county. Another sheriff reported that between January 1995 and September 1995, coordination of transportation needs allowed the county to avoid 75 trips, with a corresponding savings of 400 work hours.

During fiscal year 1996, 219 parole violators were returned to the custody of the department of corrections by the participating counties, at no expense to the department. Similarly, the department of corrections transported 390 inmates to various locations for counties and other agencies, on a cooperative exchange basis, at no cost to the county.

Conclusion

The most important lesson associated with the Transportation Assistance Program is that a cooperative transportation program should be as simple as possible. It should provide participating agencies with an immediate opportunity to offer and receive assistance with few administrative requirements. All cooperative arrangements should be done on an exchange basis within existing budgets, so that there is no need for complicated accounting systems or for special appropriations for new equipment.

In a previous effort to organize prisoner transfers, the National Sheriffs' Association set up a nationwide system for transporting prisoners across states. However, the system involved a significant amount of paperwork. Although the system was computerized, many of the operators were unable to use the software. The Transportation Assistance Program system is not complicated. Likewise, there are no stringent application or participation requirements. The participants must meet the statutory definition of a law enforcement agency, and bring with them a spirit of mutual cooperation and a desire for shared success.

A second lesson learned during the development of the Transportation Assistance Program was that agencies were able to improve the overall security of their transportation. The consolidation of trips and resources enabled agencies to transport prisoners using the equipment that is most suitable for the job. The efforts of staff can be focused more closely on doing the job right every time.

The Transportation Assistance Program received one of the Council of State Governments' 1996 innovation awards.

Authors:

Lee Cohen
Captain
Kansas Department of Corrections
Topeka, Kansas

Bill Cummins
Corrections Manager
Kansas Department of Corrections
Topeka, Kansas

Contact:

Louis Bruce
Deputy
Division of Family Management
Kansas Department of Corrections

Landon State Office Building, 4th Floor
900 SW Jackson
Topeka, Kansas 66612-1284
(785) 296-5187

Center for Women Nursery Program

Introduction

The mother-child studies of Jean Piaget, Erik Eriksen, and Anna Freud provided the impetus for the development of a program within the confines of the Nebraska Center for Women that encouraged and facilitated mother-infant bonding and improved parenting skills. The nursery program provides a firm parenting foundation for inmate mothers. The central goal was to provide an opportunity for bonding between the inmate mother and her infant with a parallel goal of changing the inmate mother's criminal behavior pattern into that of a responsible parent and citizen. As mothers attain this status, the mission statement of the department of corrections is realized.

One of the goals of social service agencies is to keep parent and child together, if at all possible. The nursery program at the Nebraska Center for Women assists in achieving this goal. Prenatal care and individual counseling aids each inmate as she reaches her delivery date. Postnatal care assists them in attaining optimum recovery. The development of appropriate parenting skills are accomplished through the nursery program. Individual deficiencies in the area of parenting are addressed for each inmate participating in the program's required courses.

Approximately 70 to 80 percent of the Nebraska Center for Women's inmate population come from abusive backgrounds. The modeling and practicing of appropriate corrective or disciplinary measures begins a necessary intervention toward breaking existing patterns of abuse. The nursery program and the Mothers' Offspring Life Development program offer a unified front providing preventative intervention for breaking the cycle of negative parenting practices. They also aid in the development of realistic expectations of the inmate mother for herself and her infant.

Development and Design

Drawing on technical assistance provided by the National Institute of Corrections, the warden and other staff at the Nebraska Center for Women visited the Bedford Hills Nursery and Children's Center in New York in 1992. Shortly thereafter, an in-house committee was formed at the Nebraska Center for Women to develop a comparable program. With support from the Director of the Department of Correctional Services, and further assistance from the National Institute of Corrections, additional staff visited the Bedford Hills facility in 1993. A needs assessment was conducted at the same time showing that between 1991 and 1993, an average of 1.24 babies were born at the Nebraska Center for Women per month. During this time frame, the average stay of the incarcerated mother was 4.5 months after the birth of her baby.

Implementation

Staff developed eligibility guidelines for the program. Inmate mothers must sign a program agreement regarding participation and affirm that they will be the primary caregiver after their release from incarceration. All applicants initially are screened by an eligibility committee of the staff who review their prior violence, social history, psychological and medical background, and overall suitability for enrollment in the program. This committee also conducts periodic reviews of the progress of each participant.

Information about the nursery program was given to all inmates. Medical staff notified nursery program staff when a pregnancy was confirmed. Each pregnant inmate received an orientation to the nursery program. Pregnant inmates who were interested in participating were required to submit an application for admission to the program.

Applicants were considered based on their history of violence, their psychological and medical background, the length of their sentence, and their availability for the program. A background investigation of each applicant was made through the Department of Social Services to determine if there was a history of child abuse or any other mitigating circumstances that should be taken into consideration. Applicants were required to meet two criteria to be eligible for consideration: (1) the inmate must have a tentative release date of no more than eighteen months after the birth of the baby; and (2) the inmate must not be in segregated status. Applications were reviewed by the warden and the nursery committee.

Continued eligibility for the participation in the nursery program requires that the inmate mother sign a program agreement affirming that she will remain the primary caregiver of her infant upon release from the Nebraska Center for Women. Additionally, she must agree to complete prenatal and Lamaze classes before the birth of the child and infant care and child development classes after the birth. She also must consent to the appropriate medical and mental health clearances.

Infants and mothers are housed in a stimulating environment on a separate floor of the East Hall Housing Unit. The nursery program ensures that the medical, nutritional, safety, and emotional needs of the participants are met. Day care services are provided for inmates so mothers can maintain job assignments and continue their education. They have to participate in mandatory parenting classes until the infant is six-months old. They have half-time morning institutional job assignments until the baby is six-months old. At that point, the mother may apply for a full-time job assignment. Inmate mothers who do not have a high school diploma or General Equivalency Diploma are required to participate in educational classes half time.

The infants are allowed to accompany their mothers outside the nursery program to participate in the Mothers' Offspring Life Development Program; to go out for recreation and meals in the dining hall; to attend religious services; to go to medical appointments, including immunizations; and to attend special programs or events. Nonetheless, the mothers in the nursery program are required to follow the same rules and regulations that apply to the general population.

Inmate mothers receive prenatal care from a contractual physician. They are transported to a designated hospital for labor and delivery and are allowed to have only medications prescribed by the physician. Well-baby checkups are made by the institutional medical department staff.

When the mothers are in school or in job assignments, inmate care providers are responsible for the infants. Care providers are required to complete special preservice training. Care providers are carefully screened, to ensure they meet the necessary qualifications.

The inmate mothers and their infants are permitted to leave the Nebraska Center for Women at the same time, following routine discharge procedures. The departing infant is provided with an inventory of permissible items. Inmate mothers who are going to community corrections or a treatment facility are required to arrange for placement of their infants during the time the mothers would be in the correctional center. Withdrawal from the nursery program may be voluntary or involuntary.

Supporting Data

Dr. Joe Carlson, Ph.D., from the University of Nebraska at Kearney, has prepared a draft evaluation to determine the effectiveness of the live-in nursery program within the Nebraska Center for Women. Only three known nursery programs exist in the United States. His survey showed that the center largely met its stated goals, and suggested strongly that misconduct reports and subsequent recidivism were positively affected. Likewise, the potential for saving taxpayer dollars through this type of program intervention is great. The survey also revealed strong feelings of accomplishment by inmate participants and staff. Those states considering methods to reduce misconduct reports, and lower recidivism rates should consider implementation of live-in nurseries within their own correctional institutions.

Conclusion

The Nebraska Department of Correctional Services and the Nebraska Center for Women program staff believe that family relationships are best strengthened through personal contact. Inmate mothers who come from abusive backgrounds usually know few effective parenting techniques. Proper instruction along with the maintenance of essential mother-child bonds while incarcerated has a significant impact on the multigenerational aspect of criminality.

To this end, the department has begun tracking infants who lived in the nursery from its beginning. Staff believe that in fifteen to twenty years, there will be a significant difference in the number of children from this program who come to prison versus children of incarcerated parents who have not been afforded this opportunity. The primary impetus, however, to maintain the program comes from the inmates themselves as, for them, the children present the primary motivation for self-improvement.

Contact:

Larry Wayne
Warden
Nebraska Center for Women

Route 1, Box 33
York, Nebraska 68467-9714
(402) 362-3317

Adult Local Detention Facility

2

Introduction

Communities across the country are faced with problems concerning exploding jail populations and deteriorating facilities. Many jail administrators need to build new structures in addition to dealing with a diverse inmate population. These problems are compounded by diminishing tax resources and the demand that administrators become more efficient in both the construction and operation of their facilities. There are approximately 3,300 jails in the United States ranging in size from the very small to those that hold 20,000 or more inmates. Regardless of capacity, the basic issues are similar in any detention center. The administration must maintain security and control, depending on the capabilities of staff and the ability of administrators to obtain optimum productivity from each employee. Some of the complexities involved in managing a modern jail are depicted in the submissions for this chapter.

Denver's Juvenile Offender Work Program. In 1993, the Denver Sheriff's Office, in anticipation of a federal court order to institute a cap on the number of juveniles in its only juvenile detention center, established a program in which the youthful offenders would provide a useful service to the community rather than serve time in a detention facility. As a result, the sheriff's office developed a work program through a collaborative effort of several city, county, and community agencies.

The juveniles who have been sentenced for municipal ordinance violations, such as curfew, graffiti, and shoplifting, are referred to the program. A deputy sheriff transports them and supervises the juveniles at various work sites throughout Denver. The deputy sheriff coordinates work assignments and also serves as a liaison to the courts, other agencies, and citizens requesting assistance, including the elderly and the disabled.

Palm Beach County—To Be The Best. In 1996, the citizens of Palm Beach County elected a new sheriff who took office with a plan to make radical changes in the structure of the organization. He determined that to be the best, an agency must have drive, vision, and goals. The sheriff revamped his command structure by establishing separate departmental directors, each of whom were given equal stature. Additionally, minorities were promoted and recruited for key positions as the human resources division was restructured. The planning and research division also incorporated the sheriff's goals in its operations.

The sheriff's values and mission statement were framed and posted in strategic locations in his department while the higher ranking administrators discussed these goals with staff. They sought recommendations on implementation of the mission. The mission was described as a road map to assist employees in becoming the best as they improved the quality of life for the citizens of the county.

Albany County, New York—Managing other Agencies' Prisoners. During the mid-1970s the Albany County Correctional Facility began to offer the use of available housing space to other jurisdictions as a way of providing mutual assistance. Eventually jail crowding led to the need to develop plans to address the conditions in the jail. Short-range plans included emergency relief by the maximum use of available space, the building of temporary housing, and the boarding out of county of inmates to other counties. Through legal action, state facilities were directed to accept state-ready inmates within ten days of notification. The Albany facility sought available space in other counties and transferred custody to the receiving county. Additional short-term solutions included the hiring of additional staff and expanding the existing facility.

Long-term plans were enhanced by legislative authorization for the construction of a 30-million-dollar facility and for support services. An agreement with the U.S. Marshal's Office resulted in $1,125,000 to be used for jail construction. Through the Work Alternative Program, individuals sentenced by the courts were assigned to work as free labor on the jail construction. The jail also realized $26,795,817 in revenue by renting out the beds that the individuals in the work program would have occupied.

Licking County, Ohio—Podular Direct-Supervision Jail. Licking County, Ohio, as many communities have discovered, found that the direct-supervision jail concept is a means to improve design, programs, and community involvement in jail construction. A 153-person panel was created to assist local officials. Local service agencies provided financial donations for an employee fitness center. The local community college donated research equipment while the public library earmarked $200,000 for a jail library. The County Ministerial Association provided funds for a variety of programs. Additionally, another critical aspect of the jail operation is a 180-member volunteer corps offering vocational, educational, and self-help programs. The county has succeeded in creating a facility that is safe, secure, and humane without sacrificing public safety.

Authors:

Colonel David Parrish
Jail Commander
Hillsborough County Jail
Tampa, Florida

Robert Lucas
Captain
Hillsborough County Sheriff's Department
Tampa, Florida

Jails and the Management of Other Agencies' Prisoners[1]

The "NO VACANCY" sign of the 1980s at the Albany County Jail and Penitentiary, located in Albany, New York now reads "VACANCY, but reservations required. Nonsmoking accommodations only."

The Albany County Correctional Facility, as it is now known, is charged with providing detention for arrested individuals as ordered by the courts within Albany County, and inmates sentenced to jail terms of less than one year. Inmates may be remanded to the facility by the local justice courts, superior, or federal courts. Currently, the facility maintains an average daily population of 783 and has a capacity of 969.

In addition to its mandated detainees, the population count includes inmates boarded-in from other counties, the State of New York, and the federal government. The federal inmate population housed at the facility includes detainees of the U.S. Immigration and Naturalization Service and the U.S. Marshals Service. The facility currently has a contract with the U.S. Marshals Service to house 55 inmates at a per diem rate of $83. Other jurisdictions pay a per diem of $90, except for the State of New York, which pays between $17 and $34 per day for each inmate housed at the county correctional facility.

Currently, New York State is negotiating a contract to board state-ready inmates in the facility for a term of less than six months per inmate. Only inmates who qualify as nonviolent and have merit time status will be kept at the facility. A per diem rate of more than $80 is being negotiated and is expected to produce increased revenues for Albany County and desperately needed beds for state-ready inmates.

The Early Days of Inmate Boarders

During the mid-1970s, the Albany County Correctional Facility began to offer the use of available housing space to other jurisdictions as a way of providing mutual assistance. This practice started as other agencies requested assistance with housing inmates who were in transit to another jurisdiction. Most of these inmates only stayed for one night. The federal government requested space primarily to house persons who were away without leave or were deserters from the military. The number of inmates boarded-in during that time was relatively small. The facility's capacity was 357 in those days. The average daily population was 125 inmates, while the staff numbered fewer than 100.

However, the inmate population began to rise dramatically with the impact of the "get tough" drug laws of the 1970s. Throughout the 1970s and 1980s, the inmate population increased steadily each year. By the late 1980s, the facility was no longer able to offer excess capacity to other agencies. Staff began to search for ways of dealing with the crowded situation. In New York State, jail space came at a premium and became a much sought after commodity.

Strategic Planning Reaps Financial Rewards

Albany County officials demonstrated keen foresight in developing short- and long-term plans to address what was becoming a severe crowding situation at the jail. For the short term, staff looked for emergency relief of such crowding by maximizing the use of available space, building temporary housing units within the facility, and boarding-out inmates to other county facilities in New York State. Boarding-out inmates proved to be a challenge in many ways.

Short-term Solutions

In addition to the tough new drug laws, the long-term stays of state inmates were another factor that contributed to facility crowding. In the late 1980s, the New York State Sheriffs' Association, along with a number of sheriffs, successfully sued the State Department of Correctional Services. In *Ayers v. Coughlin* (72 N.Y. 2d 346, 533 N.Y.S. 2d 849 (1988)), the Court of Appeals ruled that all state-ready inmates must be accepted by the Department of Correctional Services within ten days after notification of state readiness. This helped relieve crowding at local jails, but also produced bad feelings between county and state agencies.

The Albany facility remained crowded and in need of space to board-out inmates. Since most county jails in the immediate area also were crowded, staff had to branch out further within the state to find available space for the inmates. Once the space was located, approval was requested from the New York State Commission of Correction to transfer custody to the receiving county.

The staff then faced the task of selecting which inmates would be transferred. They identified sentenced inmates from the facility's population as being the best choice since they had a known term of incarceration. The decision to select from among sentenced inmates limited the potential pool to one-third of the population. Complaints were received about the inconveniences posed for attorneys, family members, and friends who had to travel great distances to visit with inmates. The staff did their best to minimize these inconveniences and recruited the most appropriate candidates for transfer.

At this time, correction officers were unhappy about the crowded and understaffed conditions. In 1988, they staged informational pickets to highlight these issues and the imposition of mandated overtime and low wages. County officials met with union representatives and made assurances that twenty-one new correctional officers would be hired and that contract negotiations would continue to address the other issues. In 1989, the facility was expanded through the creation of temporary and modular housing units in anticipation of a major expansion to begin in 1990. The short-term plans were effective in dealing with the current issues, but staff had to formulate a plan to address the future of the local correctional system.

The Long-term Plan

In 1989, the Albany County Legislature authorized funding for a $30 million construction project that would provide much needed space for secure housing and support services for staff and inmates. The expansion project is being conducted in three phases. Phases one and two have been completed successfully and have resulted in an expansion of the facility's capacity to 969 beds. Phase three is now under contract for $10.2 million and will result in the renovation of the original plant, which dates back to 1931. The completion of phase three, scheduled for December 1998, will provide additional housing for female inmates and a new medical unit for in-house health care and treatment.

The estimated capacity of the facility will grow to more than 1,030 inmates. The anticipated gender mix is 90 percent male and 10 percent female. The average daily female population has risen from 40 in 1988 to 73 in 1996. Currently, there are 68 female beds. This expansion will provide 123 female beds, which will permit the boarding-in of female inmates rather than searching for space to board them out.

In 1990, an agreement was entered into with the U.S. Marshals Service Cooperative Agreement Program (CAP). This program provided funds totaling $1,125,000 toward the capital cost of jail construction and expansion. The agreement requires that fifty-five beds be available for prisoners from the U.S. Marshals Service at the rate of $100 per day. The county also developed additional alternatives to incarceration, which complement the program of boarding-in inmates by freeing up more jail cells. The Work Alternative Program, instituted in April 1991, is a community service program to which individuals are sentenced by the court. Participants in the program report to the correctional facility at 8 A.M. Monday through Friday and work until 4 P.M. at various not-for-profit agencies under the guidance and supervision of the department. The participants provide such services as performing basic labor, painting, landscaping, and providing general maintenance to county and local governments and not-for-profit groups, such as churches and food pantries.

It is estimated that $106,346 in free labor was provided through the alternatives-to-incarceration program last year, based on the minimum wage scale of $4.25 per hour. At night and on the weekends, participants return to their homes. Thus, in addition to the labor benefits, this program has enabled the facility to realize $26,795,812.00 in revenue by renting out the beds these participants otherwise would have occupied. In addition, the not-for-profit agencies have received a service that they could not have purchased with their limited resources and funding. At the same time, these participants are paying back their debt to society for their crimes.

The success of the program to board-in inmates over the past seven years would not have been possible without the support of the courts, the county executive, the legislature, correctional staff, and the community.

Current

The expansion of the Albany County Correctional Facility was designed to accommodate the projected growth of the inmate population into the next century. In the meantime, any excess capacity allows the acceptance of inmates as boarders from other jurisdictions. The practice of recruiting for inmate boarders has become a very competitive business because it has proved to be a profitable venture for counties that are able to successfully maintain or improve their marginal costs.

Since 1990, the facility has generated more than $26 million in boarder revenues through rental of vacant cells to jurisdictions in need of space. Obviously, the ability to provide space to those in need is a great asset for public relations.

Boarding-in inmates is a major undertaking that requires the cooperation of persons involved with all aspects of the facility's operation. Facility staff must provide such mandated services as health care, safety, and security, while maintaining a balanced budget that is based on anticipated revenues and government funding. There are other stressors related to the incarceration of boarded-in inmates, many of whom may be unhappy that they are being housed outside their home jurisdiction. However, staff feel that the extra effort is worth the outcome. The facility no longer is totally reliant on tax revenues to support its operation. It actually can contribute to the general fund to the ultimate benefit of taxpayers.

Conclusion

Before a decision is made to actively pursue a business venture comparable to boarding-in inmates, the management of a facility need to consider the following questions: Will my superiors want to take on this added work and responsibility? Will the legislative body commit itself to the financial and political support? Will my staff work with me, not against me, to make it a success and not a failure? What type of reaction will surface from the community? Will the facility's physical plant provide for the required services? Will my staffing need to be increased, and if so, can I obtain new staff?

Without having a crystal ball to predict the future and wanting to be successful, it is important to rely on your experience and your staff's experience, working relations, and intuition on which direction to go.

Contact:

Edward W. Szostak
Superintendent
Albany County Correctional Facility

840 Albany-Shaker Road
Albany, New York 12211-1088
(518) 869-2600

---

[1] This essay originally appeared in the May/June 1996 issue of *American Jails*, Volume X, Number 2. It has been edited for this publication and is reprinted with permission from *American Jails*.

Juvenile Offender Work Program

Introduction

In early 1993, in anticipation of a federal court order that would institute a cap on the number of juvenile offenders allowed to be housed in Denver's only juvenile detention facility, correctional administrators confronted the fact that the city had no sanctions for juvenile offenders charged and convicted of municipal-ordinance violations. Those working in the detention arena considered various options to provide meaningful structured alternatives for this offender population. The goal was to develop a program that would allow juveniles to be involved in performing useful community service rather than serving time in a detention facility. As the result of collaboration among the Denver Sheriff's Department, the Denver juvenile courts and other agencies, the Juvenile Offender Work Program was created. This program eliminated a five-month sentencing wait and allowed juvenile offenders to do community service work the same day that they were sentenced.

The Denver Sheriff's Department operates the two adult detention facilities located in the city and county of Denver, Colorado. The county jail is a holding facility currently housing an average of 1,800 maximum- and minimum-security inmates per day. This is managed within a facility with a rated population-capacity of 1,350. The jail is located nine miles east of metropolitan Denver.

The Pre-Arraignment Detention Facility is the intake facility for all persons incarcerated within the jurisdiction. It is a forty-eight-hour holding facility for the care and custody of persons arrested and awaiting other dispositions. This facility is located in metropolitan Denver and has a design rated-capacity of 158. The average daily population is 300.

In addition, the Sheriff's Department manages the Court Services Division, wherein deputies provide courtroom security and custody of inmates awaiting court appearances, a Civil Division that is responsible for all legal processing functions, and the Impound Facility that processes the intake and release of all vehicles impounded in the city.

Development and Design

The Juvenile Offender Work Program was developed through a collaborative effort involving several city and county of Denver departments and community agencies. The city agencies included the Denver Sheriff's Department, County and District Juvenile Courts, the City Council, Public Works, the Denver Health Department's Medical Center's Code Enforcement Unit, and the Mayor's Council on Aging. The community agencies involved included the Adult Care Management, Neighborhood Support Services, and other care providers, which offer assistance to seniors and/or disabled adults.

Juvenile offenders are sentenced to the Juvenile Offender Work Program from the Denver courts for municipal ordinance violations such as curfew, simple assaults, graffiti, and shoplifting in lieu of paying a fine. A deputy sheriff picks up the daily dockets for each sentenced offender from the Juvenile Court. After checking in each juvenile, the deputy transports them to various job sites throughout the Denver area. Juveniles are directed and supervised by a sheriff. A van transports each work crew and carries the necessary paint and equipment. A deputy sheriff coordinates work assignments and serves as a liaison to the county courts, agencies, and citizens.

Work crews offer assistance to the elderly and the disabled by providing them with services such as snow removal from the sidewalks and driveways of their homes, lawn maintenance, and yard cleanups. Juveniles and their parents or guardians volunteer their services for the elderly and disabled and must sign a release-of-liability consent form.

Juvenile offenders also provide sidewalk sweeping services for public area lots. Juvenile offenders further enhance their community service by providing trash and yard cleanup for houses that have been condemned by the City's Code Enforcement Unit. The graffiti removal crews are the most recent component of the Juvenile Offender Work Program.

Implementation

The Juvenile Offender Work Program was implemented in 1993 for offenders sentenced by the Juvenile Courts. Both male and female offenders participate in the work program. In conjunction with the Denver District Juvenile Courts and the Denver Public Schools, students with truancy violations are sentenced to four Saturdays in the Juvenile Offender Work Program. They are required to attend school during the week and report to the Juvenile Court on Saturday morning for the work program.

The work program was initially done on a small scale and complemented the Sheriff's Department's Mountain Parks Program for adult offenders. In the beginning, its focus was on providing community service to the senior or disabled population. In May 1995, graffiti cleanup crews were initiated. This was due in part to a combination of the substantial increase in juvenile offenders charged with graffiti violations and an influx of federal and state monies from the "Safe City Initiatives." Job sites for the crews are located in areas throughout Denver. They are found through the Graffiti Hot Line and by referrals from agencies and citizens.

Supporting Data

Since its inception in 1993, there have been 8,704 males and 2,502 females for a total of 11,206 juvenile participants in the work program. Through November of 1997, deputy sheriffs had supervised a total of 2,156 juveniles convicted of municipal ordinance violations. This transferred into 15,092 community service hours and accounted for the removal of 8,103 square feet of graffiti from metropolitan areas.

Whether the Juvenile Offender Work Program has been successful as a deterrent to juvenile crimes has been more difficult to ascertain. There is no follow-up data on the program to measure this. However, the community members have made comments and provided positive feedback regarding the benefits derived by both the senior and disabled population from the juvenile offenders. It appears that the interaction between the juvenile offenders and these citizens has some positive benefits. The juveniles seem to respond well to these grateful groups and vice-versa. They work well with them and enjoy being able to provide them with some assistance. Observations show that the juveniles involved are productive, and the work experience and feedback may increase their self-esteem. In addition, the city and its citizens benefit from having juvenile offenders who may be responsible for the graffiti also responsible for its removal. This factor alone may contribute to ensuring for a time, a pleasant urban environment.

Conclusion

The Juvenile Offender Work Program provides the following lessons:

1. A work experience environment in the community is more beneficial for young offenders than being in the confinement area of a jail detention facility.

2. Useful community service by juvenile offenders convicted of municipal violations provides a much appreciated living assistance to seniors and handicapped citizens.

3. Participating in constructive community work assignments for juvenile offenders leads to an improvement in their self-esteem.

4. Providing a positive, structured, work experience is a more cost-effective method of managing juvenile offenders charged with and convicted of municipal ordinance violations. It further allows the community as a whole to benefit by having them perform useful and productive services, rather than allowing them to become a drain on society's resources.

Finally, a critical factor in successfully implementing and continuing a Juvenile Offender Work Program is the ongoing communication and coordination between the court judges and jail administrators. The philosophy of each actor is important and programs always are easier to implement and manage when each acts together as a partner. The program thus far has proven to have been successful and every effort must be made to continue to communicate this to those individuals who exert an impact on daily decision making.

The Juvenile Offender Work Program has received the following awards of excellence for the Graffiti Cleanup effort.

1995 "Keep Denver Beautiful" by the private Council on Keep Denver Beautiful

"Graffiti Removal Award" from the Greater Park Hill Neighborhood Inc.

1997 "Keep Denver Beautiful" by the private Council on Keep Denver Beautiful

Contact:

Orlanda Tafoya
Administrative Analyst
Denver Sheriff's Department

P. O. Box 1108
Denver, Colorado 80201
(303) 375-5664

To Be The Best

Introduction

Government and military leaders, successful business persons, sports heroes, and famous entertainers know what it takes to get ahead. They have skills and talent, but they also have drive. And, they have a vision to be the best. They know they must have a road map that will take them to the top; that is, they realize the need for a plan. This need was realized recently in the Palm Beach County, Florida Sheriff's Office.

In 1996, many citizens saw the Palm Beach County Sheriff's Office as a bloated self-serving bureaucracy. The leadership of the nearly 3,000-member office had been in place for two decades, and the voters clearly wanted a change. Bob Neumann, a retired FBI agent, promising change, was elected by soundly defeating the incumbent. Much of the old leadership retired or moved on before the new sheriff took office in January 1997.

The new sheriff immediately made radical changes in the command structure. He eliminated the position of undersheriff. Three directors for the Department of Law Enforcement, Corrections and Administration were installed. The new directors all have equal stature and report directly to the sheriff. Minorities were promoted and recruited for key slots, and the Human Resources Division was revamped. A two-year degree requirement was set for deputy sheriff in both Law Enforcement and Corrections. And, an effort to unionize the corrections deputies was defeated at a hearing with the Public Employees Relations Commission. The new sheriff envisioned excellence and knew a plan was needed to guide staff toward that goal.

Development and Design

The Planning and Research Division formalized the sheriff's goal into a business plan by incorporating a shared vision, core values and beliefs, purpose statement, mission statement, strategies, objectives, tactical action items, and benchmarking. Then, each department and division was charged with developing its own business plans. The planning and research staff provided guidebooks and much assistance, because most of the middle managers had never been confronted with such a task. The key was to have subordinate business plans complement the sheriff's plan. His plan is depicted next.

The sheriff's mission and core values and beliefs or "vision statement" was framed and posted at strategic locations around headquarters, law enforcement districts, and in the three jail facilities. The business plan also was discussed at lineups where recommendations were sought regarding the development of the business plan for the department of corrections.

The development of the plan started with a description of the operation itself: a 2,468-bed jail system operated at three sites by 645 corrections-certified deputy sheriffs and 208 support staff. Next, the department's purpose was stated: to appropriately and efficiently accept and legally confine arrestees in accordance with American Correctional Association standards. The correctional plan lists prioritized objectives that link with the sheriff's plan.

Implementation

The focus next shifted to a consideration of the following maxim: "if you can't measure it, you can't manage it." Both external and internal assessments had to be established before staff could implement tactical action items relating to the goals. The most important assessments are listed below.

External Assessments

- ACA and National Commission for Correctional Health Care Standards

- Florida model jail standards

- Policies and procedures

- Internal and external audits

Internal Assessments

- Bookings and releases

- Staff and inmate discipline

- Budgets usage

- Sick leave

- Accident rates

This is a sampling of the important assessments only. Local policies, even the political climate, can spawn numerous other measurements.

Supporting Data

The process of developing an action plan to guide the department caused staff members to look at what they were doing, how they viewed those things, to measure their actions, and to ask such fundamental questions as "can we do it better" or "why are we doing this or that?" For example, staff saw that arrestees could be booked in eight minutes at one site, yet it took up to twenty minutes at another. As a result, much unnecessary movement of inmates for health appraisals was stopped, and staff was shifted, which knocked several minutes off of the booking time at the main jail facility.

An analysis of the personnel situation was conducted, as well. This resulted in the identification of 123 deputy sheriff control room positions that could be converted to lower salaried nonsworn slots. Hiring, training, and placing of this staff is ongoing and a savings of $1.3 million dollars ultimately will be realized. The internal review did not just look at functions and personnel. A review also was conducted of the existing allocation of resources and assets. After the review, of the seventy-nine vehicles in the department, thirty-two were returned to the department. A de facto policy of assigning vehicles to certain positions or ranks had existed, and that practice seemed to have little regard for functional need or the taxpayers' dollars.

Staff also gathered cost data on inmate feeding, health care, and the commissary, and compared the findings to other facilities of a like size. Given the outcomes, a decision was made to develop requests for proposals and rebid those contracts. That process is occurring now. Outside consultants were hired to further research inmate processing and health care practices, and their analyses, when completed, will support ongoing work on the overall strategic objectives. Such analysis provides important benchmarking for the plan.

Conclusion

During January of 1998, every major division in the sheriff's office conducted the first quarterly review of its business plan. Staff had heightened anxiety over the presentations and some concerns about reaching their goals. Yet, the business plans' development through the first quarterly review has proved to be a very constructive experience. The sheriff reminded staff that the business plan is a road map to help them become the best as they improve the quality of life for the citizens of Palm Beach County.

The staff have learned that they cannot continue to throw money or people at perceived shortages. Staff involvement in the development of the business plans has allowed them to have a clear picture of the use of assets. Their involvement and empowerment has fostered the considerable talent and enthusiasm of line staff and management to surface. Finally, the public trust is being served admirably through the combined business plans.

Contact:

Harold B. Wilber
Director of Corrections
Palm Beach County Sheriff's Office

3228 Gunclub Rd.
West Palm Beach, Florida 33406
(561) 688-4410

Podular Direct-Supervision Jail

Introduction

When the time came to build a new jail in Licking County, Ohio, the sheriff decided to throw out the blueprints for a "new, old jail" and explore the possibility of planning and building a facility that would benchmark and incorporate the latest concepts in design, programs, and community involvement. The result was the 162-bed podular direct-supervision Licking County Jail.

Podular Direct-Supervision

In podular direct-supervision, housing is divided into manageable units of thirty-to-fifty rooms, arranged around a common multipurpose area. The management of inmates is proactive with constant access to staff. Officers in the pod are given broad discretionary power to solve problems, administer sanctions, and address issues. The environment and furnishings are "soft," to enhance interpersonal communications, absorb discordant sounds, reduce tension, and ease maintenance. The more normalized setting results in fewer medical complaints by inmates and reduced sick leave use by staff. There is a conspicuous absence of vandalism. The combination of physical amenities and interaction between staff and inmates characterizes the podular direct-supervision jail. Physical security is concentrated on the perimeter of the facility.

Seeking Accreditation

The Licking County Jail supervises inmates without iron bars, chain-link fences, or other stereotypical security devices commonly found in jails. The primary emphasis is placed on interpersonal communication between staff and inmates, resulting in a pleasant environment and improved behavior among the prisoners. The jail also has pursued and received accreditation from the American Correctional Association, the National Commission for Correctional Health Care, and the Commission for Accreditation of Law Enforcement Agencies—earning the "Triple Crown Award" as Ohio's first agency to achieve such a distinction.

A Community Affair

The planning for the new facility began with the creation of a diverse and active community advisory board. Public guidance and "ownership" continues to this day, offering programming ideas and local resources. Through a creative marketing strategy, a 153-member panel was created to assist local officials. Financial donations from a local service organization equipped a complete fitness center for the sheriff's office employees. The local community college donated forensic equipment for the new laboratory. The local public library earmarked more than $200,000 for the jail's library. The county ministerial association provided funding for a minister, and the county vocational school allocated staff and resources for a variety of inmate programs. One of the most critical aspects of the jail's operation is the 180-member volunteer corps, which offers educational, vocational, and self-help programs without depleting the departmental budget.

Expanding the Concept

Two unforeseen factors threatened the new jail's success. First, the population of Licking County is one of the fastest growing in the state, with a proportionate growth in crime figures. Second, Ohio's new "Truth in Sentencing" laws placed an added burden on local jails by mandating that most nonviolent offenders be sanctioned in the community rather than in state prisons. The community got to work and planned for a 168-bed expansion of the jail to accommodate the growing number of inmates. The expansion will allow the existing facility to "flex" under ever-increasing demands.

Conclusion

According to the sheriff, the benefits of the podular direct-supervision jail are obvious: it is less expensive to build, easier to maintain, improves employee morale and productivity, and reduces prisoner stress and violence. Most importantly, Licking County has succeeded in creating a facility that is safe, secure, and humane without sacrificing public safety.

Contact:

Gerry D. Billy
Sheriff
Licking County Justice Center

155 E. Main Street
Newark, Ohio 43055
(740) 349-6400

Community Corrections—
Residential

3

Introduction

Community corrections has grown into an important component of progressive correctional systems. Early in its history, community corrections programming was seen as only an alternative to incarceration, not as an important continuum of intermediate sanctions. Today, community corrections has expanded from halfway houses and parole and probation supervision to a full-range of programming, including prerelease centers, halfway houses, residential drug treatment facilities, restitution, and day reporting centers. Both residential and nonresidential services continue to grow to meet emerging needs—not just to address cost and crowding issues, but also to develop the most appropriate level of sanctioning. Matching the most appropriate community corrections program to the right offender contributes to sound correctional policy.

Increasingly, the courts, county commissioners, and legislative bodies, and departments of corrections are setting new standards for offender treatment and supervision. This is to ensure public safety while an offender is placed in a community corrections setting. Corrections professionals acknowledge that jail and prison space must be reserved for violent offenders while the most successful community corrections programs should focus on serving nonviolent offenders.

Business and community leaders also are embracing the value and benefits of well-designed community corrections programs. This is especially true when they are invited in as participants and decision makers.

The residential community corrections articles presented in this chapter were screened by a review subcommittee of the full American Correctional Association Community Corrections—Residential Committee. A total of twenty-four submissions were reviewed. The six programs that follow highlight innovative practices in residential community corrections from different jurisdictions in the United States and Canada. In California, Milestones Human Services, Inc. delivers comprehensive and innovative services to help parolees successfully reintegrate into the community. Volunteers of America of Indiana, Inc. demonstrates the importance of using an outcome measurement system to gauge the effectiveness of correctional interventions. In Dallas County, Texas, the Judicial Treatment Center offers treatment for substance abusers in the judicial system in place of regular incarceration. In Massachusetts, the Neil J. Houston House delivers a substance-abuse treatment program for pregnant women that is the only kind in the state. Summit House, in North

41

Carolina, offers female offenders the opportunity to retain primary care of their children. Then, with the Life Line Program, the Correctional Service of Canada helps long-term offenders reintegrate into society.

Committee chair:

Neil Tilow
President
Talbert House

2600 Victory Parkway
Cincinnati, Ohio 45206
(513) 751-7747

A Long-Term Approach to Residential Services Yields Reduced Offender Recidivism

Introduction

Milestones Human Services, Inc. is an award-winning, criminal justice/social service agency, committed to providing comprehensive, community-based intervention and treatment services to adult offenders, enabling them to develop strengths and acquire requisite skills for a positive, productive, and independent lifestyle. MILESTONES is a licensed seventy-six-bed residential drug and alcohol recovery program under contract to the California Department of Corrections, the San Francisco Sheriff's Department, and the San Francisco Drug Rehabilitation Court.

The parole population faces many serious barriers to successful community reintegration, resulting in a high rate of failure and return-to-custody. This continuation of the revolving-door syndrome occurs at great cost to the public and to the individual parolees. A recent survey of new commitments to the California Department of Corrections found that more than 75 percent of the offenders possessed histories of substance abuse. Further, a disproportionate number of parole revocations are due to alcohol and drug involvement. This population faces other major problems, including homelessness, lack of employment and job skills, illiteracy, and unaddressed health needs, with many parolees unaware of or incapable of effectively accessing critical social service resources in the community.

In recognition of the high economic and human costs of recidivism, the California State Legislature established and funded the Preventing Parolee Failure Program in 1990. Under this initiative, Linda Connelly and Associates, Inc., a certified woman-owned business, was awarded a contract for the San Francisco Multi-service Center for Homeless Parolees' Program in 1991 by the California Department of Corrections. This program, offering residential and nonresidential treatment services for parolees referred by parole agents, was named MILESTONES.

The Board of Directors of Linda Connelly and Associates made a decision to transfer MILESTONES to a nonprofit entity and Milestones Human Services, Inc. was incorporated in January of 1994. The 501(c)(3) status enables MILESTONES to qualify for tax-deductible donations and additional funding from public and private sources to better support client services. Linda Connelly and Associates continues to provide administrative support.

Development and Design

MILESTONES rapidly developed into a model transitional treatment program. Since the majority of its clients were long-term substance abusers, the program established a major recovery component. Additionally, MILESTONES was awarded a contract with the San Francisco Sheriff's Department in March of 1992, and, in 1995, it became a provider for the San Francisco Drug Rehabilitation Court for residential, day treatment, outpatient and relapse-prevention services. All of these contracts remain intact today. MILESTONES was awarded a drug and alcohol treatment license by the California Department of Alcohol and Drug Programs in October of 1994.

The executive management team of MILESTONES brings more than forty years of social service and criminal justice experience, both with the public and the private sector. The staff have worked in mental health, substance abuse, and prison settings. They have gained important insight into the prison culture and the fears associated with release after prison. They were challenged to design and establish a community-based intervention program to address the revolving-door syndrome and assist offenders to attain independent, productive lives in the community.

Under three contracts, MILESTONES' staff provide residential and outpatient substance abuse treatment and transitional services to a diverse group of offenders with substance abuse and other life problems and rehabilitative needs. The significant difference between this concept and traditional short-term halfway house facilities is that parolees volunteer for the program and are able to continue in the program for up to one year, followed by after-care. The greater program length and participants' commitment to personal change are the key elements needed to address the complex issues and achieve lasting change.

MILESTONES' extensive services include: residential treatment, day treatment, outpatient services, relapse prevention, and aftercare services. MILESTONES has a structured program with an established comprehensive service approach. The staff have demonstrated that through individualized case management and counseling, substance abuse treatment, educational and employment assistance, creative arts, community service, transition planning, aftercare, and collaborative efforts including the effective use of community referrals and resources, indigent parolees and other adult offenders can achieve self-sufficiency and a successful transition to independent living. These services help clients recognize and build upon their strengths, become effective self-advocates, and develop a community support system as part of their transition and long-term recovery plan.

Implementation

Comprehensive seven days per week on-site programming is offered consisting of individual, group, and family counseling. Additional counseling includes substance abuse education, relapse prevention, and 12-step groups. Life skills, General Equivalency Diploma, literacy programs, health education, vocational evaluation, job preparation, placement assistance, and creative arts also are provided. Client needs are assessed, individual treatment plans are developed, and a wide range of community resources are accessed and coordinated by case managers.

All clients perform meaningful community service twenty hours each month, allowing them to "give back" to the community, while building their skills and self-esteem. The unique creative arts program, including visual arts, creative writing, and drama, provides clients with invaluable opportunities for self-discovery and personal growth.

The case manager completes the client's individual needs assessment and individualized treatment plan within the first week, and meets with the client weekly to assess progress, assist the client in integrating treatment-group experiences, and to address any special needs. An ongoing review of client progress is conducted through case conferences every thirty days, level-advancement petitions, weekly case management meetings, weekly staff and clinical meetings, staff observation of the core treatment groups, transition planning, aftercare sessions, and the final completion.

The program uses a four-stage level system, each with specific requirements and progressively increased community plans and privileges. Initially, Level 1 clients remain in the facility for sixty-to-ninety days, participating in on-site groups and activities. Clients' progress is carefully evaluated as they progress through the level system. While the primary program focus is on recovery, clients also receive assistance with other individual identified needs, such as decision making, anger management, and other critical life skills.

To meet the special language and cultural needs of monolingual Spanish-speaking offenders and their families, MILESTONES subcontracts with the Latino Family Alcoholism Counseling Center to provide on-site substance abuse treatment, other counseling, and community referral services. This is the only residential treatment program in San Francisco providing services to this underserved population.

The ultimate goal of MILESTONES is to provide clients the requisite skills to achieve and maintain a fulfilling, clean and sober, crime-free lifestyle. Prior to leaving, clients have a solid foundation for long-term recovery. They have been drug and alcohol free for a minimum of six months. They also have a positive support system in the community, a sponsor, and a solid connection with a "home" 12-step group, and the self-esteem needed to return as independent, productive members of society.

Outcomes

MILESTONES has been recognized as a leader by the California Department of Corrections. This award-winning licensed program has become the model for other homeless parolee programs, and for the state's work-furlough programs, which now are being modified according to the MILESTONES' model. MILESTONES received the Director's Award from the department for its innovation in developing a substance abuse and multi-service treatment program.

Up to 80 percent of persons released from prison commit new crimes and return to custody. A preliminary study of 1,282 MILESTONES clients who have been released from California state prisons has shown a very low rate (21.9 percent) of recidivism, 13.4 percent for new offenses and 8.5 percent for parole revocations. As the result of MILESTONES' program and the positive working relationship with referring agencies, its contracts are fully used every year.

Conclusion

MILESTONES' successful experience proves the value and importance of providing a comprehensive, long-term program of intervention and treatment for parolees and other adult offenders.

Other lessons:

Importance of 12-step, Self-help Recovery Component

MILESTONES opened more than five years ago with an initial program mandate to help parolees obtain suitable employment as soon as possible. However, it was clear from the start that its efforts were futile without first addressing the primary problem of all MILE-STONES' clients: substance abuse. It became obvious that parolees could not handle the responsibilities of holding a job and managing money unless they were active participants in the recovery process. The program was changed to focus initially primarily on substance abuse treatment. Then, following successful progress in recovery, parolees are gradually prepared to enter the job market and become self-sufficient. Participation in 12-step programs provides a foundation for lifetime recovery and is the most likely predictor for ongoing sobriety.

Collaboration

Great emphasis is placed on collaborative efforts with the criminal justice system and other human service organizations. The clients are helped to develop a community support system for their long-term recovery plan. Providing treatment intervention to substance abusing offenders through effective community programs reduces recidivism and crime, while saving lives and freeing critical resources for desperately needed human services.

Nurturing, Structured Environment, Sense of Community

MILESTONES provides the delivery of comprehensive and innovative services needed for parolees' successful community reintegration.This has been achieved through a strong internal organization and structure, and a dedicated, diverse, culturally competent, highly skilled and well-trained staff. The staff have extensive experience in all facets of recovery treatment relative to the criminal justice and social service systems in the local community.

In addition, a primary ingredient for the program's success has been the active participation of parolees in "their" program. MILESTONES has a strong alumni association, which helps new clients see the remarkable lasting result of clients' positive change efforts. The beauty of the program is its ability to self-energize through a family culture that is unique among the criminal justice population. This individual and collective commitment by the clients makes the difference. MILESTONES' award-winning program is a cost-effective solution against crime and recidivism—providing public safety through human investment.

Contact:

Linda Connelly
Executive Director
MILESTONES Human Resources, Inc.

Suite 300, 594 Howard Street
San Francisco, California 94105
(415) 546-0603

Outcome Measurement System

Introduction

Formalized systems to gauge the positive effects of correctional interventions are uncommon in the field. Often, measures of success are limited to anecdotal evidence, or mere hunches that clients are improved in some fashion as a result of staff efforts. Staff frequently are unable to agree on the basic desired outcomes of a community corrections program. Yet, an increasing number of governmental agencies require an evaluative component for any program they fund. The American Correctional Association also is moving in the direction of mandated outcome-measurement processes for its next standards revision.

Volunteers of America of Indiana, Inc. has made a firm commitment to using correctional technologies with a strong research base and a proven track record in the field. Within the past sixteen months, it has added a new recidivism risk-assessment tool, and a cognitive-behavioral skills programming component. The risk-assessment tool serves a dual role, both to assess clients (for programmatic decision making) and to measure positive change from their point of entry in the program to their point of exit.

The plan involved using this new outcome measurement strategy with the community residential population. The residential program has a 184-bed center with contracts with the Federal Bureau of Prisons, the Indiana Department of Correction, Marion County Community Corrections, and the U.S. Federal Courts for the Probation Service. The community residential program is fully accredited by the American Correctional Association.

Development and Design

The initial outcome measurement work in the Community Residential Program has centered around use of the LSI-R (Level of Service Inventory-Revised), the new recidivism risk assessment tool. This measure is well validated by research, and is used throughout the Correctional Service of Canada. It is regarded as the world's premier recidivism risk assessment measure. Volunteers of American of Indiana received National Institute of Corrections-sponsored training in the use of the LSI-R in June 1996, and began using the tool the following month.

The agency also made the commitment to explore, and adopt for use a cognitive-behavioral skills programming component. This was brought to fruition when, in September and October 1996, T3 Associates of Ottawa, Canada trained forty Volunteers of America of Indiana staff members in their Reasoning and Rehabilitation Program. This treatment approach is well-supported by research findings, and has been implemented by correctional agencies throughout the world. The program is designed to alter criminal thinking patterns, and to provide offenders with an opportunity to acquire more normalized strategies for assessing situations, interacting with others, and considering consequences for their behaviors before they act.

The database was developed in-house by the director of clinical services. It is a comprehensive database that will allow ease of expansion to other areas of outcome measurement with this population.

Implementation

Data collection using the LSI-R began in July 1996, several months before the database was completed. This can be explained, in part, by the staff's desire to use the LSI-R data for individual program plan decisions. For example, LSI-R entry data is a major consideration in the selection of clients for the cognitive skills groups (that is, higher-risk individuals are typically selected for participation). Clients entering the community residential program are administered the LSI-R, and they are given the LSI-R once again within two weeks of their scheduled departure from the program.

The LSI-R measures recidivism risk by examining several criminogenic factors, including criminal history, education, employment, family/marital issues, companions, substance abuse issues, emotional stability, and attitude. Volunteers of America of Indiana hoped to demonstrate that by completing the residential program, the risk of recidivism would be reduced (as evidenced by total score and reduced subscale score for fluid subscales). In addition, the staff hoped to show that for those offenders who complete a cognitive-behavioral skills programming series, the degree of risk reduction for recidivism would be greater than for those not exposed to such programming.

Outcomes

At this point, there are more than 220 LSI-R "instances" in the database. More are being added each day. The LSI-R provides a comprehensive look at a particular offender, and permits targeting of services to meet the specific needs that are identified. But an examination of the aggregated data reveals a wealth of information as well. It is helpful to profile clients from the different referral sources, so staff can better understand the offenders' areas of collective need. Once these are known, programming efforts and other services can be tailored to best meet those identified needs.

There is yet another use that staff make of the LSI-R data. By comparing pre-test (entry) and post-test (exit) data, it is possible to measure the program's effectiveness in reducing the recidivism risk. Such data are available for Marion County Community Corrections, the Federal Bureau of Prisons, and the Indiana Department of Correction Zero Tolerance. The data only include clients who have both started and completed the residential program. An examination of the LSI-R subscale averages for the fluid areas (the criminal history subscale cannot change), reveals that by the time of program completion and post-test, the scores have been reduced. The reduction of the recidivism risk ranges from 29 percent for Marion County Community Corrections' clients, to 43 percent for Bureau of Prisons' referrals, and 35 percent for Zero Tolerance's cases.

It is also interesting to examine differences in the recidivism risk (and risk reduction) by gender. Pre- and post-test data were reviewed, by gender, for Bureau of Prisons' clients and Marion County Community Corrections' clients. Several areas of obvious need (and programming opportunity) stand out. For example, Marion County males have almost double the substance abuse subscale average as county females. However, issues surrounding family/marital relationships and accommodations are much more significant for the county females. This knowledge permits program staff to adjust its Women's Issue's group to address topics of maximum value to the female clients.

One additional use was made of the LSI-R data by examining the effects of participating in cognitive-behavioral skills programming. Pre- and post-test data for both cognitive skills participants and nonparticipants were reviewed. Caution must be used in interpreting this data, as the number of clients in the cognitive-skills participants' category is small. Nonetheless, an encouraging trend was noted. Cognitive-skills program participants were at a somewhat higher risk at the outset, and achieved a 36 percent decrease in their recidivism risk by the completion of their time with Volunteers of America of Indiana. Program nonparticipants achieved a lower decrease in their recidivism risk (30 percent). Staff will be able to determine if this trend continues as larger numbers of clients are included in the database.

Conclusion

Before Volunteers of America of Indiana began the new outcome-measurement process, staff believed that the program's services were of high quality, and that they truly made a difference in clients' lives. Unfortunately, they could not prove it! Now, they have the beginnings of a system that will provide an objective means to assess effectiveness. Staff have learned, to no one's surprise, that better knowledge and understanding of client needs can translate into better targeted programming. They also have learned that they can impact male and female clients differently, and that they must differentiate better between the needs of each group. The community residential program does reduce the recidivism risk (as assessed by the LSI-R). In most instances, the reduction of risk is large. Finally, even more, staff are finding that cognitive-behavioral programming may produce even greater recidivism risk reduction than participation in the general program alone.

Data collection and analysis often answers some questions, but generally leads staff to ask still more questions. Staff hope to learn more about program noncompleters, and the characteristics that may set them apart from other clients. Understanding this may enable staff to reach and retain more of these individuals. Perhaps the acid test of effectiveness, however, is evaluating reoffense data on program completers ninety days after they leave Volunteers of America of Indiana. Planning is underway to conduct such a study on a randomly selected group of clients.

In summary, outcome measurement in a community corrections setting is a necessary part of conducting business in an efficient and effective fashion. Its value to the organization offsets costs associated with the establishment of such a system.

Contact:

Timothy Campbell
Senior Vice President
Volunteers of America of Indiana, Inc.

611 North Capitol Street
Indianapolis, Indiana 46204
(317) 686-5800

Dallas County Judicial Treatment Center

Introduction

Addiction is a serious and complex disorder that has many dimensions and requires time and resources to ameliorate. Clients in the criminal justice system need a wraparound continuum of care to be successful. In 1991, a committee composed of judges from the Dallas County courts and representatives from the Dallas County Community Supervision and Corrections Department under the leadership of Judge Thomas Price decided to attempt to break the cycle of drug addiction, crime, and jail by providing effective treatment for substance abusers in the judicial system—in place of regular incarceration. After a nationwide search, they selected a private provider for the substance abuse treatment center.

The treatment program was called the Dallas County Judicial Treatment Center operated by Cornell Corrections, Inc. The administrative relationship created involved a contract from the county's Community Supervision and Corrections Department with funding provided by the state through the Texas Criminal Justice Assistance Division. The program represents a unique cooperative venture between the judiciary, a probation department, a state agency, and a treatment provider. The program opened in September 1991, and within six months the original census of 306 beds was filled.

Development and Design

The clients are not first offenders but often have had more than one felony charge; some are also on parole. Most are sentenced to the center following an unsuccessful period on probation. The probationers are characterized by needs in multiple domains such as job skills, literacy, and concurrent psychiatric disorders, in addition to problems with crime and drugs. They not only require an array of services for basic treatment but also a comprehensive continuum of care if they are to master the difficult posttreatment and postincarceration transition to the community while maintaining their recovery.

Clients sent to the Judicial Treatment Center are on probation for criminal offenses that are alcohol or other-drug related. The facility currently has 160 beds for males and 68 for females. It has three main elements. The first is a core residential six-month program of wraparound rehabilitative services with 178 beds. The second involves a six-month aftercare program in which residents work and live in the community. For clients whose return to drugs and crime is virtually certain because of absent or poor community support systems, there is a third element: a three-month live-in, work-out program with 50 beds. After completing the residential or transitional live-in-work-out program, these clients then enter the six-month aftercare program.

The clients are mandated to the program by court order. Their conditions of probation require that they complete treatment or risk revocation. Probation officers from the community supervision department have their offices on the treatment center's campus to facilitate the integration of probation and treatment system components. During the basic residential program, each client reports to a probation officer on the campus. Since the clients sent to the facility have a range of problems, in addition to criminality and substance abuse, their needs are comprehensively evaluated during the orientation phase in a number of domains. These domains include: educational, vocational, recreational, family support, social skills, medical, and psychiatric needs.

The comprehensive assessment was jointly developed by the Texas Christian University Institute of Behavioral Research and Cornell Corrections staff. The results of the assessment generate data for an individualized treatment plan, with specific goals that the client must meet to progress through the program during phase two of primary treatment. The assessment also collects demographic and clinical data to serve a dual purpose of providing outcome results and performance indicators of agency performance.

Phase three is the discharge planning and preparation phase that includes job readiness training, family sessions and contracts, integration into community based on 12-step groups, and job search. Upon gaining employment, the client either moves to community housing such as Oxford House, to their family home, or into the next phase at the center. The final or fourth phase of the program for all clients is a period of aftercare consisting of twenty-six weekly groups for support and relapse prevention, and individual sessions, when needed.

Implementation

The clients participate in modified therapeutic community programming that includes preparation of food, routine housekeeping in the facility, behavior modification procedures to resolve conflict, and group experiences. Each resident must also participate in 12-step groups such as Alcoholics Anonymous (AA) or Narcotics Anonymous (NA), and individual counseling, and daily recreational activities.

The program structure requires each client to become employed in a full-time job subsequent to completing primary treatment. In the event that a client does not have a high school diploma, the counselor requires the client to attend classes that lead to the acquisition of a general equivalency diploma (GED). On-site teachers and peer tutors work with clients to help them obtain their GEDs. The clients also may acquire job skills such as in culinary arts, computer operations, customer service, and the building trades.

The local Dallas Workforce Board, an organization supported by private and federal funds, contributes substantial continuing support for this critical job training component of the treatment program. The Judicial Treatment Center was honored by this board with outstanding contractor awards for 1994 and 1996. In 1996, the center replaced its outdated Apple IIe computers with a fifteen-station state-of-the art computer lab with funds from the board.

Learning a marketable job skill that leads to a subsistence-wage job is very important to successful recovery for the substance abuser in the criminal justice system. Job searches and placements are closely monitored by staff with the average job search lasting only ten days before the client lands a job paying a minimum wage of $7.00 per hour to the current average of $8.20 per hour.

A comprehensive discharge plan allows Cornell's staff to examine all areas of living for each client. The aftercare program includes groups in the community, probation supervision, and a continuation of 12-step groups. As clients move back into the community, they report to probation officers located in their community. The relationship continues in the aftercare elements of the treatment program as the probation department and Cornell's staff work together to monitor and assist the client in maintaining a stable recovery.

After completing this phase of treatment, each client is assigned to a probation officer in the Dallas community. To ensure the smooth integration of program elements, the Cornell's facility director and the probation department director meet with Cornell's regional director monthly to plan and problem solve.

Outcomes

Since the beginning of the program, staff have collected and analyzed client demographics and outcomes to provide a performance-feedback loop so those management decisions regarding program design would be based on accurate data. The start up of the program was so fast and success was so vital from its inception that the collection and analysis of data became an essential element of all management decisions.

In 1995, researchers, Dr. Kevin Knight and Dr. Matthew Hiller from Texas Christian University's Institute of Behavioral Research, under the direction of Dr. Dwayne D. Simpson, conducted an outcome measurement study of the 492 clients entering treatment from September 1993 to August 1994. The results indicated that 72 percent of the clients who were admitted successfully graduated from treatment. Of this group, 89 percent were not re-arrested in the first year following treatment.

After two years following treatment, the data further revealed that 73 percent of graduates had not been re-arrested. Those who did not complete the program had a significantly higher arrest rate. An additional study just completed in February 1998 of the 1994-1995 cohort indicates an 8 percent increase in positive outcomes for women and a 3 percent increase in positive discharges for younger clients than in the 1993-94 cohort. This increased positive performance was accomplished by basing program changes on outcome data.

Three articles have been published regarding the center. The first article was a descriptive article "Interventions/Wilmer: A Continuum of Care for Substance Abusers in the Criminal Justice System" published in the *Journal of Psychoactive Drugs*, January-March 1995. The second article was published in the *Journal of Psychoactive Drugs*, July-September 1996 in the "Short Communication" feature detailing the 6-month outcomes for the 1993-94 cohort. The last published article that detailed the 1-year outcomes was published in *Federal Probation*, June 1997.

Conclusion

One of the lessons learned in the development of the Judicial Treatment Center is that programs that are responsive to their contractor, their clients, and their constituency survive and continue to improve. In the last six years, the program census was reduced to accommodate funding shortages, but this was done quickly and efficiently because the reconfiguration was based on hard data. Internal monitoring of program quality indicators performed by the Total Quality Management Committee and the subcommittees, the Utilization Management Committee, and the Research and Statistical Analysis Committee, supported reductions that did not hurt program quality but hit financial targets. The most recent reconfiguration of staff reduced costs but did not increase caseloads significantly or reduce services.

Another lesson learned is that programs that can prove their outcomes are superior and set the standard for other programs. Partnering with a reputable outside research organization, (like the Texas Christian University Institute of Behavioral Research) for evaluation research adds credibility to the outcomes and increases the program's profile. The last and most important lesson is that clients in the criminal justice system need a wraparound continuum of care to be successful. Addiction is a serious and complex disorder that has many dimensions and requires time and resources to ameliorate. Short-term isolated interventions that lack the intensity and efficiency of a modified therapeutic community, amplified to include other services, are often a waste of resources for this population.

It is the consistent support and cooperation of the judges and probation department in Dallas County that has been the single largest reason that the Judicial Treatment Center has succeeded. The center's mission statement reads, "Through an interdisciplinary and cooperative approach, we provide and advocate for quality services for clients that are cost effective, benefit the community and influence social policy." Cornell Corrections has been true to that mission at the Dallas County Judicial Treatment Center.

Contact:

Julien Devereux
Facility Director, Cornell Corrections, Inc.
Dallas County Judicial Treatment Center

200 Greene Road
Wilmer, Texas 75172
(972) 441-6160 x105

The Neil J. Houston House: Social Justice for Women

Introduction

"There are more than 80,000 jailed and imprisoned mothers in the United States; these women have at least 150,000 dependent children or an average of 2.4 children each," according to the Center for Children of Incarcerated Parents (1993).

The Neil J. Houston House is a residential, prerelease substance-abuse treatment program. Houston House was created as a response to the increasing number of pregnant female offenders entering the Massachusetts Correctional Institution at Framingham. It is the only program of its kind in the state and only one of very few in the country, despite the fact that a total of 1,778 women were pregnant when admitted as inmates in 1996 (American Correctional Association, 1997).

The goals of the program are to provide community-based residential substance abuse treatment and perinatal care as an alternative to incarceration for pregnant women in conflict with the law; to assist women in attaining the optimal drug-free birth for their infants; to allow them to remain with their infants at birth to develop healthy bonding and the skills to effectively parent; to help them access early intervention services for infants, as needed; and, to provide aggressive treatment services to assist graduates to successfully reintegrate into their communities.

Most incarcerated women have a history of chronic addiction and are at high risk for contracting HIV-infection due to intravenous drug use. According to the Massachusetts Department of Health, 75-80 percent of the women incarcerated in the state have a history of polydrug abuse. Many arrive at the prison in the acute stages of withdrawal from drugs and alcohol. Many women also have preexisting medical conditions and chronic illnesses when they enter prison. Some women suffer from mental illness and neurological disorders caused or exacerbated by addiction or severe head trauma from beatings, or the traumas of physical, emotional, or sexual abuse (Wellish et al. 1994).

These conditions are compounded during incarceration due to increased exposure to infectious diseases, poor diet, crowded living conditions, violence, and traumatic stress syndrome associated with prison life. These factors, in addition to the lack of proper prenatal care, result in high-risk delivery complications and infant mortality. In contrast, a pregnant woman receiving substance abuse treatment increases her chances of delivering a healthy baby. According to one study, "the risk of low birth weight and premature birth, which often requires expensive neonatal intensive care, are minimized by drug treatment before the third trimester" (Shikes, 1990).

Development and Design

Houston House has made dramatic improvements in the living conditions and perinatal medical care for incarcerated, pregnant women. Within a structured and caring environment, it provides a woman the opportunity to deliver a healthy, drug-free infant and to build a new life with her baby. The program accommodates 15 women and infants and can administer services to 25 to 30 women per year. Since opening in February of 1989 through December 1997, it has provided services to approximately 175 women, and 136 "Houston House Babies."

A pregnant, incarcerated woman, because of her circumstances, often is motivated to change her lifestyle. Pregnancy is a time when most women are particularly motivated to improve health-related behavior (Mason, Rosett, and Weiner, 1985). However, making the transition to a drug and crime-free lifestyle requires hard work on the women's part, and a comprehensive continuum of medical and substance abuse treatment and educational services. The program allows these women to reenter society as positive, effective citizens. Substance abuse treatment, medical care, mother-child bonding, parenting education, and community reintegration constitute the primary focus.

Houston House is a program of Social Justice for Women: The Women's Division of Spectrum Health Systems, Inc. The program represents an unprecedented collaboration between the Departments of Correction and Public Health, the substance abuse treatment community, and the health care community. Houston House is the only facility in the state entirely dedicated to working with this population. The program currently is affiliated with, among others: the Beth Israel Deaconess Medical Center, Dimock Community Health Center, the Boston Medical Center, the 12-step recovery community, the Coalition on Addiction, Pregnancy and Parenting, and the Boston Food Bank.

Implementation

Substance Abuse Treatment

The Social Justice for Women programs use an eclectic blend of therapies. All services are delivered within a "relational" framework with particular attention to trauma syndrome and the mothering role. The program is structured with an orientation period and four levels of treatment.

As treatment progresses, the woman begins to see the patterns of her life and how her addiction has impacted on all its many facets. She then is able to acknowledge her part and responsibility in the negative lifestyle in which she is enmeshed. Over time, she begins to assume a peer leadership role within the house, and is expected to regularly practice appropriate behavior. Through the program, each woman develops a social recovery network and establishes external support for when she leaves the program.

Medical Services

After an initial evaluation that includes a physical exam and a psychosocial, environmental, and nutritional assessment, a comprehensive medical care plan is developed for each woman. "Providing drug treatment and prenatal care could significantly improve the health of infants born to those who use drugs and could reduce the risk of long term problems" (Shikes, 1990). Clinic visits include routine ultrasound and nonstress tests and are conducted at a local health clinic or hospital. In addition, on-site nursing care for mothers and infants is available.

Nursing/Health/Education Services

Nursing care and health-care education is a critical service provided to the Houston House residents. Most often, the women have little or no understanding of their health, their body functions, their reproductive system, or the health care needs of their infants.

Currently, Houston House provides nursing and health education ten hours per week. The nurse/health educator provides health assessments, educational classes, and individual counseling. The topics that are covered include information regarding pregnancy, infant health, HIV/AIDS, universal health precautions, sexually transmitted diseases, the resurgence of hepatitis and tuberculosis and its implications, how to access the medical community and consumer rights, family planning and contraception, and health-care maintenance as women age.

Parenting

The daily care that is required for all infants is the focus of group educational seminars, parenting support groups, and individual counseling sessions with the treatment, parenting, or medical staff. The lessons of infant care focus on both physical and emotional well-being. The program staff facilitate discussions about infant behavior. Most everyday experiences of new mothers become opportunities for teaching. The women learn that consistent, appropriate care of the baby results in a positive mother-infant relationship.

Education

While in the program, the residents must obtain their general equivalency diploma (GED). Members of the Philip Brooks House of Harvard University facilitate GED preparation. In addition, there are structured didactic sessions on topics such as nutrition, reproductive health, parenting education, and addiction education. All residents must participate.

Special Services

Birthing classes, stress-reduction workshops, smoking cessation, acupuncture, and cultural awareness activities represent some of the special services that are offered as part of the program's holistic approach.

Resettlement/Aftercare

As each woman nears the completion of her stay in the program, she begins participation in the resettlement program, and continues for one year after completing her residence. Resettlement is crucial to a woman's ongoing ability to combat substance abuse and to accept responsibility for a productive life for herself and her child. The resettlement component helps in the reintegration of Houston House residents and their infants into their home communities by facilitating access to needed community services (for example, housing, training programs, job placement, day care, parenting education, and medical care), while at the same time, providing ongoing individual and group substance abuse counseling at the program.

Outcome

Each year Houston House and Social Justice for Women staff collect and review the following statistical data:

- Total number of interviews and admissions

- Source of referral (state or county correctional system, parole, probation/other)

- Number of women who did not complete and reason (return to higher custody, left against staff advice upon completion of their sentence, referred to other programs, escape)

- Number of women delivering babies while at the Houston House

- Number of reunifications between mothers who entered postpartum and their infants

- The level and type of postcompletion participation in on-going services (Houston House resettlement or community provider in home area)

A great volume of other information regarding residents at the Houston House is obtained through program-intake forms. At present, insufficient funding precludes compilation of this data for comparative purposes. Women in residence at the program maintain "clean" urine. Likewise, parenting education and intervention results in observable improvement in parenting skills.

The figure of 136 "Houston House Babies" includes 116 births and 20 "reunifications." A reunification occurs when the woman is admitted to the program following her delivery. Of the 116 births at the program during 1989 through 1997, all but three of the babies were totally drug-free at birth. These exceptions occurred when the women were on methadone and were not able to be completely detoxified before their delivery.

Early intervention assessments of the Houston House babies found most of them to be well within the developmental norms for their ages. Anecdotally, the "babies" are doing well; the first "babies" are now in the second grade, enjoying dance class, playing sports and, in general, taking part in a full range of children's activities.

Conclusion

When a pregnant, nonviolent offender gives birth in prison, it costs taxpayers approximately $50,000 per woman and child as a result of incarceration and child placement in alternative care. Substance abuse continues to be a spiraling and chronic problem for these women.

If a pregnant, nonviolent offender goes to Neil J. Houston House, she and her baby receive pre- and postnatal care, substance abuse treatment, GED opportunities, parenting, nutrition and health education, and on-site nursing. Upon completion of her sentence, she also receives one year of counseling. Babies and mothers stay together. The women who come to the Houston House do not return to prison. They learn how to live drug and crime-free, united with their babies.

By investing in Houston House, the tools necessary to break the cycle of poverty, addiction, and crime are provided to a vulnerable population of women. Infants receive a solid foundation for growth and development with their mothers, rather than becoming entangled in the bureaucracy of the Department of Social Services and moved from one placement to another.

Houston House, through its numerous community and state collaborations, and gender-specific programming, is a progressive, effective response to address the complex needs of pregnant incarcerated women.

References

American Correctional Association. 1990. *The Female Offender: What Does the Future Hold?* Lanham, Maryland: American Correctional Association.

———. 1997. *Corrections Compendium*. Vol 24, No 11. Lanham, Maryland: American Correctional Association. November.

Blinn, Cynthia . 1997. *Maternal Ties: A Selection of Programs for Female Offenders*. Lanham, Maryland: American Correctional Association.

Center for Children of Incarcerated Parents. 1993. *How Many Are There? Data Sheets on Children of Incarcerated Parents*. Pasadena, California: Pacific Oaks College.

Mason, Edward, A. Rosett, L. Henry, and Lynn Weiner. 1985. "Training Professionals to Identify and Treat Pregnant Women Who Drink Heavily." *Alcohol Health and Research World*. 32.

McCaffrey, Barry. 1996. *Television Interview, The Today Show*. November 7. NBC News.

Sampson, Lisa. 1996. (Assistant Director of Research Operations, Massachusetts Department of Correction), *Phone Interview*. Boston, Massachusetts, October 15.

Morton, JoAnn, Editor. 1998. *Complex Challenges, Collaborative Solutions: Programs for Juvenile and Adult Female Offenders*. Lanham, Maryland: American Correctional Association.

Shikes, Janet, L. (Director for Health and Finance Policy Issues). 1990. *Human Resources Division Report to: Honorable Lloyd Bentsen, Chairman, Committee on Finance*. Washington D.C.: U.S. General Accounting Office.

Wellisch, Jean. 1994. *Drug Abusing Women Offenders, Results of a National Survey*. Department of Justice. National Institute of Justice: Washington, D.C.

Contact:

Diane Wood
Program Director
Neil J. Houston House

9 Notre Dame
Roxbury, Massachusetts 02119
(617) 445-3066

A Program for Families

Introduction

A mother imprisoned is a family fractured. Incarcerating mothers and pregnant women goes far beyond the direct impact on the mother as the children become unwitting victims of their mother's debt to society. In North Carolina, 78 percent of all incarcerated women are mothers, and 83 percent of the mothers are single parents. Perhaps more unfortunate are the cases of pregnant women who are forced to give up their newborns within 24 to 48 hours after birth, taking away the opportunity for that initial and valuable bond with their children. On any given day, more than 1,400 women are incarcerated throughout the state leaving more than 3,000 children without their mothers. The issue of justice becomes a double-edged sword as the children bear both edges, a mother incarcerated and a family separated.

In the 1970s, the need for an alternative to prison for mothers and pregnant women was discussed by the Greensboro Commission on the Status of Women. As a result of these discussions, the Commission created "Another Way," a program designed to outline the need for a vision of an alternative to prison. In the 1980s, a steering committee was established to address the needs identified by Another Way. This group evolved into a board of directors, which created a program that included residential and day-reporting elements. In 1987 the program was incorporated as the Guilford County Residential/Day Center, now known as Summit House. True to its mission, the residential and day-reporting programs allowed the female residents to retain primary care of their children.

Development and Design

In the 1980s, the steering committee that developed the original Summit House program searched for similar programs elsewhere offering front-end diversionary programming for female offenders and their children. The program development stalled temporarily due to the lack of an operating model.

The Summit House programs are now ten years old and continue to develop on an ongoing basis. The Summit House residential programs operate in a home-like setting. Dwellings with multiple bedrooms in residential communities provide women and children with housing that models a neighborhood setting. A sense of community and cooperation is fostered as the women and their children share meal preparation and dinner times, and take turns with chores and other day-to-day responsibilities.

The goals of the Summit House program are to help females in the program to:

- Improve parenting skills

- Identify and manage self-defeating behaviors

- Practice self-supporting behaviors through development of long-term goals, engage in life planning, further their education and training, learn about financial management/budgeting, and obtain employment

- Develop a healthy sense of self, family, and competency in relationships with others

Summit House provides a structured approach that blends a comprehensive selection of services. Each woman's progress is guided by a behavior modification and empowerment model where behaviors are rewarded or discouraged relative to goals set by the woman and the Summit House staff. The program uses many local agencies, professionals, and schools to provide services. The services that are provided include therapeutic intervention, classes, and workshops on major life issues such as developing positive parenting skills, practicing good health habits, completing addiction education, and then living addiction-free through involvement in 12-step programs (for example, Narcotics Anonymous). Other services include providing formal academic education; enhancing family relationships; teaching self-management skills, including job seeking and employment skills; and offering social skills training and practice.

The rehabilitation program at Summit House borrows from the most successful applications of learning and offering immediate reinforcement. Staff members serve as positive role models for appropriate behavior. This gives clients the opportunity to observe and practice positive behaviors. Staff members establish a therapeutic relationship with clients wherein unconditional positive regard is balanced with a supportive environment, one that encourages clients to take responsibility for the consequences of their behavior. The staff-client relationship is built on the principles of empowerment, where staff members support and facilitate self-sufficiency and success in clients at whatever level is needed for any given situation.

The program-management staff at Summit House are dedicated to individualized treatment with service and rehabilitation tailored to the specific needs of each mother and her children. This provides an element of empowerment to the woman entering Summit House and encourages her to participate in setting goals relevant to her needs and the needs of her family. Since each client and her children has a unique set of goals, no predetermined length of stay is set for women residing at Summit House. Depending on each woman's rate of progress, it takes between one and two years to achieve the requisite skills for graduation. These requisite skills are included in the graduation requirements for the program.

To graduate from the program, a mother must have:

- Completed her individualized treatment plan, including resolving identified criminogenic issues, progressing through the motivation system, and meeting her goals in the areas of parenting, managing finances, coping skills, and developing personal competency

- Completed counseling, including substance abuse counseling, individual and/or family counseling, (if appropriate) and continuing to be involved in her support network

- Completed her general equivalency diploma (if appropriate) or obtained her high school diploma and continued her involvement in furthering her employment opportunities either through college or advanced training

- Established employment with an income above minimum wage and arranged satisfactory child care

- Established a savings account and budget

- Located appropriate housing for her family

- Developed a homebound plan, a resource guide, and an aftercare plan with the staff

- Agreed to be involved in aftercare through her probation period or for a minimum of six months if not on probation and to seek help as needed, thereafter.

Implementation

Summit House began providing residential and day reporting services in Greensboro, North Carolina in 1987. The original program design was more punitive than the current design. The program had difficulty accessing continued funding once foundations ceased funding the start-up phase of three years. In 1990 the program closed for a five-month period. This closure allowed those involved to review the program in light of new research findings and resources in the state to assist offenders. The new program design, that of behavior modification and empowerment, evolved from this respite. The North Carolina General Assembly assisted in the reopening of the program by an increased allocation of funds. An additional focus was placed on fundraising by the board and staff.

As the General Assembly became more aware of the success that Summit House was experiencing with high-risk, nonviolent female offenders, the program was asked to expand in 1993. The General Assembly requested that Summit House establish a full day-reporting program for women in Greensboro and residential programs in the Charlotte and Raleigh areas of the state. The board of directors in Greensboro put together an ad-hoc committee to address the reorganization of Summit House into a statewide agency while consultants were hired to work with this committee and assess the feasibility of the General Assembly's request. In 1994, the board of directors in Greensboro agreed to a new governing structure for the organization. This structure includes a statewide board of governors, as the policy making board, and local boards of trustees for fundraising and local program and management oversight. There are now more than 100 volunteers involved in the oversight of Summit House statewide. Summit House currently employees more than fifty professionals working across the state.

Outcomes

During the 1997 legislative session, the General Assembly again asked Summit House to review further expansion in the Charlotte and Greensboro areas and statewide. Summit House believes the strong commitment from the General Assembly to the programs has come from three significant facts:

1) The annual cost to incarcerate a woman in North Carolina averages $33,000 ($90 per day) and the cost of building a prison cell is $13,000-$46,000. The annualized cost of providing foster care services to the at-risk children served by Summit House costs North Carolina $26,664 to $56,112 ($73 to $154 a day). The annual capital and

operating costs to provide services to a mother and a child is less at Summit House. The annual per bed cost of services at Summit House during fiscal year 1996 and 1997 was $74 a day.

2) At least 25 percent of juveniles arrested in 1995 were females. The children of incarcerated parents have been found to be much more likely to be incarcerated in the future themselves.

3) A study conducted of residents in the Summit House program between October, 1990 and October, 1995 found that only 20 percent were reincarcerated on new charges. The recidivism rate of offenders from the North Carolina Correctional Institution for Women (based on reincarceration) for the same period was 40 percent.

Summit House has been evaluated every two to three years by a well-respected expert in community corrections. In 1991 and 1993, Dr. Paul Gendreau evaluated the Greensboro program and provided staff training. In 1996, Dr. Ed Latessa evaluated both the Charlotte and Greensboro programs based on the Correctional Program Assessment Inventory developed by Drs. Paul Gendreau and Don Andrews. Dr. Latessa stated the highest scoring program nationally he had assessed prior to his visit was 71 percent. Charlotte scored 65 percent and Greensboro 58 percent. By implementing a dynamic risk assessment instrument known as the LSI-R on intake and every six months thereafter, the staff and administration believe these scores will be raised substantially upon reevaluation.

Based, in part, on the use of the LSI-R, staff now are developing a database which will include information not only on the mother and the child(ren) served, but also their families. This will provide a wealth of information for future research. Beginning in the year 2000, Summit House will begin to review recidivism results on the children housed in the program. Since children normally leave Summit House prior to their eighth birthday, adult arrest records will not be available on any children until 1999.

Summit House has been recognized statewide and nationally since its inception. In 1996 it received one of the most prestigious awards—the President's Service Award. To promote its mission, Summit House staff have made presentations at eight national conferences in the past three years. This, along with national publicity, has spawned inquiries for program models nationally and internationally. The Summit House program model has been implemented in several sites, and as far away as New Zealand. In addition, the program has been featured in the 1997 American Correctional Association publication *Maternal Ties: a Selection of Programs for Female Offenders*, and in the *Community Corrections Report* (September/October 1997).

Conclusion

Summit House staff have learned several lessons over the years. These lessons include the need to be assured that funding for continued program operations is in place. Then, always develop residential programs for high-risk offenders as a community-public-private partnership, and before responding to a community's request for a "Summit House" ask the community to provide a home properly zoned for the operation of the program.

The program's message is simple and strong—preserve the family, rehabilitate not merely habilitate, and look towards the future for the children by decreasing the likelihood they will become involved in delinquent or criminal behavior. Summit House strives daily to accomplish these goals as it reaches out to improve the outcomes of its clients—the women and their children. The significant investment in the people that Summit House serves results in their self-sufficiency and empowerment to engage in a promising, productive future.

Contact:

Karen V. Chapple
Statewide Chief Executive Officer
Summit House

612-B West Friendly Avenue
Greensboro, North Carolina 27401
(336) 691-9888

Life Line Programme

Introduction

The Mission of the Life Line Programme "is to provide, through both the in-reach and the residential component, an opportunity to motivate inmates and to marshall resources to achieve successful, supervised, gradual integration into the community."

The Life Line Programme is geared specifically towards enabling lifers and long-term offenders to reintegrate into society. It is a product of a strong partnership between the Correctional Service of Canada, St. Leonard's House, Windsor, and the National Parole Board. It is based on three important components, which are considered essential to the successful reintegration of lifers and long-term offenders: in-reach, community programming, and public education.

The first component, in-reach, consists of using the "successful" lifer or long-term offender to contact, motivate, and assist lifers to achieve optimum benefits from existing correctional programs, to contribute towards the introduction of additional programs inside the penitentiaries, and to act as a resource to institutional staff. In addition to the provision of services and support, the Life Line representative is a source of hope that there is life after life imprisonment. The in-reach worker provides support to the lifer in such processes as parole board hearings, temporary absences and unaccompanied temporary absences, and the judicial review process. The in-reach workers, who continue working with the lifer once the lifer is released, are an important link for the offender from the institution to the community. They help maintain the family connection during the long period of incarceration.

The second element, community programming, is intened to meet demonstrable needs, which were not addressed through traditional community-based facilities designed for short-term residencies. The objective is to better motivate the inmate and create better planning and management of the sentence within the institution and to provide, for selected lifers, supportive reintegration services, including a specialized residential facility in the community. The residential facility includes a community-focused program stressing individual responsibility and independence.

The third element is public education. This function is carried out by the in-reach workers, as well. It involves educating the public on the nature of the lifer and long-term offender population to increase public understanding of and support for the released offender through visiting schools, community organizations, and high-risk youth.

Several characteristics describe the uniqueness of the Life Line programme. First, Life Line employs the program involvement of lifers on parole assisting other lifers, both in the community and in the penitentiary. Second, it encompasses a partnership between offenders, community agencies, and government correctional services. Third, Life Line includes several community-based agencies each independent of one another but working towards the same goals.

While Life Line was initiated in St. Leonard's House, Windsor, Ontario, various elements of the concept have been adopted by various nongovernmental organizations across Canada. To date, there are eight in-reach workers active in four Correctional Service of Canada regions.

Development and Design

St. Leonard's House, Windsor, Ontario, was opened in 1962 and became the first halfway house in Canada, which was geared specifically to the supervision of recently released male offenders. Founded by the late Reverend T. Neil Libby, it served as the first of the several other halfway houses across Canada. Only five years after the house was opened, the National St. Leonard's Society was created. Today the Correctional Service of Canada contracts with some 170 community residential centers owned and operated by groups such as St. Leonard's.

The realization that St. Leonard's House in Windsor, perhaps could fill an even greater void in community support came in the early eighties. In Canada, there are presently approximately 3,100 lifers, of whom 2,000 are incarcerated, representing 15 percent of the total federal incarcerated population. Of these, 880 lifers are on full parole, while 220 are on day parole. One-third of all lifers are presently serving their sentences in the community under some form of supervision. Among those on parole, there exists a group of special needs lifers whose reintegration into society is more difficult. It was from this realization that in 1982, St. Leonard's House in Windsor began to set the groundwork for the development of the Life Line project.

In 1986, a research report entitled *Needs Assessment and Recommendations for Community Based Programming for Long Term Offenders* was produced by St. Leonard's with funding from the correctional service. In 1986, the Correctional Service of Canada's *Operational Review Management Report #21* entitled *Long Term Offenders* was completed. It underlined the importance of programming in the area of long-term offenders and supported the need for a focused and dedicated approach. A Federal-Voluntary Task Force was then established, which served to develop and guide what has evolved from St. Leonard's earlier groundbreaking work.

The initial response to the challenge of providing specific services to the lifer or long-term offender was a proposal from the St. Leonard's Society to the Correctional Service of Canada for the establishment of a halfway house in Windsor to serve lifers exclusively. The proposed program content was developed by a working group headed by Dr. Mary Lou Dietz of the University of Windsor and involved both the university and St. Leonard's staff with support from the Correctional Service of Canada. As funding was not immediately available, St. Leonard's submitted a proposal for a demonstration project to the Donner Foundation of Canada with the gradual phasing in of Correctional Service of Canada funding. While support was received, the foundation hoped that the idea could be developed further in partnership with the National Parole Board and the Correctional Service. A working committee, named the National Resource Group, was established under the chairmanship of John Braithwaite, past president of the American Correctional Association, and included membership from the Correctional Service of Canada, the National Parole Board, the research community, and the community correctional organizations, to develop the concept further.

In 1990, an extensive report was completed. The three well-developed components of the Life Line concept emerged as: in-reach, community programs, and public education.

In 1990, the Correctional Service of Canada agreed to provide funding for the first in-reach worker in Canada, a lifer on parole, who began entering institutions in the Ontario region to support and motivate lifers in the reintegration process starting early in their life sentence. In 1991, a second in-reach worker was introduced into the Ontario region penitentiaries.

In 1991-1992, the Life Line report commissioned by the Correctional Service of Canada, *More than a Matter of Time*, was completed and it supported the development of a comprehensive, corporate strategy for long-term offenders. It addressed several of the key recommendations of a recently completed federal *Task Force Report on the Long Term Offender* (The Perron Report). In 1992, the Correctional Service of Canada approved funding to support the following initiatives dealing with the Life Line concept:

- National consultation on the concepts developed in the Life Line project as implemented in Ontario

- The development of five beds programmed and dedicated to the lifer (St. Leonard's House in Windsor)

- A resource center for these offenders also in Windsor

Work began to develop greater operational and community support for the Life Line concept across Canada. However, the community residential aspect of Life Line did not develop as smoothly as the in-reach component. *"Halfway House for Killers Coming Here,"* was the headline that informed the citizens of Windsor, Ontario that St. Leonard's was planning to start a halfway house for lifers. A series of quiet consultations with key community groups over a two-year period resulted in a scaled-down project, which was accepted by the community. Today, the admissions committee for the halfway house is composed of various community interests, including the police and victims.

Working hand in hand with the development and promotion of Life Line was the National Resource Group, which has performed different roles throughout the years, as the concept has evolved. The National Resource Group has been active in recent times and now represents a partnership between the Correctional Service of Canada, the National Parole Board, and community-based Life Line organizations across Canada in the area of lifers' issues and programming needs. The committee's mandate includes the development of lifer strategies within the institution and the community, the monitoring of the progress of each in-reach program in the country and the formation of an important liaison between in-reach workers, lifers, and senior correctional officials. Today, membership of the National Resource Group consists of the chairman of the National Parole Board, the senior deputy commissioner of the Correctional Service, a representative of the in-reach workers, a member of the research community, and the head of a community-based organization, St. Leonard's House in Windsor.

Implementation

As stated before, the Life Line concept has been gradually implemented to different degrees across Canada. While St. Leonard's House in Windsor, is the only in-reach program to offer a residential component to date, other organizations which had been offering in-reach programs are considering the concept to varying degrees.

Under the guidance of the National Resource Group, a job description for an in-reach worker has been developed and recognized by the Correctional Service of Canada, the National Parole Board, and all the in-reach workers nationally. This brings the Life Line concept closer to full realization and provides an important tool for the further expansion of similar programs.

At St. Leonard's in Windsor, the community-based residential facility has been expanded to include four individual mini-apartments constructed specifically for the use of lifers.

In the domain of public education, in-reach workers challenge the fears of citizens and create awareness and much needed support for lifers returning to the community.

Measuring Performance

As Life Line programs are established across Canada, efforts to collect data have been expanded. In addition, a yearly evaluation of each specific program takes place.

Family Contact

While Life Line does not keep statistics on family contact, it is considered an integral part of in-reach. Contact with families occurs most often at the request of offenders and is focused on providing support and information concerning the correctional process, hearings before the National Parole Board, and private family visits.

Reduction in Institutional Incidents

In-reach workers often perform the role of intermediaries during times of conflict. These periods range from conflict between inmates, to conflicts between inmates and staff, and offer a variety of forms of mediation during major institutional disturbances. In-reach workers have achieved high credibility for their expertise in dealing with the lifer population and many times work hand in hand with the warden to alleviate frustration and remove barriers to effective programming.

Public Education

The public education activities of these in-reach workers ranged from speaking engagements at colleges and schools to presentations before the government Senate Committee in opposition to changes to the Canadian Criminal Code. The in-reach workers were invited to speak to troubled teens and youth who already had demonstrated criminal behavior. These youth were referred by social service agencies such as Children's Aid Society, by parents, probation officers, and schools.

As another example of a successful public education initiative, in Manitoba, lifers at two institutions were able to join in an activity called "Discovery Day" in April of 1997. It was a huge success as it provided a forum for lifers and citizens to meet, discuss timely topics, and have the dialog shared through television and an open-line radio show with the larger community.

Life Line and the National Resource Group have made much progress in related areas, as well. The unescorted temporary absences policy was clarified by the National Parole Board for the more appropriate use of temporary absences in developing release plans. In addition, certain federal penitentiaries have expressed interest in exploring the possibilities of special living units within their institutions geared specifically to lifers. Further, in-reach workers have been able to gain support for the greater use of the lifer population within the institution in the co-delivery of key programs with staff (e.g., peer support groups headed by lifers, or programming given by lifers for lifers).

The Correctional Service recently has established a task force to further develop and support strategies to achieve mutually defined goals, which are stated in the following terms of reference:

- The availability of an "in-reach" type worker for each offender serving a life sentence in a Canadian penitentiary

- The development of a standardized training and orientation package for all "in-reach" type workers

- The development of a set of standards and guidelines, which will form the basis for a review and evaluation of Life Line programs across Canada, the proposed approach to the conduct of such a review and evaluation

- A proposed approach to the early completion of a formal review of the potential role for life-sentenced offenders in penitentiaries including, but not limited to, access to programs, training, employment, and community service

- A proposed approach to the early completion of a review to identify key elements which contribute to the successful reintegration of life-sentenced offenders and a strategy to incorporate this into the overall approach to the management of this group of offenders

- A proposed approach to the early completion of a review of the community-based infrastructure, including residential services and programs needed to contribute to the successful reintegration of life-sentenced offenders and a strategy to incorporate this into the overall approach to management of this group of offenders

- An estimate of the type and amount of resources required to carry out its recommendations, including any long-term savings that would be gained

- Any other matters that the task force determines should be addressed in terms of the management of life-sentenced offender to ensure the highest levels of public safety consistent with the Correctional Conditional Release Act and the mission of the Correctional Service of Canada

Conclusion

It has been demonstrated that successful lifers and long-term offenders can serve as important resources within the community in enabling other offenders to reintegrate. Their ability to reach offenders on a different level than regular professional and program staff has resulted in a great degree of success.

An innovative project directed at a specific segment of the offender population, Life Line worked diligently to gain acceptance by the Correctional Service and the community and is now recognized as providing a viable service. Many years of work have resulted in the Correctional Service of Canada adopting Life Line as an official program and providing a corporate commitment to its ongoing growth.

Contacts:

Drury Allen
Director of Strategic Planning
Correctional Service of Canada

340 Laurier Avenue West
Ottawa, Ontario, Canada K1A 0P9
(613) 947-3922

John Braithwaite
Life Line Programme

RR1, Site 7C18
Gabriola Island, British Columbia, Canada V0R 1X0
(250) 247-9095

Edward Graham
Executive Director
St. Leonard's House

491 Victoria Avenue
Windsor, Ontario, Canada N9A 4N1
(519) 256-1878

Community Corrections—Residential
Additional Program Entries

Maison d'Arret/Time Out

Normand Granger, Director of East/West District, Correctional Service of Canada
Ste. 300, 222 St. Georges St., St. Jerome, Quebec J7Z 4Z9
(514) 432-3737

Maison d'Arret/Time Out opened it doors May 19, 1995 as an alternative to the recommittal of offenders whose parole has been suspended for a technical violation or due to situational difficulties. The program involves the participation of the Federal Training Centre, Laval area parole office, and the private sector. Delivered in a close environment, this short-term program uses refresher modules focusing on substance abuse, employability, violence, and emotional dependence to help offenders acquire necessary reintegration skills. The program offers a range of thirty three-hour sessions: ten on substance abuse, ten on job search, and ten on dealing with other subjects such as understanding emotional dependence, negotiating separation, and parenting skills. The program must be considered a last resort for suspension cases after all other measures have failed, such as loss of privileges, stricter supervision, or return to closed-treatment day parole. The length of stay is from fourteen to seventy-five days, and participation is voluntary.

Glenwood Jail Drug and Alcohol Treatment Program

James L. Lawrence, President, Oriana House, Inc.
P.O. Box 1501, Akron, Ohio 44305-1501
(330) 535-8116

Glenwood Jail is a full-service minimum-security jail designed primarily for offenders convicted of driving while intoxicated. It operates as a public and private partnership between the Summit County Sheriff's Office and Oriana House, Inc., in compliance with the minimum jail standards of the Ohio Department of Rehabilitation and Correction. The Glenwood Jail programs are designed to alleviate jail crowding while introducing a comprehensive education, assessment, and treatment program for substance-abusing offenders. Offenders are sentenced to the program from the court. The program has a cost to the offender on a sliding-scale fee with no cost to indigent offenders. The Summit County Sheriff's Office is responsible for the custody, and Oriana House, Inc. is responsible for the chemical dependency treatment. Glenwood Jail has a seventy-two-hour Driver Intervention Program (DIP) for first-time offenders and a Multiple Offender Program (MOP), which accepts commitments of up to 180 days. The facility is staffed by Summit County Deputy Sheriffs and Oriana House, Inc. to accommodate both the punitive and the treatment aspects of the offender's sentence.

Community Corrections—
Nonresidential

4

Introduction

While corrections as a profession is changing dramatically, perhaps the area that has been most affected is community corrections. More than 4 million offenders are under probation and parole supervision. There has been an unprecedented increase in prison populations with aggressive initiatives to build more prisons in many states. There is, however, a growing recognition that states cannot rely only on the expansion of prison capacity as the solution to the offender population explosion.

In "A Crime Control Rationale for Reinvesting in Community Corrections," Joan Petersilia (*Perspectives*, Spring 1996) points out that until dramatic efforts are made to curb the criminal activities of the three-fourths of the offenders who reside in the community, real reductions in crime or prison commitments are unlikely. Yet, the funding for community programs has diminished on the state and local level. All too often, the value of community corrections is absent from federal and state debates over where to allocate funding for solutions to the problem of crime.

Despite this absence, the field of community corrections throughout the United States and Canada continues to develop innovative programs that are making a difference. The Community Corrections Committee on Nonresidential programs had an opportunity to review many worthy programs. Five programs are highlighted in the chapter that follows. They all have one common thread: a focus on the balanced approach to community supervision that embraces a community/restorative justice model. The committee members read the various submissions and ranked them. In addition, they had an opportunity to give feedback to those programs where they needed more information. They used the core criteria established by the American Correctional Association to judge each submission.

The submissions that are included in this chapter discuss:

1. An in-house educational program in Arizona for adult probationers that has five years of recidivism data

2. An intensive-supervision program in Washington for high-profile offenders that is not office-bound but truly community-based

3. A structured system in South Carolina developed on a statewide basis to manage probation and parole violators

4. A client-services unit in Iowa that not only delivers effective treatment and supervision, but centralizes an assessment of treatment needs

5. A probation-police partnership in Boston that targets youthful at-risk offenders for special enforcement of their conditions of supervision

The committee believes that these programs represent the "cutting edge" in community corrections.

Committee chair:

John Larivee
Executive Director
Crime and Justice Foundation

95 Berkeley Street
Boston, Massachusetts 02116
(617) 426-9800

The LEARN Program—
History of Adult Probation

Introduction

A recent study from the Bureau of Justice Statistics reports that at the end of 1995, almost 3.8 million adult men and women were on probation or parole nationwide. This reflects a 3.2 percent increase since 1990. In fiscal year 1997, of approximately 44,000 adults on probation in Arizona more than 6,000 were on probation in Pima County. According to information gathered during probation presentence investigations in Pima County, more than 43 percent of defendants had not completed high school or obtained a General Equivalency Diploma (GED). These offenders were without the academic skills needed to help avoid future criminal behavior.

The Adult Probation LEARN (Literacy, Education, and Reading Network) program provides a broad spectrum of in-house educational programming for adult probationers, their families, and other adult at-risk members of the community. The program's primary purpose is to provide offenders with academic and social skills that will facilitate their reentry into the community as contributing citizens.

Classes in the LEARN program emphasize improving literacy levels, earning a GED, improving English proficiency, and training in parenting and other life skills. The program is funded through collaborative efforts from the Adult Probation Department, the Arizona Department of Education, and the Department of Economic Security.

LEARN has been providing adult education services for more than nine years. To date, 1,100 students have earned their GEDs, more than 300 have completed the literacy program, and 350 have improved their English proficiency.

Program Development and Implementation

The first LEARN lab was established in March 1988 at the Intensive Probation Supervision office in Tucson. The lab was part of a pilot project established by the administrative office of the courts and was one of six pilot sites in the state. Initially, the Principle of the Alphabet Literacy System (PALS) was the only instruction offered. Within six months, adult basic education and GED classes also were being provided, as a result of a collaboration between the probation department and Pima County Adult Education.

As the department expanded and the need for services increased, a second lab was added in January 1990 at the east probation office. Partnerships then were formed with the Arizona Department of Education, through its Adult Education Division, which continues to fund additional services in adult basic education and GED preparation.

The start of a five-year partnership between the probation department and the Arizona Department of Economic Security began in January 1992. This partnership provided services to welfare clients in the Jobs, Opportunities, and Basic Skills Program (JOBS).

In December 1993, the probation LEARN labs began instruction in English for Speakers of Other Languages (ESOL). Currently, ESOL classes are being conducted in the west and south LEARN labs. The newest LEARN lab, which opened in June 1994 at the south office, also provides literacy, adult basic education, and GED instruction. Today, three LEARN labs serve more than 1,200 students annually. A broad range of programming is provided by certified adult education instructors, support specialists, and volunteers.

LEARN uses a computerized management system that provides an individualized learning environment. During the enrollment process, a student is interviewed and given a series of adult education proficiency tests designed to establish a first-through-twelfth grade level of competence in reading, mathematics, and language skills. Based upon this assessment, the student and instructor establish an objective plan of study. The student is reevaluated after thirty hours of attendance. The degree of progress determines a student's subsequent placement in a higher level of study. The small percentage of students who enroll and immediately test into the GED level are scheduled for immediate GED testing.

Literacy instruction is provided to any student whose reading comprehension level fails to meet a sixth-grade standard of proficiency. Instruction establishes foundational skills in both reading and writing by using materials pertinent to the workplace and daily-living needs.

The Adult Basic Education (ABE) curriculum emphasizes improved reading comprehension. It also includes instruction designed to increase mathematics and writing proficiency to a sixth-through-ninth grade level.

The GED curriculum is equivalent to a tenth-through-twelfth grade level of learning. It includes instruction in writing skills; the comprehension and analysis of materials in social studies, science, and literature; and the skills required to solve problems and appropriately apply mathematical concepts.

Life skills instruction provides students with information that supplements their academic studies and positively impacts on their ability to function independently in the community. These classes include instruction on parenting, budgeting, being job ready, being AIDS aware, preparing taxes, preparing for college, and functioning in other areas. Classes are taught by community agencies and by the probation staff.

The ESOL program emphasizes survival English for the beginning student and life skills, job readiness, and pre-GED preparation. Group classes consist of communicative activities designed to develop the students' listening, speaking, reading, and writing abilities. A variety of textbooks, real-life objects, and teacher-produced materials are used in the classroom. Three levels of ESOL instruction are provided.

LEARN labs are open Monday through Thursday, with classes offered mornings and evenings at all locations. In addition, once a month, Pima Community College offers GED testing at one of the LEARN locations.

Most students in the program attend classes four hours each week. However, because of the variety of educational programming offered, students have the option of attending class up to twenty hours weekly. Students determine their schedules based on their program of instruction as well as recommendations from education and probation staff.

Program Staff

LEARN is staffed by eight certified adult-education instructors and three probation support specialists. As employees of the court, LEARN staff are required to receive sixteen hours of court-approved training annually. This includes specialized training in correctional and adult education and on mandated court requirements. In addition to workshop and conference attendance, LEARN staff present workshops at state and national conferences and are involved in community and state literacy and in correctional education associations.

Results

LEARN refutes the notion that "nothing works" in the criminal justice system. A comprehensive evaluation of LEARN demonstrated that probationers who complete the program are much less likely to commit new crimes. A study conducted in 1993 found that participation in and completion of the literacy or GED program significantly increased the probability of the successful completion of probation. More importantly, follow-up studies revealed that offenders who complete LEARN have significantly lower reoffending rates.

The Bureau of Justice Statistics reports that on a national level, 43 percent of probationers committed new crimes. However, the reoffending rate for the literacy and GED graduates of LEARN was 35 percent and 24 percent, respectively, a level far below the national average, according to a study in *Perspectives*, Winter 1994 and the *Yearbook of Correctional Education 1995-1997*. This five-year follow up on recidivism rates was completed in June 1997.

Part I of this research study demonstrated the following:

- Literacy graduates showed higher successful probation completion rates (69 percent) than the control group (47 percent) or dropouts of the program (42 percent).

- GED graduates had a higher successful probation completion rate (77 percent) compared to the control group (47 percent) and dropouts (42 percent).

Part II of this study concerned success after probation. It measured trends on probationers' recidivism rates over a five-year period. The findings demonstrate consistent trends in lower rates of new felony arrests and convictions for program graduates:

- Literacy graduates had consistently lower arrest (35 percent) and conviction rates (20 percent) as compared to the control group (46 percent and 21 percent).

- GED graduates consistently had lower new felony arrest rates (24 percent) compared to the control group (46 percent).

A second study was conducted in 1997 and examined the program's impact on probationers' employment rates, and the successful completion of probation. The outcomes of this study demonstrated:

- GED graduates who were eighteen to twenty-five years old had a higher probation completion rates than either the control group or program dropouts.

- GED graduates who were eighteen to twenty-five years old, and Hispanic, showed higher employment rates during the postprogram period.

- GED graduates showed higher job-retention rates than the control group or program dropouts.

The positive findings of these studies support the argument that ordering completion of a GED or literacy program as a condition of probation is a powerful tool to increase probationers' prosocial behavior.

Program Recognition and Replication

LEARN has received national recognition for its work with adult probationers. The Office of Correctional Education in Washington, D.C. now recognizes probation programs as a part of the correctional education continuum. Previously, all federal funding for correctional education went to institutional programs. LEARN's efforts helped change this practice, leading to new grants for community-based educational programs. On a local level, several private organizations and the local community college responded to the positive impact of LEARN by offering scholarships and other services for graduates of the program.

LEARN has been replicated in several states. Oregon, Florida, Texas, and New York have similar education programs for probationers. Additionally, Indiana, California, and Delaware have sent probation representatives to Tucson to visit the program with plans to initiate similar services in their states.

Conclusion

The success of the program itself, driven by an unfailing belief in the value of the program, has been the key to overcoming obstacles in its implementation. The local judiciary and probation department administration, including the chief justice of the state supreme court, provide strong support. Probation officers, educators, and volunteers are dedicated to providing the best services possible.

Over the course of the program's history, staff have learned several lessons. When implementing any type of program, it is imperative to develop an evaluation component at the onset of the program. Outcome data are crucial to the program's survival and improvement.

Support from the local judiciary and agency staff is essential for program referrals and success. Marketing the program and its outcomes will help facilitate ongoing support.

Finally, funding for programs always is challenging. Using creative sources, such as community, business, and corporate sponsors may be a way for many programs to survive. Promoting probation success in the community helps promote the department's mission, and educates the public about the benefits of community supervision.

LEARN staff always have believed that creative education services lead to positive changes in adult-offender behavior. While critics of rehabilitative programs continue to posit that "nothing works," this program and its evaluations offer evidence of its effectiveness as a means of enhancing the likelihood that adult offenders will complete probation successfully and thereby reduce the likelihood of repeated involvement in the criminal justice system.

Contact:

Gayle Siegel
Program Manager
Adult Probation Department of the Superior Court in Pima County

Superior Court Building
8th Floor, 110 West Congress
Tucson, Arizona 85713
(520) 740-3800

Mobile Intervention Supervision Team

Introduction

High-risk offenders need intensive supervision in the community. It is essential that the offender maintain contact with a community corrections officer who can identify dangerous patterns and intervene, when necessary. As support systems are developed within the community and the family, there will be less need for community supervision. Community placement was developed to fill this need for certain violent sexual and drug offenders who were committed after July 1, 1988.

Traditionally, supervision through the Washington State Department of Corrections has been accomplished by having offenders report to field offices. However, this approach has not always worked well. One of the more difficult aspects of monitoring offenders has been getting them to report to the field office when directed to do so. Moreover, even with regular office visits, this contact has not been enough to help a large number of these offenders stay out of trouble.

Statistical data show that offender recidivism is at its highest within the first year of release from prison. To address this alarming trend, the department has implemented an innovative solution that frees community corrections officers from their offices. This approach allows them to spend the majority of their time in the neighborhoods of the offenders they supervise.

The new initiative is referred to as MIST: the Mobile Intervention Supervision Team. MIST is a community corrections field office currently located in Seattle, Washington. MIST's focus is that of providing intensive supervision of high-risk offenders after their release from prison. The program supervises only those offenders ordered to community placement by the court at the time of their sentencing. Each of the offenders released to MIST for a supervision term of one-to-two years is released under strict conditions of supervision, usually including prohibitions against drug use and contact with victims, and requirements for completion of any treatment that is ordered. In addition, offenders must be employed, in school, or perform community service hours.

Development and Design

The staff in the northeast Washington Division of Community Corrections created a pilot program, called MIST, in June of 1994. MIST was unique because it created a mobile, self-directed work team. By forgoing the traditional setting of individual offices and working from their cars, MIST's community officers would have greater access to information. They could build relationships with the offenders, their families, their employers, businesses, service providers, and local law enforcement agencies. They could be the bridge that would help the offender build the support system that would continue after supervision expired.

MIST also was designed to pilot the concept of management by a self-directed work team. The idea of a self-directed work team comes from the principles of Total Quality Management. MIST would become the first self-directed work team in the public sector in the State of Washington.

The MIST unit was allocated a supervisor, nine community correctional officers (one of whom was also a part-time trainer), and three support staff. Equipment for the program was allocated gradually. By the end of the first year, staff had four passenger vehicles (one with a shield to be used in arrests), three laptop computers, and five cellular phones. Later, a step van was purchased and refurbished for a mobile office. The base office was small, fashioned much like a police precinct, and provided five work stations on a first-come first-serve basis. As the emphasis was on being mobile, the MIST office had less than one-third of the square footage of a traditional field office.

No additional legislation was required to implement the program, as MIST would operate under the same guidelines as other field offices, nor was any additional funding needed. As with all division field offices, MIST was funded through the department of corrections. There was no special equipment needed for this project other than the fact that MIST received laptops earlier than some of the traditional nonmobile units.

As in most new programs, some training was needed. The supervisor of the MIST team hired community corrections officers from other field offices, which made it unnecessary to do any additional corrections training. However, the team spent several all-day meetings learning the methods and concepts of self-directed work teams.

As a self-directed work team, the line staff would decide how everyday business would be done. They would have the responsibility to plan, implement, and control work processes. They would be responsible for providing quality service to their customers (offenders, other agencies, and the community). The day-to-day operation of the MIST self-directed work team is guided by the principle that if something affects the team, it must be brought to the team for discussion and development of a consensus-driven resolution.

The MIST staff built a mission statement, learned to govern themselves by consensus, and developed a list of critical success factors. The original vision was abbreviated some months later to read: "MIST is dedicated to providing opportunities for positive growth and safer communities."

The members of MIST made the decision to supervise offenders in teams of two. The mini-teams would share a caseload rather than the traditional supervision approach of one officer to one caseload. MIST found this increased offender accountability and provided for more intensive supervision than could be achieved by one officer alone. Case management is enhanced by the many diverse backgrounds and observations of the officers supervising the case.

Since MIST is a community-based program, the officers spend the majority of their time out in the field and rotate daily as the duty officer at their home office. Through this arrangement, a staff member is always in the office to maintain communication with the teams in the field, and the teams are able to provide the needed intensive supervision to high-risk offenders.

Implementation

MIST supervises offenders over a wide geographical area. This, by itself, demanded that the officers become more efficient in the way they planned their days. The officers looked for alternative work sites where they might be able to work other than the home office. They found several sites, also referred to as outstations, within local police precincts and a local housing project. They also received approval to work out of other department of corrections' field offices in the area. This not only made it more convenient for offenders to report, it also enhanced the officers' contacts in the community.

Freed from the necessity of spending many hours in the home office, the officers used their laptops teamed with cellular modems to prepare reports and access the various databases and e-mail from virtually everywhere. They no longer routinely commuted back to the office after spending the morning in the field. Instead, they found a convenient location, dialed up their computer, and went to work. They maintained vital communication with their home office via their cell phones or through e-mail using their laptops.

As the officers spent more time in the field, they looked for more effective ways to work with the offenders who still reported to the home office. MIST began to seek out more effective ways they could supervise offenders in the field and in the office—simultaneously. They expanded the scope of the duty officer's responsibilities. The duty officer became more of a dispatch officer relaying vital information through cellular phones and e-mail.

MIST officers looked further for other resources that not only would save money, and provide for more effective supervision, but avoid duplication of services. Several life skills groups such as Moral Reconation Therapy, a Victim Awareness Education Program, Transitional Resources and Community Empowerment, Helping Offenders Pursue Excellence, and other groups were held for offenders under supervision. They talked with the local employment security office and escorted offenders through the process of applying for jobs.

When offenders did not comply with conditions of their release, the MIST officers considered alternative sanctions. Alternative sanctions are those sanctions whereby an offender performs some designated task in lieu of incarceration. Given prison and jail crowding, the MIST officers looked for creative alternative sanctions that would save money, free jail beds, and provide a positive response to the offender for failure to maintain compliance with court-ordered conditions. MIST has offered sanctions ranging from attending treatment, enrolling in classes, and performing community service hours. One such sanction consisted of the offender writing a rap song against drugs for a local school.

MIST formed several partnerships with local law enforcement agencies to increase the officers' contact with offenders. Community corrections officers conducted training of police officers to be community monitors to assist in the surveillance of high-profile offenders after hours. This partnership has increased accountability for the offender, providing additional information during the hours community corrections officers normally do not work. Police officers conduct random home visits and curfew checks on high-risk offenders.

A community service program that grew out of MIST provides opportunities for offenders to complete their community service hours. The program (Washington Offenders Repaying Communities) also gives some offenders their first real taste of legitimate employment. Through the expectations of the program, offenders learn discipline, the work ethic, communication skills, and for some, employment skills. They learn how to take directions and accept personal responsibility. Lastly, it provides a vehicle where offenders of few skills can stay in compliance with the court order requiring employment, school attendance, or completion of service hours weekly. The department received the Rainier Chamber of Commerce Presidents' Award because of the community service hours program.

Outcomes

- MIST officers personally have trained more than 100 police officers from four agencies to assist in the monitoring of offenders during curfew hours.

- Through the partnerships developed with four local law enforcement agencies serving as community monitors, an average of fifty MIST offenders are being monitored by police officers at any given time.

- Between September 1996 and June 1997, MIST had 2,261 offenders, of which 1,610 were available for prosocial activities (such as employment, life skill classes, and job search). Seventy-seven percent of the 1,610 offenders were involved in thirty-two hours or more of prosocial activities per week during this time period.

- The use of alternative sanctions has saved more than one-half million dollars in jail beds. In a one year time period, MIST officers conducted 358 hearings. Of those hearings, 219 offenders were given alternative sanctions. A conservative estimate of jail beds saved, calculated at ten days saved per hearing, equals 2,190 days saved in one year. This number multiplied by $100 per day for a jail bed (a conservative estimate) equals $219,000 savings in a one-year period. In a two-year period, this would save $440,000. MIST has been in business for three years.

- In recognition of its creativity, the MIST program has won the 1995 Council of State Governments' Innovations Award and received the 1996 Washington State "Outstanding Public Service Award." Governor Lowry met with the MIST team and presented them with a certificate of appreciation for their efforts to improve the monitoring of offenders, thus ensuring the safety and well being of the parole officers, and their community.

Conclusion

On Being Mobile

The more interaction community supervision officers have with offenders, their families, treatment providers, and employers, the more familiar the officers become with the offender. They then are positioned to recognize those warning signs before something happens. Early intervention reduces the likelihood of recidivism and keeps offenders out of prison, which saves money for taxpayers, and helps keep community supervised offenders from crowding state prisons.

On Working as a Team

Forming a self-directed work team that is also a pilot for mobile supervision is not without its costs. The mobile work almost always should be considered synonymous with change. A pilot program also has "change" as its byword. This change initially produces a state much like chaos, seemingly nondirectional where new ideas are examined, adopted, and discarded in an almost bewildering kaleidoscope of confusion. And then, suddenly, there is cohesion. It all starts to gel. A wonderful sense of pride bonds the survivors together. They gather the strength and experience to attack yet another obstacle. Unless staff can develop a team spirit that brings them together during the chaotic times, being part of a self-directed work team can be very uncomfortable.

There are many details that must be handled on a daily basis. These details are what a self-directed work team manages. But as the MIST team frequently has found to their dismay, concentrating too much on the details and not enough on the process of working together as a team, can result in conflict and hard feelings. Frequent times of team building are essential to function as any type of a team, especially a team with a variety of functions.

Training in conflict negotiation is essential along with diversity training. Staff need to learn to value each other's strengths and differences. This has become a 1990s byword found in newspapers and magazine articles. Yet, despite the repetition, it is no less valuable. If a team's differences become a forum where every member tries to convince the other member to be more like him or her, new and creative solutions come to a halt. In making decisions, the majority cannot rule; instead, team consensus becomes the governing force. Team members need to be able to give up their individual preferences for the good of the team. This becomes a matter of looking at values and ethics rather than individual preferences.

By operating as a self-directed work team, staff feel empowered to provide input and make decisions for the best of the team. A result of empowerment is high motivation from staff. They enjoy coming to work—to give input, and to strive to make a difference in the world of corrections via the offender, the department, and the community.

Contact:

Tami J. Kampbell
Community Corrections Officer III
Division of Community Corrections
Washington State Department of Corrections

3600 S. Graham Street
Seattle, Washington 98118
(206) 760-2367

Improved Methods for Managing Probation and Parole Violations

Introduction

In South Carolina, all adult offenders placed on probation or parole (presently, this population is about 41,000) are supervised by the South Carolina Department of Probation, Parole and Pardon Services. Throughout the 1980s, there was a continuing rise in the offender population under supervision in the community, and a significant increase in the number of offenders who were having their probation or parole revoked.

Aside from figures telling staff how many offenders were being revoked, the department had little systematic information regarding the forces that were driving this increase in revocations. The existing policies placed considerable responsibility on probation and parole agents to identify violations of the conditions of supervision. The responsibility then was placed with the courts and the parole board to make determinations concerning these violations. By 1989, it was determined that a comprehensive review of the department's actions and policies in this area was needed.

Development and Design

With considerable assistance from the National Institute of Corrections, the Center for Effective Public Policy, and the Cosmos Corporation, management staff began their efforts in this area by assembling a team of employees from many levels of the department. First, steps were taken to understand the existing system, and the outcomes associated with the actions of those involved. They began by constructing a flow chart of the process of current violations. They then gathered information about the outcomes occurring at each stage of the process.

Staff found that the violations system was fraught with misunderstandings, that the policy objectives lent themselves to several interpretations, that the process was not efficient for staff; and that judges often disagreed with the violation recommendations. To remedy these problems, staff saw the need to undertake several specific improvements:

1. Staff determined that the response to probation and parole violations should reflect the severity of the violation and the risks posed to the community by the particular

offender, and that violation guidelines needed to be developed so that the responses to violations would be appropriate, proportional, and consistent.

2. To better use the department's internal administrative hearing officers, there was a need to empower them so that they could impose community options and various intermediate sanctions. This would eliminate the need to process certain violations further than the traditional probable cause stage.

3. Staff believed that probation and parole agents and their supervisors should be given greater authority to impose various sanctions in response to violations, and that they should become proactively involved in the resolution of violation behaviors.

4. Staff believed that by empowering them, prompt, and appropriate results for violations would be obtained, while this also would save valuable time for staff, judges, and the parole board.

5. By issuing a citation in certain cases, rather than issuing a warrant for the violation, staff could eliminate the need for many offenders to be housed in jails awaiting a disposition of their violation.

6. Finally, staff knew that information would need to be gathered so that the impact and progress of these initiatives could be determined. Methods were established for generating and collecting data for this purpose.

In short, the department set out to determine if it could implement sweeping changes to the violations' system in ways that would be beneficial to staff, the parole board, the courts, the jails, and the prisons.

Implementation

Once procedures were drafted to accomplish these objectives, the violations' team determined that it would be advisable to first try the new methods on a segment of the offender population. This would allow hearing officers, agents, and their supervisors to become familiar with the expectations and their new authority. The parole board, which was advised throughout about the project, was most supportive.

Initial work began with the parole population in approximately one-third of the state's counties in 1989. By 1990, staff were so pleased with the results that modifications were made in the policies, and the new approach to violations was expanded to all parole cases in the state. In 1991, the violation procedures were expanded to probation cases with the cooperation and assistance of judges in two judicial circuits. The expansion of the new approach to violations in all probation cases was completed in 1994.

This gradual expansion over a five-year period allowed staff to receive feedback, and make the necessary modifications to policies and procedures as they gained more information. Further modifications of specific aspects of the new approach are expected as experience dictates.

Outcomes

The impact of the violation system improvements was felt by probation and parole staff, the courts, the parole board, jails, and the department of corrections. Probation and parole staff found that many violations that were relatively minor could be handled effectively by front-line staff. This eliminated the need for these staff to initiate legal processes and to attend hearings, and it resulted in significant time savings for them. Staff also benefitted from having a clearer idea of the department's expectations, and they benefitted from being able to respond more immediately to violations. Several examples of sanctions that now can be imposed by agents and front-line supervisors include: placing the offender in a residential or nonresidential treatment facility; placing the offender in a halfway house for up to sixty days; imposing up-to-forty hours of required public service work; placing certain types of offenders on home detention; or increasing drug testing or reporting.

Courts and the parole board found that about one-half of all violation cases not resolvable at the agent or front-line supervisor level could be disposed of adequately by the administrative hearing officers. For example, last year, approximately 14,000 administrative hearings took place, and about one-half of these cases were disposed of at this hearing. This meant that 7,000 hearings did not have to occur before the courts or the parole board.

The concurrence rate between agents' recommendations in probation and parole violation cases and the outcomes imposed by the courts or the parole board more than doubled. Before this process began, the court or the parole board agreed with agents' recommendations in only about 40 percent of the cases presented. Today, the concurrence rate is over 80 percent. This outcome is especially significant for probation and parole agents who need to maintain credibility both with the offender and with the courts and the parole board. Several examples of sanctions that can be imposed by hearing officers include: placing the offender on intensive supervision; placing the offender on home detention with or without electronic monitoring; ordering the offender to perform up to 300 hours of public service work; and ordering other available community programs or services.

For jails and prisons, the main benefits have to do with the flow of offenders. Because a process was initiated that allowed for a citation instead of a warrant to be used for certain types of violations, there was a reduction of about one-half in the number of offenders who were placed in jail awaiting a violation hearing. Because more than 14,000 violations were processed last year, this meant that more than 6,000 offenders did not have to occupy a jail bed while awaiting a violation disposition. For prisons, the creative use of alternative sanctions allowed for thousands of probationers and parolees to be managed in the community in a manner that was consistent both with the risks posed by the offender and the need for public safety.

Conclusion

The revised approach to the management of probation and parole violators has netted significant advantages to the criminal justice system of the state. The development of violation guidelines, which encouraged consistency and proportionality in the response to violations, the savings of time and energy associated with the revised methods, the reduction of court and board hearings, the development of alternative placements for violators, and the development of a citation process all contributed to a more effective and efficient criminal justice system in South Carolina.

Other benefits perhaps are less visible. The department demonstrated a confidence in its front-line staff, and involved them in solutions to this difficult area. Staff developed consistency in their work and raised awareness about the actual expectations governing the violations process. Finally, by starting out rather small and gradually building its way up, the project allowed for a maximum amount of feedback and experimentation. All of these results have demonstrated the value of the improvements to the management of probation and parole violators.

Other states have been interested in these developments and conclusions. The National Institute of Corrections and the Center for Effective Public Policy, two entities which continue to stimulate and encourage jurisdictions to explore the important violations area, have referred dozens of state and county agencies to the department for information concerning this project. From the feedback received, many of these jurisdictions have used parts of this new approach as they have moved forward with their own initiatives. Although the work invested in this area is substantial, the rewards for staff and the broader criminal justice community have made the collective efforts of many most worthwhile.

Contact:

Richard P. Stroker
Deputy Director for Field Services
South Carolina Department of Probation, Parole, and Pardon Services

P. O. Box 50666
Columbia, South Carolina 29250
(803) 734-9220

Sixth Judicial District Client Services Unit

Introduction

The Client Services Unit of the Sixth Judicial District, Iowa Department of Correctional Services, is an innovative treatment-delivery system that was implemented in 1996. The Sixth Judicial District in Iowa encompasses six counties in the southeast part of the state. This includes one of the larger metropolitan jurisdictions of the state, a university town, a Native American settlement with a thriving casino, and a number of small towns and rural areas.

The Sixth Judicial District provides probation, parole, and residential supervision. In fiscal year 1996, nearly 2,000 clients were admitted to one of these units. Clients entered the system with diverse backgrounds and differing levels of risk and need. The Sixth District had made a strong commitment to implementing effective treatment and supervision strategies with offenders, based on current research. However, there was no centralized system of assessing treatment needs, delivering the various services, or evaluating the programs.

To address these gaps, a Client Services Task Force was developed to provide guidance and recommendations. Its members were recruited from the mental health, substance abuse, and education fields to provide a holistic perspective. The group developed a philosophy statement, which stated, "In partnership with the community, the philosophy of the Department of Correctional Services is to reduce crime and violence by providing offenders with a set of prosocial, anticriminal values and a subsequent belief structure that will replace procriminal, antisocial values." Goals included the incorporation of risk, need, and responsivity principles in providing services, addressing criminogenic needs, using community support systems, and offering program evaluation.

The task force also decided, during the course of its meetings, that the most effective way of meeting its goals was to hire a client-services supervisor to oversee a client-services unit made up of treatment and education specialists. This unit would assess treatment needs, coordinate needed programs both internally and in the community, and gather data for evaluation.

Development and Design

In January 1996, the client-services supervisor was hired. The client services unit consisted of a psychologist, an educator, and two community-treatment coordinators. At that time, the psychologist had been preforming mental health evaluations, the educator had been teaching life skills classes, and each community treatment coordinator had been responsible for a specialized caseload. There had been little coordination of services, and referrals to services had been done through agencies without any assessment process.

The client services unit took several steps immediately. The unit members began meeting on a weekly basis to define needs, set goals, and plan programming. They viewed the implementation of a centralized needs assessment as a top priority, and they developed a life-skills assessment. Referrals to services now were being made according to objective criteria. Agents were instructed to route all normal and high-risk clients through this assessment process to determine treatment plans.

The client services unit redefined treatment services as a continuum that clients could move through during the course of their supervision, as opposed to unrelated segments. The client services unit staff considered community-based resources when formulating a client-treatment plan, rather than confining all treatment options to on-site activities. The client services task force, which had begun as time-limited entity, was expanded to become an advisory board, with ongoing input from community-treatment providers. Finally, client services was redefined as a districtwide undertaking as opposed to separate small programming in each unit or district office.

Implementation

The client services unit currently consists of the supervisor; four community treatment coordinators, two of whom are licensed family therapists; an educator; a psychologist; a community service coordinator; and a community program monitor who facilitates some cognitive groups and coordinates recreational activities for clients. The unit operates by a shared function philosophy as much as possible. This means, for example, that both the community treatment coordinators and the psychologist do assessments, although the psychologist is able to do the more specialized ones. All staff members engage in group or individual services, again with some areas of expertise. The core functions of the client services unit include assessment, program development and delivery, partnership building, data collection, and the development of a treatment and supervision matrix.

All higher risk clients undergo a life-skills assessment done by a member of the client services unit. This includes a Level of Service Inventory (LSI), with corroboration from the presentence investigation, case management classification, and the agent. The clients have an initial screening for the presence of attention deficit disorder and can be tested further, if necessary. The psychologist is able to do IQ testing and is completing certification to administer the Hare Psychopathy Checklist. The psychologist also does mental health evaluations. Since the LSI is a dynamic risk and need measurement tool, it will be used not only for initial placement and identification of treatment needs, but also to measure client change after treatment is completed.

Program development and delivery is also a shared function in the department. Substance abuse services, batterers' education, sex-offender programming, and programming for youthful offenders all are provided, but through different departmental units. The client services unit is responsible for the cognitive-based and life skills curriculum, family therapy and other family services, workforce development, a mentoring program, community service, and building partnerships with other community agencies. The cognitive and life skills curriculum include "Positive Solutions," anger management, financial management, family dynamics, relationship building, social thinking skills, and conflict resolution. A victim empathy curriculum will be implemented soon. These services are available to probation, parole, and residential/work release clients.

Since the client services unit is so new, most of its services have been implemented only in the largest county in the district. Services are being expanded to the other counties. Services are developed and delivered as the result of needs assessments. Since each county has unique populations and needs, it is important to target services accordingly.

Because the clients are so often multineed and high risk, it is very important to use community resources in treatment planning. The community is able to offer specialized and long-term services; most clients are under supervision for twelve-to-eighteen months, and will benefit from community involvement for longer periods of time. Using community resources is also a way to target and replace the antisocial attitudes, values, behaviors, and associated risks that increase the probability of recidivism.

Community involvement offers prosocial skills, peers, and other supports to assist in the intervention process. Several examples of this community partnership include on-site substance abuse treatment for substance abusing offenders; a mental-health referral process involving the psychologist and community mental health agencies; on-site teachers from the school district to provide high school completion; widespread collaboration from education, business, and employment agencies on workforce development; and several partnership efforts with a range of social service agencies to provide comprehensive family services to correctional clients.

The supervision and treatment matrix is an effort to develop a seamless continuum of treatment and sanctions to address client's needs and community safety. It is based on the premises of intermediate sanctions and the risk/need/responsivity principles. When completed, the matrix will assist agents with supervision strategies, revocation decisions, and treatment planning, all based on assessment data. It also will serve as a data collection system, to be used for outcome and performance measurements.

Outcomes

The collection of data is a vital part of the unit's efforts. The client services unit is responsible for collecting and interpreting a variety of data, to assist in needs assessment, and outcome measures. A variety of information has been collected since the inception of the unit. The initial data dealt with client demographics, characteristics, and need, so that appropriate programs could be developed.

An initial area of concern was the number of clients referred to and completing the cognitive/life skills curriculum. With the introduction of a centralized assessment system, referrals to these programs rose 49 percent in fiscal year 1997, the number of clients completing classes increased 74 percent, and the overall completion rate grew from 61 to 71 percent. Client surveys of these classes consistently show high rankings, an interest in taking more classes, and client reports of increased knowledge, skills, and problem-solving abilities. Pre- and posttesting is used in all classes to measure the acquisition of skills and attitude change.

Because this undertaking is still so new, and because all the needed technological supports are not yet in place, long-term outcomes are not yet available. However, with the implementation of LSI retesting, continued pre- and posttesting and the monitoring of revocation rates and other important factors, outcome data can be used to guide future program decisions.

Conclusion

In review, several key factors seem vital to program success:

- Staff with a diverse professional background enrich the program development process.

- Program delivery across settings (for example, work release and probation) appears most efficient.

- Assessment-driven program planning creates more responsive treatment systems.

- Community involvement in treatment planning and the use of community resources enhances the treatment delivery system.

- Client feedback is valuable in measuring success.

- Program evaluation needs to begin immediately. The initial process and input measurements can be used in developing and measuring the longer-term outcomes and results.

Contact:

Barbara McDonald, MSW, CADC
Client Services Supervisor
Iowa Department of Corrections

951 29th Avenue, SW
Cedar Rapids, Iowa 52404
(319) 398-3675

Model for Police-Probation Partnership: Boston's Operation Night Light

Introduction

Probation departments must think strategically about the nature of the crime problem they are facing. Operation Night Light provides an excellent example of proactive responses to the increasing risk profile of those on probation.

—Donald Cochran
Commissioner of Probation for the Commonwealth of Massachusetts

Our mission is prevention of crime and fear of crime in our neighborhoods. To achieve it, we seek to work in new ways with partners from across the spectrum of the community and various institutional stakeholders. This project is significant also because it involves an innovation created by first-line officers and their peers. By working in partnership with the probation department, we are tailoring tactics down to the level of the individual offender who is most likely to be the next offender or the next victim. Night Light represents the future of public safety and criminal justice in Boston.

—Paul F. Evans
Police Commissioner, Boston Police Department

Operation Night Light is a partnership between police and probation that provides the court with a tool to enforce the terms of probation in a meaningful fashion. A simple way to capture the innovation is to note that Night Light has police engaging in community corrections and probation officers addressing community problems while probation officers remain probation officers and cops remain cops.

Night Light is driven by knowledge acquired by practitioners. The project developed from a collaboration in 1992 between probation officers in the Dorchester District Court and Boston police officers in the Anti-Gang Violence Unit. They rethought their mission and strategy as a consequence of their frustrations on the street. Their success and innovation were recognized and pushed forward by executives in both police and probation. The recognition led to the establishment of Night Light as a formal partnership between the Boston Police Department and the Office of the Commissioner of Probation for Massachusetts.

Night Light is now a central tactic in Boston's multijurisdictional, highly collaborative strategy to deter and prevent youth gang firearm violence. In addition, a dozen other probation jurisdictions throughout Massachusetts have implemented similar programs.

As a unique program, Night Light has garnered a great deal of attention from both the media in terms of favorable coverage and from the U.S. Department of Justice in terms of inquiries and site visits, including a face-to-face discussion with Attorney General Janet Reno, at the Dorchester site.

Operation Night Light is on the way to becoming a standard feature in probation practice. Aggregate crime data from the impacted areas, and anecdotal reports from officers and offenders alike, indicate that the program is working. With newly obtained grant support, data gathering began in the summer of 1995 by researchers from Northeastern University aimed at developing a more precise picture of the impact of Night Light.

Problem Statement

Communities across the country are experiencing a worrisome surge of serious violence committed by juveniles, reflected in a growing rate of homicides committed by teenagers. In the face of this disturbing trend, these same communities have been searching for policies that will stem this bloody tide. The problem becomes more urgent in the face of predictions from Professor James Fox of Northeastern University, among others, who foresees a major increase in juvenile violence occurring by the end of the decade due to demographic imperatives.

In their search for weapons to employ to decrease violence, some communities have implemented or considered citywide curfews. The notion is that by prohibiting teenagers from being on city streets during evening hours, a deterrent effect on juvenile violence will occur.

The turn toward curfews is understandable, and the early results, though questioned by some, seem encouraging. But there are some potential difficulties that a *targeted* curfew program such as Boston's Operation Night Light can overcome. General curfews, by blanketing all juveniles, can strain the resources of the local police in the process of stopping, questioning, and detaining a large number of juveniles. Secondly, in the process of targeting all youth, those who are engaged in positive, constructive, or at least harmless activities will be stopped, creating frustration on all sides. Lastly, if only a certain segment of youth (for example, those identified as potential or suspected trouble-makers) have curfews enforced against them, charges of discrimination or harassment inevitably will follow.

Operation Night Light has proven to be a sensible and workable form of a targeted curfew. By restricting enforcement to *convicted* juveniles and young adults, the enforcement task becomes manageable and the complaints about harassment essentially disappear.

Impact

What difference have the more than 5,000 Night Light contacts (for example, home visits and street contacts) made in the last three and one-half years? While direct impact is notoriously difficult to prove, the trends in the impacted areas, in terms of declining rates of homicide and other violent crimes, are encouraging. To point to some recent data, there have been no juvenile homicides involving firearms in the impacted areas since August of 1995. Data document a decline in assaults and homicides during the period in which Night Light has operated.

While no one involved with Night Light feels this positive trend is primarily attributable to Night Light, the staff involved strongly believe that compliance with probation and lessened levels of gang-related violence at least partially are attributable to the efforts of the

Night Light program. In addition, court personnel believe that probationary sentences have gained a new and enhanced credibility due to the stricter enforcement of key conditions that Night Light provides. It is clear now as it has not always been in the past—the word is on the street, so to speak—that those on probation must take their obligations seriously or they will be detected in not doing so and consequences will ensue.

There is also the hard-to-measure, but real reassurance that comes to those neighborhoods where Night Light takes place. The knowledge that probation officers are around with the police ensuring that probationers are off the streets in the evening brings a measure of relief to hard-hit communities. It is also very clear that the parents of these young people, who are often in a losing battle to keep their sons from responding to the lure of the streets, genuinely appreciate the support they receive through curfew enforcement. While this program is designed primarily to deter these young offenders from committing any new crimes, their parents recognize that it also serves to keep these same young people from being victimized themselves in the mortal combat that envelops their streets.

Obstacles

While all the staff involved in Night Light—police and probation alike—express a certain amazement at how easily the program was implemented and, even more, how much positive attention it has received both locally and nationally, candor requires discussion of both real and potential obstacles.

First, not all staff support such an approach. Officers in both agencies have questioned the wisdom of the partnership, and some of those have expressed a degree of resentment at the attention the program has received. This resistance puts a limit on the potential scope of the effort. It also must be said that not all officers are well-suited for this work. Entering the homes of citizens in the evening in a law-enforcement capacity is a delicate operation at best and only should be undertaken by officers whose interpersonal skills are well developed and whose respect for all parties involved is high.

What might have been a major obstacle—opposition to or at least skepticism from community leaders—did not emerge to any great degree. This good fortune was a product of the positive reputation of new staff among local leaders and the critical alliance with the 10 Point Coalition. Here again, the choice of officers and their personal philosophies—a mix of professionalism and support for progressive initiatives—helped eliminate any substantial friction.

A supportive judiciary is a key component. Without at least a nucleus of judges who both impose appropriate conditions and then enforce them when probation officers initiate revocation proceedings, the program would collapse. In one of the participating courts, the judges have not been so enamored of curfews for the older youthful offenders, though that department has been able to use Night Light for evening home visits, which have contained their own deterrent power, as well as for warrant apprehension.

Training to support Night Light has resulted in a three-day standardized officer safety training program rather than cobbled-together seminars, which had been the practice earlier on in the program.

Conclusion

Since its inception in Dorchester in late 1992, a total of fifteen additional courts, including four additional Boston courts, have adopted the Night Light model, with variations in some jurisdictions. In addition to the Massachusetts experience, Wisconsin and Washington State have pioneered similar efforts, referred to in some instances as "beat probation."

Indeed, a leading criminal justice text, Clear and Cole's *American Corrections*, contains the following statement:

> Another new special program is to pair the probation officer more closely with the street police officers. Officers who work in tandem with the police are often given caseloads of especially tough probationers. The special police liaison makes for more effective searches and arrests and allows probation to take advantage of information available to the police about probationers.

A recent report on the Washington experience, published in the *Community Corrections Reporter*, suggests a very positive record to date.

Jurisdictions which would seek to undertake a police-probation partnership comparable to Night Light first must ensure that: (1) the need is critical, in terms of serious juvenile crime, which, in turn, will support this intrusive, high-profile program; (2) there is a preexisting positive relationship with local law enforcement, which will be critical to sustain the close working relationship; (3) that judicial support will be forthcoming; and (4) that community resistance is not anticipated.

If these conditions can be met, the potential gains are great. Two recent and major critiques of probation have pointed, from different perspectives, to the weakness of contemporary probation practice in dealing with high-risk offenders. The charges are largely warranted. If probation is to counter these criticisms effectively and reclaim a currently eroding base of public support, it will be through programs such as Night Light. Operation Night Light has a proven record and resonates with opinion leaders and the media anxious for strategies more equal to the challenges of law enforcement in the task of working effectively with the probationer of the 1990s.

Authors:

Bernard L. Fitzgerald
Chief Probation Officer
Dorchester District Court
Dorchester, Massachusetts

James Jordan
Director of Strategic Planning and Resource Development
Boston Police Department
Boston, Massachusetts

Author/Contact:

Ronald P. Corbett, Jr.
Deputy Commissioner
Field Services Division, Office of the Commissioner of Probation
Boston Massachusetts

Room 405, One Ashburton Place
Boston, Massachusetts 02108-1612
(617) 727-5300

Community Corrections—Nonresidential
Additional Program Entries

Metropolitan Day Reporting Center

Elizabeth L. Curtin, Deputy Director
Crime and Justice Foundation
Suite 202, 95 Berkeley St., Boston, Massachusetts 02116
(617) 426-9800

In the 1980s, the Crime and Justice Foundation introduced the concept of day reporting, a correctional alternative that exercises control of offenders through attendance requirements, home confinement, and frequent monitoring, and provides treatment, education, and employment opportunities through a range of services. In partnership with the Boston Penal Institutions Commissioner, the Middlesex County Sheriff, and the Suffolk County Sheriff, the Crime and Justice Foundation designed and implemented the Metropolitan Day Reporting Center in 1987, which has served close to 2,000 clients since that time. There is also a cognitive-development component to the program, which focuses on the problem-solving capabilities of offenders by teaching them how to think before acting and by presenting techniques for effective and successful resolution of social and interpersonal problems. In addition, the Metropolitan Day Reporting Center teaches job search tactics, employment readiness, violence prevention, and health and hygiene issues. The Metropolitan Day Reporting Center has received many requests for information from around the country and from a variety of interests—probation, police, universities, nonprofit organizations, sheriffs, departments of correction, and others. There are now well over 100-day reporting centers in half of the states in the country.

Public Service Work Crew Partnerships

Thomas R. Gillam, Community Corrections Specialist
Washington State Department of Corrections
851 Poplar Pl. South, Seattle, Washington 98144
(206) 726-6719

Washington State Department of Corrections' Office of Correctional Operations, in partnership with other governmental agencies, has mobilized several offender work crews, which perform cost-effective and productive work for the community. These crews are composed of offenders released from jail under electronic home detention and from correctional caseloads in the community. Under existing law, each eight-hour day of unpaid work reduces the use of jail by one day. The Office of Correctional Operations provides crew supervision, administrative oversight, record keeping, industrial insurance for the workers, and sometimes the vehicle. The fees that are paid by participating agencies provide financial support for the correctional officers, tools, equipment, and supplies. These public service work crew partnerships have created numerous benefits for the community and for offenders including: reduction in use of limited and expensive jail space; creation of an intermediate sanction for offenders; creation of a community service work site for hard-to-place offenders; work experience for offenders; cost-effective conversion of jail time to productive work; and provision of no-cost services to the community. In addition, offenders have responded positively to the opportunity to make a contribution to their community in lieu of spending time in jail. They learn to work as a team, to follow rules of conduct and safety, and often to take pride in the fact that they were able to give something back to an appreciative community.

Community Programming: Living Skills and Personal Development Programs

Lynn Stewart, Ph.D., Manager, Living Skills and Personal Development Programs
Correctional Service of Canada
330 Keele St., Toronto, Ontario M6P 2K7
(416) 952-6497

Correctional Service of Canada has developed nationally implemented programs that address a range of needs associated with criminal behavior. The Living Skills programs provide a menu of programs that apply a cognitive-behavioral approach. The base program, Cognitive Living Skills, teaches problem solving, critical-reasoning, and interpersonal perspectives in thirty-six sessions. There is also a ten-session "booster" program derived from the longer program that is better suited for some community settings. Anger and Other Emotional Management is a twenty-five-session program that addresses problematic behavior associated with poor control over anger and other emotions. Living Without Family Violence is a ten-session awareness program for offenders who are at risk of being violent in their intimate relationships. The seventeen-session Parenting program provides male and female offenders and their partners with basic information on child development and how and when to access a broader range of services in the community. The Community Integration program is for recently released offenders who need information on how to better function in the community. Leisure Education, a ten-session program to make offenders aware of the significance of planned leisure in promoting prosocial behavior, is designed to be congenial to community delivery. CounterPoint, a twenty-session program, addresses the criminal values that support a procriminal lifestyle. In the substance abuse treatment area, the CHOICES program is a well-established short-term, moderate-intensity program with longer-term relapse prevention follow-up.

Correctional Education

5

Introduction

The Correctional Education Committee met at the American Correctional Association Congress in Orlando and again at the Winter Conference in San Antonio to make its selections for the Best Practices in Correctional Education. The committee received thirty submissions representing a wide range of programs for their review. American Correctional Association staff had assured us in advance that they anticipated that some of our own committee members might be among the authors, and they applauded that fact.

To ascertain fairness of choice, we designed a ranking form, which included a list of criteria and a scale of one to five. With the exception of committee members who had authored a submission, each member read every submission, including any supporting documentation attached by the sender. Committee members then completed a form for each. After the proposals were read and scored, a noncommittee member totaled the scores, divided the sum by the number of readers for each, and ranked them in order of the resulting scores. The instrument and process made a potentially difficult selection effort proceed smoothly and objectively.

The criteria items were as follows: (1) the program model was unique and innovative, (2) the program model included an evaluative component to measure its stated goals, (3) the program model could be replicated or generalized in another setting, and (4) the program model promoted advancement.

Submissions were judged only against each other. No attempt was made to distribute the winners evenly among various fields—juvenile, adult, state, federal, academic, or vocational. The opportunity to replicate selections in a general or specific manner should make the submissions that follow valuable to the many areas of correctional education.

All thirty of the submissions are worthy programs. If one were able to read and replicate only the goals of ANY of these authors, it would be of great inspiration and value. The committee was encouraged by the variety, the creativity, and by the obvious dedication of all of these authors, and the many practitioners in the programs they represent. They all speak well of the fine work that is done in our profession—nationwide. Many of the submissions were from the Federal Bureau of Prisons. Submissions from this agency included a wide variety of creative programs.

The program receiving our highest ranking was implemented over a decade ago and continues to be unique in Maryland and in the country. It is the model for peer tutoring in prison education.

The number two ranking went to the State of Illinois for a program that encourages job skills and employability skills both on the inside and in follow-up centers after release. Again, proponents praise this program and say it works!

The next three programs are all exemplary, as well. Nebraska has implemented a life skills program that helps prisoners acquire the skills and education necessary to fulfill their goals and objectives so there is a successful transition back into society and the workplace. For example, a HERO Skills for Life class provides inmates with positive skills and techniques for handling difficult interpersonal situations through the use of decision-making techniques and communication skills, prosocial behavior, and techniques to strengthen leadership and work relationships.

In Pennsylvania, Operation Outreach, Inc. was formed in 1973 around the truth given to aspiring entrepreneurs: "Find a need and fill it." Operation Outreach's founders identified two areas of need: the overwhelming inmate necessity to be trained in marketable skills and the shortage of affordable construction services for low-income homeowners and agencies serving this population. With the more than 1,547 inmates who have completed the program, 980 of them have obtained employment. More than 1,051 projects have been completed.

The Plainfield Correctional Facility of the Indiana Department of Correction has developed an interdisciplinary instruction program for its literacy-level classes. This has resulted not only in greater achievement for students but in greater satisfaction of the staff.

These top five of our best practices are explained in greater detail in this chapter.

Committee chair:

Diana Kim
Instructor
New Mexico State Penitentiary
Education Department

P. O. Box 109
Santa Fe, New Mexico 87504-1059
(505) 827-8550 x8336

The Correctional Education Program: Peer Tutoring

Introduction

A Brief History of Peer Tutoring

The correctional education program of the Maryland State Department of Education long ago recognized that the adult inmate population had significant numbers of illiterate and learning disabled students. In the early 1980s, the correctional education program began increasing its capability to reach the large numbers of illiterate and barely literate inmates by launching an inmate tutoring program called "Peer Tutoring." The program received national recognition from both the National Institute of Corrections (as one of the top ten adult correctional literacy programs in the United States) and the basis of a national survey of adult correctional education programs based on visits to the most promising sites.

In 1989, the Correctional Education Association and Project Literacy U.S. (ABC-TV and WQED-TV) conducted a study, *Literacy Behind Bars: Selected Education Programs for Juvenile, Jail and Prison Facilities* and, once again, two of the Maryland's Peer Tutoring program sites were nominated among the top ten adult correctional literacy programs in the nation. In 1991, the U.S. Department of Education recognized the excellent quality of the program by giving it the "Secretary's Award for Outstanding Adult Education and Literacy Programs," in a competition that looked at programs in both correctional and general adult education settings.

Since its very inception, the central focus of the peer tutoring program has been that trained inmate tutors can make a significant contribution to the correctional education program while working under the supervision of full-time trained adult basic education teachers in the regular school program. At first, the concept of inmates actually tutoring other inmates caused some consternation among correctional security officials. While the concern proved to be unfounded, it was thought that certain inmates would use their positions as tutors to gain control over their students. In actuality, the experience has been very positive. The tutors learn what it means to help someone and gain almost as much from the experience as their students.

Once the National Institute of Corrections identified the peer tutoring program as a model, the adult facilities in Maryland, which did not have a program, began to clamor for a peer tutoring program. In fact, the Maryland Commissioner of Corrections, Arnold Hopkins, nominated the literacy staff as his "Employees of the Year" in 1987 for the Excellence in Public Service Award in recognition of their contribution not only to public safety, but also to institutional management and inmate morale. This distinction was unique because the teachers and education staff are actually employees of the Maryland State Department of Education, not the Division of Correction, a fact which underlies the impact the Peer Tutoring Programming has on the atmosphere in the state prisons.

The peer tutoring instructional concept derives from a Right to Read grant given to the Johns Hopkins University Reading Center in 1980. The federal Right to Read grant targeted adult education sites for training. Correctional institutions were added as an afterthought. When the Johns Hopkins staff showed up at the Maryland House of Correction to train inmate volunteers, they were impressed because nearly eighty inmate volunteers were in attendance, a number higher than at any community site in the state. The training was based on instructional strategies taught to reading teachers in the master's of arts program at Johns Hopkins and the University of Maryland. It incorporates language experience and phonetic instructional strategies, appropriate follow-up activities, the use of positive motivation techniques, and general classroom organization.

Using state and federal funding, a master's level teacher-training program in reading education was developed in cooperation with the Johns Hopkins University in 1981. At least thirteen teachers from the Maryland correctional education program received their masters degrees in reading. Most of these teachers have remained with the correctional education program and provide the backbone for adult basic education and literacy education there.

Since the early 1990s, all major facilities have a reading lab with trained inmate tutors. At present, there are around 200 inmate tutors in the reading labs. The positive influence of these inmate aides has led to a continued expansion of the use of inmates as tutors in other areas, such as GED instruction. The institutional system recognizes the special contributions of inmate tutors by giving them extra "good time" or time off of their sentences.

A Brief History of Special Education

Simultaneously with the development of the peer tutoring program, the Maryland Correctional Education Program sought to come into compliance with the requirements of the federal special education law, 94-142. Because of the literacy program, it was obvious that there were a large number of inmates with learning disabilities. Unlike the literacy program which involves inmates of all ages, the special education program targets inmates who are twenty-one years of age or younger. The adult inmate population in Maryland currently exceeds 23,000 and about 10 percent of them fit this age category and must be screened for special education services.

Starting in the 1980s, the Maryland Department of Education's Office of Special Education provided the technical assistance of a special education specialist who worked with the correctional education program in providing awareness and identifying resources to implement the special education process. Within a few years, additional staff were hired to run the program. The staff included a special education coordinator, two full-time school psychologists, support staff, and a number of special education teachers to provide a sufficient level of service. Contracts were developed with various state and local education agencies for related services such as speech pathology.

Joint policies and procedures between the Maryland correctional education program and the division of corrections were developed, written, and endorsed by both agencies. These policies include a special education handbook. The handbook incorporates all the requirements of the reauthorized federal special education law, called Individuals with Disabilities Education Act, or IDEA.

The special education program has been fully implemented since 1985. At any given time, there are more than 100 special education students included in the state count to the United States Department of Education. The major disability areas represented in the incarcerated population are learning disabilities, mental retardation, and emotional disturbances.

The special education program is closely coordinated with the peer tutoring program. Special education students often are assigned to the lab as part of their Individual Education Plan (IEP). In the reading lab, as well as in other classes, they are given special instruction outlined in their Individual Education Plan. The special education classroom teachers have smaller numbers of students than teachers in regular classrooms so they may give students more individual attention.

The Maryland Special Education Program has been selected over the years as a model program. The National Institute of Corrections recognized the Maryland program in a 1989 national publication, *Programming Mentally Retarded and Learning Disabilities: A Guide for Correctional Administrators*, by using a number of its practices as examples to the field.

Even so, an inmate advocacy group initiated a lawsuit, alleging that a large number of inmates, otherwise eligible for special education, were not being properly screened and served with appropriate education programs. The lawsuit eventually was dismissed and an agreement was reached with the plaintiffs in 1995. The court-appointed expert who reviewed the programs, Dr. Osa Coffey, proclaimed that the Maryland special education program was in total compliance with federal and state law.

Results

Uniqueness and Effectiveness

The Maryland peer tutoring program is special because it was a pioneer in proving the feasibility and worth of inmate tutors assisting regular teaching staff in adult facilities. In an institutional setting, which usually looks at inmates in a very negative light, the peer tutoring concept was almost revolutionary. Now, peer tutoring programs can be found in nearly every state.

The Maryland peer tutoring program has greatly improved the quality, quantity, and efficiency of the adult basic education program. In the years before peer tutoring was initiated, teachers who were well-trained in literacy instruction or special education still were unable to reach most of the hundreds of low-level and educationally handicapped students in the prison system. Such students are largely incapable of working independently. Before 1980, all basic level students were mixed into regular classrooms with one teacher and an untrained inmate aide.

In contrast, in the literacy lab setting, the student works with a highly trained inmate tutor for the entire class period, five days a week. While the teacher is monitoring instruction and meeting with inmate-tutor trainees, the students continue to receive instruction and reinforcement. Most classrooms are large enough to accommodate from ten-to-fifteen tutor/student pairs as often as three times a day. In this context, it is easy to see that many more students can be accommodated. On a given day, the literacy labs serve at least 400 illiterate students.

The central measure of the effectiveness of any educational program is the educational advancement of students. Data collected by the education program indicate that, on average, literacy students gain about three months in reading skill level for every month of instruction. The Maryland special education program is one of the few programs in adult special education which has been determined to be in compliance with current state and federal laws. While many states are in compliance in juvenile correctional education, most states have only partially implemented IDEA in adult corrections.

Conclusion

Both programs, peer tutoring and special education, have been instrumental in making instruction more effective for all students. Because the staff are highly trained, all students benefit in the long run. These programs recognize the worth of every human being. Not only are students afforded a "free and appropriate education," but inmate aides are given a rare status in a prison setting, a highly regarded position as teacher aide and tutor. The Maryland peer tutoring and special education programs are examples of an important answer to the problem of breaking the crime cycle—teaching people to help people.

Contact:

Steve Steurer
Executive Director
Correctional Education Association and Correctional Academic Coordinator
Maryland State Department of Education

200 West Baltimore Street
Baltimore, Maryland 21201
(301) 918-1911 or (410) 767-0492

A Life Skills Project for Reintegration of Ex-offenders

Introduction

School District #428 offers a variety of educational options for incarcerated inmates such as adult basic education literacy training, special education, general equivalency diploma (GED) preparation, vocational training, and college classes leading toward an associate or baccalaureate degree. Most facilities offer a variety of vocational programs.

The district also incorporates a life skills curriculum into its basic education program, which includes parenting, making consumer choices, managing family resources, handling home and work responsibilities, and applying skills to jobs and careers. The life skills curriculum presents relevant issues to students that increase their overall interest, encourage group discussions, and contribute to the development of reading and critical thinking skills designed to help offenders in their successful return to their families and communities.

In 1993, School District #428 joined with the Illinois Council on Vocational Education, the Illinois State Board of Education, the Illinois Community College Board, and representatives of the Job Training Partnership Act in a collaboration, to form the Criminal Offender Coordination Committee. The Committee explored existing components of a statewide networking system to collectively deliver programs and services designed to help ex-offenders reintegrate into the community and reduce recidivism and criminal activity. Eight statewide public forums were held to explore ways to maximize resources, eliminate unnecessary duplication, and enhance the networking system for delivering services. A literature review was completed to gather information about successful local and state initiatives for the offender population.

Program Design

As a result of the recommendation of the coordination committee, in June 1994, the school district released a request for proposals to develop life skills centers during fiscal year 1995. The goal was to provide ex-offenders with the necessary life skills and services to help them successfully reintegrate into society. Services were to include vocational education; assistance with employment, housing, transportation arrangements, other subsistence needs; and counseling.

This innovative initiative established five life skills centers as pilot programs to determine their feasibility as a future statewide undertaking. The pilot sites were funded by School District #428 using the 1 percent allocation of the Carl D. Perkins Vocational and Applied Technology Education Act for corrections programs from the Illinois State Board of Education. The approximately $435,000 provided pilot sites with funding for staff and administration of the life skills centers, and funding services such as job placement, transportation, child care, emergency financial assistance, work tools, clothing, and mentors.

Life Skills Centers

The Project Kody Life Skills Center

The Project Kody Life Skills Center operates in Kane, DeKalb, and Kendall counties serving the adult and juvenile population. It offers computer-assisted instruction in a life skills lab. This allows clients to enter the program at the level appropriate to their skills and to work at an individual pace.

The Safer Foundation Life Skills Center

The Safer Foundation, located in Chicago, enrolls clients in the life skills program for seven weeks of daily class sessions, six hours a day. Clients participate in an academic skill building experience based in the real world.

The East St. Louis Township Life Skills Center

The East St. Louis Township program assists clients in acquiring the basic skills necessary for survival and for becoming productive residents of St. Clair County. The services provided include job training and placement, vocational education, entrepreneurship training, problem solving, food and shelter assistance, social interaction training, spiritual development, and community awareness. Clients also participate in group sessions that emphasize the development of basic life skills necessary for survival. The East St. Louis Township Center also administers the Illinois Department of Public Aid Earnfare Program, which allows eligible participants to receive six months of on-the-job training.

The Unlimited Community Alternative Network Project (UCAN)

The Southern Illinois Collegiate Common Market administers the Unlimited Community Alternative Network Project (UCAN). UCAN develops, monitors, and provides life skills services to ex-offenders, parolees, and probationers within twenty-one counties of Southern Illinois. Services are offered to assist with employment, education and training, housing, personal and family adjustment, health care, special treatment or therapy, substance abuse, and transportation.

The Workforce Development Council of Will County

The Workforce Development Council of Will County (formerly known as a PIC) provides support, group mentoring, and job placement activities to approximately fifty ex-offenders from Will and Cook Counties. Clients are placed in employment and mentored through small support group activities. All participants are required to be regularly involved in the Life Skills "Rebound" Program with sessions rotating on an eight-week basis. Weekly sessions offer the ex-offenders group support, addressing basic reintegration and personal issues, conflict resolution, and employment retention. After securing employment, all participants are required to report to at least one session each month for a minimum of three months. While participants are seeking employment, they must attend weekly meetings.

The Roosevelt University Employment and Referral Program

The Roosevelt University Employment and Referral Program located within Cook County is an extension of the university's community service mission and its Bachelor of General Studies/Department of Corrections degree program. The program has developed an information database of community resources for use in referrals for jobs and other services such as housing, meals, clothing, health care, and continuing education opportunities. Clients are provided transportation assistance to get them to job interviews, help in resume writing, development of job interviewing skills, and job placement. The program also provides bilingual Spanish-speaking staff and American Sign Language services.

Implementation

Each facility has a designated life-skills placement coordinator who is responsible for meeting with students who are within one to four months from release and have participated in adult basic education, general education development, or vocational programs while incarcerated, with an emphasis placed upon vocational program completers. Life skills such as parenting, self-esteem, money management, and job acquisition and retention have been integrated into the adult education curriculum.

The placement coordinator has each interested and eligible inmate complete an application for the program, which is then forwarded to the School District #428 central office for processing. The coordinator in the central office screens the applications for accuracy and forwards them to the appropriate life skills center located in the county to which the inmate will be paroled. Life skills centers then can send letters and information describing their services to the potential client shortly before release or immediately afterwards.

Referrals also are received through networking with city and county officials to serve ex-offenders on probation or parole and through probation and parole officers. When feasible, staff from the life skills centers meet with inmates to encourage their participation in the program, generally as part of the Pre-Start/pre-release program in place within all institutions in the Department of Corrections. The School District #428 coordinator works closely with the institution placement coordinators and the life skills center staff to ensure clients are referred on a regular basis and receive the services necessary for successful reintegration into society.

Results

In fiscal year 1995, 488 ex-offenders, probationers, parolees, and at-risk individuals were referred to the life-skills centers program. The number at each site ranged from 65 to 194. A total of 130 clients found full-time employment, and an additional 33 acquired part-time work. Nearly all of the clients who found employment received wages above minimum wage. The hourly wages reported by clients ranged from $4.25 per hour to $14.49 per hour.

During fiscal year 1996, the life skills centers served a total of 846 clients. This figure represents 83.5 percent adults and 16.5 percent juveniles, of whom 85.5 percent were males and 14.5 percent females. Nearly 43 percent of the clients (including juveniles) served obtained employment with an average hourly wage of $6.00. The life skills centers assisted 10.5 percent of their clients in furthering their education in adult basic education, obtaining their GED, or taking college courses. The recidivism rate was less than 5 percent for inmates who participated in the life skills centers program.

Conclusion

Life skills centers have a positive influence on probationers, ex-offenders, parolees, and other at-risk individuals. Because the criminal offender population is extremely difficult to place in an occupation, employment successes of the life skills center programs were significant. The program proves that inmates who receive an education while incarcerated have improved skills, which increases their chances of obtaining successful employment and thereby also increases their chances of becoming successful citizens.

Author:

Michelle Busher
Life Skills Coordinator
Illinois School District #428
Springfield, Illinois

Contact:

John Castro
Superintendent
Illinois School District #428

1301 Concordia Court
Springfield, Illinois 62794
(217) 522-2666 x5700

Nebraska Life Skills Program—Higher Education Reaching Out, Inc.

Introduction and Background

The Nebraska Life Skills program was funded through the U.S. Department of Education's Correctional Education Office for approximately $185,000 per year. The Life Skills Program received funds November 1, 1993 through October 31, 1996. The program was developed through the collaboration of Peru State College, the Department of Corrections, and Higher Education Reaching Out (HERO), Inc. The program was based on a Request for Proposal that called for the development and implementation of a program that would reduce recidivism by improving the life skills necessary for the reintegration of adult inmates into society.

Program Design

The target population of the program was the inmate population that was less likely to get involved with established department of corrections treatment or rehabilitation programs. This included inmates who have identified themselves or have been identified by staff as having anger control problems. The program was implemented in Nebraska State Penitentiary, Lincoln Correctional Center, the Nebraska Center for Women, and the Diagnostic Evaluation Center.

The program has served more than 632 inmates as of this date. The Nebraska Life Skills program addresses changes in the prison environment with values clarification for inmates by:

- Allowing the inmates to stop and think before they act
- Using relationship skills that are more socially acceptable
- Developing personal communication skills
- Increasing inmates' ability to handle difficult situations
- Developing their ability to forgive themselves and to move forward with self-improvement

Demographics of the Population Served

FREQUENCY BY RACE

PERCENTAGE	RACE
8.4%	Mexican American
39.1%	African American
3.5%	Native American
9.0%	Euro-American

EDUCATION COMPLETED

PERCENTAGE	EDUCATION
7%	College
16.3%	High School
39.5%	GED
43.5%	Nongraduates

CRIME RELATED*

PERCENTAGE	FACTORS
3%	Drug related
47%	Assault related
23%	Alcohol related
19%	Violence related

*CONTAINS SIMULTANEOUS FACTORS

NUMBER OF ARRESTS

PERCENTAGE	ARRESTS
30.5%	1 to 5
24.2%	6 to 10
10.2%	11 to 15
10.8%	16 to 20
12.6%	21 to 30
6.4%	31 to 40
5.7%	Over 40

INMATE AGE

PERCENTAGE	AGE
13.8%	16 to 20
25.7%	21 to 25
17.3%	26 to 30
19.3%	31 to 35
9.9%	36 to 40
10.4%	41 to 50
4.4%	Over 50

SENTENCE LENGTH

PERCENTAGE	YEARS
49.0%	1 to 5
25.2%	6 to 10
13.4%	11 to 15
2.0%	16 to 20
3.0%	21 to 30
2.0%	31 to 40
8.9%	Over 40

AGE OF ARREST

PERCENTAGE	AGE
7.1%	5 to 10
44.5%	11 to 15
32.3%	16 to 20
7.1%	21 to 25
3.2%	26 to 30
4.0%	31 to 40
3.9%	Over 40

Establishing the Program

In developing this program, Peru State College established a fifty-six-credit-hour criminal justice option within the psychology/sociology/education major that includes six upper division credit hours relating to correctional psychology and education. The psychology of correctional education and therapy (Psychology 460) had 128 students that included 12 department employees. The correctional practicum had 62 students who expended more than 2,480 tutoring hours. The program itself has several components.

Development and Design of the Nebraska Life Skills Program

The goal of Nebraska Life Skills is to offer educational programming that will help with the development and growth of inmates' life skills. The program consists of four integrated components: social skills (understanding one's self), leadership skills (communicating and developing team work), anger control (appropriately expressing anger), HERO thinking (developing positive thinking patterns), and educational planning (testing and tutoring).

Objectives

The objectives are as follows:

- To facilitate a positive change in self-concept, an understanding of learning processes, and the development of social skills literacy

- To provide offenders positive skills and techniques for handling difficult interpersonal situations

- To facilitate offenders in learning principles and communication skills that will increase their literacy and math comprehension skills and improve prosocial behavior during incarceration and after release, by strengthening relationships and overcoming obstacles in decision-making environments

Procedures

The Nebraska Life Skills program incorporates life skills. The project uses programs with individual educational testing and tutoring designed to raise the offender's literacy skills. Anger control and domestic violence therapy are designed to improve the offender's skills in domestic relations. Instructional strategies developed in literacy are designed to improve client self-esteem (in groups as well as in individuals). The social and leadership literacy curriculum includes training in: how to follow directions, how to accept criticism, how to make requests, and how to give appropriate feedback. Hero thinking focuses on learning productive thinking patterns, developing more flexible responses to situations, and restructuring the cognitive process. The I.E.P (individual educational program) is offered through student tutors (through Peru State College participation). It is designed to objectively meet and surpass individual goals in all skill levels.

Outcomes

By improving basic literacy and math comprehension skills, offenders with low academic levels and learning disabilities are able to increase their participation in other rehabilitation programs. All this improves their transition back into their communities and reduces recidivism. The program model integrates social/leadership skills and conflict resolution skills that are necessary to obtain positive goal outcomes for a targeted population of offenders.

Implementation

Educational programming helped prisoners to acquire the skills and education necessary to fulfill their goals and objectives so that they could have a successful transition back into society and the workplace. The following is a list of classes that helped with this transition.

Transitional Skills for Life—This program provides information about the correctional environment, and with activities and educational material, enables the student to make a better transition into corrections. The course enables participants to set goals for a better use of their time and efforts by using the programs offered within corrections.

HERO Skills for Life—This program facilitates a positive change in inmates' self-concept and provides an understanding of the learning processes and the development of social skills. HERO Skills for Life provides inmates with positive skills and techniques for handling difficult interpersonal situations through the use of decision-making techniques, communication skills, prosocial behavior, and techniques to strengthen leadership and work relationships.

Learning Skills for Life—This program provides for the application of the essential study skills needed to be successful in adult basic education classes, on the GED, and in college classes. It demonstrates career opportunities that will be available on completion of their degree. It helps students set goals and take responsibility for their own learning through lectures, laboratories, and tutorial programs.

Computer Skills for Life—This program provides for the application of the essential computer skills needed for success in society both at home and in the job market. It also improves the success of the students by demonstrating career opportunities that will be available on completion of the course. It helps students set goals and take responsibility for their own learning through lectures, laboratories, and tutorial programs.

Parenting Skills for Life—This program provides information about how to care for ourselves and our children with joy and without guilt. It teaches inmates about helping children develop their own internal structure of discipline, based on self-esteem rather than fear or shame. It helps students set goals and take responsibility for their own learning through lectures, laboratories, and tutorial programs.

Decision Making—This program provides instruction in the actions individuals use to make a decision.

True Colors—This is a communication program that assists in defining an individual's temperament. It allows the inmate to identify strengths, needs, joys, values, frustrations, and stressors. The model is an excellent tool for small group activity and provides reinforcement to enable the individual to develop positive alternatives to antisocial behaviors.

Evaluation and Conclusion

The evaluation process to judge the effectiveness of the Nebraska Life Skills program integrated quantitative and qualitative procedures. Seven instruments are administered to students to evaluate the impact of the program. The instruments are administered before and after the Nebraska Life Skills course. The following is a list of instruments used, what they measure, and the results of the evaluation.

Conflict Management Inventory—This instrument examines four methods of handling conflict and anger: Aggressive/Confrontative (high scores indicate a strong need to control situations and people), Assertive/Persuasive (high scores indicate a tendency to stand up for oneself without being pushy), Observant/Introspective (high scores indicate a tendency to observe others—a listening mode of behavior), Avoiding/Reactive (high scores indicate a tendency toward passivity or withdrawal in conflict situation). The scores on the Aggressive/Confrontative and Avoiding/Reactive component tend to go down after the Nebraska Life Skills program, while scores on the Assertive/Persuasive go up.

Locus of Control Inventory—This instrument examines an individual's internal and external locus of control. In other words, do persons feel like they are in control of their life or is someone and/or something else in control? The scores tend to regress after the Nebraska Life Skills program; inmates tend to feel that they have more control over their lives.

Coopersmith Inventory—This instrument examines how well individuals handle stressful situations. After the Nebraska Life Skills program, the inmates tend to show an increased ability to handle stressful situations.

Type E Stress Inventory—This instrument examines how well persons manage stress in their lives. Scores tend to regress after the Nebraska Life Skills program, demonstrating the inmates' increased ability to manage stress in their lives.

Stress Inventory—This instrument measures the number of symptoms of stress a person has and how often they occur (e.g., headaches, nervousness, sleep difficulties, and chest pain). Scores regress after the Nebraska Life Skills program, showing a reduction in the number of symptoms of stress.

Myers-Briggs Type Indicator—The Myers-Briggs Type Indicator not only measures Jung's theory of personality types, but subsequent research has found the instrument useful in identifying learning styles, coping styles, and communications styles. The sensing types were found to be twice the normal average with three types (ISTJ: 22.2 percent, ISTP: 14.1 percent, ESTJ: 11.7 percent) making up almost half of the prison population.

Conduct Reports—This is a comparison of the number of the misconduct reports an individual received six months before the participating in and six months after completing the Nebraska Life Skills program. Six months after completing the Nebraska Life Skills program, there was a 58 percent decrease of violent incidents reported and a 50 percent decrease in nonviolent incidents.

Based on all the measures, the Nebraska Life Skills program is highly successful.

Contacts:

Gene Hruza
Education Coordinator
Nebraska Department of Correctional Services

P. O. Box 94661
Lincoln, Nebraska 68509
(402) 471-2654

Contacts:

Joel Lundak
Professor of Psychology
Peru State College

P. O. Box 10
Peru, Nebraska 68410
(402) 872-2264

Vocational Training Through Community Service: Operation Outward Reach, Inc.

Introduction

Since its beginning, Operation Outward Reach has been an exercise in cooperation. It also has confirmed the truth of the familiar advice given to aspiring entrepreneurs: find a need and fill it. The founders of Operation Outward Reach identified two areas of need to fill: the overwhelming inmate need to be trained in marketable skills and the need of low-income homeowners and nonprofit agencies for affordable construction services.

In 1972, prison staff, inmates, and volunteers at the State Regional Correctional Facility at Greensburg established the Committee for Community Awareness (CCA) to meet and discuss how the prison could be more positively involved with the community. Bill Rehak, an inmate and accomplished carpenter, strongly urged the establishment of a community service program to train inmates in building skills and provide older impoverished people in the community with home repairs.

The Committee for Community Awareness presented Rehak's idea to the Superintendent at Greensburg who gave his approval for the agency to move forward. Joseph Rollins, corrections counselor and Committee for Community Awareness president, met with Michael Mulroy, director of the Westmoreland Office of Human Opportunities and secured a $2,000 grant. This small grant enabled the Committee for Community Awareness to initiate a pilot project, called Repair on Wheels. With the successful completion of the pilot project, the Redstone Presbyteriate, the regional body of the Presbyterian church, provided the Committee for Community Awareness with $8,500 as seed money to attract future government grants.

A critical step was taken in 1973, when the Committee for Community Awareness combined forces with Concerned of Pennsylvania to form Operation Outward Reach. Concerned of Pennsylvania was a nonprofit organization training the mentally disabled in the building trades and targeting the housing needs of the rural poor. The director of that organization, Father Vincent J. Rocco, became the first director of Operation Outward Reach. Supported by a $122,000 grant from the Governor's Justice Commission, Operation Outward Reach began providing services at the Greensburg Correctional Facility.

The Pennsylvania Department of Corrections is the major funder of Operation Outward Reach. This partnership between the Department of Corrections and a private nonprofit organization has been continually successful as shown in the steady growth of the organization. Operation Outward Reach was first established at the state Correctional Institution at Greensburg in 1973 and then in the state Correctional Institution at Huntingdon in 1977, in the state Regional Correctional Facility at Mercer in 1988, in the state Correctional Institution at Cresson in 1994, and in the state Correctional Institution at Somerset in 1996.

Operation Outward Reach took a giant step in 1996 when it began to operate a day treatment program for adjudicated youth in Westmoreland County, funded largely through the Department of Welfare. This program is modeled on the organization's successful adult offender program, but education and restorative justice are emphasized more. The students, all of them no longer attending the public school system, participate in education classes one day a week and in substance abuse classes. The students are held accountable through providing actual restitution for their crimes, where appropriate, and through the community service aspect of the training program.

Program Design

Adult Training

A Pennsylvania Department of Corrections' counselor facilitates the program inside the institution and provides institutional caseload management for those assigned to the program. All participating inmates must be in the prerelease program. At each prison, there are two crews of ten men each.

The actual training is conducted by two experienced tradesmen at each institution. The instructors hired have a minimum of fifteen-years experience as construction supervisors or contractors. This qualification means that the instructors are older than the average inmate so they can serve not just as a teacher, but as a role model. The instructors also must want to help people. The importance of the instructor's attitude is reflected in the comments of released inmates. They always mention the instructor by name and ask that the instructor be told that they are doing all right on the outside.

Because many of the inmates have no job experience at all, or very limited experience, the training is run as much as possible as though it were an actual job. The instructors pick up their crew each morning from the prison at 7 A.M., transport them to the work site, and return them at 3 P.M. The work week is forty hours long and projects are scheduled year around, although inmates stay in the program for only six months. Even though the instructors must enforce any security rules, they do so more as a job supervisor, and not so much as a correctional officer.

Typical projects include roofing, siding, soffit and fascia work; gutters and downspouts, porches, cement floors, block foundation, brick work, sidewalks, window replacement, and interior remodeling. During bad weather, time is used for doing estimates on future projects and for repairing and maintaining tools and equipment. Trainees also attend two hours a week of classroom training in such topics as blueprint reading, understanding math, learning safety procedures, and estimating.

The training curriculum is based on the training that would be offered in a craft apprenticeship program. The discipline and structure of this model has been effective in promoting positive work adjustment, self-discipline, and a sense of self-worth for each trainee.

A site coordinator serves as a liaison between the community, the institution, and Operation Outward Reach. A major responsibility of the site coordinator is to work with all trainees as they prepare to leave the institution. For one year after release, the site coordinator maintains contact with the inmates to provide them with transitional services.

Juvenile Training

The program for juveniles is very similar to that for adults. Each morning at 7 A.M. they are picked up at their homes and transported to the on-the-job training site. They are returned to their homes at 5 P.M. The work week is six days long for a total of sixty hours, with one day given over to education. On Saturdays, all students participate in customized general equivalency diploma (GED) classes.

The work projects are similar to those the adults participate in as well. The students work on siding, soffit, fascia, gutters, porches, cement floors, sidewalks, window replacements, and interior remodeling. An instructor's aide is scheduled at the job site to provide additional security, supervision, and training.

The juvenile site coordinator serves as a liaison between the court, the juveniles' probation officer, and their family. This day-treatment alternative program is viewed as a transitional program into adulthood because it provides not only job skills, education, and substance abuse programming, but also a path to maturation and self-esteem for these troubled youths.

Outcomes

Operation Outward Reach has been providing these services since 1972. Besides having 1,547 graduates, the program has completed 1,051 projects for low-income elderly and community groups who otherwise could not afford to have had the repairs done to their property. Of the 1,547 inmates completing the program, 980 have obtained employment; 235 have returned to prison on new charges.

A recent study was conducted by an outside evaluator for a federal demonstration project. The evaluation, using the state parole board computer system to locate dates for each experimental and control group, found significant data indicating program success. For the group of graduates from 1993-94, 83 percent remained in the community on parole versus 72 percent for the control group. Even more impressive was the group of graduates from 1991, where 74 percent remained in the community versus 59 percent of the nongraduates. Plans are underway to study eight more groups of graduates. Statistical information for the juvenile program is inconclusive due to the newness of this initiative.

Conclusion

Programs similar to Operation Outward Reach could be part of any department of corrections in appropriate institutions. Such programs can meet the needs not only of elderly citizens, the poor, and the offenders themselves, but the public relations needs of the correctional institution. Too often, correctional institutions are viewed only in a negative light. Programs where inmates can give something positive to the community demonstrate that correctional institutions can provide for the community in ways extending beyond their key role in protecting public safety.

Operation Outward Reach has received many awards over the years for its contributions to the community. The organization is proud to have met its goals: quality on-the-job vocational training through community service. The trainees receive skills and self-esteem through actual community construction projects. The construction clients have received low-cost home improvements while coming to view the prison inmate trainees in a different way than is portrayed on the evening news. The organization provides a win/win conclusion for the inmates, the public, and the correctional institution.

Contact:

Raymond Thompson
Executive Director
Operation Outward Reach

227 South 6th Street
Youngwood, Pennsylvania 15697
(724) 925-2419

Interdisciplinary Instruction at the Literacy Level

Introduction

The Plainfield Correctional Facility, Indiana Department of Correction, is a medium-security institution for adult male offenders. The population totals approximately 1,200, with an average age of thirty-four. Most men are not first-time offenders; many have not completed their high school diploma requirements.

The facility has a commitment to invest in education as the proven method for rehabilitation. Nearly 500 offenders are enrolled in the school, as a work assignment in literacy, high school curriculum, vocational classes, and postsecondary education.

Arthur Campbell High School is the only adult high school in the Indiana Department of Corrections accredited by the North Central Association of Colleges and Schools. All necessary subjects are provided to meet state-regulated requirements for achieving a high school diploma. Adult basic education courses and literacy classes are targeted for literacy-level students to prepare them for enrollment in high school. Previously, literacy teachers were responsible for teaching individual subjects in the literacy program: reading, language, and mathematics. Literacy students were enrolled on a three-period (half-day) basis.

Students test out of literacy classes at the minimum threshold of 8.0 on the Test of Adult Basic Education, indicating that these students are prepared to be successful in the high school curricula. However, an administration review of postliteracy students showed that many were not successful academically. Academic teachers commented that a lack of motivation was a significant contributing factor to this poor performance. During the course of discussion concerning specific students, it became apparent that teachers needed to have better information concerning the capabilities and interests of individual students.

Development and Design

The staff discussed various ideas for improvement in the literacy program, which resulted in the establishment of the following goals.

1. Assign one teacher to work in all literacy areas with designated groups of students. This was to provide a better opportunity for a teacher to know the educational needs of each individual student.

2. Involve other academic and vocational teachers in the total education of the student.

3. Provide students with experiential opportunities where they can participate and have success without fear of failure.

4. Provide learning activities that incorporate a variety of learning styles.

5. Make success more probable than failure.

In preparation for implementation of this program, additional goals were addressed and accomplished.

1. Teachers were cross-trained or retrained in literacy areas other than their primary area of expertise.

2. Additional classroom tutors were cross-trained or retrained in all literacy areas to assist in three of the four literacy classes. (The fourth teacher chose not to use a classroom tutor).

3. All academic and vocational teachers developed classroom activities designed to be used by literacy teachers or to be presented as in-class learning modules. The idea of interdisciplinary modules is beneficial to literacy students: it allows them to experience academic or vocational classroom ideas and techniques while still in the literacy program. These modules were designed for academic skill development, exploratory experiences, life-skills orientations, or a combination of all three.

4. All literacy teachers, counseling staff, and a number of academic teachers participated in several workshops dealing with the multiple-intelligence theory. During these workshops, they learned how to incorporate this concept of instruction into the development of daily learning activities and lesson plans.

Implementation

A class of literacy students is assigned to one teacher. Students who are having trouble in academic classes are retested, and when appropriate, removed from those classes and returned to the literacy program. An orientation program for all new literacy students was developed by student support services.

- During orientation, students watch *Renaissance Man*, a video dealing with at-risk students learning how to be successful. Students write a brief summary of the movie's content. This provides a good writing sample for the literacy teachers. Then, all students complete a learning-style inventory and discuss the best way that they learn information. The inventories are forwarded to the literacy teacher for inclusion in each student's portfolio.

Students complete an initial orientation on the use of the academic library. They are given a tour of the high school library and an explanation of the rules. Students are expected to become familiar with the collection at this institution and instructed in procedures for library access.

Two additional library modules, one on the Dewey Decimal System and the other on reference and research, are mandatory and provided to individual literacy classes as a group. Various materials are introduced: almanacs, periodical archives, microfilm collection, and card catalog listings. Card catalog worksheets and a research hunt throughout the library provide hands-on experiences with the process of conducting library research.

Students are scheduled for classes with a variety of academic and vocational instructors.

- The goal of the plant growth/metric measurement experience is to teach students to use the metric ruler to measure objects and to produce a line graph from these measurements. Skills used during this project are measuring, graphing, comprehending vocabulary, observing, and researching. Each student is responsible for planting, watering, and caring for a number of seeds. Students take daily measurements made on the plants' heights and plot them on a chart and then generate a line graph. Many of the students volunteered to plant the seedlings outdoors to help improve the school grounds for everyone to enjoy. In addition, each class was introduced to the Internet in the distance-learning room by making a virtual trip to the Missouri Botanical Garden and by accessing the Burpee Seed Catalog web page.

- Literacy and the arts are used as a way to present creative problem solving. Displays, posters, calligraphy, graphs, charts, and illustrations are combined for individual research, necessitating the use of basic drafting instruments for much of the work. Student initiative is required for all the projects.

- An initial response for many students faced with a new problem or situation is to quit. However, a four-step approach to solving problems is emphasized. First, ask questions about possible solutions. Next, make notes about the ideas uncovered regardless of the source. Third, use these ideas in a brainstorming session to further develop possible solutions. Finally, set goals to get moving toward a solution. New problems may crop up, but this time students start the process over instead of quitting. One "Literacy and the Arts" project is to research social problems and present findings in poster form. The posters and projects are displayed on bulletin boards throughout the school. Writing projects then are combined with illustrations to permit students to explore many ways of expressing their ideas.

- Vocational drafting offers a literacy module in metric use and calculation. The history and reason for metrics is related to examples familiar to students, resulting in hands-on experiences in measuring with metric units.

- *Math in Music* is a literacy module, which introduces adult literacy students to several easily recognizable mathematical constructs in the popular music they regularly enjoy. As a way of experiencing the challenge of keeping track of musical meter, students join the teacher in front of the class and play percussion instruments on prespecified beats within a song's structure. By playing along with blues and rock and roll hits, the student gets hands-on experience reinforcing newly discovered musical contexts of familiar math skills. A stated goal of this module is to guide adult literacy students to the realization that application and function of literacy skills can enhance all of life's experiences, not just academic situations.

- *Jeopardy-Grammar* is a module that students enjoy in each classroom and is developed into a competition with the winning class awarded a movie viewing. *Jeopardy-Grammar* categories include spelling, dictionary skills, abbreviations, parts of speech, and "fix-it sentences."

- A monthly calendar of learning experiences or life skills modules is scheduled. Literacy classes move as a group with the literacy teacher to the presenting classroom.

- Bulletin boards and photographic displays are maintained by literacy students. These displays are usually representative of group themes or topics. Teachers and students are encouraged to put in writing any positive observations and results.

Outcomes

The following information on literacy students covers two six-month periods.

During 1997, the average length of time to complete the literacy program ranged from 2.83 to 2.94 months. The grade point average for students completing subsequent academic or vocational classes during this period of time ranged from 2.23 to 2.30.

The following outcomes are based upon professional observations:

- The educational emphasis is refocused on total academic and vocational readiness, not just passing on tests.

- A much stronger teacher/student bond appears to have developed by having one teacher instruct a student throughout a complete literacy program. Teachers now have a much better knowledge-base concerning the potential of each student.

- Teachers no longer compare only negative notes on the common problem student. They now compare notes on the common successes of classes or students as they observe their students participating in life skill modules with other teachers.

- Students are learning to work as a group and learning how to support each other in class and in outside activities. An example of this was highly visible during class competition on language skills using the *Jeopardy* format. Teachers have observed cooperative behavior among literacy students in the library. Students are less tolerant of inappropriate classroom behavior from other students and make comments reflecting their distaste for interruptions in the learning process.

- At least one academic teacher reviewed course curriculum and made changes because students coming out of literacy could handle higher skills. Several academic teachers have developed new classes or changed existing course curricula from self-paced to taught format.

- Literacy program referrals for disciplinary problems have been reduced to a minimum.

- Students appear to have a higher level of motivation to perform and a more courteous manner of behaving in the classrooms and halls.

- Most teachers appear more satisfied with their jobs.

Conclusion

Good programs can become better. Reviews of existing programs and results must be completed periodically. Teachers should be involved in a constant review of activities as they are developed and implemented.

The goals must be defined and expectations communicated with both teachers and students. Teachers should listen to problems expressed by those involved: they are generally real. Teachers should not stop to battle individual and temporary resistance. Instead, they should focus on the goals and successes of others and the ultimate goal of what is best for student achievement. Those who are resistant either will choose to change or have little or no impact on those who are accomplishing positive, rewarding things. Resistance can be ignored and actual success can be celebrated at every opportunity.

Author:

Harry Sykes
Assistant Director of Education
Plainfield Correctional Facility
Plainfield, Indiana

Author/Contact:

Carlene Stringer
Librarian
Arthur Campbell High School
Plainfield Correctional Facility

727 Moon Road
Plainfield, Indiana 46168
(317) 839-2513 x1454

Correctional Education
Additional Program Entries

Programs at Dwight Correctional Center and Kankakee Minimum Security Unit: Illinois Department of Corrections

Gwen V. Thornton, Warden
Dwight Correctional Center, P.O. Box 5001, Dwight, Illinois 60420-5001
(815) 584-2806

Education programs at Dwight Correctional Center include basic literacy classes, General Equivalency Diploma (GED) instruction, special education classes, and college academic classes. Each program is continuously evaluated and audited to ensure current theory and practice is being used. Vocational programs include cosmetology, restaurant management, secretarial sciences, and computer technology. Apprenticeship programs include commercial cooking and baking, and various trades such as plumbing, electricity, and water/wastewater operations. At Kankakee Minimum Security Unit, a wide variety of educational programs are available, including adult basic education, GED preparation, vocational programs, and academic college programs. These programs are designed to help reduce recidivism by increasing literacy and life skills and, in the case of vocational programs, to provide marketable skills in careers available to inmates upon release. The education programs at Dwight Correctional Center and Kankakee Minimum Security Unit are a valuable tool for raising self-esteem and increasing the chances of an inmate's successful return to society. Each level, from mandatory education for those who test below the literacy level, to classes leading to a bachelor of arts degree, has a positive effect on the attitudes and behavior of the inmates.

Nebraska Project Worklink: Nebraska Department of Correctional Services and Metropolitan Community College

Marlene Rhodus, State Coordinator for Nebraska Correctional Education
Metropolitan Community College, P.O. Box 3777, Omaha, Nebraska 68103-0777
(402) 457-2605

Nebraska Project Worklink, a cooperative effort of the Nebraska Department of Correctional Services and Metropolitan Community College, provides comprehensive programs and services for the successful transition of adults from correctional facilities into productive employment within their communities. Successful transition is achieved through the development of literacy, work readiness, life skills, and community support networks prior to an inmate's release. Efforts to improve these skills include classes in five areas: education (reading, communication skills, GED, college preparation, and college credit); employment (developing work attitudes and behavior, interviewing, certification of job skills, job retention, and employer-coworker relationships); parenting (positive parenting skills and understanding the developmental stages of children); and social skills (healthy self-esteem, relationships, commitment, problem solving, and critical thinking). Upon release, Nebraska Project Worklink assists ex-offenders in identifying essential resources as they cross the bridge into the community. Those services include emergency assistance, for food, housing, and transportation; employment assistance, including job placement and mentoring; and support systems like self-help groups, problem solving, and adjustment.

A Successful Approach to Eliminating Illiteracy: Indiana Department of Corrections

Margaret M. Gisler, Institutional Teacher
Correctional Industrial Facility, P.O. Box 600, Pendleton, Indiana 46064-0600
(765) 778-8011

The literacy program at Indiana's Correctional Industrial Facility uses inmate-to-inmate tutoring to address the diverse needs of inmates whose reading skills range from total non-readers to almost the sixth-grade level. The inmate-tutors receive training in tutoring, which continues each week throughout the program to ensure that their tutoring skills keep growing. Each week, the learner works with such literacy materials as the Laubach Adult Literacy Program, Merrill Linguistics, the Language Tune-Up Kit, the Electronic Bookshelf, and several phonics programs. In addition, journal writing and keyboarding are key components of the program. Newspapers also are used to help the learners gain skills they can use after leaving the facility and to familiarize them with an excellent information resource.

Virginia's Project PROVE: Virginia Department of Correctional Education and Department of Psychology, Virginia Commonwealth University

Marilyn P. Harris, Legislative Liaison
Department of Correctional Education, James Monroe Building, 7th Floor; 101 North 14th Street, Richmond, Virginia 23219
(804) 225-3336

Project PROVE (Preventing Recidivism through Opportunities in Vocational Education) is a cooperative effort between the Virginia Department of Correctional Education and the Department of Psychology at Virginia Commonwealth University. PROVE was developed to enhance career and life planning skills in female offenders about to return to society. Graduate and undergraduate student volunteers from Virginia Commonwealth University teach the course, which soon will be replicated in the male population. PROVE is a highly structured psychoeducational program which addresses the employment needs of female offenders. It consists of twelve weekly classes lasting three hours each. Students receive out-of-class assignments each week and attendance is mandatory. The program is divided into five units focusing on responsibility, self-assessment, job search strategies, interviewing skills, and adjustment to work and home. Participants are selected on several criteria. First, they must be within six months of release. Second, they must have participated in at least one other department of correctional education course. Third, they must remain infraction free. Finally, they must express motivation and an interest in establishing employment once released.

Correctional Industries

6

Introduction

As incarcerated correctional populations increase and operational costs continue to escalate, prison and jail industries and inmate work programs are encountering ever-growing and varied demands. Correctional management and the general public expect industries and work programs to employ more inmates and respond to the expectation that inmates work. Paroling authorities are requiring that these programs produce skilled inmates who upon release can secure a job with a living wage so that they are less likely to commit a new crime. Legislators demand that industries be self-sufficient, operate like a business, and help reduce the cost of incarceration. They also look to industries and inmate work programs to assist in cleaning up the environment by recycling. However, these same legislators expect prison industries to recycle in areas that have proven unprofitable in the business community. The business community demands that industries and inmate work programs not present unfair competition and that they be a source of labor in a labor-starved economy. Customers demand quality products and services delivered on time.

The submissions included in this chapter reflect efforts by prison industries and inmate work programs in various governmental jurisdictions to respond to a number of these demands. Often, these expectations can be in conflict with each other. For example, prison management's demand to employ more inmates in industries may conflict with legislative demands that industries be self-sufficient.

The solicitation of articles for this prison industries chapter was accomplished through announcements published by the American Correctional Association, the Corrections Industries Association newsletter and web site, and through word of mouth. The result was receipt of fifteen articles from nine jurisdictions.

The committee members individually scored and ranked the articles based on a preestablished criteria and a weighted evaluation system. The criteria included those established by the American Correctional Association and program-specific criteria. Program-specific criteria included innovation, replicability, start-up costs, use of technology, interaction with education, partnership with private business, and the impact on private industry. The committee also considered each program's positive impacts on industries as a business, inmates, prison management, and the customers. A composite score from committee members was generated and an overall ranking was created.

The following seven submissions represent sound programs and practices responsive to many of the competing demands on prison industries and work programs that correctional administrators must address.

The Free Venture Program of the California Department of the Youth Authority allows the private sector to establish a work site within the department's institutions to train and hire incarcerated youth.

Pride Enterprises, in Florida, is responsible for the industrial job skill training of inmates in Florida State Prisons and for their postrelease transition support upon returning to the free community.

Computer operations in Hawaii Correctional Industries train inmates for very well-paying jobs on the outside.

Western Illinois Correctional Center's meat processing plant teaches inmates job skills.

New Jersey's prison industries, Deptcor, provides a variety of garments for the state based on an arrangement with a county jail.

Ohio Penal Industries has developed a manufacturing resources planning software package that links business planning, sales, operation planning, production planning, and support systems for capacity and materials, which insures ontime delivery, elimination of back orders, and greater efficiency in all areas.

The Mobile Home Recycling Project is one of the Wisconsin Department of Corrections' unique community service projects that creatively links the public, private nonprofit, and business sectors to rehabilitate otherwise unusable mobile homes and then turn them over to low-income individuals.

Committee chair:

Michael J. Sullivan
Secretary
Wisconsin Department of Corrections

P. O. Box 7925
Madison, Wisconsin 53707-7925
(608) 266-4548

The Free Venture Program

Introduction

The mission of the California Department of the Youth Authority (CYA) is to protect society by providing training and treatment to juvenile and young adult offenders in eleven institutions and four mountain conservation camps, with aftercare services and supervision during parole. One of the primary vehicles for achieving this mission is the preparation of youthful offenders for future employment with an emphasis on job placement and retention. To accomplish this goal and further provide for public safety and correctional accountability, the department has developed and implemented the Free Venture Program.

The Free Venture program is a unique concept that enables the private sector to set up a work site within the department's institutions to train and hire incarcerated youth. The program trains youthful offenders for meaningful jobs, teaches employer's expectations for job retention, and aids in community placement. Major components of the program involve financial restitution to victims of crime and the reduction of institutional costs.

Presently, there are Free Venture Industries at three institutions: the Herman G. Stark Youth Correctional Facility in Chino and the Ventura Youth Correctional Facility in Camarillo with two projects each involving the private sector, and the Preston Youth Correctional Facility in Ione. The latter operates the department's only interagency Free Venture project.

Development and Design

The goal of the Free Venture program is to place an increasing number of youthful offenders in realistic work and training environments in the companies' work sites within Youth Authority institutions. The program enables youthful offenders to:

1) Reduce the cost of incarceration by using a portion of their wages (20 percent of the net) to reimburse the state for room and board during their institution stay

2) Increase their accountability for their offenses by using a portion of their wages (15 percent of the gross) to pay restitution to victims of crime

3) Increase their responsibility to society through payment of taxes and family support

4) Increase their opportunities to obtain marketable employment skills by working in settings and occupations comparable to those in the communities

5) Experience the rewards of planning for their future by withholding a portion of their wages (40 percent of the net) in accumulated savings for financial responsibilities and family support when on parole

6) Increase their success on parole as a result of improved work habits and job skills, and understand personal responsibilities in realistic work settings

On October 28, 1983, a Free Venture-Private Industry Task Force was assembled to create the foundation and implementation plan for today's program. The task force had representation from private industry, labor, county government, the California Youth and Adult Correctional Agency, and the Department of the Youth Authority. The Free Venture-Private Industry Implementation Plan was adopted and approved in April 1984.

On August 1, 1985, the California Department of the Youth Authority became the first youth correctional agency in the United States to be issued a certification for interstate commerce of "prison-made" goods from the U.S. Department of Justice. This certification requires that the program be voluntary; comparable wages be paid as those in similar positions in the same locality; deductions be made from the offenders' wages for income taxes, restitution for crime victims, and reasonable room and board charges; appropriate labor unions be consulted prior to the initiation of any project; and there be no displacement of employed workers or a surplus of available workers in the community.

In November 1990, the voters of California passed legislation that enabled the adult inmate population in the department of corrections and the county jails to work for the private sector. The federal certification was then transferred to the Department of the Youth Authority from the Youth and Adult Correctional Agency.

Implementation

The Free Venture program staff is composed of an administrator, a Free Venture specialist, and a clerical support person. These personnel oversee the program, acting as troubleshooters when issues cannot be resolved at the local level. They market the program and make contacts with company executives; negotiate contracts; follow the project through its inception; and ensure that laws, regulations, policies, and procedures that impact on the program are followed.

Each institution has a Free Venture coordinator, who is appointed by the superintendent of the institution and takes on this role as a secondary assignment. The Free Venture coordinator oversees the day-to-day operation of the projects and is the first-line liaison between the on-site company supervisor and the department.

The Youth Authority markets the Free Venture program primarily by participating in institution open houses, speaking to community business groups, mailing brochures and packets to interested parties, and attending trade shows. However, most of the projects were obtained through word-of-mouth. In the case of Trans World Airlines, Inc. (TWA), the company saw a need to have an on-call work force within a half-hour's notice to staff airline reservations work stations during their peak hours. After contacting several states, TWA determined that the Youth Authority could meet these requirements best.

The Free Venture program staff target expanding or new companies with labor-intensive work. The low-cost lease and a dependable work force not requiring company health benefits, make the program attractive to these companies. Since the first two projects began in June 1985, the youthful offenders have held a variety of jobs: sheet-metal fabricator, robotics and spot welders, fork-lift operator, power-sewing and embroidery machine operators, sheet-metal and fabric cutters, packager, cement caster, electronic circuit board assembler, office worker, inventory control clerk, customer service technician, drafter, microfilm machine operator, painter, assembler of various products, and telemarketer.

After a company shows interest in participating in the Free Venture program, many issues are addressed simultaneously. The appropriate institution and potential youthful offender labor pool are located. Then, contract negotiations and the approval process are completed. The work site preparation is completed and the company moves in their equipment and supplies. After this, the institution advertises the job openings in the living units, accepts applications, and screens the applications based on California Youth Authority and company criteria. When this has been completed, the company interviews, hires, and trains the youthful offenders; and the company personnel receive orientation from institution staff.

All requirements of the federal certification must be addressed prior to the start of the project. These requirements include contacting the appropriate labor union and community business organization, contacting the Employment Development Department for the comparable pay range, obtaining the unemployment rate, and the number of surplus workers in the job classification. Then, Youth Venture must ensure that the youthful offender participants sign an authorization form to allow the required wage deductions, including restitution for crime victims, and deductions for their savings accounts.

Outcomes

From June 1985 through June 1997, more than 2,550 youthful offenders have participated in the Free Venture Program and have earned more than $7 million in wages. They have contributed $600,000 for state and federal income taxes, and more than $2 million to help defray the cost of incarceration and to pay restitution for victims of crime. Almost $2.5 million has been placed in interest-bearing savings accounts to help the youth toward a successful transition when on parole.

The savings accounts have helped the youthful offenders pay for their own eyeglasses, contact lenses, braces for their teeth, college education, family support, and airline tickets for their children and guardians to visit them while they are incarcerated. Upon release from the institution, youthful offenders are able to use these funds for rent, clothing, food, college tuition, books, and transportation. The checks are made out to the parolees and sent to the parole office. The parole agent then counsels the youth on using the funds.

Although a formal research study has not been completed, it is known that the participants selected for the TWA Free Venture Project are among the Youth Authority's youthful offenders most likely to succeed upon their return to the community. Various evaluations indicate that the overall population experiences approximately 50 percent recidivism within 24 months of release to parole. Based on 204 Free Venture participants, who had been released from the institution by September 30, 1994, 80 percent of the participants had not recidivated within 12 months. Also, based on 179 Free Venture participants, who had been released by September 30, 1993, 76 percent had not recidivated within 24 months.

Conclusion

Through its micrographics project, the Free Venture Program was a national model for the U.S. Department of Justice's Office of Juvenile Justice and Delinquency Prevention in Washington, D.C. This project was a partnership between a correctional agency, the private sector, and a Jobs Training Partnership Act (JTPA) agency. The company hired youthful offenders to operate microfilming machines, and it received Job Training Partnership Act funding to help defray the cost of training.

On May 15, 1995, the Free Venture program implemented its first project with a unionized shop. It took more than three years from the initial contact with this sheet-metal fabrication company for the project to begin. Most of the opposition came from the union's business manager. After the business manager left his position, contract negotiations went smoothly between the state and the new business manager and the owner of the company.

While they are in this program receiving training, youthful offenders are paid the minimum wage for three months. They then are paid entry-level union wages and pay union dues. The union will help the Free Venture participants obtain employment upon release from the institution. The company has hired several parolees at its Anaheim plant. One of them recently has been accepted for the apprenticeship program.

Many Free Venture program "graduates" have stated that the program helped them become responsible, law-abiding citizens. It raised their self-esteem, taught them transferable job skills, employer expectations to obtain and retain employment, and showed them how to be accountable for their actions. These "graduates" are attending college and getting degrees, working and getting promotions in their jobs, getting married, and having children. In short, they are living productive lives.

The primary purpose of the Free Venture program is to create near-normal, "real world" industrial operations inside institutions. In so doing, it causes disruptions to existing institutional relationships, raises conflicting legitimate business concerns, and introduces principles and ideas that have not been used or tried. For instance, during a lockdown, the entire institution traditionally has come to a standstill and youthful offenders are returned to their rooms. Businesses cannot operate without their workers. Youth Authority staff have been encouraged to release as soon as possible those youthful offenders who are not involved in the reason for the lockdown so that the business can continue production to meet their contract obligations.

The California Department of the Youth Authority continues to work toward eliminating obstacles to further expansion of the Free Venture program. These obstacles include Unemployment Insurance, tax credit concerns, Workers' Compensation, institutional space, and some elements of organized labor. The implications are enormous, but the program offers a great challenge to those seeking new ways to assist youthful offenders in becoming productive members of society.

Author:

Jay Aguas
Chief of Public Services and Program Support Division
Institutions and Camps Branch of the California Department of the
*   Youth Authority*
Sacramento, California

Contact:

Ed Wilder
Deputy Director
California Department of the Youth Authority
Plainfield Correctional Facility

4241 Williamsbourgh Drive
Sacramento, California 95823
(916) 262-1530

Prison Work to Community Employment: A Seamless Transition

Introduction

In today's global economy, whether in Florida or elsewhere, the labor emphasis continues its shift away from manufacturing toward the service and knowledge-producing sectors. The restructuring of the economy brought on by this phenomenon is having profound implications on the use of human capital. In today's economy, there are fewer high paying jobs; their numbers have been diminished by technological advancement and relocation to other countries. At the same time, there are fewer workers with the technical and social skills available to fill these jobs. It is against this backdrop that PRIDE Enterprises operates a comprehensive job training and community transition program designed to prepare inmate workers to meet the current and more sophisticated demands of business and industry.

PRIDE Enterprises, a private not-for-profit 501(c)(3) business, is responsible for the industrial job skill training of inmates in Florida state prisons and for their postrelease transition support upon returning to the free community. At the same time, the company is a financially independent, market-based conglomerate composed of many industries. This enables PRIDE to provide inmates with a broad spectrum of job skill paths that relate to the current job market. All of PRIDE's job training and transition programs are fully self-funded and considered integral to the company's business and operating cultures.

Since its authorization in 1981 by the Florida legislature, PRIDE has pursued its mandate—providing inmates with meaningful work, training in marketable skills, and helping them with postrelease job placement. This concept is fundamental to company operations and, when combined with a work environment comparable to that of the free world, provides inmates with the necessary tools to return successfully to free society.

Program Design

PRIDE's statewide industry operations are far-flung and diversified in both product and process. To account for this, the company developed a comprehensive process model that would satisfy not only the training and job placement needs of individual inmate workers but also the operational requirements of the business. PRIDE's process model consists of six parts.

1) *New Hire Orientation.* Newly hired inmate workers participate in a workshop introducing PRIDE's inmate programs at which time they receive a program handbook for their use.

2) *Training/Work.* Each inmate worker participates in a formal program of structured and certified on-the-job training and other related activities designed to teach workers occupational skills as well as the work ethic. The hallmark of PRIDE training is its formal recognition and certification by outside entities acknowledged as expert in the program's field. This ensures that all workers receive state-of-the-art skills training that they can carry with them out into the community to enhance their employment opportunities.

3) *Prerelease Workshop.* PRIDE staff counsel and brief workers on the postrelease process within thirty days of their release.

4) *Release to the Community.* Inmate workers contact their assigned job developer upon release to receive instructions for conducting the job search and receiving support services, if needed.

5) *Job Search and Placement.* PRIDE staff provide job leads to the participants and arrange for their interviews with prospective hiring companies using a variety of tools and techniques until a placement is confirmed.

6) *Continuing Support.* Following the initial placement, PRIDE staff offer continuing assistance through employment, social service referrals, and education assistance to encourage and support continuous employment, and to facilitate a permanent transition to the free community.

Program Implementation

Industry supervisors conduct virtually all on-the-job training with help from a small group of corporate staff for supplemental training activities and for administrative support. For every inmate worker, the company's primary focus is on technical or occupational skills training (including employability-skills counseling), preparing for jobs, and placing individuals in jobs upon release to the community. It is a holistic program in which these individual elements are integrated into a seamless process during which each individual worker participates to the degree permitted by his or her institutional environment.

Prerelease Program

Every PRIDE industry operates a formal and structured on-the-job training program patterned on the Florida Department of Education's curriculum model. Additionally, virtually all industry programs are certified by either the Florida Department of Education or other expert authority as bona fide training activities. This means that PRIDE's program graduates meet the stringent requirements of today's employers.

Each inmate worker participates in an individualized training program that may vary from 450 to 6,000 hours in duration depending on the complexity of the skill. The workers must meet the minimum skill and education-performance standards prescribed for the job skill before being awarded a certificate of achievement by the certifying authority.

Within thirty days of release, each PRIDE worker participates in a prerelease workshop to begin preparing for release and becoming employed upon return to the home community. This is a special program in which a staff member counsels workers on the job search process and gives them final instructions on how to contact a PRIDE job developer upon release.

Postrelease Program

The anchor for PRIDE's postrelease program is the job placement staff located at the company's home office. When released, inmate workers (now referred to as *participants*) contact the office by calling in on a toll-free line. The job developers give the former workers instructions that set the conditions under which both participant and job developer will operate for the duration of the job search and placement program. At this time, the job developer also assesses the participant's capacity to begin the job search. Considering individual needs, PRIDE offers temporary shelter, transportation, and clothing assistance to the participants to expedite their job search process.

The job placement process begins when the participants contact the staff job developer after release and ends with successful job placement. Each job search program is unique and special to the individual participant. During the prerelease workshop, which is conducted just prior to release, PRIDE workers complete an employment data sheet for use by the job developers during the postrelease job search. This data sheet lists variables such as home location and other contact information, education, and job skill levels, employment background and history, and other factors that are important to properly developing and carrying out a plan of action.

The job developers' objective is to assist all participants in finding a job that offers the opportunity to continue their work experience acquired while at PRIDE. The continuity of skill development, familiarity with the work environment, and use of earned training certificates in opening doors to employment opportunity can be important stabilizers in persons' transition from prison to the community. This is particularly relevant for individuals who may have had limited employment experience prior to incarceration.

Job developers often must work with several participants concurrently, meaning that they are almost always at different stages with participants on their caseloads. Certain participants need less control and direction than others. For these reasons, it makes sense for some participants to operate their job search with only general guidance and direction from the job developers. Under these circumstances, the job developer establishes an itinerary and gives the participant names and addresses of potential hiring companies. Following each interview, or at least daily, the participant provides feedback on the status and results of the search plan. The process thus described continues until the participant accepts a job offer or otherwise needs further consultation before continuing with the job search.

PRIDE's job placement staff use a variety of resources and tools with which to seek out job openings for their participants. These include networking with public and private groups, on-site data-links with the Florida Department of Labor's statewide job data bank, and heavy reliance on key employer accounts. Other resources include classified ads in the newspapers of the principal metropolitan areas, the Internet, and a variety of directories and journals.

Following initial placement, the participant enters the continuing-support phase of the process model. After thirty days of employment, the job developer follows up with the hiring company to confirm job retention and to address any problems or concerns that may have developed. PRIDE recognizes that some hiring situations do not work out and that the participant may need continuing assistance in making a permanent transition into the community.

Outcomes

The desired outcome of PRIDE's inmate programs is successful integration into free society. To this end, the company monitors the outcomes of pertinent functional activities such as job placement (as a percentage of workers released and available for employment); jobs matched to the participant's acquired job skills; and a variety of other measurable job placement performance factors. These measured outcomes are integrated with the other performance criteria contained in the company's strategic plan. Since much of the process model is unique, the company uses various relevant internal benchmarks to measure progress.

A significant measure of success is offender job placement in which individual participants and their employers enjoy a relationship that can be described as mutually productive and rewarding. PRIDE's annual report describes typical anecdotes of these "success" stories.

The ultimate benefit to the state is that fewer offenders commit new crimes and return to prison. For the past several years, former inmate workers participating in PRIDE's work and job placement programs have had a favorable record of performance and less recommitment when compared to nonparticipants.

Conclusion

PRIDE Enterprises has a multifaceted mission with intertwining business and social objectives. The PRIDE process model serves state-mandated rehabilitation goals by identifying and acting upon the social and training needs of assigned inmates. At the same time, it supports the company's business interests by providing its inmate workforce with direction, support, and skills training thereby advancing company performance in the marketplace. The success of this program depends, to a large extent, on the development of successful intracompany and intercompany relationships.

Contact:

Timothy J. Mann
Manager
On the Job Training Support
PRIDE Enterprises

Suite 103
12425 28th Street, North
St. Petersburg, Florida 33716
(813) 572-1987

Computer Operations: Partnership for Powerful Communications

Introduction

Hawaii Correctional Industries operates under the State Department of Public Safety. Like other states, Hawaii is plagued by crowded prison and jail facilities and a lack of available funds for educational and vocational programs for those who are incarcerated.

Against this backdrop, Hawaii Correctional Industries Computer Operations has enjoyed steady growth and ever-increasing educational opportunities for inmates since its inception in July of 1992. In 1991, Kapi'olani Community College established a certificate program in computer programming at Halawa Correctional Facility. It consisted of a four-course series that taught the students the fundamentals of database programming on MS-DOS based computers. When the first class completed the series in May of 1992, they were proud of their accomplishments while frustrated at not being able to continue their work with computers.

Development and Implementation

The initial computer program was developed as a partnership between Kapi'olani Community College, correctional education, and correctional industries. Similar to the California Department of Corrections' Training-Industry-Education program, it was designed as an on-the-job training program to follow the four-course certificate program already in place. Correctional industries' role in the partnership was to provide supervision, space, computer hardware and software, and to market the program statewide.

The initial effort involved the recruitment of four of the certificate students. Correctional industries staff wanted more participants, but the inmates saw the venture as risky and untested. They were reluctant to volunteer to participate. Once recruited, the inmates began by setting up their new computers and attaching to the network used by the correctional industries administrative staff. They enthusiastically grasped the tenets of networking, a complex and often frustrating facet of computing. During this time, they selected the name Paragon Microsystems for their operation.

Each student worked on small computer programs for in-house applications using Clipper, a common database query language. That completed, they were assigned the task of writing the software for the administration of databases for the Aloha State Games, a set of Olympic-style games in which people throughout the state participate. It was a rather large-scale effort for such inexperienced programmers, but it was finished in time for the games. It worked very well, and it was with great pride that they issued their first invoice.

The next project required even more programming skills. Correctional industries was asked to create a three-level system for the management of the Chapter 1 program for the Department of Education. Chapter 1 is the law governing the management of special needs' students. It has extensive reporting requirements that require database management at the school, district, state, and federal levels. The task for correctional industries was to implement a system that the state could use at the three levels over which they had control. The program, which was completed and successfully implemented, continues to provide software for more than 200 schools, 10 districts, and the state education department.

Late in the spring 1993, correctional industries began evaluating vendors for its next thrust: hardware sales and service to government and nonprofit organizations. The goal was to eventually teach the inmates to build, sell, and service computers. To move into this new arena in a stepwise fashion, the program began by reselling ready-made, factory-built systems. After three months of analysis and hands-on evaluation, Paragon Microsystems selected Gateway 2000 as the vendor. The staff felt that by using a highly regarded vendor, they could enter the market quickly and effectively with the confidence in Gateway 2000's ability to handle warranty work.

As time progressed, the inmates were trained further in hardware technology so that they could provide warranty service and telephone consultations as additional services to the customers. The inmates began producing their own private-label computers. Initially, during this phase, correctional industries staff offered prospective customers a choice between Gateway and Paragon computers. Later, the Gateway computers were phased out of the product line. This provided the inmates with more hands-on experience at building and configuring computers and the opportunity to troubleshoot and repair problems.

All inmates working in computer operations receive cross training in every area of the business. This includes hardware and software training; advanced skills training; programming; networking; handling repairs and troubleshooting; handling clerical work, customer service and sales; inventory management; and peer tutoring. The inmates in the computer program are expected to treat this business as if it were their own.

Regular meetings are held with the computer operations supervisor to discuss ideas, problems, sales promotions, training, purchases, and other issues. The inmates take an active role in most every decision made that will affect the department. With very few exceptions over the years, the inmates consistently have met and exceeded the high standards that they are expected to maintain.

Stringent state-procurement policies, private-sector unfair competition concerns, and the very nature of the correctional industries concept of training inmates in viable skills, require that the inmates in the program build all the systems from the bare case to the completed product. Hawaii Correctional Industries does not sell "pass-through" products. Every computer is custom built to the exact specifications that meet the customer's needs. If customers do not know what they need or want, they are provided with free telephone consultation to assist them in arriving at a decision. In addition, every peripheral component must be sold in conjunction with an inmate-manufactured computer. Each computer that is sold is backed by a two- or three-year onsite parts and labor warranty.

This warranty policy presented some special challenges initially. The inmates in the program are medium-custody level and, as such, are not permitted to leave the facility to service customers' systems at their site. It was necessary for the staff to find a reputable vendor with high-quality systems and components that offered an onsite warranty program. In addition, that vendor would have to agree to allow the inmate workers to build the systems rather than their own factory-trained technicians while still honoring the warranty contract. Staff members canvassed perhaps 75 to 100 computer manufacturers before they discovered the award-winning vendor with whom they have been in partnership for more than two years.

Each and every computer passes though a very comprehensive quality control procedure that was designed and implemented by the inmates in the program. This procedure is performed 100 percent of the time and is the core of the commitment to good customer service. It is because of the extra mile the program is willing to go to maintain the highest standards of product quality that the vendor remains so supportive.

The demand for programming has diminished due to easily accessible custom and commercial software. To enhance the skill level of the inmates and provide more opportunity for the individuals, Hawaii Correctional Industries has gone into partnerships with a number of state agencies, nonprofit, and private-sector companies. One of these partnerships, the C-Key program, involves the refurbishing and repair of old computers and their subsequent delivery to the department of education at no cost for use by school children.

Education

The inmates working in this program must have a high school diploma or its equivalent or must be working towards one. The inmates employed by the correctional industries computer program are actively pursuing their A+ certification credentials. They spend approximately 1.2 hours per day as workload and time permits in self- and group-study and in hands-on practice. A+ certified technicians are recognized industrywide for a standard level of competence in the servicing of PCs and PC peripherals. The candidate is required to pass two computer-delivered tests. One test covers hardware such as PC's, Mac's, monitors, printers, and modems. The second test is for the operating system specialty. Inmates have the choice of taking either Microsoft DOS/Windows or the Apple Macintosh operating system test. Certification is a stamp of approval that tells prospective clients and employers that they have verifiable, comprehensive knowledge in the area of PC repair. The going rate for PC repair technicians in the state of Hawaii is $50 to $75 per hour.

Outcomes

Since its first computer sale in June of 1993, the program has generated more than 6 million dollars in revenues. During these four years, Hawaii Correctional Industries Computer Operations has trained and employed a total of thirty-seven inmates. While this is a relatively low number of inmates in relation to the total prison population, the program is growing every year.

While no data are available as to the recidivism rate of individuals who have successfully participated in the program, thus far none of the participants who has left the facility on parole has returned. Even more, the inmates in the computer program tend to remain in contact with correctional industries' staff after they have been paroled.

At the present time, one parolee has his own computer business. Another is a network administrator for a very large corporation in Slovakia. And still another, who has been out for only a month, is attending classes provided by the Small Business Administration and other local programs to have every opportunity to establish his own successful computer sales and repair business. He also is exploring the prospects of forming a joint venture project with Hawaii Correctional Industries and the nonprofit parole program he currently is attending. This program, if implemented, will provide the parolees a guaranteed aftercare program to attend. Staff then would have trained computer technicians to provide the on-site warranty coverage for the program while at the same providing another opportunity for them to have a steady, well-paying job immediately upon their release from prison.

Conclusion

As with any business, the program's participants must build and maintain its reputation. The program achieves this by being competitive with outside vendors, producing a quality product, providing for after-the-sale service, and maintaining a skilled and competent workforce. Staff also face many of the same challenges as other computer businesses and some that are unique to the prison setting.

Two recent attempts at relieving the facility crowding problem have resulted in many of the highly skilled inmates in the program being relocated to private correctional facilities in Texas. The program frequently recruits new workers to handle the natural attrition rate.

Two years ago, security problems at the prison resulted in a two-month partial lockdown of the facility. The correctional industries workers did not report to work during this time, and the emergency hiring of civilian workers became necessary to keep up with the workload and to ensure that the customers' needs would continue to be met. This endeavor was extraordinarily costly. Since Hawaii Correctional Industries is mandated to be self-sufficient, it is imperative to have adequate resources to handle emergency situations.

While every business is susceptible to dishonest employees, the operation faces a theoretically greater risk given the background of its employees. Supervisors must work closely with security staff to be mindful of the safety and security of the facility, staff, and inmates.

Nonetheless, the Hawaii Correctional Industries Computer Operations department offers a highly innovative program, the first of its kind in the nation. It continues to generate a high level of interest as more and more businesses and individuals realize that computers are the future and the future is now.

Author:

Deborah Ross
Hawaii Department of Public Safety

Contact:

Lynn McAuley
Administrator, Correctional Industries
Hawaii Department of Public Safety

919 Ala Moana Boulevard
Honolulu, Hawaii 96814
(808) 486-4883

Meat Processing Plant

Introduction

Gross sales of more than four million dollars with production slightly over three million pounds of product would be a good set of numbers for any small industry, let alone one located within a correctional setting. The work ethic can be a focus of any correctional program, but it is unusual for the program to have such a good combination of training and production as the meat processing plant at Western Illinois Correctional Center.

Development and Design

In 1990, under the direction of Bradley, Likins, Dillow, Drayton Architects and Engineers with the services of Hendon-Lurie and Associates Process Consultants, ground was broken for a new meat processing plant at Western Illinois Correctional Center. The center itself opened in 1989 as a medium-security facility. The physical plant consists of 4,248 square feet dedicated to the production of the product; 4,050 square feet of refrigerated storage and an additional 2,000 feet for shipping and receiving.

Subsequently, an inmate work force opened the meat processing plant, which ultimately produced 225,000 pounds of product during its first eight months of operation. Since then, production has grown to 3,190,696 pounds per year, which represents the total sales of such items as beef franks, cold cuts, chicken patties, fish patties, burritos, hot wings, single-serve pizzas, sliced roast beef, and a full array of other products. There are a total of seventy-six available items. Not only do the staff and inmates of the plant produce a large number of products, they are responsible for the purchasing, controlling the inventory, labeling, and shipping of the items as any other small business in the food processing industry.

The correctional industry program at the Western Illinois Correctional Center is a success in the marketplace. Even more, it is a success with respect to training inmates about the real world. Those inmates who are employed work one of two shifts and punch in on a timeclock similar to their counterparts in the free world. Their pay is based on profit sharing for those involved on the production floor and an hourly rate for those nonproducers, who still are required to operate the plant. There are required production schedules, shipping schedules, and inventories in this operation as in the free community. The inmates learn the importance of quality control, as well.

In 1994, the plant received one award for the championship wiener and a second award for the champion ready-to-eat sausage. In 1995, the white chicken patty produced by the plant was given an award as the champion poultry product, and in 1996, the plant was honored with a reserve grand champion in the variety class of uncured meat for its beef chicken fried steak. In addition to its award-winning recognition for quality, the plant is not only a part of an American Correctional Association accredited institution, functioning within rules and guidelines of the Illinois Department of Corrections; but it also is required to meet all requirements for food production established by the Illinois Department of Agriculture. There is an inspector, as required, on site to supervise production to keep within their guidelines. The four million dollars growth in sales is a tribute to this efficient and effective correctional industry.

Conclusion

It is difficult to run any type of food processing operation given all of the community guidelines. Nonetheless, the meat processing plant at Western Illinois Correctional Center is an asset to the department of corrections and the correctional industry operation.

Author:

Jon M. Heckel
Assistant Warden
Western Illinois Correctional Center

Author/Contact:

William D. O'Sullivan
Warden
Western Illinois Correctional Center

Route 99 S., P. O. Box 1000
Mt. Sterling, Illinois 62353
(217) 773-4441

A New Partnership: Prison and Jail Industries

Introduction

As with many good ideas, this program got its start somewhat by accident. Back in late 1995, DEPTCOR's bureau chief in the New Jersey Department of Corrections received a call from the warden of the Sussex County Department of Corrections. During the course of conversation regarding starting a prison industry program, the warden stated that the facility was willing to provide a small space for an industry program. In March 1996, the department of corrections, through its bureau of state use Industries/DEPTCOR, entered into a partnership with the Sussex County Sheriff's Office, Bureau of Corrections, to produce a variety of garments for the state.

Development and Design

During the months prior to implementation, the details of the program were ironed out. DEPTCOR agreed to provide fourteen sewing machines to produce products currently manufactured by DEPTCOR (e.g., aprons, a variety of bibs, laundry bags, scuffies, and boxer shorts). The sales of these items were booming and DEPTCOR was having difficulty meeting the demand. This arrangement with Sussex County was just the answer.

DEPTCOR agreed to pay the Sussex facility on a piecework basis for its production. The warden felt that he could generate enough jobs and production to have the program pay for the cost of the officer/instructor and the inmates. Since he did not have to lay out any money for capital or a sales force, his expense to operate the program was minimal.

Based upon this understanding, DEPTCOR's bureau chief drafted a letter of agreement between the two agencies for review by each agency's head. During the development stage, DEPTCOR obtained the necessary production equipment while Sussex began minimal renovations to the shop area. When the minor electrical renovations to the shop were completed, DEPTCOR delivered and installed fourteen machines.

Implementation

After the letter of agreement was signed and the machinery was in place, operations began. The first goal was to provide intense training to the Sussex County corrections officer who was selected to supervise the program. The selection of this individual turned out to be instrumental to the program's success. DEPTCOR dedicated two weeks of intense training from their clothing shop supervisor to teach the basics of operating a sewing machine. Additional instruction also was provided in the overall management of a production shop, including record keeping, shipping, packaging, and assembling garments. DEPTCOR provided detailed, written instructions on the assembly of each item for reference. The corrections officer is responsible for planning production and assigning the inmates to specific tasks.

Outcomes

Since its inception in March of 1996, the program has proven to be very successful. By the end of 1996, the Sussex County Jail Industries program in partnership with the New Jersey Department of Corrections/DEPTCOR had produced more than 80,000 items. On a daily basis twelve-to-fifteen inmates work in the shop earning between 28 and 58 cents an hour. This is the highest-paying job in the institution and is very desirable. Through December 30, 1996, DEPTCOR paid more than $30,000 for products manufactured by Sussex inmates. Starting in July of 1997, DEPTCOR will deliver a special trimmer to Sussex County and provide instruction on the production of handmade highway brushes.

The program was a success from the start. The warden achieved his goal of putting more of his inmates to work with little or no expense to the institution, and DEPTCOR was able to find another avenue for production without the investment in civilian personnel. The commissioner of the department of corrections has presented this program to the governor as an example of the cooperative effort between state and county government.

Conclusion

The success of this program was really clear from the start. Both parties had a sincere interest in seeing this idea become a reality. There is a strong need to foster, whenever possible, intergovernmental relationships. This program satisfied the needs of both agencies and did so without any negative impact on the private sector. It is a model that can be replicated anywhere in the country, with desire to do so as the catalyst for success.

Program Specific Criteria

Innovation/high interest

Sometimes the obvious is oblivious. In this case, DEPTCOR had been seeking another source of production for various garment items. As luck would have it, Sussex County was looking to employ inmates. The match was perfect! DEPTCOR found a willing subcontractor. From an industries' perspective, this worked out well. DEPTCOR was unable to obtain additional production space in its existing institutions. In addition, the state instituted a hiring freeze and although industries was to some extent exempt from the freeze, it was still very difficult to hire staff.

In New Jersey, county correctional facilities are operated independently from the state, and oftentimes are at odds with state rules and regulations. In this instance, these two agencies were able to form a partnership between two levels of government, which had advantages for both. It is their belief that there are many jails with populations large enough to support an industry program but are without the proper resources, both knowledge and capital, to get started. DEPTCOR has opened another jail industry program in partnership with the Camden County Department of Corrections, employing more than twenty inmates. DEPTCOR is currently beginning another jail industry program with the Gloucester County Sheriff's Office, and they are evaluating the feasibility of establishing a jail industry partnership with Monmouth County. In April 1998, DEPTCOR received the Jail Industries' Innovative award for their program.

Replicability

This program is easily replicable. In fact, all it really takes is a desire among both parties to make it work. A key factor in the success of the program was the letter of agreement, which outlined the responsibilities of each agency. Although somewhat tedious, the document provided guidance to both agencies and established the parameters of a formal business relationship.

Start-up costs

Start-up costs on DEPTCOR's part were minimal. The only significant outlay was the cost of capital equipment, which averaged about $2,000 for each machine. However, DEPTCOR maintains an inventory of used equipment, and with few exceptions it was able to furnish the shop with those units. It is DEPTCOR's responsibility to maintain the equipment. There is minimal administrative expense. Since they are not dedicating a full-time instructor to the program, there is no instructor salary overhead assigned to the program.

Although it required some effort to get the program started, the agencies now have established lines of communication, which serve both parties well. DEPTCOR sends a truck to pick up the products about every two weeks. Sussex gets paid by DEPTCOR on a monthly basis. DEPTCOR requires that the money paid to Sussex for production be used to pay inmate wages, but DEPTCOR does not dictate the pay scale. Sussex uses a portion of that money to cover the expense of the officer/supervisor.

Use of technology

This particular program does not place a high emphasis on technology, but that is not to say that other programs could not. The goal was to develop, as quickly as possible, an industrial program in a county jail. From a training and cost perspective, this was the easiest and fastest industry to establish. In the future, DEPTCOR will be looking to explore other programs, which have a greater dependence upon current technologies.

Business Focus

From a correctional industries perspective, this program has many advantages. DEPTCOR is able to expand its production capacity for only the cost of capital equipment. Sales, which may have been lost due to high demand and low supply, now are captured since its production capacity has increased. In fact, DEPTCOR has found that county jail inmates are more productive than those in its state program. Part of the reason is that jail inmates can spend about seven hours a day in full production. The inmates eat in the shop and are counted in the shop allowing for greater production. In addition, they have created a great partnership with their county jail counterparts.

Inmate Focus

The inmates in this program have taken ownership of the shop. When it started, only five inmates were employed. At first, they were a bit discouraged since they were being paid by the hour with an incentive for reaching production goals. After several days, production picked up, and the inmates realized the potential for earning a decent income. When it came time to add more workers to the shop, the existing inmates took great interest in who was going to work with them. They did not want anyone who was not serious about the job since wages were tied to production incentives. All the inmates learned job skills, which are transferable to similar jobs on the outside in New York's garment district. Most importantly, it gave inmates, who would otherwise be idle, an opportunity to learn a skill and earn some income.

Prison Management Focus

This program created many additional work opportunities for state inmates housed in county jails. Without this partnership, those inmates most likely would be idle since there are no other work opportunities available to county inmates who are confined to the institution.

Customer Focus

DEPTCOR's partnership with Sussex County and Camden County has been extremely beneficial to their customers. DEPTCOR had significant backlogs for all the items they contracted for with Sussex. As a result, DEPTCOR is able to satisfy customer demand, which had been increasing steadily. The production of new goods has allowed DEPTCOR to complete customer commitments and develop inventories of products.

Contacts:

Leonard S. Black
Chief
DEPTCOR

P. O. Box 867
Trenton, New Jersey 08625-0867
(609) 292-4398

Peter Terranova
Warden
Keogh-Dwyer Correctional Facility

39 High Street
Newton, New Jersey 07860
(973) 579-0885

David Owens
Warden
Camden County Correctional Facility

330 Federal Street
Camden, New Jersey 08103
(609) 225-7632

Manufacturing Resource Planning Implementation

Introduction

The most dynamic advancement undertaken by the Ohio Department of Rehabilitation and Correction's Ohio Penal Industries in recent years is the implementation of a manufacturing resource planning software package (MRPII). MRPII software is made up of a variety of functions linked together: planning for business, sales and operations, production, and support systems for capacity and material. Output from these systems is integrated with financial reports such as the business plan, purchase commitment report, shipping budget, and inventory projections.

Historically, the state's penal industries had a reputation for being unable to fill and deliver products in a timely manner. Despite acres of raw materials and millions of dollars in finished goods on hand, it could not fill its customers' requirements on time. Too often, one crucial part remained missing. Ohio Penal Industries staff were unable to accurately answer the customers' inquiries on the status of their orders. The penal industries operation clearly needed a method of balancing inventory-tracking capacity, scheduling, and accounting for work-in-process.

In short, Ohio Penal Industries needed an integrated manufacturing information system. A search committee was formed to select an information system to enhance its business operations in the following areas:

- Controlling and tracking mechanisms for inventory, purchasing, customer-order entry, production, shipping, costing, and financial management

- Bills of material and process routings

- Work-in-process reporting

- Product costing

- Reducing paperwork and manual/redundant tasks

The committee selected the Symix Solution—an MRPII software package that integrated sixteen business functions.

Development and Design

The development of the new system began with an implementation planning and analysis effort called a Business Process Review. This review involved a twelve month in-depth analysis of the penal industries' organization, manufacturing processes, and an MRPII sizing and development study.

Ohio Penal Industries staff chose to implement twelve of the available modules with the intent of adding data collection (bar coding) and CAD interface later in the process. The plan was to bring three representative institutions on-line, along with the central offices and central distribution function.

To network all locations, a cable plant needed to be installed at all of the department's facilities. The project consisted of installing a T1 telecommunication line and an Ethernet backbone at each prison. Some locations were connected by a radio frequency local area network (LAN), which is wireless. All users are running a telephone network session on a Windows-based system connected to an Ethernet backbone. The server (SCO), which runs the database manager (PROGRESS), one corporate database and all MRP applications, has dual Pentium 90 Mhz with 256 MB of RAM and four 1 GB SCSI hard drives mirrored. All Windows users have 486 66 Mhz systems.

Implementation

Implementation began with an intense education and pilot program. Symix Systems consultants trained key central office and shop personnel on their customer-order entry, accounts payable, accounts receivable, general ledger, purchase order, inventory control, material requirements, shop floor control, and work-center capacity modules. As training sessions were completed, participants began building a pilot database to provide reinforcement for the training received and a database to test policies and procedures. The pilot database was used to develop: item master files, bills-of-material, routings scheduling techniques, and shipping processes. The decision to obtain an automated interface with the central accounting system for accounts payable and accounts receivable was a result of this process.

Once staff were comfortable with the processes and procedures developed in the training and pilot phase, the building of a solid database began. Since its product line was very simple, Ohio Penal Industries' Health Tech (janitorial chemicals) plant was selected to come online first. It was followed by the modern chair manufacturing plant, the designer furniture plant, and finally the central office/distribution functions. This was a five-month process during which staff concurrently operated the existing accounting system for all other operations. Two more plants have been added to online operations, and staff are currently in the process of upgrading to a client-server version of the software.

Data

The implementation of the Manufacturing Resource Planning information system is creating a revolution in new concepts and management techniques within the Ohio Penal Industries. For the first time, many personnel may see how their job fits into the general functioning of Ohio Penal Industries and the effect their work has on overall performance.

The most immediate advantage of the MRPII system has been the material requirements planning module. This module is changing Ohio Penal Industries' inventory-management philosophy from archaic reorder points based upon "economic" order quantities to calculating net requirements and time-phasing them to meet customer demand. Material resource planning answers the basic questions:

- What to order (or manufacture)

- How much to order

- When to order

- When to schedule delivery

Results

The five Ohio Penal Industries factories operating on the MRPII system have been able to reduce their inventories by as much as 50 percent while improving their on-time delivery performance. The designer furniture factory has reduced its open-order backlog from more than 38 percent over 120 days in June, 1995 to less than 2 percent over 90 days currently. The modern chair factory has improved inventory turns (where a turn is the return on an investment which equals the total sales divided by the inventory value) to 8+ annually and the health technology plant has achieved 12+ turns. Neither of the latter two plants has a past due customer order.

Through forecasting, even those factories that are not operating live on the system have improved their backlogs. In November, 1996, 30 percent of order backlogs were over ninety days. Currently, 76 percent of order backlogs are less than thirty days old with only 3 percent over ninety days. This improvement is possible simply because staff no longer wait to receive a customer order before beginning the material planning process.

The immediate availability of data has empowered staff at all levels. The managers no longer have to wait for a report to arrive from a factory or a salesperson to get information that is outdated even before it is received. Today, immediate access to current information is as close as the nearest terminal. Customer order information is available to everyone in Ohio Penal Industries immediately upon entry. Similarly, the availability of inventory, the status of purchase orders, the knowledge of shop operations, and more, all are consolidated at the nearest terminal. The managers are more confident in their informed decisions. Personnel at all levels find they have more time to perform their jobs because less time is spent researching data to answer inquiries.

The visibility provided by MRPII has improved teamwork, which has resulted in organizational changes. The ability to look at the bigger picture has given staff a direct understanding of the effects their activities have on others. It has become more evident that what is easier for one person may be extremely complex for everyone else. Staff understand "turf battles" and how to alleviate it by sharing information and working together to ensure that customers' needs are satisfied on time. This cooperative spirit resulted in moving the processing of purchase orders from the fiscal section to the newly formed materials management section. The move has resulted in better performance in purchasing, and in handling accounts payable and accounts receivable.

As the implementation process progresses, the system will provide ever more accurate information. System outputs will allow improved planning of order priorities, improved capacity planning, and better performance control.

Capacity-requirement planning is based upon the quantities and the due dates of both open and planned production orders. This information serves as input to the capacity-loading system, which quickly identified the finishing process at the designer furniture factory as a major bottleneck shortly after the plant came online. Information for replanning priorities alerts planners to discrepancies between open-order due dates and actual need. The system has the capability to indicate how many days each item should be rescheduled and in what direction. This enables the planner to take action to maximize the use of shop capacities.

Performance control information enables the managers to monitor the performance of planners, buyers, shops, vendors, and also monitor financial and cost performance. Control balances in the item inventory records may be used to generate reports listing variances from plans. Reports on item inactivity, inventory-investment projections, and purchase reports all may be used for performance evaluation.

Conclusion

The MRPII system holds great promise for continuously improved on-time delivery of customer orders at reduced cost. More and more productive information becomes available with each new step in the implementation process. The information provided by the system enables employees to better manage their time and efforts, and helps Ohio Penal Industries staff achieve the goal of continuous improvement.

Contact:

Tony Anderson
Director of Industries
Ohio Department of Rehabilitation and Correction

315 Phillipi Road
Columbus, Ohio 43228
(614) 752-0285

Mobile Home Recycling Project

Introduction

One of the Wisconsin Department of Corrections' unique projects—the Mobile Home Recycling Project—spans both minimum and secure facilities. The project is a joint effort of the Bureau of Correctional Enterprises, the Foundation for Rural Housing, Inc.—a statewide nonprofit corporation—and the Wisconsin Manufactured Housing Association. Inmates at the Kettle Moraine Correctional Institution, and the Black River and Gordon Correctional Centers, totally rehabilitate used mobile homes donated by the Wisconsin Manufactured Housing Association and its member organizations. The project, started in the fall of 1994, has been recognized for its creative partnership linking together the public, private non-profit, and private business sectors.

The Bureau of Correctional Enterprises is comprised of Badger State Industries, Correctional Farms, and Correctional Employment Programs. Correctional employment programs include community service programs conducted at department facilities. These community service programs sometimes serve as pilots or preindustries which, if they are financially viable, later may become an industry. The Wisconsin Mobile Home Recycling Project is one of these community service projects.

Development and Design

Ingenuity led to the inception of this project. Wisconsin Manufactured Housing approached the Foundation for Rural Housing, Inc., with the offer of older mobile homes available for donation. Fortunately, this followed a presentation by staff from the department of corrections to a statewide association of private nonprofit agencies, including the Foundation for Rural Housing. The presentation was for the purpose of expanding the department of corrections' already considerable community service program using inmate labor. The timing of these events contributed to the birth of the project.

The Foundation for Rural Housing's first grant proposal was not funded. The funding source, an agency interested in recycling, while impressed, passed the project by based on heavy competition for funding. This project was initiated ultimately through a federal grant developed by personnel of the foundation and the department. The initial eighteen-month start-up grant of $237,125 from the U.S. Department of Health and Human Services, Office of Community Services, allowed the repaired mobile homes to be given at no charge to truly low income (average less than $4,000 per annum, per person) and often homeless families. Grant funds covered the administrative and service costs of the Foundation, material costs (for example, new furnaces, new plumbing fixtures, shingles, and paint), transportation to and from the prisons, and set-up costs. The department donated its services. The Wisconsin Manufactured Housing Association through its member organizations donated the mobile homes. Though start-up was feasible without this grant, the funding provided administrative and services funds for the Foundation and allowed for the mobile homes to be given to the poor at no charge.

Implementation

The Foundation has the overall administrative responsibility for the Mobile Home Recycling project. These responsibilities include the identification of mobile homes for recycling, acceptance of the mobile home titles, payment and authorization of purchases of repair materials, arrangement for transporting mobile homes, and arrangement of the financing and identification of potential mobile home recipients. Because of the Foundation for Rural Housing's extensive administrative role, the administrative role of the department has not been substantial, taking perhaps 10 percent of a central office staff member's time. This position is charged with community service development as part of the governor and secretary's Inmate Work Initiative.

The housing association through its chief executive officer and member agencies is responsible for the donation of appropriate mobile homes. An appropriate home is one which, without prison labor, would be too expensive to repair. However, it can be rehabilitated at a materials cost of about $3,000 per home. A likely alternative for a mobile home in this shape would be landfilling, an environmental and social waste. Wisconsin has ample mobile homes which meet the "appropriate" definition.

The department's role is to repair the mobile homes. Inmates are first trained in one of the department's vocational training programs (for example, building services) and then put to work applying their new skills. The department provides the inmate wages, teacher/trainer, on-site supervision, repair scheduling, and security. It also provides the oversight staff for its share of the partnership.

Part of the reason for the recycling project's success is the existence of an ad hoc oversight work group. The group is made up of a representative of each of the major partners: the Foundation for Rural Housing, Inc; the Wisconsin Manufactured Housing Association; the Wisconsin Department of Corrections; each of the three correctional sites where recycling occurs; and Steenberg Homes. Steenberg Homes is the state's largest manufacturer of mobile homes. Steenberg's representative on the oversight work group is the immediate past chairperson of the Wisconsin Manufactured Housing Association and is a major benefactor of this recycling project, providing mobile home donations, technical knowledge of construction, and major assistance in the purchase of rehabilitation materials. The work group meets on an as-needed basis addressing such issues as fund-raising and coordination.

Outcomes

This arrangement is a winning arrangement for each of the partners. Rural Housing carries out its mission by providing low-cost housing to very needy families, at a low cost. Manufactured Housing members provide a popular public service, receive a tax benefit from the donation, and save landfill-tipping costs. The department addresses inmate idleness and performs a valuable community service by diverting waste from the landfill and providing low-cost housing for the poor. Inmates benefit by learning a viable vocational skill, by paying part of their debt to society, and by making their hours of incarceration more productive.

During the eighteen months of the grant, thirty-one homes and one transitional shelter for a Community Action Agency were provided, and three mobile homes were used as workshops at the prisons. More than sixty-six inmates were trained in the eighteen-month period. The skills that they had learned as part of the program in the three correctional facilities were applied to a visible product. Not only did that represent realistic employment, but they developed pride in assisting others. The work done met inspection standards. The materials cost was about $3,000 per home.

Since the end of the federal grant, the project has continued at a slower pace in order to make the program self-sufficient. One of the three sites has switched over to building conventional housing. Between April 1995 and April 1997, nine homes have been completed. The repair materials now are paid for by the families who will receive the homes. The average income of recipient families is slightly higher, and each placement is worked out with a local lender. There are many families who would like the mobile homes but cannot finance $5,000 and/or find the park or land on which to site the mobile home. The real problem has been in the cash flow for materials and covering the time of the Foundation staff who work with the families.

All the partners have the responsibility to raise funds for the project. For instance, the department has provided older workers as construction aides financed under a federal Older Americans Act grant and has involved local community action agencies to provide weatherization funds channeled from the federal government through the state. Weatherization funds have paid for costly items such as furnaces and also have provided for energy audits. The foundation has used Housing Cost Reduction Initiative funds from the state to help with closing and administrative costs. The department has successfully solicited the donation of building materials such as paint, electrical fixtures, and plumbing supplies to further lower the price of the project. It should be noted, however, that continuing the project is a day-by-day budgetary struggle.

Inmates have benefited from this project in a number of ways. An inmate at Kettle Moraine Correctional Institution described his feelings in this way, "Eight hours a day and you're not even in prison, as you work on the mobile home!" Another inmate expressed his appreciation for the opportunity to give something back to the community he offended when he stated that, "I like doing it for the poor people." At Black River Correctional Center, an inmate could hardly contain his enthusiasm before the first mobile home recipient officially took possession of her home. Another Black River inmate expressed a common theme in the mobile home project when he stated that the project, "gave me a little self-respect about things that I have done."

Low-income recipients have been elated in their reactions to home ownership. In a letter to Rural Housing, Lisa said in regard to her new mobile home, "Speaking for myself, it was a Godsend." Sandy, as quoted in a news article, exclaimed it was a comfort to know she could walk through her new home without worrying about falling through the floor. But Theresa perhaps stated it best when she said, "I really love it, it's great to call it my home."

Conclusion

This project is readily replicable as prisons across the United States are crowded and experience idleness problems. The project is feasible even in northern Wisconsin where one of the three sites exists and where temperatures dip to 40 degrees below zero. The work is done out-of-doors, but in inclement weather can be done in the mobile home itself. Therefore, space should not be an issue at most prisons.

Most states have vocational training programs that provide suitable training for this type of project. The Wisconsin Manufactured Housing Association is not unique, as similar associations exist in each of the fifty states and are included in the directory of the American Society of Association Executives. All states have private nonprofit and public agencies, which are committed to the provision of low-income housing and could be recruited for project administration.

While Wisconsin received a start-up grant, it was not essential. The project could have begun without the funds, albeit at a more modest level and based on a modest cost to poor families for the homes. This project can be replicated without substantial outside support. To support replication efforts, the state has developed a short video on the Wisconsin Mobile Home Recycling Project, which is available on loan. In addition, each of the partner agencies is willing to provide consultation to interested states.

An innovative staff with an entrepreneurial spirit is the key ingredient.

For the Mobile Home Recycling Project, the Wisconsin Manufactured Housing Association received the Summit Award from the American Society of Association Executives for its role in the project. The Foundation for Rural Housing, Inc., received the Fannie Mae Foundation Award of Excellence. News coverage for this project has been positive. Several newspapers have issued articles on the project, and a local TV station traveled seventy miles to cover the story on the first-completed mobile home at one of the centers.

Contact:

Art Besse
Employment Programs
Wisconsin Department of Corrections

P. O. Box 8990
Madison, Wisconsin 53708-8990
(608) 246-7576

Correctional Industries
Additional Program Entries

Rotary/Correctional Industries Mentor Program

Lynn McAuley, Administrator, Correctional Industries
Hawaii Department of Public Safety, 919 Ala Moana Blvd., Honolulu, Hawaii 96814
(808) 486-4883

There is little doubt that prison industries provide inmates with basic work and technical skills while incarcerated. However, transitioning inmates back to employment in the community upon release has proven less successful in many jurisdictions. The Hawaii Department of Public Safety has piloted a unique partnership between Rotarian clubs and its industries program. In the program, Rotary members act as mentors assisting recently released offenders to obtain and maintain employment. As part of this program, the department provided participating inmates with job seeking and job readiness skills.

TRICOR—The Vision for the Future

Senator James F. Kyle and Carle Diwota, Correctional Officer
Suite 5-A, 10 Legislative Plaza, Nashville, Tennessee 37243-0028
(615) 741-4167

Tennessee's correctional industries program is run largely by a state agency that is separate from the Department of Correction. This agency, the Tennessee Rehabilitative Initiative in Correction (TRICOR), is a unique entity combining the best of private-sector business practices and outcomes with the human development and rehabilitation aspects of a treatment program all within a government setting. For three years, TRICOR has been involved in manufacturing, business services, and agricultural jobs for inmates, as well as the sale of prison industry products and services. The sale of these products and services helps offset the cost of incarceration. TRICOR also integrates its prison industries with education and vocational training. In addition, TRICOR has a postrelease placement program for inmates leaving prison who have been trained in a TRICOR program. The program has had twenty-one referrals with eighteen inmates being placed in jobs, seventeen of whom remain employed after at least six months.

Proteus

Mary Rondou, Chief of the Financial Services Section
Bureau of Correctional Enterprises, Wisconsin Department of Corrections
P.O. Box 8990, Madison, Wisconsin 53708-8990
(608) 246-7555

The Bureau of Correctional Enterprises in the Wisconsin Department of Corrections has implemented an integrated computerized manufacturing and accounting system. This system is called "Proteus" and has resulted in better management information and control and cost savings. Since Proteus is a complete management system, all business information about the Bureau of Correctional Enterprises is readily available to management within minutes. In addition to improved management information, the implementation of automation has resulted in a major transformation of routine "paper pushing" tasks performed by central office support staff into meaningful employment opportunities for inmates in the institutions. This has generated a large number of data entry/terminal operator jobs in the correctional institutions and has reduced the need for full-time staff positions in the central office. Because of the flexibility of Proteus' operating system and the design of its software, other state correctional industry programs easily could adapt the system to fit their organizational needs.

Disturbance Preparedness

7

Introduction

There is very little more frightening to correctional administrators than the call notifying them of a disturbance in a facility for which they have responsibility. Such a situation requires an expeditious response, one that will protect persons and property, and one that may require the use of deadly force to quell. A thousand things run through the minds of correctional staff when faced with such a situation. It is impossible to personally organize the proper response when facing an immediate situation like a serious disturbance.

Correctional professionals have developed a variety of approaches to "prepare" for such a situation. This generally results in integrating staff recall procedures, using containment strategies, calling up of disturbance response teams, and using command center operations to forge a planned and practiced approach to dealing with emergencies. Over the last ten years, the "state of the art" of correctional disturbance preparedness has evolved significantly. Many agencies now have very sophisticated approaches to the preparation and management of such events.

The Disturbance Preparedness Committee reviewed nine submissions for this Best Practices project. The five submissions that are included in this chapter illustrate the various elements that must be considered in relation to disturbance preparedness, including policy development; command center management; and the training of decision makers, hostage negotiators, and emergency team responders. The committee believes these submissions represent excellence in preparation and management, and will be useful to other agencies as examples of approaches they may want to consider.

The Emergency Response Team of the Westchester County Department of Corrections was organized to handle a growing number of security-risk groups and other inmate disturbances, and as a result of its implementation has created a safer environment for both staff and inmates.

The Office of Emergency Preparedness of the Bureau of Prisons is an independent national response unit that supports the Bureau in responding to serious institutional emergencies and has formed cooperative agreements with other agencies to help when they are needed.

The Michigan Department of Corrections instituted an in-house training module on disturbance preparedness for new wardens and deputy wardens that taught them things not covered in the policies and better enabled them to handle emergency situations.

The Crisis Intervention Team of the North Dakota State Penitentiary is composed of a trained cadre of inmates who are in direct contact with suicidal inmates until the crises has passed.

The Critical Incident Management program of the Ohio Department of Rehabilitation and Correction is capable of responding to or managing any type of critical incident because of planning and training.

Committee chair:

Odie Washington
Director
Illinois Department of Corrections

P. O. Box 19277
Springfield, Illinois 62794-9277
(217) 522-2666

Westchester County, New York, Department of Correction

Emergency Response Team—Local Level

Introduction

In 1994, the Westchester County (New York) Department of Correction formally created an Emergency Response Team as a rapid-response force of correction officers and supervisors to deal with inmate fights, emergency situations, and critical incidents within its three correctional facilities. Its creation was prompted by several factors:

- A new influx of gang-affiliated members and security-risk groups in correctional custody

- An escalation in the number of inmate-initiated fights and fires that prompted the appointment of an independent inquiry panel by the county executive

- A sharp rise in the number of job-related injuries in the corrections workforce, partly attributed to training and deployment deficiencies during emergency responses

Prior to 1994, correction officers in nonhousing assignments (e.g., booking) formed the core group of security employees who would respond to emergency alarms. This deployment proved to be counterproductive in two respects. First, frequent interruption in the assigned duties of booking officers caused delays and back-ups in the admissions and discharge process of a fast-paced correctional system; and, second, the alarm response group lacked a primary focus on emergency preparedness and response, and specialized training in the handling of critical incidents in a correctional setting. Additionally, the lack of an organized, professionally trained and supervised rapid-response team risked legal liability to the county government and the department of correction for negligent assignment, failure to train, and failure to supervise.

Development and Design

The emergency response team was formed to better respond to the department's changing inmate population and to improve its alarm response process. The department's chief of operations was designated to oversee the team's functions. A team commander with the rank of captain was designated to direct day-to-day operations. Twelve supervisors and eighty officers were selected from the volunteers to become part of a highly trained emergency response team. A comprehensive mission statement to govern the activities of the team was developed and covered the following elements: conduct, physical condition, job performance, discipline, and responsibility.

Implementation

Work Schedule

A fourteen-day rotation schedule was developed to keep team members alert and attentive, while at the same time preventing staff burnout in high-stress assignments with strenuous physical activity. This rotation plan also allowed correction officers to go back to their inmate housing assignments with enhanced skills.

Training Plan

A detailed training plan was developed to comply with national standards on emergency training for adult correctional institutions, developed by the American Correctional Association. These standards recommend advanced training in firearms, crisis situations, chemical agents, defensive tactics, tactical procedures, and methods of negotiation and confrontation.

The training plan consisted of two phases: (1) an intensive five-day training program on riot control formations and drills, cell extractions, the use of the PR-24 baton, certification in the use of pepper spray, handcuffing techniques, and defensive tactics; and, (2) in-service training sessions during the fourteen-day rotation schedules on topics such as: the use of force, security-risk groups, emergency evacuations, cell searches, medical emergencies, and responses to security threats (for example, natural disasters, power failures, bomb threats, and inmate escapes). The combined preservice and in-service training plan served to upgrade the security-focused skills of the emergency response team members.

Intelligence Gathering

To enhance the department's mission of safe and secure custody, an intelligence unit was created within the team to track the movement and monitor the activities of any gang-affiliated and security risk groups within the correctional complex. A computer-based tracking system was developed to identify high-risk and violence-prone inmates and to disperse them so they would not be clustered in the various inmate housing units. Booking officers were given special orientation to acquaint them with various tattoos, items of clothing, and other identifying characteristics of gang-affiliated members and security-risk groups.

Additionally, a mutual assistance intelligence network was developed with related law enforcement agencies (e.g., New York State Police, New York City Correction Department, Westchester County District Attorney's Office, New York City Police Department, New York State Department of Correctional Services) to exchange information and intelligence within the criminal justice system.

Emergency Response Team Deployment

During the two active shifts of the department (from 7 A.M. to 3 P.M. and from 3 P.M. to 11 P.M.) an emergency response team consisting of one sergeant and six correction officers are assigned to respond to any emergency situations or critical incidents that threaten the safety and security of the local correctional system in Westchester County. They are activated at the request of the on-duty shift commander. Team responses to alarms are recorded by video camera. The presence of a video camera acts as a deterrent to correctional staff regarding excessive use of force. It is also a deterrent to inmates regarding future criminal prosecution or unfounded allegations about staff behavior.

Results

Program Cost

The 1995 operating budget of Westchester County formalized budgetary support for the emergency response team by providing funding for two sergeants and twelve correction officers ($732,940.). Additionally, the fringe benefits package for these employees amounts to $207,275. The operating expenses have been minimized by the department's access to federal surplus equipment (e.g., battle dress uniforms, gas masks, military boots, handcuffs, helmets, vests, and foul weather gear). In the 1997 operating budget, additional/replacement equipment (e.g., riot control helmets, plastic flexcuffs) totaling $4,100 has been ordered to maintain emergency preparedness.

Program Impact

The implementation of a specially trained and supervised emergency response team in the Westchester County Department of Correction has had a positive impact on correctional security, staff morale, inmate safety, and workplace injuries. As an illustration, during the first ten months of its existence (December 1994 to September 1995), the team responded to a total of 329 alarms (e.g., fights between inmates, physical attacks on correction officers) without any job-related injuries to staff and without any inmate lawsuits alleging excessive use of force or official misconduct by correctional staff.

In the two-year period before the creation of the emergency response team, lost work time due to job-related injuries escalated from 52.33 full-time equivalent positions to 112.99 such positions. During 1995, a downward trend developed, ending that year with the equivalent of 90.46 "FTE's."

In October 1996, the department's emergency response team was reorganized and its new scope included random cell searches and the discovery of contraband as part of their assigned duties. Thus far, feedback from staff indicates that creation of the emergency response team has created a safer workplace for uniformed and civilian staff. The feedback from inmates indicates that the unit is a disciplined and professional response team.

Conclusion

Because of its far-reaching impact on correctional security, staff morale, inmate safety, and workplace injuries, the emergency response team received the department's only unit citation award during a formal employee recognition and awards ceremony attended by the Westchester County Executive on August 5, 1996. The citation presented to the team stated that:

> Comprised of supervisors and officers from the Department's Tactical Unit who volunteered for this challenging assignment, ERT intervened in numerous high-risk and high-security situations with extraordinary success.

Their collective efforts over a 10-month period greatly helped to improve the safety and security of corrections as a workplace. The outstanding contributions of ERT members are a tribute to their professional training and devotion to duty.

The emergency response team in the Westchester County Department of Correction has made a significant contribution to improving staff and inmate safety and institutional security in a fast-paced and volatile work environment. The team has proven to be an important inmate management tool in a correctional setting.

Contact:

Rocco A. Pozzi
Acting Commissioner
Westchester County Department of Correction

P. O. Box 389, HQ Building
Valhalla, New York 10595
(914) 347-6020

Office of Emergency Preparedness—Federal Level

Introduction

The Office of Emergency Preparedness was created by the Bureau of Prisons' (hereafter Bureau) Executive Staff in 1990, as a result of an after-action report pertaining to the inmate riots at the United States Penitentiary in Atlanta, Georgia and the Federal Correctional Institution in Oakdale, Louisiana. The concept was for the Office of Emergency Preparedness to serve as an independent national emergency response unit to support the Bureau in responding to serious institutional emergencies, to facilitate and standardize Special Operations Response Team (SORT) training, and to establish regional logistical sites for storage of equipment for use during protracted situations. The Office of Emergency Preparedness also was created to play an active role in the field by accepting invitations to conduct emergency preparedness assessments, observe mock emergency drills and SORT exercises, and provide training.

The Bureau, as a part of its overall mission, has maintained an effective crisis management program. Crisis management involves the training of all Bureau staff for immediate response to emergencies arising during daily institutional operations. The SORT concept was developed to support disturbance control teams and hostage negotiation teams in their primary missions, not to replace them. This system provides the Bureau with a three-tier emergency response system. In all hostage situations, the hostage negotiation team is the Bureau's preferred response to safely free any hostage(s) and regain control of an institution. The negotiation process is the Bureau's primary method of responding to all hostage situations. Disturbance control teams are designed and trained to use standard disturbance control techniques professionally to both psychologically and, if necessary, physically regain control of crisis or disturbance situations. The use of chemical agents, riot control formations, and baton techniques are integral subjects of disturbance control team training.

The Special Operations Response Team is to be used only when all other avenues of resolution have been fully exhausted, and only with the warden's direct authorization. This team is activated and becomes directly involved in any situation that, in the warden's judgment, requires special tactical skills to accomplish an objective that the disturbance control and hostage negotiation teams cannot resolve. The regional deployment of the Special

Operations Response Teams requires the regional director's authorization. Its national deployment requires authorization from the director.

The Office of Emergency Preparedness is responsible for support to the institutions and regional and central office headquarters during an emergency. The office provides headquarters command center support and is charged with on-site crisis resolution at the crisis site. Additionally, the office is responsible for the development and structure of special operations and disturbance control team-training programs and certification standards.

Development and Design

During the past year, the office has been given the responsibility for coordinating several training sessions involving the command and control of crisis situations. The first session was a joint venture between the Bureau and the Federal Bureau of Investigation (FBI). This involved a mock emergency exercise at one of the Bureau of Prisons' new correctional institutions located in Beckley, West Virginia. This was the first joint training exercise between both agencies. It was designed to provide a realistic training experience for command and control staff from the local, regional, and national levels, and to offer on-site training for tactical and hostage negotiation teams.

The exercise involved the Bureau's special operations and hostage negotiation teams, FBI Negotiators and Hostage Rescue Team, as well as three FBI regional SWAT teams. The hostage situation involved two separate locations, twenty-four staff role players as hostages, and forty-five staff role players as inmates.

The exercise began at 5:00 P.M. on a Tuesday, and concluded at approximately 5:00 A.M. on the following Thursday. Over the course of the exercise, combined tactical teams from the FBI and the Bureau affected a stealth rescue of three staff who were not hostages but were trapped in close proximity to one of the crisis sites. The combined team made a dynamic, explosive entry and rescue at one site and negotiated a partial surrender and made a deliberate entry at the final crisis site. Negotiations were conducted throughout the exercise by both the Bureau and FBI hostage negotiators. The institution at Beckley was under construction and close to activation but had not yet received inmates. The scenario inside the prison provided both agencies with a realistic training opportunity.

The task of planning and directing the exercise was assigned to the Bureau's Office of Emergency Preparedness and the FBI's Crisis Management Unit. Two hundred twenty-five FBI staff responded to Beckley and participated in the exercise. Staff participants from the Bureau included 320 of the Federal Correctional Institution's Beckley staff and 100 other Bureau staff who responded from various locations. The planning staff from both agencies worked very well together. The coordination and control of the exercise was accomplished by the Bureau and the FBI controllers.

Implementation

Given the lessons learned from the Beckley exercise, the Bureau and the FBI elected to conduct the first joint-training session for select, senior officials in critical incident command. This training was designed to better prepare senior officials of both agencies and occurred at the FBI Academy in Quantico, Virginia. Upon conclusion, it provided both the Bureau and the FBI with a cadre of senior officials who can be called upon to respond to a major incident where joint crisis-resolution efforts may be necessary.

Additional training sessions similar to the training at the FBI Academy were hosted by various Bureau regional directors for wardens and FBI agents in charge, who are affiliated with each respective region. Again, these training sessions were jointly conducted by staff from the Office of Emergency Preparedness and the FBI's Crisis Management Unit.

The Bureau's headquarters hosted a training session on joint command and control of operations involving incidents at Bureau facilities where FBI resources, such as hostage response teams and engineering research may be deployed. This training was attended by select wardens, associate wardens, captains, and communication technicians. The objective of the training was to establish a cadre of personnel who can be placed on temporary duty status to serve as relief for on-scene crisis management staff.

Recently, the Bureau of Prisons signed a memorandum of understanding with the Department of Defense to provide air transportation to move material, equipment, and personnel from logistical sites or other designated facilities. Memoranda of understanding also were signed with the Federal Bureau of Investigation concerning successful resolution of hostage situations or criminal actions, which require the FBI's presence at any Bureau institution, and with the U.S. Marshals Service for the apprehension and investigation of an escaped federal prisoner and related matters.

Conclusion

The Office of Emergency Preparedness is one of the most necessary, demanding, and high profile sections in the Bureau of Prisons. The capability and preparedness of the Bureau to resolve emergencies will be due, in part, to the actions and teachings of the Office of Emergency Preparedness.

Author:

Jim Warner
Office of Emergency Preparedness
Federal Bureau of Prisons
Washington, D.C.

Contact:

Communications
Federal Bureau of Prisons

Office of Public Affairs
320 First Street, NW
Washington, D.C. 20534
(202) 307-3163

Disturbance Preparedness— State Level

Introduction

A regional prison administrator recommended the development of a training program for newly appointed wardens and deputy wardens to assist them in better understanding the administration's expectations of their roles and to provide them with the necessary knowledge of issues pertinent to the successful performance of their duties. Although the Michigan Department of Corrections historically had sent staff at various management levels to the National Institute of Corrections, state civil service, and other training programs, it was felt that training geared specifically to the wardens' and deputy wardens' role and duties in the department was needed to enhance the potential for the managers to successfully carry out their duties.

A committee consisting of wardens and deputy wardens focused on what it viewed as the critical duties, responsibilities, and issues about which a new warden and deputy warden needed training. They acknowledged that although most new wardens and deputy wardens previously have held various management positions, those positions did not completely prepare them for the scope of responsibility and decision making that would be required of them as wardens and deputy wardens.

The committee members volunteered to participate on subcommittees that addressed specific subject matters. This review led to the development of six training modules for the training program, including budget and finance, external environment, leadership and management, prisoners' special needs and programs, personnel and labor relations, and emergency preparedness. The discussion that follows presents emergency preparedness.

Development and Design

The emergency preparedness module is of four-days duration and focuses on expected responses to various emergency situations, including disturbance control. Other emergency situations addressed by the training module include managing hostage incidents; preventing escapes, reporting, and processing; and managing disasters. The training begins with discussions about the basic principles for handling and reporting all emergency situations (e.g., using deadly force, keeping the public informed about the emergency incident to achieve rumor control, and providing appropriate information to the media, and understanding the role of law enforcement agencies). The training specifically related to disturbance control addresses some of the underlying causes of disturbances and potential preventive measures, which can be taken, including the timely and proper handling of prisoner grievances, identifying and monitoring of inmate groups, and controlling tools and contraband. There also is a discussion about the development of adequate disturbance control plans and the roles of various staff in containing and terminating disturbances.

Implementation

The first training program was implemented in 1996 with twenty participants chosen by the four regional prison administrators. The participants had been appointed to their positions within three years prior to the training. The training program instructors were chosen based on their experience and depth of understanding of the department's policies regarding the handling of emergency situations. Staff who had dealt with emergency situations presented the training material, which included discussing department policies, viewing videotapes of staff responses to past emergency situations, reviewing post-incident critique documents completed on those incidents, and engaging in small group activities in which the participants in the various groups developed responses to emergency scenarios. These responses, in turn, were discussed by the entire group and the instructors.

Approximately every two months, the participants received training as a group on one of the six modules with the length of training ranging from one to five days. The six modules constituted one full training cycle.

Results

Pre- and posttests were given to the participants to assess their knowledge of various issues relating to the handling of emergency situations and the improvement in their knowledge following the completion of the training. The individual participants were not identified on their test documents to allow them to answer the questions without fear of any lack of knowledge being revealed to the administration. The posttests showed some improvement in the level of the knowledge of the participants.

The training participants also completed an evaluation of the program indicating that it was very well received. For example, out of a possible five points, the average score was five for the statement "I am glad I was able to participate in this program." The average score was 4.7 for the statement, "The program overall has increased my knowledge of emergency preparedness."

Conclusion

Training participants expressed their belief that they benefited greatly from being able to discuss the deputy director's expectations about the role of wardens and deputy wardens in handling emergency situations and learning from the successes and mistakes of other wardens and deputy wardens who handled emergency situations in the past. The participants also indicated that they better understood the nuances of handling emergency situations that are not addressed in policy.

The training module on emergency preparedness received very high praise from the participants. Along with the other five training modules, the training was found to be so beneficial that the participants, the committee which developed the overall training program, and the deputy director believed that this training program should be provided to all wardens and deputy wardens, regardless of the number of years that they have held their positions.

Given this support from both leadership and management, the training program continues today in its second cycle for employees who are newly appointed and those who have been wardens and deputy wardens for a lengthy period of time. Several of the training modules have been modified to eliminate or add issues based on the evaluations of previous participants.

Contact:

Dan L. Bolden
Deputy Director
Michigan Department of Corrections

P. O. Box 30003
Lansing, Michigan 48909
(517) 373-0287

Crisis Intervention Team for Suicide Prevention

Introduction

The crisis intervention team was developed and implemented in October, 1980. Precipitated by three inmate suicides in less than a year, the institution was faced with a need to formulate both policy and practice that would provide suitable intervention while continuing to allow for the best use of already strained staff resources. The creation of the crisis intervention team vastly increased the institution's capacity to provide face-to-face supervision of crisis inmates, while simultaneously allowing other inmates the opportunity to meaningfully assist other inmates.

Development and Design

The program was not developed to supplant the level of staff involvement, but to supplement existing efforts. The primary goal was to place another inmate in direct contact with the crisis inmate twenty-four hours per day until staff reasonably could determine that the crisis had passed. Understanding the unpredictability of each crisis, the institution pursued a program large enough to offer services ranging from several hours to several days. The result was a team of forty-two active members and ten alternates.

At the start, it was understood that it would not be practical to offer this type of program to the entire general population. A basic set of eligibility guidelines were developed to glean the most sincere, prosocial inmates for the program. To apply for the team, an inmate may have no major disciplinary reports on his or her record for a period of six months. The inmate also must demonstrate compliance with all other institutional recommendations regarding employment, education, and treatment.

Once placed on the team, inmates are provided with substantial training in crisis intervention and suicide prevention. Initially, each member is given a packet of information on suicide behaviors. After having an opportunity to read the materials, staff are available to answer any questions. New team members also are provided with an initial classroom training program, and all team members receive annual training thereafter.

The basic training regimen entails a pretest, lecture format, and posttest. The format of the lecture provides for statistical information regarding suicides, basic risk factors, warn-

173

ing signs, intervention strategies, and program rules. Of the several rules which govern the team member's behavior, the primary emphasis is placed on confidentiality. Any breach of confidentiality requires immediate dismissal from the team.

With a fully staffed, fully trained crisis intervention team, the institution was able to schedule each member for various shifts of duty, each lasting four hours. Once complete, the schedule offered team-member services twenty-four hours per day, seven days per week. The forty-two member team allowed for each member to be called on no more than once per week. The addition of ten alternates provided a two-fold benefit. First, it allowed for uninterrupted service in the event of the absence of a regularly scheduled team member, and secondly, it provided for prescreened and pretrained replacements as new members of the permanent team are needed.

Implementation

The development of the crisis intervention team partially answered the questions of who and what, but efforts to implement a working program required a concerted effort by several individual departments. In answering the question of where, the security department developed a four-celled area separate from the main population conducive to crisis situations. The observation unit allows for privacy in a safe and secure environment, yet does not unduly isolate the inmate. The security officer assigned to this area is stationed within hearing distance of the unit and provides visual staff observations each fifteen-to-thirty minutes depending on the severity of the crisis. The plant services department equipped this area with both a roving camera to observe the entire area and additional wiring for a second fixed camera to be stationed directly in front of any of the four cells. This allows for a third form of observation and is linked both to the primary officers' monitor and the institutional control room monitor.

The next most obvious question, when, began simply but has developed into a complex array of staff involvement and training. All security staff receive annual crisis intervention and suicide-prevention training. As the security staff are in contact with inmates twenty-four hours per day, they are the most likely group to recognize the various factors indicative of crisis and begin the intervention process. They are equipped with a procedure, which uses a continuum of care, matching the level of crisis to the level of intervention. At the highest level of the continuum, the inmate is moved to the observation unit, and the crisis intervention team is activated. Once the team is activated, it continues without interruption until a member of the counseling staff assesses the crisis inmate and determines that he or she no longer requires that level of intervention.

"Why have an inmate-based crisis intervention team?" This is probably the easiest question to answer. The department believes that any activity that allows inmates to involve themselves in activities that promote prosocial thoughts, values, and beliefs will be a contributing factor in the overall rehabilitative process. Many times inmates can relate much more closely to other inmates' crises as they have had similar experiences during their incarceration. Where it may be difficult for a staff member to relate to the feeling of powerlessness and guilt in losing a close family member to an unexpected death, while not having the opportunity to attend the funeral or be with other family members, a fellow inmate may know exactly how it feels and share how they dealt in a positive fashion with a similar crisis. Often, the presence of another human being and the opportunity to talk through the emotions which precipitated the crisis are all that is needed. In other cases, the extra set of eyes is critical in the prevention of suicide attempts.

Based on the institutions' belief that inmate involvement as a member of the crisis intervention team was a clear indicator of prosocial values, a reward system of "good time" credits was implemented. The successful "team" member is awarded six days of meritorious good time for the first three months of service and an additional two days for each subsequent month.

Results

Much to the credit of the crisis intervention team, the North Dakota State Penitentiary has recorded only three successful suicides in the seventeen years since the inception of the team, the last in 1988. None of the suicides occurred while the team was engaged. This not only speaks well of the crises intervention team program, but equally well of staff.

It is speculative at best to propose how many suicides have been averted due to the involvement of the team. However, several inmates who were assisted by the team while in personal crisis have commented on how helpful the process was for them. The team has been engaged in hundreds of situational crises, for thousands of hours. A typical month might reflect one to two crisis inmates requiring a total of 100 to 150 hours of team involvement. At a time when cost can determine the success or elimination of a program, institutional staff have found the crisis intervention team to be one of the least staff intensive, least costly, and most effective models available.

Conclusions

Several lessons have been learned, primarily through trial and error, which ultimately have resulted in the crisis intervention team becoming a successful and necessary part of the institution's suicide prevention plan. The most important reality is the understanding that such a team will not work without an institutionwide commitment to a "big picture" suicide-prevention plan. Several different departments play a critical role in making the plan successful, and all have learned lessons of their own.

Administrative services is responsible to track the "good time" credits earned by inmate participants. The tracking process proved to be an overwhelming experience in the beginning. It is important to establish a minimum-service criterion of at least three months. This will eliminate those inmates who lack the initiative or desire to follow through with the program. However, it is just as important to limit the initial length of service to a reasonable time frame.

At the onset, the institution required service of six months and awarded twelve days of good time for each successive six months. The greatest problem arose from the fact that many of the team members would serve four-to-five months and subsequently get transferred or discharged, and receive no good-time award. The end result, as noted earlier, is a three-month probationary period followed by an award of two good time days for each full month served. This compromise allowed the institution to meet both needs.

The treatment department has the responsibility of maintaining the overall suicide prevention plan, providing adequate training for both staff and inmates, and all crisis assessment and follow-up. Timing proved to be a critical issue for this department.

An effective reporting system followed by timely assessment and follow-up must be maintained at all times. Many of these issues have been corrected simply through the use of a designated caseload, which matches each inmate in the institution with a counselor, a weekly on-call counselor for after-hours crisis follow-up, and the writing of the crisis incident report. The crisis incident report is a documentary process, which details the known circumstances of the crisis and the level of intervention used, followed by a routing system, which places those facts directly into the hands of the primary counselor.

The lessons learned by the security department focus primarily on learning what resources were available for crisis intervention and when each resource was best used, including the use of the crisis intervention team. It increasingly became necessary for all security staff, especially supervisory staff, to become trained and comfortable with assessing crisis situations. As this process progressed, it was found that during evening and weekends, when trained counseling staff were not available, the staff were taking a "better safe than sorry" attitude and overusing the crisis intervention team. While it is typically beneficial to err on the side of safety, staff found that the extended use of the program was causing team members to experience burnout and lose interest. Training and practical experience has resulted in a staff that is much more confident in conducting primary crisis assessments and applying the appropriate level of intervention.

The crisis intervention team cannot take the place of trained staff supervision. Standards of security and safety must be kept high. This program should be viewed as one of many weapons in the institutional arsenal of suicide prevention. Other critical tools include a well-trained staff, an effective reporting system, timely assessment and followup, and a continuum that includes several levels of intervention.

Contact:

Tim Schuetzle
Warden
North Dakota State Penitentiary

P. O. Box 5521
Bismarck, North Dakota 58506-5521
(701) 328-6100

Critical Incident Management

Introduction

The Ohio Department of Rehabilitation and Correction's Critical Incident Management program was designed and developed to provide an incident-management system capable of responding to, managing, and recovering from any type or kind of critical incident. Specific focus is given to inmate disturbances, escapes, hostage situations, bomb threats, natural and human disasters, fires, prison evacuations, utility failures, and employee job actions.

The purpose of the department's critical-incident management program is to provide policy and document direction, management expectations and functions, effective resource identification and use, and regular exercise of system components. It is essential that incident-management programs identify and address significant policy issues, which provide the foundation and expectation for those responsible for implementing the program and its components.

Background

The department adopted the National Wildfire Coordinating Group Incident Command System as its incident-management model. This system provides organization, role expectations, management principles, and other necessary support concepts to effectively resolve and recover from a critical incident. The Incident Command System provides a combination of facilities, equipment, personnel, procedures, and communications, which operate within a common organizational structure. It uses assigned resources to effectively accomplish the objectives related to a critical incident. As a management system, it helps to mitigate the incident risks by providing accurate information and strict accountability necessary for planning cost-effective operations and logistical support for any incident. The incident-command system can be used on any kind or size of incident and for preplanned events.

Design and Implementation

The effective management of a critical incident involves the sound use of internal and external resources. Each prison has established letters of understanding with external support agencies such as the Ohio State Highway Patrol to provide or make available their agency resources in the event of a critical incident. Prison officials must meet annually with the local support agencies to review the prison's plans and letters of understanding.

The department also has established in policy and practice requirements for special response teams, special tactics and response teams, and hostage negotiation teams. Special tactics and response team members have received training from the Federal Bureau of Investigation (FBI), Army Special Forces, Navy Seals, and the U.S. Marine Corps. The FBI also has provided training with hostage negotiators and special response team leadership to help forge a team capable of responding to any threat. Each prison must meet monthly training standards to maintain their team's qualifications and skills.

Training

During fiscal year 1995, prison employees began receiving basic critical-incident management training. More than 1,500 supervisors and administrators participated in a twenty-four-hour, advanced incident-command system training program. The critical incident management coordinators received an additional twenty-four hours of training in incident exercise design. They are required to conduct a monthly drill and perform table top exercises, functional exercises, or full-scale exercises. Specialized training continues to be enhanced to address the needs of the program. Finally, critical incident management training is a regular component of preservice and in-service training at the corrections training academy and at the central office.

Author:

Joe McNeil
Critical Incident Administrator
Ohio Department of Rehabilitation and Correction

Contact:

Tessa Unwin
Public Affairs Liaison
Ohio Department of Rehabilitation and Correction

1050 Freeway Drive North
Columbus, Ohio, 43229
(614) 752-1157

Disturbance Preparedness
Additional Program Entries

South Carolina Department of Corrections Emergency Response Teams

Michael Moore, Director
P.O. Box 21787, Columbia, South Carolina 29221-1787
(803) 896-8555

The South Carolina Department of Corrections' philosophy regarding emergency response and preparedness is that of having sufficient highly trained personnel who can respond in a timely manner to dispel or rectify natural or human-caused situations and restore facilities to good order. In emergency situations, the overriding concern of the agency is public safety. Staff actions are guided by a desire to preserve life and prevent injuries, whenever possible. Even under emergency conditions, staff attempt to maintain and/or restore humane conditions of incarceration. Staff also are committed to the protection of community and government property. Since 1982, the South Carolina Department of Corrections has developed and expanded its Emergency Response Teams to a three-team concept with Situation Controllers (SitCon) for negotiations, Rapid Response Team (RRT) for nonlethal force, and Special Weapons and Tactics (SWAT) for lethal force. In all instances where the Emergency Response Teams have been deployed, every situation has been resolved with no loss of employee life and with minimal property damage. After every major incident, the South Carolina Department of Corrections administratively reviews the disturbance and drafts a "lessons learned" summary, which is helpful in reducing the possibility of the same causal factors occurring again.

Oklahoma Department of Corrections, Southeast Region Hostage Negotiation Team

Patricia Sorrels, Local Administrator for the Community Sentencing Division
P.O. Box 669, McAlester, Oklahoma 74502-0669
(918) 423-1668

The Southeast Region Hostage Negotiation Team of the Oklahoma Department of Corrections was created to ensure that the region could respond to hostage incidents in a consistent manner with people trained in hostage negotiation. Created in 1995, the team consists of an administrative coordinator, a team coordinator, an assistant team coordinator, and eleven team members, all of whom were chosen for their knowledge, skills, and abilities in the negotiation field. The mission of the Southeast Region Hostage Negotiation Team is the preservation of life, through a total commitment to the negotiation approach and nonviolent resolution, and to achieve this mission by a vigorous employee education program and constant team training process.

Mack Alford Correctional Emergency Response Team

Mike Talley, CERT Commander
P.O. Box 220, Stringtown, Oklahoma 74569-0220
(580) 346-7301

A 1988 riot at the Mack Alford Correctional Center indicated that extensive training was needed to bring the emergency team to a continued state of preparedness capable of responding to any incident. Today, members of the Mack Alford Correctional Emergency Response Team (CERT) are trained and highly skilled in multiple assault and rescue techniques such as repelling, shotgun rescue, and sniper deployment. The Mack Alford CERT is the current Southeastern Region CERT competition champion as well as the Southwestern Law Enforcement Emergency Response competition champion, an honor they have held since 1995. Mack Alford Correctional Center staff also include two of the most experienced hostage negotiators within the Oklahoma Department of Corrections; they are members of the Southeastern Region Hostage Negotiating Team.

Disturbance Preparedness—Federal Bureau of Prisons

Michael B. Cooksey, Assistant Director, Correctional Programs Division
320 First Street, NW, Washington, D.C. 20534
(202) 307-3226

The Federal Bureau of Prisons has developed an emergency preparedness program that provides institution staff with the necessary tools to prepare for responses to various emergencies, serving as a "blueprint" for any critical incident that may arise. The Bureau also assists institutions with contingency planning by identifying critical details that need to be addressed. Such details include the "Planning by Committee" concept, the use of memorandums of understanding with local law enforcement agencies, yearly staff training to ensure that staff know what to do during an emergency, the use of mock exercises to make sure that emergency plans are realistic and viable, and periodic testing and routine review of contingency plans.

Employee Training

8

Introduction

The Employee Training Committee received fifteen submissions from state corrections agencies, the Federal Bureau of Prisons, and the Correctional Service of Canada. The submissions were reviewed with criteria developed by the committee that emphasized originality, quality, positive impact on the originating agency, and the potential for replication in other American Correctional Association member agencies. From this process, six submittals were selected for presentation in this chapter.

The top-rated program was from the Correctional Service of Canada. This submission describes the selection and training of program delivery staff based *directly on the principles for effective correctional programs set out in research* by Ross and Gendreau. The critical objectives of the training program include selecting staff who already have and consistently demonstrate the interpersonal skills that are demonstrable in program delivery; providing thorough training to the selected staff in the knowledge and teaching skills required to deliver the specific programs; and providing for follow-up and monitoring to ensure that program staff are using the skills and techniques in an appropriate manner.

Following training, two delivery sessions are videotaped. A follow-up training session is held. The tapes are reviewed and participants are given an opportunity to view a variety of styles and levels of performance. They are provided with both positive and negative feedback. Staff who successfully perform the training requirements are certified to deliver cognitive-skills training and are deemed eligible for training in other living skills components. After seven years, there are 220 correctional services staff and 50 contract program delivery staff who are working in institutions and the community who have been trained through this process.

Region III of the Florida Department of Corrections initiated a program that formed a partnership with five local community colleges to train and certify correctional probation officers prior to employment. Prior to the implementation of this program, the regional office filled its vacancies by hiring noncertified officers. They then were sent to an academy for basic recruit training. This procedure took twenty weeks, during which time the department paid the employee's salary, benefits, and travel expenses at a cost of $14,636 per trainee. Since the region averaged hiring eighty new employees per year, the potential avings by hiring only those individuals who completed the course work and were certified by the community colleges was estimated to be $1,170,880 annually. In addition, the department now is completing background investigations before receiving exam results and, thereby, has cut the hiring-cycle time in half—to just thirty days.

The Texas Department of Criminal Justice submitted a description of their Institutional Division Training Department, which provides staff development training for some 28,000 security and nonsecurity personnel. The training department provides instruction at six regional academies and through agreements with fifteen colleges and universities. Through these facilities, the department provides preservice, inservice, instructor certification, and management training programs. As an example, the Edmundo Mireles Criminal Justice Training Academy, the nation's largest corrections academy, began a typical training day "with 537 security and nonsecurity personnel simultaneously participating in five separate and distinct training programs, ranging from preservice to management training for first-level supervisors."

While Texas presents an excellent example of training for a large department, the Virginia Department of Corrections' submission describes the development of a new corrections academy and training programs provided for a medium-sized department. The Virginia academy is designed as a five-building, 126,000 square-foot facility with an administration/classroom building, a physical skill training center, a 200-bed residence hall, a dining hall, and a maintenance shop.

The submission by the Federal Bureau of Prisons describes an "Institution Familiarization Coaching Program." It is designed to create a dynamic mentoring program to meet the needs of new staff during their probationary year. All new staff are assigned an "Institutional Familiarization Coach" within thirty days following their initial training at the Glynco Federal Law Enforcement Training Center. The coaches receive specialized training in the area of counseling skills, interpersonal communications, probationary concerns, and institution services. New staff are allowed to meet all the coaches and then choose whom they feel most comfortable in approaching. The coaches then make themselves available on an as-needed basis.

Finally, Ohio's submission describes its Leadership Training Program, which is an intense, three-month course that teaches its participants to work as a team through innovative techniques borrowed from the business world. Courses on quality, creative thinking, management, career development, media training, and other subjects give the participants a broad learning base.

The six entries selected span the full range of correctional training activities: from a multifaceted program for a large agency to a less complex mentoring program in an institution; from a community college certification program that saves an agency potentially millions of dollars to a program that uses the latest research to select and train program service providers. The committee hopes that these selections provide readers with examples of programs worthy of replication in their respective agencies.

Committee chair:

Dr. Allen Ault
Chief
National Institute of Corrections Academy

1960 Industrial Circle, Suite A
Longmont, Colorado 80501
(303) 682-0382

Selection and Training of Program Delivery Staff

Introduction

When the Correctional Service of Canada decided in 1989-90 to develop a broader range of correctional programs, it also had to determine how delivery staff should be trained. The selection and training of delivery personnel for the Living Skills, Offender Substance Abuse Pre-release Program (OSAPP) and Choices (Community Correctional Brief Treatment Relapse Prevention and Maintenance Program) programs is based directly on principles for effective correctional programs set out by Ross and Gendreau. As their research shows, the effectiveness of programs is partly dependent on the quality of staff delivering them. The careful selection of staff, good training, and good supervision are the keys. Other research shows that staff who demonstrate and model the prosocial behaviors and the specific skills they are teaching are essential to effective programs.

The critical objectives of a staff selection and training program are to address the following things:

- To select staff who already have and consistently demonstrate the interpersonal skills and/or behaviors they will be expected to model during program delivery

- To train staff with a thorough grounding in the knowledge and teaching skills that are required to deliver the specific programs (including offender assessment, presentation of program materials, group facilitation skills, and reporting on program outcome)

- To follow-up and monitor to ensure that program staff are using the skills and techniques of program delivery in the appropriate manner

Design and Implementation

There are some minor differences between the approaches for living skills and substance abuse programs, but they follow the same model, which is described next.

1. Staff are chosen for training based on a set of criteria covering the basic behaviors and personal attributes that have been shown in research to contribute to effective programming.

2. These candidates attend an initial training program, at least two weeks in length, which provides:

    *   A basic theoretical grounding in the models underlying the program

    *   An opportunity to prepare and deliver specific program sessions, with immediate and detailed feedback, to develop or refresh their group facilitation skills

    *   A review of all sessions in the program

    *   Training in how to assess offenders for the program (pre- and posttesting), and an understanding of the purpose and process of effectiveness in evaluation research

    *   Immediate verbal feedback on their training performance, and a written recommendation for the future

3. Those who are recommended to proceed to deliver programs normally deliver two program offerings, which are videotaped. The individual who trained the staff reviews the tapes, and provides feedback on areas to be improved or praised.

4. After two delivery sessions, a follow-up training session is held, with a group of staff in one region, normally over three days. This session consists of:

    *   A review of key parts of each person's tapes, allowing all participants the opportunity to view a variety of styles and levels of performance and to hear both positive and negative feedback

    *   Additional information sessions or workshops on key aspects of the program or new developments in treatment

5. Following this session, staff who have performed successfully are certified to deliver cognitive skills training and are eligible for training in other components of Living Skills. In the case of the Offender Substance Abuse Pre-release Program or Choices, they are certified to deliver these programs.

6. Training sessions for other Living Skills programs (Living Without Violence, Parenting, and Leisure Education) are shorter, normally four or five days, since they deal only with the specific program content and in the case of Living Without Violence, the theory and background on family violence. Those certified in cognitive-skills training already have the facilitation skills and background knowledge on the cognitive-behavioral model required to deliver these programs. Training for Anger and Emotions Management is longer (ten days), as additional content information, facilitation, and counseling skills are required to deliver this program.

7. Staff training for other national Correctional Service of Canada substance abuse programs follows a similar model. However, the initial training varies in length according to the intensity of the program and the skills required to deliver it.

Conclusion

After over seven years of working with this model, the department is considering or will be adopting several changes. In general, however, the "learning by doing" approach, along with careful guidance and supervision, produces excellent program delivery. There are 220 correctional services staff working in institutions and the community to deliver programs, and approximately 50 program deliverers working under contract. Most of these staff have been trained through this process.

A number of lessons have been learned during this period of time. These lessons are summarized below.

- *The training and certification process could be more flexible in timing; however, it is critical to maintain standards of quality.*

Operational managers have raised two issues here. First, some think it is too long. Depending on the operational unit's scheduling of programs, it can take many months and in some cases up to a year, for newly trained staff to deliver two complete offerings. In addition, scheduling difficulties can cause long waits between offerings of follow-up training. It can take up to two years to complete the process.

Second, community operational managers feel quite hampered in their ability to get staff who qualify to deliver other living skills components, because of the requirement to be certified in cognitive-skills training before training in other components can take place. This approach uses the certification process for cognitive-skills training to be relatively certain that staff are able to deliver programs effectively before training them in additional components. However, some community operational units find it difficult to offer this training frequently enough to ensure staff are certified within a relatively short time. They also feel that some of the other components are much more likely to be delivered in the community than this training.

The Correctional Service of Canada is considering allowing staff who have not completed certification in cognitive-skills training, but who are demonstrating good potential as a deliverer, to be trained in other components and begin delivering them. This would allow them to deliver more programs and gain more experience. It also would help community units expand their capacity to deliver programs. The correctional services still would retain the basic standards for certification.

- *The training process should emphasize program facilitation skills*

The initial training programs (at least two weeks in length) provide a great deal of training on how to facilitate learning by offender participants in the program. The staff's facilitation skills are developed and refined through the entire certification process, and these skills are relatively generic in nature. While program content is important, the method of delivery is crucial to meeting the goals of adult-oriented, cognitive-behavioral programming, that is, to guide the practical learning by adults of new attitudes, behaviors, and interpersonal skills, while respecting the background and experience adults have.

- *Applicability of the process to full-time, part-time, or contract program delivery staff*

The model that is relied on is used whether program deliverers are appointed to work full-time, appointed for determined periods, redeployed within their job category, or hired under contract. This is unlikely to change even when the Correctional Service of Canada has implemented a national policy that all program delivery staff be permanently appointed to full-time positions with a common job description. The leadership is committed to a model that emphasizes on-the-job learning and demonstrated abilities leading to certification. The experience with this process also leads to the conclusion that in contracting for program delivery, corrections agencies must set specific standards regarding staff qualifications and/or training and monitoring to ensure these standards are met.

- *Training should be a continuous activity that requires management attention*

The successful implementation of correctional programs requires more than sending staff to a one-shot training session. Consistent, high-quality delivery requires a commitment within the correctional agency to establish a function to provide ongoing monitoring, support, and management. The size of this commitment depends on the scope of implementation of the program. Even if an agency is only implementing a new program in one unit, this ongoing function still should be in place. The Correctional Service of Canada assigns approximately ten regional employees directly to this activity, including providing direct training, to support the implementation of living skills and substance abuse programs in all its operational units. Part of five regional managers' time is devoted to the management function, supported by two small staff teams at the national level.

Author:

Linda McLaren, Senior Project Officer of Institutional
    Reintegration
Correctional Operations and Programs
Correctional Service of Canada

Contacts:

John R. Weekes, Ph.D.
Manager, Substance Abuse Programs
Correctional Service of Canada

---

340 Laurier Avenue West
Ottawa, Ontario, Canada K1A OP9
(613) 947-0587

Lynn Stewart
Manager, Living Skills and Personal Development Programs and Family
    Violence Prevention Programs
Correctional Service of Canada

---

330 Kele Street
Toronto, Ontario, Canada M6P 2K7
(416) 952-6497

Local Community Colleges for Probation Officer Basic Training

Introduction

Due to the high cost of training new correctional probation officers at satellite academies, compounded by budget constraints, an action team was formed to study the feasibility of a local recruit academy. The recommendation of this team, based on the use of quality management tools, was to form a partnership with local community colleges to conduct the academy. Partnerships were initiated with Seminole Community College, Brevard Community College, Withlacoochee Technical Institute, Lake Vocational/Technical College, and Central Florida Community College. A further decision was made that as of January 1996 only those applicants would be hired who have graduated from a basic recruit academy and have passed the Florida Department of Law Enforcement exam to become a Certified Correctional Probation Officer.

Development

Prior to the implementation of this project, Community Corrections Region III within the Florida Department of Corrections filled its vacancies by hiring noncertified officers. This allowed the vacancy to be filled, but the new employees were not trained to perform their job functions. Once hired, the employees were sent to one of the two satellite academies (Vero Beach or Lake City) for basic recruit training. The procedure took approximately twenty weeks, during which time the department paid for the employee's salary, benefits, travel expenses, training costs, hotel accommodations, and meals. The completion of basic training cost the department of corrections (and taxpayers) $14,636 per trainee.

Over the three-year period prior to the start of this project, Region III sent an average of eighty new employees a year to the satellite academies. A potential savings of $1,170,880 annually was projected to be the result of not hiring anyone until after they had graduated and passed the state certification exam.

Implementation

Region III hired its first "certified officer" community college basic recruit graduate in December 1995. The classes, taught by Florida Department of Law Enforcement certified instructors, include required subjects, such as human diversity, interpersonal communication skills, supervision, operations, defensive tactics, firearms, and first aid. Basic recruit classes have been completed at Seminole Community College, Brevard Community College, and Withlacoochee Technical Institute. To date, Region III has hired thirty-two graduates. In March, 1997, both Brevard and Withlacooche had graduating classes with an expectation of filling twenty-five vacancies from those classes. Seminole Community College concluded another basic recruit class in April, 1997. Withlacoochee started another class in July, 1997, and both community colleges started their next classes in August, 1997.

Supporting Data

Region III thus far has saved approximately $468,352 in salaries, training costs, mileage, per diem, and overtime by using the local community colleges. By the end of the fiscal year (June 30, 1997), at least twenty-five more positions are expected to be filled for a total saving of $834,252. It is anticipated that future yearly savings will be in excess of $1 million. In an effort to reduce the amount of time from the date of graduation to the date of hire, background investigations now are conducted on the students while they are attending the academies. In the past two graduating classes, it has taken approximately sixty days to process the applicants for hire. By completing background investigations before receiving the exam results, it is estimated that the hiring cycle should be reduced by thirty days.

Conclusion

Using local community colleges to provide the basic recruit training creates a pool of certified officers at virtually no cost to the department. College graduates who are interested in becoming probation officers now can greatly improve their chances of employment by obtaining certification prior to application, even if they decide to apply in another region. Local community colleges that have developed correctional probation officer academies have improved and expanded their criminal justice programs and now offer a better range of services to their customers. In addition to cost savings, training has been improved by using local certified instructors who have direct job-related experience. Officers, likewise, are able to perform their job functions in a reduced time frame.

If the other four regions in the department were to implement this localized training concept, the projected regional savings of $1 million could be expanded to a statewide savings of more than $7 million annually. This project's impact on training is consistent with the "vision" of the Florida Department of Corrections, which emphasizes public safety and a highly trained ethical and dynamic workforce. It is also an excellent example of making the department's strategic plan, mission, and values statement work in partnership with community resources.

Authors:

Barbara Scala
Assistant to the Division Director
Florida Department of Corrections
Orlando Florida

Richard W. Hoehn
Correctional Services Administrator
Florida Department of Corrections
Orlando, Florida

Contact:

Joseph F. Hatem, Jr.
Division Director
Florida Department of Corrections

Suite N-909
400 W. Robinson Avenue
Orlando, Florida
(407) 245-0840

Texas Department of Criminal Justice

Institutional Division Training

Introduction

The Institutional Division Training Department of the Texas Department of Criminal Justice provides staff-development training for security and nonsecurity personnel assigned to institutional and state jail facilities. The training department operates six regional academies covering the state. It currently maintains agreements with fifteen colleges and universities to meet the training needs of approximately 28,000 correctional personnel.

The training department is headquartered at the Chase Field Criminal Justice Center in Beeville, Texas. Administrative support operations include coordinating and monitoring college programs, word processing, developing curriculum, and managing human resources.

The Edmundo Mireles Criminal Justice Training Academy, adjacent to the Training Department's administrative headquarters, is the nation's largest academy for correctional employees. The Mireles Academy provides facilities for preservice, inservice, instructor certification, and management training programs. On December 2, 1996, the Edmundo Mireles Academy began the day with 537 security and nonsecurity personnel simultaneously participating in five separate and distinct training programs, ranging from preservice to management training for first-level supervisors.

In-service programs also are conducted at the Sam Houston State University Criminal Justice Center, the Ellis I Unit, the Coffield Unit, the Hilltop Unit, and Ramsey I Unit regional academies.

Development

The preservice program provides new correctional employees with the training necessary to develop the foundation required for them to begin their assigned duties in an appropriate and professional manner. The training serves as an orientation period for the new employees and familiarizes them with agency policies and procedures.

Preservice academy graduates are provided a two-week period of on-the-job training at their assigned facility. This period of supervised, practical instruction is designed to provide new officers with opportunities to apply the lessons they have learned at the academy.

The forty-hour in-service training program, for security (correctional officer through captain) and selected nonsecurity personnel, is designed to ensure the efficient operation of correctional facilities. The program focuses on the primary issues of concern to the Texas Department of Criminal Justice's institutions through job-related training.

The basic curriculum for supervisory and nonsupervisory classes is divided into two primary segments: core courses and specialized training. Core courses are those deemed necessary for annual security and health services training. Specialized courses are designed to provide the flexibility to respond to the changing needs of the attendees.

The specialized training programs are designed to provide employees with the necessary skills to become effective instructors. The courses include certification as a trainer for staff trainers in firearms, chemical agents, and defensive tactics. After successful completion of the course(s), employees are allowed to teach classes for the department.

The management training programs provide the Texas Department of Criminal Justice employees with the opportunity to develop supervisory and management skills from basic through advanced levels. The courses include the following topics: principles of supervision for first-level supervisors with no prior supervisory training; basic management, for supervisors who previously have completed the prior course, and advanced management, for majors and other designated supervisory personnel.

Implementation

The training department began in 1959 when the personnel department established a preservice training school. However, it was not until 1972 that all employees hired in security positions were required to attend preservice training. Today, both security and selected nonsecurity personnel are required to attend preservice training. In March 1995, the training department expanded the security preservice program from a 3-week 120-hour academic program to a 6-week 240-hour academic training program. The second part of security preservice training consists of 2 weeks (80 hours) of on-the-job training conducted at the unit of assignment. Nonsecurity personnel attend a 3-week 120-hour academic preservice training program designed to improve their awareness of security issues and inmate management.

The annual in-service training program of the training department was created in May 1984. Prior to that time, in-service training was provided by the personnel and training lieutenants at each facility. In-service training is provided by the six regional academies and participating colleges.

The management training programs were developed in the late 1980s and early 1990s to improve the supervisory and management skills of both correctional and nonsecurity personnel. Other specialized programs (such as those in chemical agents, firearms, and for a defensive tactics instructor) were developed to meet specific unit-level training requirements. These programs are conducted annually on an as-needed basis.

Outcomes

In response to the largest correctional facility growth the nation has ever experienced, the training department provided training to 21,460 personnel in fiscal year 1996. These personnel are responsible for operating 89 institutional and 16 state jail facilities. These numbers are expected to increase by approximately 10 percent during fiscal year 1997, as new facilities open and more employees are eligible for inservice training. On January 15, 1996, the Texas

Department of Criminal Justice's Institutional Training Division was accredited by the American Correctional Association's Commission on Accreditation for Corrections.

Conclusion

Training continues to be the foundation upon which successful corrections operations are based. Correctional training continually must evolve to meet the changing needs of the user community to ensure the safety and stability of correctional facilities and at the same time to minimize potential liabilities.

The revamping of the preservice curriculum and updating of the inservice curriculums proves that the first approach may not always be the best. During the evolution of these programs, staff found that what may appear to meet the needs of the audience on paper may fall short when presented in the classroom environment. Flexibility is the key to the continuing strength of a successful program. Administrators and instructors alike must be willing to accept change to meet future challenges in the ever-changing world of correctional operations.

Author:

Taylor J. Huddleston
Curriculum Coordinator
Chase Field Criminal Justice Center
Beeville, Texas

Author/Contact:

Charles D. Godwin
Director of Training
Chase Field Criminal Justice Center

HC-02, Box 955
Beeville, Texas 78102-9802
(512) 362-6458

Academy for Staff Development

Introduction

The Virginia Department of Corrections places a strong value on developing and supporting its most important resource—its employees. The Academy for Staff Development is the heart of the department's employee training and development program. It is committed to providing high quality human resource development services for more than 11,000 employees, in support of the department's overall mission to meet the public safety needs of Virginia's citizens.

The Academy recognizes that to achieve its mission, it is essential that a total employee development delivery system be established. This system includes three equally important elements that are necessary in providing high quality training programs and services:

1) Highly qualified staff who understand the mission and goals of the Academy and who are dedicated to providing quality services

2) A curriculum development and delivery process that includes ongoing needs assessment, use of the most effective methods of training presentation, and multifaceted program evaluation

3) Academy facilities that provide a physical and psychological environment, thereby enhancing the total learning experience of the adult learner

What follows focuses on the third element, the academy's facilities: an overview of the facility, its design and creation, and what is most important, its role in creating an effective learning environment.

Design and Implementation

Initially, the academy provided training programs for correctional officers, counselors, and institution and community corrections managers in a leased facility that was built in 1891 as a resort hotel. From the very beginning, the Virginia Department of Corrections recognized that a permanent location with additional capacity eventually would be needed. The scope of academy training and services increased dramatically over the next thirteen years. The need for training space that was larger and more flexible increasingly became apparent.

In 1989, the department began an unprecedented period of system expansion including both new prison construction and growth in community corrections programs. As the need for employee training increased, it became evident that there was an urgent need for a larger residential facility capable of meeting long-term training requirements. In 1990, based on the recommendations of a legislatively funded study, funding was provided to construct a new residential academy on department of corrections property in Goochland County, Virginia. The Academy for Staff Development moved into the new facilities and began operation in May 1993.

Planning and Design Process

The planning and design process for the new academy involved a number of steps, including:

A clear understanding of the academy's role in supporting the mission and philosophy of the department of corrections.

The academy's mission always has been to serve all employees. This factor was significant in the design process, as it was necessary that employees view the academy as a learning facility with specialized space for simulation and specific skill development, and classroom space for didactic training.

The projection of future program needs relative to training volume, presentation methodologies, and use of new technology for program delivery.

The projected use of the academy to meet future program needs was included in the pre-planning study. This study also identified the need for space that would accommodate a diversity of training methodologies, including lecture, small group exercise, role play, demonstration, and practice of various physical skills, and specialized training in a broad range of skills from use of firearms to computer programs. The planners also recognized the need to be prepared to accommodate future technology.

Input from department of corrections' staff, particularly academy staff.

The academy staff and other department employees received the first-draft design for their review and comment. This feedback provided a collective perception of the positive and negative features of the initial draft design. This "end user" input was invaluable and led to a number of significant design changes that enhanced the academy's overall learning environment.

Partnership with the department's project engineer, architectural firm, and building contractor ensuring input into the design and construction modifications throughout the project.

As the design of the new facility was completed and the construction phase began, administrative staff closely monitored the progress to ensure that any change order or design modification did not occur without their input. This monitoring process was critical throughout the construction phase as numerous problems and changes occurred, which could have inadvertently had a great impact on the future use of the facility.

Academy Physical Facilities

The academy is designed as a modern 200-bed full-service training facility. The physical facilities consist of five buildings (totaling 126,000 square feet) on the academy campus, and a state-of-the art firearms' range located on the grounds of a correctional facility adjacent to the academy. The facilities on the main campus include the administration/classroom building, a physical skills training center, the residence hall, the dining hall, and the maintenance shop.

Administration/Classroom Building

In the hub of academy activities are the administrative and training staff offices; the registrar and training records unit; eight classrooms separated by "storage alleys," and a large conference room with movable partitions that allow for configurations ranging from four forty-to-fifty-person classroom-size spaces to one large area with a capacity of 200 persons. Training support areas (such as copy center, audiovisual support, and the armory) and the library are located in close proximity to the classrooms and office areas.

The academy's library is fully automated and services the entire department. The library is highly specialized in the areas of corrections, criminal justice, treatment theory and methods, management, and staff training and development. The library's resources include current texts, periodicals, videos, and Internet access. Interlibrary loan access provides the academy with the ability to obtain materials from libraries across the Commonwealth and around the world.

The registrar and training records section is responsible for all program registration, training records, and documentation. The automated registration program receives approximately 1,000 registrations monthly. The system registers, wait lists, confirms, and prints class rosters and transcripts. The academy maintains training records for approximately 29,000 current and former department of corrections' employees.

Physical Skills Training Center

This facility is a large multipurpose building with a design very similar to a gymnasium. The large main room can be partitioned into three separate physical training areas that can be used simultaneously. This facility also has a two-tiered, four-cell mock cell block with a fully functional control center. The cell block gets very heavy use for role play simulations, skill evaluations in areas such as cell search, crime scene preservation, and inmate extrication. It also is used extensively for canine training. The center, which has an exercise room and locker rooms for men and women, is used in the evenings for recreational purposes.

Residence Hall

The residence hall is designed to house 200 participants in two-bedroom, four-person suites. Study and television lounges are available in each wing of the building with a large game room and lounge area over the main lobby. The residential unit as well as all academy facilities are handicap accessible. Eight handicap rooms are available for use upon request.

Dining Hall

The dining hall can accommodate up to 165 persons at one seating. The food storage, preparation, and service areas are designed to enhance efficiency to accommodate the serving of large groups as expeditiously as possible. In 1997, 106,278 meals were served in the food service unit.

The food service staff also serve special banquets and prepare meeting accommodations. The annual department of corrections' service awards banquet (for twenty-five-year and above recipients), and catered breaks for special events (such as Board of Corrections meetings). Legislative hearings conducted at the academy and picnics are also accommodated, upon request.

Maintenance Shop Building

The maintenance shop supports the buildings and grounds unit in managing the overall operation of the physical plant. The academy has an automated environmental management system that monitors all heating and air conditioning, fire suppression, and security locks throughout the academy.

Firearms Range

The firearms range consists of four independent ranges that can be used simultaneously. Two twenty-five yard 12-point handgun ranges, a fifty yard 2-point handgun range, a fifty yard rifle range with a tower and four firing points, and a shotgun range are available. The target systems are fully automated. The facility has a classroom equipped with a laser-driven firearms training simulator (F.A.T.S.) system for judgmental (shoot-don't shoot) training.

Academy Training and Development Programs

Since opening its doors, the academy has provided a significant amount of training and development services to department employees. The facility also has been used by various other state agencies for training or meetings. In 1997, the academy presented and accommodated 874 programs. The sheer number of these programs demonstrates the breadth and depth of the training and development services provided by the academy. Many of these programs would not have been presented without the physical resources the new academy is very fortunate to have.

Conclusion

The Academy for Staff Development continues to do what it was designed to do, provide a total learning environment for each departmental employee during his or her training. Since opening its doors in 1993, the academy has received numerous accolades from various training and criminal justice professionals. The academy has been contacted and visited by a number of individuals interested or involved in designing a criminal justice training facility. Feedback from these individuals and other colleagues specifically has noted the design features that enhance the flexibility of the facility relative to promoting effective training activities.

Although many positive comments have been received, modifications continue to be made to address the many opportunities and challenges experienced in meeting the tremendous growth and expansion of the department of corrections. In the future, the academy anticipates a greater use of distance education technology and the provision of high quality training and development that all employees deserve.

Contact:

Jerry Eggleston
Manager
Academy for Staff Development
Virginia Department of Corrections

1900 River Road W.
Crozier, Virginia 23039
(804) 784-6802

Institution Familiarization Coaching Program

Introduction

The Federal Correctional Institution, at Three Rivers, Texas, developed an Institutional Familiarization Coaching Program in 1992. It is well known that some new employees (not all) often have difficulty adjusting to the complex work and multifaceted work environment of a correctional institution. To assist in their integration into the workforce and to aid in their career development, the administration viewed the establishment of a coaching program as essential. The goals of the program were to create a strong and dynamic mentoring initiative to meet the needs of new staff during their probationary year, while empowering local staff to be innovative in the program design and implementation.

In activating this program, a plan of action with associated deadlines and designated responsible staff was established on July 11, 1992. The first phase called for educating staff and advertising. The second phase involved the selection and announcement of institution coaches. The third phase required that a mentoring committee be established and convened. The fourth step called for the assignment of the coaches. The final phase required a program assessment and follow-up training sessions for all coaches.

Implementation

Beginning October 1, 1992, all new staff were assigned an institutional familiarization coach within thirty days of their return from the Glynco Federal Law Enforcement Training Center. Though monitored by the employee development department, the executive assistant to the warden is responsible for the overall program. Initially, five staff members were selected through a training opportunity announcement for the collateral duty position of coach. Four more staff members were selected subsequently through the same process.

During institution familiarization, a two-week introductory course in the Bureau of Prisons, the employee development specialist explains the program. The coaches introduce themselves and give a brief history of their career with the Bureau of Prisons. The coaches then make themselves available to new employees on an "as needed" basis. Each coach makes contact with all new staff members on the telephone or in-person. The employee development specialist contacts each coach by the telephone or in-person to discuss any problems or concerns new staff may have. The coaches submit a quarterly report detailing their activities for the previous quarter. These reports assist in determining the quality and quantity of the coaches' work. They also assist in assessing common problems and concerns.

To ensure that the most qualified staff are selected as coaches, this collateral duty position must be considered very desirable and marketed well. Coaches represent the diverse workforce of the institution relative to gender, race, creed, and more. The coaches who are selected receive specialized training in counseling skills, interpersonal communications, probationary concerns, and the institution's range of services.

Conclusion

Under this program, new employees meet with a coach when there is a need to do so. For some, this may be more than once a month. For others, it may be less. The need for consultation is determined by the new employee. All coaches take an active role in the institution familiarization coaching program by talking with new staff as often as possible. This usually occurs while standing in the key line, in the staff lounge during lunch, during institution mail distribution, and through brief telephone calls. This program was designed to allow new staff to meet all the coaches and to choose whom they feel most comfortable in approaching.

Author:

Michael Purdy
Acting Warden
Federal Correctional Institution
Three Rivers, Texas

Contact:

Communications
Federal Bureau of Prisons

Office of Public Affairs
320 First Street, NW
Washington, D.C. 20534
(202) 307-3163

Training Leaders

Introduction

Developing future leaders is a solemn responsibility of existing managers. Selecting, training, shaping, and nurturing tomorrow's leaders is both challenging and fulfilling. In the Ohio Department of Rehabilitation and Correction, completing the intense, three-month leadership training program is considered a privilege and is taken seriously by participants.

Development

The department began by opening the training process, sharing resources, and networking with others. By continuing this process, the department continuously expands and enhances training. Experts from inside and outside the agency contribute to the knowledge base and offer students a fresh perspective on management and leadership. The presenters range from the director of the department, the governor's executive assistant who teaches a course on political realities, representatives from other state agencies, and managers from the private sector. An active oversight committee with wide-ranging interests and experience contributes to the program's vitality and diversity.

Content

The department's best and brightest first learn to work as a team through innovative techniques borrowed from the business world. For example, the program opens with a rope course in which students offer assistance and support to fellow students. As in the business world, the ropes' challenge contributes a strong esprit de corps among the students. Dangling from a rope sixty feet up in the treetops is a powerful incentive for cooperation among the students.

Other courses are offered to give the participants a broad learning base. These courses include the following topics: managing through quality creative thinking, benchmarking, facilitating, managing change, transforming the organization, and developing your career. The students often point to the intense, two-day media training course provided by the Ohio State Highway Patrol as the most feared and invigorating segment of the training. Within this segment, they experience lifelike scenarios in which they survive (or fail) at ambush interviews, trick questions, and opportunistic talk-show interviewers.

Each student selects a mentor from a field in which he or she is interested. These coaches and their proteges learn from each other to appreciate the challenges inherent in different areas of corrections. The bond between coach and protégé often extends past the formal training period.

Results

The leadership classes are divided into four small groups. Each group is assigned a project. These projects are submitted by department staff, and are real-life problems that require real-life solutions. The projects involve researching, benchmarking, using Total Quality Management processes, and employing teamwork, showing responsibility and, above all, achieving results. Project presentations, in which teams display the results of their work, are well-attended events. The department has adopted recommendations from several teams, including work on managing critical incidents, tracking critical resources, developing an academy multimedia center, understanding victims' issues, "super max" prison programming, revising employee performance evaluations, employing a centralized recruitment process and centralized quartermaster, developing policy implementation strategies, and more.

Rather than relying on simple classroom presentations, the leadership training program challenges students in a variety of ways. All participants are required to complete the course while maintaining a regular workload. They are exposed to a dizzying array of concepts and training techniques. Project completion imposes all the stresses inherent in real-life corrections management. Learning is accomplished through various mediums including public speaking presentations, information fairs, written and verbal communications, teamwork, and computer technology. Each participant evaluates the course, adding ideas and enhancing the experience for future classes. Even more, the contacts made through networking remain with the graduates throughout their careers.

Leadership-course outcomes include the opportunity to work with others, to learn new and creative leadership skills, to be exposed to group dynamics, and to have the experience of challenging one's professional and personal growth.

Author:

Dr. Bob C. Rice
Superintendent for the Corrections Training Academy
Ohio Department of Rehabilitation and Correction
Columbus, Ohio

Author/Contact:

Tessa Unwin
Public Affairs Liaison
Ohio Department of Rehabilitation and Correction

1050 Freeway Drive North
Columbus, Ohio, 43229
(614) 752-1157

Employee Training
Additional Program Entries

Management Development: Utah Department of Corrections

Author: Abdul Baksh, Contact: Joe M. Borich, Correctional Academy Director
Fred F. House Training Academy, 14727 S. Minuteman Dr., Draper, Utah 84020
(801) 495-6600

To fulfill the philosophies and objectives of management development, the Utah Department of Corrections uses job rotation, acting appointment, and educational and professional degrees to prepare its managers to assume progressively increased responsibilities. Job rotation is one of the most effective management-development tools. It broadens employees' experience, provides a testing ground for potential managers, and motivates staff to perform at higher levels. Acting appointment is an invaluable strategy in which an individual who shows potential for advancement is placed in a higher-level position when the incumbent is absent, on an extended period of vacation, or on sick leave. This gives the individual the opportunity to function in the more senior position, and senior management can better assess the individual's potential for growth. It also provides the organization with a valuable source of people to fill managerial positions. The Utah Department of Corrections has one of the best educational assistance programs in the state. Staff with high managerial potential may be sent to one of several Utah universities to pursue an advanced job-related degree as part of a total development strategy. Expenses over and above $1,500 per annum are absorbed by the department. The staff member, in turn, signs a contract to remain with the department for three years after successful completion of the advanced degree. The department also provides training courses in such subjects as leadership, time management, problem solving, long-range planning, conflict management, and various areas of human resource law.

Employee Development Initiatives: Federal Correctional Institution, El Reno, Oklahoma

A. M. Flowers, Warden
Federal Correctional Institution, El Reno, Oklahoma 73036-1000
(405) 262-4875

In February of 1996, the Bureau of Prisons staff and representatives of the Oklahoma Department of Corrections established the Interagency Development Council. Membership in the council is open to all local, state, and federal law enforcement agencies. The purpose of the council is to keep agencies informed of available training and developmental activities in which they can participate at little or no cost. The establishment of the Interagency Development Council is a step forward in sharing ideas and technology for the benefit of local, state, and federal law enforcement personnel.

Diversity Advisory Board: Nebraska Department of Corrections

Joy Shalla-Glenn, Personnel Manager
Nebraska Department of Correctional Services, Building 15, Folsom and Prospector Place,
Lincoln, Nebraska 68509-4661
(402) 471-2654

The Nebraska Department of Correctional Services' Diversity Advisory Board was started by Director Harold W. Clarke as a unique approach to employee development, training, and interpersonal relations. Diversity in the work force is a significant factor in strengthening human relationships and in maximizing individual and organizational capabilities. The Diversity Advisory Board acts as a lightning rod for the director, assistant directors, and division heads on diversity issues; establishes contacts with subcommittees on diversity-related issues; functions as the core group to push the departmental diversity effort; performs an annual evaluation of the department's diversity efforts; and provides a written report annually to the director on the department's diversity activities. The Diversity Advisory Board's subcommittees include workplace harassment, employee selection, recruiting, mentorship, and promotion board. In addition, the board has had significant success in keeping the diversity initiative before the department and its staff. Posters, training, diversity potluck lunches, presentations, and critical support from the department's leadership are but a few of the activities that continually keep the effort in the forefront.

Safety Awareness Week: Louisiana Correctional Institute for Women

Johnnie W. Jones, Warden
Louisiana Correctional Institute for Women, P.O. Box 26, St. Gabriel, Louisiana 70776
(504) 342-6298

Safety Awareness Week began in November of 1993 as a unique and innovative approach to promoting and enhancing staff knowledge of various safety issues. It consists of a week-long program of safety activities, skits, and training sessions covering safety topics. The program was designed to address safety issues, which are especially applicable to the Louisiana Correctional Institute for Women, given the nature of the facility (adult correctional), the geographical location (near chemical plants and railroads), and the weather (hurricane-prone area). The purpose of the program is to enhance staff knowledge of safety issues within the context of their specific jobs by involving them in the preparation and delivery of safety talks, skits, and training sessions. The course promotes a safer correctional environment and emphasizes management's commitment to safety by devoting an entire week annually to a discussion of safety topics in addition to ongoing in-service training. Its purpose is to provide staff with information on a variety of safety topics that would be useful to them in their personal lives, and to enhance the facility's relationship with agencies and industries in the private sector by including them in a program of mutual concern and interest.

Facility Design

9

Introduction

In the past decade, more correctional facilities have been designed and built than ever before in the history of the field, and there seems to be no end in sight. Design options are also more numerous than ever previously anticipated.

The Committee on Facility Design was charged with determining what constitutes "best practices" relative to correctional facility design and to select programs within this category. The committee developed evaluation criteria and parameters for reviewing submissions. Program submissions were solicited nationally for consideration. Following their review by a panel representative of a cross section of appropriate professionals and the concurrence of the Facility Design Committee, the projects selected as "best" are included in this chapter.

The committee acknowledges that there are numerous and varied methods for design development and selection within the various corrections entities and that many persons (e.g., corrections staff, architects, engineers, planners, politicians, and contractors) play major roles with regard to correctional facility design. These same players also exert an influence in the processes of determining what, who, how, when, how much, for whom, and why.

Nevertheless, major steps in the traditional design process should include consideration of alternative construction methods and the funding process, which may differ depending on the jurisdiction. The end result should be a functional facility. Regardless of the facility needed, the design process should be the first step and should include an appropriate planning phase prior to determining the budget for the project. The programs that follow meet these expectations.

The Colorado State Penitentiary has been recognized internationally as a leader in the management of high-risk administrative segregation inmates. This is due both to its architectural design and to its level system of programming. The Florida Department of Corrections met its need for a greatly increased number of facilities in very quick order through the use of precast concrete and strong teamwork on the part of the contractors and the department of corrections.

The Arlington Detention Facility in Virginia is a high-rise vertical facility, which has the ability to offer a wide range of inmate services in a cost-effective manner. These services are enhanced through a combination of centralized administration, decentralized programming, and security control.

The Washington State Department of Corrections has taken a fresh approach to the process of facility design at its correctional center located on McNeil Island. The new approach incorporates inmate education and development into the process of facility construction and has resulted in a savings of at least 35 percent over otherwise-anticipated costs of construction, as well as teaching inmates specific construction skills that they can use on the outside.

The Hamilton County Juvenile Court Youth Center is a model of a participatory design process based on clearly identified design objectives developed through an end-user participation process.

Committee chair:

Michael W. Moore
Director
South Carolina Department of Corrections

P. O. Box 21787
Columbia, South Carolina 29221-1787
(803) 896-8555

The Colorado State High Security Penitentiary

Introduction

In 1990, the Colorado State Legislature approved funding for a 500-bed close-custody facility. The Department of Corrections subsequently contracted with Daniel Mann Johnson Mendenhall Architects and the Correctional Services Group to provide the initial design for the facility. After acceptance of the original design, the department determined there was a priority need for high-security beds. The executive staff decided to use the close-custody design for these beds.

The department reviewed the existing close-custody design, made minimal modifications (e.g., adding noncontact visiting booths), and determined the operational needs for the higher-custody level inmates. The resulting concept presumed that by developing operational plans using physical plant attributes, the Colorado Department of Corrections could create a safe environment for the management of the most difficult inmate population while encouraging their successful reintegration into less secure facilities.

Design and Development

The initial operating plan for the Colorado State Penitentiary was based on standards derived from departmental administrative regulations, the American Correctional Association Standards for Adult Institutions, the American Medical Association Standards, and federal, state and local life, safety, and environmental requirements.

The concept of administrative-segregation security guided the planning for the penitentiary and required several components: security zoning, electronic technology, and perimeter security. Various levels of internal security were attained through the use of materials, furnishings, and design principles that contribute to secure, safe, and humane living and working environments for inmates and staff alike.

Even though the original design was for close-custody management, the physical plant design contributed to the successful management of inmates requiring a high-security environment. This included restricting inmate movement to a minimum by providing the majority of services at individual cells or within the pod area, by providing excellent lines of sight between individual cells and the pod office/control centers, and by providing interconnecting doors between day halls for efficiency of the cell meal service and safe and secure movement of inmates in emergency evacuation situations.

The department of corrections realizes that staff are its greatest resource. It was this recognition that informed the development of the penitentiary. The department used staff input in the design and development by activating user groups. These user groups were composed of staff from various facilities within the department and represented all aspects of facility operations. The user groups were charged with reviewing the plans for the facility, recommending policy and procedures, and ordering adequate equipment to ensure the secure operation of their area of expertise.

Implementation

The principle of "security zoning" was applied in the development of the site plan and the functional relations of the operational components. This minimized inmate movement and facilitated control within the secure perimeter.

The first level of zoning is the buffer area, which extends approximately 200 feet outward from the perimeter security fencing, exclusive of the facility parking area. The second level of zoning is defined as the perimeter fence, and the area between the physical plant and the fence.

The third zone of control is defined as the penitentiary building's exterior perimeter and the associated space. This third level of security is established by hardened exterior walls with controlled access into the zone through the facility's main control room, vehicle entry, and the delivery dock control room.

The fourth level of zoning is known as the operational floor levels, and there are operational subzones on each floor. This fourth level of security is established by controlled access through elevators and stairwells to each of the three floor levels and by controlled access in and out of subzones on each floor level.

The fifth level of zoning is referred to as housing unit access by sallyports and is enclosed by security-hardened barriers, which contain the total space for each housing unit. This fifth level is controlled by both master and pod control room operations and by the monitoring of stairwells, elevators, and main corridor-entry doors.

The sixth level of zoning is referred to as the day hall and is defined by hardened walls and ceilings enclosing each sixteen-cell day hall within the housing unit. This sixth level is controlled by floor officers and pod control room operations of entry and interior doors.

The seventh and innermost zone is referred to as inmate cells and is defined by hardened cell walls, floors, and ceilings with a mechanically operated, sliding entry/exit door. Control is maintained by unit floor offices and pod control room staff.

To enhance direct staff supervision, the design and construction of the penitentiary lends itself well to the use of correctional technology. Security electronics include: security monitoring and recording cameras, personal alarm systems, an 800 MHZ radio system with emergency buttons, fluoroscope, biometric palm identifier, and a computer-enhanced, touch-screen inmate movement control system.

The complexity of the touch-screen electronic door control resulted in inadvertent staff error in opening and closing cell doors. Switching to track-ball operation specifically adapted for the penitentiary simplified this task resulting in greatly reduced staff error and creating a safer, more secure operation. Door openings and closures are tracked and recorded by a computerized data logging system, which provides a verification of activities and staff passage.

Electronic monitoring via closed circuit television is used for monitoring living unit day halls, living unit access sallyports, vehicle and pedestrian sallyports, pedestrian circulation corridors, elevators, and other key access points. Doors that limit access but need not necessarily be constantly monitored allow staff access to various areas of the facility through a magnetic reader-card system. Reader cards restrict staff access by limiting doors that can be opened by that specific reader card. Additionally, the reader-card access system provides a computerized record of when and by whom each designated door was used.

The marriage of the design, construction, and operations of the penitentiary supports an inmate-incentive program that allows inmates to demonstrate their willingness and readiness to progress to lower-security facilities. As the level of trust increases, there are improvements in their quality of life, greater independence for movement, socialization, and more opportunities for work and recreation. Staff are trained in specific methods of inmate management designed to maintain control while reducing the potential for staff or inmate injury.

The staff have developed constructive and meaningful contemporary programs based on academic, religious, recreational, and personal needs for inmates classified for placement in administrative segregation. The delivery of programming occurs in three phases: closed circuit television presentation, cell-to-cell instruction, and private individual counseling. The intense program presentation includes the following: anger management, passive recreation programs, education, gang intervention, stress management, mental health, religion, library/law library, case management, drug/alcohol, and life skills.

The conditions of confinement are managed with an incentive quality-of-life program, based on an increased level of privileges. The program is behavior driven and consists of the following four levels:

> *Punitive Segregation:* This is the short-term assignment of an inmate to disciplinary detention as a result of a conviction based on a due process code of penal discipline.

> *Quality Level One:* This is the entry level to the stratified-incentive program for inmates classified as administrative segregation who have proven by their institutional adjustment an unwillingness to conform to the regulations and procedures of the department. Inmates at this level enjoy the fewest privileges of the program. Inmates may remain at this level indefinitely if their behavior warrants.

> *Quality Level Two:* This is the second level of the stratified incentive program. These inmates may have exhibited a propensity towards violence, escape, and/or a disrespect for facility safety, security, and order.

> *Quality Level Three:* This is the level for inmates classified as administrative segregation who have demonstrated appropriate adjustment to the penitentiary. They have shown proper interaction with staff and other inmates, an absence of misconduct, suitable cell conditions, and overall positive behavior.

Inmates are assigned to Quality Level I upon entry to the penitentiary. Through demonstrated appropriate behavior, they may progress through the Quality of Life Program. The inmates are held accountable for irresponsible behavior and recognized for appropriate, responsible behavior. Appropriate behavior may be rewarded by consideration for placement in less-restrictive facilities consistent with applicable procedures.

Data Collected and Results

The Colorado State Penitentiary opened in August 1993 and was fully operational by November 1993 with a capacity of 504. The facility houses both male and female offenders who have been placed in administrative segregation. On June 30, 1994, there were 489 offenders housed at the penitentiary, nearly 5 percent of the jurisdictional population. The facility's mission to house administrative segregation offenders has enabled other facilities to be less tolerant of violent behavior and maintain a zero tolerance of active gang involvement.

The effects of the close-custody program on offender behavior has been measured by a research brief prepared by the department's Office of Planning and Analysis. This brief showed the program's impact on offender behavior systemwide as measured by incidents of violence.

Six key categories were chosen to measure the program's effect on systemwide rates of violent incidents. The number of use of force incidents, fights, self-inflicted injuries, inmate deaths, assaults on inmates, and assaults on staff were compared for similar time periods before and after the opening of the penitentiary. This data indicated a continual decrease in fights, self-inflicted injuries and assaults on staff subsequent to its opening. The level of use-of-force incidents was reduced from an average of twenty-two per quarter to sixteen per quarter. The only category of violent incidents that increased after the opening of the penitentiary was assaults on inmates.

The Colorado State Penitentiary is seen as a deterrent to violence within the correctional system and is used to house predators and active gang members. A reduced rate of violent incidents, therefore, is expected among the other facilities. The increase in inmate assaults may indicate that not all predators or active gang offenders have been removed totally from the system.

The results of this analysis reflect a systemwide reduction of incidents of violence since the penitentiary's opening. The presence of a dedicated facility to segregate the most difficult-to-manage offenders appears to be a deterrent to violent-offender behavior. The ability to remove and safely house these offenders away from the general population has reduced the pool of offenders creating management problems. The results of this research strongly suggest that the reduced rate of violent incidents has been the result of housing violent behavior offenders within the penitentiary. The structured control imposed by its operations has resulted in no violent inmate deaths, suicides, or serious staff or inmate injuries, and no escapes in the four years since its opening.

Conclusion

The blending of physical plant design with interdisciplinary operations has created an integrated program structure. The close-custody program has proven itself successful in managing a difficult inmate population. In fact, the Colorado State Penitentiary has been recognized internationally as a leader in the management of high-risk administrative segregation inmates. The National Institute of Corrections regularly suggests that correctional professionals tour the program when they are developing an administrative segregation ("supermax") facility.

The Colorado State Penitentiary received the American Correctional Association's accreditation status from the Commission on Accreditation for Corrections in August of 1996. During their audit, the auditors commented that the penitentiary would serve as a model for other systems in the management of high-risk offenders. Two other state systems have purchased the building design and are implementing the basic premises of the program.

The original design and construction of the penitentiary infrastructure allowed for additional bed-space capacity. In the spring of 1996, construction began on an additional 252 single-bunk cells. The completion of the expansion will enable the penitentiary to meet a recognized need for transitioning inmates from a tightly controlled, highly secure environment to a less secure general population setting. Consequently, the program has been expanded to include the Progressive Reintegration Opportunity unit.

The Progressive Reintegration Opportunity unit is a continuation of the penitentiary's inmate management philosophy to provide a behavior-driven program for the structured transition of inmates from administrative segregation to a general population facility. It also serves as a diversionary program for inmates at general population facilities who need intervention to modify problematic behaviors. Levels IV and V of the Progressive Reintegration Opportunity unit will operate as a continuation of the Quality of Life Levels I, II, and III currently in place. In this system, inmates work their way to increased incentive levels, which offer increased privileges through demonstration of appropriate behavior and self-discipline.

Psycho-educational, vocational, and structured active recreational programs for Level IV and V inmates will serve several purposes. The inmate's successful completion of the Progressive Reintegration Opportunity unit program will offer the administration an opportunity to assess an inmate's behavior in small group settings and provide an objective basis for decisions concerning progression to less secure facilities. The programs will help increase the inmate's successful reintegration into a less secure facility and, ultimately, back into society. The behaviors and self-responsibilities instilled by this program will serve as the cornerstone for further personal growth. The unit was completed in late spring of 1998.

Contacts:

Aristedes W. Zavaras
Executive Director
Colorado Department of Corrections

Carl Zenon
Region I Director
Colorado Department of Corrections

Suite 400, 2862 S Circle Drive
Colorado Springs, Colorado 80906-4195
(719) 579-9580 / (719) 540-4845

Donice Neal
Superintendent
Colorado State Penitentiary

P. O. Box 777
Canon Cirty, Colorado 81215-0777
(719) 269-5120

Prison Design for the Future: Precast Concrete

Introduction

When Florida Governor Lawton Chiles made a promise through his Safe Streets Program to eliminate the forced early-release of inmates in his state due to housing shortages and to institute longer sentences for repeat offenders, the question was how to construct the forty-five new housing units needed to meet the required number of beds. The requirements went well beyond the issues of construction speed and cost efficiency. The design had to allow the prisons to adapt to different uses, including general population sections, confinement areas with administrative and disciplinary segregation sections, and sections for lockdown situations.

The prisons also had to meet the demands of the Florida environment: an effective ventilation system since the state's prisons are not air-conditioned; the ability to stand up to heavy rains, salty air, and wind; and the capacity to resist a hurricane. They also needed to be easy to repair and to retain durability for a long period of time. This was quite a challenge even when the aggressive schedule was not added into the equation.

The Bureau of Facilities Services of the Florida Department of Corrections had planned to use an existing design for a 112 single-cell housing unit nicknamed "the butterfly dorm." This bowtie-shaped structure was designed in the early 1980s and was both safe and effective. However, it also was relatively expensive and time consuming to construct. The bureau staff determined that they had to find a less expensive and faster way to accomplish the job. Their goals included a housing unit that would be safe for staff and inmates, easy to maintain, fast to build, and simple to operate. To facilitate the design process, the bureau solicited input from representatives of the department's security and maintenance staff. This truly would be an opportunity to improve the efficiency of the building.

Development and Design

The chief of the bureau was the leading force behind the breakaway design. According to then Chief Randall Dender, the "facilities services had gradually replaced outside A/E firms by doing work in-house. With the repetitive nature of our building program, this was extremely cost and time efficient for the department and no reuse fees were paid. The decision was made to redesign the single cell housing unit inhouse, with speed of construction and cost per bed as primary objectives."

The department explored various options. The short construction window lent an edge to prefabricated construction methods such as precast concrete. Precast pieces could be manufactured at central plants and transported to the various sites. The pieces then could be produced during site preparation and concurrently during all phases of construction, meeting the aggressive time frame.

Speed although critical was not the only issue. Precast concrete worked well with the challenges of the Florida environment. Choosing between steel and precast concrete manufacturers, state officials determined the best bet was precast concrete. State officials visited several Precast/Prestressed Concrete Institute certified plants to look at cell modules and manufacturing techniques. Precast manufacturers assisted the state in the design phase and suggested changes and new ideas.

The new T-building concept was born from this research for prison design in Florida. The precast methodology specified was the same modular process used in the construction of bridges and parking garages. The key to precast's value came in taking advantage of its ability to replicate one form many times.

The use of precast was not a new construction method. The Bureau of Facilities Services had used precast in the past in the butterfly dorm. And it has been used in many jails and prisons across the country. What is unique about the Florida T-building is the extent to which precast concrete elements are used, not just for cell modules, but for the entire building. In other prison systems, precast is limited to cell modules, flat roofs, and floors. The rest of the building usually is completed using conventional on-site construction techniques.

Architects are reluctant to design in all precast, feeling that their creativity is restrained. As a result, they do not take advantage of precast's most valuable attribute—repetition. Not all cells are alike in conventional construction. Plans for conventional construction call for cells which are rights, lefts, shaped to fit a building shape, corners, and odd numbers, instead of repeatable sequences.

Implementation

The T-building has three identical wings. Each cell is identical to the others with none specifically designed for left or right sides, up or down, inside or outside corners, or any other configuration. The only alteration is in one module composed of two cells and a four-shower bay. Six of these are included in each building, one on each of the two levels of the three wings. Cells are delivered to the site completely finished and ready for installation. All fixtures and furnishings are supplied in place, including entry doors and mechanisms, sinks, toilets, lavatories, wiring, and lighting. Shower modules also are delivered completely plumbed, wired, and ducted. Only bunks and mirrors need to be installed and exteriors painted. All other rooms and sections in the T-building are built from precast, including control rooms, clothing-issue rooms, hearing rooms, interview rooms, storage rooms, mechanical spaces and overhead, and attic maintenance rooms.

The roof system was one of the many design options left to the manufacturers. Prior to the award of the bid, six manufacturers were identified as meeting qualifications to complete the job requirements. One of the two who eventually won an award of twenty-eight buildings is RPPD Cell Manufacturers Ltd. (RPPD), a limited partnership comprised of Rotondo Weirich of Lederach, Pennsylvania, who provided expertise in module cell design, production, and finishing; Perry-Parrish, Inc. of Gainesville, Florida, which provided administrative support and general contracting duties; and prestress manufacturer Dura-Stress, Inc. of

Leesburg, Florida. It was at this point in the bid process that Rotondo Weirich determined that engineering and design experience in total precast structures, as opposed to just cell modules, was needed and contacted LEAP Associates International, Inc. of Tampa, Florida.

LEAP Associates worked with the preliminary plans and helped design the totally precast prototype framing and roof. The president of LEAP met with members of Rotondo Weirich's design team and created a working plan for the roof and framing. A few weeks later, Bureau of Facilities Services' staff reviewed the preliminary plans. Although LEAP had changed some of the dimensions to improve the layout, the bureau staff liked the concept and requested additional changes. LEAP Associates then value engineered the floor plan providing more space than the previous plan, while reducing the size of the T-building's footprint, thus improving site clearances. The department of corrections felt the concept embodied all the tenets it was trying to achieve and included the specifications in its contract documents.

During the bidding phase, LEAP Associates created three roofing designs, then settled on a hollowcore roof system that "pops up" where the buildings come together. The hollowcore roof is covered with a composite panel made of plywood and rigid insulation, then shingles. To meet the demanding design schedule, LEAP Associates started shop drawings thirty days prior to the contract award to keep the project on its accelerated track.

RPPD won twenty-eight of the buildings with LEAP's framing and roof design. The new T-buildings allowed the greatest use of the cell module designed by Rotondo Weirich. As discussions with bureau staff continued, improvements and changes were made. The bureau also took advantage of precast production time and redesigned the mechanical system to complement the new configuration of the mechanical spaces.

Data Collected

There were more benefits of precast manufacture than anticipated. Precast allows the shell of an entire T-building to be erected in two-to-three weeks, instead of months, as needed in conventional construction. Cells come in even numbers to share a service chase. Upper floors are the same as lower floors. One wing is like all the others. Maintenance areas are accessed through a seven-foot tall attic thereby ensuring that staff do not need to stoop or crawl to reach mechanical systems and will not bang their heads on trusses. The attics include entrances away from the inmate-occupied sections, increasing security, and running over the dayrooms into the attic space above each wing of cells.

The basic construction approach is the same for each facility. Cell blocks are trucked to the site where a concrete slab has been prepared. Cranes place the cells into position, two cells high, with a separate balcony included on the fronts to allow access. While additional cell modules are brought in, precast framing is completed on those already set. Precast end walls are installed and additional precast walls are erected for interior control rooms. Finally, composite material is used to complete the roof and miscellaneous metal pieces, such as staircases, are added.

The finished precast T-building was subjected to hurricane tests to ensure it could withstand fluctuations in air pressure. Staff concluded that the buildings were very secure and very weather resistant.

By using prefabricated cells, the state will save $17 million in total construction costs and be able to lock up 8,000 more prisoners at the program's completion. Construction time is cut in half, from ten to five months per building. Inmates lay underground utilities, paint the exterior, and install electrical wiring, bunks, and shingles. Eighteen of the buildings were built using force account labor, in which prisoners serve as labor to finish construction after the precast is erected. Estimates of savings were approximately $500,000 per project using force account labor compared to having outside contractors do the work. Inmate labor would have been used for more of the projects, but the department of corrections was building 24,000 beds in one year and could not do it by itself. Bureau staff believe that the inmate work force offsets more than 90 percent of the total labor cost of such projects.

In a breakdown of conventional construction versus precast, it is easy to see why the T-building was, and is, a success.

Table 1: Comparison of Conventional versus Precast Concrete Construction

	Butterfly Dorm	T-building
Number of Cells	112	132
Lawful Capacity	149	176
Maximum Capacity	222	258
Cost (1993)	$1.9-$2.75M	$1.9-$2.2M
Tool Area Per Building	22,000 sq. ft.	24,352 sq. ft.
Time of Construction	10 months*	5 months*
Design and Construction Document Fees	$35,675	$0
Bidding Fee	$5,529	$0
Construction Administration Fee	$33,427	$0
Cost Per Bed	$12,387	$8,527

The construction time is for the actual erection of the building. Approximately two months of preparation time is required to set up the project, process contracts, and prepare shop drawings, among other tasks, prior to erection as defined by Florida statutes.

Using the new 132-cell T-building design in the five-year plan saves approximately $7,000,000 in reuse fees alone. The T-building's design accounts for ease of construction and improved observation from the control room. The door-locking system was simplified to reduce cost and maintenance.

While it takes more area to accommodate the T-building, two outdoor recreation areas are created by the space between any two of the T-building's wings and may be fenced off easily. Considering how the building is to be used and initial comments from officers, the superintendent, and operations staff during programming for the building, these two areas provided by each T-building will make the different classifications easier to manage. The design of the T-building also allows the department to reduce its operating costs by improving the correctional officer to inmate ratio to 3 officers for every 258 prisoners.

Further comparison widens the gulf between conventional and precast construction when it is considered that the eighty-two butterfly dorms required by the five-year plan yields 12,218 lawful beds while eighty-two T-buildings yield 14,432 beds. The extra 2,214 beds provided by the T-building eliminates the need to construct 1.68 single cell institutions.

Assuming a single cell institution costs $35 million to build and $15.8 million to operate, the T-building will save $58.8 million in construction and $531 million in operating expenses over a 20-year period by virtue of its design, not factoring in the previously mentioned cost savings.

Additionally, conventional construction usually carries with it incentive clauses for early completion, which may amount to more than $2,500 per day. Precast, as a result of its manufacture and design process, saves more than $1.4 million in early construction incentive bonuses by cutting construction time in half. This, coupled with the fact that 2,816 lawful precast construction single beds are brought on-line compared to zero conventional construction beds in the same building-schedule timeline, makes a strong case for precast construction. The bureau, likewise, had difficulty in finding masons in the construction year beginning the program. If the buildings had been constructed using conventional methods, the entire program would have suffered significantly and been behind schedule. Remarkably, the average precast erection takes only fifteen days, with the fastest being built in only nine days.

Conclusion

The development of the concept and the speedy construction of individual facilities would not have been possible without a dedicated team. Once the state had chosen precast concrete, bureau officials worked well with the contractor because both were dedicated to solving problems. A shared commitment was the final factor in the project's success. The manufacturers, project managers, and engineers began design work over a month prior to the bid date and began production long before the contracts were approved. This was how the projects met the one-year-to-completion time frame.

Precast manufacturers worked as prime contractors on the project instead of as subcontractors. They worked directly with the state and were called in early enough to give the project the flexibility of a design/build project. By January 6, 1994, six of the facilities were occupied. The state met Governor Chiles' target of having prisoners serve 75 percent of their sentence by January 1995, nearly one year ahead of schedule.

The Florida prison success story can be repeated all over the country. When the cost effectiveness of a standard design is shown to corrections officials and the right team members are assembled, safe, efficient, cost-effective housing units can be erected in as few as nine days, leaving only the interior finishing to be completed.

Contacts:

Steve Watson
Architectural Supervisor
Florida Department of Corrections

2601 Blair Stone Road
Tallahassee, Florida 32399-2500
(850) 410-4210

Cindy-Jo Thomas
Marketing Manager
LEAP Associates

P. O. Box 16007
Tampa, Florida 33687
(813) 988-6870

An Urban High-rise Jail

Introduction

Faced with serious crowding of the old county jail, Arlington County, Virginia had to consider options for expanding its jail capacity. This need was exacerbated by the very small land area constituting the county (twenty-six square miles), and its location within a highly urban setting, just outside of Washington, D.C. The growth in Arlington County was not limited to its jailed population. The county population increased by more than 11 percent during the previous ten years, with much of the growth from immigrant populations. The options for expanding the county jail were limited by space considerations and the concurrent expansion of other county offices and services at the existing courthouse/police/detention facility complex. As with any correctional facility, residents and community groups resisted relocating the site elsewhere in the county.

The existing facility was of a linear design with limited inmate-management flexibility. Thus, not only was the old jail crowded and somewhat dated, operational requirements, terms of inmate management, and levels of programming could not be met. Though it is a highly transient community, the Arlington County citizenry has high expectations for its government agencies. Fortunately, comprehensive programming always has been supported by the citizens both financially and by their direct participation in jail programming activities.

Development and Design

The selected site was adjacent to the old jail/courthouse complex. The size of the site was a typical city block on which both the detention facility and the future courts/police building must rest. Thus, a small facility footprint was imperative which, coupled with the commercial development in the surrounding area, suggested a high-rise facility design. With no space for future expansion around the site, space would need to be provided at the planned site. The facility required space for an initial 500-bed capacity plus shell space for additional cells for future expansion within the building footprint. Support services would require space to serve the facility's ultimate capacity of 800 inmates.

The sheriff's office and county staff worked with consultants to determine the best design approach. The experience of those working in high-rise correctional facilities that were built in recent years had led to the development of the mini-jail concept. Early high-rise jail designs attempted to provide many centralized services and activities, and it was soon discovered that their vertical transportation systems were overwhelmed by the volume of movement which, in turn, forced serious curtailment of many activities. In New York City, the renovation of the Tombs into a modern correctional facility created the first mini-jail concept. The building was divided into a stack of three autonomous units, each managed separately, each with a program or mini-center, which served a number of housing units directly by stairs rather than by elevators.

The Arlington County Detention Facility used this mini-jail concept to enhance the vertical design requirement and to strengthen programming and services both to inmates and staff. Four mini-jails were created, which house a total of 509 inmates. Mini-jails 1, 2, and 3 contain 144 beds each for a total of 432. Mini-jail 4 consists of 72 beds subdivided into three 24-bed housing units for special jail populations. These groups include the mentally ill, aggressive and disorderly inmates, and inmates who require separation from the general population. Anticipating fluctuations in the population and future expansion, the general population cells were sized to 80-square feet to allow for double celling.

With the exception of visitation, law library services, and specialized medical care, all services are provided within each mini-jail. Sick call, medication administration, commissary, academic education, and individual and group counseling are all located adjacent to the housing units. Dining, exercising areas, and some counseling services occur within the housing units. In fact, an outdoor recreation yard was designed at each housing unit to allow direct access to recreation, and to allow for borrowed light in each cell.

It was not cost efficient to decentralize all programs and services. The visiting area, law library, and specialized medical services were centralized to limit duplication of staff, supplies, and equipment. There was a need, however, to find a safe and secure means for inmates to travel to these locations. Requirements to ensure the facility provided for the appropriate accessibility under the Americans with Disabilities Act, and the desire to limit the use of stairs in the facility made the use of elevators a necessity. The system had to ensure the security of the elevator and allow access only to authorized locations, but without overburdening staff to control each elevator.

Due to the small amount of space available at the site, wherever possible the detention facility and the future courts/police building would have to share functional areas. The most obvious of these was the loading dock. The design of the loading dock needed to provide access from the courts/police building without breaching the perimeter of the detention facility. This was accomplished by designing a double sallyport at the loading dock, whereby the loading dock itself was essentially a sallyport. A complete sallyport was designed from the loading dock into the detention facility to address the issue of facility security. A separate entrance into the loading dock was provided to access the courts/police building.

The compatibility of the facility with its residential and business neighbors was critical to the design process. The facility had to be designed to provide unification and cohesion for the courthouse area complex—it had to be a bonus rather than a detriment to the neighborhood. The design of the new facility needed to understate its high-security aspects while still providing the requisite security for a broad range of custody levels.

Implementation

The twelve-story detention facility is organized into five, two-story "mini-jails" served by three stories of support space located in the base of the building. Each mini-jail operates as a semi-autonomous grouping. Service delivery is maximized while inmate movement is minimized. One of the mini-jails has been retained as shell space with rough-ins for future plumbing and electrical needs.

Case managers and zone supervisors have offices in their respective mini-jail to ensure they are in a better position to identify and address needs of both the inmates and staff assigned. Using the direct supervision management style, supervisors are more adjacent and thus provide support to their staff in the housing units. Case-management staff are now more aware if inmates do not attend requested programming. Though the facility is managed under the assumption of inmate self-sufficiency, responsibility, and accountability, the case managers and supervisors can provide immediate reinforcement and intervention to ensure program opportunities are maximized.

Inmate movement to centralized programs and services is accomplished through a pass system, issued by the housing unit staff. The elevators are programmed to allow inmates relatively free access to authorized floors, but controlled access to unauthorized floors through a card-access system. Each elevator is equipped with a camera that can be monitored by central control. Additionally, central control staff, at any time, can take manual control of any elevator in the secure perimeter.

Operationally, security staff are responsible for viewing the passes of inmates they encounter. Rarely is there an incident where an inmate violates the privilege of unescorted movement to authorized locations. This system of inmate movement allows for greater, more secure movement within the secure perimeter of the facility, but does not require significant intervention by central control staff, nor escort staff from one floor to another.

The courthouse/detention facility tunnel is a secure area that eliminates the need for outside court transportation. Inmates are moved to staging areas prior to court, and are moved by only two escorts to court lockups. No incidents (attempted escapes, assaultive behavior) have occurred when moving inmates to court. The reduced need for security staff is apparent here. Despite the ease in which inmates can be taken to court, video arraignment also is available at the mini-jail level to limit inmate movement even further.

To respond to the requirement for pleasing aesthetics, which were vital to the community's acceptance, the facility's facade is constructed of limestone-colored, precast concrete-insulated panels that are visually compatible with the surrounding commercial and office buildings. Furthermore, secure narrow cell windows are concealed behind vision and spandrel glass panels which, when viewed from the street, create the appearance of a large window in a typical office building.

Outcomes

Consistent with national figures, while the number of persons committed to the detention facility has grown slightly, the average length of stay has increased significantly. Thus, the need for longer term programs and services also has increased. Through the facility design, the sheriff's office was able to expand and improve program delivery. The chart on page 224 depicts some of the increases in programming in terms of percentages of inmates participating (calculated from the average daily population at the time of the data collection). Other indicators of overall facility operations also are listed.

Table 1: Programming and Disciplinary Issues by Percentage of Inmates Participating

Activity	Prior Facility	Current Facility
Disciplinary Action Reports	16	23
Inmate Assaults	11	5
Work Force	16	25
Academic Education	20	21
Substance Abuse Programs	39	54
Therapeutic Community	5	6
Vocational Education	2	8
Religious programs	71	90

While there is a clear increase in disciplinary action reports issued, this speaks primarily to the increased level of staff supervision and accountability of inmates. The incidents of assaults decreased, suggesting the facility is safer. Most notable is the increased percentage of inmates participating in activities, which reduces idle time and provides tools for successful reintegration back to the community. This could not have been accomplished without a dedicated and professional staff; however, despite quality staff, the level of programming could not be accomplished without a facility design that fostered offering a wide range of services and programs in a cost-effective manner.

The planning for double celling in combination with building shell space for expansion was sound. The facility planned in 1988 was not opened until 1994. By the time staff moved in the first inmates, 100 additional bunks were mounted in the cells. An additional 60 bunks were added immediately following occupancy.

The Arlington County Detention Facility is proud of its accreditation by the American Correctional Association, the Virginia Department of Corrections, and the National Commission on Correctional Health Care, which is made possible in part by a design that supports operations.

Conclusion

In a vertical facility, the ability to offer a wide range of inmate services in a cost-effective manner is enhanced through a combination of centralized administration, decentralized programming, and security control. The detention-facility design enhances security by limiting movement, and the delivery of program services by bringing these functions to the inmate rather than bringing the inmate to the source. Thus, the mini-jail design has allowed the Arlington County Detention Facility to expand its operation, and more specifically the programming for the inmates, while enhancing security in the facility. Staff can more effectively supervise and manage inmates in their living units rather than escorting inmates throughout the facility to services and programs.

Sharing operations with the courthouse reduced the footprint of the Justice Center Complex, allowing the facilities to be built adjacent to other county offices and services.

Through design features, functions can be successfully shared between buildings requiring different levels of security.

The community response has been positive; in fact, most are not aware that the building is a correctional facility—even after visiting the courts and police building that face the detention facility. The increase in level of participation at the facility by the citizens demonstrates the continuing commitment of the community to a professional and progressive corrections operation.

Contact:

Thomas N. Faust
Arlington County Sheriff

1435 North Courthouse Road
Arlington, Virginia 22201
(703) 228-4460

McNeil Island Corrections Center,
Washington State Department of Corrections

Work Ethic Camp: Inmates Construct Facility

The Washington State Department of Corrections has taken a fresh approach to the process of facility design at its correctional center located on McNeil Island. The new approach incorporates inmate education and development into the process of facility construction. The success of this program has been positive and is continually increasing.

McNeil Island Corrections Center began construction of a new Work Ethic Camp in April, 1996. The camp will function as a four-month "boot camp" facility upon its completion. The difference with this camp is that it is being constructed solely with inmate labor. Construction consists of an 11,000 square-foot administration/education building, a 6,800 square-foot covered fitness building, and two 100-bed housing units which total 27,000 square-feet. Thus, the total area of construction that is being completed using inmate labor exceeds 44,000 square feet.

The goals of this project were to incorporate inmate programming and vocational training into the entire construction process, benefiting both the institution and the inmate workers. The institution hoped to take advantage of some of the inmates' construction expertise, while also providing meaningful skills to inmates who had no construction experience. Staff felt that the project would build self-esteem and a positive self-image for the inmates working on the construction crews. They also felt that they could maximize taxpayer dollars through the use of inmate labor in the construction process.

Initial feedback on the success of this project has been phenomenal. The goals are being met with incredible success. The inmates are learning all aspects of the construction process, and taking a surprising amount of pride in their work. In addition, construction is only a fraction of what it would cost to contract out the project.

Many of the inmates working on this project have had no prior construction experience; not surprisingly, several never have held any meaningful employment. When the inmates are assigned to this program, they each are evaluated to identify specific job skills and whether they possess any actual construction experience. Those inmates who lack the necessary construction expertise are assigned to a vocational training program incorporating classroom and on-the-job training and instruction. These sessions teach the inmates basic construction and safety principles, which enables them to work safely and productively on the job site.

When inmates reach an acceptable level of proficiency, they are assigned to a work crew supervisor. Inmates identified as already possessing the required job skills when they enter the program are assigned directly to a crew supervisor. Those inmates who become part of a work crew are assigned by the crew supervisor to an appropriate area, which best uses their talents.

Since a majority of the inmates assigned to the work crews have only a basic understanding of the construction trades, the staff members on the construction sites act as both supervisors and vocational trainers. The crew supervisors have used the construction site as a training room. They have incorporated on-the-job-training into the complete construction process, teaching the many different trades required to complete the buildings. The supervisor demonstrates a task and then lets the inmate crews complete that section of the job, checking back periodically to ensure quality control. This process has proved to be very successful. The inmates feel they have a certain sense of freedom in their work, and they take a great deal of pride in their production.

Many of the inmates working on this project are seeing for the first time that their hard work can accomplish something of value. It is hoped that by providing job skills they can use upon their release, and by letting them realize what they can accomplish with dedication and hard work, these inmates will leave the institution and lead productive lives.

Estimates at the beginning of this project were that the institution could save more than 35 percent of the total cost of the buildings by using inmate labor instead of contracting out the project. At the project's completion, cost savings exceeded this estimate. The institution also has been able to exert greater control over construction schedules, material purchasing, completion dates, and various other tasks that would not have been possible if the project had been contracted out. This project has proved to be a great success for the inmates, the institution, the taxpayers, and everyone involved.

Authors:

Gary D. Jones
Associate Supervisor
Washington Corrections Center
formerly of the McNeil Island Correctional Center

Steve Anderson
Associate Director
KMB Justice Facilities Group
Olympia, Washington

Author/Contact:

Willie Dixon
Project Plant Manager
McNeil Island Correctional Center

P. O. Box 88900
Stillacoom, Washington 98388
(253) 512-6550

A Juvenile Detention Facility that Works

Introduction

In 1989, the Hamilton County, Ohio, Board of County Commissioners authorized the planning for construction of a new Hamilton County Juvenile Court Youth Center. The site for the new facility was the same site as the old facility, which had been constructed in the early 1950s. The site is located in a diversified neighborhood in the Mt. Auburn area of Cincinnati, Ohio. The old detention center was a two and one-half story, 42,000 square-foot structure placed in the middle of a 4.8 acre site. Immediately adjacent neighbors include the William Howard Taft House, a national park historic site, a public elementary school, a community recreation center, a city-operated health clinic, a senior citizens' center, and many multifamily residences.

The site was bisected by two separate zoning districts, which would prohibit the construction of a new facility without obtaining a zoning variance. A portion of the western part of the site is included within the Auburn Avenue Historic District boundary.

Design and Development

Glaser Associates, in conjunction with the staff of the Hamilton County Juvenile Court Youth Center, spent many meetings in the programming phase for the new facility. The project team was fortunate to have the time to develop a thorough programming document that was grounded in the facility mission statement. Clearly identified design objectives were developed through an end-user participatory process that invited each participant to articulate their process requirements.

Some of the design objectives included the following:

- To provide for flexible and adaptable space that can be responsive to possible changes in legislative policies and practices

- To design for decentralization of as many facility support services as permitted by security schematics

- To minimize, when possible, the movement of residents to services or programs, rather taking services or programs to living units

- To provide for a wide range of youth classification and youth segregation capable of responding to possible changes in legislative or judicial policies or practices

Another significant component of the programming process was a thorough review of critical regulatory standards that would have an impact on the project. The following standards were reviewed and analyzed to assure that the design process would be inclusive of all critical points: the Ohio Basic Building Code, NFPA Life Safety Code, American Correctional Association Standards, Ohio Department of Youth Services Standards, Ohio Department of Youth Services Design Guide, Auburn Avenue Historic District Guidelines, and the City of Cincinnati's Zoning Code.

The zoning review highlighted the need to obtain a zoning variance to build on the existing site and the need to obtain approval of the Historic Conservation Board. These obstacles were addressed by initiating a door-to-door community informational/marketing campaign with neighbors identifying and explaining what the existing facility limitations were and how the design team hoped to address them. This process involved three months of contacting neighbors, inviting them to tour the existing facility, asking them to identify concerns that they had about the old facility and what they might see as concerns or requests for a new facility. Staff made a series of presentations to the community council, prior to any public pursuit of a zoning variance. Ultimately, this plan of action allowed for a unanimous endorsement from the community council, prior to maneuvering through the zoning variance process and obtaining Historic Preservation District approval.

The design of the facility commenced in earnest in August 1992 with the award of the architectural contract to Glaser Associates and the construction management contract to Turner Construction Company in association with D. E. Foxx and Associates. Construction commenced in December 1993, with demolition of the existing facility gymnasium and an eight-bed housing unit to obtain an optimal footprint for the new facility. The new facility was occupied in November 1995, followed by the demolition of the existing facility and completion of site work.

The Hamilton County Juvenile Court Youth Center is a 164,000 square-foot, five-story concrete frame structure built into a hillside that has a thirty-foot differential from east to west. The lower level is predominantly services (food service, laundry, loading dock) and includes a vehicular sallyport for law enforcement. The main level is the hub of the facility—incorporating intake, medical, administration, and the courts. The facility design consists of three floors of housing. Housing consists of eight units, with each unit consisting of two pods, containing ten single sleeping rooms, one quiet room, an interview room, dayroom, two shower rooms, clean and dirty linen closets, and a shared multipurpose room. The dayroom area within each pod accommodates a designated leisure area for group activities and television viewing and designated space for meals, which are served in each housing pod. The unit/pod design provides sixteen distinct ten-bed pods for the application of the facility classification system.

Multipurpose rooms and visitation pods contain large curtain walls with security glazing to maximize the introduction of natural light and a view created by the high-elevation site. Multipurpose room space is specifically dedicated for the facilities' mobile-educational curriculum, recreation programming, religious programming, informational programming, and group sessions. The facility has a full-size gymnasium, exercise room, and two secure outdoor recreation yards.

This project was a joint venture among the Hamilton County Juvenile Court, the Ohio Department of Youth Services, and Hamilton County, Ohio. The total project budget of $24,950,000 included $8,500,000 from the Ohio Department of Youth Services through County Capital Projects H.B. 812.

The budget is broken down in the following way:

Construction cost	$ 19,800,000
Fees	$ 3,200,000
Equipment and furniture	$ 1,370,000
Miscellaneous county costs	$ 580,000
Total project budget	$ 24,950,000

Implementation

Bid Package

The design team believed that one of the most critical bid packages for the success of the project would be the detention-security package. To maximize the probability of obtaining a competent contractor, the security-detention bidders were prequalified as approved bidders. The prequalified security contractors were required to identify who they would team with to provide the electronic-security component for the project. Firms had to respond to a questionnaire, which asked them to identify technological competency, scope of work force, history of meeting schedules and budgets, percentage of change order costs in previous projects, outstanding project litigation, and references.

The early development of the electronic-security control system was required by bid specification. A demonstration touch screen that was loaded with a prototype of the facility schematic was available within four months of the groundbreaking ceremony. This early schedule allowed for a review of the screen graphics for clarity, color, process logic, and the ergonomics of design, thereby eliminating end-of-schedule change orders.

Partnering Sessions

To develop a common goal and vision for the project, the various project players were involved in a two-day partnering session. Office and field representatives from all twenty-four bid packages, owners' representatives, the architect, construction manager, building inspectors, and OSHA staff participated. This process created a forum to address concerns and perspectives of all the various representatives.

The outcome of this session was the following vision statement (see page 231).

This partnering process was summarized in the project slogan: "Model of Excellence." When it was completed, the project was within budget and free of litigation.

> ## Vision Statement
>
> *THE PROJECT:* Make profit with pride by instilling commitment to excellence by all members of the project team. With "2020 VISION," the goal is to provide a quality product to the community, which results in the best juvenile detention center in the nation. Give constant attention to budget, coordination, and project schedules.
>
> *THE TEAM:* A globally minded team is characterized by mutual trust and respect for one another. The team cooperates fully to achieve intended goals through multilateral work. Positive, skilled, experienced, highly professional craftspeople compose the team and their talents are well utilized. Team members are friendly and caring.
>
> Stewardship is held by all for the model project. A positive atmosphere is created that stimulates enjoyment and satisfaction in each individual's work.
>
> *THE CUSTOMER:* The major goal is customer satisfaction, and combined efforts that exceed owner and team expectations. The primary focus is to safely construct a well designed, functional, quality facility, as envisaged and needed by the owner, ahead of schedule and under budget.
>
> *COMMUNICATION:* Honest, open and effective communications are maintained and team members are responsive to each other in a timely fashion. This environment enables everyone to fairly and amicably resolve problems and disputes. An exchange of ideas and information is encouraged.

Development of Process Teams

The scope of change and transition that was undertaken required the involvement of as many people as possible to become infused with the vision for change and to help plan how that process would happen. As most in this field, the participants were challenged by the concrete thinking that is often the benchmark of those who work in corrections and the criminal justice system. The opportunity to step out of the traditional box and investigate and experience a change process was exhilarating to some, and immobilizing to others. Process teams started thirty-six to twenty-four months before facility activation.

Process teams were established for eight different areas: activation, classification, facility control, intake, programming, reception and release, support services, and unit management. Team leaders were assigned, but team membership was both on a voluntary and invitational basis to balance the abstract and concrete thinkers from our staff. The visionaries and the pragmatists, and sometimes pessimists, were needed to make the process realistic and, in hindsight, extremely effective. These teams dealt with every process issue from resident clothing, to telephone access, to departmental processes, and departmental training.

One of the most challenging components of the individual process teams was cross communication among the teams to reflect the importance of the interdependence that existed among them and to prevent any one team from developing processes unilaterally.

Mock-up Pod

The bid packages were established with the provision for a semi-operational mock-up pod to be incorporated within the schedule of the building process. With the realization that some aspects of the pod operations would be inoperable, the advantage of fast tracking a pod would allow for a prototype pod for various contractors' long-lead items, such as custom supply and return-air fixtures. The mock-up pod allowed for benchmarks to be established for installation and quality expectations. Final finishes were excluded from this mock-up process, but frames, doors, ceilings, lighting fixtures, and plumbing fixtures allowed for installation problem solving.

From an operational standpoint, the mock-up pod allowed the ability to plan, schedule, and analyze training opportunities. Operational process teams had access to the pod throughout construction. This allowed for the development of transitional on-the-job training processes creating accurate and realistic task analysis.

Although there was a real but unspecified cost for this component of the project, it allowed for on-site problem solving of a design process that would occur multiple times directing a path toward efficiency and quality. Without question, this reduced change orders.

Suicide Monitoring Data

Within the organizational culture, technology and data were used as management tools to ensure that youth were monitored in a way that was consistent with standards, policies, and procedures. The critical issue to be addressed was consistent staff performance in monitoring youth in a timely process consistent with the youth's assigned suicide-risk level. The facility has been designed with great attention to architectural detail to reduce any fixtures that might allow for a ligature point. Ultimately, the success in keeping the population safe rests with the consistent application of assessing, monitoring, and observing standards.

A system was designed for a graphic panel and correctional officer tour interface, which allowed for each sleeping and holding room within the facility to be set as either a high- or low-suicide-risk room dependent upon the assigned suicide-risk level of the youth assigned to that room. High-risk rooms are monitored randomly in five-minute intervals, and low-risk rooms are monitored randomly in fifteen-minute intervals. The system is designed so that a high-risk room experiences an audible alarm at four minutes and a low-risk room experiences an audible alarm at thirteen minutes. The alarm prompts staff to monitor.

When staff members monitor the room, they document that monitoring by pressing a nightlight button that silences the audible alarm and simultaneously records the date, time, unit, pod location, room number, risk level, and the monitoring time. This information is downloaded into a relational database that may be accessed through a number of search fields. To maintain quality assurance, random snapshots of monitoring sequences are taken throughout the facility everyday. Although the monitoring sequence was not a change from policies in the old facility, the new technology process and data recording was.

Conclusion

No matter in what era, facilities do not work unless they are thoughtfully designed and supportive of the culture, mission, and professionalism of the staff who comprise the organization. The areas that have been addressed all contributed to the success of this project. The process facilitated a tremendous maturation to occur on the part of the facility management team. The things that were done and the processes that were undertaken all would have been for naught if not for the commitment of a talented work force, and the acceptance and support of the community. Working together, an environment and culture was created that is safe and secure for the community, residents, staff, and visitors. These combined factors are truly what make "a facility that works".

ACA Facility Design Criteria: Responses to Design Criteria

1. The design meets or exceeds all American Correctional Association (ACA) physical-design requirements. Programming space exceeds design capacity by almost 30 percent.

2. The Youth Center exceeds the Americans with Disabilities Act (ADA) requirements for all resident, staff, and visitor areas. Each housing pod has at a minimum one resident room that is ADA-compliant. Shower rooms, living units, and all facility signage are ADA-compliant.

3. The Youth Center meets requirements for fire safety. The City of Cincinnati Fire Department and City of Cincinnati Building Department were heavily involved in the early stage of building plan development to ensure code compliance. All emergency evacuation plans were reviewed by the Cincinnati Fire Department. The facility smoke-compartmentalization and smoke-evacuation process were tested multiple times during the testing phase of the construction process.

4. The design meets all federal, state, and local environmental requirements, storm water permits, wastewater permits, air-discharge permits, and all other code requirements of the Ohio State Building code, and the City of Cincinnati Building Code.

5. The design of the facility allows for efficient handling of crowding through the use of one extra sleeping room beyond rated-bed capacity in each of the sixteen housing pods, creating a 10 percent overpopulation buffer. The facility programming space exceeds ACA requirements based on bed capacity.

6. The facility is designed to accommodate the addition of one unit, which would increase bed capacity by 12.5 percent. The mechanical systems of the building were designed to handle this addition. The space was wired and roughed out for a possible addition. Programming and support space were designed to handle additional beds.

7. The design of the facility blends with the topography of the area and the masonry colors of the neighboring structures. All external appearances of a secure correctional facility were minimized to integrate with the diversity of the neighboring residents and businesses. The western border of the site sits within a historic preservation designation and required review and approval of the Cincinnati Historic Preservation Board. Site landscaping and the renovation of the original rock perimeter retaining walls were identified as a critical component in the aesthetic appeal of the structure and the site.

8. The facility design introduces natural light into every sleeping room, housing pod, and with the use of curtain walls with security glazing in all multipurpose rooms and visitation pods. The use of the large glazed areas maximizes the introduction of natural light and with a high-site elevation creates an expansive panoramic view.

9. The design maximizes the use of line-of-sight for all direct service staff, support personnel, and educational personnel. The podular design of housing units creates direct line-of-sight on all resident sleeping rooms.

10. Accessible and well-maintained mechanical systems was a facility-design priority. Consequently, location and access to mechanical systems were critically analyzed and reviewed both for design and constructability. Design and construction phases were reviewed by the facility engineer for operational effectiveness and efficiency. All major mechanical areas are located outside the resident-security perimeter. Plumbing chases are accessible at waist height, with minimal extension to reach valves and fittings.

11. The facility housing design consists of eight housing units, with each unit divided into two separate housing pods. This design provides sixteen distinct separate physical areas for the application of the facility classification system.

12. All spaces within the facility were carefully designed to minimize the use of any architectural design or finish that would contribute to a youth-suicide attempt. Supply- and return-air vents were designed to significantly reduce the possibility of using them as a ligature point. All sprinkler heads and supply and return ducts were positioned directly in the line of sight of a resident's room door. All towel hooks were designed with a half-inch length and five-pound breakaway pressure.

13. The facility more than meets normal life-cycle requirements with special consideration given to mechanical applications, roofing, and finishes.

14. The design provides flexibility for a wide range of programming activities to occur without compromising the facility classification system. Facility programming space allows for maximum-time usage in distinct and common areas.

15. The design of the facility is that of a multistory (5) structure. The facility has three stair towers, one centrally located within the security perimeter and two that have the ability to be accessed outside of the perimeter. The facility has four elevators, two designated for resident movement, one for visitation, and one for law enforcement access to the facility's intake department. The central stair tower allows for access and staged evacuation of all staff and residents in an emergency situation. Facility control can continue to operate during such an emergency status.

16. The facility is designed to minimize resident movement through the facility. Most services and programs are mobile and are delivered in housing units or in multipurpose rooms immediately adjacent to the housing pods. When resident movement occurs for programming and visitation purposes, these activities are scheduled consistent with resident-housing classification.

17. The youth center electronic security system operates from two distinct facility-control rooms. The touchscreen system controls doors, cameras, all egress and ingress to the security perimeter, police sallyports, and delivery sallyports. All elevator controls are managed by facility control. Presently, the facility does not operate on the full range of remote-security controls for which the system has the capacity.

18. Entrances and egress points to the youth center were designed to coincide with user processes. A staff entrance is separate from a public entrance. Police vehicular traffic is designed to enter the facility through accessing a secure vehicular

garage. Deliveries occur in a separate delivery sallyport. The entrance and egress design exceed applicable standards.

19. The youth center design has created multipurpose room space for each of the eight-housing units. This space is specifically dedicated for the facility mobile-educational curriculum, recreation programming, religious programming, informational programming, and group sessions. The facility has a full-size gymnasium, exercise room, and two secure outdoor recreation yards.

20. The facility design consists of three floors of housing. Housing consists of eight units, with each unit consisting of two pods, containing ten single sleeping rooms, one quiet room, one dayroom, two shower rooms, clean and dirty linen closets, and a shared multipurpose room. The dayroom area within each pod accommodates a designated leisure area for group activities and television viewing and designated space for meals, which are served in each housing pod. The design supports all existing programming and future programming initiatives.

21. The youth center design incorporates appropriate storage areas for all functional units and departments. The facility design provides for storage space for clothing, materials, and supplies on each housing pod, separate storage for dirty clothing, a large storage room on each housing unit, and utility closets on each housing pod. Janitorial closets are on each floor or functional area. The facility storage and central supply is of a significant size to allow for a full inventory of facility supplies to be maintained. Resident personal clothing and articles are stored separately in the reception-release department.

22. The youth center design and operations has allowed for optimal energy conservation and usage. The facility cooling towers have been designed and set for minimal-water consumption. The laundry equipment has been purchased for maximum-water conservation. The facility toilets have had flush timing set for minimal but yet effective water usage. The building has a sophisticated building controls system that has been adjusted to optimize HVAC performance. The facility operates below the projected utility consumption as designated by the utility supplier engineers.

23. The facility is designed as a direct-supervision unit-management operation. Youth are directly supervised at all times. Movement of youth outside of housing pods is supervised by staff. Unit manager's offices are within multipurpose rooms of each housing unit. Direct care staff maintain a direct presence in each housing pod. There are no unit offices for direct care staff.

24. The youth center is a safe and secure environment for residents, staff, and visitors. After several years of operations, it continues to be the foundation of our ability to successfully meet our mission.

25. The youth center is a safe, secure, clean and well-maintained juvenile detention facility. The design and application of technology promotes and emphasizes the commitment to providing the highest quality of care to be found in a juvenile correctional facility.

26. The youth center's main entrance provides a reception area and lobby for parents and visitors. The lobby has a dedicated reception desk for the greeting and registering of all parents, visitors, and agency personnel. Public bathrooms and vending and phone areas are provided immediately adjacent to the lobby.

27. The youth center has been designed with visitation pods located on each housing floor for contact visitation between residents and authorized visitors. The facility design also provides for the ability to provide noncontact visitation when classification or security risks dictate.

28. The youth center design includes offices for the manager in each functional unit and housing unit. Unit housing mangers' offices are located in the multipurpose rooms of the managers' assigned housing unit. All support services also have designed office or work area spaces.

Contact:

Robert J. Dugan
Superintendent
Hamilton County Juvenile Court Youth Center

2020 Auburn Avenue
Cincinnati, Ohio 45219
(513) 946-2644

Health Care

10

Introduction

Correctional health care administrators recognize that many factors influence the cost of care within correctional facilities. Among these factors are tighter budgetary constraints and escalating costs for services in inmate populations that are confined for ever-longer periods of time. Health care administrators face other issues as well, including prison litigation; changes in technologies; an increase in the number of offenders with contagious and infectious diseases; and, geriatric offenders in prison and in community-based programs. In response, administrators with health care responsibilities must develop a health care delivery system that relies on a comprehensive, holistic approach to providing health and mental health care services. These services must be sensitive to the cultural, subcultural, age, and gender specific needs of a growing and diverse offender population.

The correctional health care delivery system confronts many issues in providing appropriate access to quality, cost-effective health care. Given the poor physical and mental health of the inmates entering correctional settings, the provision of adequate health and mental health care necessarily must become a higher priority in the years ahead. In this era of cost containment, all correctional agencies continue to have a moral and constitutional obligation to provide appropriate clinical care. Correctional health care administrators are remiss in their obligation if they do not rise to the challenges associated with providing appropriate access to clinical care, and a consistent quality of care, in a cost-effective manner.

The Health Care Committee reviewed nine submissions, selecting five for inclusion as major entries in this chapter. The programs that follow describe efforts by correctional health care administrators to respond to the many demands facing the correctional health care delivery system. In seeking to meet these demands, the administrators and jurisdictions in question have sought to balance the needs of the offender with the needs of the institution and the community to ensure that the services provided are consistent with contemporary health care standards.

Two entries are from the Federal Bureau of Prisons Health Services Division—one on tuberculosis prophylaxis and the other on the Heart Healthy Program, which concerns providing healthy eating choices for inmates and convincing them to eat in a healthier way.

The Texas Correctional Managed Health Care is an innovative partnership of the state's prison systems with two leading health science centers and community hospitals.

The Parole and Community Services Division of the California Department of Corrections links inmates with HIV/AIDS to medical and support services upon their release to parole and thus prevents many inmates from committing new crimes simply to continue getting health care.

The Ohio Department of Rehabilitation and Correction's telemedicine program has reduced costs and the number of potentially dangerous offenders in transit by linking, through telecommunications, the Ohio State University Medical Center with prisons throughout the state.

Committee chair:

Kenneth P. Moritsugu, M.D.
Medical Director, Health Services Division
Federal Bureau of Prisons

Suite 1000, 320 First Street NW
Washington, D.C. 20534
(202) 307-3055 x0826

Tuberculosis Prophylaxis

Introduction

Inmate populations are at high risk of developing active contagious tuberculosis due to multiple-risk factors, including poor access to medical care prior to incarceration, impoverishment, malnutrition, increased rates of drug use by injection, and Human Immunodeficiency Virus (HIV) infection. In addition, 25 percent of federal inmates are foreign-born, mostly from countries where tuberculosis infection is highly prevalent and inadequately treated.

More than 100,000 inmates are housed in approximately 90 Federal Bureau of Prisons' facilities throughout the United States. All inmates are screened for tuberculosis infection at intake, and annually thereafter, by the intradermal injection of purified protein derivative (PPD) tuberculin by the Mantoux method. Inmates with positive tuberculin skin tests, in accordance with the Centers for Disease Control criteria, or who have symptoms of active tuberculosis, are further evaluated radiographically with a chest x-ray. Individuals identified as having the active disease are immediately confined in a negative-pressure room until arrangements can be made to hospitalize them. Inmates who have a positive skin test, but do not exhibit any signs of active tuberculosis, are referred to as tuberculosis-infected or "PPD positive." It is the function of the tuberculosis prophylaxis program to prevent these inmates from becoming contagious, thereby presenting a risk to other inmates or correctional staff.

Design and Development

Inmates entering a Federal Bureau of Prisons facility are given an intake screening within two hours of arrival. Part of that physical includes a PPD skin test, a medical history, and a medical examination, as outlined on the tuberculosis chemoprophylaxis record to rule out the presence of tuberculosis.

Inmates who are transferred from one Bureau of Prisons facility to another are required to have had a PPD skin test and/or a chest x-ray during the previous year. This prevents inmates with active tuberculosis from infecting correctional staff or other inmates who are transported with them.

The most effective method of preventing someone who is PPD positive from becoming infectious is by treating them with an antibiotic for at least six months. In most cases, the antibiotic of choice is isoniazid (INH). It is very important to the success of the treatment that the inmate takes INH at the proper dosage for the full-time period without missing doses. If this does not happen, several outcomes might occur—all of them undesirable. The inmate may not complete the full dosage regimen and so the infection is not successfully treated, the bacterium could become resistant to INH so that the antibiotic is not effective on that strain of the bacterium, and the improperly treated inmate could convert to the active disease state and infect other inmates or staff.

With some frequency, inmates do not take their INH properly, thereby setting the stage for further problems. Additionally, INH can cause liver damage, sometimes progressing to liver failure and death. To ensure successful treatment, the Bureau's tuberculosis prophylaxis program has taken several steps: directly observed preventive therapy (DOPT), monthly patient screening, and a consolidated monthly INH prophylaxis-medication administration record (MAR).

All inmates who are undergoing tuberculosis prophylaxis are required to come to the pharmacy window twice a week for the administration of isoniazid under the direct observation of the pharmacy staff. Not only does this afford the pharmacist an opportunity to monitor the inmates' compliance with the treatment regimen, but this encounter also provides an opportunity to ask inmates about any symptoms they may be having regarding drug side effects and allergies. It is also the best time to check on whether inmates are experiencing any symptoms that might indicate a progression toward active tuberculosis (for example, night sweats, a bloody cough, difficulty in breathing).

To facilitate this process, the chief pharmacist at the Federal Correctional Institution in Englewood, Colorado developed a monthly INH side-effect interview and monitoring form. The program consists of the pharmacist giving inmates a questionnaire once a month to determine if they have early symptoms of isoniazid-induced hepatitis, a potentially life-threatening side effect to drug therapy. The questionnaire is available in both English and Spanish, and asks the inmate to respond yes or no to a checklist of side effects, which they have experienced in the past month (for example, fatigue and weight loss, brown urine, and loss of appetite). An affirmative response requires that the inmate see a staff physician for further evaluation.

This program was presented to the National Jewish Center for Immunology and Respiratory Medicine in April 1996, in Denver, Colorado, to broad appreciation by the clinician audience. In May 1996, the program was adopted by all Bureau of Prisons' pharmacists as a method to help them discover drug toxicity problems before they become severe. In September 1996, the program was presented to the Federal Pharmacy Conference at the University of Wisconsin. The attendees included pharmacists from the Veterans Administration, the military services, and the U.S. Public Health Service. Again, the response was overwhelmingly favorable.

For quite some time, Bureau pharmacists tracked inmate compliance with INH prophylaxis on a standard monthly medication administration record. A major disadvantage of this record is that it was necessary to complete and file at least six separate monthly forms for each inmate undergoing INH prophylaxis. Reviewing patients' medical records to discover when they began INH treatment and whether they had been compliant was a difficult task when at least six documents had to be evaluated.

In March 1997, the pharmacy staff at the Federal Medical Center in Carswell, Texas, developed a six-month tuberculosis preventive treatment program. The form for this program contained a consolidated record of the entire treatment protocol. In addition, the form had a section that addressed recent laboratory findings related to liver enzymes. The laboratory information related to liver enzymes allowed the pharmacist to review and track all pertinent data that might have an impact on the current liver status of the inmate.

The Joint Commission on the Accreditation of Health Care Organizations has commented quite favorably on the Bureau's tuberculosis prophylaxis program during numerous accreditation reviews. Further, these program changes have been cited by the Bureau as examples of disease prevention tactics to U.S. Attorney's offices, federal courts, members of Congress, and to interested American citizens.

Results

The low number of cases of active tuberculosis in the Bureau of Prisons in part may reflect the success of this program. In 1996, the Bureau of Prisons had only sixteen cases of active tuberculosis, despite having an inmate population at significant risk for the disease. In addition, since the initiation of the monthly patient screening program, no inmate has been hospitalized as a result of inadequacies in recognizing symptoms of INH-induced liver failure. This is also remarkable in view of the fact that between 0.3 and 2.6 percent of all patients who take isoniazid have clinical hepatitis, depending on age, liver status, and alcohol use.

Annually, the Bureau treats between 4,000 and 5,000 inmates with six months of isoniazid. Given this usage level, between 12 and 130 inmates could be expected to have clinical hepatitis in any one year. Prompt identification of the early symptoms of hepatitis and a corresponding intervention by bureau pharmacists have prevented any problems with more severe cases. While the Bureau houses more than 100,000 inmates at any one point in time, approximately 200,000 inmates go through the prison system during a calendar year. Despite this huge movement of individuals at risk for tuberculosis, the Bureau experiences very few cases of the active disease.

Conclusion

The pharmacy tuberculosis prophylaxis program is a vital contributor to that success. A program of this sort is difficult to administer unless the organization has a cadre of dedicated professionals who are willing to take ownership. Because the Bureau has at least one pharmacist at each of its facilities, the coordination of this nationwide program was relatively simple. A large correctional organization would need a similar group of employees to duplicate this success.

The importance of doing an immediate intake screening cannot be overstated. Inmates who exhibit suspicious symptoms of tuberculosis can be isolated at that early stage, thereby avoiding possible infection of large groups of inmates and staff. The requirement that inmates in the transport system must be tested within one year of movement is also important. An additional benefit from this emphasis is that it makes all correctional employees—whether custody or health services—more aware of the risk of tuberculosis. All

Contact:

Communications
Federal Bureau of Prisons

Office of Public Affairs
320 First Street, NW
Washington, D.C. 20534
(202) 307-3163

Heart Healthy Eating Program

Introduction

In 1989, the Bureau of Prisons identified a need to address the eating habits of inmates incarcerated in the Bureau of Prisons through reviews of nutritional analysis and increased requests for medical diets. Due to new sentencing guidelines, inmates were staying in prison longer, and the aging population was increasing medical costs relative to age. The Bureau's accelerated population growth and increasing numbers of medical diets placed an additional burden on limited staff and financial resources. Given these developments and because of the documented linkage between diets high in fat, cholesterol, and salt with an increased need for medical intervention, the Bureau designed a nutritionally balanced alternative heart-healthy meal plan.

Development and Design

The primary goals of the Heart Healthy program were to address the issues of inmate health and increasing medical costs. A training curriculum was developed for institution food service administrators, and nutritional information was shared with staff and inmates. A policy was implemented requiring alternative food items to replace food high in calories and fat. Nutritional information cards providing information regarding portion size, calories, cholesterol, sodium, and fat also were developed.

Through nutritional education, the Heart Healthy program provides everyone (especially those with medical concerns), with medical diet information that allows them to self-select healthy alternatives to mainline food items. The Heart Healthy program promotes healthy eating habits that can impact positively on the inmates' health care needs while incarcerated and into the community when released.

In 1990, the Bureau of Prisons provided nutritional training to all food service administrators as the first step in implementing its Heart Healthy program. Nutritional information (for example, a "Healthy Eating in the 1990s" packet) was developed for staff and inmates. The institutions developed a nutrition-information bulletin board and started posting nutritional information for inmate review. In 1992, the Bureau implemented the nutritional information card. These cards show the recommended portion size, and provide the amount of calories, cholesterol, sodium, and fat for that portion. In 1995, the bureau updated its medical policy and required food service to provide alternative choices for food high in fat, sodium, and calories.

Results

Nutritional analysis indicates that the nutrition training provided to all food service staff administrators has been beneficial. The analysis of the institution master menus revealed the following reductions.

Statistical Results from Heart Healthy Program

	1989 Daily Average	1995 Daily Average
Available calories	5,400	3,360
Calories from fat	44%	32%
Cholesterol available	847 mg	433 mg
Sodium average available	10,500 mg	6,500 mg

Conclusion

The use of Heart Healthy menus, alternative foods, nutritional information cards, and inmate education have eliminated special diets in most institutions apart from medical centers, where inmates with special dietary needs receive meals prescribed by staff dietitians. Nutritional analysis supports the benefits of staff nutritional training. The lack of formal inmate grievances regarding medical diets supports the success of the Bureau of Prisons' Heart Healthy and self-selection programs. The success of the Heart Healthy program rests with the nutrition training provided to the institution food administrators, staff, and inmates.

Contact:

Communications
Federal Bureau of Prisons

Office of Public Affairs
320 First Street, NW
Washington, D.C. 20534
(202) 307-3163

Correctional Managed Health Care Partnership

Introduction

The Texas Correctional Managed Health Care innovative partnership exemplifies the success that is possible by redefining traditional roles. It represents a unique collaboration between the state's prison system, two leading health science centers and a number of community hospitals. The Texas Department of Criminal Justice, the University of Texas Medical Branch at Galveston, and the Texas Tech University Health Sciences Center joined forces to form the Correctional Managed Health Care Advisory Committee.

The Correctional Managed Health Care Advisory Committee and its partners have developed a statewide provider network offering medical services to inmates. Its primary purpose is improving access to quality health care while containing cost by maximizing the use of the state's medical schools, securing efficiencies through improved intergovernmental collaboration, and using managed care tools.

In Texas, costs for prison medical care had been increasing at a rate of 6 percent per year and represented 10 to 14 percent of the state prison system's operating costs. Additionally, in response to crowding, Texas had embarked on an aggressive prison construction program that soon will confine nearly 140,000 prisoners. Since many new prison locations are in rural areas, the economic problems faced by rural hospitals further impact upon the state's ability to provide cost-effective health care. Traditional delivery systems also have been strained by increased rates of infectious diseases such as HIV, hepatitis B, and tuberculosis.

Development and Design

From its inception, the Correctional Managed Health Care program has operated as a cooperative partnership among the Texas Department of Criminal Justice, the University of Texas Medical Branch, and Texas Tech University Health Sciences Center. This partnership is embodied in the legislation that formed the committee through equal representation from each entity. The Correctional Managed Health Care Advisory Committee is established by the provisions of Section 501.059 of the Texas Government Code. This legislation, originally enacted by the 73rd Texas Legislature and amended by the 74th Texas Legislature, provides the structure for the correctional health care system now in place.

Implementation

This partnership significantly changed how medical care is delivered. Traditionally, inmate health care was provided by employees of the prison system and through fee-for-service arrangements with hospital providers. These arrangements offered little incentive to control costs. Under the managed care plan, complete medical services are provided through contracts with the universities for a fixed sum per prisoner. In accordance with statute, the department contracts for these services with the Correctional Managed Health Care Advisory Committee, which, in turn, contracts with the University of Texas Medical Branch and Texas Tech University Health Sciences Center on a capitated (fee-per-offender) basis for the provision of health care services for their assigned prison population.

The inmates for which the University of Texas Medical Branch and the Texas Tech University Health Sciences Center receive payment are determined by the geographic location of the prison units. Texas Tech University Health Sciences Center contracts with the Correctional Managed Health Care Advisory Committee for defined regions in West Texas (approximately 20 percent of the offenders), while the University of Texas Medical Branch contracts for all remaining defined regions (and the remaining 80 percent of the offenders). The Texas Department of Criminal Justice Health Services Division retains the functions of preventive medicine, inmate grievances, operational review, and coordination of offender transfers for medical reasons.

The capitation amounts negotiated by the Correctional Managed Health Care Advisory Committee with the University of Texas Medical Branch and the Texas Tech University Health Sciences Center vary by the services provided and by the differences in the demographics and health status of the inmates. Both entities are responsible for the provision of medically necessary health care services covered by the contract fee. Their responsibilities include recruiting and hiring health care personnel to staff the prison infirmary, diagnosing prisoners' health problems, providing treatment, and making referrals to specialists.

These services include primary care services, all specialty care services, community provider outpatient and ancillary services, and all inpatient hospital services. Both the University of Texas Medical Branch and the Texas Tech University Health Sciences Center vary in the services they provide. The University of Texas Medical Branch and the Texas Tech University Health Sciences Center enter into subcontracts and capitated or discounted "fee-for-service" arrangements with community providers to provide locally based services when they determine such action is warranted.

Effective, January 1, 1996, the University of Texas Medical Branch and the Texas Tech University Health Sciences Center assumed operational responsibility for all of the Texas Department of Criminal Justice mental health services in their respective university sectors. All psychiatrists and former Texas Department of Criminal Justice mental health staff have been transitioned to the university systems. These arrangements provide incentives for controlling use and generate an increased interest in preventive care. Use of telemedicine technologies also enable cost-effective access to specialty care.

Results

The partnership has resulted in lower medical costs, the establishment of a statewide network of providers, and a uniform standard of care. While maintaining a commitment to accreditation and significantly improving access to care, the Texas State Comptroller has estimated that the correctional health care partnership will save the state's taxpayers at least $125 million over a five-year period. It also serves as a model of intergovernmental collaboration for other states to use to manage access, quality, and costs of correctional health care.

247

In fiscal year 1996 and 1997, an additional $24.5 million in savings were returned to the state as a result of the cost-control methodologies employed by the partnership. Fiscal year 1997 medical costs were $5.23 per offender per day. In fiscal year 1993, those costs had been $5.99 per offender per day (a 12.7 percent reduction).

At the same time, vacancy rates of health care providers have dropped significantly; the average number of days spent waiting for a specialty clinic appointment has dropped by more than 50 percent; access-to-care indicators show marked improvement, and every Texas Department of Criminal Justice health care facility has received national accreditation. In fiscal year 1997, the health care system recorded 3.6 million medical encounters.

Since the implementation of the managed care system, and based on a review of medical records conducted by the Texas State Auditor, access to care compliance improved 27.7 percent, clinical encounter compliance has increased by 35.7 percent, and most dramatically, chronic care compliance rose 158 percent. In all, twenty-two individual performance indicators showed statistically significant gains. It is also important that these positive results were obtained at the same time that the correctional population to be served more than doubled.

In 1995, the Correctional Managed Health Care Advisory Committee partnership was awarded "special mention" by the National Managed Health Care Congress in their annual Astra Merck/National Managed Health Care Congress Partnership Award program. Even though the program traditionally focused on private-sector partnerships, the judges noted that the Texas Department of Criminal Justice-Correctional Managed Health Care Advisory Committee partnership "does reflect the innovative spirit celebrated by the awards, and therefore has grabbed our attention as deserving of a special mention."

Conclusion

The Correctional Managed Health Care Advisory Committee partners believe that the results of their cooperative venture represent long-term benefits to the state and each respective partner. The partnership emphasizes "win-win" scenarios where the motivations for the participation of each partner are recognized and addressed. The criminal justice agency is seeking quality, cost-effective medical services and provider risk-sharing arrangements. The universities are seeking teaching and placement opportunities and financial support. The participating hospitals are seeking financial stability. By understanding these motivating factors and integrating them into the work of the partnership, a successful venture has been formed.

Author:

Darin George
Assistant Director for Administrative Services
Correctional Managed Health Care

Author/Contact:

James E. Riley
Executive Director
Correctional Managed Health Care

Suite 415 1300 11th Street,
Huntsville, Texas 77340
(409) 294-2972

Prerelease Program for Inmates with HIV: Cost-effective Case Management

Introduction

The California Department of Corrections administers the Transitional Case Management program. This program was developed to link inmates with HIV/AIDS to medical and support services upon their release to parole. These transitional services provide HIV/AIDS-infected prisoners released to parole the specialized care required for their illness, and reduces or eliminates instances in which individuals intentionally return to prison with a new crime to obtain HIV/AIDS-related care.

The program evaluation data suggest that the Transition Case Management program reduces the rate of recidivism of the more seriously ill who are the most costly to house in prison. The subsequent savings generated by this program were found to substantially exceed the costs of the program. This management and health care innovation involved contracting with a private vendor to provide case managers for the offenders with AIDS. The costly problem of parolees returning to prison for treatment could be prevented or reduced by making community-based treatment more available through better case management.

Background

In October 1992, the research branch of the department conducted a follow-up study of 520 inmates with HIV/AIDS who had been released to parole between 1989 and 1991. Seventy-one percent of these inmates were returned to prison within one year of their release. The return rate for all felons in the department released to parole during 1990 was 53 percent.

In response to the identified higher recidivism rate for parolees with HIV/AIDS, the department's Parole and Community Services Division developed and implemented the Transitional Case Management program.

Development

During the program-development stage, staff conducted a literature search for any interventions designed to prevent offenders' return to prison simply for HIV/AIDS treatment service. In addition, federal, state, and county correctional agencies were surveyed to identify if such programs existed. No such programs could be found.

As of January 1, 1997, the California Department of Corrections housed 145,565 inmates in 32 state prisons and supervised 100,935 parolees at 119 parole offices in 65 locations throughout the state. All HIV/AIDS inmates are confined at 9 of the 32 state prisons. However, they are paroled to all locations throughout the state. The logistics involved in the development of the program were of considerable magnitude.

Asked to develop an innovative program, the parole division contacted individuals and agencies within the state's AIDS community known for their leadership and cutting-edge response to the AIDS' epidemic. Their expertise combined with staff knowledge of the offender led to the design of this highly successful program.

Program Design

The Parole and Community Service Division contracts with two service providers for transitional case management services. The first is the Tarzana Treatment Center, serving HIV/AIDS inmates paroled to Los Angeles and Orange Counties. The second is through the Volunteers of America, serving individuals paroled to Alameda, San Francisco, and Contra Costa Counties. These counties were selected because a majority of the target group are paroled to them.

Each service provider offers an interdisciplinary team consisting of a registered nurse case manager, a social worker, and a benefits counselor. Their services include:

- The scheduling of meetings with identified inmates ninety days prior to parole

- The provision of comprehensive medical and psychosocial assessments

- The development of a service plan based on the needs identified in the comprehensive assessments

- The linkage of HIV/AIDS parolees with services in the community upon release to parole

- The provision of assistance to parolees with their transition into the community, until the individuals are assigned to a long-term HIV/AIDS case manager

The teams work closely with correctional and medical staff within the institution, the parole agent of record, the client, and the client's family in the development of the service plan using existing community resources. The service providers participate in Title 11 HIV Comprehensive Care Consortia meetings. Title 11 HIV Comprehensive Care Consortia are federal- and state-mandated HIV/AIDS program planning bodies in local service areas.

The program was implemented through the support of the department's director, and was introduced to prison and parole administrators. In addition, advisory committees were formed consisting of department staff, local community representatives, and program participants, to guide the program's overall implementation.

Program Evaluation

Service providers submit monthly reports that include a client roster, documentation of the level of the disease's progression based on the categories defined by the Centers for

Disease Control and Prevention, and a record of the services provided. These data were used in the department's evaluation.

The evaluation used a quasi-experimental design to assess the effectiveness of the program. A classical experimental/control design would have denied treatment to the control group since there is no alternative program available. The evaluations showed that the program lowered the recidivism rate of HIV/AIDS positive parolees by nearly 20 percent over six months and 12 percent over one year. The program will be expanded based on those results.

Conclusion

This program is relevant to adult correctional management in several ways. First, it involves a partnership with nongovernmental bodies for services the private sector can provide better. Second, it expands the use of private case management services in the adult correctional system, thereby displaying the benefits of partnerships between community-based agencies and correctional systems. Third, the program generates correctional costs savings and reduces the demand for prison beds. Fourth, the success of this demonstration project triggered other funding streams for inmates with HIV/AIDS (for example, AIDS Education and Prevention Grants). Finally, the decision to continue and expand the program resulted in an administrative management policy that program decisions be based, in part, on cost-effectiveness as determined by acceptable research methods.

Program Recognition

The California Probation, Parole and Correctional Association has acknowledged the importance of the Transitional Case Management Program. In addition, the program was recognized in the American Correctional Association's October 1996 issue of *Corrections Today*.

Author:

Vicki Sanderford-O'Connor
Parole Agent
California Department of Corrections
Sacramento, California

Contact:

Marisela Montes
Deputy Director
Parole and Community Services Division
California Department of Corrections

P. O. Box 942883
Sacramento, California 94283-0001
(916) 323-0576

Telemedicine

Introduction

The Ohio Department of Rehabilitation and Correction's telemedicine pilot project was launched in 1994. This initiative linked the Ohio State University Medical Center with the Southern Ohio Correctional Facility, Ohio's maximum-security prison. The purpose of the program was to replace the transportation of some dangerous offenders through state highways with the transportation of medical information on those offenders via telecommunications links. The department also expected to improve on the timeliness and efficiency of health care delivery and save on transportation and overtime costs by eliminating unnecessary round-trip hospital visits.

Benefits

The benefits of telemedicine have exceeded all expectations. The reduction in numbers of potentially dangerous offenders in transit indeed was realized, as was the cost-benefit derived by shifting transportation officers and vehicles to other uses. Inmates hoping to angle a free ride to the doctor by faking medical problems have had the magic carpet ride pulled out from under them. As a bonus, institutional medical staff benefit by increased access to Ohio State University Medical Center's vast medical resources. For example, every Friday at noon, correctional nurses and physicians are invited to participate in live, interactive, fully accredited medical education programs emanating from the Medical Center's Ohio Medical Education Network programs (OMEN). Other sites nationwide access the programs through satellite, but Ohio correctional sites get them over a dedicated T-1 system, right into their clinics.

Telemedicine has been expanded to include telepsychiatry. The hardware now is used for complete psychiatric assessments using experts across the state, and for discussing specific cases between two or more psychiatric units. It has become a very important timesaving tool for conducting commitment and retention hearings to determine whether inmates' mental conditions are such that they should be retained involuntarily at the psychiatric facility. A hearing officer or judge can preside over the session from a distant location while still being able to maintain eye contact with the patient. A similar process is used to convene three-judge panels from various sites to conduct involuntary medication hearings.

Clinicians note that the overall reaction of patients to telemedicine has been positive. Most patients state that they feel very comfortable during the procedure, and appreciate not having to go through the handcuffing, shackling, enduring long drives and hours of waiting involved in traditional medical visits. The department's security staff also support telemedicine, pointing out that it decreases the security risks inherent in inmate transportation.

Teleconferencing substantially can reduce the need for many types of inmate "road trips." The equipment also can be used to conduct disciplinary hearings on inmates who have been transferred. Likewise, prisoners can testify and participate in formal court arraignments without ever leaving the confines of the prison. Case managers may conduct conferences, medical and otherwise, from one site to another.

The teleconferencing avenue is a two-way street. Not only does it cut down on the number of inmates on the road; it also helps reduce the number of road trips taken by professional staff. Using "distance learning" teleconferencing techniques, instructors at one site can teach or attend classes at several locations. Interactive video gives students a front row seat for asking questions and participating in discussions whether they are in the classroom or one hundred miles away. Specialized courses, such as those offered on OMEN and on the Law Enforcement Television Network, can be broadcast to a wide range of professionals. This calendar year, the department will offer physicians forty hours of continuing education on-site at no cost to staff. This amounts to a full 85 percent of the hours required for certification.

Results

In just a couple of years, the department has become a leader in telemedicine. Seven prisons now are linked to the Ohio State University Medical Center, averaging 225 consults per month. With more than 4,000 consults since 1994, staff are preparing to extend the network to each of the prisons. Telemedicine has moved from a tentative pilot project to a full-blown medical services management process. While telemedicine may not employ the traditional "hands on" medical methodology, staff have no reason to believe it is not equally effective.

Contacts:

Michelle Gailiun
Director of Telemedicine
Ohio State University Medical Center

A348 Starling-Loving Hall
320 West 10th Avenue
Columbus, Ohio 43210
(614) 293-3776

Chris Lizza
Administrator, Video Conferencing System
Ohio Department of Rehabilitation and Correction

Dr. Larry Mendel
Medical Director
Ohio Department of Rehabilitation and Correction

1050 Freeway Drive North
Columbus, Ohio 43229
(614) 752-2942

Health Care
Additional Program Entries

Central Florida Reception Center

Ronald McAndrew, Superintendent
Florida Department of Corrections, PO Box 628040, Orlando, Florida 32862-8040
(407) 282-3053

The Florida Reception Center was not initially designed to provide comprehensive medical services. However, due to the rapid increase in the state inmate population and the influx of inmates with special needs, the mission requirements were changed to that of a medical diagnostic and reception processing center.

Management, Administration, and Operation Review

Bob Duncan, Senior Project Officer, Health Services
Correctional Service of Canada, Sir Wilfred Laurier Bldg, 340 Laurier Ave W, Ottawa, Ontario, Canada K1A 0P9
(613) 996-0959

The Correctional Service of Canada established the Management, Administration, and Operation Review (MAOR) process in June of 1993, in response to a federal government requirement to identify areas of expenditure savings. This initiative provided the introduction of health services delivery within an overall policy and program framework for effecting changes aimed at producing cost savings.

Federal Medical Center Mental Health Patient Care

Communications
Federal Bureau of Prisons, 320 First Street NW, Washington, DC 20534
(202) 307-3163

The Federal Medical Center in Rochester, Minnesota serves as a major psychiatric and medical referral/treatment center for all federal inmates of the Bureau of Prisons. Activity therapy plays an important role in the multidisciplinary services offered to inpatient medical and psychiatric patients.

Community Youth Drug Awareness

Communications
Federal Bureau of Prisons, 320 First Street NW, Washington, DC 20534
(202) 307-3163

Several facilities within the Bureau of Prisons are offering programs in which inmates speak to community groups—especially youth groups—about the importance of staying in school and avoiding drugs and the consequences of criminal activity. The goal of the program is to help young people become more aware of the impact their lifestyle choices have on themselves, their families, the community, and society.

Juvenile Corrections

11

Introduction

The programs selected for inclusion in this chapter share a clear and well-thought out process for creating and implementing innovative management practices within juvenile justice systems. Even more, they each provide for the standardization of practices within statewide systems. The programs that are highlighted are suitable for replication and implementation by other corrections' consumers who may be interested in developing comparable practices and procedures within their own jurisdiction.

The Juvenile Corrections Committee established a three-pronged set of selection criteria. These included a review of each submission's basic format, its content, and finally whether the submitted programs received recognition from agencies other than their own. Submissions were solicited through a request for proposal process from juvenile corrections systems throughout the country. The key to the selection of those submissions that follow was whether they described an initiative that was primarily management-based rather than programmatic in focus. In addition, the winning submissions were those that had innovative methods of managing a change process within juvenile justice systems.

The three programs that follow illustrate systemwide management processes that allow for the more effective use of resources, both financial and human. They enable correctional administrators to provide better and more comprehensive services to the entire spectrum of juvenile justice stakeholders.

The first program that is described is known as RECLAIM Ohio from the Ohio Department of Youth Services. Through this initiative, the state overhauled and creatively redesigned its procedures for allocating funding to juvenile courts at the county level. In doing so, it brought all state and local juvenile justice stakeholders into an interactive partnership that benefits the entire system.

The California Department of the Youth Authority's Personnel Security Monitoring System allows all of the state's juvenile corrections institutions and camps to effectively monitor the comings and goings of staff, volunteers, and visitors. Its purpose is to increase the security of staff, volunteers, and visitors who work for or otherwise come into contact with the Youth Authority. It is a technologically advanced system that is suitable for replication in other governmental agencies.

The final submission describes the creation and initial implementation of a major change initiative by the New York State Division for Youth referred to as the "Youth Development System." The goal of this undertaking is to implement a single behavior-management system for all youth, and to adopt a shared model of intervention to be used by correctional staff across the entire spectrum of the division's facilities.

Committee chair:

Jesse E. Williams, Jr.
Chief Probation Officer
San Francisco Juvenile Probation Department

375 Woodside Avenue
San Francisco, California 94127
(415) 753-7556

Ohio Department of Youth Services

RECLAIM Ohio

Introduction

Historically, the State of Ohio saw two primary trends in its juvenile justice system that led to the development of RECLAIM Ohio (Reasoned and Equitable Community and Local Alternatives to the Incarceration of Minors). First, juvenile courts lacked adequate resources for local alternatives. Second, state institutions were seriously crowded, operating at 175 percent of design capacity. The department lacked the resources to hold youth accountable and to provide meaningful competency building programs.

While state funding for county-based juvenile justice and correctional services was in place, it was embedded in a line item within the department's budget. Rather than creating an alliance between state and local juvenile justice and correctional entities, this set up a competition for scarce resources. When juvenile court judges pled for increased funding for local alternatives, the legislature considered shifting funds from the department's institutional operation. When the department pled for additional operating money for crowded facilities, the obvious place to find funding was to debit the juvenile court subsidies. Past experience with subsidies to juvenile courts and the lessons learned from benchmarking with other systems triggered the decision to develop a strategy for juvenile corrections that tied the state and juvenile courts together as partners.

Development and Design

The result was the development of RECLAIM Ohio—a new way of handling the business of juvenile corrections. Under RECLAIM Ohio, the majority of funds allocated by the state legislature to the Department of Youth Services are distributed based on the level of delinquency adjudications in each county. The judges then can "purchase" a state commitment or purchase, expand, or develop local services. It is a local choice based on the needs of the individual youth and public safety.

Putting the fiscal resources into the hands of decision makers has made the cost of state secure incarceration viable to all. It also has fostered a sense of joint ownership of the delinquency problem and developed a partnership between state and local juvenile justice systems.

Through RECLAIM Ohio, each county receives a percentage of the RECLAIM allocation based on the percentage of Ohio's felony-level delinquents adjudicated in their county. Adjudication, the juvenile equivalent of conviction, is used in the funding formula because it means that counties are allocated money on the basis of how many criminal youth they have, not on the number of judicial commitments to the department. In this way, funds are distributed on the basis of criminal conviction, not on judicial sentencing patterns. While other factors, such as juvenile filings or population were considered, adjudication was selected because of the existence of accurate data and its applicability to the purpose of the funding.

RECLAIM Ohio provides counties with a pool of state funds, sufficient to pay for commitments for 25 percent of the juvenile felony offenders. If the county commits, it must pay the state for each commitment out of its RECLAIM allocation. If the county reduces commitments to some lower percentage, that money follows those diverted youth to fund local alternatives.

Several safeguards are built in to ensure that this program remains a positive, and never a negative, fiscal incentive. If a county runs out of the state RECLAIM Ohio allocation, no county money ever has to be used to pay for a commitment. RECLAIM Ohio has a contingency fund, so if judges already have expended all of their state money, they still can commit the youth to the department and the per diem is paid through the contingency.

Implementation

The test phase for RECLAIM Ohio began in 1994. House Bill 152, which became effective on July 1, 1993, established the Felony Delinquent Care and Custody program (or RECLAIM Ohio). Among other things, this bill outlined the formula by which counties would be allocated funds under RECLAIM Ohio and debited for institutional commitments, created the Care and Custody Oversight Committee, set up a pilot program, and provided for full implementation on January 1, 1995. In the six months prior to the implementation of the pilot program, the Care and Custody Oversight Committee met to select the volunteer counties, which would participate in the pilot project. The pilot project began on January 1, 1994, and lasted one year. Nine counties varying in size and population demographics were selected. During the pilot phase of the program and the first few months of full implementation, the oversight committee and the department identified aspects of the program that needed to be modified or fine-tuned.

On the technical side, these nine counties worked with department staff to keep rules, forms, reporting requirements, and procedures customer friendly and simple. On the programmatic side, these same counties reduced their commitment to the department by nearly 43 percent. More than 1,000 youth were served in RECLAIM Ohio programs. Taking the RECLAIM Ohio program statewide, however, meant shifting the culture of 88 county juvenile courts and a state department into a business mind-set.

In 1995, the department had a budget of $186 million, $110 million of which was allocated to RECLAIM Ohio. Fiscal structures were set in place to deal with the new market-driven institutions. Every month, department staff worked with the county to calculate and verify the number of state bed days purchased by each county. A responsive payment system was created, which promptly provided each county with a check for the difference between the allocation and the debit for the state bed days.

At the county level under RECLAIM Ohio, county commissioners became the fiscal agents with the programs administered by the juvenile court. It was left up to the courts whether they chose to purchase services through contracts or to develop and expand court-operated programs. Rather than have state administrators pass judgment on the types of programs counties planned to use, county juvenile court staff were given the freedom to select local programs. Accountability was product driven. If the program failed to produce good results, then the offender would continue delinquent activity, and the county eventually would commit the youth to the department and pay the state per diem. Therefore, it was in the best interest of the county to hold the vendor of service accountable for the success of the program.

As a condition of receiving RECLAIM funds, counties were required to aggregate and relay to the Ohio Department of Youth Services basic information on the youthful offender target population—all adjudicated felony-level offenders, the number committed to the department, and the number served in local RECLAIM programs.

Results

As mentioned, the pilot phase of RECLAIM, implemented in nine counties, allowed those counties to cut commitments by 43 percent and serve more than 1,000 youth locally. Those nine counties were able to keep more than $3 million in state funds to use locally. Additional data were gathered through a study conducted by the University of Cincinnati. During an average follow-up period of 47 weeks, 87.4 percent of youth in local RECLAIM pilot programs were diverted successfully from the Department of Youth Services.

As part of that study, county officials also were asked about their satisfaction with the program. According to the evaluation, "Overall, 85 percent were very satisfied, and 15 percent were somewhat satisfied being a pilot county for RECLAIM Ohio."

During 1995, the first full year of implementation, more than 9,000 youth were served locally with RECLAIM funds and admissions to the department decreased by 6 percent. In total, the counties retained $17 million new state dollars for local programming. This continued in 1996 when the counties retained a similar amount and funded local programs for approximately 12,600 youthful offenders.

Many counties used RECLAIM Ohio funds to expand or enhance traditional services such as probation or out-of-home placement. Other counties created or contracted for innovative services such as twenty-four hours a day domestic-violence intervention, Afrocentric mentoring programs, and after-hours probation monitoring.

The impact on the department can be seen in the adjudication and commitment statistics. In the 1990s, the number of felony-level delinquency adjudications continued to rise, from 14,388 in 1991 to 15,857 in 1996. However, the percentage of adjudicated felony-level delinquents committed to the department has continued to drop from the 1991 commitment rate of 22.4 percent, to only 17.4 percent in 1996.

For the department, this means a drop in admissions to state-secure institutions and hence, a drop in crowding. From 1991 when the daily population exceeded 2,500, the 1997 population hovered around 2,000. This constitutes a 20 percent reduction in the population of teens locked away in a secure state institution each day. This shift from commitment to a greater reliance on community-based services has dropped the crowding level from the high of 175 percent down to an average hovering around 120 percent.

This decrease has made a tremendous difference in the department's ability to provide good, consistent, basic services such as security and humane living conditions. Beyond that, it has allowed the department to develop needed processes to deal with different aspects of its "product line," including a sex-offender specific institution, enhanced mental health units, and a central reception process center.

These services also can be targeted better since counties now more consistently are committing the more serious, violent, repetitive offender. From 1990 to 1995, the percentage of lower-level, property offenders versus more serious, violent delinquents has dropped from 75 percent to 65 percent of admissions.

Conclusion

Some of the most successful counties are those that have an established infrastructure and successful history with community corrections. The state has a long tradition of providing a subsidy to the juvenile courts based solely on the population of the county. This support remains constant and is unaffected by the RECLAIM Ohio program. The degree to which the county government takes a true financial partnership role with the state in addressing juvenile justice issues influences the county's ability to develop and support a broad range of local alternatives.

To enhance the effectiveness of the RECLAIM Ohio program, the department holds voluntary RECLAIM meetings with court staff at least every other month, and holds an annual statewide conference to share information on programs that work. It also has established challenge grants to award to counties having difficulties implementing effective local options.

Judges have reported to program evaluators that they now are better able to see the costs versus the benefits of various corrections' products and to gauge cost and benefits for individual cases. Judges, county commissioners, and the legislature are beginning to see state-secure incapacitation as an expensive product.

Not only does this help the funding of secure institutions at the state level, but it has brought community corrections into focus for local and state decision makers. A prison cell or a perimeter fence is easy to see, understand, and fund. RECLAIM Ohio has made community corrections programs not only visible, but attractive to decision makers.

Contact:

Carol Rapp Zimmermann
Assistant Director
Ohio Department of Youth Services

51 North High Street
Columbus, Ohio 43215
(614) 466-8733

Security Monitoring System for Personnel

Introduction

The California Department of the Youth Authority is in the process of installing a personnel security monitoring system at each institution. The system electronically records the entrance and departure of staff, volunteers, and business visitors as they enter and exit a Youth Authority facility. The purpose of the system is to increase the security of staff, volunteers, and visitors by ensuring that they have exited the institution at their expected departure time. The system is designed to ensure that preestablished security procedures will be activated if a person does not depart the institution in a timely manner, and, thereby, the system reduces the opportunity for assaults on staff, volunteers, and visitors.

Development and Design

The department has more than 4,300 staff and hundreds of volunteers and business visitors entering and exiting the 11 institutions and 4 mountain camps on a daily basis. These institutions house approximately 9,200 offenders. Of the latter, 63.8 percent have been committed for violent offenses, including murder and assault. Prior to the introduction of the new system, the methods and procedures for accounting for staff, volunteers, and business visitors entering and exiting varied somewhat by institution. However, most facilities relied either on the exchange of an identification card or name tag for institution keys, a sign in/out sheet, use of a staff roster, or in-and-out boards.

To be effective, these methods required individuals entering a Youth Authority institution or mountain camp to follow rules and procedures strictly and consistently. Yet, none of these methods was found to be satisfactory from a security perspective. They could be circumvented in a variety of ways. There also was a recognized need to develop a standardized methodology for responding to circumstances where employees and others did not exit the institution in a prescribed and timely manner.

With these concerns in mind, the Institutions and Camps Branch LAN Manager for the Youth Authority coordinated the complex task of defining the needs of the twelve sites throughout the state. The steps necessary to implement an automated personnel security monitoring system were determined in concert with control agencies, such as the Department of General Services.

Together, the participating agencies developed a massive bid document to secure a capable vendor and to ensure the timely installation of the proposed system. Several vendors proposed systems to better meet the needs of the institutions and camps branch than their present system. The presentations were followed by a review of the proposals' in-and-out systems against the department's security and physical plant needs. The vendor was chosen and the new system was implemented in November 1997.

The new personnel security monitoring system uses electronic fingerprint capture technology. This technology was chosen because, from a procedural perspective, it takes all the guesswork out of knowing who has entered and exited. Personnel are positively identified. The technology is easy for personnel to use and has an excellent accuracy ratings. At the time of enrollment in the system, the fingerprint scanner records a template of the fingerprint. The template is stored with a personal identification number (PIN). Personnel are issued access cards with the PIN barcoded on the back.

At the time of entry or exit, the equipment then can read the barcode and quickly identify personnel. When the finger is placed on the fingerprint scanner, that image is then compared to the stored template for verification. Records of entry and exit transactions are stored on a host computer, which then compiles reports and provides alerts to security personnel about any personnel who are beyond his or her expected departure time.

Conclusion

Though there are no specific data yet collected through this project, the outcome measures will be gauged by the system's ability to properly account for staff entering and exiting Youth Authority institutions. Other measures will consider the extent to which injuries have been minimized to staff or others having contact with the various facilities.

Youth Authority staff believe the personnel security monitoring system represents the first major implementation of such an identification system in California. They expect to participate in substantial interaction with other governmental jurisdictions when the system becomes fully operational.

Contact:

Bill Goff
Automation Project Manager
Institutions and Camp Branch
California Department of the Youth Authority

Suite 224
4241 Williamsbourgh Drive
Sacramento, California 95823
(916) 262-1541

Youth Development System

Introduction

Behavior management systems in residential facilities are a reflection of a program's overall philosophy and provide the context for general service delivery and control. How a program views its residents determines how it provides services and shapes control systems.

Historically, each of the residential facilities operated by the New York State Division for Youth has operated with an independently developed behavior management system. Each system evolved largely from the personal philosophy of the facility director or senior program staff. There was no common philosophy of child care or youth development that tied these systems together. These differences were problematic due to the fact that most residents of division facilities are likely to be transferred between facilities during their placement. Since facilities operated different behavior management systems, residents generally began their stay at a new facility at the entry level, regardless of progress or development at the sending facility. The resident was required to learn new norms and expectations.

A 1995 report on the division's secure facilities conducted by the New York State Commission of Correction gave management the impetus to change. The review found the following:

> The Behavior Level System is not implemented in a standard fashion . . . [It went on to recommend] The Division should restructure its Behavior Level System to one which focuses primarily on positive reinforcement of developmental progress in social and rehabilitative skills. . . . In revising the Behavior Level System, the Division should take steps to standardize this operation in all secure facilities.

The Youth Development System is the division's response to this recommendation, and it applies not only to secure facilities, as recommended by the Commission report, but to limited secure and nonsecure facilities, as well.

Development and Design

Goal: Given the commitment to change, the division's goal was to have a single behavior management system for all facilities that would clearly define the agency's rehabilitative philosophy, be consistent with the agency's counseling program, and provide a rationale for dealing with residents' behavior that was founded in specific behavior/developmental theory.

General Background

Program Development: The deputy director for residential services appointed a project coordinator and charged the directors of the division's six secure facilities, along with representatives of the office of program development and evaluation, to achieve a consensus on a single behavior-management system for the agency that would meet these goals. The resulting model, referred to as the Youth Development System (YDS), provided the foundation for what is used in limited secure and nonsecure facilities.

General system concept: As its title implies, the Youth Development System is based on principles of youth development. Unlike behavior management systems where residents begin with a full array of privileges, which may be lost, or systems where residents gain privileges by not breaking rules, residents under the Youth Development System begin with only basic privileges. They advance and earn status and privileges by learning specific prosocial skills, and by demonstrating increased self-control and problem-solving skills.

Stages: The Youth Development System has four stages: orientation, adjustment, transition, and honors. Each stage makes assumptions about the residents' social skills and ability to accept responsibility for their behavior. A resident's stage is a sign of status. It also determines privileges and how staff interact with him or her. A resident's stage is identified by his or her shoelace color, with a different color used for each stage. The stages concept standardizes residents' privileges. Each stage has specific privileges associated with it. The residents gain privileges only by advancing to the next stage.

The Youth Development System is a developmental system based on residents learning and demonstrating specific skills and responsibilities. When staff agree that a resident has mastered the skills of the current stage and is beginning to demonstrate the skills of the next stage, the resident is advanced to the next stage. The resident then is entitled to the privileges and is subject to the expectations of that stage. If residents regress, the assumption is that they are not using the skills acquired at the previous stage(s), not that they have unlearned them. Therefore, residents may lose privileges of a stage (and earn them back through a "Behavior Improvement Plan" described later), but they do not lose the stage they have achieved.

Staff Interaction Styles: Given the demonstrated skills and expectations of residents at each stage, staff interact with residents at each stage using appropriate styles. As a resident advances, staff styles move from being highly directive (for the orientation-stage residents) to a delegating style (for the honors-stage residents).

Mentor: Each resident is assigned a mentor to explain the Youth Development System and to keep the resident focused on developing the skills needed for advancement. The mentor evaluates the resident each week on the expectations associated with that particular stage. This weekly mentor review is placed in the resident's youth development log.

Behavior Improvement Plan (BIP): A behavior improvement plan is a means of focusing the attention of all facility staff and the resident on specific behavior that is in need of improvement. The Behavior Improvement Plan is a one-page document that specifies a goal

266

for the plan, expectations for both staff and residents, and a plan-review date. A Behavior Improvement Plan is required if a resident will lose specific privilege(s). The privilege(s) lost and the plan of action for the resident relate to the behavior problem. A Behavior Improvement Plan need not be for negative reasons. It also may be used to help a resident focus on specific skills needed to advance to the next stage in the Youth Development System.

Stage Advancement: Each stage specifies resident responsibilities, which translate into criteria for advancement to the next stage. Advancement decisions are made at a stage-advancement meeting. Since criteria for advancement are clear and widely understood, any facility staff may request a stage-advancement meeting. Residents' counselors are responsible for ensuring that a review is scheduled when they believe the residents meet the criteria for advancement. All staff are welcome to participate in the meeting, but only the counselor and representative of the education program are required to attend. The decision to advance a resident to the next stage requires an agreement by all attending the meeting; one negative evaluation will keep the resident from advancing. The reason for advancing or not advancing a resident must be based on documentation in the youth development log.

Documentation: An essential element of the Youth Development System is that the rules and expectations for residents are clear to all staff and residents, and that program efforts and progress are well documented. Staff and resident manuals and the youth development log promote these functions.

All residents receive a resident manual and a resident rule book for which they must sign a receipt. Staff are provided with these manuals; in addition, they receive a staff manual and copies of forms and system diagrams.

A youth development log is maintained on each resident by staff on the unit. The youth development log contains all information relevant to the resident's progress in the Youth Development System. It contains the following sections:

- Room Condition Agreement—a checklist used as a baseline for assessing responsibility for damage to the room at a later date

- Aggression Replacement Training (ART) reports—which contain progress reports on the agency's Aggression Replacement Training counseling program (one of the requirements to advance from the orientation [lowest] stage)

- Activity reports—reports on any behavior incidents

- Mentor reports—completed weekly

- Education evaluation reports—required every two weeks to assess a resident's functioning in school

- Log entries—staff on the 12 P.M. to 8 A.M. shift transcribe resident-specific notes from the general unit log into the youth development log

- Advancement worksheet—results of meetings that assess a resident for advancement

- Behavior Improvement Plans (BIPs)—all behavior improvement plans are compiled in the youth development log

Implementation

The implementation challenge was to introduce, with minimal disruption, a new and highly structured youth development system into facilities of different sizes, configurations, populations, and behavior management systems. The program has been introduced into the division's six secure facilities to date, with other levels of security to follow.

The first step was to introduce a resident rule book. This book provided standard rules and behavior expectations for residents in each area of the facility program. Resident rules were introduced prior to the full Youth Development System implementation to reduce the overall impact of the system and to begin to establish an expectation of change for staff and residents. The rules were enforced through existing facility behavior management systems until the Youth Development System was implemented.

To promote consistency in all of the division's facilities, secure facility directors, as a group, trained the senior staff of all secure facilities during a two-day training session. The purpose of the session was to introduce facility managers to the Youth Development System, get feedback on the system from managers, field test the training design, and demonstrate the training model that individual facility directors and their management staff would use to train all staff in their respective facilities.

Each facility developed its own implementation plan within general time constraints. An emphasis was placed on the comprehensive training of all facility staff, including youth division aides (child care staff), teachers, counselors, maintenance workers, cooks, clerical staff, and health services staff. The facilities were granted additional time for implementation, if warranted. The quality of implementation was given a higher priority than speed of implementation.

Following the training of all facility staff, the residents were trained in the system. The residents already present at the facility during the transition were evaluated by their treatment team according to the criteria for stage advancement and their new stage in the Youth Development System was determined. A process was established to give residents the opportunity to appeal their initial-stage designation. Although most residents lost status and privileges during the transition, few appealed their stage assignment, and those who did appeal generally accepted the outcome.

There were very few problems associated with the transition of residents to the new system. This is attributed largely to the explicit criteria for stage advancement, and the fair and consistent way of applying them.

To improve the chances for a successful implementation of the program, an expectation of change was promoted within each facility before implementation began. Staff meetings, ongoing feedback from staff on draft elements of the system, and written communication helped promote the expectation of change among staff. To set the stage for change for residents, signs were posted throughout the facilities with such sayings as "the YDS is coming." The intent was to share information as early as possible with staff and residents to avoid surprises, establish the fact that a change would take place, that the change was positive, and that it was supported by facility administration.

Results

Since the Youth Development System only recently has been implemented in secure centers, limited data are available. Nonetheless, informal reports from facility directors indicate that the system has been well received by staff and that residents have accepted it.

Although not necessarily representative of all facilities, the MacCormick Secure Center, the first facility to fully implement the system on December 24, 1996, has monitored the number of restraints used on residents as an indicator of problems associated with the transition to the Youth Development System. These results show a decrease in the number of restraints each month from twenty-six in December to five in April. Note that the number of restraints used continued to decline in April despite the admission of seven residents, a large number for one month at MacCormick. All but two were sent to MacCormick as a result of disturbances in another facility and one was from a psychiatric center.

Planners expected that the number of restraints needed initially would increase when the Youth Development System was implemented since residents would be under greater control and have fewer privileges than under the prior behavior management system. The initial data from MacCormick and verbal reports from other facilities suggest that the transition to the Youth Development System has proceeded smoothly.

A monitoring instrument has been drafted and will be field tested shortly. In addition, indicators of program success will be developed in conjunction with program evaluation efforts.

Conclusion

The division believes several key ingredients are essential to manage a change process of this scale and to properly implement a systemwide programming philosophy. The first ingredient is to involve directly top-level managers in the design process. The second ingredient is to ensure that information flows from system design meetings to senior management, to line staff, and to residents as it becomes available. The final ingredient is to have the facility director and senior staff provide direct, visible, and unequivocal support for the system. The system should be presented as their own, and something they believe in, not something handed down to them to implement.

Contact:

Louis F. Mann
Deputy Commissioner for Rehabilitative Services
New York State Office of Children and Family Services

52 Washington Street
Rensselaer, New York 12144-2735
(518) 473-1786

Juvenile Corrections
Additional Program Entries

Illinois Department of Corrections Juvenile Division

John R. Platt, Acting Deputy Director
Washington Cottage, 3802 Lincoln Highway,
St. Charles, Illinois 60175
(630) 584-0750

The Juvenile Division of the Illinois Department of Corrections has benefited from a management process whose well-defined structure has a system of controls in place, which promotes the achievement of agency goals. Policies and procedures to comply with state law, operational requirements, American Correctional Association standards, and administrative decision making are conveyed to staff in a standard format. Staff are responsible for implementing these procedures. However, the process is dynamic to respond to needed revisions, which test the validity of the procedures in achieving compliance with policies. Both internal and external management audits within the juvenile division, and random and systematic spot checks, assess the implementation of policies. The results are provided to policymakers to determine their effectiveness. Having established a management and organizational process, the Illinois Department of Corrections has a firm foundation for confronting the challenges related to increasing population levels, crowding, competition for resources, and the increasing aggressiveness of the youth served.

Project Zero Tolerance: A Balanced Approach to Reducing Violence—Louisiana Department of Public Safety and Corrections

Dora Wheat, Executive Management Officer
Office of the Secretary, PO Box 94304, Capital Station, Baton Rouge, Louisana 70804
(504) 342-6794

Project Zero Tolerance is a comprehensive project throughout the Louisiana Department of Public Safety and Corrections designed to reduce the number of offender-on-offender, staff-on-offender, and offender-on-staff acts of violence. Project Zero Tolerance was implemented on August 1, 1996. Its strategies include: (1) communication and education for all staff, juveniles, parents, and juvenile judges regarding the department's commitment to reducing acts of violence; (2) intensive training for both staff and juveniles; (3) formal on-site monitoring by top-level institutional administrative and clinical staff; (4) establishment of an independent, objective project team to review current policies and practices and to investigate acts of violence and allegations of violence; and (5) establishment of a toll-free hotline for reporting incidents or allegations of violence. A task force currently is being assembled to make recommendations on the effectiveness of Project Zero Tolerance and to suggest changes that can be made to reduce further the occurrence of acts of violence in secure institutions.

The Career Systems Development/Weaversville Intensive Treatment Unit—Pennsylvania Department of Corrections

Arthur Eisenbuch, Director
Weaversville Intensive Treatment Unit, 6710 Weaversville Road,
Northampton, Pennsylvania 18067
(610) 262-1591

The Career Systems Development Corporation/Weaversville Intensive Treatment Unit is widely regarded as one of the nation's oldest and most successful public-private sector partnerships in the field of secure juvenile corrections. The program operates on a contract between Career Systems Development Corporation and the Commonwealth of Pennsylvania and provides secure care for adjudicated male juvenile offenders. The correctional treatment services provided by the program include intensive individual counseling, group counseling, family therapy, and academic and vocational education. The program also offers residents numerous recreational, social, religious, and work-study programs. The Career Systems Development Corporation/Weaversville Intensive Treatment Unit can accommodate twenty-three youth and employs thirty full-time staff.

Correctional Mental Health

12

Introduction

In this opening section of the chapter on correctional mental health, the chair of the Correctional Mental Health committee offers something that stylistically diverges somewhat from the other chapters. It is a fairly complete outline of a model or comprehensive program in correctional mental health. The model is a compendium of judicial requirements; a review of judicial studies on point; a survey of other model criteria or standards; and the collective experience, and perhaps wisdom, of the committee.

No effort is made here to distinguish adult from juvenile systems or jails from prisons. Since this material is addressed to the practitioner, the committee is confident that the user will understand, at least as well as the committee does, the distinguishing factors involved.

The chapter well might have begun with a concern for diversion of at least some persons with mental illness from the correctional system. A justice system that attempts to divert prisoners who are impaired from incarceration or correctional supervision is desirable to many. However, the boundaries of the assignment begin with the inmate at the door. The criteria in the outline thus takes the confined population as it exists in myriad correctional jurisdictions across the country. A brief rationale is given, where appropriate, to provide somewhat more guidance than an unadorned outline.

A concern for comprehensive mental health services in prisons, jails, and while offenders are under supervision is a relatively new phenomenon. Though no one system may be found that represents an all-inclusive mental health model, five programs follow that variously offer striking innovations in assessing, intervening, or tracking offenders suffering from mental disabilities. These are programs not only on the right path, but which have design features and component parts worthy of emulation.

Each of the following programs offers an approach that others may wish to replicate. The Cook County, Illinois, Probation Department offers a unique casework program that responds to the mental health needs of adult probationers that is administered solely through a probation department. The Michigan Department of Community Health through its Bureau of Forensic Mental Health Services delivers mental health services to the Michigan Department of Corrections through a management information system that provides a variety of daily reports to clinicians, including data for performance measurement and quality improvements. The Washington State Department of Corrections screens all offenders entering the system through its Offender Profile Report that provides information on each offender's violence potential, suicide risk, victimization potential, substance abuse issues and treatment needs, and mental health and education program needs.

The California Department of the Youth Authority implemented its Continuum of Care model to provide better coordination of institutional treatment and parole supervision services to at-risk sex offenders, and so far, none of the offenders who have completed the program has been arrested for any subsequent sexual offenses. The model demonstrates that sex offenders are more capable of changing their inappropriate sexual behaviors than previously thought, but it requires use of a relapse-prevention model and other treatment principles. The last essay discusses the Bureau of Mental Health Services of the Ohio Department of Rehabilitation and Correction. Through the recent settlement of a consent decree, it has established a continuum of care using a multidisciplinary approach to developing a holistic intervention ranging from outpatient to residential services.

Criteria for a Comprehensive Correctional Mental Health System[1]

Basic Criteria

System compliance with basic legal requirements mandate the following three requirements:

1) Availability of adequate human resource individuals who are properly trained in the identification and treatment of mental illness

2) Availability of adequate physical resources that are designed to meet the varying mental health needs of the subject population

3) Adequate access to these human and physical resources

Rationale: At a minimum, a correctional mental health program must meet the rather nominal demands of the Eighth and Fourteenth Amendments. This is simply a threshold, and obviously one must address the meaning of "adequate," "properly trained" and the like.

There is a considerable literature on point (see, for example, Fred Cohen, Captives' Legal Right to Mental Health Care, 17 *Law and Psychology Review*, 1 (1993); Thomas L. Hafemeister and John Petrila, Treating the Mentally Disordered Offender: Society's Uncertain, Conflicted, and Changing Views, 21 *Florida State University Law Review* 731 (1994)).

Specific Criteria

1) Identify inmates with mental illness

Rationale: Unless the system has in place mechanisms to identify those needing care, either at reception or after confinement, it simply cannot meet its treatment obligations. Better systems will have a computerized classification and tracking system.

2) Identify appropriate care of those inmates suffering from alcoholism, drug addiction, some form of sexual dysfunction, or problems associated with the "battered woman syndrome"

Rationale: The conditions noted here generally fall outside of legally mandated care. However, a correctional system that is responsive to these individuals is one that is a "full service" system and that is deemed desirable. Compliance with basic legal requirements would encompass only the seriously mentally ill. However, a comprehensive system would have a fully integrated system and not draw artificial distinctions between "special needs" categories.

3) Train staff on the signs and symptoms of mental disorder and those inmates with "special needs"

Rationale: The identification of those who need care does not end at the front door, nor is it limited to specialists. Security staff, especially those assigned to mental health special care units, and to segregation units must be able to identify those who need care and understand the behavior associated with the condition or any medications involved. Such training should be subjected to rigorous evaluation on the information conveyed, and attitudes and behavior changed.

4) Ensure the quantity and quality of human resources available for the various tasks associated with mental health treatment

Rationale: Mental health staff should be appropriately licensed, multidisciplined, and function administratively in an integrated fashion. Staffing ratios for psychiatrists, psychologists, social workers, and others should be established and used as at least a rough guide for judging the quality of a system.

Opportunities will exist for staff development and enrichment. "Burn out" and "dry out" seem endemic to staff members in this highly charged environment. Comprehensive programs will provide opportunities for growth and respite.

5) Ensure the quantity and quality of physical resources available

Rationale: Obviously, a certain amount of physical space should be designed and available to meet various treatment needs or program objectives. The available space should be designed to meet the need for the following: hospitalization; longer-term care needs but not necessitating hospitalization; crisis care (for example, suicide-watch placements); transitional care units; and perhaps, a special needs unit (for example, housing the dual-diagnosed inmate). Use of a "least-restrictive environment" approach suggests enhanced concern for the inmates' needs.

6) Ensure access to care

Rationale: Without ready access to diagnosis and care, the human and physical resources that are available become virtually meaningless. This calls for a study of waiting lists, knowledge by security staff and inmates on how to gain access, and appropriate training and orientation of inmates on gaining access.

From the standpoint of actually auditing a system, access must be evaluated on site. Cells, beds, and staff may be counted, but access is a dynamic concept and must be observed. A model system would perform regular audits, question inmates and staff, assess the orientation process, and even do emergency "trial runs." In evaluating access, one necessarily also evaluates the relationship between security and mental health staff. Without a collaborative approach, no system will function very well.

7) Keep records with appropriate content

Rationale: Records are crucial to the continuity of care. They are also a barometer of the quality of care provided in that without regular progress notes and a comprehensible individual treatment plan, there is no way to be certain if care is given and no easy way to accommodate personnel changes, which are endemic to corrections. The legal concern here is with the continuity of care, and it is the mental health record that is a necessary, although not sufficient, factor in meeting that obligation.

8) Provide medication management

Rationale: Without necessarily endorsing the practice, we recognize that medication is the treatment of choice for the mentally ill inmate. There should be reasonable access, then, to the psychiatrist; a formulary that does not restrict access to the newer psychopharmacological agents, which are emerging at a rapid pace, and there must be regular monitoring and testing. In systems with rapid turnover, or the use of locum tenens psychiatrists, special attention must be paid to medication practices, especially changes in medication.

9) Provide restorative opportunities

Rationale: For the seriously mentally ill, medication well may be the treatment of choice, but it should not be the only treatment or program. For those not taking medication then, it is even more important to have a full-range of activities, along with individual and group therapy.

Comprehensive programs offer work opportunities along with structured physical activities, horticultural programs, guide-dog training, vocational training, and more. Programs dealing with anger management, and social skills, along with educational opportunities, often enhance restorative opportunities.

10) Use a Management Information System

Rationale: A model MIS should be computerized and used for needs assessment, continuous quality improvement, and tracking. Model programs will produce concrete examples of how MIS is best used in the system.

11) Provide data/research on treatment outcomes

Rationale: Comprehensive programs will not be content to simply "build, hire, and provide access." They will be concerned with the articulation of treatment objectives and be engaged in acceptable research on outcomes. Articles in peer-reviewed publications would be extremely good evidence on point.

12) Consider economies of scale

Rationale: Is the administrative and organizational structure designed to provide the maximum care for the funds allocated? Are services regionalized (or clustered)? Are services shared and accessible? Are actual costs known?

13) Develop policy and procedures that are contemporary, comprehensive, and accessible

Rationale: In the interest of uniformity and consistency of practice, a system must have contemporary policy and procedures on point. They should be available and understandable. Special attention will be paid to transfers from correctional settings to mental hospitals, forced medication, and suicide. These three areas generate the most legal concern and have the clearest legal mandates. In addition, a policy on the use of restraints is most important for its humane implications, although the law on point is not so clear.

14) Provide discharge planning

Rationale: A comprehensive-care system should not end at the institution's walls. Inmates needing care inside are not magically going to not need care on release. Discharge planning begins inside, and appropriate community care, including medication and housing arrangements, are the hallmark of a comprehensive system.

Committee chair:

Professor Fred Cohen
Adjunct Professor of Law
University of Arizona Law School

9771 East Vista Montanas
Tucson, Arizona 85749
(520) 760-1143

[1]Fred Cohen is the principal author of this section.

Casework Practice with Mentally Ill Probationers

Introduction

One of the most disturbing and unbidden consequences of transferring persons with mental illnesses from state hospitals to community-based treatment facilities has been the criminalization of the mentally ill (Torrey, 1997). As research has shown, persons displaying the signs and symptoms of mental illnesses are more likely to be arrested than members of the general population (for example, Teplin, 1984). The linkages between the criminal justice and mental health systems are either tenuous or nonexistent; hence, the mentally ill involved in these systems often fall through the cracks. As a result, their conditions are exacerbated, and they frequently become both chronic arrestees and psychiatric patients (Lurigio and Lewis, 1987).

Persons on probation with serious mental illnesses have been an especially neglected group (Lurigio, 1996b). In general, mental disorders in community corrections' populations are likely to be ignored unless an offender's psychiatric symptoms are an explicit part of the offense or are florid at the time of sentencing. Mentally ill offenders with less outwardly disruptive symptoms or signs of mental illness may receive scanty attention from community corrections staff. Probation officers generally lack the experience and backgrounds necessary to deal effectively with emotionally troubled clients. In short, probationers with mental illnesses are an underidentified, understudied, and underserved population, and most probation officers are unable to handle successfully the problems of these offenders (Veysey, 1994).

This article describes a program designed to respond to the mental health needs of adult probationers. The program, which started in 1988, has been implemented by the Cook County Adult Probation Department in Chicago. The initiative is unique and exemplary in several ways. It is one of the few specialized probation programs for the mentally ill that is administered solely through a probation department. As Boone (1996) reported in his national survey of probation and parole agencies, only 15 percent of the departments responding indicated that they operated such programs. It is the only externally funded program of its kind in Illinois and the only county-run criminal justice program in the state to receive funding from the Illinois Department of Mental Health and Developmental Disabilities.

Over the years, the program has served approximately 3,000 clients and has been lauded by the Department of Mental Health and Developmental Disabilities, the Cook County Department of Corrections, and the forensic community in Illinois for its outstanding work with mentally ill offenders. It also has been the topic of numerous professional conference presentations (for example, Lurigio, 1993, 1995, 1996; Spica and Lurigio, 1991).

Program Origins

In the late 1980s, a governor's task force in Illinois elucidated the special problems of offenders with mental illnesses. The task force made several recommendations relating to probation and court services. In response to the task force's suggestions, a probation department, with the assistance of the Administrative Office of the Illinois Courts, submitted a proposal to initiate a special unit of probation officers responsible for supervising and referring for services offenders with mental illnesses. The proposal was submitted in October 1988 (Lurigio and Klimusko, 1988). Shortly thereafter, the probation department received a grant from the Department of Mental Health and Developmental Disabilities to implement the program, called the Mental Health Unit. The program began accepting cases in 1989 and has been funded by the Department of Mental Health and Developmental Disabilities each year since then.

Program Implementation

The mental health unit consists of five probation officers and one supervisor, each with a background in mental health. The officers spend the majority of their time managing their caseloads, which are significantly smaller than standard probation caseloads. Potential clients can be referred to the unit by judges or other probation officers working in Chicago and in surrounding suburban court locations.

The officers initially screen probationers to determine their eligibility for the unit, basing their decisions mostly on the probationer's previous psychiatric histories and hospitalizations. Mental health unit officers gather this information from probationers, hospital and mental health treatment records, from probationers themselves, and from probationers' families. Rapport between officers and clients develops very slowly, and the mental health unit's clients, unlike the clients in regular caseloads, take a long time to adjust to their probation.

The officers refer probationers for mental health services, matching them with treatment facilities and changing services if a different treatment is indicated. Mental health services can involve outpatient or inpatient treatment and longer-term residential care. The probationers most often are referred to community mental health centers in the areas where they live.

Probation officers engage in a number of activities to assist clients in fulfilling their treatment mandates. They counsel probationers, help them to budget their time and resources, and support them with any difficulties they may be experiencing in treatment. The officers also help clients to access disability benefits, to get Supplemental Security Income, and to obtain medical cards. Through the unit's efforts, the probation department has been approved as a site for Medicaid reimbursements.

Outcomes

The probation department has undertaken studies of the mental health unit's operations and clients through records analyses, interviews, and case studies. Interviews have shown that probation officers bring a good deal of mental health-related experiences and training to the unit, such as previous work with mentally ill persons in residential and substance abuse treatment, and experiences with developmentally disabled persons and sex offenders. The officers advocate strenuously for their clients to obtain clinical services for them. They provide resources for probationers and determine what services exist in the community to help probationers recover.

The most difficult aspects of the officers' jobs is trying to find resources for clients who are very difficult to place in community treatment programs because of their serious mental illnesses, substance abuse problems, criminal histories, or dual diagnoses. In addition, the officers periodically become frustrated with clients who do not comply with treatment and reject the assistance that is offered to them. Nevertheless, the officers believe that they generally are making a difference in their clients' lives.

The analyses of the mental health unit's cases demonstrated that the most common diagnoses, given to three-fourths of the program's participants, are Axis I psychotic disorders (e.g., the schizophrenics, severe mood disorders, and bipolar disorder). Clients' psychotic symptoms often are related to long-term drug use such as PCP-induced psychosis. About fifty of the probationers in the mental health unit have been dually diagnosed with substance abuse problems and mental illnesses. Between 5 to 10 percent of probation officers' caseloads include probationers with developmental disabilities and organic brain defects or damage.

Almost all probationers in the mental health unit are on psychotropic medications. They are mandated by the court to receive mental health services, ranging from individual outpatient psychotherapy to inpatient psychiatric hospitalization. The bulk of the unit's clients have probation sentences of eighteen months or more, and treatment tends to span the entire length of their sentences.

The vast majority of mental health unit clients are male (84 percent) and two-thirds are African American. A large percentage of them (85 percent) have never been married, and nearly three-fourths (74 percent) are unemployed. The majority of probationers in the program (73 percent) have prior arrests, and more than half (54 percent) have prior convictions. Two-thirds of the unit's clients have been hospitalized previously for serious mental illnesses. On average, those with histories of in-patient care have been hospitalized four times. In addition, 68 percent of the clients have received prior outpatient care, and 77 percent have had prior counseling for mental health problems.

Conclusion

The unit staff work with probationers who present a variety of challenges. Clients' difficulties include psychiatric, economic, and social problems, and many have histories of substance abuse. Mental health agencies sometimes are reluctant to accept such probationers due to their criminal backgrounds; others reject them because of their dual diagnoses or lack of insurance.

The serious mental illnesses of mental health unit clients frequently complicate case assessments and require officers to proceed with caution when attempting to build relationships and trust with them. Despite these difficulties, program officers are committed to their clients, to help them deal more effectively with everyday problems and to maintain their treatment and medication regimens. Furthermore, the officers have a knowledge of both the clinical and criminogenic issues confronting their clients and know how to strike a balance between these two areas.

Several suggestions are offered for probation departments that are planning to address the difficulties of offenders with serious mental illnesses. Services for mentally ill probationers should be provided through special programs that are staffed by officers with educational backgrounds and experience in the mental health domain. Specialized units can monitor smaller caseloads, which is crucial because probationers with mental illnesses require a great deal of time and attention. In general, they have multiple problems: comorbidity with substance abuse disorders and developmental disabilities, poor health, housing and financial difficulties, homelessness, joblessness, and a lack of social support. These clients need habilitation as much as rehabilitation.

Cross-training for mental health and correctional staff goes a long way toward increasing their mutual understanding and respect. Moreover, cross-training greatly improves the working relationships between the two groups. Most important, cross-training encourages a team approach to working with clients.

Finally, probation officers should find alternative strategies for handling the technical violations of probationers with mental illnesses. These violations are often a function of the clients' symptoms, problems with treatment compliance, or difficulties following directions. For example, the failure to report may result from cognitive impairment, delusions, confusion, or the side-effects of medication. As a rule, incarceration or other punitive sanctions should be avoided when responding to such instances. More effective options include relapse-prevention techniques and systems of progressive sanctions. Probation officers can view technical violations as opportunities to forge closer alliances with clients and to assist them in avoiding future, and more serious problems, including subsequent criminal activity.

References

Boone, H. B. 1996. Mental Illness in Probation and Parole Populations: Results from a National Survey. *Perspectives.* 19, 14-26.

Lurigio, A. J. 1993, April. *The Criminalization of the Mentally Ill: Correlates and Recommended Solutions.* Paper presented before the Justinian Society, John Marshall Law School, Chicago, Illinois.

————. 1995, September. *The Mentally Ill on Probation and Parole: Overview and Prescriptions for Change.* Opening address to the National Coalition on Mental and Substance Abuse Health Care in the Justice System's Working Session, Chicago, Illinois.

————. 1996a. October. *Criminalization of the Mentally Ill.* Paper presented at the Eleventh Annual Statewide Forensic Conference, Chicago, Illinois.

————. Ed. 1996b. *Community Corrections in America: New Directions and Sounder Investments for Persons with Mental Illness and Codisorders.* Seattle, Washington: National Coalition for Mental and Substance Abuse Health Care in the Justice System.

Lurigio, A. J., and K. L. Klimusko. 1988. *Effective Supervision and Case Management for Mentally Ill and/or Mentally Retarded Offenders on Probation.* Springfield, Illinois: Administrative Office of the Illinois Courts.

Lurigio, A. J., and D. A. Lewis. 1987. The Criminal Mental Patient: A Descriptive Analysis and Suggestions for Future Research. *Criminal Justice and Behavior.* 14, 268-287.

Spica, A. R., and A. J. Lurigio. 1991, October. *Probation's Response to the Mentally Ill/Mentally Retarded Offender in the Criminal Justice System.* Paper presented at the Sixth Annual Statewide Forensic Conference. Hines, Illinois.

Teplin, L. 1984. Criminalizing Mental Disorder: The Comparative Arrest Rate of the Mentally Ill. *American Psychologist.* 39, 794-803.

Torrey, E. F. 1997. *Out of the Shadows: Confronting America's Mental Illness Crisis.* New York: John Wiley & Sons.

Veysey, B. 1994. Challenges for the Future. In *Topics in Community Corrections* (pp. 3-10). Longmont, Colorado: National Institute of Corrections.

Author:

Arthur J. Lurigio
Professor and Chair of the Criminal Justice Department
Loyola University
Chicago, Illinois

Author/Contact:

Nancy Martin
Chief Probation Officer
Circuit Court of Cook County
Adult Probation Department

Suite 2000
69 West Washington,
Chicago, Illinois 60602
(312) 603-0258

Implementing an MIS System for Planning Program Capacity and Validating Service Utilization

Introduction

The Michigan Department of Community Health has provided mental health services to the state's prison population under agreement with the Michigan Department of Corrections since 1992. During the early stages of implementing this agreement, the Michigan Department of Community Health formed the Bureau of Forensic Mental Health Services to oversee the transition and delivery of mental health services. This new bureau has worked productively with the Bureau of Health Care Services of the Michigan Department of Corrections to improve program models, integrate health care and mental health services, and improve management information and reporting systems to assist in decision-making for both departments.

These recent changes in service-delivery arrangements and improvements in programs and information systems occurred within the context of a long-standing consent decree, *United States v. Michigan*, regarding mental health services and several other issue areas. Under this decree, the state improved mental health staffing levels, developed a full continuum of mental health services, built an accredited psychiatric inpatient hospital, and developed an automated system for tracking referrals and evaluations and entry/exit from mental health programs across the corrections system.

A key component of this consent decree requires that 1 percent of Michigan's total prison population be devoted to acute psychiatric hospital beds with an additional 2.2 percent of prison beds to be maintained for long-term rehabilitation and residential beds. These so called fixed-percentage requirements were to be implemented several years ago, unless the state was able to develop an alternate plan acceptable to the federal court. However, with progress in developing the new hospital and adding intermediate capacity as needed, the fixed percentage requirements have been deferred while state officials continue to work on the alternate plan.

Development and Design

During the past two years, staff from the two bureaus have worked closely with federal district court experts, F. Warren Benton, Ph.D. and J. Franklin James, M.D., and U.S.

Department of Justice expert, Jeffrey Metzner, M.D., to develop an acceptable alternative to the fixed percentage requirements for determining program capacity. These efforts have produced a methodological approach for projecting bedspace requirements based on recent mental health service utilization data, an interdepartmental process for continuously reviewing and maintaining the validity of clinical decisions, and a series of improvements in management information and reporting that facilitates clinical management by field staff.

The model relied on for projecting the number of needed inpatient, rehabilitation, and residential beds emphasizes short-term (one-year and two-year) projections from recent or current service-utilization experience. This approach also incorporates a review of service utilization experience for newly committed prisoners to the state's prison system.

The utility of the state's bedspace projections for planning future capacity and resource needs depends on both the reliability and validity of service utilization data on which projections are based. A major challenge has been to devise a process that incorporates monitoring and systematic data collecting to identify problems and take corrective action, as needed.

This has been accomplished in part by developing an interdepartmental continuous quality improvement (CQI) process that provides staff at the local facility, regional, and department central office levels opportunities to meet regularly and discuss systems and patient-management issues. The activities of field staff also have been guided by a comprehensive plan for reviewing clinical decisions, including case-findings and referrals, evaluation, and placement of mentally ill prisoners throughout the prison system.

Enhancements in management information and reporting have made important service utilization and patient management information available to the central office, and to regional and local program staff. Following a collaborative process to assess information needs, a series of output reports were developed or existing reports improved to ensure that field staff had access daily to the following types of information:

- Listings of prisoner referrals requiring evaluation in either general population or segregation settings—the segregation reports list "at-risk" prisoners whenever they enter control or segregation units

- Detailed report of patients by program unit with information about custody level, DSM IV axis I-V, psychotropic medications and compliance, group and individual therapies, service utilization, and other characteristics

- Listings of prisoners transferred to the particular facility since the previous day who need to be assessed and admitted to the program

- Separate listings of active and inactive mentally ill prisoners in segregation units, including characteristics such as major mental disorders and other mental health attributes

These reports enable the bureaus to make information for the management of patients available at the level at which such management is most effective. Facility clinical staff are able to track active patients and at-risk prisoners at their facilities and to respond to prisoners in need of evaluation or referral.

Implementation of Continuous Quality Improvement and Data Review

The remainder of this discussion focuses on the state's recently implemented system for projecting bedspace, reviewing performance measures, and conducting continuous quality improvement studies. A two-tiered review of data and information sources has been implemented to ensure that clinical practice and operations are scrutinized in a comprehensive manner. In the first or broad level of analysis, data are collected and reviewed each quarter on a series of performance measures relating to service utilization and various validation activities. At this level of the review, the focus is on variations among programs and providers in the particular quarterly period, and also on longitudinal comparisons to identify major changes in performance across quarters. Problematic findings during this phase of the review process may prompt immediate supervisory action or an in-depth "look behind" studies of a particular finding or condition to assist in understanding and resolving potential problems. The interdepartmental continuous quality improvement process is used to guide the analytic and follow-up activities, which may be necessary as part of this review.

At the second level of review, scheduled reviews or studies are completed of major clinical activities, including but not limited to referrals, assessments, diagnostic practices and treatment, and placement recommendations. These in-depth reviews are conducted through the interdepartmental continuous quality improvement process and rely on efforts by staff from the two bureaus to collect and analyze data and make recommendations regarding changes in practice, procedures or other adjustments, and suggest corrections that may be necessary to solve problems and improve performance.

The implementation plan which follows is divided in two parts. Part I outlines the key components of the bed-need projection methodology, while Part II lays out validation activities, continuous quality improvement studies, performance measures, and data sources. Full implementation is well underway.

Part I. Analysis of Utilization and Projection of Bed Need

Purpose: Project bedspace requirements for the inmate population requiring mental health services and guide planning and budgeting efforts by using valid information on utilization of program resources. Based on findings, review options. Options include continuing to monitor utilization, making changes in programs, or adding program resources or capacity. Then, staff are to submit recommendations through channels.

Major steps to be followed in projecting utilization and in determining bedspace requirements:

- Review recent (three-year) trends in mental health service utilization by level of care; focus on monthly averages for the most recent year and quarter.

- Review and incorporate recent trends in service utilization by the intake population; analyze trends in this population group for the most recent year and quarter and compare this to systemwide trends.

- Use actual department of corrections' prisoner population figures to obtain the percentages of the prisoner population being served by level of care for recent years and quarters.

- Calculate projected utilization figures by multiplying the percentage(s) in the previous step by the department of corrections' projected prisoner population for the next two years.

- Determine bedspace planning target figures by adjusting utilization figures in the previous step for 95 percent occupancy. Performance measures are the number of days utilization exceeds 95 or 100 percent of capacity.

Part II. Validation Activities

1. Maintain validity of Psychological Services Unit (PSU) assessments in reception/ intake, segregation, and general population settings.

Performance measures include dispersion of psychological services unit referral recommendations by the provider and the number of prisoners found in the category of treatment not required (TNR) or not evaluated (at reception) and admitted to care within sixty days.

On the quarterly review of performance measures, tabulate information using available screens/output reports and compare this information to earlier quarters; if major changes or problems are indicated, conduct an in-depth review through the interdepartmental continuous quality improvement process.

Continuous quality improvement studies include the following items: (1) Review referral decisions by provider and diagnostic category; (2) Assess level of care recommendations including the recommendation of treatment not required (TNR) for patients with major mental disorders and admitted to care within sixty days; (3) For individuals who receive no psychological services or unit evaluation in reception, review admissions to care within sixty days following reception for individuals with a major mental disorder.

The screens/output reports include the following:

- Summary of psychological services unit referrals by facility, provider ID, and disposition

- Listing of psychological services unit referrals by facility and setting

- Listing of referrals with a disposition of treatment not required subsequently deemed major mental disorders and admitted to treatment within sixty days

- Listing of prisoners with major mental disorders admitted to care within sixty days of reception after receiving no evaluation in reception

- Inactive at-risk prisoners placed in segregation

- Long-term segregation prisoners

- Prisoners not at risk in segregation

2. Maintain the validity of outpatient team assessments and dispositions within reception/intake, segregation, and general population settings. The performance measures include the number of prisoners deemed treatment not required admitted to care with major mental disorders within sixty days of disposition and the number of patients admitted to outpatient care followed by admission to inpatient care within sixty days.

On the quarterly review of performance measures, tabulate information using available screens/output reports; review variation among providers and compare results to earlier quarters. If major changes or problems are indicated, conduct an in-depth review through the interdepartmental continuous quality improvement process.

Continuous quality improvement studies include the following: a review of the level of care recommendations by outpatient providers and an assessment of the level of care recommendations including treatment not required (TNR) with care received during a subsequent sixty-day period.

The screens/output reports include the following:

- Summary of outpatient recommendations by provider ID and setting

- Detail of outpatient team recommendations by provider ID and setting

- Listing of referrals with a disposition of treatment not required subsequently denied major mental disorders and admitted to treatment within sixty days

- Prisoners receiving mental health services during a requested time period

3. Reconcile referrals by psychological services unit with admissions to the mental health continuum. The performance measure is the number of instances in which admissions are not preceded by documented case finding (referral) by the psychological services unit.

On the quarterly review of performance measures, tabulate information using available screens/output reports; review variation among facilities and changes from earlier quarters. If major changes or problems are indicated, conduct an in-depth review through the interdepartmental continuous quality improvement process. The continuous quality improvement study is a review by the facility of whether patients admitted to care have a documented referral in the referral and evaluation system.

The screens/reports include a listing of psychological services unit referrals by facility and setting and a summary of mental health referrals and entry into the continuum for the prison and camp population.

4. Monitor access to appropriate levels of care and department of corrections' "overrides" of mental health referrals in all settings. Performance measures include the following:

- Number of automated referrals in segregation not seen by psychological services unit or outpatient team in required time frames

- Number of days admissions to acute care are delayed

- Number of instances in which required levels of care are different than actual placements

- Number of prisoners with undetected major mental disorders within sixty days

- Number of prisoners in override status at the end of the quarter

- Number of new overrides in the quarter

- Number of prisoners in segregation with major mental disorders

- Number of prisoners in protective custody/segregation with major mental disorders

On the quarterly review of performance measures; tabulate information using available screens/output reports; review variation among facilities and changes from earlier quarters. If major changes or problems are indicated, conduct in-depth review through the interdepartmental continuous quality improvement process.

The continuous quality improvement studies include the following:

- Assess whether computer generated referrals (in segregation) are being evaluated by the psychological services unit and outpatient team in a timely fashion

- Review waiting list information to ensure that beds are available in acute care

- Assess whether treatment team recommendations are in accord with actual placement

- Review a sample of recently committed prisoners who have not been admitted to mental health care to determine whether these prisoners have unmet mental health needs

The screens/output reports include:

- Mental health evaluation summary

- Mental health utilization

- Mental health alternate dispositions

- Mental health census utilization report

- Daily listing of active mentally ill prisoners in segregation

- Daily listing of inactive mentally ill prisoners in segregation

- Sample of newly committed prisoners not admitted to mental health treatment

- Summary of active patients/inactive patients by facility, treatment unit, and egregation status

- Summary of psychological services unit referrals by facility, provider ID, and disposition

5. Review appropriateness of level of care in terms of the level of patient functioning

The performance measure is the number of patients with Global Assessment of Functioning (GAF) scores lower than is indicated as appropriate in the criteria.

On the quarterly review of performance measures, using the appropriate and/or other output reports, identify the number of individuals by facility with Global Assessment of Functioning scores that are below the level indicated for the level of care; have regional managers check to determine if there is a problem. Make immediate mental health referrals if prisoners are not at appropriate levels of care. Compare results with earlier quarters. If major problems are indicated, conduct an in-depth review though the interdepartmental continuous quality improvement process. For the past eighteen months, this review has been completed as part of the Bureau of Forensic Mental Health Services continuous quality improvement plan.

The continuous quality improvement study is to assess whether the the level of functioning is consistent with the the prescribed level of care. The screens/output reports include the mental health utilization report.

6. Maintain validity of clinical decisions, including diagnoses and placement, discharge and movement in the continuum. Performance measures include the following:

- Number of instances of possible problematic patterns of diagnoses in the quarter

- Number of patient records found with major documentation deficiencies

- Number of prisoners with major mental disorders who have four or more moves in the continuum during a designated time period

- Number of patients who move from acute to outpatient and back to acute care within a sixty day period

- Number of patients admitted to care after leaving reception

- Number and proportion of patients in segregation at the end of the quarter

On the quarterly review of performance measures, tabulate information using available screens/output reports or information provided by the team/unit staff. Review variation among providers and facilities and changes from the earlier quarter. If major changes or problems are indicated, conduct an in-depth review through the continuous quality improvement process to:

- Assess whether potentially problematic patterns of diagnoses are valid

- Assess whether medical records documentation supports clinical decisions

- Assess whether recommended level of care is appropriate to the mental health needs of individuals by reviewing level of care decisions and subsequent placements

The screens/output reports include the following:

- Prisoners with Axis I code indicating major mental disorders, malingerers, major mental disorders progression

- Prisoners with major mental disorders who have four or more moves in the continuum

- Prisoners receiving services during a requested time period by facility and unit

- Mental health utilization

- Listing of patients who move from acute care to outpatient team to acute care levels of care, within sixty days, while in the mental health continuum

- Patients admitted to care after leaving reception

- Daily listing of active prisoners in segregation

- Daily listing of inactive prisoners in segregation

Conclusion

The management information system developed by the Bureau of Forensic Mental Health Services in conjunction with the Michigan Department of Corrections' Bureau of Health Care Services serves three broad purposes. First, it provides a variety of daily reports to clinicians at each level of the treatment continuum. Second, it provides data which are used to review specific performance measures and to conduct a two-tiered continuous quality improvement process. Finally, it generates the data necessary to conduct future bed-need projections. In so doing, it provides comprehensive and timely management and health care information for decision makers in both departments.

Contact:

Dr. Roger C. Smith
Director
Bureau of Forensic Mental Health Services

3511 Bemis Road
Ypsilanti, Michigan 48197
(313) 434-9506

Offender Profile Report

Introduction

The Washington State Department of Corrections screens all offenders entering the correctional system to identify those in need of mental health services, substance abuse services, or specific security precautions. In addition to screening for mental health treatment needs, information derived from this screening process is used by classification counselors to make decisions about the placement of offenders. The Offender Profile Report system provides an assessment of each offender's violence potential, risk of suicide, risk of victimization while incarcerated, vulnerability to substance abuse and need for substance-abuse treatment, as well as mental health and educational programming needs.

This screening process takes place at the reception centers for men and women. A psychologist, nurse, or social worker conducts a brief (five- to fifteen-minute) mental-health screening interview with all offenders, usually on their first day at the reception center. The interview responses cover the following areas and are recorded on a scannable computer form:

- Mental health history

- Suicide

- Symptoms of major psychiatric disorders

- Offense history

- Family history (criminal and mental health)

- Level of functioning

Offenders with emergent mental health needs may be identified through this process, and, if necessary, referred directly to mental health services for further evaluation and treatment. This is rare. The majority of offenders remain at the reception center for processing, and within the first week of their stay complete a battery of psychological and educational tests. The tests include the Revised Beta IQ Exam and the Test of Adult Basic Education

(TABE) for educational placement purposes, the Suicide Risk Screen (SRS), the Buss-Durkee Hostility Inventory (BDHI), the Monroe Dyscontrol Scale (MDS), and two brief substance-abuse screening measures, the Veterans Administration Alcohol Screening Test, and a drug abuse screening test. These instruments were chosen for (1) the content domains they address; (2) their ease of administration; (3) the fact that most are public domain instruments, and thus economical, and (4) the fact that the underlying psychometric properties (reliability and validity) of these instruments are well-documented in the professional literature.

Test results, interview responses, and other needed information are recorded on machine-readable forms, and an optical scanner is used to enter the data into a personal computer, where software does all scoring, data manipulating, and report generating.

A set of rules or algorithms is applied to each offender's test-scale scores, specific test item responses, structured interview responses, and personal and demographic data to produce rankings on five-point scales for each offender's potential for violence and substance abuse, risk for suicide and victimization, and possible evaluation and treatment needs. A series of predictive and diagnostic statements are synthesized into a written two-to-four page mental health screening report designed to assist in decisions regarding an offender's mental health status, educational placement, potential management and treatment considerations, and classification and placement needs within the system. The specific areas addressed by the report include the following:

- Demographic information

- Test validity

- Psychiatric diagnosis

- Suicide potential

- Victimization potential

- Violence potential

- Substance abuse potential

- Intelligence

- Educational/academic achievement

- Psychotropic medication

- Management and treatment considerations

    —Requiring immediate attention

    —Special programming considerations

    —Megargee classifications, if the MMPI is administered

- Summary of alcohol and drug history and the individual's stated interest in treatment (if the Oregon Alcohol and Drug History form is administered)

Development and Design

The development of the Offender Profile Report began in 1984, when the Department of Corrections began discussions with Dr. Eric Trupin and Dr. Ron Jemelka, faculty members in the Department of Psychiatry and Behavioral Sciences at the University of Washington, to address concerns about adequate mental health care within corrections. The concern was that resources for mental health were limited, growing numbers of incoming offenders appeared to be mentally ill, the number of offenders was increasing dramatically, and federal court opinions, such as *Ruiz v. Estelle*, were establishing minimal standards for mental health care within prisons. Further, policy analyses indicated these trends would continue.

The National Institute of Corrections provided summaries of federal case law on mentally disordered offenders, written primarily by Dr. Fred Cohen, which detailed issues of "deliberate indifference" to the mental health care needs of offenders, right-to-treatment, and the ancillary right to assessment issues. These documents served as a backdrop for the development of an assessment system that would be both economical, and meet these developing standards for mental health screening.

Validation

The fact that someone can generate a report from interview and test scores is of little value, if the accuracy of that report is poor or is unknown The next step in the development of the Offender Profile Report was to validate these screening procedures and to make changes, where needed, to improve its clinical accuracy. To accomplish this goal, Dr. Jemelka was awarded a series of two National Institute of Justice grants (86-IJ-CX-0072 and 90-IJ-CX-0020) to validate the Offender Profile Report and to develop improvements to this screening approach. As a result of this work, as well as continued support from the department of corrections, and the assistance and support of the Oregon and Georgia Departments of Corrections, fully validated versions of the Offender Profile Report were implemented in Washington in 1989, in Oregon in 1990, and in Georgia in 1991.

The National Institute of Justice-funded research studies produced refinements that resulted in the Offender Profile Report better duplicating clinical judgments of offenders' mental health needs and risk potentials at intake. Importantly, this diagnostic accuracy is achieved at a fraction of the cost of conducting thorough evaluations by mental health professionals at intake. Descriptions of these studies on the reliability and validity of this assessment process were published in the professional literature. Further developments and enhancements to the profile report, particularly in the area of drug and alcohol screening, have been implemented in the Oregon State Department of Corrections' version of this instrument.

It was apparent early on that an intake assessment validated on male samples would not be adequate for female offenders. In 1994 through 1996, the Department of Corrections funded a study by Dr. Jemelka at the Washington Institute to extend this work to female offenders, to achieve parity in intake assessment procedures for women. That work has resulted in an equivalent fully validated form of the Offender Profile Report for Females.

The current tasks in the ongoing development of the Offender Profile Report are to develop Windows 95 versions of these programs. Much of the original development was conducted in an MS-DOS operating environment for PCs, before Windows even existed. As almost all computers now use a Windows operating system, there is a need to update these programs. The department also is working to integrate the Offender Profile Report into a larger risk-assessment process to be used with offenders leaving the department's jurisdiction.

Results

How Does the Offender Profile Report Perform?

The Offender Profile Report has proven to be very effective as an initial screen in identifying mental health needs and risk potentials in incoming offenders. While it cannot make distinctions between diagnostic categories and specific levels of risk for all offenders, it has proven quite accurate in identifying those offenders where some mental health or behavioral problem exists. This allows the department to focus limited resources on incoming offenders who appear to be in need of a more thorough evaluation, and possibly mental health treatment.

For men, about 25 percent of incoming offenders are screened as having a potentially serious mental disorder. Follow-up evaluations by mental health professionals usually confirm that at least half of these are "true" cases (significant mental health problems confirmed by a mental health professional). The false-negative rate appears to be very low for men (very few "true" cases are missed).

The Offender Profile Report has good predictive accuracy for women, as well. The Offender Profile Report "flags" just under 50 percent of women for significant mental health problems, and these results are confirmed approximately 60 percent of the time. Since it is an initial screening instrument, its most important asset is that it identifies almost all offenders who need mental health resources.

Conclusion

The Offender Profile Report now has been in use in Washington State for more than ten years. Through federal and state support, it represents the only fully validated computerized assessment process available. To date there are no other validated computerized mental health assessment processes in prison settings. The Offender Profile Report accomplishes the following for the department.

- It provides an objective, reliable assessment of all incoming offenders. All offenders are evaluated in the same manner.

- It provides an assessment supported by an established research base, regarding reliability and validity.

- Taken together, the process provides the department a legally defensible approach to mental health screening.

- It permits the department to target mental health resources on those most in need.

- It addresses federal standards for adequate mental health treatment and screening in a cost-efficient manner. All forms are machine-readable and read by an optical scanner. Thus, there is no labor intensive data entry, and minimal clerical resources are required. The time spent by the mental health staff in intake assessment and clerical functions is reduced significantly.

- The Offender Profile Report yields a wealth of data on mental health and behavior which is of use to classification and custody staff, and mental health professionals.

- It permits the maintenance of a database, which can be used to analyze trends in the number of offenders who meet mental health and behavioral risk criteria. This information can be invaluable in planning services, budgeting expenditures, responding to legislative inquiries, and shaping mental health policy. Quarterly reports on the number of offenders assessed and meeting certain diagnostic, behavioral, criminal and demographic criteria are routinely provided.

- Through the working relationship with the Washington Institute for Mental Illness, Research and Training, which is affiliated with the University of Washington, the Offender Profile Report provides an adaptable, approach to mental health screening that can be modified as department needs change.

Author:

Ron Jemelka
Senior Research Scientist
The Washington Institute for Mental Illness Research and
Training

9601 Steilacoom Boulevard, SW
Tacoma, Washington 98498-7213
(253) 756-3996

Author/Contact:

David Lovell
Assistant Research Professor
University of Washington

P.O. Box 357263
Seattle, Washington 98195
(206) 543-3108

Continuum of Care for Adolescent Sex Offenders

Introduction

In July 1994, the California Department of the Youth Authority implemented the Continuum of Care model to provide better coordination of institutional treatment and parole supervision services to at-risk sex offenders. The Continuum of Care project was implemented because it was determined that there were too few treatment resources for high-risk and dangerous sex offenders committed to the Youth Authority. The resources that had been developed were not used in a manner that ensured the continuity of treatment. Wards who had undergone treatment in the institution needed to receive services in the community that maintained and reinforced the gains they made while they were committed.

The availability of a continuum of treatment resources for wards who exhibit addictive or compulsive sexually assaultive behavior is essential for treatment effectiveness. Youth Authority staff determined that at any given time, 74 percent of the most dangerous sex offenders in the institutions and 88 percent of the sex offenders on parole were not receiving the kinds of treatment interventions believed to be most effective in helping to prevent future victimization.

The shortage of treatment slots also led to waiting lists for sex offender treatment. National research over the last decade indicated that, left untreated, high-risk sex offenders become more dangerous to public safety. Therefore, the Youthful Offender Parole Board was reluctant to parole sex offenders without specialized intervention. Because of this, sex offenders had one of the longest average lengths of stay; the length of stay for violent sex offenders averaged 50.8 months, and is second only to those committed for homicide.

The objectives of the Continuum of Care project are to provide improved public protection, to develop a more efficient method of coordinating, planning, and managing appropriate interventions for sex offenders, to develop a viable mechanism for increased quality control, and to attempt to reduce the length of stay by augmenting specialized resources for the sex offender population in a more efficient and coordinated way.

Development and Design

The Continuum of Care project was funded by the governor for implementation in the 1994-1995 budget. By adding a 60-bed program in northern California to the already existing 80 beds in southern California, the number of sex-offender beds was increased to 140 statewide. Both programs used similar treatment models. A cognitive-behavioral approach using relapse-prevention principles was adopted at both sites. Field parole agent specialists became active members of the treatment teams at the two institutionally based programs.

Institutional Treatment Programs

Treatment at the two institutional programs is implemented at the direction of a professional treatment team consisting of clinical psychologists, clinical social workers, parole agents, and correctional youth counselors. Group therapy is the primary method of delivering services. Family and individual therapy also are used.

Both the northern and southern institutional programs were able to reduce the average time for completion of those programs from twenty-three to nineteen months. This occurred as a result of better coordination between parole and institution staff, and by "front loading" offenders into the program. This means that offenders selected for this programs were placed into the sex-offender program within six months of their entry into the system. Front loading in this way minimizes the denial in the offender, which becomes strengthened the longer the offender remains untreated.

Community Parole Supervision

This project provided for four sex-offender specialist field parole agents in both northern and southern California. The eight parole agents were trained in the same treatment principles (relapse prevention) as the institutional staff. The sex-offender specialist parole agents carry reduced caseloads, which allow for more intensive supervision and closer coordination with local police and sexual-assault investigators. The parole agents also use electronic monitoring and other state-of-the art intensive supervision techniques to maximize public safety.

All offenders released to parole supervision are required to continue sex-offender specific treatment in the community. The community-based therapists also use relapse-prevention principles in their ongoing weekly group therapy sessions. Ongoing communication occurs between the institutional treatment staff, the parole staff, and the community therapists to ensure the continuity of treatment.

Program Evaluation and Research

A full-time research specialist was assigned to assess the effectiveness of the treatment and supervision of the high-risk sex offenders. Prior to the Continuum of Care project there had been no comprehensive study that assessed a coordinated service-delivery approach for the high-risk sex offenders. This project provided an opportunity to measure the impact of this effort. The research component uses a random selection process for choosing both the experimental and control groups. This may be the most appropriate way to truly measure the value of these intervention strategies. It is important to emphasize, however, that those individuals placed in the control group are not "denied" treatment. They still receive the full range of services currently offered to offenders who are not chosen to participate in this intensive program.

Implementation

Once the program proposal was approved and funded by the governor, the Youth Authority implemented the Continuum of Care Project for Sex Offenders. Staff were assigned to the various parts of the project and were trained in the principles of relapse prevention. Once staff were in place, the Youth Authority sponsored a week-long training session for staff involved in the Continuum of Care project. This helped to ensure the continuity of treatment. Principles such as relapse prevention, sexual-assault cycles, victim empathy, and thinking errors were taught. A Continuum of Care advisory committee meets on an ongoing basis to discuss the continuity of treatment, and to recommend solutions to problems.

Data Collected

Staff are collecting data which will lead to an accurate profile of the characteristics of the sex-offender population and provide an extensive program evaluation. At the present time, the data are considered preliminary in nature due to the relatively short period that the project has been operating. While it is still too early to make any quantitative judgments on recidivism rates or program effectiveness, initial test results show promise.

The results of the Multiphasic Sex Inventory were used to measure progress in treatment. At the beginning of the study, there were no differences between the experimental group and the control group. However, after two years in treatment, the experimental group has shown improvement in several areas. There is significantly less voyeuristic behavior (especially among rapists), and participants are experiencing less sexual dysfunction (a result of feeling more hopeful and less helpless in controlling their behavior). They display more honesty in disclosing sexual obsessions and less cognitive distortion and immaturity. Participants demonstrate an increasing willingness to take responsibility for their behavior, and significantly more motivation for treatment. The experimental group also has demonstrated more appropriate sexual knowledge and beliefs.

At the beginning of treatment, the child molesters tended to be honest in describing their inappropriate sexual behavior, but failed to see the inappropriateness of it. With treatment, the child molesters began to see their behavior as deviant. The rapists, as a group, were less honest in describing their sexual behavior. When aggressively confronted by staff and peers, rapists are significantly more honest and complete in describing their sex crimes. This information can be helpful during program development and selection.

Those in the experimental treatment program experience significantly less gang activity than those in other living units. A supportive and therapeutic environment had been established on the treatment unit. Prosocial behavior is rewarded, and there is less need to act in an antisocial manner or maintain gang relationships. A common treatment experience had drawn the group together on therapeutic terms. Sex offenders effectively can complete a sex-offender specific treatment program and gain release in less time that other Youth Authority sex offenders who do not have this treatment experience.

Research also is being conducted by Dr. Hans Steiner, a research psychiatrist from Stanford University. He compared the characteristics of a nondelinquent adolescent population, the Continuum of Care sex-offender population and offenders from the Youth Authority's general population. The preliminary findings indicate that after two years of treatment in the Continuum of Care project, the characteristics of the sex offenders more closely resembled the nondelinquents than the delinquents in the Youth Authority's general population.

Conclusion

After three years of providing Continuum of Care services the following trends have emerged.

1) None of the offenders who have completed the program has been arrested for any subsequent sexual offense.

2) The length of stay for the experimental group of offenders has been slightly less than the length of stay for the control group of offenders.

3) The relapse-prevention model and other treatment principles appear to be effective in reducing future sexual victimizations by these offenders.

4) Staff need continued training, support, and clinical collaboration to minimize stress and avoid burnout.

5) The new violations that paroled offenders committed were generally for property and drug offenses.

6) Sex offenders are more capable of changing their inappropriate sexual behaviors than previously thought.

7) Treatment needs to be individualized because deficits vary across persons and cultures.

Author:

Jay Aguas
Chief of Public Services and Program Support Division
Institutions and Camps Branch of the California Department of the
    Youth Authority
Sacramento, California

Contact:

Ed Wilder
Deputy Director
California Department of the Youth Authority

4241 Williamsbourgh Drive
Sacramento, California 95823
(916) 262-1467

Bureau of Mental Health Services

Introduction

In 1991, a class action lawsuit, *Dunn v. Voinovich*, was filed in federal court, alleging inadequate mental health care in Ohio's prisons. Rather than fighting the suit, the Ohio Department of Rehabilitation and Correction adopted a collaborative strategy. Central to this approach was engaging a team of outside experts led by Fred Cohen, L.L.B., L.L.M., to conduct a detailed audit and inspection of mental health care in every State of Ohio prison. This team of experts issued an 800-page report in August of 1994, which recommended specific changes to substantially improve the service delivery system.

By February 1995, nearly all substantive issues were resolved, and the consent decree was being finalized. During this time, the department asked Mr. Cohen to serve as the monitor of the decree and to provide consultation in developing the new system to ensure it was consistent with the goals and specific provisions of the consent decree. Mr. Cohen participated in strategic planning with department staff, visited all potential treatment sites, and consulted regarding specific policies. In July 1995, the consent decree was signed and implementation of the improved system began.

Development of New Initiatives

Ohio's approach to settling the *Dunn v. Voinovich* lawsuit provided a catalyst to develop new initiatives in prison mental health care. This approach also enabled the state to avoid tremendous litigation costs and to build a strong collaborative relationship with the monitor and his team focused on improving services and care while avoiding unnecessary conflict. An article published in the October/November 1995 issue of the *Correctional Law Reporter*, entitled, "Ohio's Mentally Ill Prisoners Get Historic Consent Decree: Both Sides Agree," described the amicable nature by which *Dunn* was resolved. The article states:

> . . . Ohio seems headed in the direction of creating the finest prison mental health care in the country. Director Wilkinson, who already distinguished himself in handling the Lucasville uprising, once again shows his leadership and understanding of how to use the legal process. . . .

The department's approach to developing a service system is consistent with a community mental health model. The revamped system provides a continuum of care and treatment of mentally ill inmates from the time they set foot in prison to parole supervision in the community when they are released. Because mental illness is generally a lifelong condition, continuity is extremely important to ensure that the right care is provided.

Identification. An improvement in the early identification of mental illness has taken place. All inmates received by the department or transferred to other institutions within the system are screened by medical and mental health staff for the presence of mental illness. This promotes appropriate placement in the institution and is vital to meeting inmates' programmatic needs. Additionally, mental health staff conduct weekly rounds in segregation units to identify inmates in need of services.

Tracking. Once identified, it is important to track inmates with mental illnesses. A computerized classification system has been developed that identifies the current level of mental health care. The mental health classification is verified on all inmates prior to transfer to ensure that they are housed in institutions with appropriate levels of care. Inmates needing higher levels of care are transferred within seventy-two hours. This classification system allows the department to track the movement of inmates with particular mental health needs and assists in analyzing systemwide use patterns and future needs.

Oakwood Correctional Facility. The Oakwood Correctional Facility, accredited by a Joint Commission on Accreditation of Healthcare Organizations, provides acute care for male and female prisoners. This care may include short-term aggressive treatment for persons who, because of mental illness, represent a substantial risk of physical harm to themselves or others or housing for persons who are gravely ill and unable to function in the prison environment.

Clusters. The prison system is now subdivided into clusters. Each cluster is made up of one-to-five correctional institutions. Clusters are designed to operate like catchment areas in a community mental health model. Cluster mental health teams use a multidisciplinary approach to developing holistic interventions ranging from outpatient to residential services. The mental health team works jointly with medical, recovery services, and sex-offender programming staff.

Residential Treatment Units. Residential treatment units exist in one prison within each cluster. These units house prisoners with mental illness who do not need inpatient care but require the therapeutic milieu and full range of services and variable security that are offered.

Psychiatric Outpatient Services. Mental health care and support services are offered for prisoners with serious mental illness who can function satisfactorily in the general population.

In the Community. The department collaborates with the Department of Mental Health to provide community linkages for inmates with mental illness leaving prison. Twelve community linkage social workers assist inmates prior to release to set up appointments with mental health agencies to ensure continuity of care.

Implementation

The department strives to integrate inmates with mental illness into the prison community in the same manner that the Department of Mental Health has endeavored to integrate nonincarcerated persons with mental illness into their communities. In this way, inmates with mental illness are distributed throughout the system so that they may have access to the same programs and services available to other inmates.

Services are brought to the offenders, whenever possible. These services assist them to function more effectively in the "natural" environment, that is, the general population. When individuals are taken out of their natural environment for services, they often have difficulty transitioning from the treatment environment back to their natural environment, and this is a source of considerable stress. This approach not only helps prisoners adjust more effectively to their environment but also is cost-effective because hospital care is considerably more expensive.

Staff recognize that services should be appropriate to the current level of need and not more or less restrictive than is necessary, based on the treatment needs of the prisoner and the safety of the institution. Mental illness is not static. Inmates with mental illness require different levels of care at different times. It is important not to underutilize or overutilize various levels of care. Overuse results in wasted resources, while underuse results in a person not receiving necessary care. The careful placement of prisoners based on their level of need results in cost-effective, quality care.

All staff, psychiatrists, psychologists, nurses, social workers, unit managers, case managers, and corrections officers have a role in ensuring a quality system of mental health care. The department's new hires receive eight hours of preservice training on mental health issues, and existing institution staff receive six hours of annual inservice training.

The department is also a provider of continuing education credits for social workers and counselors and has provided a three-day specialized mental health training seminar for more than 1,200 corrections officers and institution staff during the past two years. Furthermore, a statewide Training Oversight Committee regularly meets to identify training needs and plan training programs. This committee involves clinicians, support staff, bargaining unit representatives, and managers.

The National Coalition on Mental and Substance Abuse Health Care in Criminal Justice sponsored a policy design academy in September 1994. An "Ohio Team" led by the Governor's Executive Assistant for Public Safety included representatives from the Department of Rehabilitation and Correction, the Department of Mental Health, the Ohio Department of Alcohol and Drug Addiction Services, the Department of Youth Services, a community mental health board, an alcohol and drug addiction services board, a sheriff, and a family member of one of the mentally ill inmates. Ohio's team developed a vision statement that reads:

> To develop an organized approach for the continuity of holistic, quality treatment for juveniles and adults who come into contact with the criminal justice, mental health and substance abuse systems.

A follow-up work group of these departments held an Ohio Policy Academy, "Linkages for the Future," in which several counties participated. A Request for Proposals was sent to participating counties with the specific goal of assisting them in developing community options for nonviolent, mentally ill or chemically dependent offenders. Five of the counties that participated received funding to design programs to decrease the number of substance abusers and mentally ill offenders who were incarcerated and to increase the number of treatment slots available for criminal justice referrals.

Conclusion

Quality mental health care can best be described as providing the right service, to the right person, by the right person, at the right time, in the right place. The continuity of care is critical to effective management of the symptoms of mental illness. Such care must be coordinated by all persons providing treatment to the prisoner and between various levels of care to ensure the person's history of mental illness, symptoms, and response to various treatments can be considered in developing a treatment plan and successfully managing the illness.

Contact:

Tessa Unwin
Public Affairs Liaison
Ohio Department of Rehabilitation and Correction

1050 Freeway Drive North
Columbus, Ohio, 43229
(614) 752-1157

Mental Health
Additional Program Entries

Mental Health Services in Summit County, Ohio Jail

Michael Mullin, Mental Health Coordinator
Summit County Sheriff's Office, 205 East Crosier St., Akron, Ohio 44311
(330) 643-2145

Summit County has a continuum of care for the mentally ill of the county, from emergency services through hospitalization. Summit County Jail is part of that continuum of care by offering a comprehensive array of services for the severely and moderately mentally ill offender and for the emotionally distressed or mentally retarded offender. Services are provided within the jail and include an assessment of each individual who shows signs of mental illness, individual counseling, psychiatric evaluation and prescription of medications, specialized housing for inmates in need of such an arrangement, anger control groups, chemical dependency groups, HIV education groups, and referrals for continuing care in the community, whenever necessary and possible. Summit County Jail also has an intensive chemical dependency pod, which is a thirty-day modified therapeutic community within the jail. With these services, Summit County Jail is able to offer the mentally ill offender at least the same level of care as that which is available in the community.

Mental Health Care Delivery in an Adult Corrections System

Gail Fricks, Deputy Director for Health Services
South Carolina Department of Corrections, P.O. Box 21787, Columbia, South Carolina 29221
(803) 896-2241

The South Carolina Department of Corrections has restructured its mental health care delivery to use resources more effectively and, where possible, maintain a community model. The resulting changes are responsible for the economy of scale being realized at the South Carolina Department of Corrections. The department has developed a complete continuum of care, which includes a complete mental health evaluation, screening tests for particular problems, and assignment to an appropriate bed. Inmates with similar mental health problems are clustered to match the level of professional care needed. In addition, the department has established a psychosocial branch of mental health care delivery, which includes substance abuse and cognitive restructuring programs and therapeutic communities, sex offender services, and youthful offender programming. This program has been in place for more than a year. Since the restructuring of delivery services, there has been no increase in staff size. This effort has resulted in movement of resources and the right sizing of staff to meet the increased need at specific sites.

The Changing Face of Mental Health Services in Kansas

Elizabeth Gillespie, Warden
Larned Correctional Mental Health Facility, P.O. Box E, Larned, Kansas 67550
(316) 285-8039

The Larned Correctional Mental Health Facility was opened in January of 1992. The current capacity is 174, with 120 maximum-security beds and a unit for 54 minimum-security inmates who perform work for the facility and the community. The facility has the following program objectives: (1) to provide psychiatric and other services required to treat and monitor inmates who are significantly impaired by chronic mental disorders or organic dysfunction; (2) to provide an environment that is the least restrictive possible within the requirements of appropriate security and custody; and (3) to assist inmates in reaching a level of mental health wellness and stability that will allow them to return to general population status in a regular Kansas correctional facility. The program is not designed for long-term placement of mentally ill inmates. The facility is accredited by the American Correctional Association, and the medical program has been certified by the National Commission on Correctional Health Care.

Assessing the Needs of Ohio's Incarcerated Youth

Cheri Walter, Deputy Director of Program Services
Ohio Department of Youth Services, 51 North High Street, Columbus, Ohio 43215-3098
(614) 466-9318

In an attempt to address the program needs of juveniles confined in Ohio's state-operated correctional facilities, the Ohio Department of Youth Services developed the Circleville Youth Center, Diagnostic and Assessment Center. Juvenile offenders spend approximately three weeks at the center and receive a battery of assessments that cover mental health, substance abuse, sex offense, education, medical concerns, dental concerns, psychosocial concerns, and religion. The results are summarized and forwarded to the parent institution and the juvenile courts. The array of assessments provides the staff with a clear and definable overview of the youth's emotional, behavioral, and medical issues. Ohio's institutions use the assessment results for classification and assignment on living units, and in planning for treatment, and aftercare.

Public Information

13

Introduction

Keeping the public informed about the actual work and the real world of corrections is a challenging task. At one level, every corrections employee is a public relations staff member, representing the agency and the profession to the public. But there also is a place for specific staff and programs, dedicated to informing the public about corrections.

Over the years, many standard public information programs have evolved—programs intended to make sure that corrections gets its message out to the public. These include the establishment of public information officer positions, offering institution tours, and a variety of activities, most of which are oriented toward members of the news media, but some of which also involve direct public contact. Many agencies and individual institutions have established additional outreach and information programs, to more completely communicate their mission and activities to the public.

The best of such programs contain new, innovative, and particularly effective methods to educate, promote, and inform the media, other relevant audiences, or the general public about correctional processes, operations, or programmatic initiatives. These programs also include a clear method for describing or assessing the problem area, accompanied by measurable goals and an evaluation plan that monitors the way it promotes and creates public support. Finally, they highlight how the program was implemented and how it might be replicated.

Making a decision about which of the many such programs around the nation represents a "Best Practice" is a difficult process. The five programs that are included in this chapter meet these criteria. They are more than worthy of consideration by any correctional agency that is trying to expand its public outreach and do a more effective job of conveying its value and importance to the many communities it serves.

Because the majority of inmates in prison eventually will return to the community, it is important that the community understand the correctional systems for which they are paying taxes and which support the economic life of many communities in which correctional facilities are located. It is much better to be proactive—involve the community in a positive way before there are problems—rather than in a reactive posture, after problems occur. The Correctional Service of Canada is attempting to do this. It has advisory committees of more than 500 citizens who discuss various aspects of the criminal justice system.

Most of these other programs deal with the media and the public at large. They are programs that have garnered media attention and public involvement. In Texas, the Department of Criminal Justice in partnership with Habitat for Humanity allows inmates the opportunity to build homes for low-income individuals, and simultaneously the inmates learn home-building skills that they can use after their incarceration ends. The Louisiana Department of Public Safety and Corrections keeps the state beautiful by cleaning up litter along highways so that tourists can enjoy the natural beauty of the state.

Inmates in the Illinois Department of Corrections have assisted the Illinois Emergency Management Agency in disaster-assistance relief. In Ohio, inmates participate in a variety of public service programs, including Adopt-A-School, animal care, and art programs including the creation of signage for nonprofit causes.

Committee chair:

Joyce Jackson
Deputy Director for Communications
Illinois Department of Corrections

P. O. Box 19277
Springfield, Illinois 62794-9277
(217) 522-2666

Citizens' Advisory Committees

Introduction

Communities and their citizens have an important role to play in the criminal justice system. As part of the Canadian correctional process, the Correctional Service of Canada is the federal agency responsible for the administration of the sentences, the management of federal correctional facilities, and the supervision of offenders serving terms of two years or more. Over time, the interaction between the correctional service and concerned members of the community has evolved into an organized means for community involvement in the Canadian correctional system through Citizens' Advisory Committees.

While the concept of citizen participation within the correctional service originally began in the early 1960s, its formal recognition came through a Parliamentary Sub-Committee Report on Federal Penitentiaries (1977), which was issued following several serious prison disturbances across Canada. The study acknowledged a need for the involvement of citizens, as representatives of communities, who would have access to institutions to monitor and evaluate correctional policies and procedures. Subsequently, the correctional service has made Citizens' Advisory Committees mandatory for every federal institution in Canada and, eventually, for parole offices.

Over the years, the advisory committees have helped to inform communities about the correctional process, to provide a vehicle for the community to represent and express itself in the core work of the correctional service, and to contribute to the overall development of correctional facilities and programs. Managed by committed individuals who volunteer their time and skills to provide a valuable public service, some 500 citizens now are active in its ranks, with currently more than 60 advisory committees across Canada.

Development and Design

Citizens' Advisory Committees are organized on local, regional, and national levels. The local committees, typically are made up of five-to-eight members and headed by an elected chairperson. Each committee is associated with a correctional services' operational unit across Canada. The responsibility for recruiting, training, coordinating, and maintaining these local committees rests with the head of each operational unit.

All local advisory committees are members of a regional citizen advisory committee in each of the five administrative regions of the correctional service (i.e., Atlantic, Quebec, Ontario, Prairies, and Pacific). The local advisory committees are represented on the regional committee either by the chairperson of each local committee or by an executive committee elected by the members of the region.

The (elected) regional chairperson is automatically a member of the Citizens' Advisory Committee National Executive Committee. The regional chairperson, along with a coordinator from each of the regional headquarters within the correctional service, is responsible for the administration of each regional Citizens' Advisory Committee.

At the national level, the National Executive Committee is made up of one representative from each regional Citizens' Advisory Committee and is headed by an elected executive chairperson. The national executive, through a national advisory committee coordinator from the correctional service's national headquarters in Ottawa, is responsible for the national coordination of all such advisory committees across Canada.

The national executive is responsible for the coordination of recommendations made by local and regional advisory committees on policies and programs that affect all operational units of the correctional service. These recommendations then are presented by the national executive committee to the commissioner of corrections. The national executive committee meets three to four times per year. The National Citizen's Advisory Committee conferences are held every two years during which general action strategies are set for the next two years.

Appointments are made for a period of two years and are based on consultation with the local advisory committee, as appropriate, with the recommendation of the operational unit and consent of the regional deputy commissioner. The guidelines for recruitment are directed at representing the community served by the correctional service program or facility (e.g., social, cultural, and demographic backgrounds) and, as much as possible, any regional variations of the specific local offender population.

Implementation

With the introduction of the correctional service's mission in 1989, the Citizens' Advisory Committees have experienced an atmosphere of increasing cooperation and involvement. This was further enhanced through the *Corrections and Conditional Release Act of 1992*, which facilitates the ". . . involvement of members of the public in matters relating to the operation of the Correctional Service."

Through voluntary participation in the Canadian correctional process, and guided by their mission, the Citizens' Advisory Committees serve as:

Advisors—Through open discussion with the correctional service, these committees provide consultation and advice, which contributes to the operation and development of programs and policies.

Independent observers—The advisory committee members act as independent observers of the day-to-day activities and operations of the correctional service.

Liaison—They serve as a communication link with the community, by actively interacting with the correctional service's staff, the public, and the offenders.

Mission of the Citizens' Advisory Committees

The mission was formally adopted by the Citizens' Advisory Committees and the commissioner of corrections on May 31, 1994. It reflects the belief in the right of all citizens to become informed participants in the correctional process, to contribute to the quality of that process and of the decisions made. The mission states:

> Citizens' Advisory Committees, through voluntary participation in the Canadian federal correctional process, contribute to the protection of society by actively interacting with staff of the Correctional Service of Canada, the public and offenders, providing impartial advice and recommendations, thereby contributing to the quality of the correctional process.

Results

Correctional facilities and programs are part of the community and cannot exist in a vacuum. Through ongoing dialog and consultation with the community, the advisory committees play a vital role in assisting the correctional service to become more responsive to all Canadians.

The general activities by which these committees accomplish their mission and role include the following:

- Advising and assisting the local, regional, and national managers on the overall development of correctional facilities and programs, and their impact on the community

- Providing advice and recommendations to the local, regional, and national managers on community issues, problems and needs

- Meeting regularly with the offender committees, the local union representatives, and with the local management and the employees

- Facilitating the development of community-based resources supportive of correctional programs

- Educating the local community in correctional objectives and programs; developing and implementing the means to enhance communication with the local community

- Contributing to the role of volunteers and encouraging public participation in the correctional process

Conclusion

Implications for Other Organizations

Citizens' advisory committees can provide an important link with the local community (general public). In being informed participants in any government process, such committees can contribute to the following:

- Creating a climate in which the government and the public can exchange views, ideas, and information that can result in policies and programs responsive to public priorities, needs, and concerns

- Providing the public with a better understanding of policy and program options and government constraints

- Providing an opportunity for an informed public to support and participate in achieving the goals of government

Outlook for the Future

The Correctional Service of Canada is committed to recruiting volunteers from all cultural and socioeconomic segments of the community and to foster their services. The future of corrections will depend very much on the community's support and participation, and the Citizens' Advisory Committees are a vital part of that participation.

Canadians want to know and have a right to know why and how the correctional service does what it does. The informed involvement and support of the community is critical to the success of correctional work.

Through its determination to better receive and incorporate public views into its policy and program development, the correctional service hopes to promote public knowledge and understanding of corrections, contribute to the overall development of correctional facilities and programs, and foster even greater public participation in the correctional process.

Contact:

Jim Davidson
Director General
Correctional Service of Canada

1045 Main Street, Unit 102
Moncton, New Brunswick, Canada E1C 1H1
(506) 851-3461

A Partnership with Habitat for Humanity

Introduction

Almost four years ago, in August 1994, the Texas Department of Criminal Justice's Robertson Unit in Abilene participated in its first project with Habitat for Humanity, contributing 420 offender hours to construct a house in one week during a "Blitz Build" program. A year later, they did it again. During December 1995, the Hutchins State Jail worked with Habitat volunteers to construct a house in Dallas. The success of the relationship between the Dallas Area Habitat program and Hutchins prompted the formation of the nation's first correctional chapter of Habitat for Humanity.

Currently, almost one in five of the department's facilities—some twenty at the latest count—participate in Habitat for Humanity projects. Five are state jails, thirteen are institutional division prisons, one is a substance-abuse treatment facility, and one is located at a state prison but is actually part of a faith-based program, which is privately operated.

The Dallas Experience

It was the hope of everyone involved that the Dallas Area Habitat for Humanity-Department of Criminal Justice partnership would be unique in several respects. There were three major components to the vision. First, that a long-term relationship with a department facility (in this case, the Hutchins State Jail) would be developed along the lines of a campus Habitat chapter; second, that a consistent training and experience program could be developed to enhance the relationship for both parties; and third, that the Dallas Area Habitat affiliate would serve as a copartner in the development of a new, innovative approach to affordable housing and the incubation of a new entity devoted to increasing the rehabilitative opportunities for newly released residents.

The partnership with the Hutchins State Jail provided important volunteer assistance to the Dallas Area Habitat during their "Blitz Build." It was a very positive experience for the Hutchins State Jail residents and staff, and one that provided outstanding positive media coverage for both partners.

The campus-chapter design is pertinent because this structure operates on a long-term basis within an institution (such as a college), and yet the volunteer population (the students) is transient. The situation is the same within a correctional unit. The typical campus chapter achieves continuity through the commitment of a faculty or staff person to interface with the local Habitat affiliate or Habitat International. The corollary for a correctional chapter is the involvement of a staff person on an ongoing basis.

Implementing the First Correctional Chapter

The department's relationship in the Dallas Area Habitat is with the Irving Chapter. After review by the appropriate staff at both agencies, a "Chapter Partnership Agreement and Policy" was approved and signed. The Hutchins State Jail Chapter of Habitat for Humanity was officially chartered on June 26, 1996.

The members of the Dallas Area Habitat help conduct monthly chapter meetings at the Hutchins State Jail, and inmate work crews have continued to help build new houses, along with various other related projects. Inmates who work on Habitat projects can be certified in various house-building skills if they gain enough hours in a specific area. They also may begin the process of qualifying for a Habitat house of their own.

Results

Some Lessons Learned

The establishment of an affiliate-chapter relationship between a local Habitat affiliate and prison chapter should not be started without significant commitments by both the affiliate and the prison. It is not the intent of this relationship simply to provide the local affiliate with an additional source of volunteer labor on an as-needed basis. The relationship should be of long-term benefit to all participants. It should enhance the capacity of the affiliate to construct Habitat homes and provide an effective program to address recidivism. It also should offer hope to the residents of the institution because they will have received skill training and skill certification. Then, the program offers participating inmates an opportunity to network and meet with potential postincarceration employers. More importantly, it should provide a sense of self-worth and discipline related to community service and the satisfaction of building a home for a deserving family.

The local affiliate must provide the following:

- A formal board commitment to enter into the relationship

- A task force or committee devoted to the relationship

- A commitment to provide for regular chapter meetings, probably monthly

- A commitment to regular work opportunities if house construction is not available, then in other tasks, which provide the opportunity for skills training and certification

- Participation and skills certification

- A basic tool chest (nail aprons, hammers, and so forth)

- Transportation for offenders (if needed)

- Construction supervision by qualified personnel

- Volunteer insurance

- Lunches (probably) and coffee (optional)

There is one other major requirement for the affiliate and that is a sense of respect for the prison-chapter participants. These participants are volunteers and deserve that recognition. It is encouraged that the affiliate volunteers recognize the offender volunteers by name and greet them with friendship and an open hand. The affiliate, however, must abide by the rules of the institution governing "free world" contact (e.g., no use of tobacco products by the offender volunteers).

The local prison chapter must provide the following:

- A formal agreement with the local affiliate

- Prison chapter governance with an administrative sponsor

- Appropriate supervision

- Provision of chapter-meeting space

- Storage of the chapter toolbox

- Flexibility for the prison-chapter participants in terms of work hours (for instance, by allowing a late dinner) and attendance at Habitat dedications

With commitment and good faith on the part of both the affiliate and the correctional institution, the affiliate/prison chapter relationship should be a fulfilling experience for all involved.

Expansion of the Partnership

While the first correctional chapter was in formation, work continued on individual projects and more prison units volunteered to help local Habitat chapters and affiliates. During 1996, the Robertson Unit, Hutchins State Jail, Cole State Jail, and the Venus Pre-Release Center participated in various Habitat projects. A total of 25,000 volunteer hours were spent by residents of these four department facilities.

In 1997, a total of twenty facilities worked with Habitat for Humanity in some way. Several units built trusses and cabinets within the confines of the institution, through the Windham School District's vocational training classes. Several other facilities built an entire house inside a confined area, which Habitat then moved to the site. Still other facilities sent crews to the actual Habitat construction site to assist in the building of the houses. In fact, one facility sent a crew to the Jimmy Carter "A 100 Houses in 100 Days" blitz build in Houston.

In another instance, six units helped in the building of a Habitat house. While the components of the modular house were being built inside a prison, at the actual construction site a second unit did the plumbing, a third completed the electrical work, still others did the foundation work, and another unit completed the odd jobs at the site. They all worked together to complete the house.

The Habitat affiliates, which have worked with inmate offenders, have expressed their pleasure at the fine attitude and work ethic of the residents and their supervisors. Additionally, no disciplinary problems yet have been encountered. The high degree of ownership and commitment of the residents has impressed everyone, especially the "free-world" volunteers.

In discussing their thoughts and ideas after participating in a project that provides decent, affordable housing to needy families, almost all of the offenders have expressed a positive feeling of "giving something back" to the community and showing pride in producing something of permanence.

Conclusion

Media Involvement

Throughout the growth of Habitat partnerships with the Department of Criminal Justice facilities, the media has had a very significant impact on the success of these endeavors. Newspaper articles have lauded the efforts of local Habitat affiliates in getting offenders involved. In many cases, local newspapers have run feature articles on the Habitat for Humanity work projects, and on other community work projects in which offenders are involved. This type of coverage keeps community residents informed of the positive things being accomplished by confined individuals. It makes them aware of programs, which have had a positive impact on offenders, and may help them become constructive members of society and decrease the likelihood of recidivism.

At a recent workshop at the Habitat for Humanity's Southwest Regional Conference, participants learned about the use of the media in promoting Habitat projects. Department offenders were highlighted as examples of the type of unique information that the media is seeking.

The Hutchins State Jail Chapter of the Dallas Area Habitat for Humanity was chosen as the "1997 Outstanding Volunteer Group of this Year" by the Volunteer Center of Dallas County. This award was created to identify and recognize outstanding and innovative volunteer efforts in Dallas County. The award honors those individuals, companies, and groups who exemplify the role of the volunteer and make a significant positive impact on the lives of other Dallas County residents. Winners are selected by a panel of judges representing the Dallas nonprofit, civic, and business communities.

Contact:

Sharon B. Keilin
Assistant Director for Operational Support
Texas Department of Criminal Justice

P. O. Box 99
Huntsville, Texas 77342-0099
(409) 437-2523

*Louisiana Department of Public Safety
and Corrections*

Roadway Beautification

Introduction

Under the direction of its secretary, the Louisiana Department of Public Safety and Corrections began a major project to clean up litter throughout the state. Louisiana is a state which takes pride in its ability to encourage tourism because of its vast natural resources. The state often is referred to as the "Sportsman's Paradise," and it is rich in bayous, swampland, and other breathtaking natural settings. The efforts to keep it beautiful accelerated when Governor Mike Foster announced his major antilitter project in July, 1996. His support provided additional impetus to the department's mandate to improve the state's image.

Development and Design

The project was enhanced by the coordination of several state and local agencies. The state departments joining efforts included the Department of Public Safety and Corrections, the Department of Transportation and Development, and the Department of Environmental Quality. Local governmental entities which routinely participate include the local parish and county sheriffs. The latter operate parish and county jails.

This partnership of state and local government has resulted in the project's ability to provide a comprehensive approach to a statewide problem. The efforts of the Department of Public Safety and Corrections in coordinating the project has been one of the governor's most successful initiatives on behalf of the citizenry.

Implementation

Each of the state's fifteen secure institutions is involved in the daily task of providing crews on major highways to clean up debris and trash along the roadway. The Department of Transportation and Development assists through a daily pick-up of the bagged and stacked debris. A tremendous amount of coordination is involved around the state to ensure that the two departments are scheduled to provide services along the same route.

To assist the state agencies and the citizens in maintaining their highways and byways, a toll-free telephone hotline has been established for reporting littered roadways, litter law offenders, and illegal dump sites. The hotline began operations in January 1997 and received more than 800 calls during its first year. The hotline is under the auspices of the Department of Environmental Quality and is a twenty-four-hour service that is answered by employees eight hours a day and by an answering machine at all other times. Upon receipt of a complaint regarding a littered highway, coordination with the Departments of Public Safety and Corrections and Transportation and Development begins with the objective of eliminating the problem. Illegal dump site problems are handled by the Department of Environmental Quality. Reports regarding motorists who are observed littering require providing the vehicle license plate number. A letter subsequently is sent to the motorist along with a litter bag.

Outcomes

Reports are submitted weekly by the institutions to the Office of the Secretary, which provide data regarding areas where clean-up activities were done, the number of inmates and supervisory staff involved, hours of work performed, and the volume of litter collected. Thus far, the reports have shown an average of 17,000 hours of community service work performed by the Department of Public Safety and Corrections per week.

Conclusion

"Project Clean Up" is a coordinated statewide litter removal program, which uses state inmate labor in all of its eight highway districts. The state's clean-up efforts are widely publicized in newspaper articles, television and radio public service announcements, car bumper stickers, a video produced by the local capitol area cable television station that details the inmate clean-up efforts, billboards throughout the state featuring the governor and his wife reminding citizens to help in this endeavor, and a Department of Environmental Quality newsletter that is published quarterly.

The Louisiana State Senate Litter Task Force was formed to work toward combating the state's litter problem. The group is made up of legislators, state agency representatives, and citizens. They are involved currently in developing a plan to provide education and information to citizens as a means of increasing their interest and participation in keeping the state clean.

The department has diligently sought success by ensuring that only those inmates who pose the least threat to public safety are permitted to participate. The classification system is monitored vigorously to help meet project goals.

The uniqueness of this project is exemplified by the partnership formed by the Department of Public Safety and Corrections and the Department of Transportation and Development, two state agencies that have not had common interests and goals in the past.

Because of the critical need for close coordination between state and local government in the management of prison and jail space, local law enforcement agencies (through their sheriffs) have joined in the statewide effort to maintain litter-free highways. It is a rarity to travel Louisiana's highways on any day of the week and not experience the sight of state inmates "giving back to the community" by helping to ensure a litter-free state highway system. Inmates who participate in the project and supervising employees must participate in a highway safety training class provided by the Department of Transportation and Development.

This project is also unique in that it involves all state adult and juvenile correctional institutions. The success is measured not just by the sheer volume of litter collected, nor the huge number of inmate work hours expended weekly, nor in the lack of threats to public safety, nor in the tremendous cooperation between state and local governments. Rather, it is measured by the luxury of touring the state's major highways and recognizing the beauty of the land rather than the litter of the people who access those highways.

Contact:

Jannitta Antoine
Deputy Secretary
Louisiana Department of Public Safety and Corrections

504 Mayflower Street
Baton Rouge, Louisiana 70802
(504) 342-6744

Weathering the Storm: A Team Effort

Introduction

In late fall 1992, when the Illinois Emergency Management Agency was revising its state emergency operations plan, they discussed the labor force available for disaster assistance and began considering ways state agencies could help in emergency situations. During January 1993, while work continued on the plan revisions, some levees in Illinois along the Mississippi River developed problems with water seepage due to weeks of heavy rainfall. The Illinois Emergency Management Agency attempted to correct seepage problems during February, March, and April, 1993. Fighting the seepage problem literally drained the Governor's Disaster Fund.

Levee districts had pumped continuously and were reimbursed for their expenses from the fund. The problems with the levees continued. By June 30, 1993—the last day of the state's fiscal year—problems had escalated. With the fund depleted, sandbags were direly needed on a levee in Niota, Illinois, a small community in Hancock County on the Mississippi River. Illinois Emergency Management Agency officials were at a loss as to how to proceed.

Since there was no money to activate the National Guard, sandbags would not get to the levee or be placed where they were needed. Then, as a last resort, someone suggested using prison inmates—an untested resource—to do the job. In the waning moments of the fiscal year, an Illinois Emergency Management Agency official contacted an Illinois Department of Corrections' official who would be their liaison for getting inmates deployed in the flood control efforts. Within an hour, the chief administrative officer of the Western Illinois Correctional Center—located two counties away from Niota—had sent nearly 70 inmates to the site. Due to the quick response, this levee was able to be saved for a few more weeks.

Expansion

During this time, Governor Jim Edgar convened a task force of all state agencies, with imperative instructions that there be full cooperation among the agencies to help the flood victims. This task force was to review all areas, including agriculture, infrastructure, acquisition/relocation, business recovery-mitigation, flood control, and housing needs. As a result of this cooperation, the Illinois Department of Corrections made a legitimate response and became a recovery agency in the flood control efforts.

Many sparsely populated communities along the Mississippi River were threatened by the rising flood waters. Many of the people in these communities never had imagined the threat of losing their farmland and homes, and were caught completely off guard. In addition to inmate work crews, agency staff provided assistance and ingenuity in tackling the flood.

Sometimes, the worst of times brings out the best of ideas. At the onset of the great flood of 1993 along the Mississippi River, sandbags quickly became a valuable tool with which to hold back flood waters. And, the more expeditiously that bags could be filled, the greater the number of bags that could be produced and the more areas that could be saved.

The Illinois Correctional Industries program at Shawnee Correctional Center developed and mass produced an ingenious "funnel on a stand" for filling sandbags. The "old way" of filling sandbags was for one person to hold the bag open with bare hands, while another person—shovel in hand—filled the bag with sand. Often, hands were cut with the shovel, and inevitably not all the sand would make it into the bag.

With the funnel, or "shoot," one person holds the bag under the bottom of the device while the shoveler loads sand into the funnel. This method results in a production rate at least twice as fast as the old way. It is a safer way to fill bags, and a much more efficient system of making sandbags where nearly all of the sand actually winds up in the bag. According to the Acting Superintendent of Shawnee Industries, "hundreds" of the funnels have been constructed and provided to almost all area municipalities along the Mississippi and Ohio Rivers, which had experienced major flooding again in 1997.

The impact of prison inmates serving several communities and working side by side with many citizens also is overwhelming. A good example of the relationship between local citizens and inmates was realized by an inmate in a song he wrote that was sung on the levee while the inmates worked: "They say in Niota the eatin's mighty fine; they feed me twice a day, and now they're friends of mine. Oh, Lord, we won't let you flood, cause there is lots of love. They say in Niota, the people's mighty fine; our skin's a differ'nt color, they don't pay it no mind."

This song is suggestive of the relationships that formed between the citizens and inmates during the disaster work. Most of the inmates were minorities serving sentences for crimes committed in Chicago. Many were from housing projects there, and now they were in southern and southwestern Illinois battling mother nature. These inmates never heard any negative comments from the citizens, never were called any derogatory names, and were well treated.

Even though the levees broke in Niota, the townspeople thanked the inmates. This tended to confuse some inmates. Some of them wondered why they were being thanked when many townspeople lost their homes to the flood. The locals appreciated the inmates' assistance so much that a permanent bond was established between them.

The flood control efforts of 1993 were repeated in 1994; this time, inmates assisted along tributary rivers rather than along the Illinois and Mississippi Rivers. During peak flood control efforts, between 700 and 1,000 inmates were used on a daily basis. Inmates have been used to fight flooding and in flood cleanup efforts every year since 1993.

Inmate workers also are used for relief in other natural disasters. The word has spread throughout various communities as to how inmate labor can be very useful. Inmates often have been used to assist in tornado and severe storm cleanup since 1993, activities which also are coordinated through the Illinois Emergency Management Agency.

Implementation

What follows explains the implementation process of communities requesting assistance from the Illinois Department of Corrections and why the implementation process needs to run its course during times of state emergencies:

1) The Illinois Emergency Management Agency statutorily is responsible for managing and coordinating any state-supported response to an emergency situation.

2) The Illinois Emergency Management Agency is in direct contact with the governor's office either by phone or the staff of the governor's office will be present within the State Emergency Operation Center during the emergency. Additionally, the emergency center provides the governor's office with frequent updates of written reports of progress; therefore, reports must reflect very specific and factual information.

3) All state agencies have a liaison appointed by the agency director to coordinate their agency's function with the Illinois Emergency Management Agency.

4) County Emergency Services and Disaster Agency Coordinators (each county is mandated by law to have one) immediately coordinate their needs through the Illinois Emergency Management Agency. Because there are only limited resources available, depending upon the nature and extent of the emergency, areas requiring the use of state resources must be prioritized by order of need, rather than on a first-come, first-serve basis. The governor, through the Illinois Emergency Management Agency, monitors the total disaster and establishes the priorities for resource management. A local emergency services and disaster agency coordinator cannot see the entire scope of the problem; the Illinois Emergency Management Agency establishes control over state resources so that they are not misdirected to units of government needing them less than others. There must be control so that the locals do not "grab up the resources" for less consequential matters.

5) Resource management by the Illinois Emergency Management Agency is a key factor, which also takes the burden off a facility administrator.

6) Overtime costs are another reason the Illinois Emergency Management Agency monitors disaster assistance, as in state-declared disaster areas. The money to pay for many resources can be provided by other budgets, including federal disaster assistance, if the area is declared a federal disaster area. Besides fighting floods and cleaning up tornado debris, inmates are prepared to do a multitude of things. Over a year ago, the Illinois Department of Corrections provided the Illinois Emergency Management Agency with a list of services it could provide in the event of severe cold and hot weather emergencies. Such services include but are not limited to providing the following: transportation for displaced persons to shelters, providing ice and/or water to those in need; inmate work crews to load and unload supply trucks; telecommunication equipment; meal preparation for emergency shelters; work release inmates to assist the American Red Cross, Salvation Army, and other organizations in distributing food and supplies to citizens/workers; air conditioned buildings to allow temporary relief from extreme heat (select facilities only); staff assistance in door-to-door checking on the well being of citizens during periods of brownouts; refrigeration units to store food products; and crews for snow removal for city, county, or state property.

The department of correction's involvement with the Illinois Emergency Management Agency has become so extensive and the coordination efforts of both units were working so well, that the director felt the need to appoint a permanent State Emergency Operations Center liaison to deploy inmate work crews on a statewide basis, and oversee the department's involvement. During disasters, the liaison is assigned to the emergency operations center with the other state agency liaisons to coordinate efforts.

Throughout the period of the emergency response, data are collected by the liaison from all of the participating facilities to document the number of staff, inmates, and hours worked at each site. After compiling this information from each facility, it can be used later for annual reports, and comparative studies. These studies vividly outline the cost savings experienced by the state through the use of inmate labor compared to hired labor, in such disasters or emergencies. In the last few years alone, more than 250,000 inmate-labor hours have been expended on floods and tornado cleanup.

Results

Media Coverage

Media coverage of this major catastrophe was extensive. Periodicals such as *The New York Times, Newsweek*, and numerous other media outlets nationwide wrote lengthy articles about this inmate labor. A wide variety of stories filled the newspapers, from human interest accounts to reports on all of the different ways the flood had affected various situations. The media prominently carried these stories.

The publicity that the Illinois Department of Corrections received from all of this attention was positive and extensive. Word quickly spread to other communities that needed this invaluable resource. To this day, communities rely heavily on inmate labor to assist them in related activities. This has aided in strengthening the agency's image in the eyes of the public. With the ever-increasing inmate population and the rising need for more prisons and prison work camps, many communities now will vie for a new facility in their area. Over the years, communities have gained firsthand knowledge of the value of having a correctional facility close enough to provide assistance when the need arises.

Conclusion

The state now has a unified system. The cohesiveness of the task force is what makes the system work so well. It provides a model from which all states could benefit. This model easily can be applied to existing programs used by other states. The current system now is used even in preparations for future disasters.

More than a dozen state agency liaisons spent a week in Little Rock, Arkansas, in February, 1997, at a seminar designed to respond to a New Madrid seismic zone earthquake. This involved the assembling of state officials from a seven-state area along with Federal Emergency Management Agency officials and other federal officials, scrutinizing step-by-step the aftermath of a simulated 7.6 level earthquake. The corrections department was involved in this initiative to gain insight into the role it would need to play in the event of a catastrophic event of this nature.

Corrections in Illinois has become an intricate part of the emergency management system. It provides valuable assistance to help the citizens of the state. The state has learned a great deal from these experiences in the last several years, primarily that valuable resources can be found if the time is taken to find them.

Even the inmates have learned from their experiences. Most inmates who have participated in these disaster responses have commented on how good they feel to be able to help in such worthwhile activities. They like to see the fruits of their labor and can feel good about themselves because they are able to give something back to the community. The Illinois Emergency Management Agency and the Department of Corrections' connection has been and continues to be a great success.

Contact:

Augustus Scott, Jr.
Warden
Lincoln Correctional Center
Illinois Department of Corrections

P. O. Box 549
Lincoln, Illinois 62656
(217) 735-5411

Ohio Department of Rehabilitation and Correction

Community Service by Inmates

Introduction

Corrections historically has been a field buffeted by public opinion. Correctional administrators either bask in anonymity or face reform depending on the public mood. The traditional response to these winds of change has been to acquiesce and adapt accordingly. Recently, however, correctional agencies have opted to take over the reins and drive public opinion by trumpeting their successes. One area that naturally lends itself to positive public opinion is the time-honored tradition of having prisoners perform community service.

In January 1996, the Ohio Department of Rehabilitation and Correction made a remarkable commitment to the expansion of community service by inmates. With assistance from the governor, the wardens, and several Adopt-A-School partners, the department kicked-off a massive community service campaign called, "A Million Hours . . . It's in the Works." The effort mirrored the 1996 Olympics, with each prison attaining new levels of success on their Olympic "torches." Thanks to the Olympian efforts of inmates and staff, the department completed more than 1.54 million hours of community service by the end of October 1996.

Implementation

Each of the twenty-nine wardens made a commitment to enhancing their community by devoting inmate labor to nonprofit organizations, government agencies, and local schools. Screened prisoners under escort work outside the fence, while higher-security inmates contribute through projects that can be done on the inside. Help arrives in many ways: inmate crews build school playgrounds, raise puppies for Pilot Dog, Inc., wash laundry for the homeless, and renovate housing for sale to families of limited income. The only caution placed on the campaign is that no working Ohioan be deprived of work.

The strong partnerships resulting from these efforts have resulted in significant change. Communities in which prisons are located have come to acknowledge and appreciate the help provided by inmates. Fellow state and local agencies have been able to complete projects, which otherwise would have been postponed for lack of funds or personnel. Positive news coverage of success stories has emerged statewide and even nationally, and the public's image of idle inmates has been challenged. Finally, prisoners have learned the many benefits, both practical and spiritual, of paying back to society.

Areas of Focus

Education—Every prison and the central office participates in the Adopt-A-School program. Through these partnerships, inmates repair computers, make learning aids, restore desks, print materials, design award certificates, paint classrooms, maintain school grounds, and build reading lofts for young students.

Animal Care—Inmates in fifteen prisons raise puppies in partnership with the Pilot Dog, Inc. program for the visually impaired. Inmates in two prisons care for animals who have wound up in county Humane Society kennels. In partnership with the Ohio Wildlife Center, inmates at the Ohio Reformatory for Women care for injured and orphaned animals until they can be returned to their natural habitat. Prisoners at the Oakwood Correctional Facility train puppies to work with physically handicapped people for the Companion Dog Service.

Art—Existing artistic abilities have been encouraged and groomed among the inmate population. Several public agencies, including the Capitol Square Review and the Advisory Board for the Ohio Statehouse, display exhibits of inmate artwork. Often, the exhibits are focused on anticrime and antiviolence themes. Inmates screen T-shirts and print posters and other signage for nonprofit causes. Some organizations have commissioned inmates to make "thank you" gifts for community volunteers.

The department's Bureau of Community Service works with staff in each of the state's 29 prisons to carry out the program. Prisoners have performed more than 4.4 million hours of service since community service was formally tracked in 1991. The department looks forward to an even more successful year in 1998.

Conclusion

Productive community service offers many benefits. Nonprofit and government agency recipients of the labor and resources provided by community service programs achieve results that would have been impossible under today's budgetary constraints. Prisoner participants learn the intrinsic value of a job well done. They also receive the gratitude and praise of those they assist. Prisons benefit by fielding programs that entail productive work, ease tension, and promote positive feedback. Also, correctional agencies benefit from the positive public perception and the immeasurable good will resulting from these programs.

A positive feature story in the local newspaper about prisoners refurbishing school lockers and building a ball field makes a solid impression on the taxpayer. The positive public relations value of a segment on a national television news magazine touting the success of inmate-trained guide dogs cannot be measured. A populace that has directly benefited from community services programs will not readily agree to knee-jerk "tough on crime" legislation. Communities that benefit from the work done by inmates and supervised by professional staff are ambassadors for the corrections profession. Like a pebble dropped into a pond, the concentric waves of good will emanating from community service are endless.

Contact:

Bill Thoroman
Chief, Community Services
Ohio Department of Rehabilitation and Correction

970 Freeway Drive North
Columbus, Ohio 43229
(614) 752-1158

Public Information
Additional Program Entries

Computers for Schools Program

Sylvia Ortiz, Special Assistant to the Chief Deputy Director of Support Services
California Department of Corrections, P.O. Box 942883, Sacramento, California 94283
(916) 327-4904

The California Department of Corrections took a unique approach to stretching tax dollars in a state that ranked forty-eighth in the nation in ratio of students per computer. California is also faced with scarce state funding for educational technology. In a program that is a partnership between the California Department of Corrections, the nonprofit Detwiler Foundation, California schools and businesses, inmates repair donated computers for the state's public school system. Obsolete computers are obtained from businesses and refurbished by inmates in the Department of Corrections' vocational education/industry program. This helps meet the technology needs of schools and the Department of Corrections' need to provide meaningful employment for inmates. The program has expanded from four institutions to thirteen, and in 1996, 16,500 computers were recovered for schools. This effort is an excellent example of a corrections department developing partnerships with different segments of the community in a relevant program that is successful for all parties.

A Balanced Portrayal of a Critical Correctional Program

Thomas R. Kane, Assistant Director, Information, Policy, and Public Affairs
Federal Bureau of Prisons, 320 First Street, NW, Washington, D.C. 20534
(202) 514-6537

The Bureau of Prisons worked extensively and diligently with the producer and reporters of a CBS *60 Minutes* segment on Federal Prison Industries, known as Unicor. The resulting news piece was a balanced portrayal of this critical correctional program. The coverage of Unicor was an important public relations effort. Millions of people had the opportunity to see what every correctional professional wants the public to know about correctional industries—how they are keeping inmates busy and preparing them for life after incarceration.

Sight for the World

Keith Cooper, Warden
Sheridan Correctional Center, P.O. Box 38, Sheridan, Illinois 60551
(815) 496-2311

In 1995, the Sheridan Correctional Center entered into a partnership with "I Care International" to assist in the processing of used eyeglasses for donation to people in need of eye care who live in impoverished areas around the world. Inmates at the Sheridan Correctional Center clean, sort, mark, inventory, and pack glasses that ultimately will provide sight to individuals who may be unable to afford glasses. In addition to sorting and packing, Sheridan Correctional Center inmates inspect the frames and classify the glasses by prescription strength. The lens prescriptions are determined on eleven Lensmeters that were donated by Wal-Mart Vision Centers. Accompanying the Lensmeters was the personalized attention and training of the director of technical support for the Wal-Mart Vision Centers. The inmates who have been trained on the Lensmeter have become skilled in determining lens' prescription strength. When the glasses are ready, they are given to "I Care," who distribute them around the world. To date, more than 70,000 pairs of glasses have been processed.

Vandalia Correctional Center Work Camp

Michael W. Baker, Warden
P.O. Box 500, Vandalia, Illinois 62471
(618) 283-4170

For the past fifteen years, Vandalia Correctional Center has been involved in the Work Camp Project, a program that uses supervised inmate work crews to provide public services to Vandalia and neighboring communities. Today, Vandalia Correctional Center fields more than 200 supervised inmates who work on labor-intensive projects such as picking up litter along state and federal highways; mowing and lawn care for court houses, airports, municipal cemeteries, and Chamber of Commerce property; assisting in the preparation for county fairs; and cleaning up and maintaining state parks. During the floods of 1993 and 1994, inmates provided thousands of hours of inmate labor, working around the clock to assist others fighting the effects of the floods. In 1993, Vandalia Correctional Center adopted a park, which had been closed for lack of funds. It remains one of the best maintained parks in the community. The Work Camp Project is very well received by the neighboring communities.

Research

14

Introduction

Notwithstanding periodic decreases in crime, the growth in the number of offenders in correctional custody, whether in the community or in facilities, continues to escalate. Along with this growth comes an increased need for funds. Correctional systems represent the fastest growing item in the budgets of many jurisdictions across the country. The more extensive use of research can assist corrections professionals in meeting the challenge of doing more with less or making more efficient use of available resources.

The careful selection of research topics and appropriate follow-up relative to the results can have a dramatic impact on the operations of institutional and community corrections. Research may play an important role in relation to such issues as classification decisions regarding custody; housing, and work assignments; determining which programs should be eliminated, modified, or initiated; and, how to best justify requests for additional resources. Overall, research figures prominently in identifying the extent and frequency of operational problems, assessing appropriate strategies to deal with difficulties, and evaluating programs.

The American Correctional Association's correctional policy has maintained that the findings from research and evaluation are essential to informed correctional policy, program development, and decision making. Consistent with the Association's efforts to encourage and disseminate correctional research and evaluation findings, four program descriptions are provided in this chapter. A fifth program was selected by both the Research Council and the Health Committee. It discusses a quasi-experimental study designed by the California Department of Corrections to evaluate community-based treatment services to inmates with HIV/AIDS. Though it is a good example of the value of applied research, it is included in the chapter on health programs.

The selection of programs by the Research Council to be included in this chapter involved: (1) the development of criteria unique to research, to be used in conjunction with the American Correctional Association's core criteria for best practices submissions; (2) the review of twenty-one program submissions by the council; and (3) the selection, which consisted of a more detailed review and refinement of the most promising programs by active council members.

The criteria unique to research used by the council to evaluate the various submissions involved a review of the following: (1) whether collaboration between correctional practitioners and research personnel resulted in a research product that had an impact on correctional policy and practice; (2) whether the research program significantly advanced correctional knowledge in a way that allows correctional administrators to create new programs or improve existing ones; (3) the soundness and transferability of the research design and methodology; (4) whether the research, published or nonpublished, had been conducted within the last five years and, (5) consistent with quality and availability of program information, diversity was sought relative to topics; geographical areas; adult and juvenile institutions; and community, state, federal, and local jurisdictions.

The four programs that are covered address a range of topics, including: (1) classification, (2) education, (3) work and vocational training, and (4) the drug testing of parolees. A brief description of each program is provided next.

- The first study from Canada resulted in the development of an Offender Intake Assessment Model. It was designed to standardize orientation, and integrated an offender risk and needs assessment process throughout the correctional agency. This device enabled the agency to "forecast the growth of its prison population, monitor changes in composition, improve risk management procedures, and measure correctional performance."

- The second study from Ohio examines the impact of prison education programs on recidivism. Positive results were found for certain subgroups of offenders, which "helped ensure continued funding of college programs." Additionally, existing programs and current programs were modified to better serve the needs of the offender population.

- The third, a longitudinal study by the Federal Bureau of Prisons, evaluates the impact of participation in work and vocational training programs on the postrelease recidivism of 7,000 adult offenders.

- The final program discusses a four-year experimental study by the California Department of the Youth Authority involving youthful offenders released to parole. The study's objective was to determine how much drug testing should be part of regular parole supervision, with no reduction in caseload size and no access to additional outside resources.

Committee chair:

Helen Corrothers
U.S. Sentencing Commissioner (Ret.)

3104 Beaverwood Lane
Silver Spring, Maryland 20906
(301) 871-6685

The Offender Intake Assessment Process

Introduction

The Correctional Service of Canada recognized that an offender's needs should be the basis for programming, and that service delivery should focus primarily on successful reintegration into the community. Consequently, an Offender Intake Assessment model was developed to standardize an overall orientation and to integrate risk and needs assessment throughout the correctional service.

The Offender Intake Assessment process is a comprehensive and integrated evaluation of the offender at the time of admission to the federal system. It involves the collection and analysis of information on the offender's criminal and mental health history, social situation, education, and other factors relevant to determining risk and needs. This provides a basis for determining institutional placement and for establishing the offender's correctional plan.

The objective was to ensure that offenders' needs, risk of reoffending, and any other factor that might affect their successful reintegration into the community are systematically identified upon admission to the federal system. The assessment process represents the latest generation of correctional assessment technology. Moreover, it aligns itself directly with the community version of an offender risk/needs assessment tool. The results of the offender intake assessment and community-based reassessments were incorporated into the nationwide computer-based Offender Management System.

Development and Design

Beginning at the commencement of the sentence, case managers coordinate the collection of all relevant information about offenders from sources within and outside the correctional service. This information forms the basis for all future decisions and recommendations that case managers must provide throughout the course of managing the offender's sentence. In addition to being the central figure in the front-end assessment process, case managers play a major role in correctional planning; supervising institutions; preparing cases for decision (parole board and release); and supervising individuals in the community.

Upon receiving a federal sentence (two years or more), the offender is interviewed by a case manager (parole officer). Whether the recently sentenced offender is at a local jail, or in a remand or detention facility, the case manager begins the intake-assessment process by orienting the offender to the federal correctional system. First, and foremost, case managers start with identifying any critical concerns (e.g., suicide, security, and health). Then, the case manager collects the offender's records from court, police, probation, forensic evaluation, and jail. Shortly thereafter, this information is transferred, along with the offender, to a federal institution, which has a specialized unit designated as the intake assessment unit.

Even after the offender has been transferred, a postsentence community investigation is initiated by a case manager located in the community from which the offender came. The postsentence community assessment report contains collateral sources of information. The report contains knowledge of the offender's relationship with significant others (e.g., family, employers), and the liklihood of their future contacts with the offender during incarceration or at the time of release, and the degree of support that others are prepared to offer to the offender upon the offender's return to the community. Moreover, collateral perceptions of the offender's needs are obtained in relation to employment, marital/family relations, substance abuse, and more.

Upon arrival at an intake assessment unit, the offender undergoes an admission interview and orientation session. During this period, the offender receives an initial assessment, which is a screen for concerns about immediate physical health needs, security (personal and safety of others), mental health, and suicide. At this stage of the assessment process, should any concerns arise, a psychological referral is made, followed by an appropriate intervention, if required.

After having passed through an initial assessment, the offender then proceeds to the two core components of the intake assessment process: (1) criminal risk assessment and (2) case needs identification and analysis. A rating of criminal risk for every federal offender is based on the following: the criminal history record, the offense severity record, the sex offense history checklist, whether detention criteria are met, the result of the statistical information on recidivism scale, and any other risk factors as detailed in a criminal profile report, which provides details of the crime(s) for which the offender is currently sentenced.

Implementation

In 1991, a national working group was assembled to design, develop, and implement a front-end assessment process. Because of its complexity and its decisive role in shaping the subsequent phases of the offender's sentence, the Offender Intake Assessment project has demanded a sizable investment of research energy and has continued to be a priority throughout its implementation.

Data Collected

The Correctional Service of Canada's new Case Needs Identification and Analysis protocol identifies seven need dimensions. These include: employment, marital/family, associates/social interaction, substance abuse, community functioning, personal/emotional orientation, and attitude. A list of indicators (about 200 in total) and rating guidelines are provided for each of the seven need dimensions. In rating each need area during assessment, the offender's entire background is considered. This includes personal characteristics, interpersonal influences, situational determinants, and environmental conditions.

Psychological evaluations, behavioral observations of the intake assessment unit staff, and supplementary assessments (e.g., education, substance abuse) are added to the intake assessment process. All of this case-based information then is brought together at a case conference, which is attended by a multidisciplinary intake assessment unit team. It is recognized that any consensus reached by the team about the offender's risk and needs should result in significant improvements in the predictive validity of the intake assessments.

The end product of this process is a summary report about the offender. This report contains, for each offender, a bottomline or overall risk/needs level ranging from low-risk/low-need to high-risk/high-need; a statement on each of the seven need areas ranging from "factor seen as an asset to community adjustment" to "considerable need for improvement;" a prioritization of needs; an estimate of motivation; a custody-rating designation ranging from minimum-, medium-, to maximum-security; a complete social history; and an institutional placement decision. This comprehensive and integrated assessment package serves as the basis for formulating a correctional plan for the offender.

Conclusion

In 1992-93, the Offender Intake Assessment process was piloted in all Correctional Service of Canada regions. On the basis of this trial exercise, refinements have been made, and work which began in 1993-94 has addressed the training of staff, the establishment of technological support, and data collection and analysis as a means of measuring correctional performance.

In 1994, the new assessment protocol was implemented in all regions. Since implementation, nearly 11,000 full offender-intake assessments have been completed and entered into the Offender Management System. Until recently, the situation existed where about one-half of the institutional population had comprehensive risk/need assessment information derived from the Offender Intake Assessment.

While this information is organized in a systematic fashion and available on the Offender Management System, to be able to profile the entire institution population would entail a case-by-case review of the existing population who have not undergone the new assessment process. Such an exercise was accomplished by means of a streamlined assessment process whereby the bottom-line risk/needs rating (criminal risk and case needs), a Statistical Information on Recidivism Scale-Revised (SIR-R1) score and ratings on each of the seven criminogenic need areas (employment, marital/family, associates, substance abuse, community functioning, personal/emotional, attitude) were made available on all offenders.

By having assessed the entire federal offender population upon admission in a comprehensive, integrated, and systematic fashion, the correctional service can forecast the growth of its prison population, monitor changes in composition, improve risk-management procedures, and measure correctional performance. This new technology should improve release rates by systematically identifying lower risk offenders earlier in their sentence, thereby reducing the costs of incarceration and providing a more humane response to offenders. Moreover, this approach also may bring about a reduced requirement for higher security. It also can yield useful information for evaluative purposes. This, in turn, has the potential to improve operations and reduce costs for the correctional service.

Faced with the correctional challenges of the late-1990s, the Correctional Service of Canada is able to assess offenders upon admission to correctional facilities in a comprehensive, integrated and systematic fashion and routinely reassess them thereafter. A nationwide computer-based structure for systematically collecting and integrating offender evaluations has been designed for conducting population forecasts and impact analyses. This will yield important information for strategic planning purposes. Finally, a fully automated offender-intake assessment and community-based reassessment process can improve the way correctional agencies manage risk.

Contact:

Larry Motiuk
Director General of Research Branch
Correctional Service of Canada

340 Laurier Avenue West
Ottawa, Ontario, Canada K1A 0P9
(613) 995-4694

Impact of Participation in Correctional Education Programs on Recidivism

Introduction

Interest in correctional education programs, particularly those at the postsecondary level, has been heightened by challenges to Pell grants for inmates on the federal level, and by the removal of instructional grants at the state level. The Ohio Department of Rehabilitation and Correction realized that a large-scale study of the impact of education programs on recidivism would be a valuable tool not only for meeting those challenges, but also for internal program modification. While previous studies indicated that the delivery of educational programs in prisons enrich the students and help in the management of prisons, this was the first report on the impact of state educational programs on recidivism.

Development and Design

The department's research team evaluated all offenders released from prison in fiscal year 1992, using information from several internal databases and inmate files. Educational achievement was defined as any of the following: the attainment of a vocational certificate; a GED; a high school diploma; or a certificate or degree from a college program during incarceration. Participation was defined as an official assignment to Adult Basic Education (ABE), vocational, GED, or a college program for ninety days or more. Recidivism was defined as a recommitment to the Ohio prison system within two years of release, either through a technical violation or a new sentence.

Implementation

The data that were collected included basic demographics, information about current conviction and sentence, the Test of Adult Basic Education (TABE) score at admission, program participation and achievement, and return to prison.

Major Findings

The report, "Evaluation of the Impact of Correctional Education Programs on Recidivism" indicated that involvement in an educational program in prison does appear to reduce recidivism slightly overall, and significantly among specific prison populations. While education could not be seen as a "magic bullet" that can reduce recidivism systemwide, it provides many benefits to the prison system, prisoners, and the society as a whole.

- Three-fourths of the new inmates received by the department each year are less serious offenders. The study shows that recidivism rates for this group are substantially lower if they achieve a vocational certificate or educational degree during their relatively short prison terms. In fiscal year 1995, there were 14,359 inmates admitted to the prison system with third and fourth degree determinate or fourth degree indeterminate sentences. The study indicates that the achievement of a certificate or degree had a substantial positive effect on this type of offender.

- At any given time, approximately two-thirds of the inmate population can be described as serious offenders. Recidivism rates for these serious offenders were substantially reduced if they participated in an educational program during their prison terms. While more serious offenders represent only about one-fourth of yearly intake, they make up approximately two-thirds of the inmate population on any given day. These offenders are incarcerated for longer periods of time. They "stack up" in numbers and are considered more dangerous than others.

- Female offenders involved in educational programs had a one-third lower return rate than those not involved. This finding remained true whether the prisoner completed or just participated in a program, and for every type of educational program examined by the study.

- Certain educational programs appeared to be well suited to distinct age groups. Adult Basic Education programs had a greater impact on older inmates. Vocational programs, general equivalency diplomas (GED), and college programming tended to have a more positive effect on younger inmates.

- For those who received a GED or college degree, the closer the achievement date was to the release date, the less likely the offender was to return to prison.

Since participation in educational programming is only one variable affecting recidivism, it cannot be seen as a complete solution to the problem. For example, sex offenders, as a group, tend to recidivate more often than others. For this and various other subgroups, participation in educational programming had a lesser impact.

Conclusion

The study was completed at a critical time for correctional education programs, in general, and college programs, in particular. As a result of the findings, the department made significant changes in its management of educational resources:

- Educational staff were increased at locations where less serious offenders were incarcerated, specifically at reception, minimum-security camps, and boot camps

- Policy changes were implemented to give priority in educational programming to inmates closest to release

- The department transferred the high school programs from a high-security facility to a lower-security institution. Educational programs available to female inmates were increased

- Contracts for evening ABE/GED programs and "mini" vocational programs were boosted

- Guidance and counseling staff were instructed to direct younger offenders toward appropriate educational programming.

The study enabled the department to make sound, empirically based decisions regarding the deployment of resources and to ensure the continued funding of effective educational programs.

Contact:

Tessa Unwin
Public Affairs Liaison
Ohio Department of Rehabilitation and Correction

1050 Freeway Drive North
Columbus, Ohio, 43229
(614) 752-1157

The Effect of Prison Work Experience, Vocational and Apprenticeship Training on Recidivism

Introduction

The Post-Release Employment Project (PREP) was designed to evaluate the impact of prison work experience and vocational training on offenders' behavior following their release to the community. The evaluation began in 1983 and data were collected through October 1987 on more than 7,000 offenders. Preliminary findings were reported in 1991, when all offenders in the study had been released to the community for at least one year. The present report looks at a much longer release horizon, covering ten years for many of the offenders. What follows reviews the study design and methodology, briefly lists the initial findings, and then provides greater detail on the long-term results.

Development and Design

Unlike most studies of prison vocational training or work experience, PREP was designed as a prospective longitudinal evaluation. Inmates were selected as study group members prior to their release if they had participated in industrial work within the institution setting or had received in-prison vocational instruction or apprenticeship training. Based on these criteria, 57 percent of the study group participants worked exclusively in prison industries, 19 percent had a combination of work experience and vocational training, and the remaining 24 percent had received either vocational or apprenticeship training, or a combination of the two.

Since it was not possible to assign inmates randomly to a study or control group, a quasi-experimental design was used in which comparison subjects were chosen from the "reservoir" of all other inmates released in the same calendar quarter as study group members. The nature of participation in industrial work and vocational training programs imposes a significant problem for this and other evaluations, which precludes the use of random assignment techniques. Instead, alternative techniques were relied on to control the potential bias resulting from the way in which participants were selected.

This is a common problem in evaluation studies and has been termed selection bias. Selection bias implies that there is a process which determines how people are selected (or self-selected) to participate in a particular program. It also implies there may be unique characteristics of the selected group that increase the probability of a successful outcome even in the absence of any program intervention.

To overcome this problem, a statistical matching procedure was adopted. It was developed by William G. Cochran and Donald B. Rubin and further refined by the latter and Paul R. Rosenbaum. The procedure is a two-step approach. In the first step, the researcher models the selection process, contrasting program participants and nonparticipants on variables related to their participation. As a result of the modeling, a "propensity score" is generated, indicating the likelihood that an offender would be selected for participation in prison industry or vocational training. In the second step, the propensity score is used in conjunction with other variables to select matched comparison subjects. Theoretically, the matched comparison subjects are equivalent to the study group participants in every respect, except for their participation in the work or vocational training program.

Previously Reported Findings

The findings from previous reports can be grouped into institutional adjustment, halfway house, and postrelease results. In terms of the first group, the PREP results demonstrated that inmates who participated in the work, vocational training, or apprenticeship programs, or a combination of these programs were less likely than comparison group members to have a misconduct report during their last year of incarceration. When program participants did receive a misconduct report, it was less likely to have been for serious misconduct. Program participants also were thought by their unit teams to be more responsible.

Many federal inmates are released to a halfway house rather than directly to supervision in their community. A halfway house provides a structured setting that allows an inmate to work in the community yet receive closer supervision than under ordinary postrelease supervision. Comparison subjects were just as likely as study group participants to complete their halfway house stay without committing misconduct, which would warrant their return to prison. Study group participants were 24 percent more likely than comparison subjects to obtain a full-time job or a day labor job at some point during their halfway house stay.

After inmates were released to the community, researchers gathered initial postrelease outcome data by calling supervising probation officers. In the U.S. federal criminal justice system, probation officers supervise and monitor offenders who receive sentences of probation, and offenders who receive prison sentences and are subsequently released to a term of supervision. Information was gathered on rearrest and supervision revocation, whether offenders were able to gain employment, and the legal wages they earned during the period. The offenders were followed for one year during their supervised release.

By the end of the year, 6.6 percent of the study group and 10.1 percent of the comparison group had been rearrested or had their supervision revoked. This was statistically significant. Furthermore, by the end of the year of supervision, 72 percent of the study group and 63 percent of the comparison group had found and maintained employment. This difference also achieved statistical significance. Finally, although not statistically significant, study group members who were working at the end of one year were earning, on average, $821 per month, while comparison subjects who were working were earning $769 per month.

Implementation

Although the initial results of the PREP project were encouraging, research staff were interested in whether the study-comparison group differences would hold up over a much longer time period. Although not able to reassess employment and earnings, the researchers were able to analyze recidivism among the study and comparison group members.

For this analysis, research staff culled the automated Bureau of Prisons' records to determine whether the study or comparison group participants had been recommitted to a federal facility for a new offense or had been returned due to a supervision-revocation violation. Most of the participants in this follow-up study had been released for at least eight years, some for as long as twelve years.

It was possible for offenders in this study to be convicted and committed for a state offense, a status that could not be recorded or evaluated using federal data exclusively. However, there is no theoretical reason to believe that offenders would be prosecuted and convicted contingent upon their status as study or comparison group members, thus introducing some unknown bias into the follow-up data.

Data Collected

The analysis examined the amount of time offenders were in the community prior to their recommitment. If industrial work experience and vocational training had a salutary effect, study group members should have spent a longer time in the community. The analysis was conducted on males and females as separate strata, since it is well known that women are less likely to recidivate than men. Confirming these expectations, the findings revealed that 19.3 percent of the women and 31.6 percent of the men followed for this study were recommitted within the follow-up period. When the survival times were compared for men and women who were recommitted, on average, men had a much longer survival time (811 days) than women (647 days). Thus, although fewer women were likely to fail, those who did failed much earlier than their male counterparts. This may have some interesting implications for the design of men's and women's programs.

The study group participants were divided into three subgroups representing participation in prison industries exclusively (57 percent), training programs—vocational and apprenticeship (24 percent), and participation in both prison industries and training programs (19 percent).

There were two different recidivism measures that could be culled from the automated records—recommitment based upon a new offense or recommitment based upon a supervision revocation. Several analyses were conducted that examined the different program effects for men and women separately and which analyzed the program effect with respect to the different recidivism measures.

Conclusion

For males, there were significant program effects when recidivism was defined as a recommitment based upon a new offense. Specifically, men employed in prison industries improved their probability of survival by 20 percent over comparison group members. Furthermore, men completing vocational or apprenticeship training improved their probability of survival by 28 percent relative to comparison members. Although the effects for men who participated in both work and training programs did not reach statistical significance, the results indicated that the effect was consistent with the other two program groups. It is likely that this latter group did not reach statistical significance because it was a relatively small group of participants. When recidivism was defined as recommitment for a new offense or supervision revocation, there were no program effects for men.

For women, as with men, the training did not increase their survival probability in the community when the outcome was defined as either a revocation or a new offense combined. However, contrary to the finding for men, the training did not increase women's probability of survival in the community when the outcome was defined as commission of a new offense only. Although the effect of vocational and apprenticeship training was in the desired direction, it did not achieve statistical significance due to the small number of study group women involved in this type of training.

The inability to find any program effect may be related to the small number of women in this research study who were recommitted for a new offense (only 52 women out of 913, or about 6 percent, during the eight-to-twelve-year follow up). The method of analysis that was used is designed to summarize the influence of individual characteristics or experiences on failure rates (i.e., recommitments). However, of the women in this study, 94 percent did not fail; consequently, there is little information for the statistical procedure to analyze. The method does not provide any information about the study and comparison group members who did not fail (virtually all of the women in this research study). Further analysis of the women is required to understand any differences that may exist between the study and comparison groups. Additional analysis also may require the collection of additional outcome measures (for example, related to employment). It is plausible that while the training does not make any difference in the rate of recommitments, because of the small incidence of recommitments among women in general, the training could have significant effects that are not detected by the particular outcome measures and statistical methods used in this analysis.

In summary, it appears that the impact of in-prison employment in an industrial work setting and vocational or apprenticeship training can have both short- and long-term effects reducing the likelihood of recidivism, especially for men. Although the program effects do not seem to have an impact on supervision revocations in the long term, they have an important impact on recommitment for new offenses. On average, offenders who receive new sentences will spend a much longer time in prison than those who only have their supervision revoked. Thus, in-prison work and training programs could have a benefit in reducing prison populations due to recidivism.

Contact:

William G. Saylor
Deputy Chief
Office of Research and Evaluation Federal Bureau of Prisons

320 First Street, NW
Washington, D.C. 20534
(202) 307-3871

Evaluation of Drug Testing for Parolees

Introduction

The California Department of the Youth Authority recently completed a four-year, experimental study of drug testing for youthful offenders released to parole. The intent of this study was to determine how much drug testing should be part of regular parole supervision—that is, carried out by parole agents in the context of their regular duties with no reduction in caseload size and no access to additional outside resources, such as testing facilities.

Development and Design

The study was designed to assess differences in outcome for comparable groups that differed in the amount of drug testing but not in other aspects of supervision. The levels were chosen to provide a reasonable range of possible drug-testing frequencies, from "no testing" up to two tests per month. Of primary interest were the crime-reduction, or public safety, benefits of these drug testing levels: reduced criminal behavior and increases in the number successfully completing parole.

Drug use is believed to contribute to criminal behavior, both directly and indirectly, and to hinder the establishment of prosocial relationships and lifestyles. Reduced drug use is thought to lead to a reduction in criminal behavior. Drug testing is believed to reduce drug use among offenders through deterrence and detection. The threat of detection through drug testing may deter offenders from using drugs. For offenders who are not deterred, drug testing aids in the detection of substance abuse, and sets the stage for treatment or sanctions, which may reduce drug use directly and/or bolster future deterrence.

Implementation

The analysis of descriptive data across groups, drug-test information, and supervision levels suggests that the study was implemented as designed. In fact, the study was an overwhelming success, and stands as one of the few successful large-scale experimental studies of correctional interventions.

Parolees were accepted into the study based upon preestablished eligibility criteria. These criteria excluded only those parolees for whom the policies regarding routine drug testing would not apply (e.g., parolees who were participating in special programs or residing in rural areas). No evidence of a breakdown in the sampling procedure, intentional or otherwise, was found, and the number of those eligible actually exceeded the estimated proportion of total parole releases. A total of 1,958 parolees was included in the study.

Group assignments were based on a computerized random assignment procedure that placed parolees in each of the five testing conditions based on predetermined probabilities. Testing levels included no-testing, one test every two months, one test per month, and two tests per month. During the initial three-month period (reentry), the testing levels were enhanced to twice that level, consistent with other aspects of supervision. During this period, one of the no-test groups was tested once every two months.

The goal of the random assignment was to establish groups that were similar in all major respects, thereby minimizing the likelihood that preexisting group differences would affect outcomes. Comparisons across groups on important background characteristics identified no significant differences, and led to the conclusion that the groups were essentially equivalent. This similarity meant that any differences in outcome among the groups could be attributed to differences in the experiences of the parolees in the groups after entering the study.

The groups were tested at different levels throughout parole, although the magnitude of the differences was less than anticipated from the design. The "no testing" group actually turned out to be a "minimal testing" group, with about one in twelve of the parolees tested each month. The high-test group was tested less than once per month, on average, during the period following reentry (case management). Further, there was a considerable amount of variation in testing within groups. However, differences in overall testing levels were statistically significant. In addition, analysis of testing for each month of parole indicated that differences did not erode appreciably over time—that is, the groups were tested at different levels throughout the offenders' period of parole.

Audits and interviews with parole agents suggested that the failure to reach and maintain anticipated levels had more to do with the practical difficulties of maintaining particular, predefined testing levels than it did with good faith efforts to comply with the study protocol. They seemed to reflect, for the most part, a good faith effort to comply with difficult expectations that ran counter to normal casework decision making (e.g., not being able to test Group 1 parolees suspected of drug use and not being able to reward parolees who refrain from drug use by reducing the amount of testing).

Other aspects of supervision, such as the number of contacts, did not differ across groups. Data on supervision levels and numbers of face-to-face contacts revealed no tendency to vary other aspects of supervision to accommodate the different testing levels. The only aspect of parole that differed across groups was the amount of drug testing.

The groups can be thought of as representing clusters of drug-testing policies involving overall investments in drug testing. Within each group (policy), some were tested more than others, and some parole agents were more diligent and consistent than others at following the policy. The policies can be compared in terms of the outcomes for the parolees in the groups.

Data Collected

The comparisons of parole outcomes (that is, types of removal from parole) indicated no overall differences across groups in level of "adjustment:"

Good adjustment (on parole at twenty-four months or discharged for reasons other than a parole violation);

Marginal adjustment (missing, dishonorably discharged, or revoked for a technical violation of parole); or

Poor adjustment (removed from parole because of criminal behavior or incarcerated for an arrest at twenty-four months).

There was a slight tendency for the groups with more frequent testing to have fewer cases remaining on parole and, therefore, to have a lower proportion with "good" adjustment.

An analysis of arrests showed no reduction for the higher test groups in the average numbers of arrests or the proportions of each group with any arrests. There was a slight tendency for arrests to be higher for groups with more testing during the parole period and over a full twenty-four months (which may have extended beyond the parole period). These differences were found to be statistically significant at forty-two months.

The analyses of parole handling of positive tests indicated that the lack of a positive relationship between drug-testing levels and parole adjustment or criminal behavior could not be attributed simply to a failure to use the drug-testing information in accordance with the model of change (deterrence/detection). Parole agents paid attention to the drug test results, considered the results when making casework decisions about parolees, and responded to positive tests with increased sanctions and increased drug treatment. As testing levels increased, more parolees were identified as drug users, and this information was used by agents, who applied both sanctions and treatment in an effort to reduce the substance-abuse problem.

Parole agents did not rely solely on the drug-testing information for identifying and assessing substance-abuse problems among parolees, however. The agents identified some parolees as needing treatment despite having no positive tests. They also determined that some parolees who did have positive tests did not have a substance-abuse problem that interfered with their functioning enough to warrant service.

Exploratory analyses focused on the potential value of drug testing for identifying parolees who pose a greater risk to public safety. Positive drug tests during the first three months of parole (reentry) were found to indicate higher levels of arrest over the follow-up period up to forty-two months. These results suggest that drug testing might be used as a risk-assessment tool to identify parolees who demonstrate their higher criminal propensity by submitting positive urine samples early during parole.

Conclusion

The data did not permit an assessment of the impact of drug-testing differences on drug use, but it did permit an assessment of these differences on criminal behavior. Parolees tested at higher levels did not perform better on parole or afterward. If anything, the differences were in the opposite direction: over the longer follow-up periods, parolees at higher-testing levels performed more poorly. At the very least, there was no evidence that higher levels of drug testing led to a greater positive impact on public safety than testing at lower levels.

Based on the results of this study, the general answer to the question of how much drug testing to include as part of routine parole supervision would be minimal surprise testing, but perhaps regular, frequent testing during the first three months of parole (reentry). This recommendation is based on the general results of the study and on results of various specific analyses. It also is based on insights regarding drug testing that were gained through interviews with agents and the experiences associated with implementing the study.

This recommendation, however, does not imply that drug use by parolees should no longer be considered a problem. The present study did not address whether drug use information was important or whether attending to the substance-abuse problems of parolees had any effect.

Minimal Drug Testing

The outcome comparisons showed no public safety benefit associated with levels of testing beyond that which was given to the no-test groups. From a public safety perspective, therefore, there is little justification for testing beyond a minimum level. Because some testing went on for these no-test groups, the study cannot, technically, permit conclusions about a true no-test condition. Further, because all of the parolees in this study were subject to testing (whether tested or not), the threat of testing must be included in any recommendation following from the results. For that threat to be credible, however, there must be some testing occurring.

By keeping drug testing at a minimum, the agency can avoid unnecessary costs associated with drug testing. The agency also can avoid other opportunity costs associated with the potential overreliance on drug testing: agent/parolee relationships that favor control at the expense of service and support and which are structured around a failure-oriented, relatively distasteful activity.

To the extent that agents are expected to monitor the drug-use behavior of their parolees, other monitoring methods would have to be used to a greater extent. The results of the process analysis, noted previously, suggest that such methods are available and are being used in lieu of, or in combination with, drug tests. Agencies also may have to rely on other methods of documenting the need for intervention with parolees or monitoring the progress of parolees, and evaluating the job performance of parole agents.

Drug Testing During Reentry

While the findings suggest little public safety benefit for testing above a minimum level, the predictive value of early drug use on parole suggests the potential value of regular, fairly frequent drug testing during the reentry period. The lack of a good understanding of what to do with parolees who test positive early, however, along with the tendency for parolees to go AWOL after submitting a positive test, suggests a certain caution in this regard.

Offenders testing positive in the first three months of parole were much more likely to be arrested during parole and later, indicating that an early positive test is a good indicator of increased risk for subsequent criminal behavior. Parolees testing positive only after the first three months were no different from parolees who never tested positive. This finding suggests that a positive drug test early in parole is a powerful indicator of criminal propensity and that regular, frequent drug testing can provide a relatively straightforward risk-assessment procedure.

A note of caution is called for, however. In the first place, it is not at all clear what should be done with parolees who demonstrate their higher-than-average criminal propensity through testing positive early in parole. There is no research to suggest how best to reduce the future danger posed by these parolees. While it may be tempting to respond to these parolees with increased incarceration (to protect the public for as long as possible) or to require intensive drug treatment (to try to reduce whatever influence drug use may have on their behavior), it was common for parolees to be "missing" after submitting a positive test. If "missing" was in anticipation of the possible consequences of getting caught using drugs, increasing the sanctions or the treatment associated with positive tests could exacerbate this problem. Parole agents may lose whatever influence they have with such parolees, and the parolees may become even more unstable and irresponsible. In short, "getting tough" with these parolees may create unanticipated consequences, resulting in bigger problems than drug use.

While drug testing appears to have some utility for identifying parolees with higher future arrest rates, the benefits of increased testing for this purpose are not clear. A better understanding of how to respond effectively to this indicator of criminal propensity without, literally, scaring the parolees off is required.

Contact:

Michael Gallegos
Deputy Director
Parole Services and Community Corrections
California Department of the Youth Authority

4241 Williamsbourgh Drive
Sacramento, California 95823
(916) 262-1363

Research
Additional Program Entries

Criminal Career Profile: A Qualitative Index of Criminal Violence

Steve Wong, Director of Research
Correctional Service of Canada, Regional Psychiatric Centre (Prairies)
P.O. Box 9243, Saskatoon, Saskatchewan, Canada S7K 3X5
(306) 975-5400

Research has found that a key predictor of future violence is the extent of past violence. To predict future violent behaviors, it is essential that reliable and valid measures of past violence be identified. The "Criminal Career Profile (CCP)" examines a graphical representation of the amount of time spent incarcerated and not incarcerated since the offender's age at first conviction. The authors suggest that the Criminal Career Profile is useful in clinical risk assessments, criminal justice research, and program evaluation.

Validation of the Pennsylvania Addictive Classification Screening Instrument

William Harrison, Director of the Bureau of Inmate Services
Pennsylvania Department of Correction, Box 598, Camp Hill, Pennsylvania 17001-0598
(717) 730-2707

This study validated the Pennsylvania Department of Corrections Screening Instrument (PACSI) by comparing scores on 120 new prison admissions with two other validated screening tools measuring substance dependence. The PACSI was found to correlate highly with other known measures and is now used to screen inmates for drug and alcohol abuse upon intake.

Residential Facilities for Juvenile Offenders

Daniel Storkamp, Director of the Office of Planning and Research
Minnesota Department of Corrections, Suite 200, 1450 Energy Park Dr., St. Paul,
Minnesota 55108-5219
(612) 603-0194

This research on juvenile offenders, mandated by the state's legislature, was the first systematic study of juvenile recidivism rates in Minnesota using statewide court and law enforcement data. The Minnesota Legislative Auditor's Office analyzed rearrest rates for 1,472 offenders released from selected residential facilities in 1991 (this included state, county, and private facilities). Surveys also were conducted to collect the perceptions of county supervisors and social service directors concerning juvenile residential facilities. The study highlighted the need for offender-tracking systems and ongoing evaluation of programs and facilities. Data from this study is being used by the legislature in weighing decisions to close or privatize some of the facilities and to determine additional research needs.

Restorative Justice

15

Introduction

Considered by many justice practitioners and community activists as a "new" approach to dealing with crime and delinquency, restorative justice is, in reality, an age-old concept deeply rooted in both biblical and ancient African cultures. The Code of Hammurabi (c. 1700 B.C.) included victim restitution among its many tenets. The concept of a village being damaged by the detrimental actions of one of its members against another is deeply imbedded in early African mores.

Restorative justice is emerging "back to the future" in America today. Beginning in the late 1970s, programs that focused on offender accountability and repairing harm to both the victim and community emerged, first in the form of victim/offender mediation in Elkhart, Indiana. The increasing power and expanding voice of our nation's victim advocacy movement has made both victim involvement and offender accountability key goals that can be reached through restorative justice approaches. And communities' frustrations with crime, delinquency, and soaring recidivism rates are leading their members to become part of the solution, instead of merely critics of the problem.

Seven guiding principles of restorative justice were identified by panelists at a national teleconference sponsored by the National Institute of Justice in December, 1996:

1. Crime is an offense against human relationships.

2. Victims and the community are central to justice processes.

3. The first priority of the justice process is to assist victims.

4. The second priority is to restore the community, to the degree possible.

5. The offender has personal responsibility to victims and to the community for crimes committed.

6. The offender will develop improved competency and understanding as a result of the restorative justice experience.

7. Stakeholders share responsibility for restorative justice through partnerships for action.

In considering these guiding principles, one thing is clear: restorative justice principles and practices offer a markedly different approach to crime, delinquency, community protection, and victim assistance than our historical and current approaches to justice practices. As America seeks to balance the rights and interests of victims, offenders, and the community in systemic and consistent ways, time and experience will tell if restorative justice is the viable solution that is needed to address the root problems of crime and delinquency today.

There are several challenges to restorative justice proponents and practitioners:

- While community involvement is integral to the success of restorative justice, it is difficult to come by in some regions. "Communities" must be defined by the persons who comprise them, not merely by geography. Individuals who have isolated themselves behind alarm systems, security bars, and locked doors must be coaxed out to assume their rightful ownership of justice.

- For some offenders, accountability is much more difficult than retributive punishment. Taking responsibility for wrongdoing and making amends for harm caused can make incarceration or detention seem like the easier alternative.

- Accustomed to being left out of the development of programs and policies that directly affect them, crime victims may be rightfully suspect of restorative justice approaches. Victims and their advocates must be involved in every step of planning and implementing restorative justice protocols and programs.

- Justice practitioners must be willing to share power with key justice stakeholders, chief among them the members of the community.

- Systematic program evaluation is lacking, although early research shows tremendous promise. What are presented in this paper as "best practices" should, in reality, be considered "promising practices" until thorough evaluations are conducted for each innovative approach.

Restorative Justice in Corrections: Measuring Success

The effectiveness of any correctional program should be judged in the same way the effectiveness of any product or service is judged. Cost, or even results, taken alone are never enough to truly gauge the efficiency or quality of a program, product, or service. The cost of achieving the desired outcome without creating a new cost or problem is the way customers intuitively judge what is the best value for their investment.

In judging restorative justice programs, a variety of measures to evaluate performance should be considered:

Decrease in the offender's harmful acts (recidivism)

To be judged successful, a restorative justice program should be able to document a reduction in the likelihood that an offender again will cause harm. This can be thought of as a measure of decreased recidivism. Conviction on a new charge is a most narrow indicator of crime and, therefore, harm. Broader indicators, such as rearrest, parole violations, absconding from parole, and even death in the commission of a crime are more useful in refining measures to indicate that the offender is continuing in harmful behavior patterns. The longer the period in which these behaviors are tracked, the more compelling the performance measure becomes.

Decrease in criminogenic risks

To be judged successful, a restorative justice program should be able to document that, using a dynamic risk-assessment instrument, reduces the risk that an offender will engage in criminal, delinquent and/or harmful behaviors. Objective, dynamic-risk instruments assess the level of criminal risk posed by offenders, even if the offenders have had no formal encounter with law enforcement or the court system. Measuring the risk before, and tracking the change in that risk over time, is one indicator that the program has reduced the probability that the offender will again cause harm.

Increase in victim satisfaction and involvement with the justice/corrections processes

To be judged successful, a restorative justice program should be able to document that the program increases victim satisfaction with the justice and/or corrections system. For any restorative justice process to engender the political support to continue, the stakeholders must see it as having value for the key consumers of the service, chief among them—victims. Surveying victims to assess their satisfaction level and involvement is a key way to measure success.

Increase in community satisfaction and involvement with the justice/corrections process

To be judged successful, a restorative justice program should be able to document that it increases the community's satisfaction and involvement with the justice and/or corrections system. As with victim satisfaction, community approval of this inclusive justice/corrections strategy is critical to the political and functional viability of the process.

Increase in offender accountability and competency development

These two core tenets of restorative justice provide appropriate measures of program success. Increases in victim restitution and community service hours performed highlight increases in accountability. Similarly, the number of offenders who learn something positive through their participation in justice processes—through programs such as victim/offender mediation, community service, mentoring, victim awareness classes, family group conferencing, and myriad treatment modalities—point to measures that can pave the path to productive, law-abiding lives for offenders.

Cost effectiveness

To be judged successful, a restorative justice program must be able to document that, under clearly defined circumstances, the program is the best value when compared to traditional retributive strategies. Defining the circumstances (e.g., type of offender, circumstances of the harm to victims and community, resources available, and scope of the program) is critical to obtain a measure of best value. The program then must be able to show that retributive and more traditional justice/corrections protocols are either less effective or more costly for their target group. A restorative justice protocol that can show that it lowers the chance of crime, delinquency, and/or harm over the long term should factor in the costs of the program over an offender's lifetime and compare that to the lifetime costs and crime costs of offenders receiving other sanctions. The soaring costs of crime to victims and society that are reduced by restorative justice approaches are also appropriate measures of cost effectiveness.

Best Practices

The American Correctional Association's Restorative Justice Committee has identified four programs that it considers to be "promising practices" for other jurisdictions to replicate. These include the comprehensive policies and programs implemented by the Dakota County, Minnesota Community Corrections Department; the "Impact of Crime on Victims" classes/panels initiated by the California Department of the Youth Authority that have been replicated in more than twenty states; the Community Reparative Boards sponsored by the Vermont Department of Corrections; and the vision statement and programs adopted by the Minnesota Correctional Facility for Women at Shakopee. These innovative restorative justice approaches involve both institutional and community corrections, and adult and juvenile corrections.

Committee chair:

Anne Seymour
Consultant

746 9th Street, SE
Washington, D.C. 20003
(202) 547-1732

A Comprehensive Restorative Justice Model

Background

Dakota County, Minnesota, consists of the first ring of suburbs south of Minneapolis and St. Paul. Its population is approximately 340,000, and it is among the fastest-growing areas in the Midwest. The county is comprised of urban, suburban, and rural communities, and stretches over a large geographic area. Its Community Corrections Department is operated through the elected county board (seven commissioners). The services include juvenile and adult probation/parole, juvenile institutions (secure and nonsecure), and adult alternatives to jail. Staff and volunteers in the department annually supervise approximately 12,000 individuals.

Development and Design

Through a technical assistance grant from the federal Office of Juvenile Justice and Delinquency Prevention, Dakota County became one of three pilot sites selected to examine and implement the Balanced Approach to Restorative Justice. The project began in 1992 and is ongoing, although no additional technical assistance is being provided. Most of the following program enhancements are a direct result of the Office of Juvenile Justice and Delinquency Prevention's assistance, and the work of a progressive slate of elected officials (the county board, judges, the county attorney, and the sheriff).

Implementation

To be effective and consistent, it is imperative that the department adopt a singular conceptual framework to mold current and future practice. Through the Balanced Approach to Restorative Justice project, this framework took on a restorative-justice foundation. The following were some of the action steps taken to create a single-minded restorative justice approach to how the department addresses crime and delinquency.

Mission and Subsequent Administrative Steps

Upon examining restorative justice principles, it soon became apparent that the existing department mission needed to be changed. A year-long planning process ensued, which included the creation of a staff planning team, surveys of primary stakeholders, and a survey of 700 citizens. Most controversial was the role the department was to take with victims of crime. After much input and discussion, the following mission statement was adopted:

> We are committed to preventing crime and repairing harm caused by crime. We promote: public safety and crime prevention in the community; accountability and opportunity for positive change of the offender; justice for the victims; and, respectful treatment for all involved.

Vision and Action Plan: From the mission statement came a planning process for developing a compelling vision. Approximately 50 percent of the staff participated in the formation of a vision that provided a direction for the department's future. The net result was a specific twenty-one point action plan. Many of the program and policy changes noted emerged from this plan.

Training and Orientation: For the department to carry out the vision, all staff needed to be provided with orientation and ongoing training. To promote this, the department hired a training coordinator whose responsibility includes the facilitation of staff development and the development of orientation plans consistent with the department's initiatives.

Job Descriptions and Performance Evaluation: Staff job descriptions and performance-evaluation measures needed to be changed to reflect new expectations. Some of these have been accomplished, with the rest targeted for the end of 1998.

Outcome Measures: If "organizations are what they measure," then outcome measures must change to reflect new expectations. Perhaps of most importance, the mission clarified that the department had three customers (not just the traditional offender): the victim, the offender, and the community. Specific outcomes are sought for each customer. The department's information system does not even have data fields on two of the customers (the victim and the community). New measurements now have been identified, and steps are being taken to accommodate collection of these data.

Victim-centered Programs and Practices

The following are actions taken to promote the objective of repairing harm caused to victims, providing victims with input into decision making, and improving victim satisfaction with the justice process.

Victim-offender Meetings (Face-To-Face): This is a program whereby the victim is given the opportunity to meet with the offender face-to-face to express emotions, get questions answered, hold the offender accountable, and determine the amount and method of restitution payment (financially and otherwise).

Crime Repair Crew: This is a service to victims whereby individuals (or their representatives, such as an advocate or police officer) can call for assistance in repairing property damage caused by crime. A supervised crew of lower-risk offenders will repair the damage within twenty-four to forty-eight hours at no charge to the victim.

Victim Impact Panels: A panel of victims, usually from drunk-driving crashes, tell their stories to a group of offenders. They describe the personal impact an offense had on them and others. It provides victims with an opportunity to express themselves and gives them a positive outlet for an otherwise tragic event. For offenders, it is designed to help them understand the consequences of their actions, and to increase their empathy for others.

Youth Repay Crews: Since many offenders are unemployed or underemployed, or do not hold a regular job (such as a young juvenile offender), repay crews offer an opportunity for them to earn money for restitution. These crews are comprised of offenders who are responsible for restitution but have no financial means to make payment. For every hour they work, $5.00 is designated to their restitution account. The funds come from a sentencing system, whereby the courts order payment to the fund by those youthful offenders who have the means to pay.

Enhanced Restitution Collection Procedures: The Restitution program consists of staff who create procedures and policies to improve the collection of funds. The staff serve in a supportive role to the probation officers who need to ensure that payment is made. Several examples of techniques to improve restitution collection include a policy that restitution is to be disbursed before other financial obligations (such as fines, surcharges, and/or fees); use of garnishment and wage assignments; use of credit cards; use of revenue recapture methods; and the use of billing procedures.

Victim Restoration Program and Hotline: A specific Victim Restoration program unit was established to reduce the frustration victims often face in obtaining information, and in providing a more focused attention to victims. Among other functions, the staff provide a hotline service through which a victim can call one phone number, and a staff member will track down the information and persons needed to take action and bring about a speedy resolution of the matter.

Offender-centered Programs and Practices

The following actions are taken to promote the objective of holding offenders directly accountable to the victim and the community that they harmed, and improving their positive competencies.

Cognitive/Behavioral Programming: New assessment tools identify the criminogenic needs of the offenders and provide targeted intervention to address those needs. Successful application of cognitive programming nationally has reduced recidivism by 25 to 50 percent, on average. Locally, offenders are meeting in groups of ten to twelve with trained facilitators, and complete a curriculum of cognitive-skills training.

Restorative Case Plans: The department objectives include more than public safety or recidivism reduction. Sometimes, however, other objectives can be diminished as these goals are emphasized. To be balanced and comprehensive, the department has begun to develop case plans where each customer (victim, offender, and community) and the restorative goals are given equal attention and importance.

Intensive Supervision: Serious offenders coming out of prison need special and intensive attention due to their risk of harming the public. Two probation officers are assigned small caseloads of fifteen offenders each to provide heightened surveillance and monitoring services.

Reintegrative Community Work Service: Although community-work service projects provide valuable opportunities for offenders to contribute to the well-being of their communities, the sheer number of offenders limit the department's ability to assess and individualize these placements. Through an innovative grant, the department is embarking on a new project of also using community-work service for revenue purposes. The revenue will be used, in part, to provide the department with the opportunity to place certain offenders on projects that are more restorative in nature.

Specialized Programming: If the department is to be able to provide offenders with the tools they need to be successful in society, its approaches need to be individualized. Not all offenders are alike, and their needs require a flexible, individualized response. The department has created a number of specialized programs to deal with the varied needs of the offenders, some of which include sex offender programs; a domestic violence program; New Chance nonresidential; Youth Challenge motivational programming; Safe Streets First program for repeat drunk drivers; youth Wrap Around Services; School Success; and the extensive use of intermediate sanctions, such as electronic home monitoring, Jobs Not Jail, and Sentenced To Service work crews.

Community Centered Programs and Practices

The following actions are taken to promote the objective of directly involving the community in addressing and preventing crime.

Family Group Conferencing: Conferencing is a form of youth diversion whereby the local community representative and victim meet with the offender in a face-to-face setting, along with a trained facilitator and a law enforcement staffer. The victim and community representative describe how the offense affected them, and an accountability plan is developed. In most cases, the community provides the monitoring function to ensure that the offender completes the agreed-upon conditions.

Volunteer Program: The department is involved in recruiting, screening, training, and providing placement services for more than 100 volunteers and interns who provide direct victim/offender services.

Law Enforcement Partnerships: Efforts are underway to improve information sharing and collaboration between the department and law enforcement. In one project (Operation Network), community corrections is providing the Apple Valley Police Department with computerized information that includes: names, addresses, sentencing conditions, and special concerns for law enforcement officers. This report is updated monthly. Law enforcement and community corrections staff meet monthly to discuss the report and specific cases. The department also meets with law enforcement and the community to notify local communities when a dangerous sex offender is released from prison.

School-based Probation: To move probation officers out of the office and into the community, a pilot project has begun that houses juvenile probation officers in local schools to assist the schools in handling probationers in a more timely fashion.

Community and Volunteer Involvement in Policy Development: The department has two policy committees composed of justice system personnel and community members to assist in the development of policies. They are the Community Corrections Advisory Board and the Victims Committee.

Conclusion

It is important to note that there are now examples of justice processes that move beyond an offender-centered approach to one that is inclusive of victims and the community. Such an approach, ironically, helps the offender, as well.

Author:

Mark Carry
Community Corrections Director
Dakota County Community Corrections
Hastings, Minnesota

Contact:

Tom Adkins
Deputy Director
Dakota County Community Corrections

Judicial Center
1560 West Highway 55
Hastings, Minnesota 55035
(612) 552-3065

Impact of Crime on Victims Classes/Panels for Offenders

Background

In 1984, the California Department of the Youth Authority implemented an innovative educational strategy that stressed the impact of offenders' crimes on victims. As a recognized leader in the movement to bring victims into the correctional arena, the Youth Authority used this unique relationship to develop one of the most powerful programs for juvenile offenders—Victim Impact Classes/Panels for Offenders. The Victim Impact Classes/Panels for Offenders program, which is currently operating in all Youth Authority facilities, brings courageous victims and/or survivors of crime into the institutions, camps, and parole offices to share their personal tragedies and thereby educate offenders about the emotional, psychological, physical, and financial impact of their victimization.

Development and Design

In the early 1980s, a core group of Youth Authority staff asserted that traditional models of offender programming were ineffective in curbing delinquent behavior. Program developers claimed that youth service workers had "missed the boat." Their premise was that it was not enough to teach offenders to read or to become welders if they returned to the community with no respect for other people's bodies or property. They claimed that a full-service youth program must address what an offender has *done*, just as vigorously as it addresses what they *need*.

The primary goal of the Victim Impact Classes/Panels for Offenders program, as developed by this core group, was to prevent further victimization by creating offender awareness of the impact that crime has on victims, families, and the community. The program was structured to hold juvenile offenders accountable by stressing their personal responsibility for the human consequences of their crimes, and to develop both cognitive and emotional empathy toward crime victims.

The literature suggests that empathy is a key factor in the development and understanding of aggressive behavior. Children who possess little or no empathy often engage in violent and aggressive tendencies. Low levels of empathy lead to the inability to understand another's feelings. This has stimulated additional research showing that children with aggressive tendencies tend to commit acts of violence against innocent victims that may lead to involvement in the juvenile justice system.

Many researchers have proposed that empathy is a skill that can be learned. Studies suggest that empathy can be learned at a young age, and then further developed by training.

If it is true that offenders incarcerated with the Youth Authority have low levels of empathy, and that empathy can be increased or improved through training, then a program that stresses the impact of crime on victims might increase levels of empathy and decrease the percentage of violent and personal offenses committed by youthful offenders in the future.

The challenge of empathy development in youthful offenders is addressed in the two primary components of the Victim Impact Classes/Panels for Offenders program: the educational curriculum and the victim speakers.

Youthful offenders enrolled in the Victim Impact Classes/Panels for Offenders are taught by Youth Authority instructors and guest lecturers. These instructors receive a minimum of forty hours of intensive training, and annually forty hours of refresher training to develop and enhance the unique knowledge and skills needed to teach this powerful curriculum. The program consists of thirty-five to sixty hours of an experiential curriculum over a period of six-to-twelve weeks.

The topic areas that are covered include property crimes, domestic violence, crimes against the elderly, child abuse, sexual assault, assault, robbery, drunk driving deaths and injuries, drug dealing, victims of gang violence, and homicides. The course begins with property crimes and moves through other crimes, with homicides as the final chapter. The order allows for the establishment of adequate understanding and rapport before entering the more sensitive areas of the program.

Each part of the curriculum includes readings, audiovisual presentations, and interactive teaching strategies to engage the offenders in cognitive and emotional contact with the consequences of their criminal actions, particularly the consequences paid by the victims. Crime-specific chapters include information about the crime, the accountability statement, the impact on victims, and sources of help.

There is no better way to impress upon offenders the human consequences of their criminal actions than to personalize and humanize the crime by bringing an actual crime victim face-to-face with youthful offenders in the classroom. The guest-speakers' component is undoubtedly the most important and powerful aspect of the Victim Impact Classes/Panels for Offenders.

In observing a Victim Impact/Panels for Offenders class, one first notes the serious and somber tone. When a victim presenter speaks, every word weighs heavily on those witnessing the presentation. It is an unusual quiet that lasts sometimes much longer than the actual class period. Eyes are fixed on the presenter and, often, offenders can be seen fighting back tears that are both inevitable and appropriate. During these powerful moments, empathic thoughts and feelings become evident as the youth ask questions or discuss their concerns about what happened to the speaker. In addition to crime victims often representing such groups as Mothers Against Drunk Driving and Parents of Murdered Children, victim advocates from child abuse, rape crisis, and domestic violence programs also participate in the program.

Implementation

The Victim Impact/Panels for Offenders classes are incorporated into the institution education section and taught by credentialed academic instructors in the majority of Youth Authority facilities. The program is structured as "education" versus "therapy." The boundary between education and therapy often is blurred when dealing with a topic with such rich emotional impact. However, its placement in the educational arena provided access to skilled instructors to teach the educational curriculum and facilitate the emotionally laden guest-speakers' presentations. Trained Victim Impact Classes/Panels for Offenders instructors develop close working relationships with treatment counselors and professional staff to provide individual treatment services, as needed, to offenders participating in the program.

A typical Victim Impact/Panels for Offenders class consists of fifteen to twenty offenders facilitated by one trained instructor in sessions lasting one to two hours. The program objectives are to:

- Prevent further victimization

- Create offender awareness of the impact that crime has on victims, families, and the community

- Teach positive decision-making skills

Offenders are selected for participation in the program in one of three ways. Their participation may be mandated by the agency's paroling authority, the Youthful Offender Parole Board. The offender may be recommended by the offender's treatment team. Finally, the offender may volunteer. The Victim Impact Classes/Panels for Offenders program is a very popular program for offenders. Filling-up class space is never a problem or issue.

Program Evaluation

There has been limited research on the relationship between offender participation in victim awareness educational programming and an offender's subsequent criminal behavior. A formal evaluation was conducted by the Washington Department of Corrections that assessed the effect of its victim awareness program (modeled after the California Youth Authority program) on offender reoffense rates and offender payment of restitution obligations. This was a single component study that only measured data associated with completion of the program against nonparticipation. Although not totally conclusive, the study did show that the reoffense rate and payment of victim restitution obligations of those offenders who successfully completed the program were positively affected. Overall, these offenders were less likely to reoffend, and were likely to fulfill their restitution obligations. An additional benefit of the program, as noted by the Washington study, was the participation of victims and victim advocates in the course. Victim participation provided victims with a sense that they were positively affecting the accountability of the offender, and reducing further victimization.

The results of a cognitive empathy study comparing an experimental group of offenders participating in a Victim Impact Class/Panel for Offenders program at one of the California Youth Authority's institutions with a control group of nonparticipants indicated that the Victim Impact Classes/Panels for Offenders-group demonstrated a significant positive change in cognitive empathy toward crime victims.

Conclusion

The Victim Impact Classes/Panels for Offenders program has been heralded as an innovative approach to working with youthful offenders. The essential, powerful combination of an experiential curriculum taught by trained instructors and victim-speaker presentations has resulted in both national recognition and replication.

Beginning in 1990, the Youth Authority participated in a national training and technical assistance project, "Crime Victims and Corrections: Implementing the Agenda for the 1990s," sponsored by the U.S. Department of Justice's Office for Victims of Crime, and presented by the National Victim Center, the National Organization for Victim Assistance, the American Correctional Association, and the California Department of Corrections. Additionally, the Youth Authority's program was one of three training tracks offered to participants in conferences held in eight states. The California Department of the Youth Authority Office of Victims Services conducted training programs for the Federal Bureau of Prisons and the U.S. Department of Defense. Six states and the four branches of the military have completed one or more agency-facilitated week-long intensive training sessions for their Victim Impact Classes/Panels for Offenders instructors. In 1997-1998, Youth Authority staff are showcasing the Victim Impact Classes/Panels for Offenders program as one of three training tracks in the Office for Victims of Crime-sponsored training and technical assistance project, "Promising Practices and Strategies for Victim Services in Corrections," which is in eight states.

National recognition has resulted in numerous requests for training and technical assistance. This prompted the agency to submit a joint proposal with the national office of Mothers Against Drunk Driving to conduct the first Victim Impact Classes/Panels for Offenders training for instructors for a national audience. Sponsored by the Office for Victims of Crime, more than 200 corrections professionals, community-based program staff, victim/witness staff, and other volunteers will be trained throughout 1997-1998, with an advanced training program planned for February 1998.

The Victim Impact Classes/Panels for Offenders program was awarded the prestigious "Innovative Program Award" by the National Victim Center in 1988, was the subject of a CNN Special Report, a *Time* magazine article in 1989, and was featured by CBS's *60 Minutes* in 1992. It is cited by the American Correctional Association Victims' Committee as a model program, and is listed in the 1997 National Institute of Corrections' *Cognitive-Behavioral Programs: A Resource Guide to Existing Services.*

Contact:

Sharon English
Deputy Director
Office of Victims Services
California Department of the Youth Authority

4241 Williamsbourgh Drive
Sacramento, California 95823
(916) 262-1392

Community Reparative Boards

Introduction

Community involvement in the justice system is a process that is rapidly gaining interest among many criminal and juvenile justice agencies, communities, and the public. While not an entirely new concept, it takes several forms. It may be a program through which members from the community sit on a board, and meet with victims and offenders with a focus on holding offenders accountable to the victim and the community. Vermont's Reparative Probation Board is another expression of this movement.

Recognizing that "the community has been missing from our criminal sanctions," the Vermont Department of Corrections, with the support of a Bureau of Justice Assistance grant, initiated the Community Reparative Board (Probation) program in September 1995. Citizens from local communities comprise the boards and meet with offenders and victims.

The primary purpose of a community board program is to have an offender come face-to-face with the *community*—a meeting around which an agreement is negotiated specifying ways that the offender will make reparation to the victims and the community. The intent is to shift from an offender-focused "retributive" form of justice, to a "restorative" model that views crime as a personal violation, and promotes a problem-solving focus based on dialog that brings offenders, victims, and the community together to address the harm caused by the offender. The community plays a facilitative role in the restorative process of righting the harm and injuries caused by the offender.

Direct participation of the community in the justice process is strongly favored by the public. This has been validated through several public opinion studies, including one conducted in Vermont in the spring of 1994. The results from this survey indicate support for programs with a reparative emphasis, and which involve the community and citizens in the process.

Program Goals

The goals of the Community Reparative Board program consist of the following:

1) Promotes citizens' ownership of justice by involving them directly in the justice process

2) Provides opportunities for offenders to take personal responsibility and be held directly accountable for the harm they caused to victims and communities

3) Generates meaningful "community-driven" consequences for criminal actions that reduce costly reliance on formal criminal justice processing

4) Provides opportunities for victims and community citizens to confront offenders in a constructive manner about their behavior

5) Effects a high degree of victim and community compensation and resolution

6) Allows offenders to complete the program in a short period of time with minimal official involvement

7) Secures offenders acceptance back into communities as responsible and productive citizens

Program Implementation

Offenders are referred to the program through the traditional sentencing process. There is no formal "referral" process. Following an adjudication of guilt, offenders are given a suspended sentence and placed on probation using an "Administrative Probation Order" with a condition that states: "You shall actively participate in and complete the Reparative Probation program."

The offender, then, is scheduled to appear before a community reparative board consisting of several citizens from the offender's respective community. It is this step, meeting the board, which is the innovation that distinguishes this program from other traditional programs. The specifics of the sentence are in the hands of a board of community citizens—volunteers—the offender, and possibly a victim who wishes to participate in the process. The result of the meeting is an agreement between the board and the offender stipulating specific activities that the offender will do to complete the program. The agreement must focus on activities that are related to the following four goal areas: (1) restore and make whole the victims of crime, (2) make amends to the community, (3) learn about the impact of crime on victims and the community, and (4) learn ways to avoid reoffending in the future.

Reparative activities may include, but are not limited to the following: making restitution to victims; family-group conferencing; and participating in community work service, victim-offender mediation, cognitive skills development sessions, victim empathy programs, decision-making programs, and driver improvement courses.

The person on reparative probation is not under traditional supervision. Compliance with the terms and agreement is the responsibility of the offenders, including adequate verification and documentation of the completion of their activities. Once the sanctions are agreed upon and assigned by the citizen board, offenders have ninety days to fulfill their agreements and complete the program. Upon completion, the board may recommend discharge from probation. If offenders fail to successfully complete the program activities within the ninety-day period, they may be returned to the court for further action. Offenders' relationships with the community reparative board would end at this point.

Population Served

The Community Reparative Board program is intended to be used for offenders convicted of nonviolent offenses. These may be misdemeanor or felony crimes, and consist of a host of offenses ranging from retail theft to burglary. While community reparative boards generally are best suited for offenders convicted of nonviolent and low-level offenses, having community members involved in the process of dealing with serious offenders can be equally effective, as demonstrated in the sentencing circles conducted in Western Canada and Minnesota.

Evaluation

There is little quantitative research and data on the effectiveness of community reparative boards. There is a growing concern and understanding that evaluation and assessment must consider different measures than the standard offender-focused measure of recidivism. These measures must include such things as victim and community responsivity and satisfaction, and a movement from negative measures (reoffending) to positive measures such as community value, or various indicators of healthy-citizen relationships within the community. At this point, experiential and anecdotal information show a great deal of promise for community reparative boards as an effective response to crime.

Budget

No definitive budget exists exclusively for the program at this point. However, the program has been staffed, with the interest and support of Vermont's State Legislature, with reparative board coordinators. These positions are part of the correctional staff and are dedicated to the program on a full-time basis. Additionally, the local operating units around the state have been directed to begin preparing specific budget details and requests exclusively for the program.

Conclusion

Community reparative boards can offer courts a viable sentencing option for offenders. The intent is to have a sanction that responds to crime victims and communities at the same time that it does not burden the criminal justice system. Such boards also provide the offender with a reparative experience without expending needed justice resources that can be used more effectively for serious criminal offenders.

Author:

Michael J. Dooley
Correctional Program Specialist
National Institute of Corrections
Washington, D.C.

Contact:

John Gorczyk
Commissioner
Vermont Department of Corrections

103 South Main Street
Waterbury, Vermont 05671-1001
(800)241-2442

Restorative Justice: A Correctional Institution's Approach

Introduction

The Minnesota Correctional Facility-Shakopee is the only state facility for female felons. It houses all classifications of offenders, and has a 243-bed capacity. In 1996, the Minnesota Correctional Facility-Shakopee developed a vision statement that included a restorative justice philosophy: "To create an atmosphere where individual differences are recognized and respected and each of us is challenged to work toward a commitment to restorative justice."

The development of this vision statement involved a two-year process that included staff training on the principles and application of restorative justice. The trainers were professionals who had experience outside of the Minnesota Correctional Facility-Shakopee. The subsequent exploration of how these principles of restorative justice discussed in class could be applied to an institutional setting was conducted by a committee of correctional officers, caseworkers, social service staff, and administrative staff. The implementation of restorative justice practices in the facility resulted from the program development of this committee. The evolution of restorative justice practices at the Minnesota Correctional Facility-Shakopee is a work in progress with room to grow and modify.

The committee identified five restorative justice principles as applicable to an institutional setting:

1. Developing offender awareness of injury to victims

2. Involving the offender in repairing harm

3. Involving the community in the process of holding the offender accountable

4. Increasing offender competency

5. Increasing offender connections to conventional community members

Development and Design

Offender Awareness of Injury to Victims

In August 1996, two staff from the Minnesota Correctional Facility-Shakopee received scholarships to be trained as trainers in the Impact of Crime on Victims' classes sponsored by the California Youth Authority and Mothers Against Drunk Driving, in conjunction with the U.S. Department of Justice, Office for Victims of Crime. Upon completion of their training, they, in turn, trained numerous social service staff and correctional officers to run victim-impact classes. In November 1996, the inmate reception and orientation program was expanded to include twenty hours of victim-impact programming. The goal of this victim-centered curriculum is for the offender to begin to:

- Understand the impact of her crime upon victims

- Accept responsibility for past criminal actions

- Develop personal safety skills with a focus on crime prevention

- Learn how to bond with positive, healthy people

- Contribute to her community in a way that will prevent future victimization

The teaching methods include short reading assignments, large and small group discussions, writing exercises, and discussing videotapes and case examples presented in person by victim speakers. The curriculum covers eleven topics: property crime, drugs and society, violent crime, domestic violence, crimes against the elderly, child maltreatment, assault, sexual assault, robbery, drunk driving/death and injury, and homicide. The order of presentation begins with the least sensitive areas (property offenses) and concludes with homicide. This is done to build rapport and openness with offenders and to establish an adequate understanding before entering into more sensitive areas.

The victim-impact class curriculum incorporates pretesting and posttesting of empathy levels. To date, administrators note higher levels of empathy in posttesting; however, it is too early to tell the longevity of the raised empathy levels.

The recruitment of victim speakers has proven to be a long process of building relationships with organizations and agencies that provide victim support services. It has broken new ground with victims' coalitions and specialized victims' groups in building bridges to offenders and correctional institutions.

The efforts to build these relationships have involved individual meetings with victim/witness program coordinators, representatives of specialized support groups for victims, and crime-victim coalition coordinators. Along with the victim-impact classes, the chemical dependency and sex offender treatment programs have incorporated victim-impact components into their curriculum.

Involving the Offender in Repairing Harm

Repairing the harm caused by the offender's crime required a creative approach for an institution. The approach chosen was based upon the concept of giving back to the community in the form of service projects. Two long-term projects are underway. The first involves a partnership with Canine Companions for Independence, which provides the service of dogs to people with disabilities other than blindness. The second involved adopting the West Central Academy public grade school in the Minneapolis area.

Canine Companions for Independence is a national, nonprofit agency that uses volunteer puppy raisers to take an eight-week-old puppy into their home and teach it basic obedience skills, and socialize it to the many settings a service dog would be exposed to in its work with a person with a disability. At sixteen-to-eighteen months, the puppy is returned to one of the Canine Companions' regional training centers to receive advanced training to be of service to a person who is mobility or hearing impaired.

Presently, the Minnesota Correctional Facility-Shakopee has puppies number four and five being raised by two inmates. Obedience-training classes for the puppies are conducted by community volunteers who are also puppy raisers for Canine Companions. The puppies go to work, school, programs, and meals with the inmates to develop socialization skills. Community volunteers also connected to the company take the puppies out of the institution on an occasional basis to socialize the puppies in stores and to provide city-street training. The first three puppies raised by inmates at the Minnesota Correctional Facility-Shakopee have made a difference for their new masters/mistresses. Rearing them also has provided a sense of giving back and accomplishment to the inmates who raised them.

The projects completed so far by the inmates for West Central Academy include repairing the students' school uniforms, building play equipment, creating a school banner, sewing costumes for a school play, and providing minimum-security inmates to clean up the school grounds periodically throughout the school year. For the holidays in 1996, the inmates raised funds to buy material to sew winter headbands for every student in the school.

Giving back to the community also is evidenced through the institution's construction technology class, which has built storage sheds, chairs, tables, and planters for a battered women's shelter, a youth program, flood victims, and children's programs in the community. During the floods in the spring of 1997, inmates sandbagged for the community and, in the fall, emptied sandbags and cleaned-up from the flood. Inmates have sewn quilts for shelters, knitted mittens for the homeless, and sewed clothing for a children's home.

Since state monies cannot be used, funding for these activities has been a challenge. Financial support has come from collaboration with local churches, social service agencies, and through inmates donating money themselves through doughnut sales within the institution with the help of a local bakery.

Other forms of "giving back" that have been a traditional part of the Minnesota Correctional Facility-Shakopee include inmate speakers who go to schools and churches to talk about their experiences; restitution from inmate pay; inmates organizing and implementing the March of Dimes telethon; and Prison Fellowship community projects to help the elderly or other people in poverty.

Involving the Community in the Process of Holding the Offender Accountable

Currently, the Minnesota Correctional Facility-Shakopee has representatives from agencies in the community providing either one-to-one or group contact with inmates, with the goal of maintaining this connection after release. Various agencies specializing in the African-American community, Native-American community, and Hispanic-American community currently provide services to the inmates. Prerelease planning is provided by two agencies, which also are providing community follow-up.

Increasing Offender Competency

Along with the victim-impact classes described earlier, twenty hours of cognitive restructuring classes were added to the inmate reception and orientation program. Inmates are taught to identify errors in their thinking, belief systems, and attitudes and to be aware of those errors as they are manifested in daily living situations. The key concept of cognitive restructuring is that relevant correctional change must include a change in the offenders' fundamental concepts and perceptions of authority, rules, and accountability. These concepts mark the essential difference between prosocial and antisocial attitudes and behaviors.

The cognitive restructuring program works hand-in-glove with the Minnesota Correctional Facility-Shakopee's critical thinking program, which is offered later in the inmates' incarceration. This program teaches problem solving, being assertive, negotiating, interacting with groups, handling relationships, and managing emotions.

Group conferencing represents another initiative to increase offender competency through instruction on how to settle differences between inmates. Staff have been trained in this method of mediation and negotiation to work with the inmates when volatile issues arise between them as an alternative to administrative segregation or a change of placement. The goal of group conferencing is to demonstrate through role modeling and experiential activities an alternative way to solve a problem with an individual or a group.

Increasing Offender Connections to Conventional Community Members

Historically, religious volunteers have been one of the few connections inmates have had to the conventional community. The service projects described earlier and creative efforts by the recreation department have significantly increased these connections with the community. The volunteers with Canine Companions for Independence who provide obedience training by taking the puppies home for further training, and agencies receiving services from the inmates, have provided valuable connections. The recreation department also has invited community softball and volleyball teams to play against the inmates at the Minnesota Correctional Facility-Shakopee.

What Are the Results?

The linkage between restorative justice practices and lower recidivism rates is too early to discern at the Minnesota Correctional Facility-Shakopee. The victim-impact classes demonstrate an immediate higher empathy level among inmates. Victim coalition groups have reported a more positive view towards the Minnesota Correctional Facility-Shakopee and its effort to focus on perpetuating positive behavior. Inmates report a sense of giving back to the community when participating in the projects. Though not always successful, staff report that inmates are trying out their newly acquired cognitive skills. There also has been an increased community interest in offenders and their potential for rejoining the community through increased media attention to the Minnesota Correctional Facility-Shakopee's efforts in building restorative justice practices in an institutional setting.

Conclusion

Restorative justice attempts to balance the rights of victims, offenders, and the community. This different approach to justice helps represent the interest of all three groups. By helping the offender to realize the injury caused to victims, by involving the offender in repairing harm, by getting the community involved in holding the offender accountable, and by increasing the offender's competency and connections to conventional community members, the Minnesota Correctional Facility-Shakopee is attempting to fulfill its restorative justice philosophy.

Contact:

Connie Roehrich
Warden
Minnesota Correctional Facility—Shakopee

1010 W. 6th Avenue
Shakopee, Minnesota 55379
(612) 496-4459

Shock Incarceration

16

Introduction

The first modern boot camps were established in Georgia and Oklahoma in 1983. Other states began to follow suit, and by 1987 this military model of corrections was being praised as the answer to the problem of systems bursting at the seams with escalating prison populations. Since then more than 100 programs have opened and closed throughout the country, with mixed success, resulting in a great deal of controversy about the benefits of this short-term, intensive approach to offender treatment.

A few programs have achieved notable success. These successful programs share several features in common. They have been well documented and thoroughly researched for several years. They have clearly articulated goals and mission statements. They are committed to the education and treatment of offenders, and they have strong staff-training components.

This chapter focuses on the best practices in boot camp/shock incarceration programs in the country. It describes those programs which have, through evaluations, demonstrated the most positive results. Those program characteristics that appear to ensure lasting positive effects include the following items: (1) staff training, (2) a comprehensive program for offenders emphasizing substance abuse treatment, academics, and life skills training, and (3) a dedicated aftercare program, which supports the reintegration of the young offenders into society through job development, follow-up substance abuse treatment, and family support.

There were both general and specific criteria used to select the programs submitted for consideration as a "Best Practice in Shock Incarceration Program." First, all nominations had to be approved by the head of the submitting agency and not be directly involved in litigation. In addition, the committee determined that to be considered a "Best Practice" the program:

1. Should be able to be replicated and implemented by other corrections agencies seeking to modify or develop their own program

2. Should have been operating at least three years and be able to show significant, well-documented, measurable results

3. Have a strong aftercare component providing follow-up services

The committee received submissions from agencies throughout the country and was impressed with the quality of the programs reviewed and the commitment to effective correctional practices demonstrated by the programs. Some programs had to be eliminated either because there was no documented research or the program had not been operating for a sufficient period of time to show results. Indeed, a few of those programs closed prior to the completion of the review, or did not respond to the follow-up request for documentation of results. Some programs, which the committee knows to be operating effectively, did not respond to requests to submit their programs for review and, therefore, could not be included here.

Five programs are highlighted in this chapter. They include the Arkansas Department of Corrections' Boot Camp Program; the IMPACT Program at the Elayn Hunt Correctional Center of the Louisiana Department of Corrections; the New York State Department of Correctional Services' Shock Incarceration program which operates in four shock incarceration correctional facilities and has been modified for the department's Willard Drug Treatment Center; and the SUMMIT Boot Camp Program operated at the Shutter Creek Correctional Facility of the Oregon Department of Corrections. The fifth program, the Youth Leadership Academy (YLA) and the City Challenge Program of the New York State Division of Children and Family Services, (formerly New York State Division for Youth), has been included as an example of a well-designed program for juvenile offenders. Though it has been nationally recognized as a model for juvenile boot camp programs, no research data are available on program outcomes. However, the program has been awarded funding for research by the Federal Office of Justice Programs to commence in 1997.

This introduction will review the historical development of this type of programming. It also will focus on those characteristics which the committee believes contribute to the success of outstanding shock incarceration programs. The well-known criticisms of shock incarceration and boot camp programs also are discussed. Of the programs selected as "Best Practices," most had been operating continuously from four-to-ten years by 1997, with aftercare components providing follow-up services for graduates. The Shock Incarceration program in New York had the most thorough documentation of success over a ten-year period of operation, the only dedicated staff training component, a long-term, comprehensive internal and external research component, and has served as a model for many other agencies throughout the country.

Historical Context

Mandatory drug sentencing laws of the 1970s resulted in prisons increasingly crowded with offenders committed for nonviolent offenses, generally drug-related crimes. In the ten-year period between 1973 and 1983, with the "war on drugs" accelerating, the prison population doubled, In the next ten years, it doubled again. By October 1994, more than one million men and women were incarcerated in the United States. More than four million swelled the ranks of probation and parole. The majority of these offenders were convicted for nonviolent, drug-related offenses. By the end of 1997, the incarcerated population had reached 1.7 million, or one in 155 people in the United States.

In an effort to stem the rising tide of prison crowding, criminal justice officials, legislators, and the public sought effective solutions. In 1983, Oklahoma and Georgia simultaneously implemented a new approach to dealing with young, nonviolent drug offenders—correctional "boot camps." The programs were short-term, 90 to 120 days, regimented, and modeled after a military boot camp for new recruits. The belief was that a highly intensive, brief incarceration period might be a more effective means of dealing with this increasingly young, nonviolent population. Early intervention, a "Scared Straight" approach that lasted for longer than an afternoon, coupled with teaching self-discipline, became the leading edge of incarceration programs.

Legislators saw boot camps as a means of having an impact on crime while, at the same time, conserving scarce tax dollars because of the shorter duration of the programs. Those who had served in the military remembered with fondness how the military "made a man" out of them. The public liked the "get tough on crime" message from media presentations featuring "in your face" drill instructors shouting at young offenders blamed for the lack of safety in their communities. Conservatives appreciated the "tough, no nonsense" approach to the problem of drugs in the community. Liberals liked the idea that young, nonviolent offenders were being incarcerated for less time. It seemed the "perfect" solution.

By the end of 1986, Louisiana became the eighth state to open a "boot camp" program, lasting from 90 to 180 days, depending upon evaluations of participants' progress. Initially, the emphasis was on hard work. Education and other treatment programs were limited in the IMPACT program, partly because to that point, the guiding philosophy was that there was not enough time in these short-term, high-impact programs to have much of an effect through treatment and education. Within a year after opening, optional education programs were added, offering willing participants an opportunity to study for a GED and participate in drug treatment groups. Since then, mandatory programming for all participants is a requirement for successful completion. The IMPACT program is distinguished by its emphasis on continuous improvement. The program has been modified and expanded throughout its operation, developing into a comprehensive approach to treating the young offenders participating in the program.

In August of 1987, the Department of Correctional Services in New York State became the ninth agency to implement the phenomenon, but with a new twist. Rather than relying solely on military components, hard labor, physical training, drill and ceremony, New York's Shock Incarceration developed a holistic model. This model focused on developing the physical, mental, emotional, and spiritual dimensions of participants through intensive substance abuse treatment, academic education, decision making and life skills training, for a full 6 months, rather than the average 90 to 120 days then common for most boot camps. It also included an intensified aftercare program. New York was the first to make "intensive substance abuse treatment and education" mandatory for all participants. Another key addition was a requirement for an intensive, one-month training period for all staff who work in the program.

This became the first of what has since been called the "second generation" of boot camps, and is a model for others to follow. New York's program also emphasized the importance of comprehensive research. Its annual legislative report documents the progress and success of graduates and the program. That research has served as the basis for continuous improvements in program delivery. Like Louisiana, New York also has continuously modified and expanded treatment and education components.

By the end of 1995, more than 55 jurisdictions had implemented some type of boot camp for offenders. The Office of Justice Programs had awarded $24 million dollars for planning and construction grants to another 44 jurisdictions. In addition, the American Correctional Association had published *Standards for Adult Correctional Boot Camp Programs* and *Standards for Juvenile Correctional Boot Camp Programs* and had produced two videotapes addressing the issues of adult and juvenile boot camp programs.

In 1996, the American Correctional Association published an excellent planning guide for developing effective shock incarceration programs, *Juvenile and Adult Boot Camps*. This is a collection of papers by nationally recognized leaders in the field and is an excellent reference for those interested in developing, improving, or expanding shock incarceration programs. It is a hands-on guide, providing step-by-step suggestions for practitioners. It is, likewise, an invaluable resource for identifying the programmatic characteristics shown to produce excellent results.

In recent years, criticism of boot camps has emerged as their "promise" has not been realized universally. Some of this has been warranted by poorly designed and implemented programs, eager to "jump on the boot camp bandwagon." Often, however, the inappropriate actions of a few individuals have been cited as examples of why boot camps are not effective. Poorly planned programs, emphasizing compliance and control as the principal aspects, with no attention paid to the need for education and substance abuse treatment and no after-care support, have not proved to be effective.

Unfortunately, effective programs have been grouped with ineffective ones in these criticisms, and no distinctions are made about how programs differ in intent, population served, focus, and direction. Generally, the critics are concerned about the same short-sighted misconduct, which equally concerns the leaders of the most effective shock incarceration programs.

Some policymakers and staff of a few programs appear genuinely to believe that it is their job to punish offenders and those programs reflect that philosophy. In general, these are also the programs which close because their recidivism rates tend to be higher than comparison groups, they do not prove to be cost effective, and they show poor results. Punishment and intimidation do not work in these programs any more than they do in any other correctional program.

Critics of shock incarceration programs, objecting to what is considered unnecessarily cruel treatment of young offenders, have blamed the military components for what they believe to be harsh and even brutal methods. "Military" has been equated with abuse. Punishment, abuse, harassment, and intimidation are not "military." That is a gross misunderstanding of the focus on self-discipline espoused by effective programs and a disservice to programs that effectively use the military model. The media contributes to some of the misunderstanding by highlighting extremes of behavior, which appeal to the more jaded, cynical public, eager to see offenders "punished." Media features of boot camp programs often focus on drill sergeants shouting, punishing, and demeaning young, scared offenders to the satisfaction of those who believe these offenders are to blame for robbing them of their freedom and safety.

Shock Incarceration/Boot Camp Programs: Purpose and Goals

The term "boot camp" was coined by the military, to identify a six-to-eight-week period of intensive training designed to turn young recruits into disciplined, effective soldiers. The term "boot" designates the newest member of the armed forces. Basic training is designed to teach "boots" military bearing and discipline, how to take care of body and mind, personal hygiene, problem solving skills, teamwork, and respect for authority. In addition, recruits learn how to move with pride and dignity; cooperate with those around them, develope esprit de corps and gain in physical fitness, knowledge, skills, and abilities. After the initial period of instruction, advanced training focuses on developing skills, including learning leadership skills and other specialized skills.

The "war on drugs" was a natural for borrowing the terminology and methods of military boot camps and incorporating them into a similar program for drug offenders. The inner cities, where most of these young offenders come from, are referred to as "combat zones" where weapons abound. The guilty and the innocent, children, and senior citizens alike, are killed along with young people engaged in "turf wars" in the struggle for power that the drug trade feeds. The desire to end the senseless violence associated with drugs, and the need to do it in a cost-effective way, contributed to the development of shock incarceration programs.

The rationale for using a military model is based in sound corrections practice. Corrections agencies are paramilitary organizations, with rank structures, hierarchy, and procedures based on a military model. The goals of a military boot camp are consistent with the goals of an effective shock incarceration program. John Zachariah, chief court administrator and director of administrative services of Cuyahoga County Juvenile Court, Ohio was formerly regional administrator for the American Correctional Association. While in that position, he directed the development of boot camp national standards. In the 1996 National Institute of Justice research report, "*An Overview of Boot Camp Goals, Components and Results*," Mr. Zachariah reports:

The Armed Forces manual explicitly states several key issues that are essential to military boot camp training goals:

- *Organization.* The program must be organized with formal intermediate goals or progressive phases so that the conversion process can be properly structured and both the trainer and new soldier are clear on progress.

- *The dignity of the new soldier.* Every effort must be made to instill a sense of identification with . . . the training unit, and the leaders of that unit. This cannot be accomplished in an atmosphere of "we/they." From the start of the training cycle, the new soldier must be presented an atmosphere that says "leader/soldier," where the drill sergeant . . . and officers are seen as role models to emulate rather than people to be feared and avoided.

- *Degree of control.* The leaders of training units must continue to develop self-discipline in their soldiers. Self-discipline begins early in boot camp by ensuring . . . total control over . . . activities. This control is relaxed over time as soldiers demonstrate their willingness to accept responsibility for their actions.

- *Responsibility.* If new soldiers are to be successful and productive members in (the) future . . . they must learn responsibility for others as well as themselves. Every work detail, every period of instruction, and every opportunity to reinforce leadership should emphasize the necessity for cooperation and teamwork.

- *Training cadre role.* The . . . operative philosophy is to train soldiers by building on their strengths and shoring up their weaknesses. It is not to "tear them down and build them up again." (Department of the Army, *Basic Combat Training Program of Instruction*, 1991)

These goals are the essence of any good correctional boot camp program. They encourage self-discipline, respect, and physical, mental, and spiritual development. These key issues address the importance of having clearly stated goals; building life skills; developing self-esteem, and displaying cooperation, teamwork, self-discipline, and productivity. Staff should be "role models to emulate rather than people to be feared." It is incumbent upon proponents of the "military model" to ensure that correctional boot camp programs strictly adhere to these standards through effective program methods. Those who operate harsh, punishing programs must rethink their goals, objectives, and methods, or they will continue to fail to have an impact on offenders and crime. Critics need to be educated about the goals and direction of an effective shock incarceration program and the purpose of the military model.

But Do Shock Incarceration Programs Work?
—The Debate

In *Shock Incarceration: Rehabilitation or Retribution?* Doris MacKenzie said ". . . there is little evidence that the getting tough element of shock incarceration will, by itself, lead to behavioral change." Many heard, "Boot camps don't work!" (A.P. headline, 1995) Those who operate successful correctional programs long have known that a single focus is not effective in changing offenders' lives. The multisite evaluation of shock incarceration (MacKenzie and Souryal, 1994, *Multisite Evaluation of Shock Incarceration: A Final Report.* Washington, D.C.: National Institute of Justice) cited Louisiana and New York as two programs which did have a significant impact on lowering recidivism and demonstrated positive, postrelease community adjustment of graduates. Both of these programs have comprehensive educational and treatment programs and dedicated aftercare programs.

According to Doris MacKenzie and Dale Parent, for shock programs to be effective, these programs must include:

1) A sufficient number of eligible inmates who are recommended for the program

2) A large enough number of offenders completing the program

3) A true reduction in the length of time offenders spend in prison

4) Offender-participants who are drawn from those who would normally be incarcerated rather than those who would normally be sentenced to probation (or no net widening) (MacKenzie and Parent, 1991, "Shock Incarceration and Prison Crowding In Louisiana." *Journal of Criminal Justice.* Vol. 19).

In remarks made to a National Institute of Corrections' Intensive Skills Workshop presented at the American Correctional Association Congress of Correction in 1991, Dale Parent cited the New York State Shock Incarceration program as a model which contains all of the features necessary if boot camps are to have the capacity to reduce prison bed space needs and to cut both operational and capital costs.

When designing programs, the content of the program has to serve its purpose and goals. Methods that may work for one program may not translate to another setting. Programs for adults and juveniles differ in the population served, demographics of the participants, offense type included, cultural differences, and age and sophistication of the clients, and goals. Those methods that may be effective for adults may not work for juveniles. The methods that are selected must have serve a clear purpose.

A structured period of aftercare is essential in boot camp programs. Drug abuse is a lifelong disease. Relapse prevention does not happen in a vacuum. It takes time and the commitment of resources. Aftercare requires an investment of resources, but the results of programs with strong aftercare components establish the cost-effectiveness of such an investment.

Even with good aftercare programs though, it is ultimately the offender who decides success or failure, not the program. Zachariah cautions that hospitals are not blamed if patients relapse after they are discharged when they no longer need hospital care. If a patient does not follow the recommendations of the doctor and refuses to take prescriptions, hospitals are not blamed if the patient gets sick again. Corrections is not forgiven in the same way if parolees refuse to follow the programs prescribed for them while they were in the system. In the course of educating society, legislators, and critics of the system, it is important to remind them that continuing treatment and resources in the community are as important as the institutional phase.

Many shock incarceration programs have shown themselves to be very effective. With the right people in charge, with committed, well-trained staff, good supervision, and, for a select population of inmates, they are powerful tools. There are many excellent models for change. Shock incarceration is not for everyone, neither inmates nor staff. They are not THE ANSWER to the many problems of the correctional system.

The members of the Shock Incarceration Committee are proponents of shock incarceration. They also have seen poor examples of programs, which contribute to the negative reputation that unfortunately affects all such programs, the good with the bad. However, the committee members know how effective well-run programs can be.

References

American Correctional Association. 1995. *Juvenile and Adult Boot Camp Programs.* Lanham, Maryland: American Correctional Association.

———. 1995. *Standards for Adult Correctional Boot Camp Programs.* Lanham, Maryland: American Correctional Association.

———. 1995. *Standards for Juvenile Correctional Boot Camp Programs.* Lanham, Maryland: American Correctional Association.

MacKenzie, Doris L., et al. 1989. Shock Incarceration: Rehabilitation or Retribution? *Journal of Counseling Services and Rehabilitation.* 14 (2).

MacKenzie, Doris L. and Dale Parent. 1991. Shock Incarceration and Prison Crowding In Louisiana. *Journal of Criminal Justice.* Vol. 19.

MacKenzie, Doris L. and Claire C. Souryal. 1994. *Multisite Evaluation of Shock Incarceration: A Final Report.* Washington, D.C.: National Institute of Justice.

Zachariah, John. 1996. An Overview of Boot Camp Goals, Components and Results. *National Institute of Justice Research Report.* Washington, D.C.: National Institute of Justice.

Committee chair:

Cheryl Clark
Director for Shock Incarceration
New York State Department of Correctional Services

Building 2, State Office Building Campus
Albany, New York 12226
(518) 457-8144

*New York State Department of
Correctional Services*

Shock Incarceration in New York: A Comprehensive Program

Introduction

New York State's Shock Incarceration program was established by enabling legislation on July 13, 1987 (Chapter 261 of the Laws of New York). Two weeks later, the program opened at the Monterey Shock Incarceration Correctional Facility. From one 250-bed facility for males, the program expanded over the next two years to become the largest shock incarceration program for sentenced state prisoners in the nation, with a capacity of 1,390 male inmates and 180 female inmates in four facilities located throughout the state. Female inmates are lodged in the largest of the facilities, Lakeview Shock Incarceration Correctional Facility, where 540 male inmates also participate in the six-month institutional phase of the program. In 1995, legislation mandated the creation of the Willard Drug Treatment Center, an 850-bed program for second-felony offenders and parole violators, which operates under the "shock" model in a 90-day institutional phase and a one-year, graduated period of aftercare.

New York's program is a holistic model, addressing physical, mental, emotional, and spiritual dimensions of participants within the context of a therapeutic community. Due to the documented substance-abuse histories of the majority of program participants, a major emphasis is placed on substance-abuse treatment through its foundation in the Network and Alcohol and Substance Abuse Treatment programs. The shock incarceration program is delivered in two phases: a six-month institutional phase, followed by a six-month, intensive aftershock phase of parole supervision in the community, offering a continuum of treatment services.

Legislative restrictions require that all participants (except in the Williard Drug Treatment Center) be sentenced to their first term of state incarceration for nonviolent felony offenses and within three years of parole eligibility at the time they are in reception. Initially established for offenders between the ages of sixteen to twenty-four, the age range has been increased three times, to age thirty-five. "Shock" has the largest population of participants between the ages of sixteen to twenty-one in the country.

Statement of Purpose

The expressed purpose of the omnibus bill establishing shock incarceration was "to enable the state to protect the public safety by combining the surety of imprisonment with opportunities for the timely release of inmates who have demonstrated their readiness for return to society." The legislation specifically stated:

> Certain young inmates will benefit from a special six-month period of intensive incarceration. Such incarceration should be provided to carefully selected inmates committed to the Department of Correctional Services who are in need of substance abuse treatment and rehabilitation. An alternative form of incarceration stressing a highly structured and regimented routine, which will include extensive discipline, considerable physical work and exercise and intensive drug rehabilitation, is needed to build character, instill a sense of maturity and responsibility and promote a positive self-image for these offenders so that they will be able to return to society as law-abiding citizens.

Implementation

Staff Training

All staff of the Shock Incarceration program are departmental employees who have completed mandatory training at the Department of Correctional Services Training Academy. In addition to this basic training, all staff, in any capacity, who choose to work in shock incarceration facilities are required to attend a month-long, comprehensive training program, that prepares them to teach the program's concepts to participants.

The therapeutic community philosophy emphasizes that all staff are involved in creating the therapeutic milieu and are role models for participants. Equally, all staff are part of the treatment team. Shock incarceration staff training includes instruction on: presentation and instructor development skills; control theory; life skills; decision making; accelerated learning techniques; alcohol and substance abuse treatment; the elements and dynamics of a therapeutic community; team building; physical training; military bearing; drill and ceremony; command presence; cognitive, affective, and behavioral treatment philosophy and methods; and leadership and group process.

The course is offered at least once annually and has been certified for both undergraduate and graduate credit by the state education department. To date, more than 3,000 staff have been trained in the program. New York State is nationally recognized for this staff-training component. Many agencies of other jurisdictions, including other countries, have sent staff to shock incarceration training in New York or have contracted for on-site training in their locations. This training is generally two weeks in duration.

Treatment and Education Program

Shock incarceration is a rigorous, multitreatment program, emphasizing discipline, substance abuse treatment, and education, with group and individual counseling, all within a military model. Inmates are in treatment, and education programs daily throughout the six-month program, for a minimum of forty hours per week of treatment, education, decision making, and life skills. Academic classes include adult basic education, GED preparation, English as a Second Language, and special education, and are scheduled for one day and two evenings each week. The other five evenings include Network, alcohol and substance abuse programs, and prerelease classes or group counseling sessions.

Network, a decision making and life skills program, forms the foundation of the therapeutic community. An underlying basis for the Network philosophy is control theory, which proposes that nonconformity is a product of the failure of the social bond. It assumes that inmates entering the department are individuals whose bonds to society are weakened or broken, and exposure to the shock incarceration program will help restore these bonds. Daily community meetings provide a forum for resolving problems and noting progress.

Despite the limited time spent in academic classes, the average increase in math scores is 1.8 years and two or more years for reading. The passing rate for the GED test has increased from 40 percent in 1990 to 75.5 percent in 1996. Inmates who already have high school diplomas are trained as literacy volunteers, serving as peer tutors for Adult Basic Education, math, reading, and English as a Second Language classes.

The Alcohol and Substance Abuse Treatment program is based on the 12 Steps to Recovery of Alcoholics Anonymous and Narcotics Anonymous and is a primary focus of the program.

Prerelease classes are offered throughout the six-month institutional phase and include preparing for a job, budgeting, parenting, managing anger, and using alternatives to violence.

Work and Community Service Program

Community service is another key component of shock incarceration. Each year, supervised crews of inmates from the program perform thousands of hours of community service as part of the daily routine of the facilities. Community service provided by the four facilities is estimated to total 1.2 million hours annually. Cash-strapped rural communities would not have been able to provide these services if they did not receive assistance from staff and inmates in the shock program. Inmates learn a work ethic and valuable skills through these services and from the jobs they perform as part of the daily work program in maintenance, kitchen and food service, maintenance of lawns and grounds in the facilities, and snow removal in facilities and neighboring communities. They also provide emergency and disaster relief to areas, whenever the need arises.

Physical Training, Drill, and Ceremony

The military components of shock incarceration are a key to teaching self-discipline, pride, and dignity. They also promote physical health (woefully inadequate in most inmates entering the program), teamwork, cooperation, and self-esteem. Evidence also suggests that the improvements in physical health support the significant advances in learning documented in the academic program. The physical training program includes calisthenics, based on the *Army Field Manual* and a platoon run, led by drill instructors. The program takes into account the very poor physical health of most offenders and builds gradually, increasing in intensity as inmates build fitness levels and progress through the program.

All movement is in formation, with inmates marching as a platoon, reciting platoon mottoes and cadences, which reinforce the message of the treatment program and teach inmates to carry themselves with pride and dignity, "standing tall and looking good." A very practical reason for maintaining military discipline is that the program is very large, platoons average sixty inmates each, with one drill instructor. Formal movement is efficient for getting to classes, meals, work, and group activities on time.

The drill instructor is one of the principal change agents on the mutlidisciplinary team. Another benefit is the span of control afforded the drill instructor assigned to the platoon. Inmates come from every ethnic background, neighborhoods, even different countries. They often enter the program with a history of rivalry and conflict, some of which began in their neighborhoods, some in the jails where they were incarcerated previously. The military components provide a safe structure for reinforcing cooperation and eliminating problems.

Aftercare

New York State was the first state to emphasize and build into the program design dedicated, intensive aftercare, which has been operating continuously since the first graduates were released in March 1988. Planning for parole begins within two weeks of entering the program, with prerelease classes scheduled for three hours every other week throughout the six months. Parole staff develop an aftercare plan with each participant prior to the participant's release to the community and supervise parolees in the six-month aftershock program. Community-based service providers deliver vocational training, job development and placement, continuing substance-abuse treatment, and support groups. In addition, parolees are encouraged to attend Alcoholics Anonymous, Narcotics Anonymous, and other support groups, for at least ninety meetings in ninety days, to support their transition and develop new habits.

Results

For every 100 shock incarceration inmates released, it is estimated that the department saves $2.4 million, which it otherwise would have had to expend for the care and custody of these inmates. For the first 18,269 releases from the program, the department saved an estimated $537.6 million in both operating and capital costs. For each graduate there was an average net savings of 350 days or 11.5 months from their actual date of release from the program to his/her court-determined parole eligibility date. After one year, 90 percent of the program graduates remained in the community. After two years, the success rate (71 percent) was 6 percent to 12 percent better than comparison groups. Shock incarceration graduates are more likely than comparison groups to be employed and more often involved in personal growth activities, including recovery groups like Alcoholics Anonymous.

Since the program began, the department's Division of Program Planning and Research and the New York State Division of Parole have produced an annual report to the legislature. This report consistently shows that while shock incarceration costs slightly more than general confinement, the considerable cost-savings are realized because of shortened lengths of stay and the fact that the program's graduates are more likely than comparison groups to be successful on parole supervision, despite remaining at risk for longer periods of time.

In addition, other agencies have conducted independent evaluations of shock incarceration. A 1993 national review of boot camp programs conducted by the U.S. General Accounting Office (GAO) noted that of the jurisdictions studied, "New York is the best example of reported cost savings." New York was one of eight programs in the National Institute of Justice's multisite evaluation of shock incarceration and was found to have the lowest rate of recidivism of the states in the study. The study also noted that it was one of only three programs having a positive impact on program participants' recidivism and prison crowding.

Conclusion

New York State's shock incarceration has been nationally recognized as a model correctional program by the American Correctional Association, the National Institute of Justice, and other independent organizations. Lakeview was the first stand-alone shock incarceration facility in the nation to receive American Correctional Association accreditation, being reaccredited for the second time in October 1996.

Contact:

Cheryl Clark
Director for Shock Incarceration
New York State Department of Correctional Services

Building 2, State Office Building Campus
Albany, New York 12226
(518) 457-8144

Oregon's SUMMIT

Introduction

The Oregon Department of Corrections' boot camp for adult male and female felony offenders is located at Shutter Creek Correctional Institution in North Bend, Oregon. It was mandated by the 1993 Oregon Legislature in House Bill 2481. Oregon SUMMIT was established in March 1994 and was designed to ease prison crowding and have an impact on criminal recidivism. The program is a two-phased program, six months in the institutional setting, followed by transitional leave and an aftercare program supervised by parole officers throughout the state.

The program includes both male and female offenders from the age of juvenile remand through age forty, and has a program capacity of 150 males and 16 females. Shutter Creek Correctional Institution also houses 100 general population male inmates. Program eligibility requirements exclude those convicted of sex offenses, most first-degree crimes, and mandatory minimum sentences. Offenders with recent escape histories and unresolved detainers are also excluded. Eligibility screening is done on site. After being screened for eligibility, inmates must volunteer to participate.

Statement of Purpose

SUMMIT is an acronym for "Success Using Motivation, Morale, Intensity and Treatment." The program emphasizes cognitive change, basic education and work skills, discipline, teamwork, and responsibility in a military framework. The SUMMIT philosophy states the direction of the program. "A place where what we believe and say is what we do." The SUMMIT program is demanding and rigorous physically, mentally, and emotionally. It is designed to support inmates who make positive changes in their lives and learn life skills, which lead to success.

Implementation

Staff Training

Staff development training is held twice a year for sixteen hours each session and serves to keep the program focused. SUMMIT Academy, a forty-hour reprise of the initial immersion training for new staff, is held once a year. The program is modeled after the Shock Incarceration program in New York. Prior to the opening of SUMMIT, consultants from New York provided immersion-style training for administrators, supervisors, and all staff in two sessions, one in September of 1993 and the second in March 1994, after which the first group of inmates arrived. Since that time, managers have provided in-house training for staff transferring to work in the program. Drill instructors also were trained in the U.S. Army Rehabilitation Training Instructors Course (RTIC) at Ft. McClellan, Alabama. Program staff at SUMMIT also are required by department regulations to complete all mandatory departmental training.

Treatment and Education Program

Within the military framework, the heart of the program is a modified therapeutic community, centered on the concept of cognitive change: the idea that changing thinking results in a change of behavior. The cognitive change basis of the Oregon SUMMIT program draws from the pioneering work on the criminal personality by Drs. Yochelson and Samenow. Their work identified patterns of thinking called "thinking errors" common in the thinking of criminals.

SUMMIT brings together several cognitive approaches for maximum effectiveness, in 8.5 hours of classes each week. Gordon Graham's video and activity program "Breaking Barriers" engages inmates in hands-on exercises, which assists them to make positive changes in their lives. The Franklin Reality Model encourages inmates to examine their limiting beliefs and implement new ones, which support their success. Dr. Merry Hansen's Pathfinders, a cognitive skills-cognitive restructuring program, covers such topics as team-building, communication, job readiness, anger management, time management, and problem solving.

Alcohol and drug services consist of twelve hours per week of alcohol and drug education, discussion groups, and 12 step meetings. An emphasis is placed on the key concepts of addiction, the physical and social effects of alcohol and drug abuse, and recovery planning. Spiritual wellness is another key component of the program, with religious services available on weekends.

Education classes at SUMMIT consist of approximately thirteen hours a week of adult basic education and work towards GED certificates, computer skills, and resume writing. Each inmate is also given Dr. Mary Meeker's Structure of Intellect (SOI) test, which measures abilities for learning and includes follow-up modules designed to develop and enhance learning abilities.

Work and Community Service Program

Inmates work off-site three days a week, performing community service work and physical labor for nonprofit agencies, under the direction of correctional work crew supervisors. The skills gained working cooperatively and improving community resources, through projects such as beach clean-up, stream enhancement, forest preservation, and playground repair, support inmates in learning pride in accomplishments, time management, decision making, and teamwork.

Physical Training, Drill, and Ceremony

Each day begins early in the morning with a motivating physical training session and run, designed to set the tone for the day. The physical training program is based on the one learned from the Army's U.S. Army Rehabilitation Training Instructors' Course program. Physical training is an integral part of the personal wellness program. Fitness evaluations are performed at intervals during the program to measure inmates' progress.

Personal wellness classes are held weekly, delivered by the facility's health services staff. Inmates are taught how to evaluate their health needs, how to access heath care, and how to identify lifestyle choices that affect their health. They learn skills to integrate positive health practices into their lives.

During the day, as inmates move about the facility, they do so in formation, either as a platoon or in squads. As motivation, cadences are used, which are created largely by the inmates themselves, with approval from the program manager and drill sergeant. Cadences with prosocial messages are beneficial in keeping the inmates' minds on the change process and motivating them as a group.

Aftercare

After graduation, inmates leave with their families and return to their communities for ninety days of transitional leave. This transitional period allows them to practice their new behaviors and attitudes in their communities, under the supervision of parole officers. During this period, they are still technically inmates and the responsibility of the SUMMIT program. If they do not abide by the conditions of transitional leave, including attending all required parole officer meetings and mandated treatment, maintaining appropriate housing and obtaining full-time jobs, they are returned to the SUMMIT program. Those returned are reviewed by the superintendent's committee, which makes a recommendation to the superintendent on their program status. Inmates who successfully complete the ninety-day transitional leave then are placed on postprison supervision for the period ordered by the sentencing judge.

A strong link between the SUMMIT program and parole officers is necessary for the success of inmates during the transitional leave period, and during postprison supervision. Cognitive change groups are available in many communities. The participants are encouraged to attend Alcoholics Anonymous and Narcotics Anonymous. Some parole offices make use of their day reporting centers to supervise SUMMIT graduates. Parole officers attended the initial immersion training with SUMMIT staff. Periodic meetings are held to network with parole officers assigned to supervise the program's graduates.

Since October 1996, SUMMIT has been working with Oxford House, a federally funded program through the State Alcohol and Drug Services. Oxford House provides no-interest loans to graduates for security deposits and down payments for rent, to be repaid over two years. Arrangements are made for groups of graduates from the same locations to rent housing together. This gives them an opportunity to live independently during the transition phase, and beyond, if required, in an environment which supports and reinforces the lifestyle they learned at SUMMIT.

Results

As of October 1997, eighteen platoons had completed the program, and three more were currently active. Of the 1,136 total participants, 606 have completed the institutional phase of the program and another 19 remain eligible to do so, having recycled into a later platoon where they remained active. Of the 606 who completed the institutional portion, 510 have graduated from the transitional leave portion. Another thirty-eight were currently on transitional leave, remaining eligible to graduate. Based on this data, the institutional phase completion rate is 54 percent and the program graduation rate is 47 percent.

SUMMIT graduates receive an average "time cut" of 331 days, from the date of graduation from transitional leave, to their projected release date had they not participated in the program. As with the other intensive treatment models discussed in this publication, the SUMMIT program is somewhat more expensive to operate than a general-confinement program. These costs have been accounted for in estimating the total savings realized from releasing graduates almost one year earlier than their terms of incarceration. For each successful inmate, the department estimates a cost savings of $15,528. Based on the number of successful graduates, the total cost savings to the department has been $7.9 million since 1994, or 168,814 bed days.

The recidivism of SUMMIT graduates is significantly less than recidivism among comparable inmates who did not participate. For those released as of October 1997, the probability of recidivism for a new felony conviction within the first year following release from SUMMIT is 10 percent. The comparable rate for released SUMMIT-eligible inmates who did not attend the program is 19 percent within the same time period. This group was also in prison an average of ten months longer than a SUMMIT graduate. At two years, the contrast is 20 percent for SUMMIT graduates and 33 percent for nonparticipants.

At an October 1996 reunion of SUMMIT graduates, they shared the following feedback:

> I'm involved in college, NA and AA meetings, church, volunteering . . . no longer have anything in common with old friends, we're different people. . . I'm a hotel manger. I use the tools . . . to motivate my employees. "Get your hands out of your pockets, walk with purpose, look professional." . . . The number of [aftercare] meetings seemed daunting at first. I didn't realize how much I'd need them. I actually enjoyed them . . . I didn't get really Honest, Open and Willing until after the program. It didn't sink in until then. I needed a ladder for work, saw one, thought about taking it . . . didn't . . . I had ignored my family for ten years . . . never had a girlfriend for more than a month . . . now my fiancé and I hold "community meetings" to solve problems.

A twenty-six-year-old graduate described by her first parole officer as "a nightmare to supervise" was an addict, shoplifter, and runaway by age sixteen, and neglected her children. She volunteered for SUMMIT for the fourteen-month time cut, graduating in 1995. Now, her same parole officer says, "I was struck by her willingness to take personal responsibility . . . she attends AA and NA meetings, never misses appointments and is a positive mother and provider . . . Summit has worked."

Conclusion

The Oregon Department of Correction Boot Camp program is committed to continuous improvement and development of this very important initiative. Since February 1996,

SUMMIT staff have been supporting the Oregon Youth Authority with staff training and the development of the Tillamook Youth Accountability Camp. This camp provides a program for boys ages fourteen to twenty-one modeled after SUMMIT, with a capacity of fifty.

Author:

David S. Cook
Director
Oregon Department of Corrections

Contact:

William Beers
Superintendent
Shutter Creek Correctional Institute

2000 Shutter's Landing Road
North Bend, Oregon 97459-0303
(541) 756-6666

Arkansas' Boot Camp

Introduction

The Arkansas Department of Correction's Boot Camp was created by Act 492, which state lawmakers passed during the 1989 General Assembly. The boot camp is located at the Wrightsville Correctional Institution, in Wrightsville, Arkansas. Since its creation, the program has shown increased growth, from an initial group of 60 inmates and a staff of 8 when the unit opened in 1990. The program had expanded to an inmate population of 150, with 46 staff in 1991. By 1994, the program once again had expanded to accommodate 30 female inmates, though with no increase in staff.

Statement of Purpose

The Arkansas Boot Camp Act was passed to relieve the skyrocketing cost of incarcerating the expanding number of offenders in conventional penitentiaries. The General Assembly decided to implement a more regimented, military-like program. The boot camp program is intended to teach self-control, responsibility, and the skills and habits needed for a productive life to individuals who have shown they lack such skills. The drill and work portions of the program are designed to provide structure and discipline for individuals who may have been irresponsible and unmotivated in the past. The treatment portion of the program stresses internalizing positive values, developing internal controls, and setting positive goals, while providing the skills needed to pursue those goals.

Implementation

Staff Training

All newly hired drill instructors attend the Arkansas Department of Correction Training Academy and receive 240 classroom hours of corrections, weapons training and qualification, and first-aid certification. Upon graduation from the training academy, drill instructors receive forty hours of on-the-job training from certified field training officers. They then have thirty days to complete the Positive Mental Attitude course conducted by the unit training officer. Based on availability of funds for travel, new drill instructors are enrolled in the U.S. Army Rehabilitation Training Instructors' Course at Ft. McClellan.

All officers and support personnel receive mandatory ancillary training of at least forty hours each year, and annual weapons requalification and firearm safety training. Selected officers also receive specialized training as members of the emergency services team to support the department with tactical recovery operations. All officers receive annual evaluations and certifications as drill instructors from their immediate supervisors and the boot camp training officer.

Treatment and Education Program

The boot camp is designed as a total treatment program, followed by a supportive aftercare program in the community. The substance abuse treatment program is licensed by the Bureau of Drug and Alcohol Abuse Prevention to provide comprehensive substance abuse services to the incarcerated population. The program is built on a triad—discipline, academic education, and substance abuse training. Since its inception, the boot camp program has provided offenders with the substance abuse treatment program and the responsible actions program.

The mission of the substance abuse treatment program is threefold: to remediate chemical dependency and substance abuse problems; to aid offenders in living chemical free, productive lives in the community; and, to reduce offender recidivism. The array of services provided through this program includes education in the 12 step program; psychoeducational groups on the 12 steps; group and individual counseling; prevention for those who are at risk for becoming substance abusers; and, random drug screens and relapse-prevention therapy.

The responsible actions program is part of an intensive correctional program and provides essential treatment. The program blends a variety of tools from Alcoholics Anonymous, psychological counseling, class exercises, homework assignments, and assessment techniques.

Academic education prepares inmates for their general equivalency diploma (GED). Since the start of the boot camp program, 706 inmates have received their GED through the Arkansas Department of Correction School District. The boot camp currently employs two full-time teachers and provides lecturers from other agencies to provide inmates with a broad spectrum of self-improvement classes.

The boot camp provides a life skills program to assist inmates with life after they have been graduated from the program. Food service teaches food preparation and inventory skills, sanitation standards, dietetic requirements, and proper procedures for food serving. Inmates working with laundry and supply learn inventory, chemical use, and uniform pressing and altering. This program also provides inmates with communication skills and skills for job-interviews, job-application completion help, and stress management. These skills provide them with essential elements for a productive postincarceration life, while providing the department with effective workers.

Work and Community Service Program

Work activities are designed to instill a work ethic and teach inmates the value of physical labor. Additionally, teamwork, a sense of accomplishment, and self-pride become ingrained as important. Community service activities include maintaining the cleanliness of state highways; working on facility lawns and grounds; and providing maintenance, kitchen, laundry, and other services.

Physical Training, Drill, and Ceremony

The boot camp program provides a rigorous, but controlled physical fitness program that helps inmates develop a healthy drug-free body and a sound mind. The morning physical training session consists of push-ups, sit-ups, and side straddle hop, followed by a daily run. This very important part of the boot camp program instills self-drive, motivation, and determination to meet the day's challenges. Inmates run an obstacle course to develop agility, motor skills, hand/eye coordination, and endurance. On weekends, they play team sports that create a competitive spirit, while teaching teamwork and good sportsmanship. Each week the group that best demonstrates esprit de corps, high morale, and discipline, while moving in formation from one place to another receives a ribbon.

Aftercare

Aftercare plans are developed with each participant by the substance abuse program staff prior to release to the community. From these, referrals are made to diverse groups such as Alcoholics Anonymous, Narcotics Anonymous, Chemicals Anonymous, mental health centers, vocational rehabilitation, and other programs as indicated by the individual aftercare plan. Follow-up options for daycare (thirty days), intense outpatient treatment (three-to-four days each week for thirty-to-forty-five days), and outpatient treatment (once a week for as long as needed) are available for offenders under the auspices of the substance abuse treatment program. Relapse-prevention therapy is an important part of the aftercare plan and begins while inmates are in boot camp.

Research and Evaluation

Under contract, Arkansas State University's Office of Educational Research and Services conducted an external, independent evaluation of the boot camp from March 1992 through December 1993 to provide department officials with information about program effectiveness in modifying selected inmate behaviors. The research concluded that the program was successful in modifying selected behaviors in positive ways.

As of August 1997, a total of 3,704 male inmates had participated in this 105-day program and 2,250 had graduated. A total of 232 female inmates had participated and 116 had graduated. Of the 2,250 male graduates, 902 (40 percent) were returned to incarceration for parole violations. Of the 232 women graduates, 15 (6.4 percent) were returned to custody.

Each case of a returning inmate is reviewed by the boot camp administrator and staff to identify shortfalls that the inmate encountered while on administrative transfer. They attempt to identify any trends in violations committed by boot camp graduates. This information is conveyed to staff at all levels and passed on to inmates preparing for graduation and transfer to parole.

A cost savings analysis for the years 1994 through 1996 indicated an estimated savings of $17,809,481. While the average cost of treatment in the boot camp program is higher ($36.90 per day) than for general confinement ($27.85 per day), the savings resulting from a shorter confinement in the boot camp (105 days as compared with an average of 791 days had they served their full sentence) is estimated at $18,150 per year for each inmate who successfully completes the program. In 1994, 368 inmates graduated, 136 returned to incarceration (37 percent). In 1995, 347 graduated, with 109 returning to incarceration (31.4 percent). In 1996, 368 graduated and as of July 1997, about 87 had been returned (23.6 percent). After deducting savings for returned inmates from the total estimated savings, the department projected an average annual net savings of $5,936, 493.

Anecdotal statements of successful graduates released from boot camp from June 1992 through August 1996 also were collected. The offenders quoted share their gratitude for what the program taught them and how the skills they learned in boot camp have supported their success postrelease. They say:

> I've turned my life around from the fast money on the street corner, to an intelligent businessman in . . . society. . . . Had I never participated in the boot camp program, my life was on the way down a deadend street. Also, the aftercare meetings helped me to cope with being in society again. . . . The program has allowed me to rebuild my self-esteem, my body, mind, character, family and public relations. The education I got . . . has allowed me to go further with my learning. Since my release . . . I now manage a vending machine company . . . I take care of rental property [businesses, car washes, and storage rentals] . . . I just finished the firefighter I and II nationally certified school . . . I completed the EMT course . . . Without the great people of Boot Camp taking the time to rebuild my life, I don't know where I would be today. I have tried to show my thanks by continuing my education and . . . helping others. . . . I won't deny that it was the hardest 105 days I ever went through. Making it through meant everything to me. It shows in the life I have now. I . . . have (worked) for a year. . . . I owe my life to [so many people at Boot Camp] . . . I learned how to stay out of trouble and maintain a job for over two years . . . being polite, saying "Yes sir" or "Yes ma'am" can carry you a long way . . . respect for others and mostly for myself. . . . The program helped me in all areas of my life. . . . it taught me that I do not need alcohol to solve my problems. . . . I have to take one step at a time, one day at a time.

Conclusion

The Arkansas Department of Correction's Boot Camp program is recognized for its commitment to effectiveness throughout its seven years of operation. The department and staff are committed to continual quality improvement.

Contact:

Tom Rochelle
Boot Camp Administrator
Wrightsville Correctional Institution

P. O. Box 1010
Wrightsville, Arkansas 72183-0407
(501) 897-5806 x301

Louisiana Department of Public Safety and Corrections

IMPACT Program

Introduction

The Intensive Motivational Program for Alternative Correctional Treatment (IMPACT) is a rigorous, multifaceted, six-month program emphasizing discipline, education, and substance abuse counseling, all within a military model. This coeducational program, which operates at the Elayn Hunt Correctional Center in St. Gabriel, Louisiana, began in 1987. It had a capacity of 136 males and was available to females housed at the adjacent Louisiana Correctional Institute for Women, the only state prison for women.

In the summer of 1997, the program expanded to accommodate 200 males, and is continuing to accommodate all eligible females who volunteer to participate. Women are transported to the IMPACT program each morning at 5:00 A.M. for physical training and returned to the women's correctional center after the program ends each evening.

Initially, the target population was first-felony offenders committed to state custody for seven years or less for an offense carrying parole eligibility. In 1989, statutory eligibility was expanded to include second offenders who previously have not been incarcerated. The statute also provides that offenders sent to IMPACT must agree to enter the program. From its inception until late August 1992, entry into IMPACT required the positive recommendation of three independent decision makers: the Division of Probation and Parole, the sentencing court, and the secretary of the department or his designee. Under this arrangement, the court surrendered jurisdiction over the offender from the point of sentencing or probation revocation, when it formally recommended an offender for IMPACT.

In August 1992, the law was amended in two ways. One revision added the option of allowing the court to directly sentence an offender to IMPACT and retain jurisdiction if the offender was refused entry or removed from the program for any reason other than a violation of institution or program rules. A second revision authorized staff of the Adult Reception and Diagnostic Center, with the warden's approval, to identify and recommend suitable offenders for participation in IMPACT. The final decision to participate remains with the offender, who must indicate a willingness to participate in writing.

Program Purpose

IMPACT was authorized by statute in 1986. One of the goals of the program is to prevent the process of deviant acculturation or "hardening" through lengthy involvement in the usual prison experience. The program is premised on a treatment model within a military setting. IMPACT is a two-part program, consisting of a period of 180 days of highly regimented, tightly structured incarceration, followed by at least six months of intensive parole supervision.

IMPACT has been developed around three goals: to provide a suitable alternative to long-term incarceration for primarily youthful first- and second-offenders; to reduce the department's financial cost without undue risk to public safety; and to equip inmate participants with the life skills necessary for their success in life. Based on these goals, IMPACT is organized and operated to help offenders develop self-confidence, self-respect, a sense of personal responsibility, and respect for others' attitudes and value systems. It also serves to enhance life skills, and the ability to self-evaluate based on a treatment program premised on cognitive restructuring.

Implementation

Staff Training

All IMPACT staff are departmental employees who have completed mandated training at the Department of Correction Training Academy. In addition, all drill instructors and supervisors complete the U.S. Army Rehabilitation Training Instructors' Course (RTIC) at Ft. McClellan. All personnel receive in-service training of at least forty hours each year. In addition, selected supervisory staff participate in the shock incarceration staff training operated by the New York State Department of Correctional Services. Interagency training in after-care planning was provided to all program and key parole staff by consultants from New York in September 1996.

Treatment and Education Program

The intensive incarceration phase initially varied in length from 90 to 180 days, depending on participant's progress. Now it is six months. IMPACT includes strict discipline, physical exertion, community service and, most importantly, rehabilitative therapeutic regimes in substance abuse, value reorientation, self-discipline, and responsibility. Once the incarceration phase is completed, inmates enter into an intensive parole phase lasting a minimum of six months and then continue on parole supervision until their full-term date expires.

In May of 1995, the Job Skills Education Program was incorporated into the treatment phase of IMPACT. This is a self-motivated, computer-based instructional program that has an excess of 220 job prescriptions including GED and college preparatory prescriptions. As of May 1997, 132 GED diplomas had been awarded to participants and 401 certificates were issued for various job skills prescriptions.

The Louisiana Department of Public Safety and Corrections recently has been awarded a residential substance abuse treatment grant to enhance the substance abuse treatment within the program. In addition to 140 hours of other forms of rehabilitative treatment, each inmate receives approximately 200 hours of substance-abuse treatment during the institutional phase. Substance-abuse treatment continues while the inmate is in a community residential unit, provided on a statewide basis by the Office of Alcohol and Substance Abuse. Until 1996, substance-abuse treatment was offered to offenders approaching the end of the institutional phase, during the last month of the program.

Work and Community Service Program

Inmates learn work ethics and skills by participating in work projects for the correctional center and through job skills training while in the institutional phase of the program. Contacts with the Department of Labor begin while inmates are in the program and placement services are available to them upon release. Selected inmates are involved in a mentorship program established by the Louisiana Department of Health and Hospitals; they learn CPR, communication skills, self-esteem, trust, and character building skills.

In 1998, a new program is planned to train IMPACT participants in the shipbuilding trade, to fill the estimated 6,000 vacancies in the industry. IMPACT will offer training in shipfitting, welding, and surface preparation. Upon successful completion, graduates will be paroled to one of two work release centers, which will continue the treatment begun in IMPACT for up to six months, and offer employment in the shipbuilding trade.

Physical Training, Drill, and Ceremony

The IMPACT program is based on a military model, with inmates assigned to platoons and squads within the company. All movement is in military formation, with positive, motivational cadences. Each day begins with calisthenics based on the *Army Field Manual* and a platoon run, led by drill instructors. The program is geared to build strength, endurance, and cardiovascular fitness in a graduated manner, and to accommodate fitness levels (or lack thereof) as inmates progress through the program. The military components of the program build confidence and physical health, and teach cooperation and teamwork.

Initially, IMPACT was first conceived to be a "military program in a treatment model" and has evolved into a "treatment program in a military model." Changing needs, review, updated analysis, and statistics, along with national popularity influenced changes in the program.

Aftercare

Although there has always been some aftercare support for graduates, the program has been greatly enhanced in the past two years. The IMPACT Aftercare Task Force has been in place since the first planning session in September of 1996 and continues to convene regularly. This committee is comprised of representatives of several state agencies, including the Departments of Labor, Alcohol and Substance Abuse, and Probation and Parole. The task force is responsible for developing and implementing strategies to ensure the success of the aftercare phase of the program.

Aftercare plans are developed with each participant prior to release to the community. The Division of Parole supervises all aftercare components, which are provided jointly by the Departments of Labor, Alcohol and Substance Abuse, Probation and Parole, and community service agencies and providers. Because offenders are released to areas throughout the state, parole creates linkages between the institutional phase and the community residential phase.

Results

IMPACT saves the State of Louisiana $750,000 for every 100 inmates who complete the program. Over the ten-year history of IMPACT, this translates into an allowance of over $13 million in operating funds and $20 million in construction costs for approximately 700 cells to house long-term, violent, predatory criminals. Approximately 45 percent of inmates entering the IMPACT program do not complete it. The program is designed to eliminate individuals who are not receptive to change. According to an internal study done for the Department of Public Safety and Corrections, at the end of 1996, 56 percent of 1,993 graduates had not returned to state institutional supervision, nor had they been given probation for a new crime.

A 1991 evaluation of shock incarceration in Louisiana showed that the program is meeting its primary goal of creating a new sentencing option that would provide placement for inmates who otherwise would be sent to the state's crowded prisons. The report stated:

> There appear to be some benefits for individual inmates who complete IMPACT. They report more positive attitudes, are more optimistic about their futures, have more positive attitudes toward staff than other inmates, and state that the shock incarceration experience was beneficial. Due to the regime of physical exercise and the drug-free environment, many inmates also reported that shock incarceration was a healthy experience. Additionally, upon release they became involved in more positive social activities (MacKenzie, Shaw, and Gowdy, 1991, *NIJ Research in Brief*).

That same report included comments from inmate participants concerning their feelings about the benefits of the program:

> I volunteered because I wanted rehabilitation that I wouldn't receive in prison. . . . This program teaches me to respect others and to work with them. I learned confidence. . . . Classes teach how to take care of body, personal hygiene, how to tell the old gang "NO" . . . how to deal with peer pressure. . . . What is good about IMPACT is the form of discipline. It teaches you to use your ears instead of your mouth. . . . This program . . . changes people. [It teaches you to] look out for yourself so you don't go downhill. . . . The program's main thing is to teach you to stay out of trouble.

This evaluation led to the Louisiana program's inclusion as one of eight programs in the National Institute of Justice multisite evaluation of shock incarceration. IMPACT was reported as one of only three programs having a positive impact on participants, recidivism, and prison crowding. IMPACT graduates had a low rate of recidivism for new felony convictions. With the emphasis on education and treatment added in 1995-1996 and the enhanced aftercare components added in 1997, staff anticipate even lower recidivism rates in the future.

Conclusion

The IMPACT program has been nationally recognized as a model correctional program by the American Correctional Association. In October of 1996, the IMPACT program was reaccredited by the American Correctional Association, scoring 100 percent on all accreditation standards. The program continues to evolve, demonstrating a commitment to growth by the leadership, which has a positive impact on the program, staff, and inmates.

Author/Contact:

C. M. Lensing
Warden
Elayn Hunt Correctional Center

P. O. Box 174
St. Gabriel, Louisiana 70776
(504) 642-3306

Youth Leadership Academy and City Challenge

Introduction

In 1991, the New York State Division for Youth explored the development of a military boot camp model as an alternative to the traditional residential care for juvenile delinquents. With assistance from the state's Division of Military and Naval Affairs and its successful military leadership model, the Youth Leadership Academy and its aftercare component, City Challenge, were developed.

The Sergeant Henry Johnson Youth Leadership Academy, located in Delaware County, New York, is a thirty-bed "boot camp" for male juvenile delinquents from New York City, fourteen to seventeen years old, who require restrictive out-of-community placement in a limited secure facility. The academy provides a six-month program followed by an intensive aftercare program called City Challenge, which is located in Brooklyn.

Statement of Purpose

The Youth Leadership Academy and City Challenge programs are based on an empowerment philosophy centered around four values: self-discipline (accountability), affiliation (trust and relationships), self-esteem (competence), and self-worth (worthiness). These four values are further defined through twenty-five subcomponents from which cadets develop positive self-concepts through a cognitive restructuring process. The City Challenge aftercare component is designed to help cadets practice and retain the prosocial skills and attitudes they learned while at the Youth Leadership Academy; to assist, counsel, and facilitate their movement back to families and communities; and to reaffirm the Youth Leadership Academy's program values.

Staff relationships with cadets are built through a leadership model that requires positive assumptions about cadets, visualizes positive outcomes, rewards successes, and counsels youth about shortcomings. Cadets are not punished, demeaned, nor diminished in any manner. This "value building process" begins immediately when the cadet arrives at the academy. Using a Cadet Development System, which describes program procedures and establishes roles and responsibilities, all decisions about advancement, empowerment, and release are tied to the program's twenty-five value components. This design creates the positive, dynamic culture in which positive outcomes are achieved.

Implementation

Staff Training Programs

The program staff are either Division for Youth employees or are retired from the military. The staff are selected especially for this assignment. The academic teachers are all credentialed by the New York State Education Department. Psychologists, counselors, and other treatment staff are credentialed in their areas of expertise. The custody staff (cadet leaders) are retired from the military. In addition, the youth division has a training unit that conducts or coordinates training for division-mandated staff training. In-house training specific to the academy is conducted there.

Treatment and Education Program

The academy is an intensive, highly structured, and physically rigorous six-month training program. The daily routine and discipline, while rigorous, are supportive and enabling rather than punitive. Cadets are measured for their improvements in personal behavior, thinking processes, self-concept, educational attainment, and job skills. Family involvement is a significant part of the program.

The academy is divided into three phases: Basic Challenge, Adventure Challenge, and Advanced Challenge. Basic Challenge is basic training. A highly normal, directive form of leadership is used and cadets earn trust. A system of merits and demerits records behavior.

Adventure Challenge is an Outward Bound-type program in which cadets learn more about themselves and their abilities to overcome barriers. Advanced Challenge is a program designed to teach work skills, develop self-discipline, and build esteem through the accomplishment of difficult and complex building tasks.

Education is one of the key themes running through the academy's program. Everything is viewed as a learning experience. Teachers, including special education and secondary education teachers, and a vocational specialist, provide daily classroom instruction to each cadet. The cadet leaders (line staff) assist teachers and conduct instruction in the absence of a teacher. Specified classroom norms are established and enforced.

Two programs were designed specifically for the academy: the Magic Within and the Job Book. The Magic Within is a sixty-module group counseling program that provides self-awareness, values, and goal setting. The Magic program gives young people the ability and responsibility to declare themselves competent and worthy. This approach stresses individual accountability and the capacity to improve. Many elements in the program are drawn from the Total Quality Management philosophy, adapted to the needs of a high-risk youth population.

The Job Book provides experiential training based on 200 performance-based tasks designed to build personal competence and enhance esteem. The direct care staff teach a specific skill, model it, supervise cadet practice of the task, and evaluate performance. Representative tasks include: passing physical performance standards, identifying trees and wildlife, writing a business letter, demonstrating first aid, understanding due process, and participating in community service.

Group counseling is conducted daily based on The Magic Within and aggression replacement training (ART). ART is a behavior modification strategy that includes structured learning therapy, anger control techniques, and moral reasoning. Aggression replacement training teaches behavior and The Magic Within provides a reason why. Other groups also are conducted on AIDS prevention, substance abuse, and law-related education.

Families are brought into the cadet's development process. Parents are consulted and mentored by staff. When the family is not available or presents no hope for the cadet, an alternative is developed with the cadet as a full participant in his future. Under these circumstances, an extended family member or a variety of other resources are used.

Work and Community Service Program

Because cadets are juveniles, their work while at the Youth Leadership Academy is to study in academic classes. They maintain their housing unit and are responsible for personal care, and performing chores typical of those appropriate for teenagers. They learn skills that will prepare them for the world of work during Advanced Challenge.

Community service is a vital component of the City Challenge program. The New York City Parks provide a rewarding outlet for cadets as they are able to make a lasting and visible contribution to their environment while receiving training. City recreation programs are accessed through the involvement with the parks, opening a variety of alternatives for leisure time, critical to every youth's effort to remain positive and productive.

Physical Training, Drill, and Ceremony

The academy uses a variety of military-style training programs through which skill levels are achieved and relationships with staff mentors are solidified. These programs combine 290 performance-based stress reducers, fitness skills, and skills associated with strengthening families. The direct care staff teach, model, and evaluate cadets in these programs.

The academy provides an intense, achievement-oriented environment, relevant to the lives of the residents it services. A ropes course is used to teach skills, build confidence, and help cadets learn to overcome barriers. Cadets do not march or engage in any other exercises designed to demonstrate compliance. In accordance with signed conditions of participation, cadets wear military uniforms (battle dress fatigues) and surrender all personal clothing and equipment, except family photographs and religious artifacts.

Aftercare

Youth participate on a daily basis in the City Challenge aftercare program for five months, Monday through Friday. Through partnership with the New York City Board of Education, an alternative high school is offered on-site at City Challenge, which also has its own career education center. New partnerships with LaGuardia Community College and the city's Career Employment Opportunities office are creating a foundation for work readiness programs. Home and family assessments also are offered, including family reintegration programs, crisis intervention, and classes in independent living.

The New York City Board of Education provides a minimum of 3.5 hours of instruction a day. The fact that City Challenge is fully integrated with the board of education allows access to a wide range of services. The most critical of these services is the broader alternative high school system, which includes open access to vocational programs.

It is the intent of City Challenge to move youth into a city-based educational program tailored to the needs and desires established while in residential treatment. The opportunity to earn a GED is seen as a major part of that program. The New York City Department of Transportation Green Team stipend program is used extensively. This program allows youth to complete their GED, gain work experience, and enter a community college. The participants also have the option of moving out of the City Challenge program into city-sponsored alternative programs in their local community.

At the conclusion of the City Challenge placement, the youth generally enter the Division for Youth Aftercare program until such time as their court assignment ends. Funds from the W. T. Grant Foundation augment the City Challenge services. These services are provided by the Children's Aide Society of New York and include clinical support, program enrichment, service linkages, family linkages, training, case management, career readiness, alumni leadership organization, comprehensive health care and psychiatric referrals, and ongoing program and clinical consultation.

Results

As of 1997, since opening in 1991, the Youth Leadership Academy has served 245 youth. The City Challenge program, which opened in 1992, has provided services for 203 youth. A formal evaluation of the academy and the City Challenge program is currently being conducted by the University of Maryland. Comprehensive data on program outcomes and effectiveness are being collected through this research initiative.

The federal Office of Juvenile Justice and Delinquency Prevention, as part of its efforts to improve program outcomes, has conducted extensive research demonstrating the importance of the transition stage of youths' rehabilitation to their success. It has provided the services of a national expert, David Altschuler from the Johns Hopkins University, to assist in designing a model juvenile aftercare program to match the model juvenile boot camp. In addition, it is providing support to obtain private foundation and federal funds to conduct a thorough evaluation and documentation of both phases to become a national demonstration project.

Conclusion

The Youth Leadership Academy and City Challenge programs together have become a model for other programs in the country. The programs have been a centerpiece for two Office of Justice Programs Boot Camp Planning Conferences. The academy has been visited by more than seventy national and international jurisdictions.

Both the academy and City Challenge have been accredited by the American Correctional Association under the Boot Camp and Day Placement standards. The Youth Leadership Academy was, in fact, the first juvenile boot camp accredited by the American Correctional Association. The program represents a considerable investment of resources in this juvenile population, a demonstration of the commitment of the state's Division for Youth in providing quality services to adjudicated juvenile offenders.

Contact:

Louis F. Mann
Deputy Commissioner for Rehabilitative Services
New York State Office of Children and Family Services

52 Washington Street
Rensselaer, New York 12144-2735
(518) 473-1786

Substance Abuse Treatment

17

Introduction

The field of correctional intervention now is being heavily influenced by a wealth of high quality research that has amassed in recent years. Perhaps, for the first time, correctional intervention is being grounded firmly in sound, testable psychological and criminal justice theory. This research confirms that some approaches to correctional intervention are effective in reducing offenders' risk for future criminal conduct. The dimensions of risk, need, and responsivity provide the conceptual foundation for developing effective correctional intervention (e.g., Andrews, Bonta, and Hoge, 1990).

Briefly, the "risk principle" dictates that the most intensive and multifaceted intervention should be reserved for the highest risk offenders—those who stand the most to gain (in terms of risk reduction) from treatment. The "need principle" indicates that intervention specifically should target "criminogenic factors"—factors that are linked to the offender's criminal behavior and are amenable to influence and change. Substance abuse is a primary example of a criminogenic factor. Finally, the "responsivity principle" emphasizes that the approach and modalities used in the treatment process should be based on sound theory and research and should fit closely with the offender's characteristics, orientation, and interpersonal style to maximize the benefit to the offender and the overall effectiveness of treatment. As a general rule, approaches to treatment that make use of behavioral and cognitive-behavioral techniques are best suited for use with offenders.

These principles provide clear guidance to correctional agencies regarding the design and content of effective correctional intervention. Many correctional jurisdictions have been very active in developing and implementing treatment programs and intervention models that draw from solid criminal justice and correctional theory and research; others are just commencing this challenging process.

The treatment of offenders' substance abuse problems is an excellent example of this process in action. In many instances, the program content, structure, and service delivery models of substance abuse treatment currently available for criminal justice clients do not reflect the basic risk, need, and responsivity principles. The substance abuse treatment that is widely available to offenders, especially in the United States, continues to reflect traditional thinking regarding the nature and origins of offenders' alcohol and other drug problems. Specifically, most programs currently available embrace the position that alcohol and drug-use behavior is a disease process that, by definition, evolves in a progressive and chronic fashion (e.g., Jellinek, 1960). This perspective holds that clients need to be actively (and sometimes aggressively) confronted about the existence of substance use problems because they are in a state of "denial" and fail to acknowledge the presence and true seriousness of their problem.

However, recent advances in both correctional and noncorrectional substance abuse treatment fields provide solid direction to correctional program developers and administrators regarding the design and content of effective substance abuse treatment. Importantly, a convincing body of research supports the conclusion that the disease perspective lacks a solid theoretical frame and empirical basis. It has been referred to by some researchers in the area (e.g., Sobell and Sobell, 1993) as a "belief-based" approach due to the lack of substantive theory and supporting research. Others have suggested that notions of a disease have little clinical utility (e.g., Ogborne, 1997) and actually may impede treatment (e.g., Miller and Rollnick, 1991; Peele, 1989) by placing individuals who believe they are subject to a disease, at *increased* risk for relapse (see Miller, Westerberg, Harris, and Tonigan, 1996).

Moreover, recent research uncovering genetic predispositional factors and neurochemical factors associated with alcohol and other drug use (for reviews see Ellinwood and King, 1995; Ray and Ksir, 1996), and a wide range of gastrointestinal, cardiovascular, neurological, and oncological conditions that are the result of chronic abuse and dependence frequently are misused as evidence for the existence of substance use disease. Taken together, as scientific attention on substance abuse treatment has increased, both within and outside of the correctional realm, a number of criteria (with theoretical and empirical support) have emerged and are now available to guide the design of effective substance abuse treatment for offenders.

Best Practices

The following criteria for identifying "best practice" substance abuse programs are drawn from a detailed examination of the relevant correctional and noncorrectional substance abuse treatment and research literature. These criteria served as the basis against which each of the programs presented in this chapter were evaluated. Numerous programs from across North America were submitted for consideration. The three programs presented below were deemed acceptable for inclusion because they met either most or all of the criteria.

The criteria reflect the current state of knowledge of effective corrections-based substance abuse treatment. The dimensions were blended from program standards and guidelines for general program accreditation currently in use by *Her Majesty's Prison Service* in England (*Her Majesty's Prison Service*, 1996), the *Scottish Prison Service* (*Scottish Prison Service*, 1997), and the *Correctional Service of Canada* (Porporino, 1997). The criteria were adapted for direct application to the specific area of substance abuse treatment.

- *Explicit, Theoretical and Empirically Based Treatment Model and Model of Change.* There must be an explicit theoretical model of how the program facilitates change in problematic offender behavior. There must also be evidence to justify the assumptions of the model.

- *Target Criminogenic Factors.* The program must be designed to change factors that have been shown to be closely linked to the participants' criminal behavior.

- *Responsivity Principle.* The treatment techniques and modalities used to target these criminogenic factors must be ones to which offender participants are responsive. The conditions necessary for these techniques and modalities to operate effectively must be specified as part of the program.

- *Cognitive-behavioral/Relapse Prevention.* Programs must combine both cognitive and behavioral techniques drawn from social learning theory. Cognitive-behavioral-oriented relapse prevention is at the heart of this approach for the treatment of substance abusing offenders.

- *Skill-development Oriented.* Programs must teach and practice skills that participants can use to avoid future criminal activities and to engage successfully in legitimate and socially appropriate behavior (e.g., relapse prevention).

- *Multifaceted/Multimodal.* Programs must address a range of criminogenic factors that are linked to substance abuse in an integrated and mutually reinforcing way.

- *Dose.* The amount, intensity, sequencing, and spacing of treatment should be related to the seriousness of the criminogenic factor and the risk and persistence of offending.

- *The Continuum of Care From Institution to Community.* Treatment gains made during incarceration need to be reinforced and strengthened by intervention efforts in the community.

- *Ongoing Monitoring.* Programs must have a built-in commitment to monitoring their operation, and correcting and improving their performance when they deviate from required standards and procedures.

- *Ongoing Evaluation.* A commitment to ongoing quantitative program evaluation of treatment effectiveness must be built into the program.

The first of the three programs that follow is actually a summary of the comprehensive treatment model and range of interventions applied to offenders by the Correctional Service of Canada. It presents a systemic approach within a national correctional system. The second program offers a description of the philosophy and practice of drug treatment programming within the Federal Bureau of Prisons. The final program describes an intensive and comprehensive treatment program for the substance abusing offender by the Center for Interdisciplinary Studies in Denver, Colorado. These programs show that it is possible to provide effective intervention for substance abusing offenders when program design and implementation draw from the principles of risk, need, and responsivity.

The references listed next pertain to all the essays in this section.

References

Andrews, D. A., and J. Bonta. 1994. *The Psychology of Criminal Conduct.* Cincinnati, Ohio: Anderson.

Andrews, D. A., J. Bonta, and R. Hoge. 1990. Classification for Effective Rehabilitation: Rediscovering Psychology. *Criminal Justice and Behavior.* 17, 19-52.

Andrews, D. A., K. I. Zinger, R. D. Hoge, P. Gendreau, and F. T. Cullen. 1990. Does Correctional Treatment Work? A Clinically-relevant and Psychologically-informed Meta-analysis. *Criminology.* 28, 369-404.

Bush, J. M., and B. C. Bilodeau.1993. *Options: A Cognitive Change Program* (Prepared by J. M. Bush and B. C. Bilodeau for the National Institute of Corrections and the U.S. Department of the Navy). Washington, D.C.: National Institute of Corrections.

Collins, J. J., and M. Allison.1983. Legal Coercion and Retention in Drug Abuse Treatment. *Hospital and Community Psychiatry.* 34, 1145-1149.

Collins, J. J., R. L. Hubbard, J. V. Rachal, and E. Cavanaugh.1988. Effects of Legal Coercion on Drug Abuse Treatment. In M. D. Anglin, ed. *Compulsory Treatment of Opiate Dependence.* New York: Haworth.

Correctional Service of Canada. 1991. *Task Force Report on the Reduction of Substance Abuse.* Ottawa: Correctional Service of Canada.

Dolan, K., and A. Wodak.1996. An International Review of Methadone Provision in Prisons. *Addiction Research.* 4, 85-97.

Ellinwood, E. H., and G. R. King.1995. Drug Effects and Biological Factors. In J. Jaffe, ed. *Encyclopedia of Drugs and Alcohol.* Macmillan Library Reference.

Field, G. 1989. A Study of the Effects of Intensive Treatment on Reducing the Criminal Recidivism of Addicted Offenders. *Federal Probation.* 53, 51-56.

Ginsburg, J., and J. R. Weekes.1998. Unpublished raw data. Ottawa: Correctional Service of Canada.

Her Majesty's Prison Service. 1996. *Criteria for Accrediting Programmes - 1996/1997.* London: Her Majesty's Prison Service.

Hubbard, R. L., J. J. Collins, J. V. Rachal, and E. R. Cavanaugh.1988. The Criminal Justice Client in Drug Abuse Treatment. In C. G. Leukefeld and F. M. Tims, eds. *Compulsory Treatment of Drug Abuse: Research and Clinical Practice* (DHHS Publication No. ADM 88-1578, pp. 57- 80). Rockville, Maryland: National Institute on Drug Abuse.

Izzo, R. L., and R. R. Ross.1990. Meta-analysis of Rehabilitation Programs for Juvenile Delinquents. *Criminal Justice and Behavior.* 17, 134-142.

Jellinek, E. M. 1960. *The Disease Concept of Alcoholism.* New Brunswick, New Jersey: Hillhouse Press.

Kadden, R., K. Carroll, D. Donovan, N. Cooney, P. Monti, D. Abrams, M. Litt, and R. Hester. 1992. *Cognitive-behavioral Coping Skills Therapy Manual: A Clinical Research Guide for Therapists Treating Individuals with Alcohol Abuse and Dependence* (Project MATCH Monograph Series, Vol. 3). Rockville, Maryland: National Institutes on Alcohol Abuse and Alcoholism.

King, K., S. Rene, J. Schmidt, E. Stipetich, and N. Woldsweth. 1994. *Cognitive Intervention Program.* Madison, Wisconsin: Wisconsin Department of Corrections.

Lipsey, M. W. 1992. Juvenile Delinquency Treatment: A Meta-analytic Inquiry into the Variability of Effects. In T. D. Cook, H. Cooper, D. S. Cordray, H. Hartmann, L. V. Hedges, R. J. Light, T. A. Louis, and F. Mosteller, eds. *Meta-analysis for Explanation* (pp. 83-127). New York: Russell Sage Foundation.

Lipsey, M. W., and D. B. Wilson. 1993. The Efficacy of Psychological, Educational and Behavioral Treatment: Confirmation from Meta-analysis. *American Psychologist.* 48, 1181- 1209.

Lipton, D. S. 1994. The Correctional Opportunity: Pathways to Drug Treatment for Offenders. *Journal of Drug Issues.* 24, 331-348.

Marlatt, G. A. and J. R. Gordon, eds. 1985. *Relapse Prevention: Maintenance Strategies in the Treatment of Addictive Behaviors.* New York: Guilford.

McDermott, S. P. and F. D. Wright. 1992. Cognitive Therapy: Long-term Outlook for a Short-term Psychotherapy. In J. S. Ruttan, ed. *Psychotherapy for the 1990s* (pp. 61-99). New York: Guilford.

McGuire, J. and P. Priestley. 1995. Reviewing "What works": Past, Present and Future. In J. McGuire, ed. What Works: Reducing Reoffending (pp. 3-34). New York: Wiley.

Miller, W. R. and S. Rollnick, eds. 1991. *Motivational Interviewing: Preparing People to Change Addictive Behavior.* New York: Guilford Press.

Miller, W. R., V. S. Westerberg, R. J. Harris, and J. S. Tonigan.1996. What Predicts Relapse? Prospective Testing of Antecedent Models. *Addiction.* 91, 155-171.

Miller, W. R., A. D. Zweben, C. C. DiClemente, and R. G. Rychtarik.1994. *Motivational Enhancement Therapy Manual: A Clinical Research Guide for Therapists Treating Individuals with Alcohol Abuse and Dependence* (Project MATCH Monograph Series, Vol. 2). Rockville, Maryland: National Institute on Alcohol Abuse and Alcoholism.

Millson, W. A. 1996. *Evaluation of the Recovery Program at Collins Bay Institution: Final Report.* Ottawa: Correctional Service of Canada.

Millson, W. A., J. R. Weekes, and L. O. Lightfoot.1995. *The Offender Substance Abuse Pre-Release Program: Analysis of Intermediate and Post-release Outcomes* (Research Report, No.: R-40). Ottawa: Correctional Service of Canada.

Monti, P. M., D. B. Abrams, R. M. Kadden, and N. L. Cooney.1989. *Treating Alcohol Dependence: A Coping Skills Training Guide.* New York: Guilford.

Monti, P. M., D. J. Rohsenow, S. M. Colby, and D. B. Abrams.1995. Coping and Social Skills Training. In R. K. Hester and W. R. Miller, eds. *Handbook of Alcoholism Treatment Approaches: Effective Alternatives* (pp. 221-241). Boston: Allyn and Bacon.

Ogborne, A. C. 1997. Theories of "Addiction" and Implications for Counseling. In S. Harrison and V. Carver, eds. *Alcohol and Drug Problems: A Practical Guide for Counselors, 2nd Edition* (pp. 3-18). Toronto: Addiction Research Foundation.

Parks, G. A., and G. A. Marlatt. 1997. Keeping "What Works" Working: Cognitive-behavioral Relapse Prevention with Substance-abusing Offenders. *In What Works: Critical Issues Research and Best Practices in Community Corrections.* International Community Corrections Association Conference, Cleveland, Ohio (October 5-8, 1997).

Peele, S. 1989. *Diseasing of America: Addiction Treatment Out of Control.* Boston, Massachusetts: Houghton Mifflin.

Porporino, F. J. 1997. *Developing Program Accreditation Criteria for the Correctional Service of Canada: Issues and a Suggested Approach.* Ottawa: Correctional Service of Canada.

Prochaska, J. O. and C. C. DiClemente. 1992. Stages of Change in the Modification of Problem Behavior. In M. Hersen, R. Eisler, and P. M. Miller, eds. *Progress in Behavior Modification* (pp. 184-214). Sycamore, Illinois; Sycamore Publishing.

Prochaska, J. O., C. C. DiClemente, and J. C. Norcross. 1992. In Search of How People Change: Applications to Addictive Behaviors. *American Psychologist.* 47, 1102-1114.

Ray, O. and C. Ksir. 1996. *Drugs, Society, and Human Behavior.* St. Louis, Missouri: Mosby.

Ross, R. R., E. A. Fabiano, and R. D. Ross.1986. *Reasoning and Rehabilitation: A Handbook for Teaching Cognitive Skills.* Ottawa, Ontario: University of Ottawa.

Ross, R. R. and L. O. Lightfoot.1985. *Treatment of the Alcohol Abusing Offender.* Springfield, Illinois: Charles C Thomas.

Ross, R. R., and R. D. Ross.1988. *Cognitive Skills: A Training Manual for Living Skills-Phase 1.* Ottawa, Ontario: Correctional Service of Canada.

Rotgers, F. Manuscript in preparation. Harm Reduction in Corrections: Adopting a Pragmatic Approach to Substance Users. In J. R. Weekes, ed. *Components of Effective Substance Abuse Treatment for Offenders: A Correctional Practitioner's Guide.* Lanham, Maryland: American Correctional Association.

Scottish Prison Service. 1997. *Prisoner Programme Accreditation.* Edinburgh: Scottish Prison Service.

Sobell, M. B. and L. C. Sobell. 1993. *Problem Drinkers: Guided Self-change Treatment.* New York: Guilford.

Van Voorhis, P. 1987. Correctional Effectiveness: The Cost of Ignoring Success. *Federal Probation.* 51, 56-62.

Vigdal, G. L. and D. W. Stadler. 1992. Comprehensive System Development in Corrections for Drug Abusing Offenders: The Wisconsin Department of Corrections. In C. G. Leukefield and F. M. Tims, eds. *Drug Abuse Treatment in Prisons and Jails* (pp. 126-141). Washington, D.C.: U.S. Government Printing Office.

Wanberg, K. W. and J. L. Horn.1983. Assessment of Alcohol Use with Multidimensional Concepts and Measures. *American Psychologist.* 38, 1055-1069.

———. 1987. The Assessment of Multiple Conditions in Persons with Alcohol Problems. In W. M. Cox, ed. *Treatment and Prevention of Alcohol Problems* (pp. 27-56). New York: Academic Press.

Wanberg, K. W. and H. B. Milkman. 1997. *Criminal Conduct and Substance Abuse Treatment: Strategies for Self-Improvement and Change.* Thousand Oaks, California: Sage Publications.

Weekes, J. R. 1997. Substance Abuse Treatment for Offenders. *Corrections Today.* 59, 12-14.

Weekes, J. R., E. Fabiano, F. J. Porporino, D. Robinson, and W. A. Millson.1993. *Assessment of Substance Abuse in Offenders: The Computerized Lifestyle Assessment Instrument.* Paper presented at the annual meeting of the Canadian Psychological Association, Montreal, Quebec.

Weekes, J. R., A. E. Moser, and C. M. Langevin. 1997. Assessing Substance Abusing Offenders for Treatment. In *What Works: Critical Issues Research and Best Practices in Community Corrections.* International Community Corrections Association Conference, Cleveland, Ohio (October 5-8, 1997).

Committee chair:

John R. Weekes, Ph.D.
Research Manager
Correctional Service of Canada

340 Laurier Avenue West
Ottawa, Ontario, Canada K1A OP9
(613) 947-0587

Substance Abuse Treatment: Canada's Approach

Introduction

In 1989, the Commissioner of the Correctional Service of Canada commissioned a Task Force on the Reduction of Substance Abuse. The Task Force's Final Report (Correctional Service of Canada, 1991) recommended the development and implementation of an elaborate, multifaceted assessment and treatment model to meet the diverse treatment needs of incarcerated offenders and offenders on release. Integral to this approach was the recognition that offenders who abuse alcohol and other drugs represent a heterogeneous group with respect to the nature and severity of the substance abuse problems—ranging from relatively minor problematic substance use to severe and debilitating, polydrug abuse. Accordingly, to fully meet offenders' treatment needs, a range of programs were needed that varied in terms of intensity, duration, and cost. The report also emphasized the need for interventions to be tailored to meet the specific treatment needs of women and Aboriginal offenders.

Prevalence of Offender Problems with Alcohol and Other Drugs

United States and Canadian research repeatedly has demonstrated that a staggering number of offenders have substance abuse problems relative to the general population. Indeed, data with Canadian federal offenders indicate that about seven-out-of-ten offenders exhibit problematic use of alcohol and other drugs (Weekes, Fabiano, Porporino, Robinson, and Millson, 1993; Weekes, Moser, and Langevin, 1997).[1] Moreover, substance use and abuse is somehow related to more than 50 percent of the crime committed by these individuals.

However, not all offenders evidence chronic, serious problems. Correctional Service of Canada data on the prevalence and seriousness of offenders' substance abuse problems indicate that only about one-third of offenders have serious problems. A third have low-severity problems. Finally, and perhaps surprising to some, a full third of offenders do not present significant problems warranting treatment. The data also indicate that the relationship between substance use and crime strengthens dramatically with increasing severity, both for present offences and past criminal behavior.

These patterns of substance abuse characteristics underscore the need for differential treatment models to: (1) ensure that offenders receive appropriate and sufficient "dosages" of treatment; (2) prioritize offenders according to risk and need; (3) target substance abuse that is clearly linked with criminal behavior; (4) avoid the "over-prescription" of treatment; and (5) ensure the timely and cost-effective delivery of intervention services during incarceration and following release into the community.

Implementation

Correctional Service of Canada's Treatment Model

Since the formation of the task force and the publication of its final report, the Correctional Service of Canada has actively undertaken the development and implementation of a range of substance abuse programs to meet offenders' treatment needs. These programs were developed following a detailed examination of contemporary theory, research, and practice in the treatment of individuals with substance abuse problems (correctional and noncorrectional literatures), and research on the characteristics of effective correctional treatment.

The current model, which is the result of an iterative process over the past few years, offers an array of institutional- and community-based program options that are delivered nationally to offenders in federal correctional institutions and on conditional release in the community. Overall, these interventions are a blend of national "core" programs and other programs and treatment services that are provided on contract by various agencies and organizations to offenders under the Correctional Service of Canada's jurisdiction.

A "Harm Reduction" Approach

The national "core" substance abuse programs that were developed and implemented across Canada are founded on the principles of harm reduction (e.g., Rotgers, in press). As such, the programs do not consider total abstinence as the only positive outcome for treatment. While abstinence is the preferred outcome for many, if not most offenders, the model recognizes that some individuals can moderate their alcohol use successfully and that the reduction of high-risk drug use behaviors is a solid indicator of success. Importantly, while many offenders commence treatment with the goal of moderating their future alcohol and drug use at safer levels, by the end of the treatment process, the majority of these program participants make the *voluntary* decision to abstain from all intoxicants.

Consistent with the harm reduction approach, the Correctional Service of Canada employs an institutional bleach program to reduce the risks associated with offenders sharing contaminated needles. In addition, it recently has implemented the use of methadone for the treatment of serious opiate use of incarcerated offenders. Methadone maintenance treatment is a well-recognized and effective long-term treatment for individuals who are at high risk for infectious disease transmission. Some former heroin addicts have been maintained successfully on methadone for decades and have led productive lives free of the dangers associated with injecting heroin.

It is noteworthy to point out that methadone maintenance treatment has been used successfully by a number of correctional agencies including New South Wales (Australia), Spain, Switzerland, and Denmark (see Dolan and Wodak, 1996). At present, the New York City correctional complex on Riker's Island is the only prison site in the United States to offer methadone maintenance treatment to incarcerated offenders.

The Role of Assessment

The heterogeneity of offenders' substance abuse problems leading to differential treatment emphasizes the need for comprehensive assessment. Whereas many existing programs purport to assess offenders' substance abuse problems, few models result in the development of truly individualized treatment plans. Frequently, offenders who participate and undergo assessment of their substance abuse problems then are admitted into the one and only substance abuse program offered by the institution or halfway house.

Alternatively, in the Correctional Service of Canada's model, assessment leads to clear decisions regarding the intensity and duration of treatment that is delivered to the offender. As outlined next, the model does not make use of lengthy and costly therapeutic community programs. Instead, the primary or intensive phase of treatment is delivered in a focused and time-limited manner. In most cases, the intensive phase is strongly oriented around developing skills, modeling, role-playing, and practicing. The structure of the intensive phase varies according to the overall intensity and the intended client population for each program. The intensive phase is followed closely by ongoing maintenance follow-up sessions that serve to expand and reinforce the principles delivered to offenders during the initial stages.

The Computerized Lifestyle Assessment Instrument or CLAI serves as the primary screening device to identify offenders with alcohol and other drug problems. The CLAI has been subjected to extensive research to confirm the accuracy of offenders' responses (summarized in Weekes, et al., 1997). The overarching strategy employed by this research was to examine issues related to the validity and reliability of offender self-reported information on substance use behaviors. The studies analyzed a variety of independent sources of information including collateral data, in-person interviews, other independent assessments and measurement approaches, and a range of psychometric analyses and checks. The results of these investigations converge in support of the conclusion that, contrary to popular belief, offender-generated information about substance use is a sufficiently accurate reflection of the nature and severity of the offenders' problems with alcohol and other drugs.

Assessment information provided by the CLAI screening process forms the basis for case management referrals to substance abuse treatment providers. In the Correctional Service of Canada, institutional case workers are referred to as parole officers, or institutions parole officers (POIs), reflecting the Service's emphasis on preparing and reintegrating offenders safely back into the community at the earliest possible time. After receiving the referral, program delivery officers (correctional staff who have received specialized training in substance abuse treatment) undertake further assessment using structured interviews and other tools to confirm the individual's suitability for treatment, to enhance the offender's readiness to change, and to finalize the substance abuse treatment plan in collaboration with the offender.

Once the program has commenced, program delivery officers maintain attendance and performance records for each offender. In addition, final reports are completed and forwarded to the offenders' institutions parole officers for inclusion in the documentation that is assembled for review by the National Parole Board. The final report analyzes and summarizes the offender's performance in treatment and makes suggestions regarding the need for further treatment.

Cognitive-behavioral Treatment (CBT)

The Service's model for substance abuse treatment is based on social learning theory that explains the genesis of adult problems with the consumption of alcohol and other drugs. This approach acknowledges the role of a variety of genetic and physiological predisposing factors. The individual's social learning underscores the influence of environmental factors that contribute to the development and maintenance of substance abuse problems. Extending from the social-learning theoretical approach, the Service's programs incorporate a range of behavioral and cognitive-behavioral intervention modalities, and various complementary client-centered approaches (e.g., "motivational interviewing") to foster offenders' commitment to change and to maximize the effectiveness of corrections-based substance abuse treatment (e.g., Miller and Rollnick, 1991; Prochaska and DiClemente, 1992).

The cognitive-behavioral approach employed by the Service's programs also emphasizes the use of structured relapse prevention (Marlatt and Gordon, 1985; Parks and Marlatt, 1997). Structured relapse prevention is a skill-development approach that teaches participants about the relapse process, how to identify and handle high-risk situations, and how to deal with urges and cravings, slips, lapses, and relapses.

Current Regimen of Substance Abuse Programs

At present, the Service's inventory of national substance abuse programs consist of the programs that are described next. All programs with the exception of the Alcohol, Drugs and Personal Choice program incorporate postintensive phase-maintenance sessions that are designed to build on the skills taught during the session and to provide offenders with the opportunity to share their experience since completing the program.

Alcohol, Drugs, and Personal Choice

Alcohol, Drugs, and Personal Choice is a prevention program consisting of nine half-day sessions offered to incarcerated offenders with no significant substance abuse problem. It also serves as a primer for offenders with more serious problems who go on to participate in more intensive intervention. The program aims to provide offenders with accurate information on the harmful effects of alcohol and other drugs and to foster changes in offenders' attitudes towards substance use and abuse.

Offender Substance Abuse Pre-Release Program

The Offender Substance Abuse Pre-Release Program consists of twenty-six half-day sessions in an institution using cognitive-behavioral treatment techniques. The program strives to facilitate knowledge acquisition, attitudinal shift, and the development of solid cognitive-behavioral, relapse prevention skills prior to an offender's release into the community. The Offender Substance Abuse Pre-Release Program currently accepts offenders with intermediate-to-severe substance abuse problems and offenders with a high rate of low-severity problems. In general, the program targets offenders who are within six months of release.

Programme ALTO

ALTO is a twenty-session institutional program that is offered in French to offenders incarcerated in the Quebec region. The theoretical and clinical basis for ALTO is the same as the Offender Substance Abuse Pre-Release Program. ALTO is a prerelease program that accepts offenders with intermediate to severe substance abuse problems and offenders with a high rate of low-severity problems.

Women's Institutional Substance Abuse Program

The Substance Abuse Program for Federally Sentenced Women is a moderate intensity, twenty-one-session program offered to incarcerated female offenders. The sessions are divided into two phases, and the women are assessed and placed in either phase one or phase two based on where they are in the change process. Phase one of the program is composed of eleven group sessions offered on a weekly basis, and three individual counseling sessions. Individuals with minimal motivation, and limited skills and knowledge about substance abuse issues and relapse prevention are referred to phase one. The focus of phase one is to provide basic drug and alcohol education and exercises designed to move the client along in the change process (e.g., decisional balance). Phase two includes three individual sessions and ten weekly sessions. The goal of phase two is to provide the women with basic information on relapse prevention and an opportunity to develop the skills necessary to maintain their lifestyle changes.

Women's Community Substance Abuse Program

The Women's Substance Abuse Program—Community Component is a brief intervention of low-moderate intensity. The most appropriate candidates are women who have successfully completed the institutional program and require ongoing participation in treatment, or women whose risk and need levels are suggestive of someone who would benefit from a low-intensity community intervention. The program was adapted from Choices by adding information deemed necessary to meet the needs of women and, for continuity, by making links to information provided in the institutional women's program. This program is delivered in a five full-day or ten half-day format and is followed by weekly maintenance sessions for three to six months. The goals of the intensive phase are to introduce skills and cognitive-behavioral relapse prevention concepts. The women practice and enhance the skills through their participation in the maintenance phase.

Brief, Community-based Relapse Prevention Program (Choices)

Choices offers a brief-intervention program to offenders on release in the community or incarcerated in a minimum-security setting. The program is delivered either across five full-day or ten half-day sessions followed by weekly maintenance sessions for a minimum of three months. The program focuses on teaching cognitive-behavioral relapse prevention techniques to offenders. The program is intended for offenders who have completed institutionally based treatment to extend and enhance their treatment gains and as a primary treatment for offenders who can be safely treated in the community.

Other Substance Abuse Programs

The Service relies on a broad range of other substance abuse programs across the country to make substance abuse treatment fully available to offenders. However, recent reviews of these programs indicate that they vary widely on many dimensions including structure, duration, intensity and quality of treatment services, theoretical base, extent of focus on the link between substance abuse and criminal behavior, cost, and likely effectiveness.

Program Evaluation Methodologies and Preliminary Results

The analysis of treatment effectiveness is a key component of every national program implemented by the Correctional Service. As a result, program evaluation and effectiveness methodologies are designed into each program from the outset. The analyses are intended to provide both intermediate treatment outcomes (pre- to postprogram) and longer term posttreatment outcomes measured relative to substance abuse-related readmissions, parole suspensions and cancellations, and new criminal behavior.

Typically, intermediate outcomes are assessed using a battery of measures. On a group basis, the instruments specifically are designed to measure and assess key program targets (such as skills acquisition). On an individual basis, the measures are designed to evaluate each offender's performance in treatment. Posttreatment and postrelease outcome measures are provided by the Correctional Service's extensive offender management databases, which track offenders following release until the expiration of the warrant of committal.

A major analysis of the Offender Substance Abuse Pre-Release Program, ALTO, and the Choices programs is currently underway. The aggregate databases for these programs represent offenders from across the country who participated in these programs, while incarcerated and in the community. It is anticipated that findings for both intermediate and postrelease outcomes will be available during the fall of 1998. In the meantime, several studies of the Offender Substance Abuse Pre-Release Program provide a glimpse into the effectiveness of this intervention.

Prior to the national implementation of the Offender Substance Abuse Pre-Release Program, a pilot initiative was conducted at a single site between 1990 and 1992 (Millson, Weekes, and Lightfoot, 1995). Offenders were followed for an average of fifteen months after release from custody. The results from this study indicated that 31 percent of offenders who completed the program were readmitted back into custody for technical violations (20 percent) and/or new criminal convictions (13.6 percent). Further analysis confirmed that offenders with low-severity problems were readmitted at a lower rate (21-22 percent) than offenders with more serious problems (24-44 percent). Offenders' performance in treatment was measured using a battery of pre- and postprogram self-report instruments that were designed to measure treatment gains on specific targets of intervention.

Offenders who evidenced good performance in treatment were the least likely to be readmitted over the course of the follow-up period compared with offenders who performed more poorly. By the end of the follow-up period, almost 90 percent of the offenders who performed optimally were still in the community versus just over 50 percent for those who performed the poorest. These findings underscore the ability of intermediate measurement of program performance to reliably predict future behavior and add further evidence for the value of self-reported information on substance abuse provided by the offenders.

Conclusion

Comparison of Cognitive-behavioral Treatment and Disease-model Program Approaches

Millson (1996) compared the effectiveness of the Offender Substance Abuse Pre-Release Program with a traditional recovery program that used many "belief-based" intervention modalities. The latter was premised on the notion that substance abuse is the result of a disease process. Two groups of offenders who were matched on key treatment-relevant characteristics (e.g., severity of substance abuse problem) were assigned to one of the two programs. Program participation was monitored and each offender was tracked for twelve months after release. The results consistently indicated that offenders who participated in the cognitive-behaviorally oriented program yielded higher rates of success in terms of lower rates of readmission and new convictions than those who completed the recovery program. Further, offenders who completed the Offender Substance Abuse Pre-Release Program were more likely to remain in the community over the course of the follow-up period compared to offenders who participated in the recovery program.

New Program Developments

The Service recognizes that providing high quality substance abuse treatment services to offenders is not a static process. New developments in substance abuse assessment and treatment services, both inside and outside of the correctional arena, appear regularly. Staff believe it is critical that they remain abreast of and, where possible, contribute to advances in treatment. The following are representative of research and development efforts in progress.

Specialized Treatment for the Most Serious Abusers

Presently, the Correctional Service is developing an intervention designed to provide intensive focused intervention for offenders with severe substance abuse problems on admission, including active users. The intent is to assist them in developing the short-term goal of successfully modifying their substance use during incarceration, and in fostering the long-term goal of controlling or eliminating substance use after release. This new component of the Correctional Service of Canada's model will be combined with existing institutional and community programs and maintenance components to form a consistent, long-term treatment plan that provides a clear continuum of care that begins during incarceration and extends solidly into the community.

Pre-treatment Priming Using Motivational Interviewing

In many correctional settings, offenders who are not fully prepared to begin in the treatment are either turned away from much needed treatment or are placed in a program before they are fully committed to the process of changing longstanding habitual behavior patterns. The Correctional Service is in the process of developing and implementing a brief intervention using the principles of motivational interviewing to enhance the treatment readiness of offenders who reject the notion that they have a substance abuse problem or who are ambivalent about the need for treatment (see Prochaska and DiClemente, 1992).

Offenders who are at the "precontemplative" or "contemplative" stages of change (Prochaska and DiClemente, 1992) will participate in the program to foster readiness and commitment for treatment. It is anticipated that by moving them to more treatment amenable stages such as the "preparation" or "action" stages, they will derive greater benefit from the treatment experience. Moreover, the motivational interviewing approach already embedded in the Correctional Service's existing substance abuse programs will further reinforce these efforts to maintain offenders' motivation and openness for treatment.

Preliminary data from a study examining the efficacy of the motivational interviewing approach with alcohol abusing offenders (Ginsburg and Weekes, 1998) suggests that about 40 percent of offenders who were pretested at the precontemplative and contemplative levels moved into either the preparation or action stages after participating in one motivational interviewing session.

---

[1]References are listed in the bibliography at the end of the introductory chapter (see p. 415).

Contacts:

John R. Weekes, Ph.D.
Research Manager
Correctional Service of Canada

Carmen Long
Project Manager, Community Substance Abuse Programs
Offender Programs and Reintegration Branch
Correctional Service of Canada

340 Laurier Avenue West
Ottawa, Ontario, Canada K1A OP9
(613) 947-0587 / (613)996-8508

Drug Abuse Treatment Programs in Federal Prisons

Introduction

The purpose of the Federal Bureau of Prisons' Drug Abuse Treatment programs is to provide quality, empirically based drug abuse treatment services to all inmates with a demonstrated need and interest in such treatment. This commitment to provide opportunities for self-improvement is articulated in the Bureau of Prisons' mission statement and, most notably, in the agency's strategic goals.

The philosophy underlying all of the Bureau of Prisons' drug abuse treatment programs is that individuals must assume personal responsibility for their behavior. Despite the influence of environmental conditions and circumstances, the primary target for change is the individual's conscious decision to engage in drug-taking and criminal behavior. Therefore, the principal goal of treatment is to equip the individual with the cognitive, emotional, and behavioral skills necessary to choose and maintain a drug-free and crime-free lifestyle.

The bureau subscribes to a biopsychosocial model of treatment that guides interventions in all of the bureau's drug abuse treatment programs. This holistic approach emphasizes comprehensive lifestyle change as the key to treatment success. Issues such as physical well-being, family relationships, and criminality are targeted for change, in addition to the traditional treatment goals of relapse prevention and abstinence.

The bureau maintains that the acquisition of positive life skills is the means through which drug abuse treatment program participants can change the negative thinking and behavior patterns that led to their drug use and criminality in the past. Through individual and/or group counseling, participants can gain awareness of the negative consequences of their previous thinking and behavior patterns and can learn and develop alternative skills.

Program Design and Development

The Federal Bureau of Prisons has provided drug abuse treatment in various forms for decades. Since the passage of the Anti-Drug Abuse Acts of 1986 and 1988, and with an increased emphasis on and resources for drug treatment, the bureau redesigned its treatment programs. With the help of the National Institute on Drug Abuse and after careful review of drug treatment programs around the country, the bureau developed a drug treatment strategy that incorporates the "proven effective" elements found through this review. Generally speaking, the bureau's strategy is to address inmate drug abuse by:

- Screening all incoming inmates for substance abuse problems to match specific, individualized treatment services to the unique treatment needs of any given offender

- Ensuring that all inmates are aware of the treatment opportunities available to them while in the bureau's facilities

- Placing each eligible inmate in treatment according to his or her need

- Providing continuity of care both during the offender's incarceration and while in the community

To accomplish these objectives, the bureau employs a five-part treatment strategy that includes:

- Orientation, screening, and referral

- Drug abuse education

- Nonresidential drug abuse treatment services

- Residential drug abuse treatment

- Transitional services

The bureau's residential drug abuse treatment program is the flagship of its drug abuse program strategy. Currently, 42 Bureau of Prisons institutions operate residential drug abuse treatment programs, with a combined annual capacity of nearly 6,000 inmates. The programs are 6-, 9-, or 12-months long and provide a minimum of 500 hours of drug abuse treatment. The bureau has a three-phase treatment curriculum that is followed in every residential drug abuse treatment program. The bureau places tremendous emphasis on the transitional component so that inmates become engaged in continuing treatment as they return to their home communities.

Inmates participating in a residential drug abuse treatment program reside in a treatment unit, separate from the general population. Typically, treatment is conducted no less than four hours a day, five days a week. The remainder of the day is spent in education, work skills training, recreation, and other complementary programs such as disease prevention and health promotion instruction, or English as a Second Language. Each residential drug abuse treatment program is staffed by a doctoral-level psychologist who supervises the drug abuse treatment staff, each of whom carries a caseload of no more that twenty-four inmates.

Implementation of the Program Design

The current drug abuse treatment program design became operational in 1989. Since implementation of the program, the most significant impact on the Bureau of Prisons' drug abuse treatment programs occurred in 1994 with the passage of the Violent Crime Control and Law Enforcement Act. This legislation required the Bureau of Prisons to provide residential drug-abuse treatment, the most intensive and comprehensive component of the drug abuse program strategy, to 100 percent of all eligible inmates by the end of fiscal year 1997 and every year thereafter.

In response, the bureau commenced an ambitious expansion plan, which involved redoubling its efforts in recruiting and developing new drug abuse treatment staff, redesigning and testing the most efficacious staff training approaches, refining and implementing the standardized drug treatment curriculum, expanding the transitional services component to keep offenders engaged in treatment as they return to their home communities, and developing a host of other strategies to successfully accomplish the largest drug abuse program expansion in the history of corrections. By the close of fiscal year 1997, the Bureau of Prisons satisfied the requirement of providing treatment to all eligible inmates.

Program Monitoring and Evaluation

The hallmark of any good drug treatment program is the parallel application of a strong evaluation component to assess the effectiveness of the intervention. The Bureau of Prisons recently completed an interim evaluation of its residential drug abuse treatment program. This comprehensive evaluation, conducted with funds and assistance from the National Institute of Drug Abuse, reveals that in the first six months after release from bureau custody:

1. Inmates who completed the residential drug abuse treatment program were 73 percent less likely to be arrested for a new offense than those who did not participate in a residential drug abuse treatment program.

2. Inmates who completed the residential drug abuse treatment programs were 44 percent less likely to use drugs or alcohol than those who did not participate in a residential drug abuse treatment program.

This interim report is based on offenders who had been released from bureau custody and were in the community for six months. The findings of this preliminary evaluation are noteworthy because of the sample size involved (1,866 inmates), a rigorous research design, and the uniqueness of a multisite sample (20 programs at various institutions).

These findings, which suggest that drug abuse treatment assists inmates during this initial transition period, offer encouragement for the conclusion that another correctional program works, breaking the cycle between drug use and criminal activity. The final study will include approximately 3,000 offenders who will have been released to the community for a minimum of three years.

Equally important, the Bureau's Office of Research and Evaluation completed an evaluation of inmates housed in high-security institutions who completed a bureau residential drug abuse program. The findings indicate that for a two-year period following treatment, institutional misconduct among inmates who completed the residential drug abuse treatment program was reduced by 50 percent. These results demonstrate that drug abuse treatment in corrections-based settings assists in the management of inmates. These results underscore the notion that treatment has a vital impact on institution safety and security.

Conclusion

Providing drug abuse treatment in correctional institutions poses significant challenges. The Bureau of Prisons, like other correctional agencies, must respond to shifting public priorities, new legislative mandates, institution mission changes, staff turnover, and other factors that challenge effective drug abuse treatment. Given these challenges, for drug abuse treatment programs to be effective, they must be planned carefully and implemented in accordance with the following principles:

- Strong support from top management staff establishes the importance of the program within the agency.

- A specific treatment orthodoxy, supported by scientific evidence of its effectiveness, must be established (e.g., length of time in treatment, treatment philosophy).

- Systematic treatment documentation must be provided to foster replicability across institutions (such as assessment, curricula, treatment plans, treatment summaries, and program policies). Specific program documentation affords program consistency across the entire correctional system.

- A clearly defined system of incentives and sanctions must be in place. Incentives and sanctions promote an inmate's motivation for treatment. This system rewards positive behaviors and deters undesirable behaviors.

- A qualified, well-trained staff is essential. Clinical training for drug abuse treatment staff should be conducted regularly as should cross-training between treatment and corrections staff. This ensures all staff understand their contribution to the treatment of individuals in the correctional setting.

- A transitional services component must continue the established treatment regimen in the community and combine treatment with community supervision.

- A commitment to outcome and process evaluation is essential to maintain effectiveness. Program administrators, funders, and staff require constant feedback on the successes and deficiencies of the program. This allows the program to be adjusted in response to measured results.

The Bureau of Prisons' drug abuse treatment program has undergone the review of Congress, federal regulators, independent evaluators, and the Department of Justice leadership. The program has been found to be effective in positively changing inmate behavior both in the institution and upon release to the community.

Contact:

Communications
Federal Bureau of Prisons

Office of Public Affairs
320 First Street, NW
Washington, D.C. 20534
(202) 307-3163

Criminal Conduct and Substance Abuse Treatment Strategies

Introduction

The relationship between criminal conduct and alcohol and other drug use is robust and well documented (see Wanberg and Milkman, 1997; Weekes, Moser and Langevin, 1997).[1] Statistics range from 60 to 80 percent with respect to offenders who are reported to have substance abuse histories, offenders who commit crimes while under the influence of drugs, and the percentage of recidivists who have substance abuse histories. Postrehabilitation outcomes are similar with both recidivism and relapse rates (returning to prior alcohol and other drug abuse pattern) each ranging from 50 to 70 percent.

The interaction patterns between criminal conduct and alcohol and other drug abuse are complex and varied. Drugs change or modify mood, thought, and behavior. Compulsive substance use can result in a loss of control and heightened impulsivity—subsequently interacting with criminal conduct. The economic "benefits" of criminal conduct fit into the economic consequences of drug disruption, which places a high financial burden on the substance abuser. The internal result of criminal conduct (such as the fear of getting caught) can be relieved with alcohol and other drug use. With some offenders, such use leads to or precedes criminal conduct. With others, criminal conduct leads to or precedes alcohol and other drug use.

Although the interaction between substance abuse and criminal conduct is complex, what is simple and straightforward is the fact that there is a distinct group of individuals who are dually affected and have a history of alcohol and other drug use and criminal conduct. What is also clear is that legislative bodies, the criminal justice community, the treatment and research communities and society at large have identified this dually affected group— the *substance-abusing offender*—as a major target for intervention and treatment.

Does treatment work for the substance-abusing offender? First, with respect to alcohol and other drug treatment outcomes, the findings are clear: treated clients do better than non-treated clients; treatment does reduce the drinking severity; treatment contributes significantly to alcohol and other drug behavioral change; a majority of outcome studies report a significant positive outcome effect; and even brief intervention is more effective than no treatment at all with respect to changing drinking patterns (see Wanberg and Milkman, 1997, for a review of these findings). The literature is also clear that what works are a wide variety of communication skills and cognitive-behavioral training (Monti, Rohsenow, Colby, and Abrams, 1995).

There is also a significant body of literature to support the efficacy of the treatment of the offender (Andrews et al., 1990; Izzo and Ross, 1990; Lipsey, 1992; Lipsey and Wilson, 1993; Lipton, 1994; McGuire and Priestley, 1995; Van Voorhis, 1987). As to what works best for offenders, those features that stand out are cognitive-behavioral and skills-training oriented approaches (e.g., Andrews and Bonta, 1994; Andrews, Bonta, and Hoge, 1990).

Finally, there are numerous studies that support the efficacy of the treatment of the substance-abusing offender (Collins et al., 1988; Collins and Allison, 1983; Field, 1989; Hubbard et al., 1988; Vigdal and Stadler, 1992; Weekes, 1997). These studies have shown that criminal justice clients do as well if not better than other clients in drug abuse treatment, that criminal justice system involvement helps clients stay in drug abuse treatment, and that coping skills training and therapies are more effective than interactional-interpersonal therapies with the dually affected group.

These findings became the basis for the development of an intense, comprehensive treatment program for the substance-abusing offender—*Criminal Conduct and Substance Abuse Treatment: Strategies for Self-Improvement and Change* (Wanberg and Milkman, 1997). The purpose of this article is to briefly describe this program and approach. The program contains the following parts: a provider's manual, including a thorough literature review pertinent to the treatment of the substance-abusing offender; an outline of the treatment program covering basic elements of the treatment platform upon which the program is structured; a description of characteristics of effective counseling; principles of assessment; operational guidelines for treatment; and a treatment curriculum, including fifty sessions of specialized programs to bring about cognitive and behavioral changes in the substance-abusing offender's substance use and criminal conduct. A participant's manual outlines all treatment sessions and provides classroom exercises, homework assignments, schematic illustrations, and photographs for improved subject clarity and ease of comprehension.

Implementation

Underlying Assumptions and Key Principles of Strategies for Self-improvement and Change

A number of important developments in recent years in the area of implementing improvement and change in substance abuse and criminal justice clients provided the basis upon which *Strategies for Self-improvement and Change* was developed.

The role of substance-abusing offender providers is multidimensional: Although the term "treatment" is used in various portions of the manual, substance-abusing offender service providers are seen as educators and skill trainers, rather than traditional treatment providers as narrowly defined by the disciplines of psychiatry, psychology, social work, and substance abuse counselors.

Multidimensional assessment is a platform for implementing change: Research over the past thirty years clearly has indicated that there is a significant degree of variance found among individuals with alcohol and other drug problems. Awareness of this variation has indicated multiple alcohol and other drug use patterns and types. This finding has called for a multidimensional, differential assessment approach to both the evaluation and diagnosis of alcohol and other drug abuse clients. Such assessment goes beyond seeing alcohol and other drug abuse as a unitary or single condition. There are multiple conditions of the client's life adjustment problems that need to be identified. This approach provides a basis for applying different treatment approaches to different types and patterns of addictions.

The substance-abusing offenders are individuals with a history of substance abuse: Although reference is made throughout this article to the "substance-abusing offender," to be brief, it is more meaningful to think in terms of an individual with a history of criminal conduct or an individual with substance abuse behavior. This view separates the person from the problem. It allows for a clearer focus on changing the person's thinking and behavior. It sees the person as having the power to change behaviors or thoughts and not necessarily as having to change his or her very self.

Engaging the client's primary social unit: Treatment must engage the client's significant others and the client's primary social unit. Treatment needs to enlist the support, understanding, and the reinforcement power of the family and significant others in the person's effort to make change.

Cognitive-behavioral therapy or treatment is a key approach for implementing change: Cognitive-behavioral therapy or treatment approaches are indicated to be effective in the intervention with those who have alcohol and other drug abuse and criminal conduct. These approaches vary from a strong focus on behavioral therapy, a strong focus on cognitive-therapy, or a focus on the combination of the two. Although many cognitive-behavioral therapy or treatment approaches are described in treating alcohol and other drug abusers and offenders, cognitive restructuring and coping and social skills training seem to be the two most commonly applied. These two elements of cognitive-behavioral therapy or treatment are basic to the Strategies for Self-improvement and Change program.

Relapse and recidivism prevention are essential components of treatment: The research and clinical literature are clear: effective treatment must build specific programs and approaches to address relapse and recidivism. Over the past twenty years, clear and distinct treatment protocols have been developed to formally address these issues in treatment.

Individuals go through stages when making changes in their life-adjustment problems: Research during the 1980s and 1990s in the area of the psychology of change (e.g., Prochaska and DiClemente, 1992; Prochaska, DiClemente and Norcross, 1992) has indicated that individuals go through relatively identifiable stages when changing psychosocial and behavioral patterns and problems. Individuals differ with respect to this change process, particularly as to the degree of readiness and motivation to engage in a formal change process. Drawing upon the concepts of change in the literature, the authors have developed a model for change upon which this treatment program has been built.

The implementation of change is based on the key principles of therapeutic support and motivation, therapeutic confrontation, and therapeutic reinforcement. Efforts to bring about change begin with developing a therapeutic alliance with the client—a climate of rapport, trust, and openness. Change is further enhanced through the methods of therapeutic feedback and confrontation. Change is strengthened through methods of therapeutic reinforcement.

The integration of therapeutic and correctional approaches: With the substance-abusing offender, it is essential to integrate the methods and concepts of therapeutic and correctional treatment approaches, namely, therapeutic and correctional confrontation. Therapeutic confrontation treatment confronts the client with the client—the client's need to change, the client's agenda, and the client's ambivalence and contradictions. Correctional treatment confronts the client with society—society's expectations and the contradictions between those expectations and the client's behavior. Thus, effective substance-abusing offender treatment is both client-centered and society-centered. Treatment addresses both the agenda of the client and the agenda of society with respect to behavioral change and correction.

Effective treatment capitalizes on the strengths of diversity: Treatment is culturally responsive and sensitive and addresses the client's cultural values, competencies, and strengths. Treatment uses these strengths and competencies to enhance growth and change. Treatment acknowledges that strengths are found in the diversity of gender, age, ethnic groups, and lifespan experiences.

With these concepts and principles in mind, the authors developed Strategies for Self-improvement and Change for the substance-abusing offender. The program uses the principles of differential assessment, the key concepts and approaches of cognitive behavioral therapy, and the principles of the psychology of change in the development of the process, structure, and content of the program. The program is client-oriented but provider-directed.

The authors reduced the psychology of change to a three stage model: *Challenge to Change, Commitment to Change,* and *Ownership of Change.* It is assumed that individuals first must be challenged to make changes and improvement in their lives. This challenge may be from within, from without, or a combination of both. For many of the program's clients, it will be the legal-sanctioning system. Once challenged, the goal is to reduce ambivalence and to get the commitment of the client to make change. Once change takes place, those individuals who maintain their changes are those who feel a sense of ownership of that change. "It's mine."

Resources for the Development of the Treatment Curriculum

A number of resources were used in developing the Strategies for Self-Improvement and Change treatment curriculum. Experts in the field were interviewed as to what they felt were important components for a cognitive-behavioral therapy or treatment program for substance-abusing offenders. About twenty experts working in substance abuse and correctional programs in Colorado reviewed the manual.

A number of treatment manuals were reviewed. These included manuals developed by Bush and Bilodeau (1993), Kadden and associates (Kadden, Carroll, Donovan, Cooney, Monti, Abrams, Litt, and Hester, 1992), King and associates (King, Rene, Schmidt, Stipetich, and Woldsweth, 1994), Miller and associates (Miller, Zweben, DiClemente, and Rychtarik, 1994), Monti and associates (Monti, Abrams, Kadden, and Cooney, 1989, Monti, et al., 1995), and Ross and associates (Ross and Lightfoot, 1985; Ross and Ross, 1988; Ross et al., 1986). The clinical, research, and academic experience of the authors provided the most substantive basis for the development of the treatment curriculum. Finally, the Strategies for Self-improvement and Change manual was reviewed by a number of experts in the treatment of substance abuse and criminal conduct who provided valuable input in the development of the program structure, process, and curriculum content.

Assessment as a Key Foundation of Strategies for Self-Improvement and Change

An important component of Strategies for Self-improvement and Change is the screening and assessment process. The client is engaged in the assessment process as a partner with the understanding that assessment information is just as valuable to the client as to the provider and that change is based on self-awareness. One module is devoted to engaging the client in an in-depth, differential assessment process, having the client investigate areas of change that are needed and then to construct a master profile and a master assessment plan that the client can use as a guide for change. A variety of instruments and procedures are recommended to enhance this partnership-assessment approach.

An effective assessment approach recognizes that there is a general influence of a certain problem area on a person's life and within the problem area there occurs a wide variety of differences among people (Wanberg and Horn, 1987; Weekes, et al., 1997). For example, alcohol has a general influence on the life of the alcohol-dependent individual. Yet, individuals who have alcohol problems differ greatly. Some are solo drinkers and others drink at bars; some have physical problems from drinking and others do not; some drink continuously, some only periodically.

Assessment, then, must consider two levels of evaluation: (1) the general effect of a certain problem area, (e.g., alcohol and other drug abuse, criminal conduct); and (2) the specific ways that these problem areas affect the person's life. An assessment of the general influence is the basis of screening. Looking at the more specific influences and problem areas involves the application of a differential or multidimensional assessment.

The Strategies for Self-improvement and Change manual structures the differential and in-depth assessment around five broad areas. Each of these is briefly discussed.

Assessment of alcohol and other drug use and abuse: Strategies for Self-improvement and Change spells out both screening and in-depth, differential assessment approaches. Inclusion guidelines for alcohol and other drug services are provided with both minimum-symptom criteria and psychometric approaches described. The conceptual framework for alcohol and other drug differential assessment includes identifying the types of drugs used and the benefits, styles, consequences, and concerns around their use. A variety of tools are used in this assessment process, including self-report questionnaires, collateral reports, reflection groups, and thinking reports.

Assessment of criminal conduct: The key foci in this assessment area are the extent of antisocial patterns including criminal associations and criminal attitudes. Dynamic risk-factor assessment focuses on the modifiable criminogenic needs of the offender. Another area of assessment is the identification of patterns of criminal thinking and thinking errors. The thinking report is a foundational assessment tool used throughout the treatment process.

Assessment of cognitive and affective processing: Since the rationale behind cognitive therapy is that emotions and actions are determined by the way individuals structure their world, then the task of assessment is to understand the way the individuals structure that world (McDermott and Wright, 1992). The primary window for such an assessment is that of examining individuals' cognitions. Through assessment, understanding, conceptualizing, and intervening, treatment helps clients understand and control emotions and actions which, in turn, will influence their cognitive world.

Assessment of Life-situation Problems: There are several areas of assessment, outside of the alcohol and other drug abuse, and legal and criminal conduct area. Strategies for Self-Improvement and Change addresses these at both the screening and more in-depth levels of evaluation. These pertain to current life-problems, which the client may be experiencing. These areas include the following:

- Social-interpersonal adjustment

- Productivity, job and economic adjustment

- Marital, family, and relationship adjustment

- Health adjustment

- Psychological-emotional adjustment

Assessment of Motivation and Readiness for Treatment: The work on stages of change (Prochaska and DiClemente, 1992; Prochaska, DiClemente and Norcross, 1992) has made it clear that an essential component of assessment is that of determining the client's readiness and motivation for treatment. The area of treatment motivation and readiness should be assessed during the clinical intake interview. A number of questions and issues can be addressed to evaluate this area:

- Willingness to be involved in treatment

- Whether the person feels a need for help at this time

- Whether the client has thought about making changes in particular areas

- Whether the client actually has made deliberate changes

- Degree of problem awareness

- Whether others feel that the client should make changes or that the client needs help

Structure of Treatment Program

Strategies for Self-Improvement and Change provides a standardized, structured, and well-defined approach to the treatment of the substance-abusing offender client. It is a long-term (nine-months to one-year) intensive, cognitive-behavioral oriented treatment program for *adult substance-abusing offenders.* The recommended client age is eighteen years or above. However, some older adolescents may benefit from portions of the curriculum.

Strategies for Self-improvement and Change can be delivered effectively within the framework of the sanctioning process, either in a community or incarcerated setting. Some providers may find it difficult to extend a particular treatment program over a period of nine months to one-year. Modifications may be made to shorten the time period of treatment. Following Phase I, where sessions are delivered twice a week, providers may continue to deliver sessions on a twice-a-week basis. This would shorten the formal presentation by three months.

Strategies for Self-improvement and Change is behaviorally oriented, skill-based, and multimodal. Strategies for Self-improvement and Change attends to both extrapersonal circumstances (events that led to criminal conduct and substance abuse) and intrapersonal processes (thoughts, emotions, beliefs, attitudes) that led to criminal conduct and substance abuse.

The treatment curriculum for Strategies for Self-improvement and Change is comprised of twelve treatment modules that are structured around three phases of treatment. These treatment phases are premised on the conceptual framework of the *Challenge to Change,* or the reflective-contemplative phase, the *Commitment to Change* or the determination and action stage, and the *Ownership of Change* or the stabilization of change. The rationale and purpose of each phase are outlined. Each module provides an overall statement of purpose, contextual explanation, and is subdivided into a series of discrete sessions (lesson plans) with specific learning objectives and strategies to achieve those objectives. Each module with its discrete session plan is taught in a logical sequence with basic topics covered first, serving as the foundation for more difficult concepts covered later. Each session is broken into six discrete parts: (1) the rationale of the session; (2) the objectives of the session; (3) the session content and process; (4) the classroom and homework assignments; (5) the summary review; and, (6) the session evaluation and client evaluation.

The Themes of the Treatment Curriculum

Building on the findings of the historical and theoretical review, the treatment curriculum is built around key themes for self-improvement and change. These themes are not necessarily presented in sequence, but are imbued in the treatment curriculum content and process. These themes are the following:

- Building trust and rapport with the client

- Enhancing motivation and readiness for treatment involvement

- Developing knowledge about the process of change and about drug abuse, criminal conduct, and the cycles of drug abuse and criminal conduct

- Enhancing self-awareness through self-assessment and self-disclosure

- Enhancing self-awareness through the assessment of others and feedback

- Developing and strengthening the basic skills for coping with and managing intrapersonal and interpersonal relationships and problems

- Engaging in prosocial behavior and community responsibility

- Using moral reasoning and values

- Preventing relapse and recidivism

- Developing a healthy life style

Overview of the Treatment Program

Phase I: Challenge to Change involves the client in a reflective-contemplative process. A series of lesson experiences are used to build a working relationship with the client and to help the client develop the motivation to change. The sessions also are directed at providing basic information on how people change, the role of thought and behavior in change, and basic information about substance abuse and criminal conduct. A major focus of Phase I is helping the client develop self-awareness through engaging in self-disclosure and receiving feedback. The assumption underlying this approach is that self-disclosure leads to self-awareness, which in turn leads to self-improvement and change. The clients are confronted with their own past and then challenged to bring that past into a present change-focus. The goal is to get the clients to define the specific areas of change and to commit to that change. This phase includes a review of the client's current alcohol and other drug and criminal conduct with the results of this review becoming a focus of the reflective-contemplative process. Phase I has the following modules:

Module 1: Building trust and harmony

Module 2: Building a desire and motivation to change

Module 3: Building the knowledge base for change

Module 4: Self-disclosing and receiving feedback

Module 5: Preventing relapse and recidivism

Module 6: Understanding the change process

Phase II: Commitment to Change involves the client in an active demonstration of implementing and practicing change. All clients undergo an in-depth assessment of their life situation and problems and look carefully at the critical areas that need change and improvement. The targets of change are identified.

Then, a later module has eighteen sessions that focus on strengthening basic skills for change and helping the client learn key cognitive-behavioral therapy or treatment methods for changing thought and behavior that contribute to substance abuse and criminal conduct. Themes of these sessions include coping and social skills training with an emphasis on communication skills; managing and changing negative thoughts and thinking errors; recognizing and managing high-risk situations; managing cravings and urges that lead to alcohol and other drug use and criminal conduct; developing self-control through problem solving and assertiveness; managing thoughts and feelings related to anger, aggression, guilt and depression; understanding and developing close relationships; understanding and practicing empathy and prosocial values; and moral development. The specific modules comprising this phase include the following:

Module 7: Developing a commitment to change

Module 8: In-depth assessment: Looking at the areas that need to change

Module 9: Strengthening basic skills for self-improvement and change

Phase III: Ownership of Change or the stabilization and maintenance phase involves the client's demonstration of ownership of change over time. This involves treatment experiences designed to reinforce and strengthen this commitment and establish changes. The concepts of relapse and recidivism prevention are reviewed. This phase includes sessions on critical reasoning, resolving conflicts, and establishing and maintaining a healthy life style. Change is strengthened through helping the client become involved in a variety of auxiliary methods including mentoring, role modeling, and using self-help groups and other community-based recovery maintenance resources.

Current Delivery Sites and Provider Training

Strategies for Self-improvement and Change is being used statewide in Colorado for offenders in various components of the adult criminal justice system. Several pilot sites have delivered the program within both community and incarcerated settings. The program has been successfully delivered to a number of groups within these two settings.

A concentrated effort has been made to train and certify providers in Colorado. The certification process involves the completion of a four-day intensive training program, supervised implementation of the delivery of Strategies for Self-improvement and Change as it is outlined in the manual, attendance at a two-day follow-up training program, and participation in evaluation of clients who have enrolled in the program.

Basic Beliefs Underlying Work With Substance-abusing Offenders

A basic belief underlying the development of Strategies for Self-improvement and Change is that the clients—the substance-abusing offenders—have the same human needs as everyone in society. It is important that substance-abusing offender clients be approached with respect and as persons who deserve to have the benefits of what those working with them know and have learned about the psychology of change. Society typically "looks down" upon this particular group of clients and often views them as hopeless with respect to rehabilitation and change. As this message is heard and as staff themselves at times feel the discouragement, it is important to remember two important facts.

First, the most human of qualities is the capacity to think. All persons have this unique and human capacity, which is different from all other species on earth. The greatest hope for improving ourselves and becoming better persons is to use our mind and capacity to think. *Everyone can capitalize on the strengths of this unique capacity, including individuals with substance abuse problems and a history of criminal behavior.* This program capitalizes on this strength. It takes the capacity to think and makes it the pinnacle for change. It is through thinking that individuals have the most hope for change. That hope for change is just as great with the substance abuser and the offender as with any other person. The challenge is to capitalize to the fullest extent on this capacity.

The second basis for hope is understanding that change is natural. Change is built into nature. Nothing remains the same. "Everything has its season." The most real aspect of living is change. The fact of change becomes the basis of hope. For if change is natural, then it is natural for the substance-abusing offender to change. The challenge is for staff to use their skills and knowledge to capitalize on and direct the inherent capacity for change in positive, constructive, and healthy directions.

---

[1]References are listed in the bibliography at the end of the introductory chapter (see p. 415).

Contacts:

Kenneth W. Wanberg, Th.D., Ph.D.
Director
Center for Addictions Research and Evaluation (CARE)

16050 West 69th Place
Arvada, Colorado 80007
(303) 421-1261

Harvey B. Milkman, Ph.D.
Director
Center for Interdisciplinary Studies

889 Logan Street, Suite 207
Denver, Colorado 80203
(303) 830-8500

439

Substance Abuse
Additional Program Entries

Ohio Department of Youth Services, Substance Abuse Services

Cheri Walter, Deputy Director
51 North High Street, Columbus, Ohio 43215-3098
(614) 466-9318

The Ohio Department of Youth Services provides substance abuse services in varying degrees to all youth committed to the department's care. Since the inception of the Office of Substance Abuse Services in 1985, significant enhancement and expansion has transpired, leading to a comprehensive array of services designed to address the diverse needs of the substance-abusing juvenile offender. Institutional and parole programs have been established that incorporate a broad range of departmental objectives and state-of-the art intervention strategies. Current service delivery is as follows:

Assessment—While at the Ohio Department of Youth Services Reception Center, youth are administered the Juvenile Automated Substance Abuse Evaluation (JASAE) to determine their current level of alcohol and other drug use.

Education/Intervention Program—Also while at the Reception Center, youth are required to complete substance abuse education. The program is based on the "Design for Living" curriculum developed by the Hazelden Foundation.

Substance Abuse Specific Units—All Ohio Department of Youth Services institutions have specific dormitories that provide psychoeducational substance abuse programming.

Residential Treatment Centers—The Ohio Department of Youth Services provides drug and alcohol treatment to youth who need a structured residential program.

Aftercare—The youth's transition from an institution to the community is facilitated by substance abuse parole officers. These specialists provide linkage with community-based agencies and other recovery activities to ensure the youth receives a continuum of care.

Drug Trafficker Program—The department has framed a special drug traffickers program that has institutional, parole, and community-based service components.

Substance Abuse Staff Training—The purpose of this training is to increase staff knowledge and recognition of the nature of substance abuse and delinquency issues of the juvenile population.

Bradenton Drug Treatment Community

Diane G. Lee, Project Director
Bradenton Drug Treatment Community
P.O. Box 1406, Oneco, Florida 34264-1406
(941) 751-7605

The Bradenton Drug Treatment Community is a community-based, intensively supervised alternative program for drug-dependent youthful offenders committed to the Florida

Department of Corrections. The program targets male offenders, ages sixteen to twenty-four, with chronic substance abuse problems. The three-phase, eighteen-month-long prison diversion program integrates intensive residential treatment, reentry planning, and aftercare services to reduce the incidence of substance abuse and the likelihood of recidivism. It brings together a multidisciplinary team of corrections and treatment professionals to offer services through all stages of the offender's journey back to a meaningful life. The overall goals of the program are (1) to provide a degree of security and discipline appropriate for the offenders involved; (2) to provide diagnosis, treatment, and services to assist offenders in pursuing a course of lawful and productive conduct following release; (3) to reduce criminal recidivism by offenders; (4) to lower the cost of correctional services and facilities by reducing criminal recidivism; and (5) to provide work that promotes development of industrial and service skills.

Technology

18

Introduction

Technology continues to emerge as a critical issue in corrections. The need to evaluate, select, and use technology in corrections is now and will continue to be a valuable tool to enhance staff safety and the security of both correctional institutions and the general public. It also may serve as a cost saver in certain applications.

Less than ten years ago, it was not uncommon for entire corrections agencies to be void of computers, technology review committees, or technology products of any kind. Strolling through an American Correctional Association conference exhibitors area a decade ago, one found plenty of construction materials, fencing, clothing, even food products but little emerging technology. Individuals used to be able to spend an hour or two in the exhibit area and see all the technology that was there. Now, it takes them every minute that the exhibit area is open to view the technology and then they may not see it all. The use of technology will continue to grow exponentially in the future.

The American Correctional Association has recognized the importance that technology plays in corrections and has made a concerted effort to facilitate a better understanding of it within the correctional community during previous conferences. Over the past two years, each conference has had either a technology workshop or an entire technology track, all of which have been heavily attended. There is a complete track on technology at the 1998 Annual Congress of Correction in Detroit. Federal agencies such as the National Institute of Justice and the federal Bureau of Prisons are actively involved with technology initiatives in cooperation with state and local corrections agencies.

This chapter includes "Best Practices" in the area of technology. There were many submittals from the field in a broad band of subject areas. Due to the expansive range and breadth of technology, it took some time to review the various submittals. Virtually all of the submittals addressed a new way to apply technology within a respective agency to either enhance efficiency, save money, or improve public safety. It was difficult to narrow it down to just five programs. There were many submittals deserving of mention, including the numerous correctional agencies that have created technology review committees to better address technology needs, test equipment, and procure technology for future use.

This chapter describes five programs selected as "Best Practices." The first selection is a telemedicine initiative submitted by the Louisiana Department of Public Safety and

Corrections. This initiative enhances safety by reducing the transport of inmates for medical reasons. It also saves in labor and transportation costs. The second selection is a utilities management initiative submitted by the Texas Department of Criminal Justice. Its implementation enhanced the monitoring of utility costs, thus enabling cost savings by rescheduling inmate work programs and other functions to nonpeak hours. The third selection features a video conferencing and communications program submitted by the Illinois Department of Corrections. This initiative increased communications by connecting the department, state facilities, and the courts through video technology, thereby reducing costs and enhancing security.

The fourth selection is a Felony Offender Reporting System submitted by the Washington Department of Corrections. This initiative established a system for disclosable public information regarding felony offenders and saves time on presentence reports. It also increased communications among criminal justice entities. The final selection describes an intranet usage initiative submitted by the Correctional Service of Canada. This program improved the dissemination of information and policies to all employees, thus saving time and money.

Other agencies may benefit from the initiatives presented in this chapter. Sometimes resistance to change or the fear of the unknown prevents an agency from looking at emerging technologies as a solution or part of a solution to a particular problem. The key is to evaluate technology for its most appropriate uses and apply it accordingly. Technology is not the cure-all for the many problems faced by corrections today. It can, however, serve as a valuable tool to use in improving safety and security, cost savings, and time savings for the staff.

Committee chair:

Kevin Jackson
Technology Centers Program Manager
National Institute of Justice

633 Indiana Avenue, NW
Washington, D.C. 20531
(202) 307-0645

Louisiana Department of Public Safety and Corrections

Network Telemedicine: Louisiana State Penitentiary

Introduction

The telemedicine program underway at the Louisiana State Penitentiary is an outgrowth of the Louisiana State University Medical Center's telemedicine initiative, which began in 1995. The goals of this project are to:

- Reduce the number of prisoner transports from Louisiana State Penitentiary to the secondary- and tertiary-health care service centers

- Reinforce the security parameters and performance objectives of the department of corrections

- Reduce the physical presence of inmates in the general civilian population served by the hospital-based clinics

The targets for cost savings included:

- A reduction in the transportation expenses of vehicle use and fuel, and overtime for security staff

- A reduction in administrative and logistical efforts on the prison site for scheduling and moving inmates

- An anticipated future potential savings to be generated as a result of earlier intervention in medical cases prior to conditions developing into more serious situations

Through this program, the population at the Louisiana State Penitentiary is receiving medical services in several specialty areas in a fashion comparable to previous methods, but in a more efficient and cost-effective manner.

Background

The Louisiana State Penitentiary at Angola is the largest state facility, housing roughly 5,000 inmates. The facility is located along the banks of the Mississippi River, approximately forty miles north of Baton Rouge. The majority of its inmates are classified as long-term residents.

The prison compound maintains a fully staffed treatment center and satellite infirmaries on the 18,000-acre institution. The medical resources include seven physicians, thirty-eight nurses, a lab, a pharmacy, an x-ray unit, a thirty-bed in-patient center, and satellite infirmaries at various camps throughout the prison.

Currently, inmates proceed from an infirmary to the treatment center for addressing their medical needs. Once it is determined that the progression of health care requires services from one of the off-site hospitals, the inmate is scheduled for the next available appointment at the appropriate clinic. This holds true for initial clinic examinations and follow-up care for chronic, postoperative, and recurring conditions.

In the past, the transportation of inmates from Louisiana State Penitentiary for medical-related reasons to the secondary- and tertiary-hospitals totaled approximately 3,000 in a six-month period. An analysis of this total reflected that two out of three of these transports were directed to the Charity Hospital in New Orleans, and the other third went to the Earl K. Long Hospital in Baton Rouge. The driving time to New Orleans from the Angola area is approximately two hours. The driving time to Baton Rouge is approximately sixty minutes.

Implementation

Telemedicine Operations at the Louisiana State University Medical Center

The Telemedicine Program, based at the Louisiana State University Medical Center in New Orleans, began in August of 1994. With a mission of facilitating statewide development of medical telecommunications programming, the goal of the project was to improve the access to, and quality of health care for all residents of Louisiana. Begun as a cooperative project between the Louisiana State University School of Medicine and the Louisiana Health Care Authority, now the Louisiana State University Medical Care Health Care Service Division, this program has expanded from its original three sites (New Orleans, Lake Charles, and South Cameron) to a ten-site network spanning the I-10 corridor (Iota, Lafayette, Church Point, Villa Feliciana, Baton Rouge, Angola, and the Orleans Parish Prison). Tertiary consultations are provided by Louisiana State University specialists.

Since August of 1994, 750 patient encounters have been held using fifteen different Louisiana State University specialists, both adult and pediatric. Major specialties using the network are neurology, psychiatry, orthopedics, dermatology, and cardiology. The feedback from both patients and physicians has been positive, with access to specialty care and saved travel time cited as the most important benefits of the encounters.

This network currently uses compressed video equipment running at both half and full T-1 bandwidth. Using a variety of specialized patient cameras, comprehensive patient examinations can be performed, including diagnostic cardiac echocardiology and ultrasound imaging. High-definition monitors allow the patient and the physician to interact as if they were in the same room. With the primary care physician and the specialist both involved in a medical consultation, pertinent history can be discussed and interventional therapies agreed upon. Follow-up encounters, scheduled on a regular basis, give the specialist an opportunity to evaluate interventions and make any necessary adjustments in a timely manner. Store and forward (in other words, videotape) videoconferencing furnish a health care provider with the videotape of the patient for viewing by a specialist at a later time.

Continuing education programs for physicians, nurses, and auxiliary health care providers form another component of the telemedicine program. Recognizing that it is often difficult for medical personnel to travel to metropolitan areas to attend seminars and keep up with current trends in medicine, the telemedicine network attempts to bridge the educational gap across the state by transmitting educational conferences such as grand rounds to various hospitals on the network. The equipment deployed in this operation is state-of-the-art. The equipment used in this phase of the project was based on V-tel Codecs supplied by Hughes Training, Inc.

The Beginning

At the start of the fiscal year 1997-1998, the medical staff at the Earl K. Long Hospital, a part of the Louisiana State University Medical Center, in Baton Rouge, entered into a contract with the department of corrections to provide a comprehensive plan for health care for the inmate population. The project centered on the population at the Louisiana State Prison and included reliance on telemedicine as a significant component in the overall delivery of health services. Under the direction of Dr. Karam, the Internal Medicine Department at the Earl K. Long Hospital developed several clinics for the Louisiana State Prison. These clinics included diabetes, hypertension, HIV, pulmonary, case management, and chest conference.

The interesting element of the telemedicine linking between Louisiana State Prison and the Earl K. Long Hospital is that the videoconferencing equipment at the latter was based on the CLI CODEC. As a result, the connections between the Louisiana State Prison and the Earl K. Long Hospital had to be industry standard format (FCIF), providing for compatibility between equipment from two different vendors.

Results

To date, the telemedicine program at the Louisiana State Prison has conducted a total of 52 clinics and processed 273 inmate encounters—including at least one inmate from the death-row population. The impact of this operation on the routine transportation activity of the institution is still being measured. Though it is apparent that the overall volume of inmate transportation has been reduced, a detailed analysis of the number of vehicle runs and staff requirements is still incomplete.

Of the clinics scheduled, approximately 10 percent have been canceled for nonmedical or nonprison-related reasons. Generally, the cause of the failed clinics has been service disruptions to the telephone circuits, or to a lesser extent, equipment problems. Changes to the procedures used for linking the Louisiana State Prison to the Earl K. Long Hospital are expected to reduce some of the network problems. It is anticipated that increased familiarity with the videoconferencing equipment by the end users at both the Louisiana State Prison and the hospital will help minimize the equipment-related difficulties.

Conclusion and Future Plans

Future developments call for an expansion into additional clinics, efforts to increase the volume of participation, and the use of store and forward technology. Also, plans are underway to offer educational classes for the staff at the Louisiana State Prison using the videoconferencing equipment.

In addition, given the initial results of the telemedicine project, plans are in development to expand the deployment of telemedicine into other correctional facilities in the state. At this time, the David Wade Correctional Center has been participating in telemedicine for more than two years. Correctional administrators at the Dixon Correctional, the Washington Correctional, and the Louisiana Correctional Institute for Women also are exploring the concept for use in those settings.

Contact:

Terry Clair
IS Site Manager
Louisiana Department of Public Safety and Corrections

P. O. Box 94304, Capitol Station
Baton Rouge, Louisiana 70804-9304
(504) 342-8782

Integrated Facilities Information

Introduction

The State of Texas has experienced a rapid growth in its prison system leading the national trend of increasing facility construction for offenders. The Texas Department of Criminal Justice approached this construction task using prototypical designs for maximum- and medium-security facilities and state jails.

The system capacity increased from 40,000 in 1987 to just under 140,000 in 1996 (see Figure 1a). The growth in the capacity, reflected in all aspects of budget expenditures and utilities, is no exception. The utility expenditures rose from $15,000,000 to $60,000,000 during the same time period (see Figure 1b).

Figure 1a: System Capacity Growth

Figure 1b: System Utility Expenditures

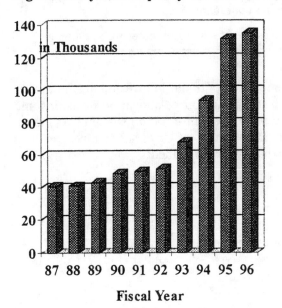

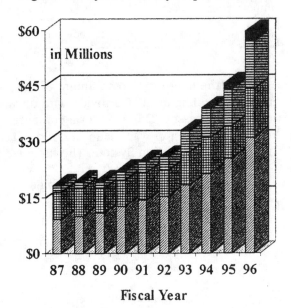

The expansion program at the Texas Department of Criminal Justice was nearing completion in 1995 and the result was 34,000,000 square feet of prison facilities to maintain and operate in the most cost-effective method. These facilities cover the state from El Paso to Beaumont, and the Texas Panhandle to the Rio Grande Valley. The Texas Department of Criminal Justice had grown to be the largest state agency and the number one energy consumer among state agencies. In January 1995, a partnership began with the Texas State Energy Conservation Office to build a proactive utilities and energy department within the Texas Department of Criminal Justice that would reduce costs and save natural resources.

Development and Design

The method used to track utility expenditures, equipment maintenance, and repairs on the prison units was labor intensive and ineffective. The analysis of energy consumption and energy costs was difficult due to the manual entry of utility-billing data on ledgers. Operations and maintenance had similar practices with equipment lists recorded on cards at the individual prison unit along with the corrective and preventive maintenance work orders. Access to this information is critical to energy-resource management. Additional information can be gained by metering individual buildings within the prison complex. Operations and maintenance have a parallel story. The need for information to allocate capital and human resources in the rapidly expanding prison system was critical.

Table 1. Information provided by implementing these technologies

Submetering of Buildings	Computerized Maintenance Management System
Identify major energy users by department	Identify departments requiring maintenance
Trending and load profiles	Workload profiles—based on craft or buildings
Establish energy performance standards	Establish standards for preventive maintenance
Identify operational changes that may adversely impact energy costs	Identify operational changes that may signal equipment failure
Verify savings from energy efficiency projects	Be aware of expiration dates for equipment

With the long-term commitment of management to continual improvement, the metering and trending systems provide data on which to base resource-allocation decisions and improve processes. The need for a computerized integrated information system was identified, and a decision was made to build a Texas Department of Criminal Justice Facilities Integrated Information System. The modules of that system included:

- Utilities and energy monthly bills

- Metered data—energy profiles

- Computerized maintenance management system

- Finance

- Design, construction

- Inventory

The intent was to build each module with links to a core database such that information could be accessed easily by all departments. Users would have unimpeded access to the information they needed to complete their jobs.

A pilot program of twenty-five prototypical units, comprising approximately 25 percent of the Texas Department of Criminal Justice's square footage, was kicked off in the summer of 1995. Thirteen medium-security prisons (1,000 beds) were included in the program, along with five state jails (2,000 beds) and five transfer facilities. Prototypes were chosen for ease of implementation and for analysis.

Implementation

Submetering

A metering subcontractor was hired to train two Texas Department of Criminal Justice staff electricians to install watt-hour transducers that would meter electrical consumption. The eight meters installed on each unit are connected to a data logger for remote metering through a modem. Only electrical consumption was metered since the facilities were operational, and this would have the least impact on operations and security. Also, electrical costs are 50 percent of utility costs and monitoring of these costs would provide the greatest return on the initial investment. The staff electricians have completed the installation at eleven of the twenty-five sites. The rest will be on line within the year.

The Monitoring and Analysis Program (MAP) is a software package that automatically polls all loggers through a modem from Huntsville and downloads the data weekly. Hourly weather data are polled weekly to provide an additional component needed for a comprehensive analysis of energy consumption and energy loads. MAP is an integrated system that combines energy consumption monitoring at remote locations, data storage, analysis, and reporting.

Utility Billing Database

Texas A&M Energy Systems Lab (TAMU) was contracted to develop a utility billing audit program in the Microsoft Access database that was available at the Texas Department of Criminal Justice Facilities Division. The Texas A&M Energy Systems Lab team assessed the database requirements after meeting with the accounts payable personnel responsible for all utility bills. Within two weeks of the initial meeting, the Texas A&M Energy Systems Lab determined that Microsoft Access was not the long-term solution to the development of a comprehensive integrated database. So, they continued to develop a utility accounting software in Microsoft Access while the Facilities Division Data Resource Team researched the acquisition of a more robust database. The intention was to rewrite the Microsoft Access code in the new application in the next fiscal year using it as a bridge or a fix.

Students from the Sam Houston State University were hired through the funds provided by the Texas State Energy Conservation Office to input the utility bills that had amassed throughout the fiscal year. The initial application had some major bugs, however. After several crashes, the application was stabilized and data were stored. The need to provide consistent data streams for like utilities, so that comparisons and standards could be made, was brought to light early in the data entry process. A conversion factor was built into the application so that all consumption units would be standardized. The implementation process for this utility accounting software brought insight to the initial design process and produced many changes that were core to the integrated information system, mainly the new and more robust database software.

Computerized Maintenance Management System (CMMS)

A team of maintenance personnel from various crafts were charged with getting the foundation needed at each unit so that the Computerized Maintenance Management System could be used. Their tasks included tagging all equipment using a coding system that would establish standards across prototypes. Each unit received hardware. Unit staff were trained as other team members tagged equipment. The Huntsville staff received additional training so that users could interact and network with each other. The resistance by some maintenance staff to try automation was and still is the biggest hurdle.

Results

Submetering

The weekly data have provided load-profile information. This enables staff to investigate low-cost or no-cost operations and maintenance measures. These include such things as night setback of air-conditioning systems and shifting hours of the laundry operation, which are both simple cost-reduction measures. Figure 2a is a sample report that will be going out to the wardens at each prison currently being metered. Each building will have a profile that compares to the overall unit profile thus identifying the impact on monthly electrical costs.

Figure 2a: Metered Data Output—Unit Load Profile

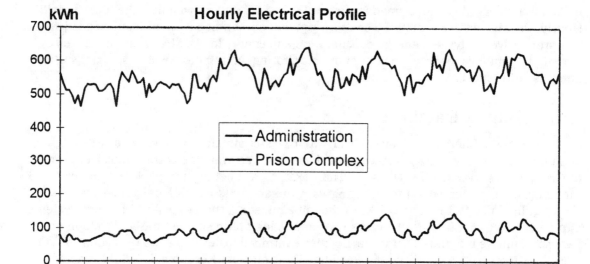

Two metering technicians, originally trained by an outside subcontractor, are now conducting in-house training to six more metering technicians. One metering technician compiled an installation manual, which the facilities division electrical engineer reviewed. The most impressive result has been the increased computer literacy by the metering specialists. The technology transfer and upgrade of skills are a win-win for the agency and the employees.

Utility Billing Database

The utility billing section has identified billing errors that would have cost more than $690,000 in the last two fiscal years. The availability of electronic data has allowed for the development of comparative graphs so that the wardens can see how consumption has changed. The graphs will include a three-year cycle similar to the graph in Figure 2b. Currently, monthly reports that include nine graphs are sent to the wardens involved in the pilot program. The utility billing database has made preparing the annual management reports less time consuming. The fiscal year 1996 reports were ready within two months of the fiscal year close-out as a result of this project.

Figure 2b: Utility Billing Database Output—Monthly Electrical Consumption

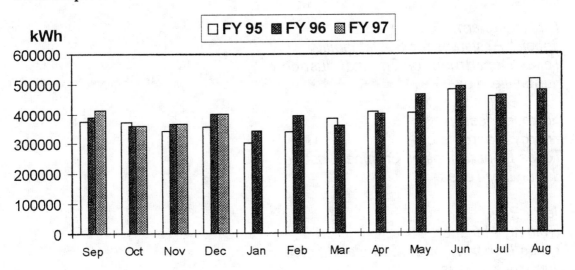

Computerized Maintenance Management System: Application

The data is now being analyzed for comparisons between like units and the impact of age on the corrective workload order. On the unit level, the results have been varied based on the staff use of this powerful tool. Junior Lapaglia, the unit maintenance supervisor at the Terrell Unit, Livingston, Texas, has used this tool to improve his operations and reports:

> The monthly report prepared through CMMS for Warden Treon, gives an accurate account of our maintenance department and the work performed by the employees throughout the course of the month. It gives us an accounting of where the maintenance budget is going and which departments are having the most calls. We have solved grievances, Level 1 and Level 2, through this program and have determined whether the abuse is inmate or employee. In some instances, repayment for abuse is being collected.

> The employees are the key developers of CMMS at the Unit level. As a Unit Supervisor, I must depend on them for input.

> If, in the future, each department must establish a yearly budget, the Maintenance Department will have a comprehensive history of each department's maintenance cost and we can determine how much of their yearly budget should be applied to maintenance problems.

Conclusion

The rapidly changing field of computer technology has been a blessing and a curse during this process. The good points are that the costs go down over time and the machines are faster. However, the time period between the original research and the approval "through channels" often results in conflicting hardware and software issues because of evolving technology. Nonetheless, the effort has been worthwhile because information is being made available that will help meet the goal of continual improvement and resource allocation. Data provides information that is used to gain knowledge. Knowledge can generate wisdom after many "challenges" all of which have an impact on the bottom line.

Authors:

Tia Henegham
Special Assistant for Sustainability
Texas Department of Criminal Justice
Huntsville, Texas

Norman Pleasant
Energy Coordinator
Texas Department of Criminal Justice
Huntsville, Texas

Jerry Reed
Training Manager
Texas Department of Criminal Justice
Huntsville, Texas

Contact:

Tom Merka
Program Director
Facilities Division, Utilities and Energy
Texas Department of Criminal Justice

P. O. Box 99
Huntsville, Texas 77342-0099
(409) 437-5649

Videoconferencing

Introduction

One area of technology that presently is being used and fine tuned by the Illinois Department of Corrections is the application of videoconferencing. Stateville Penitentiary currently is linked into a statewide network with sites at Springfield, the central office in Chicago, other state facilities, and the federal circuit courts. Each center is designed to serve a multitude of applications. Numerous opportunities are available for using this technology, including: training of employees, holding of business meetings, court hearings, and parole and deportation hearings.

Through this technology, the department is able to link all its sites together or in any combination. The videoconferencing equipment allows for multiple conferences to be conducted at the same time. The department also has the ability to connect to other agencies, universities, and entities nationwide with the same video capability, even though they may have different vendor equipment.

Development and Design

The videoconferencing equipment that has been installed is from the V-Tel corporation, a leader in such equipment. All equipment has been installed in a secure setting and is completely interactive. The operation of the video network is the full responsibility of the department.

The design employs a single customized cabinet holding dual-monitor configurations. The lower unit of the cabinet houses all electronic equipment. The upper unit of the cabinet houses the monitors and camera. The customized cabinet was constructed by the Illinois Department of Corrections from materials that met prison specifications. All wiring is located within the cabinet, with the exception of auxiliary equipment such as the document camera or control table and keyboard. These are within the designated area. The camera and audio also may be controlled by a wireless, handheld remote. Microphones have been mounted in the ceiling, with a conduit back to the base unit.

Implementation

Staff scheduling for the use of the video network is coordinated by a video conference coordinator at each site with a central coordinator located in Springfield. All scheduling is done on a first-come first-serve basis. Emergency scheduling only is permitted if authorized by the director of the department. Any scheduling to arrange an inmate's appearance in court is coordinated between the institution and the legal process video coordinator in Chicago. These individuals, in turn, coordinate the use of the rooms with the central video coordinator. Those staff designated as video coordinators and various selected employees receive training in the basic use and maintenance of the equipment and the procedures to be followed when problems arise.

Results

The V-Tel large group conferencing system has provided unmatched conferencing flexibility for the department. It has allowed staff to personalize the configuration to fit their needs. Most centers have been designed to provide access to staff and inmates for purposes such as immigration/deportation hearings, parole board hearings, interviewing and meetings with legal representatives, staff training, and facilitating inmate appearances in federal court. The use of videoconferencing has impacted significantly on the safety and security problems associated with the transportation of inmates by staff and their physical presence in courtrooms and the community. It also has reduced labor costs and the ancillary expenditures normally incurred by the department.

Conclusion

It is the intention at Stateville to take full advantage of the technological innovations and applications of videoconferencing for use in a correctional setting. Reducing contact with inmates and limiting transportation of inmates within the general community significantly reduces the possibility of escapes. It does not jeopardize security. In fact, it provides the opportunity to evaluate and implement changes in existing practices that may result in a safer and more secure work environment.

Contact:

Dwayne Clark
Warden
Stateville Correctional Center

Route 53, P. O. Box 112
Joliet, Illinois 60434
(815) 727-3607

Felony Offender Reporting System

Introduction

Since 1995, the Washington State Felony Offender Reporting System has been providing on-line access to publicly disclosable information concerning felony offenders. The information can be queried by name and date of birth, by social security number, by the Washington State Patrol, by identification number, or by the Washington Department of Corrections' identification number.

The information available to the public includes the offender's demographics (e.g., age, height, and weight); supervising office, officer, and dates of supervision, if in the community; conviction history, dates of incarceration, institution, and projected release date, if incarcerated; identification as a serious, violent, or sex offender, and aliases. The information that is available only to law enforcement includes the offender's mailing address, gang affiliation, FBI number, and incarcerated behavior characteristics, such as infractions.

The Washington State Felony Offender Reporting System concept originated in 1991 in response to an identified department need to share information with the Washington Office of the Administrator for the Courts. Community corrections personnel within the department needed access to information in the files of the administrator for the courts to conduct presentence investigations and to monitor offenders under supervision.

Court clerks and other users of the office of the administrator of the courts' system needed access to information in department of corrections' files to locate offenders owing court fees. In addition to responding to information requests from the office of the administrator for the courts' system users, department personnel also were responding to requests from federal criminal justice agencies (e.g., the FBI; the Bureau of Alcohol, Tobacco and Firearms; and the Immigration and Naturalization Service), local criminal justice agencies, and the general public. The volume of requests from all the sources combined was running at about 2,500 requests per month.

An agreement was reached whereby the department obtained free on-line access to the office of the administrator for the courts' files in return for agreeing to provide their system users with on-line access to department file information. Both organizations felt that once the agreement was fully implemented there would be a significant time savings for both the department of corrections' personnel and the various office of the administrator for the courts' system users.

Development and Design

At the start of the development, a decision was made to meet departmental needs (e.g., cut down on time spent responding to inquiries), the needs of the larger criminal justice community, and the disclosure needs of the general public—to the extent practical. To determine these needs, staff reviewed ongoing requests for information. They compiled and reviewed a tentative list of data elements with a sample of potential users, including representatives from local law enforcement, court clerks, prosecuting attorneys, public defenders, and jail administrators.

The resulting list of data elements then was reviewed with the department's assistant attorney general to get an opinion on the disclosability of each. To simplify administration, a decision was made to only make available those data elements which fell into one of two groups. The first group included data about offenders and their sentences, information that was always disclosable. The second group involved data that always were disclosable to law enforcement, but not to the general public. Data that did not fall into one of these groups were excluded from consideration. Since implementation, a third category has been added for data disclosable to state government agencies but not to the general public. Such data already were available to law enforcement.

Implementation

The implementation of the system consisted of writing six new inquiry screens, and then providing on-line access to the screens for personnel not from the department of corrections. In response to an analysis of potential system users, three primary means of accessing the Washington State Felony Offender Reporting System information were provided.

The office of the administrator for the courts, which serves court clerks in all counties and also provides access to their system to various businesses and other users, has a direct connection to the Washington State Felony Offender Reporting System from their central computer.

The Washington State Patrol added a new inquiry code to the network they provide for accessing, among other things, criminal history files, drivers' license information, and outstanding warrants. Queries, which come from users of this network, are considered to be from law enforcement and are provided access to the "law enforcement only" data in the Washington State Felony Offender Reporting System.

Other state agencies or anyone having access to the Washington State Department of Information Services computer also can gain access to the Washington State Felony Offender Reporting System with prior approval from the department. At least one member of the news media has taken advantage of this capability.

Results

The free and full exchange of information that was envisioned between the office of the administrator of the court and the department of corrections is occurring. Authorized users of the office of the administrator of the court's system access the Washington State Felony

Offender Reporting System without the need for department identification. Personnel from the department of corrections access the office of the administrator of the court's systems without the need for the office of the administrator of the court's identification.

All users of the Washington State Patrol law enforcement network access the Washington State Felony Offender Reporting System without the need for department of corrections' identification. As a result, the parties involved are realizing significant time savings by not having to research and respond to as many requests from each other. Even more, the desired information now is available in a more timely manner.

After more than a year of operation, the Washington State Felony Offender Reporting System is responding to 1,300 queries per month from the office of the administrator of the court's system users, and about 14,000 queries per month from law enforcement. Department personnel believe that a number of these queries concern ongoing criminal investigations where detectives wish to determine if a previously convicted felon was incarcerated or "on the street" when a crime was committed. Thanks to checking with local law enforcement during its design, the Washington State Felony Offender Reporting System query screen is formatted specifically to answer this question.

The availability of the Washington State Felony Offender Reporting System has removed the necessity for the department to develop programs to meet the special needs of other state agencies. For example, access to the system has been provided to support enforcement officers in the Division of Child Support in the Department of Social and Health Services. This reinforces the officers' efforts to minimize state costs by tracking parents behind in payments. Upon request, access also has been provided to the offices of federal agencies located within the state.

Conclusion

The benefits to the department from time savings alone have far exceeded the cost of the development of the Washington State Felony Offender Reporting System. By keeping the design concept simple and having only three classes of users, administrative costs for the system are minimal. Nonetheless, making potential users of the system aware of its availability, and providing them with operating instructions, a description of each screen and the data elements it contains, has been a continuing challenge.

Law enforcement, criminal justice, and other users now have access to, and the benefit of, information, which was formerly unavailable. A steady increase in the number of queries is expected as more potential users become aware of the Washington State Felony Offender Reporting System and the information it contains. At some point, handling a larger volume of queries may become a cost issue.

Prior to implementation of the Washington State Felony Offender Reporting System, the department had direct connections to both the office of the administrator for the courts and the Washington State Patrol computers. Providing for access to the system for other than the office of the administrator for the courts or Washington State Police system users posed a major problem. It was addressed by working closely with the Washington Department of Information Services. As a result, anyone having access to the Department of Information Services can access the Washington State Felony Offender Reporting System following approval by the department of corrections. In addition, the department of information services also handles the administration of dial-in access following set-up.

The sharing of information within the criminal justice community has been encouraged by the state Criminal Justice Information Act Executive Committee, and is in direct support of one of its business requirements. Further sharing within the community is expected.

Author:

Dale Putnam
Former Chief of Information Services
Washington Department of Corrections
Olympia, Washington

Contact:

Don Price
Chief, Information Technology
Washington Department of Corrections

P. O. Box 41100
Olympia, Washington 98504-1100
(360) 586-6396

Intranet Technology for Dissemination of Policy and Legislation

Introduction

As is the case with all correctional organizations, the Correctional Service of Canada operates under a huge umbrella of policy and legislation. On occassion, ensuring that this vital, yet dynamic, information is available to every employee who needs it in a timely and effective manner has proven to be a daunting task. A paper-based distribution system is cumbersome, prone to error, and can be anything but timely. On the other hand, having the information available in an electronic format only is useful if the people who need the information have an effective vehicle at their disposal for retrieving and viewing it.

The Correctional Service of Canada prides itself on being an adopter of information technologies that support its corporate mission. Over the past several years, the Correctional Service of Canada has established a robust network of 8,000 desktop computers, linking 170 institutional, parole office, and administrative locations across the country. It recently deployed a corporate intranet, called InfoNet, across its entire network. Intranets employ the same technology as the internet ("web" technology), and have proven, in their short period of existence, to be cost-effective, and process-effective vehicles for distributing information throughout an organization.

Even though InfoNet was designed to allow for the dissemination of all kinds of information, its most important role has been to become the Correctional Service of Canada's primary vehicle for ensuring that all staff have access to the policy and legislative documentation that governs its operation.

Development and Design

The initial design specifications for the corporate intranet called for technology components that would ensure efficient access to InfoNet from all sites across the country. The design defined the base content that would be acceptable prior to its implementation.

The Correctional Service of Canada's governing policy and legislative documentation consists of the Corrections and Conditional Release Act and Regulations, the commissioner's directives, and various operational manuals, instructions, and standing orders. From a content-collection point of view, the challenge was not great—all of these documents already were available in electronic format. During the past several years, the Correctional Service of Canada's information distribution process had evolved from a hard copy mailed across the country, to electronic copies transferred electronically and printed locally. With InfoNet, the objective was to eliminate the need for printing by providing a computer interface that allowed for search, retrieval, and direct viewing.

An important decision made early on in the developmental phase of InfoNet was that the "owner" of any particular document would retain the responsibility for the currency and accuracy of its content. This ensured that the staff responsible for content were an integral part of the overall process. In addition, content committees were formed, both at the national level and in the regions. These committees continue to be active and provide invaluable feedback for ongoing improvements.

A key element of the design was a "link" that was constructed between InfoNet and the Correctional Service of Canada's primary business application—the Offender Management System. From any screen within the Offender Management System, the user has instant access to policy and legislative information contained on the InfoNet. While this feature is currently not context-sensitive, work will begin shortly on making it so.

The real challenge in the design and development of InfoNet was at the technical level. Internet technology is still at an early stage and constantly continues to evolve. The addition of InfoNet on the Correctional Service of Canada's network could not decrease the performance and/or availability of other existing corporate applications using the same infrastructure. To maximize the chance of success, intranet design information was gathered from other government departments and agencies, and from the private sector, and suppliers.

One of the design solutions that came out of these discussions was the use of proxy servers to dynamically "replicate" the information stored on a central intranet server sent out to the Correctional Service of Canada's five regions. Designers believed that the use of proxy servers was a proactive way to minimize the impact of additional traffic on the network. Since these proxy servers also could be used as regional web servers, this allowed for the efficient distribution of regional and local content (such as regional instructions and standing orders that are derived from the commissioner's directives).

Implementation

The full implementation of InfoNet began on February 14, 1997. This national roll-out was preceded though by a six-month pilot study at the Correctional Service of Canada's national headquarters. The pilot phase provided the implementation team with many important suggestions for improving both the "look and feel" of InfoNet and its content. It also allowed for the assessment of the proper level of training that was required. From this, it was decided to use both formal training and extensive on-line help. Formal training was made available in both a classroom setting and through "expert users," on a case-by-case basis.

The feedback from users was considered crucial at both the pilot stage, and after national implementation. For example, even though a great deal of effort went into the implementation of an initial search technology for electronic documents, the decision to use this product was revisited based on user feedback. The product was not well received by the user community and had to be replaced with another search engine that was easier to use. The lesson learned was that the "best" tool, if not well understood, provides little functionality.

No discussion of the implementation of InfoNet would be complete without highlighting the "team" aspect of the project. The Correctional Service of Canada was fortunate enough to have professional and dedicated resources assigned to this project—a project manager, a production supervisor, two production workers, a quality assurance specialist (very important to establish and maintain the credibility of the intranet content), and "web" specialists for the engineering and ongoing production of the site.

Results

The benefits from the introduction of InfoNet can be seen at different levels. In the short term, we now have a new and effective medium for the communication of policy and legislation. Within minutes, updated information is available from coast to coast to all 8,000 networked computers. Notification of new information is handled through the "What's New" feature of InfoNet. The ability to search the site means that access to required information for the conduct of any particular job function is just a few keystrokes away.

Over the mid-term, the requirement for the production of hard copy has been reduced, and continues to decrease, as growing numbers of staff become comfortable with a new way to access and view information. This not only has led to a reduction in costs, but it makes the Correctional Service of Canada a responsible corporate organization because of its protection of the environment.

As for the future, the introduction of web technology at the Correctional Service of Canada has opened up many other opportunities for the effective use of technology. Some of the most promising currently being evaluated include: data-based information dissemination, computer-based training on a mass scale, electronic bulletin boards, and electronic commerce.

Conclusion

As with the implementation of any new technology, it is important to avoid pitfalls, learn from problems, and build upon previous success. Several factors formed the key to the success of the Correctional Service of Canada's corporate intranet as a medium for the dissemination of policy and legislation. These factors included working as a team, senior management supporting the project, the effective marketing of the project, the training offered to staff, the availability and the quality of the Correctional Service of Canada's basic network infrastructure, and last, but not least, involving of the end-users in providing constructive feedback.

Contact:

Louise Saint-Laurent
Assistant Commissioner
Correctional Service of Canada

Sir Wilfred Laurier Building
340 Laurier Avenue W.
Ottawa, Ontario K1A 0P9

Technology
Additional Program Entries

Electronically Enhanced Early Release Program

Michael Gallegos, Deputy Director, Parole Services and Community Corrections
California Department of the Youth Authority, 4241 Williamsbourgh Drive, Sacramento, California 95823
(916) 262-1363

In 1991, the California Department of the Youth Authority began a pilot program in four parole offices using electronic monitors to provide a supervised sixty-day early release program. The Electronically Enhanced Parole Release Program was initiated to save institutional beds while at the same time enhancing the department's ability to provide public protection. It also affords the parolee a greater opportunity for success by providing support and control during the difficult transition and adjustment period from the institution into the community. Wards can be paroled up to sixty days prior to the projected release date in addition to any good time they have earned. They are placed on intensive supervision, contacted weekly, and drug tested, as indicated or required. Supervision is enhanced substantially through the use of electronic monitoring. Response time to suspected violations or schedule infractions is timely, as dictated by the ward's risk level, degree of infraction, and adjustment to parole. Sanctions for repeat violations or schedule infractions range from a case conference to return to an institutional program. Those successfully completing the sixty days are assigned to regular reentry supervision and services. In 1994, the program was expanded and now encompasses all sixteen California Department of the Youth Authority parole offices statewide.

Automated Electronic Mapping and Surveying Institution Light Levels Using Satellite Positioning Systems

Jim Mahan, Chief, Office of Security Technology
Federal Bureau of Prisons, 320 First Street, N.W., Washington, D.C. 20534
(202) 307-3191

In the past, the Bureau of Prisons evaluated outdoor lighting surveys using manual measurement methods. Using facility blueprints as a base map, the surveyor collected a relatively small number of light measurements with a handheld light meter. This manual method is tedious and labor intensive. The Bureau of Prisons has developed an automated method of electronically mapping and surveying the light levels of an institution using the latest in satellite positioning systems. The final output from the system is an easy-to-read contour map of the lit and unlit areas of an institution. The color map clearly identifies lighting deficiencies and potential areas of security concerns. The Bureau of Prisons worked jointly with the U.S. Department of Defense to fund and develop this unique technology as a system with multiple applications for organizations with an interest in the physical security of their facility.

Digitized Fingerprint and Photograph System

Dwayne Clark, Warden
Illinois Department of Corrections, Stateville Correctional Center, Route 53, P.O. Box 112, Joliet, Illinois 60434
(815) 727-3607

The Illinois Department of Corrections is in the process of implementing a digitized fingerprint and photograph system that produces high-quality photo IDs and fingerprints. The process uses less labor, fewer materials, and is accomplished at a lower cost to the facility. With basic computer skills, operators can design cards, print full-color ID cards, and revise and reissue existing cards. The digitized fingerprint system allows staff to identify quickly and accurately individuals who come to visit inmates.This technology will allow staff to take digitized fingerprints of inmates in the same manner as visitors. It is designed to accurately identify inmates, store information, and quickly retrieve it at various locations.The implementation of this technology makes the process of taking, developing, storing, and retrieving inmate mug shots and visitor information obsolete. Future plans for this system include integration with outside law enforcement agencies to alert those agencies when a wanted individual or fugitive attempts to visit an inmate.

ProDES: The Program Development and Evaluation System

Philip W. Harris, Ph.D., Associate Professor of Criminal Justice,
Department of Criminal Justice, Gladfelter Hall, Room 512, Temple University, Philadelphia, Pennsylvania 19122
(215) 204-5267

ProDES is an outcome-based information system that tracks all Philadelphia delinquents for the duration of their involvement with the juvenile justice system. Its primary focus is to provide a continuous flow of information that is used for developing programs, matching youths to programs, and assessing available program resources. ProDES has three goals: (1) to facilitate the development of intervention programs for delinquent youths by providing those programs with continuous outcome information that is relevant to the ways in which program personnel think about change; (2) to facilitate planning of the entire array of delinquency services provided by the Department of Juvenile Justice Services through the provision of program-level outcome information that identifies program strengths and weaknesses in the entire array of services; and (3) to facilitate the rational matching by probation officers and judges of adjudicated youths to programs that can meet their needs and the needs of the community. ProDES is a valuable and important information system that monitors the kinds of programs that best serve the needs of Philadelphia's juvenile justice system and the youths, families, and communities assisted by its interventions.

The Use of Technology in the Management of the Juvenile Parole Population

John R. Platt, Acting Deputy Director, Juvenile Division
Illinois Department of Corrections, 3802 Lincoln Highway, St. Charles, Illinois 60175
(630) 584-0750

The juvenile field services staff of the Illinois Department of Corrections are responsible for supervising all youth paroled from the juvenile division's six facilities. Parole services are divided into three separate districts that encompass Illinois' 102 counties. The ability to access and share information on every parolee within the system is a critical need for agents who must oversee the juveniles' compliance with their parole plans while attempting to manage their public risk. For timely and accessible information on every parolee, the Juvenile Division of the Illinois Department of Corrections uses two data/communications systems: the Juvenile Tracking System and "Profs," which is a form of electronic mail. The Juvenile Tracking System is a comprehensive, online control, tracking, and reporting system. More than 600 Illinois Department of Corrections' staff, located at juvenile facilities and field offices throughout the state, are authorized to use the system. The Juvenile Division also uses "Profs" electronic mail to enable all juvenile division staff to communicate with one another through access to a computer terminal. Critical information can be moved almost immediately through the "Profs" system so that staff can stay current on developments in a juvenile's case at any time. The use of the Juvenile Tracking System and "Profs" in combination with one another provides the juvenile division with a method of comprehensive data collection and a valuable communication system.

Victims

19

Introduction

In 1986, the issue of corrections-based victim services was first raised by the American Correctional Association in a broad policy statement. It said that victims should be treated with dignity and respect and should be notified about the status of their offender.

Correction-based victim services are a relatively new phenomenon in the United States. Historically, crime victims and those working with them focused on the "front end" of the criminal justice system—law enforcement, prosecution, and the court. At best, victims were notified of available community programs and received notification of arraignment, trial, and sentencing hearings. In some cases, victims were permitted to submit victim-impact statements.

More recently, many states have adopted victims' rights amendments, legislation, and policies that have enhanced victims' rights and services in adult and juvenile corrections agencies, and paroling authorities. With these steps, crime victims began to have a voice in the postsentence phase of their cases.

This shift in philosophy and attitude has changed the focus of attention from a sole concern with the rehabilitation of the offender to a more inclusive commitment to responding to victims as clients of corrections agencies, too. Increasingly, victims are viewed as individuals who deserve rights and services from the justice system; not simply protection from offenders but accountability as well.

In 1997, the Association of State Correctional Administrators identified ten core elements for corrections-based victim services as essential for good practice. These elements include:

1. Incorporating victims' rights and needs into the overall agency mission statement

2. Designating a full-time staff member to plan and implement a comprehensive victim-service program with representatives at institutions and regional offices

3. Providing core services to victims of crime that include notification, protection, input, restitution, and information and referral

4. Creating a victim advisory council to guide program implementation

5. Establishing written policies and procedures for victims' rights and services

6. Developing a public information plan and outreach program that describes the services and assistance provided by the agency

7. Developing and using a training curriculum for orientation and continuing education for all agency staff

8. Developing and implementing policies, procedures, and protocols on responding to staff victimization

9. Implementing victim-impact classes and panels for offenders

10. Designating an agency representative to participate in local, state, and regional victim-service coalitions

In selecting the most promising corrections-based programs for victims for inclusion in this chapter, the committee considered these elements. In addition, it also reviewed whether the program submitted had clearly defined goals or measurable outcomes; if the program were replicable; if cultural competency issues were considered in the program design; the level of innovation; and, whether program staff collaborated with other groups. The American Correctional Association's Victims Committee selected the following five programs that it considers to be Best Practices.

The Victim/Witness Notification Program of the Washington State Department of Corrections is an integral part of the overall operation of the department of corrections and serves the victim community as a clearinghouse in addressing victim issues regarding the release and placement of offenders. The program permits notification to victims and witnesses who choose such notification about almost all state-committed offenders; it also contains a ten-week module that teaches offenders about the impact of their crimes.

The Victims Services Program of the California Department of Corrections uses notification, a restitution program, and training to respond to the various needs of crime victims, and it helps to ensure that everyone recognizes and understands the impact of crime on victims.

The California Department of the Youth Authority's Victims Services Division offers a model program of victim notification; restitution collection and disbursement; classes on the impact of crime on victims for youthful offenders; victim-offender meetings; and observations of National Crime Victims' Rights Week.

The Victim Service Division of the South Carolina Department of Corrections has learned that including victims in its decision-making process is not problematic. The inclusion of victims—including staff victims—in decision making and providing victims with information has had a positive effect.

The Office of Victim Services of the Ohio Department of Rehabilitation and Correction is only staffed by survivors of crime and victim advocates. The mission of this office is to give victims the opportunities to participate in decisions concerning an offender's liberty and to provide support and information.

Committee chair:

Gail Heller
Executive Director
CHOICES

P. O. Box 06157
Columbus, Ohio 43206-0157
(614) 258-6080

Victim/Witness Notification Program

Introduction

The Washington State Department of Corrections' Victim/Witness Notification Program was created in 1983 with the passage of state laws supporting the right of crime victims and witnesses to be informed of the status of offenders committed to the department. The change in the state statute was a response to the brutal murder of a rape victim who had testified against her offender. The offender was serving a sentence for the rape and was on a work-release program when he returned to the victim's home.

The legislation and the department's subsequent implementation of the laws acknowledged that both the victims of crime and those who witnessed the crimes are impacted and are deserving of the same rights regarding information about the offender. The initial legislation extended such rights only to victims and witnesses of violent crimes. However, through the department's initiative in partnership with victims and witnesses of other crimes, the laws have been enhanced, and afford the right of notification to all victims and witnesses of sex, serious drug, and felony-harassment crimes. This comprehensive list of eligible offenses for notification covers almost all crimes for which individuals are committed to prison under state law for their first offense.

The Washington Department of Corrections' Victim/Witness Notification Program is the oldest program in the nation. It has been used as a model for other states interested in implementing a notification process for those impacted by crime.

Development and Design

The department of corrections' headquarters administers the program. All offender-movement information from the department's twelve prison facilities, two prerelease facilities, and sixteen work-release facilities are sent to the Victim Witness Unit. From there, notifications are made to eligible individuals who choose to participate in the program. Participation in the program is voluntary and victims and witnesses must request notification.

When the offender is convicted of the offense and committed to a facility, all victims and witnesses of that crime receive an invitation letter, which outlines their right to receive notification from the department. The names, addresses, and telephone numbers of eligible participants are obtained from prosecutors, law enforcement officials, and other criminal justice agencies. All personal information about participants in the program is confidential and not released to anyone. This is one advantage of the program's centralized operation. Offenders cannot get direct access to information about those in the program. The department's policy is that all eligible offenders will be treated as if there are individuals to notify to protect those who actually are enrolled in the program.

The underlying principle of the program centers around the rights of victims and witnesses to receive timely and accurate information about offenders. They are informed of the status of offenders during incarceration, including any proposed release plans developed by sex offenders, specific release addresses, and actual release dates. Other types of notifications provided include offender transfers from prison to a community-based work-release facility, furloughs, appeals, and deaths during confinement. The program has an ongoing escape procedure in which victims and witnesses are notified by telephone within four hours of an escape occurring. They then are notified when the offender is recaptured.

Implementation

After the request for notification is received from the victim or witness, program staff verify the status of the offender relative to the offender's current incarceration. Once it is determined that the victim or witness meets the criteria for participation in the program, the offender has been committed to the department as a component of the sentence, and the offender is still in confinement, the victims or witnesses receive a confirmation letter. This letter officially confirms their participation in the program and provides them with a toll-free telephone number if they need to contact program staff.

All offender-movement information received in the Victim Witness Unit from correctional facilities statewide is handled on-line. The automation of the information coming into the unit ensures that it is received in a timely manner and that confidentiality is maintained. Likewise, all of the information relating to those participating in the program is automated to ensure quick access for notification purposes. This information is protected. Only program staff have access to names, addresses, and telephone numbers of participants.

Once the offender-movement information is received, staff verify whether there are individuals requiring notification. Generally, notifications are made by letter, and enrollees receive information at least thirty days prior to an offender's movement, except for cases involving escapes and deaths. Victims and witnesses have an opportunity to provide information about safety concerns with regard to an offender's placement and release.

The Victim Witness Unit serves as a liaison between the supervising community-corrections officers and facility staff in communicating the concerns that are expressed by those receiving notification. This information is used in the release planning of the offender and in determining the best supervision strategies after the offender is released. The partnership that exists between the department and the community through this process has enhanced public safety by allowing victims and witnesses a formal process to express potential safety concerns prior to the offender's release.

An added component of the Victim Witness Unit was the development and implementation of the Victim Awareness Educational Program in 1991. This program teaches offenders through an educational model about the actual impact their crime had not only on the primary victim, but also the secondary victims of the offense. It is not enough to teach offenders life and employment skills, when they make the transition from supervision to independence, if they do not understand what impact their behavior had on the victims and the community.

This program is taught in concert with selected crime victims who tell real stories of the impact of crime in their lives. Offenders are given classroom work and "homework" assignments that address victim issues. During the ten-week course, eight subjects are covered ranging from property crime to homicide. The educational program is offered in both the department's correctional facilities and to offenders under community supervision.

The Victim Witness Unit also provides victims and witnesses a centralized location where they may address issues when they feel harassed, intimidated, or threatened by an offender under the department's jurisdiction. It serves as a liaison between the facility where the offender is incarcerated and the victim alleging the harassment.

Currently, there are more than 11,000 victims and witnesses enrolled in the department's notification program. On average, 180 notifications are made each month, and 170 new requests for notifications are received each month.

Conclusion

The Victim Witness Unit is an integral part of the overall operation of the department of corrections and serves the victim community as a clearinghouse in addressing victim issues regarding the release and placement of offenders. It assists in building a collaborative effort with those in the community, thereby facilitating the exchange of information between correctional facilities and department staff responsible for the supervision of the offender following release. Without this partnership between the department's operation and input from the victim, valuable information is lost that supports public safety and assists offenders in their return to the community. The Victim Witness Unit also provides a place where victim and witness issues are heard and advocacy occurs. This becomes an important link for those impacted by crime, for in many instances, victims and witnesses are no longer the "forgotten element of the criminal justice system."

Author:

Bill Stutz
Manager, Witness Notification Program
Washington State Department of Corrections
Olympia, Washington

Contact:

Marianne McNabb
Assistant Director
Washington State Department of Corrections

P. O. Box 41100
Olympia, Washington 98504-1119
(360) 753-3016

Victim Services Program

Introduction

In 1982, the California State Legislature amended the state constitution to include crime victims' rights. The enactment of subsequent penal, civil, and government codes guaranteed victims the rights to be heard throughout the criminal justice process and to receive notification and restitution. The California Department of Corrections' Victim Services Program was established in 1988 as part of a growing commitment to victim awareness and assistance. The mission of the program is to examine and respond to the various needs of crime victims. It also is responsible for ensuring that inmates and parolees, correctional staff, and the general public recognize and understand the impact of crime on victims. The program is a function of the Special Projects Branch, Evaluation, Compliance and Information Systems Division.

Design and Development

The director of the department of corrections created the goal of establishing a comprehensive victim services program within California and requested support and assistance from top management. This five-year workplan identified current resources and considered the scope of future services and made projections about the resources necessary to implement the five-year plan. Staff discovered that full program development would extend far into the future and would require high maintenance. These observations were based on experience with the fluid nature of program components and the fact that the department was dealing with a very litigious population of adult inmates with more rights than victims have.

Implementation

Although the scope of the Victim Services Program continues to grow, its core focus is on providing services that target victims' rights and needs. The program is committed to improving the treatment of victims at all levels of involvement with the department. It also ensures that inmates, parolees, staff, and the general public understand the impact of crime on victims.

The current activities of the program include providing notification to victims, offering victims direct services, managing the collection of restitution, and developing and distributing victim services information. It also provides training for the staff on victims' issues, conducts an annual forum, offers presentations to a variety of organizations, supports institution and parole-based fundraising and other activities, places victims on advisory committees, and provides them with information about the workings of the correctional system. Finally, the program has involved victims in addressing high-notoriety cases, created partnerships with other states in resolving crime victims/corrections issues, and focuses on staff-victimization concerns.

A wide array of notifications are made to victims, witnesses, family members, and concerned citizens regarding an offender's release to parole, parole suitability hearings for lifers, any change in custody or supervision status, death, escape and/or capture. More than 15,000 notifications are provided per year.

Direct referral and other information services are available to crime victims, witnesses, family members, victims' advocacy organizations, institutions, and those involved in parole. The program office receives approximately 150 new telephone calls and letters each week mainly regarding offender location, special conditions of parole, speaking at lifer hearings, threats, intimidation, or harassment, and assistance with HIV/AIDS court-ordered testing. The majority of clients are victims of violent crime such as domestic violence, sexual assault, and homicide. Direct services also are provided to staff victims. The program lets them know what resources are available to them other than those provided by the Employee Assistance Program and the department.

A restitution program, established in 1992, is managed by the Victim Services Program from a centralized, coordinated perspective. To date, the department has collected more than $11 million from inmate wages and other trust account deposits. Revenues from restitution fines are distributed to the State Board of Control and deposited into the Victim Compensation Fund. In addition, the department now has statutory authority to collect on direct orders of restitution payable to crime victims, and to make restitution a condition of parole. Currently, administrative fees collected from inmates are paying for four positions associated with inmate-restitution collection. More positions paid for by inmates and parolees are anticipated to be included in this pool of money for parole and community corrections facilities.

Victims' services information is developed and distributed as part of the comprehensive services provided within the department. This includes the distribution of brochures and forms associated with notification and restitution to more than 1,500 victim-service agencies per year. It also includes department-produced videos, which have been recognized nationally and are distributed throughout the country to other correctional and parole agencies.

Department training is offered regarding the impact of crime on victims, including crimes of domestic violence, stalking, child molestation, and rape. Staff receive training on victimization issues at the academies, in new employee training, and at annual training sessions. External training at the national level is provided to other departments of correction. Statewide training is facilitated for various agencies and groups including the California District Attorneys Association, the Chief Probation Officers Association, judges, the Board of Control, victim-witness agencies, the Victim Resource Center of the McGeorge School of Law and other advocacy programs, and legislators. Staff of the Victim Services Program are consultants to the National Victim Center, the National Organization for Victim Assistance, and the Federal Office for Victims of Crime. Several program staff currently are registered with the National Institute of Corrections as technical experts and trainers.

The Victim Services Program staff conducts an annual forum using resources from throughout the department and the state. Attendees at this forum are the approximately eighty department staff who are also "victim services' representatives." They are appointed to this position by their wardens and regional parole administrators. Training allows for networking, sharing of ideas and experiences, and receiving updates on changes in laws and input of staff towards departmentwide program development.

Program support that is provided to the various institutions and parole divisions concerns fundraising, inmate-impact groups, Victims' Rights Week, and local victim-net- working activities. Such activities include walk-a-thons, Kid's Day, a Giving Tree, mentor projects, and resource allocations for such things as printing and staff volunteer time. The thirty-two prisons and four parole regions raise more than $215,000 per year from fundraising by staff and offenders and return it to the communities surrounding them for victim services.

Staff participate in various prison, parole, and citizen advisory committees to encourage an open exchange of information and education and the sharing of ideas on how to better serve and interact with one another. The Victim Services Program coordinates and works with the institutions, parole divisions, and the director's office on high notoriety and public interest cases. They lend support to the department when an offender continues to harass or intimidate a victim.

Conclusion

The Victim Services program illustrates that the success of comprehensive victim services within a corrections environment must be supported from the top down. The program manager must have the support of top management and direct lines of communication to accomplish the task. Program development and maintenance are in a constant state of flux and require monitoring and modifying.

The program also shows that ongoing training of staff and the public are critical to the success of program activities. Public relations, political involvement in the legislative arena, involvement in the grass roots crime victim advocacy groups, and visibility of the program are essential to maintain the momentum of services.

An awareness of sensitive issues at the front end of program development such as staff victims, cultural issues, litigation potential, and involvement of all "users" from within and external to the department, is mandatory. Finally, the success of this initiative demonstrates that appropriate resource allocations for personnel, operations, program activity development, and maintenance are critical to sustaining a forward momentum.

Authors/Contacts:

Sandi Menefee
Chief, The Office of Victim Services and Restitution
California Department of Corrections

P. O. Box 942883
Sacramento, California 94283
(916) 358-2436

Sylvia Ortiz
Special Assistant to the Chief
The Office of Victim Services and Restitution
California Department of Corrections

P. O. Box 942883
Sacramento, California 94283
(916) 327-4901

Victim Services Division

Introduction

The California Department of the Youth Authority's Victims Services Division provides comprehensive coordinated services to institution and parole staff, victims, local victim-assistance agencies, the judicial system, and nationally recognized victims groups. The program is premised on the Youth Authority's belief that the justice system is accountable to victims and has a responsibility to implement programs that will address the long-term impact of crime on victims. It also is the Youth Authority's policy to offer offenders treatment opportunities and instill in them an awareness of the impact of their behavior on others.

The Victim Services Division provides assistance to victims by advocating for victims, providing direct services to victims, training staff on victims' legal rights and how to be sensitive to victims' issues, and holding offenders accountable for their behavior and educating them on the impact of crime on victims.

The Victims Services Division is housed in the Youth Authority's Office of Prevention and Victims Services in Sacramento. Providing this comprehensive statewide victim services program through a central professional victim services unit ensures that confidential information is secure, victim interactions are skillfully conducted, and that the professionalism of victim services staff is enhanced.

The Youth Authority is composed of eleven institutions, five youth conservation camps, and nineteen parole offices throughout the state. The designated victims services coordinator at each location acts as a liaison between the worksite and the division.

Development

The Youth Authority designated its first victims' services specialist in 1983. Since that time, efforts to establish and coordinate statewide victims' programs have proven fruitful and are recognized throughout the state and the nation. The division has implemented a variety of victim-oriented models where offenders are held accountable, crime is personalized, and victims can be heard. These program and services include the following items.

Victim Notification

In accordance with California state laws, victims have the right to certain allowable offender information per their request. All victims and potential victims have the right to be notified about annual reviews, escapes and recaptures, parole dates and subsequent changes, and parole consideration hearing dates. In addition, in cases identified as "serious and violent" offenses, victims have the right to be notified about the discharge date and reason, furlough or day pass consideration, release dates, release to reentry, work furlough programs, and transfers to another institution.

The division assists each Youth Authority facility in the development of an automated tracking system to ensure that victims who have requested information receive timely notification of the offender's status. The Victim Services Division maintains a centrally located database which houses confidential victim information and case specifics, and tracks notification efforts.

Restitution Collection and Disbursement

The division is responsible for verifying court-ordered victim restitution and fines, researching any discrepancies, and requesting amended court orders from the county of commitment. It distributes all victims' restitution checks directly to the victims, or to their designee. The Youth Authority takes the collection of restitution very seriously and pursues it as an effective means of holding offenders accountable for the financial losses their behavior has incurred and as a gesture of amends for the consequences of their actions.

Impact of Crime on Victims Classes

The "Impact of Crime on Victims" classes began in 1984. The program was developed to expose youthful offenders to the long-range harm their actions cause their victims, to hold offenders accountable for these actions, and to teach offenders better ways to handle conflict and violence.

Currently, all Youth Authority institutions and camps offer the classes. The course includes thirty-five-to-sixty hours of an experiential curriculum over a period of six-to-twelve weeks. Impact speakers are an essential component and are often actual crime victims or victims' services providers.

In 1985, the first annual training for trainers was held to educate youth authority staff and invited guests on victims' services and the impact curriculum. The number of participants per training has doubled over the last ten years.

External Activities

Division staff are actively involved in a variety of external activities. Staff serve as members and/or support for the activities of California's Youth and Adult Correctional Agency Victim Task Force and the Task Force to Review Juvenile Crime. In addition, staff frequently are called upon to give educational presentations on victim awareness, violence prevention, and crisis intervention to community-based organizations, schools, victim's services providers, law enforcement personnel, correctional staff, and the judiciary

Victim-Offender Meetings

In a continued commitment to enhance direct services to victims, the Youth Authority has developed and recently implemented policy and procedure requirements necessary for safe and productive victim-offender meetings. Such meetings afford the opportunity for victims to come face-to-face with the offender responsible for the crime against them and their family. Such meetings allow victims the opportunity to express feelings and opinions and to ask questions raised by the offense, directly to the person responsible. In turn, offenders broaden their understanding of the consequences of their behavior through the power of the victim's statements. Victim-offender meetings humanize the criminal justice process and provide the possibility for necessary closure and healing for both victims and offenders.

National Crime Victims' Rights Week

The California Department of the Youth Authority observes National Crime Victims' Rights Week through a variety of local site activities. These activities include fundraisers for local victim's services organizations and victim awareness presentations throughout the state. The division serves as a resource for all local sites and assists each site in developing its plans to commemorate crime victims, by publishing and distributing material, conducting site visits throughout the state, and representing the Youth Authority at all functions.

Outcomes

The Victims Services Division currently serves 14,962 offenders under the jurisdiction of the Youth Authority. Of those offenders, almost 10,000 currently are registered in the database and have obligations to just over 12,000 victims. There are currently 6,127 offenders who have an obligation to pay a restitution fine to the California State Victims of Crime Fund. It is estimated that approximately $4 million is owed in victims' restitution and another $2 million in fines. More than 100 victims appear before the Youthful Offender Parole Board each year and approximately 45 requests are made each month for direct services to victims.

Conclusion

Establishing victims services in juvenile corrections is innovative and serves as a model and valuable asset to the nation. The impact of the Crime on Victims' program has been replicated in several states across the nation. In addition, a modified curriculum in victims' awareness education has been developed and implemented in county camps, county court, schools, and probation departments in northern California.

Contact:

Sharon English
Deputy Director
Office of Victims Services
California Department of the Youth Authority

4241 Williamsbourgh Drive
Sacramento, California 95823
(916) 262-1392

Division of Victim Services: A Comprehensive Approach

Introduction

The South Carolina Department of Corrections offers a comprehensive victim-service program and shares the distinction of being one of the first corrections-based victim notification programs in the country. In operation since 1985, the program consistently has been cited as a model by the Office for Victims of Crime of the U.S. Department of Justice.

The Division of Victims Services consists of three full-time employees. The program is housed in the Office of Executive Affairs, which reports directly to the director. The organizational placement of the program is important. Having Victim Services on the director's executive staff sends the message throughout the 32 institutions and among the 6,700 employees that they are to carry out their responsibilities with sensitivity and special attention to the rights of crime victims. Elevation of the program to division-level status gave victim services status equal to that of programs for inmates.

Another key aspect of placement is autonomy. The Division of Victim Services is independent of programs for inmates. There is no structural influence, and as advocates for victims, the staff may intervene on any level and may cross all organizational lines of authority.

The agency is serious about its commitment to crime victims, and it has put that commitment into writing. The agency mission statement and goals have been rewritten to include consideration of victims. These statements hang on the walls of each institution and in each of the division offices.

Development and Design

What may distinguish the South Carolina Department of Corrections from other corrections-based victim notification programs is that the concept of victims services permeates the entire agency. The victim emphasis is pervasive in all agency decision making and program-implementation activities. Victims want more than just information about a release or an escape. They want information and inclusion in the criminal justice system. Victims want to know about and understand the programs of corrections; they expect corrections to listen when told about the impact of those programs on their lives. Several examples are provided next that illustrate how victims have been included in departmental decisions and activities.

- Face-to-face media interviews and photographs of inmates have been stopped so as not to glamorize the crimes of the offenders, and not to revictimize the victims and their family members.

- Violent offenders have been removed from community-based programs such as work release.

- Furloughs have been stopped.

- Prior to offender placements in designated facilities, each registered victim is contacted for input and concurrence.

- A toll-free telephone number has been installed strictly for use by victims and their families.

- Inmate organizations are required to give 15 percent of their fundraising proceeds to victim service organizations or to a charity.

- Work-release inmates are assessed 5 percent of their gross wages for the Victim Assistance Program that awards grants to victim-service organizations.

- Prison industries inmates are assessed 15 percent of their gross wages for the Victim Compensation Fund that awards financial assistance to crime victims, according to state law.

- In 1995 and 1996, the sale of confiscated inmate jewelry raised more than $12,000, which was given to the South Carolina Victim Assistance Network for victim scholarships.

The South Carolina Code of Laws requires the department to a provide notice of release—a temporary provisional or final release from custody—and to a provide notice of escape. A constitutional amendment for crime victims is pending ratification in the legislature.

The program is designed to offer information to the victim and, where appropriate, to provide for the victim's inclusion in the decision-making process. Emphasis is placed on a full and complete up-front contact that is attractively presented and in language that a layperson can understand.

The notification program provides information about changes in the status of an identified inmate, and offers an avenue for the victim or victim's family to raise considerations regarding those changes. Notices of release from custody are given by letter. Telephone calls are immediate with information about escapes and subsequent apprehension. Special attention is provided to victims during the time the offender is on escape status.

With regard to executions, special briefings are held with the victim's families. With the uniqueness of this event, special procedures are in place and thoughtful attention is given to them. The South Carolina Code of Laws now allows for three of the victim's family representatives to witness the execution as a result of the efforts from the department of corrections working with the General Assembly.

Complaints are received and acted on. All inquiries are answered by telephone or letter. The installation of a toll-free telephone line provides easier access to the agency for victims and their families. Special meetings, upon victims' requests, can be arranged with wardens, other institutional staff, or inmates. Harassing mail and telephone calls are stopped. To further enhance inmate accountability, victim impact panels and classes will be introduced in 1998.

The law was amended in 1991 to allow for greater protection of victim's records and thus provide confidentiality. This legislation gives privileged status to the address and telephone numbers of victims registered with the department.

A telephone status check also is offered. Any time victims want to check on an inmate's location and eligibility dates, they may do so by telephoning the office. This service helps to eliminate some of the fear that so many crime victims feel. It gives the victim a point of entry into a system that previously was complex, confusing, sometimes hostile, and often closed.

Upon receipt of a request for registration, the request is verified and eligibility criteria are checked. A search is conducted for the correct offender, and the victim data are entered. The victim/witness forms are printed, the documentation letter is prepared and sent to the victim, and appropriate internal documentation and flagging occurs.

Prior to the release of an inmate, the registered victim is notified in writing, and the record is documented. In cases where the release is immediate or a letter would be arriving too late, the registered victim is phoned. These procedures meet all American Correctional Association accreditation standards.

Also important are services to employees assaulted on the job. The comprehensive program is an institution-based peer response with outside counseling services provided, where needed. A Task Force on Workplace Violence has been appointed and challenged to enhance and expand the present service for assaulted employees to include traumatic and criminal acts away from the workplace.

Outcomes

There are more than 11,500 active victims registered for notification. There are more than 6,000 inactive victim records that are automatically reactivated upon the return of the offender. The number of registered victims has grown by an average of 28 percent in each of the last five years. The department of corrections maintains the largest data bank of crime victims in the state and makes it available on a confidential basis to other state agencies.

The victims of both violent and nonviolent cases are registered. Of the total inmate population, 31 percent of all inmate records have registered victims.

Conclusion

The South Carolina Department of Corrections has learned that including victims in its decision-making process is not problematic and has had a positive effect. The department also learned that having a Division of Victim Services provides wardens and institutional staff a referral resource so their time can be spent better on matters of security and operation of the institution. The victim services staff are trained to handle inquiries calls, letters, and special requests.

Contact:

Barbara Grissom
Director of Victims Services
South Carolina Department of Corrections

P. O. Box 21787
Columbia, South Carolina 29221
(803) 896-1733

Office of Victim Services

Introduction

Although the Office of Victim Services within the Ohio Department of Rehabilitation and Correction was not formally created until 1995, the department's commitment to providing services to victims of crime began in the early 1980s when the Ohio Parole Board's Victim Notification Section was created. This section began notifying victims, upon request, of upcoming parole hearings, escapes or deaths, releases from prison to community supervision, and pending executions.

Following on the heels of victim notification was an invitation to victims to share information with the Ohio Parole Board on the impact of the crime they had experienced. This information is considered a vital factor in the board's decision making regarding an inmate's release.

In the early 1990s, the department's director recognized that there was a need in the corrections' process to provide even more comprehensive services to survivors of crime. Subsequently, the Office of Victim Services was codified as part of Senate Bill 2, Ohio's "Truth in Sentencing Law," in July 1996. The actual composition of the Ohio Parole Board also was impacted by Senate Bill 2, which mandated that a crime victim or advocate be appointed as a board member to represent victims' issues.

Development and Design

The creation of the Office of Victim Services marked a milestone in the department's movement to replace the criminal justice system with a victim justice system. Ohio incorporates the voice of victims in a very unique way by selecting only survivors of crime and victim advocates to staff this sensitive office. It is the mission of the Office:

> To build mutual understanding and open communication among Department of Rehabilitation and Correction employees, victims, their families and community victim groups. The office facilitates victims' access to the Department by giving them opportunities to participate in decisions concerning an offender's liberty, and by providing them support and information, as needed.

The goals of the office are the following:

- Ensure that all employees understand and respond to victims in a timely and sensitive manner

- Include victim-input in the decision-making process regarding an inmate's status

- Minimize trauma to victims and their families by providing advocacy and support throughout the system

- Strengthen the partnership between the department and victims, advocates, and community groups to improve service delivery

To better serve crime victims, the Parole Board and the Office of Victim Services launched an even stronger outreach program to increase the community's awareness of services available throughout the department. Through this increased visibility and the relationships forged with local and state advocacy groups, the number of victims registered for notification more than doubled in two years' time, from approximately 6,500 at the end of 1996 to almost 14,000 at the end of 1997.

Results

Networking

The victims of crime are benefiting currently from a strong relationship forged between the department and the Ohio Victims of Crime Compensation program administered by the Court of Claims and the Crime Victims Services Section of the Attorney General's Office. This partnership among agencies serves to synchronize victim services at the state level.

The Office of Victim Services collaborates with various statewide victim services' coalitions to improve the overall quality of services provided to Ohio's crime victims. These coalitions along with local prosecutors, sheriffs, and the U.S. Attorney's offices are represented on the department's Ohio Council on Victims' Justice. The council was created to ensure victim input into operational changes that impact on victims and to serve as liaisons between the department and the constituents of council members.

Impact

An important function of the Office of Victim Services is to assist the Parole Board in ascertaining the feeling of victims and learning about the physical, emotional, financial, and other impacts of the crime prior to the board's release decisions. In cases where no victim is registered formally for notification with the office, the relationships with local victim assistance programs are invaluable in searching for crime survivors.

Registered victims are notified of pending hearings on their offenders and invited to schedule a meeting or arrange a phone call with a hearing officer during Victim Conference Day, a day set aside each month for the board to meet with crime survivors prior to a hearing. This is the victim's opportunity to make the parole board aware of the full impact of the crime and provide any information they would like the board members to consider in their case. In addition to meeting in person or talking by phone to a representative of the parole board, victims are invited to send any written materials, photos, or video and/or audio tapes that might be relevant to the board's deliberations.

Effective in 1996, crime victims could, through the office, petition the parole board to have a full board hearing for any case where a panel has recommended the inmate for parole. In addition, at this hearing, after a recommendation to release has been issued, the victim, sentencing judge, prosecutor, inmate representative, and a representative of the law enforcement agency that assisted in the prosecution of the case may offer relevant testimony regarding the possible release of the offender. Offenders are not permitted to attend these hearings.

Structure

The staff of victim advocates are central to the operation of the Office of Victim Services. These individuals, who are themselves crime victims and/or previously have worked in the field of victim advocacy, are vital links in providing education and intervention services, and provide further insight to the department. One advocate is in charge of victim notification, and works from the central office location. These advocates are often a lifeline for the victims, and they spend the majority of their workdays providing direct information and assurance to crime victims, either by phone or in person.

Victim coordinators provide a much-needed service in each of Ohio's prisons and regional parole offices. These individuals are existing employees appointed by the director to provide specialized services to victims. Since it is vital for all employees of the department to understand and respond to a victim's needs, the coordinators provide in-service training and ongoing victim services information to staff. The coordinators meet quarterly to train and strengthen their skills and are in regular communication with the office regarding situations within their institution or parole regions.

New Horizons

The Office of Victim Services has begun to facilitate victim-sensitive offender dialog in certain violent offenses. This dialog involves a process in which the victim and offender meet to discuss the impact of the crime. A specially trained mediator who works for several weeks or months to prepare participants for the actual face-to-face meeting facilitates the process. While this type of meeting is not appropriate in all cases, this experience can be very healing for the victim, providing answers to burning questions and offering some measure of closure and control. This process in no way influences potential inmate benefits such as parole, good time, or access to other programming.

The staff of the Office of Victim Services also are working to strengthen its relationship with family members of victims of inmates sentenced to death. It is important that families wanting to participate be kept informed of the appeal status of their offenders. This effort also involves the attorney general's capital crimes section and the governor's office.

As part of the community outreach effort and to provide the best services possible for victims, the office has created varied materials, including a pamphlet outlining the services that it provides, a series of videos used to explain the correctional process and services available to victims, names of community groups or other interested individuals, an office of victim services on-line web site, and a comprehensive booklet explaining the functions of the office.

Conclusion

The department's efforts toward enabling victims to have the involvement they deserve in the correctional process and to receive the consideration, respect, and dignity that is their right is very much in keeping with the community justice process. Community justice strives to repair the harm done to victims and the community through negotiation, mediation, victim empowerment, and reparation. The offender, the victim, the community, and the relationship among the three are involved in the community justice process. The Ohio Department of Rehabilitation and Correction and within it, the Office of Victim Services, is committed to continuing and improving the services provided to crime victims.

Contact:

Tessa Unwin
Public Affairs Liaison
Ohio Department of Rehabilitation and Correction

1050 Freeway Drive North
Columbus, Ohio, 43229
(614) 752-1157

Victims

Additional Program Entries

Post Trauma Staff Support Program

Wayne Scott, Executive Director
Texas Department of Criminal Justice, P.O. Box 99, Huntsville, Texas 77342-0099
(409) 294-2101

The Post Trauma Staff Support Program of the Texas Department of Criminal Justice establishes a uniform procedure that provides immediate peer support to employees who experience emotional trauma following a work-related critical incident. Incidents may include physical or sexual assault, the death of a staff member or an inmate, psychological assault or death threat, hostage or riot situation, the witnessing of an attempted suicide, exposure to potentially life-threatening disease, natural disaster, or fire. The Post Trauma Staff Support Program is staffed by employee volunteers who have received post trauma response training and who exhibit professional standards of conduct. The goal of the program is to minimize the effects that the trauma of a critical incident may have on employees. The program has received a "STAR" award from the Texas Corrections Association.

Crime Victims Services Bureau

Jean S. Wall, Director, Crime Victims Services Bureau
Louisiana Department of Public Safety and Corrections
P.O. Box 94304, Capitol Station, Baton Rouge, Louisana 70804-9304
(504) 342-6740

The Crime Victims Services Bureau enables victims, their families, witnesses, and other affected persons to track the movement of inmates in state custody. By making a formal request, victims will be notified of a particular inmate's sentence change, if he or she is scheduled for a possible release hearing, escapes, or is released from institutional custody. Persons receiving unsolicited communications from inmates or having questions about laws and policies governing inmate participation in programs also are encouraged to contact the bureau. When a person makes a notification request regarding a particular inmate, his or her name is entered into a controlled-access database. The program raises a "flag" which appears on several key computer screens and computer-generated reports built from the inmate database. A copy of the request is sent to the institution where the inmate is housed and becomes part of the inmate's permanent record. The Louisiana Department of Public Safety and Corrections implemented the Crime Victims Services Bureau without additional expenditure of funds by incorporating the new duties into the employees' daily operations.

Afterword

During the past three decades, the corrections community has been buffeted by wide-ranging changes unprecedented in the history of the field. Landmark Supreme Court rulings affecting all aspects of prison administration, the adoption in many states of determinate or "truth-in-sentencing" reforms, the loss of faith in rehabilitation, and growing demands for results-driven management have redefined the expectations governing the correctional landscape. Those correctional leaders who have been most successful in both the adult and juvenile justice systems have shown a willingness to reexamine how they do business. In so doing, they have adopted far-reaching strategies enabling them to navigate through the white waters created by the constancy of change.

It is well known that over 1.5 million adult offenders are in prison or jail. Another 4 million offenders are under community supervision—either on probation or parole. Though the total numbers may pale in comparison, the past decade has witnessed an alarming escalation in the rate of juvenile violence, as well as a significant increase in the percentage of youthful offenders falling under the jurisdiction of juvenile corrections. It is likely in the years ahead that the number of adults and juveniles experiencing some form of retributive sanctioning will continue to increase. What happens to these offenders matters a great deal relative to the development of credible correctional policy and the preservation of community order.

Fortunately, as the preceding chapters demonstrate, there is an abundance of "good work" going on in the field of corrections; best practices contributes tangibly to community well being, effective programmatic intervention, and sound public policy. Alongside the incessant and often unsettling changes noted above, there has been a sustained commitment to implementing programs and practices that make a difference to offenders, staff, and the various constituencies served by corrections practitioners. In myriad jurisdictions across the United States and Canada, at the federal, state and local level, in both the public and private sector, programmatic initiatives are underway that address public safety, competency development, and offender accountability. Many of the more promising initiatives represent empirically based practices that draw on research findings and evaluation studies.

One of the more significant themes that emerges from the best practices presented herein is that of community partnering and collaboration. Whether through increased victim involvement in various facets of correctional decision making, the incorporation of restorative justice principles emphasizing offender reparation for the harm caused by crime, reliance on citizen advisory committees, or fruitful collaboration between law enforcement and community supervision agencies, correctional systems are moving towards a more inclusive, community-centered focus. There is a growing recognition as evidenced throughout this monograph that the system is strengthened when community representatives are brought in as full participants in the correctional process.

This publication represents an encyclopedia of best practices in many areas of correctional operation. Any person seeking an understanding of the field of corrections today must first recognize the sheer breadth and diversity of programming that exists. Even more, as the various chapters show, the development of a program that may be described as a best practice in corrections is not an aberration. The presence of a best practice in any given jurisdiction requires highly motivated practitioners with the will to make a difference, a knowledge of what works or what is effective, thoughtful planning, the establishment of well-defined outcomes, and a desire to know whether these outcomes, in fact, are achieved over time. In essence, the leadership and staff of the program must embrace accountability and seek by their efforts to produce results that create clear public value.

The best practices discussed in the preceding chapters incorporate many of these features. They are worthy of replication. Yet, they are not exhaustive of what might be referred to as a best practice. No doubt, many correctional agencies not represented in this publication have promising initiatives or programs that warrant such a designation. For those who wish to develop sound programming, or simply to know where such programs might be found, the submissions included in this book provide only a starting point for discussion, not the end of the journey. The search for lasting solutions to the troubling, yet persistent problems that beset those who deal with adult and juvenile crime is a perpetual one. If *Best Practices* offers some assistance in identifying viable strategies and practices with regard to such problems, then it will have served its purpose for those corrections practitioners who believe firmly that the work they do, if done well, contributes directly to the public good.

Edward E. Rhine
Deputy Director
Division of Parole, Courts and Community Services
Ohio Department of Youth Services

Chair
ACA Best Practices Coordinating Council

ACA Organization

Executive Committee

American Correctional Association, 1996-1998

President
Reginald A. Wilkinson

President-elect
Richard L. Stalder

Past President
Bobbie L. Huskey

Vice President
Victoria C. Myers

Treasurer
Charles J. Kehoe

Executive Director
James A. Gondles, Jr.

Board of Governors Representative
Dennis Avery

Board of Governors Representative
Gwendolyn C. Chunn

Board of Governors

American Correctional Association, 1996-1998

Board of Governors

Judy C. Anderson, South Carolina

Dennis Avery, Minnesota

Parkes Casselbury, Tennessee

Gwendolyn C. Chunn, North Carolina

Harold W. Clarke, Nebraska

Jesse W. Doyle, Illinois

David R. Jaso, Texas

James F. Kyle, Tennessee

James J. Lawrence, Ohio

Mae B. McLendon, North Carolina

Eloy L. Mondragon, New Mexico

Ralph Moulder, Florida

Sharon R. Neumann, Oklahoma

Jay M. Newberger, South Dakota

Joanne G. Perkins, Illinois

T. A. Ryan, South Carolina

John Sheridan, New Hampshire

John L. Simonet, Colorado

Delegate Assembly

Delegate Assembly—Elected

Carolyn V. Atkins, Missouri
Samuel Bachelor, Tennessee
Dan Richard Beto, Texas
Paul E. Bollwahn, Virginia
Luella Burke, Michigan
James L. Clark, Maryland
Missy Creed, Ohio
Larry DiStefano, New York
Barbara C. Dooley, Tennessee
Deborah Elijah, Tennessee
Joyce G. Fogg, Virginia
Patrick W. Foley, North Dakota
Bridget P. Gladwin, New York
Charles Thomas Haynes, Tennessee
Bryan Hill, Pennsylvania
Gary Hill, Nebraska
Joyce Jackson, Oklahoma
Shirley J. Johnson, Missouri
Diana Kim, New Mexico
Bernie Kroeker, Canada
Mary L. Livers, Oklahoma
Cathy E. Mansell, Mississippi
Marjorie Marlette, Nebraska
Lynn McAuley, Hawaii
Fred M. Mosely, Ohio
Albert Murray, Tennessee
Anne M. Nelson, Utah
Greg Pease, Alaska

Mary Ann Saar, Maine
George W. Sherlock, Kansas
Mary Sillman, Iowa
Carla J. Smalls, South Carolina
Patrick J. Sullivan, Jr., Colorado
Barbara L. Sutton, Wisconsin
John V. Vollmann, Jr., Florida
Anne S. Walker, South Carolina
Kelly D. Ward, Louisiana
Clarence B. Williamson, Illinois
Bruce Wolford, Kentucky
Ginny L. Wood, Missouri
Alan R. Wright, Arizona
Vicki Wright, Texas

Delegate Assembly—Appointed

Linda Albrecht, Colorado (NAJCA)
Scott Anders, Missouri (MCA)
Jerry Armijo, Colorado (CCA)
Roy Bohrer, Texas (TCA)
Ken Burger, Iowa (ICA)
Michael Burnett, Kentucky (KCCD)
Jerry Butler, Illinois (ICA)
Mary Leftridge Byrd, Pennsylvania (APFO)
George Camp, Connecticut (ASCA)
James Cook, Connecticut (ACCA)
Olivia Craven, Idaho (APAI)
Ellen Czaplewski, Washington, D.C. (AIA)
Anthony Czarnecki, New York (MASCA)

Richard Darling, Maryland (MCJA)
Nancy Dibenedetto, Wisconsin (WCA)
Earl Dunlap, Kentucky (NJDA)
Dick Edwards, Minnestoa (NCRA)
Bob Ekman, Utah (UCA)
Dave Glenwick, New York (AACP)
Chuck Gould, Virginia (VA)
Mel Grieshaber, Michigan (IACO)
Matthew Hamidullah, North Carolina (NABCJ)
Steve Hanrahan, Nevada (NACJP)
Gail Heller, Ohio (CSCA)
Mike Holloway, Tennessee (TCA)
Bob Houston, Nebraska (NCA)
Steve Ingley, Maryland (AJA)
Pat Keohane, Missouri (NAAWS)
Peter Kinziger, Wisconsin (ICCA)
Barry Krisberg, California (NCCD)
C. Martin Lensing, Louisana (LCA)
Cindy Liebe, Oregon (OCJA)
Edward Loughran, Massachusetts (NCJCA)
Kevin Manley, Massachusetts (CCJA)
Joe Marchese, New York, (IACTP)
Ray McCleese, Florida (FCCD)
Jim Mustin, Virginia (FCN)
Barbara Neff, Massachusetts (CAM)
Carl Nink, Arizona (APPCA)
Greg Owen, Michigan (MCA)
Barbara Pierce, North Carolina (NCCA)

Sherry Pilkington, North Carolina (PPCAA)
Bud Potter, Ohio (OCCSA)
Bill Reznor, Pennsylvania (PAPPC)
Bernie Rhodes, Virginia (VCA)
Burt Rosefield, Ohio (ACHSA)
Burt Rosen, Pennsylvania (PF)
Susan Rotenberg, Washington (NCMSAHCJS)
Ronnie Scotkin, Maryland (ACRIM)
Jerome Scruggs, Oklahoma (OCA)
John Sheridan, New Hampshire (ICAN)
Marvin Shimabukuro, Hawaii (HCJA)
Cathy Slack, Colorado (CAMA)
Gale Smith, New York (JJTA)
Carole Smith, Minnestoa (MCA)
Gwyn Smith-Ingley, Maryland (CIA)
Patrick Snedeker, New Mexico (NMCA)
Dottie Stanfill, Indiana (ICA)
Stephen Steurer, Maryland (CEA)
Barbara Strecker-Gaudreau, Kansas (KCA)
Richard Stroker, South Carolina (SCCA)
Lawrence Vaults, Texas (SSCA)
VeLinda Weatherly, Alabama (ACCD)
Karen Wesloh, Minnesota (ACFSA)
Carl Wicklund, Kentucky (APPA)
Diane Wiley, Utah (WCA)
Linda Willenberg, Washington (WCA)
Mel Williams, New York (NYCYSA)
George Yefchak, New Jersey (NJCA)

Participating Committees

Adult Corrections

Chair:
Ronald Angelone, Virginia

Vice Chair:
Kenneth L. McGinnis, Michigan

Members:
Wilson C. Bell, Florida
Al Bennett, Indiana
Michael Bradley, Kentucky
Camille G. Camp, New York
Donal Campbell, Tennessee
Sharon E. Fairchild, Missouri
Bridget P. Gladwin, New York
Todd L. Guelker, Mississippi
Robert D. Hannigan, Oklahoma
Robert Matthews, Georgia
Dave McKune, Kansas
Raymond P. Mulally, Florida
Carl Nink, Arizona
Michael J. O'Dea, III, Kentucky
Ted Sakai, Hawaii,
Ari Zavaras, Colorado

Adult Local Detention

Chair:
Patrick J. Sullivan, Colorado

Vice Chair:
Michael O'Toole, Colorado

Members:
Frances W. Clark, Georgia
Ray J. Coleman, Washington
Bryan Hill, Pennsylvania
Robert Lucas, Florida
Margaret A. Moore, Washington, D.C.
David S. Owens, Jr., New Jersey
Alice F. Pollard, Missouri
Walter R. Smith, Colorado
Robert O. Viterna, Texas
John W. Welch, Jr., Maryland
Harold B. Wilber, Florida
Marvin J. Wilson, Iowa

Community Corrections— Nonresidential

Chair:
John J. Larivee, Massachusetts

Vice Chair:
Jan P. Autery, Alabama

Members:
Jasper R. Clay, Jr., Maryland
Alton Daniels, Louisana
Donald G. Evans, Ontario, Canada
William G. Grosshans, Wisconsin
Gail D. Hughes, Missouri
Kermit Humphries, Washington, D.C.
Nancy Martin, Illinois
Matt Novak, Ohio

Mario Paparozzi, New Jersey
Paula G. Pumphrey, Arkansas
Joseph A. Ruskowitz, Kansas
Hugh J. Turcotte, Connecticut
Ray Wahl, Utah
Vicki Wright, Texas

Correctional Education

Chair: Diana Kim, New Mexico

Vice Chair: Steve Steurer, Maryland

Members:
Barbara Baethe, Texas
Dr. Carolyn Eggleston, California
Jack Littlefield, Ohio
Marilyn McAuley, Hawaii
Joann B. Morton, South Carolina
Dr. Kenneth Robinson, Tennessee
Christina Rutland, New Mexico
T. A. Ryan, South Carolina
Mary Sillman, Iowa
Bruce Wolford, Kentucky
Alan R. Wright, Arizona

Community Corrections— Residential

Chair:
Neil Tilow, Ohio

Vice Chair:
Robert M. Balboni, Connecticut

Members:
Lynne Marie Bielecki, Connecticut
Richard J. Billak, Ohio
John H. Clark, California
Robert L. Gloeckner, Ohio
Kathryn Boggs-Gray, Alaska
Al Hall, Washington, D.C.
M. Tamara Holden, Oregon
Jan Kempf, Kentucky
June Koegel, Maine
Daniel Lombardo, New Jersey
John McMahon, Florida
David J. Meyer, Missouri
Claudia Rowland, Chicago
Dennis Schrantz, Michigan
S. Anne Walker, South Carolina
John Wynbeek, Michigan

Correctional Industries

Chair:
Michael J. Sullivan, Wisconsin

Vice Chair:
Gwyn Smith Ingley, Maryland

Members:
Thomas Albrecht, Washington, D.C.
Anthony Anderson, Ohio
Joan E. Baker, Washington
Leonard S. Black, New Jersey
Tom G. Crago, Colorado
Pamela Jo Davis, Florida
Randall Guynes, Virginia
James M. LeBlanc, Louisiana
Lynn McAuley, Hawaii
Rod Miller, Maryland
Linda Morrison, Pennsylvania
Michael Quinlan, Virginia
R. Dale Riley, Missouri
Knut A. Rostad, Washington, D.C.
Steve Schwalb, Washington, D.C.
Thomas Townsend, Ontario, Canada
Don Waggoner, Oregon

Disturbance Preparedness

Chair: Odie Washington, Illinois

Vice Chair: Richard P. Seiter, Illinois

Members:
Phil Armold, Washington, D.C.
John D. Brush, Mississippi
Calvin Edwards, Pennsylvania
Bill Hedrick, Illinois
Arthur A. Leonardo, New York
Charles E. Lister, Florida
John D. Morgan, Ohio
Dennis Sherman, New York
Ronald L. Stepanik, Tennessee

Employee Training

Chair:
Dr. Allen Ault, Colorado

Vice Chair:
Sally Halford, Iowa

Members:
Nancy Cook, Tennessee
Gary Cornelius, Virginia

Kathy Black-Dennis, Kentucky
Larry A. Fields, Oklahoma
Dr. Ida Halasz, Colorado
Susan M. Hunter, Washington, D.C.
Randy Johnson, Kentucky
Alton Lick, North Dakota
Joe Marchese, New York
Tommy Norris, Washington, D.C.
Steve Norris, Tennessee
Sheila Siddiqui, Florida
John J. Vollmann, Jr., Florida
Susan Yeres, California

Facility Design

Chair:
Michael W. Moore, South Carolina

Vice Chair:
Paul Donnelly, New Jersey

Members:
Kendal L. Ball, Ohio
David M. Bogard, Virginia
Ron Budzinski, Illinois
G. Kevin Carruth, California
Jack Chapman, Oregon
Anthony D'Aquila, North Carolina
Glenn Gauger, Missouri
Joe Hopper, Alabama
James B. Jones, Washington, D.C.
James Moynihan, Georgia
Allen L. Patrick, Ohio
Marcella C. Rapp, Colorado
John D. Rees, Tennessee
Frank H. Roberts, Arizona
William B. Robinson, Pennsylvania
Francis J. Sheridan, New York
Rob Speitly, Florida
Eugene Walker, Georgia
Norman Wirkler, Colorado

Health Care

Chair:
Kenneth P. Moritsugu, Washington, D.C.

Vice Chair:
John H. Clark, California

Members:
Robert L. Brutsche, Virginia
Richard Kiel, Maryland

John R. Miles, Georgia
Cassandra F. Newkirk, New Jersey
Herbert Rosefield, North Carolina
Allen D. Sapp, Jr., Texas
Vicki Verdeyen, Washington, D.C.
Edward C. Wolahan, Colorado

Juvenile Corrections

Chair:
Jesse E. Williams, Jr., California

Vice Chair:
Geno Natalucci-Persichetti, Ohio

Members:
Francisco J. Alarcon, California
James Ball, Tennessee
Flora Brooks Boyd, South Carolina
Michael Bryant, North Carolina
Karen Leah Chinn, South Carolina
Gary K. Dalton, Utah
Larry DiStefano, New York
Barbara C. Dooley, Tennessee
Kurt C. Friedenauer, Illinois
Wayne R. Liddell, Michigan
Richard Luchansky, Connecticut
James Martin, Texas
Lloyd Mixdorf, Arizona
Albert Murray, Kansas
Anne M. Nelsen, Utah
Nervie Oliver, Michigan
Gale Smith, New York
Patricia West, Virginia
Michael White, Washington, D.C.
Daniel Williamson, Okalahoma
John K. Zachariah, Ohio

Mental Health

Chair:
Fred Cohen, Arizona

Vice Chair:
Joel A. Dvoskin, Arizona

Members:
Sharon Aungst, Ohio
Gary Dennis, Kentucky
J. L. Glass, Kansas
Ivan Godfrey, New York
Jane Haddad, Virginia
Jeffrey L. Metzer, Colorado

Dr. S. Hunter Rentz, South Carolina
Susan Rotenberg, Washington
Susan Salasin, Maryland
Dr. Chester E. Sigafoos, South Carolina
Cheri L. Walter, Ohio
Linda A. Wood, Florida

Public Information

Chair:
Joyce Jackson, Illinois

Vice Chair:
Susan W. McCampbell, Florida

Members:
David S. Cook, Oregon
Daniel R. Dunne, Washington, D.C.
Nicholas J. Hun, West Virginia
Veltry Johnson, Washington
Peggy G. Kanche, Arizona
Tip Kindel, California
Tim Kniest, Missouri
Sharron Kornegay, Ohio
Heather Lockwood, Ontario, Canada
Jerry Massie, Oklahoma
Eugene Morris, Florida
Greg R. Pease, Alaska
Richard Phillips, Colorado

Research

Chair:
Helen Corrothers, Maryland

Vice Chair:
Peggy Ritchie-Matsumoto, Ohio

Members:
Israel Barak, Jerusalem
James L. Beck, Washington, D.C.
Lawrence Bennett, California
Gerald G. Gaes, Washington, D.C.
Don Gottfredson, California
James P. Harris, Connecticut
Raymond A. Helgemoe, New Hampshire
Pamela K. Lattimore, Washington, D.C.
Doris Layton MacKenzie, Maryland
Leonard I. Morgenbesser, New York
Dr. David Robinson, Ontario, Canada
Ronnie Scotkin, Maryland
Richard Tewksbury, Kentucky

Honorary Members:
James Austin, California
Lorraine T. Fowler, South Carolina
Lawrence Greenfeld, Washington, D.C.
Paul H. Hahn, Ohio
Peter B. Hoffman, Maryland
Joann B. Morton, South Carolina
Frank J. Porporino, Ontario, Canada
T. A. Ryan, South Carolina

Restorative Justice

Chair:
Anne Seymour, Washington, D.C.

Vice Chair:
John F. Gorczyk, Vermont

Members:
J. Otis Davis, Michigan
Michael Dooley, Colorado
Charles W. Gould, Virginia
Margaret Pugh, Alaska
Greg D. Richardson, Washington, D.C.
Mary Ann Saar, Maine
Dora B. Schriro, Missouri
Stuart Simms, Maryland
Chiquita A. Sipos, California
Carol Rapp-Zimmermann, Ohio

Shock Incarceration

Co-chair:
Cheryl Clark, New York

Co-chair:
Ray Hobbs, Arizona

Members:
William S. Beers, Oregon
Marjorie L. Brown, Illinois
Stephen J. Huffman, Ohio
Betty Mitchell, Ohio
Ronald W. Moscicki, New York
Joshua Perry, Alabama
Ted Shumaker, Pennsylvania
Clifford Terry, Arizona
Walter D. Thorne, New York

Substance Abuse

Chair:
John R. Weekes, Ontario, Canada

Vice Chair:
Barry Bloomfield, New Jersey

Members:
Donna Bailey, Texas
Lt. James L. Clark, Maryland
Michael Collins, Massachusetts
Rick Dillner, Minnesota
Anthony C. Ealey, Illinois
Earl C. Huch, Maryland
Scott Johnston, Missouri
M. Patrick McCabe, Florida
Dr. Steve Valle, Massachusetts
Gerald L. Vigdal, Wisconsin
Beth A. Weinman, Washington, D.C.

Technology

Chair:
Kevin Jackson, Washington, D.C.

Vice Chair:
Larry Dubois, Massachusetts

Members:
David H. Bland, Alabama
Paul E. Brodeur, New Hampshire
Joseph R. Claffy, Illinois
Francis R. Ford, Maryland
Rod Hurley, Arizona
David W. Linn, Maryland
Charles W. Moore, Alabama

G. Steve Morrison, South Carolina
Charlie Raubacher, Washington, D.C.
Henry Risley, Kansas
Samuel F. Saxton, Maryland
Thomas J. Sexton, South Carolina
Howard L. Skolnik, Nevada
Debra D. Spencer, New Mexico
Donald Stading, Illinois
David E. Wilkins, Florida
Leonard R. Witke, Wisconsin

Victims

Chair:
Gail M. Heller, Ohio

Vice Chair:
Sharon J. English, California

Members:
Mary Achilles, Pennsylvania
Lt. Col. Harold Anderson, Georgia
Ronald L. Bartee, Nebraska
Jane Nady Burnley, Virginia
Linda Connelly, California
Tracy Godwin, Kentucky
Trudy Gregorie, Virginia
Ellen Halbert, Texas
David Jordan, South Carolina
Annesley K. Schmidt, Washington, D.C.
Marlene A. Young, Washington, D.C.

American Correctional Association Accomplishments August 1996—August 1998

On behalf of the Executive Committee, the Delegate Assembly, the Board of Governors, ACA Past Presidents, James A. Gondles Jr., and the ACA staff, it is a pleasure for me to report on the accomplishments of the association during my term as ACA President. It has been an enjoyable and productive two years; I look forward to serving the ACA on the Executive Committee for the next two years as past president.

Once again, I would like to express my gratitude to the aforementioned and others for their contribution to the success of the American Correctional Association.

Accreditation

ACA was awarded a grant by the U.S. Department of Justice, Office of Justice Programs, the Bureau of Justice Assistance for the development of performance-based standards for the Adult Community Residential Standards manual.

Several state departments of corrections have entered into the accreditation process for the first time: adult—Mississippi, Texas, and Virginia; juvenile—California. Many jails also have contracted for initial accreditation.

The Hawaii Department of Public Safety was the first agency to be awarded accreditation in the prison-industries category.

Chapter/Affiliates

ACA welcomed two new associations into the ACA chapter/affiliate family: the Hawaii Criminal Justice Association and the International Correctional Arts Network.

Conferences

Enhancements to the conference program book included the addition of a second color, use of user-friendly icons, and tabs (which are included in the Detroit Congress of Correction program for the first time).

The 1998 Winter Conference in San Antonio witnessed a record attendance for a Winter Conference: 3,400.

Also, in San Antonio, ACA had its largest exhibitor registration ever for a Winter Conference.

At the Congress of Correction in Orlando, for the first time, a public health fair was conducted for conference attendees.

International Relations

ACA participated in international corrections and criminal justice events in six foreign countries: Canada, Hungary, Israel, Italy, Mexico, South Africa, and the Commonwealth of the Marianas in Saipan.

ACA continued to receive an increased number of international delegates at both the Winter Conferences and the Congresses of Correction.

Management

The ACA warehouse staff implemented aggressive cost-saving strategies with major transportation companies in 1997, which have kept shipping-costs at the lowest level possible.

The conversion from the AS400 Membership/Order Entry System to iMIS was completed at the end of June 1998. This change now enables ACA to better serve members and will improve the effectiveness of reporting in the financial sector and other areas.

Since the beginning of ACA's investment relationship with Legg Mason on December 6, 1996, an increase in investment value from $219,818.40 initially invested to the current value as of April 30, 1998, of $1,749,993.75 was realized. Because of this significant growth, ACA was able to reach its set-aside fund goal of six-months reserve by January 1998. We are now pursuing a nine-month goal.

Organizational

ACA membership ratified a new Constitution and Bylaws in November 1996, which was implemented January 1, 1997.

Several new committees, councils and task forces were formed to address various correctional issues. These groups included: the Best Practices Coordinating Council, Disturbance Preparedness, Correctional Education, Employee Training, Facility Design, Correctional Industries, Mental Health, Health Care, Restorative Justice, Shock Incarceration, and Youthful Offender Task Force. The community corrections committee was split into two separate committees: Residential and Nonresidential.

Publications

For the first time, ACA published this book entitled *Best Practices: Excellence in Corrections*. Overall, more than twenty-five new publications were introduced in the last two years.

Reform and Retribution: An Illustrated History of American Prisons was featured in an issue of Publishers Weekly on small publishers. *Reform and Retribution* also received a 1998 Award of Publication Excellence.

ACA publications had a record-breaking year in 1997 both in orders processed and in sales of books, correspondence courses, and videos.

Corrections Today was redesigned in 1998 with a new masthead and internal page design. *Corrections Today* received three 1998 Awards of Publication Excellence.

Corrections Compendium was added to the association's menu of publications in October 1997. It is projected that through marketing efforts, subscriptions for this publication will double in the first year of ACA publication.

Scholarship

ACA enacted a student scholarship program enabling full-time criminal justice students in local colleges and universities to attend ACA conferences on a complementary basis.

Technology

For the first time ever, ACA, via satellite, broadcast five videoconference workshops from the Orlando Congress of Correction. Also, for the first time, from the Congress of Correction in Detroit, ACA will broadcast six live audio conferences.

ACA introduced its new internet site: www.corrections.com/aca

The "technology pavilion" was introduced at ACA conferences in Orlando and San Antonio. Internet access, an automated exhibit hall map, among other hands-on technology, was available for the first time to conference attendees.

The first-ever video teleconference of a Commission on Accreditation for Corrections' hearing panel occurred at the Congress of Correction in Orlando. A Lima, Ohio prison subsequently was awarded accreditation.

Training

Corrections employees enrolled in ACA correspondence courses increased from 7,200 per year in 1996 to 10,200 in 1998.

One new and four revised correspondence courses and nine new video-based training series were developed. ACA's courses and videos won a total of four Awards for Publication Excellence during this period.

ACA provided in 1997 an 80 hour on-site training to a Saipan delegation.

The U.S. Department of Justice, Office of Justice Programs, National Institute of Justice awarded a contract to ACA to study correctional technologies. A successful technology conference was held in Baltimore in 1997. This project now has been refunded. Plans are underway to conduct another conference in the fall of 1998.

Successful juvenile forums were conducted in Orlando and Cleveland.

Another U.S. Department of Justice, Office of Justice Programs, National Institute of Justice grant was awarded to ACA on a project entitled "New Boys on the Block." National data concerning management (including classification, discipline, housing, and so forth) of juvenile offenders being housed in adult facilities will be studied.

Summary

As you can see, the list of accomplishments by the American Correctional Association in the last two years is impressive. As president of the world's largest and oldest correctional association, I am humbled by the professionalism and knowledge of my correctional colleagues throughout the world. Serving as president of this illustrious organization is the icing on my correctional career cake.

Thank you for making the past two years productive and memorable.

Reginald A. Wilkinson
President

Biography of
Reginald A. Wilkinson

President Reggie Wilkinson has a long and proud history of involvement with the American Correctional Association. In the early 1980s, he represented the Ohio Correctional and Court Services Association both as vice president and president at the ACA Delegate Assembly. He also served on the Delegate Assembly for many years as Past President of the Ohio Correctional and Court Services Association.

Wilkinson has chaired numerous ACA committees: the Chapter Presidents' Development Committee, the Council of State and Regional Chapters, the Long-Term Institutions Committee, and the Affirmative Action Committee. He also has served as a member of many other committees: Constitution and By Laws, Membership, Long-Range Planning, Organizational Affiliates, and Professional Development. Moreover, he was the Ohio state chairman of the National Conference on Correctional Policy (Williamsburg II).

In addition to serving as president of one of the oldest and largest dual-membership chapters, he has been active with other ACA affiliate partners. Specifically, he was a founder and first president of the Ohio Chapter of the National Association of Blacks in Criminal Justice. He later served several terms as a member of the Board of Directors of the National Association of Blacks in Criminal Justice. Wilkinson also has been very active with the Association of State Correctional Administrators. For two terms, he chaired the program and training committee of the Association of State Correctional Administrators, was a member of several other committees, served as a trainer in both the All Directors' and New Directors' training programs, and moderated the All Directors' Training Institute for two consecutive years.

Wilkinson also has participated in many ACA-affiliated and some non-ACA affiliated corrections and justice organizations such as: the North American Association of Wardens and Superintendents, the Correctional Education Association, the American Association of Correctional Training Personnel, and many others. Additionally, both prior to and during his term as ACA president, he has given keynote speeches and conducted workshops at many correctional conferences (see some of these speeches in this volume).

Throughout his career, President Wilkinson has championed correctional accreditation. He was the warden of the first ACA-accredited prison in Ohio: the Dayton Correctional Institution. Currently in Ohio, all but five adult prisons are accredited. In addition to the twenty-five accredited correctional institutions, the central office, two boot camps, the parole board, probation and parole services, and the training academy all are ACA-accredited. The unaccredited prisons and prison industries are scheduled to be accredited within the year. Ohio may become the first "fully" accredited Department of Corrections in the nation.

Additionally, Reggie Wilkinson has served as an auditor/consultant for the Commission on Accreditation for Corrections. He continually has supported the efforts of the Correctional Accreditation Managers Association. In Ohio, efforts are underway to form the nation's first statewide accreditation association.

Wilkinson serves as the Director of the Ohio Department of Rehabilitation and Correction, the fifth largest state correctional system in the United States. Governor George V. Voinovich appointed him to this post in February 1991. He has worked in the field of corrections since 1973 in a number of administrative capacities including volunteer coordinator, administrative assistant, strategic planning coordinator, superintendent of training, warden, and deputy/regional director.

Numerous awards, both local and national, have been bestowed upon Mr. Wilkinson. Nationally, he has received the Michael Francke Award, the Association of State Correctional Administrators' highest honor. The National Association of Blacks in Criminal Justice awarded him their highest recognition: the William H. Hastie Award as well as the National Association of Blacks in Criminal Justice Chairman's Award. The Justice George Lewis Ruffin Society bestowed the Justice George Lewis Ruffin Society Award upon Wilkinson. Further, the International Community Corrections Association named him winner of the Distinguished Service Award.

Locally, Reggie has received both the President's Award and the Joseph A. Janesz Correctional Achievement Award from the Ohio Correctional and Court Services Association. The Community Corrections Association, Inc. awarded him the Public Service Award. The Ohio Community Corrections Organization recognized him with the Dr. Bennet J. Cooper Award. Many other organizations and associations have recognized Wilkinson for his contributions to the corrections field and to the community.

Reginald A. Wilkinson believes in a "balanced approach" to corrections, which advocates that certain nonviolent offenders, both adult and juvenile, be punished and treated in the community, while violent offenders require incarceration and extensive programming to prevent recidivism. He also has embraced the philosophy of community justice as a theoretical underpinning for correctional operations. In his assessment, despite significant gains, a more balanced and holistic approach to the justice process is still much needed to augment correctional management and leadership.

Presidential Addresses

Speeches and Writings of
Reginald A. Wilkinson,
1996-1998

Introduction

The ten following speeches and writings provide a background for the events during the tenure of American Correctional Association President Reginald A. Wilkinson. During the two years that he led the American Correctional Association, he promised that at the end of his tenure as president, there would be a best practices book, and this book is proof of that pledge. Also, as a result of his leadership, we have best practices from some of the new committees that he established: mental health, medical health care, technology, facility design, shock incarceration, and disturbance preparedness that complement the contributions from the other committees. The speeches and writings reflect his interest in technology and the benefits of technology, especially computers and the internet, that enable the paperless office, teleconferencing, and distance learning.

He also is concerned with greater choices for victims, greater opportunities for inmates to better themselves, interagency partnerships, alternatives to incarceration, critical incident management, and community service. He reminds us of the importance of successful treatment programs that reduce recidivism and lessen the chances of future victimization. He is further concerned with the development of prototype prisons for specialized populations that enhance security and program delivery.

He asks if there is justice in a society where more young African Americans languish in jail than attend college. "As a society, we need to wrestle [the] child away from the counterfeit family of gangs. We need to make each child a participant in our culture."

President Wilkinson reminds us that correctional accreditation not only helps us gain public confidence but that being accredited is synonymous with correctional best practices. He congratulates the many corrections professionals who have succeeded despite awesome odds, but he cautions us that "the only way we can face the challenges of the next century is to work together for the continuous improvement of our proud profession."

What Works?
by Reginald A. Wilkinson

Corrections Today Editorial

August 1996

"Knowledge is power," has been a traditional mantra in our business. It refers to the practice of keeping information to ourselves until it can be used to our best personal advantage. Today, knowledge still is power—but it is only powerful if you give it away. In the age of information technology and team awareness, we have learned that the product generated by a group of individuals is much better than the product generated by one.

I recently participated in a national video conference sponsored by the National Institute of Corrections titled, "What Works and What Doesn't in Correctional Practice?" Corrections leaders Bobbie Huskey, Alan Ault, and others discussed what may be one of the most important topics in our profession. I commend the National Institute of Corrections for their leadership.

There are many examples of "what works" or "best practices" in correctional agencies internationally. The following are programs and initiatives that, in my experience, work:

Programming works. We house, supervise, and treat a variety of people. In order to concentrate programming in areas where it will do the most good, some departments have created prisons and dormitories for "special needs" groups of inmates. Examples range from boot camps for young street toughs to dormitories for illiterate substance abusers. The idea applies to sex offenders, high school dropouts, the mentally ill and retarded, the elderly, and others. In building "supermax" prisons, agencies acknowledge the security requirements of violent, predatory, and repeat offenders. In most cases, putting people with similar profiles together makes sense. We can target security, programming, staff, and training to better serve these populations.

Community corrections works. While many new laws call for longer, more definite sentences for violent and repeat offenders, some also contain a "presumption for local punishment" for many nonviolent offenders. States can network with local jurisdictions to create and expand residential and nonresidential community sanctions.

Meaningful work works. Learning essential job skills in a realistic work environment should improve an inmate's chance of getting a job and becoming a productive citizen upon release to society. Many jurisdictions are implementing community service projects both inside and outside of jail and prison confines. The inmates benefit, the agency benefits, and the recipients of the labor benefit. If the assigned work is tied to learning good work habits and responsibility, the chance of success is further enhanced.

Technology works. It helps us work harder and smarter. For example, several states have successfully implemented telemedicine, in which inmates participate in medical conferences with doctors and specialists in another location via video cameras. While these projects can be expensive to implement, they save thousands of dollars a year in transportation costs. Video conferencing can be applied to staff meetings, parole hearings, and more. And, there is no question that computers and databases are substantially more efficient than typewriters and paper. Then, there are the more fantastic aspects of technology, such as nonlethal weapons. The future of corrections is inextricably linked to technology, and we risk being left behind if we don't take advantage of it.

Involvement works. Many of us involve ourselves in societal concerns such as victims' issues, assisting "at risk" youth, adopt-a-school programs, and more. Forward-thinking correctional agencies, anticipating public moods and trends, are proactive rather than reactive in addressing them.

Lifelong learning works. Offering professional development opportunities to employees is crucial. If it's agreed that the next century will bring about even more change, then preparing for change must be a main ingredient of professional growth. Stagnation leads to complacency and a lack of vigilance, which is perhaps even more dangerous. Lifelong learning energizes the individual and the entire system.

Participatory management works. Looking to the business world for trends in leading people, many of us use principles of "TQM" or Total Quality Management in our agencies. Employees from all levels can serve on high-performance work groups or problem-solving teams. For example, when we write new post orders, we solicit input from the people who work that post, and write the post order so it works to the advantage of the employee, the offenders, and the agency. Teams make us more efficient and effective. Teamwork gives workers ownership. Belonging to a team boosts an employee's morale.

This edition of *Corrections Today* is dedicated to the best practices in the business. One of the most important benefits of a professional publication like *Corrections Today* is that it enables us to share ideas and borrow from the best. Many of the programs mentioned in this issue employ some or all of the strategies I have mentioned. As director of a large correctional agency, I know how important it is to search for benchmarks such as these.

For a long time, we in corrections lived by the motto: "If it ain't broke, don't fix it." I say, "If it ain't broke, fix it anyway." You may end up with a terrific new approach to an old problem.

As I begin my two years as president of the American Correctional Association, I would like to introduce you to a primary theme of my term: "Find the best, use the best, share the best, be the best."

Presidential Acceptance Speech by Reginald A. Wilkinson

American Correctional Association
126th Congress of Correction
Nashville, Tennessee
August 21, 1996

It is an honor for me to accept the position of president of the American Correctional Association. It is particularly a pleasure for me to do it, as is the tradition, here at the Delegate Assembly, for it was here as president-elect of the Ohio Correctional and Court Services Association that I first experienced the inner workings of this august body. Some of those early deliberations were a tad bit feisty.

I consider the American Correctional Association to be one of the more stalwart organizations in the nation. It will be my personal delight to serve you as ACA's ninety-fourth president. I am especially elated to be an ACA president from the State of Ohio. As you certainly are aware, ACA's first and longest reigning president was a Buckeye (OSU): former Ohio governor and nineteenth president of the United States of America, Rutherford B. Hayes. I have come to know President Hayes rather well, having visited the Rutherford B. Hayes Presidential Center, located in Freemont, Ohio, on several occasions recently. ACA Executive Director Jim Gondles accompanied me there earlier this year. I even spent the night at the Dillon House, the home of a Hayes' family friend across the street from the Hayes complex, entitled Spiegel Grove. If you are ever in Northwest Ohio, I suggest you consider touring the Hayes Center.

I also am excited to be an ACA president from Ohio because, as you are aware, our first Congress took place in Cincinnati. ACA, at that time, was named the National Prison Association. It was a pleasure for me to preside over the Opening Session of the 125th Anniversary Congress of Correction last August in the Ohio River City I call home. The play that was presented depicting how President Hayes would react to correctional practices today truly was exhilarating.

As many of you know, I have been a very active participant in ACA for many years. I want you to know, however, that I am not naive enough to believe that I can achieve an agenda without your support. I have the utmost respect for the decision-making bodies of this organization. I also have tremendous regard for all of you individually—not just because you are voting members of the Delegate Assembly, but because I know all too well the challenges you and I face as corrections professionals. As director of the Ohio Department of Rehabilitation and Correction, I know that what you do is value added to a very honorable profession. In fact, whenever I am confronted by persons who might suggest that corrections is a less-than-noble occupation, I look them in the eye and explain that correctional workers make a major contribution to our respective communities. I want ACA to continue making that contribution as well.

I want you to know that I have thoroughly enjoyed working with President Bobbie Huskey and the ACA Executive Committee for the past two years. I am particularly appreciative of Bobbie's leadership; her insight and commitment truly are commendable. I plan to build upon many of the contributions made during the Huskey administration. I would like now to share a few preliminary thoughts with you regarding priorities that I have conceptualized for the next two years:

I have decided to adopt the theme of this month's (August 1996) *Corrections Today*— "Programs That Work"—as a foundation. In the editorial column of *Corrections Today*, I wrote: "For a long time, we in corrections lived by the motto, 'If it ain't broke, don't fix it.' I say, 'If it ain't broke, fix it anyway.'" I also suggested that we must "Find the best, use the best, share the best, (and) be the best." To this end, let me briefly point out a few specific initiatives:

I will work with a total of thirty-eight committees. One-half of these committees will participate in what I consider to be a very exciting activity. Each will be responsible for identifying a number of "best practices" in their specific disciplines. For example, the Victims' Committee will, after reviewing survey data, document correctional victims' programs that make a difference. Even though I use the phrase "best practices," I am not suggesting a competition. Instead, I am asking for a diverse list of programs that would cross geographical regions and program types such as juvenile or adult, prison or community supervision. The chairs of these committees would form the ad hoc Best Practices Coordinating Council that I have asked Ed Rhine to chair. When all of the best practices vignettes have been compiled, the plan is to publish them. The book should be ready to give to Congress attendees in August 1998. I also think that it will be important that the Program Council gives consideration to highlighting some of these documented promising programs in conference workshops.

Furthermore, I would like to let you know that there will be several new ad hoc committees. For the first time there will be a committee on restorative justice, which is an emerging criminal justice—or shall I say victims' justice—concept. I am sure we will hear more about restorative justice in months to come. I have decided to have two community corrections committees: one to address residential options and the other to focus on nonresidential sanctions. Of course, these two committees will need to work closely together. There will be a Correctional Industries Committee. I also have named a Committee on Mental Health, as well as a Medical Health Care Committee. I have divided the Technology and Design Committee into two separate committees; there now will be both a Technology Committee and a Facility Design Committee. Also, for the first time, there will be a committee on shock incarceration and another on disturbance preparedness. All of the aforementioned new committees will participate in the best practices project. I am looking forward to the accomplishments of all our committees and councils.

You might want to know as well that, in the process of picking persons to serve on committees, I made sure that persons who represent corresponding ACA affiliates are members of these committees. For instance, the Correctional Industries Committee would have representation from the Correctional Industries Association. I also have included representatives on committees from other organizations such as the National Institute of Corrections and the Office of Justice Programs.

As I indicated previously, existing programs and initiatives shall continue to be a priority. We now have a visioning document which outlines some very important values for ACA. We need to continue our efforts to promote legislative activities, especially our legislative position statements. Updated policies and resolutions should continue to be advanced. News releases about correctional current events also help shape stakeholder views about our craft. Developing and nurturing relationships with affiliate organizations and even some nontraditional associations also will help foster good communication.

The accreditation process is critical to the future of this association. Our continued support of the Commission on Accreditation for Corrections, the Standards Committee, and the Division of Standards and Accreditation will help ensure a positive future for the American Correctional Association. Efforts to develop performance-based standards are continually progressing.

I am looking forward to an exciting two years as president of this illustrious and historic association. As we go about the business of trying to do the right thing for our society, I am hopeful that you will join me in my excitement. It once was said that there are several kinds of people in our world: there are those people who make things happen; there are those people who watch things happen; and, there are those people who wonder what happened. I would like for you to help make things happen. Thank you.

A Tribute to ACA Past Presidents
Presidential Address
by Reginald A. Wilkinson

American Correctional Association
Winter Conference
Indianapolis, Indiana
January 27-29, 1997

Standing before you today, my esteemed colleagues and friends, is without a doubt one of the most gratifying and stellar moments of my corrections career. Affording the president the opportunity to express his or her correctional credo on such an occasion is a unique moment of distinction. Many a time, as a member of the association, I have sat and listened to the statements of my distinguished predecessors. I therefore realize the magnitude of my responsibility this morning (Lejins, 1963).

In preparing my remarks, I reread a number of previous presidential addresses—some recent, some historical. When read in sequence, those speeches provide an excellent chronology of corrections. They describe problems and concerns, frustrations and disappointments—as well as hopes and dreams (Carlson, 1979).

I am certain that every president over the history of the ACA believed that he or she presided during a particularly difficult and challenging period. I want to assure you that I am no exception to that rule. The last two years have been a time of substantial challenge as well as considerable progress (Carlson, 1980).

If Thomas Paine were alive today, writing pamphlets about corrections instead of taxation, he would again be saying, "These are the times that try men's souls." Police and corrections cannot stop street crime. Street crime is the product of serious social and economic ills in our country (Keller, 1976).

I say to you that the leadership role is ours if we will take it. I say to you that the progress of criminology and criminal rehabilitation over the next half century lies in our hands. What we do in the next few years, the steps we take, the methods we pursue, will affect our nation for many years to come (Hancock, 1968).

The unfortunate thing is that we have been at a crisis level for so long that we have become jaded in our response to the situation. We were once shocked and angry about what was happening to us. The capabilities of law enforcement and the judicial system produced commitments that far outstripped corrections' ability to absorb. A good number of today's black infants will have . . . a heritage of having a father who was in prison. Not only is race a factor in the population that we serve, but it is also obvious that economic status, educational level, and a number of other social factors characterized those committed to our custody. These problems cannot be solved by corrections (Sublett, 1990).

To the extent that sentences are unjust, we who carry them out become agents of injustice. To the extent that sentences are irrational, we will lack purpose and reason in what we do. Developing a system that says to every convicted criminal, "you will be punished in a just and reasonable manner without bias," and then proves it, is hardly soft on crime. And if we combine that with real opportunity for positive change for self-improvement, the public will be well-served (Johnson, 1993).

It has been said that no other business or profession is told to run an effective, cost-efficient, safe, humane, and legal organization while being denied the power to control their programs, products, and finance let alone production goals (intake), quality control (capacity), and sales (output). Unity and consensus on common goals will give us the necessary power to have an impact on public policy and significantly affect the course of our destiny (Corrothers, 1992).

We should say to the legislatures, the community, the sentencing authorities, "Don't send us people so that they can go to school. Send them to school. Don't send us people so that they can be vocationally trained. Send them to vocational trainers. Don't send us people so that they can have psychiatric care, be spiritually regenerated, medically restored, or conquer their drinking habits. Send us only the people the community rightly fears and because there is no place for them. Allow us and expect us to run programs designed to meet the needs of these kinds of people" (Wheeler, 1973).

Corrections is moving, but how far, how fast, depends to a large extent on our abilities to act as social action stimulators, community planners, and advocates rather than [acting] alone on our skills as correctional administrators in the traditional sense. We have tended to defend our failings with "we do the best we can with what we have." That is not an adequate excuse. We have what we have in large part because of our defensiveness and failure to develop the strength to demand more (Coughlin, 1974).

The correctional sky is filled with the flutter of wings. Waves of hawks and doves are continuously calling to us their opposing criticisms. We have, as a result of the swing of the public mood or the political pendulum, been at times, too lax, or too rigid; too rehabilitative, or too punitive; too caught up with institutions, or about to give them up entirely. At one time or other . . . we have been moved by every possible product of institution imagination and even idiocy. The time has come to develop a balanced, rational approach to the total criminal justice system (Braithwaite, 1975).

The fact is, it is time, long past time, for change in corrections. Our critics may have the facts wrong and some of their assumptions are wrong, but the thrust of what they are saying is correct. We know—all of us know that corrections has not kept up with the times (Attica aftermath, Sigler, 1972).

We cannot and should not accept the entire blame (for our failings), not by a long shot . . . but . . . we must forget about the past . . . and take the leadership in moving out and moving ahead. I recall in my penitentiary days that nothing changed from one day to another, from one year to another or even one decade to another. However, we are living in a time of accelerating change and we . . . have to take the ball and start running (Sigler, 1972).

We, along with the prisoners we supervise, all too often become institutionalized, accustomed to a given way of doing things, threatened by change, preferring routine to thinking, satisfied to do today as we did yesterday, to do tomorrow what we did today. We have been able in a rapidly changing world to keep alive at least some remnants of the good old days, some nostalgic Shangrilas behind stone walls where we have been successful in slowing the march of time and progress. I don't know whether you call this complacency, or apathy or institutionalization. I think it is the latter. Corrections can be as good as we want it to be or as shoddy as the public will tolerate! The choice is really ours to make. There need be no such word as "can't" in our corrections vocabulary (Powers, 1961).

I believe one of the most important questions we can ask ourselves wherever we are in the system is: "Why are we doing this?" If we get the answer "because we have always done it this way," . . . then we need to dig deeper. There are many challenges for corrections. Let us ensure that we not only make the challenges, but that we are also equal to them (Leeke, 1978).

Change can be brought about by one of two ways, either leadership from within directing the change or outside pressures forcing the change. In the latter case, where change is forced upon us from outside the field, it is often chaotic and uncontrolled. Leadership in corrections has and should continue to control change from within the system (Wainwright, 1971).

Policy can be implemented only by influencing and changing the perceptions of the public. Changing these perceptions, often in the face of politically motivated rhetoric, is a monumental task (Hutto, 1985).

The public does have a stake in what we do, say and believe about corrections. Not only should we educate and talk to our fellow citizens, but we must also listen to them more. To our surprise, we may learn as much from them as they from us (Hutto, 1986).

In my opinion, the majority of Americans very simply want potential offenders to feel that it's not a good idea to commit crimes. And when a crime is committed, they want a reaction. They want the offender to be held accountable. They want to feel certain that there's been some type of punishment, some type of deprivation. They have a further interest in seeing something happen to dissuade further criminality. These expectations . . . are entirely reasonable and attainable (Corrothers, 1991).

The old saying that we should "walk the walk and talk the talk" . . . is a good one. Those of us who have undergone accreditation in our facilities, or have audited for others, have seen the dramatic impact these written standards can have on prison conditions. Accreditation is a dynamic, evolutionary process . . . the phenomenal progress of putting those words into action is the Association's most important accomplishment in this century (Johnson, 1994).

Accreditation is probably the foremost accomplishment of the corrections community and we need to move ahead with dexterity and aggressiveness to ensure that the process continues to exist and thrive (Cunningham, 1986).

What can we offer the line personnel? I say that we can offer the line officer in corrections . . . the ability to protect their jobs, to offer them training . . . to have more funding to allow them to do their job better. An ACA that will offer line personnel an opportunity to participate (MacDougall, 1969).

Among the many and varied functions which our association performs, that of providing a national forum for the exchange of experiences, knowledge and ideas by all those who are engaged in correctional work is, in my opinion . . . the most important one (Lejins, 1963).

I see for the ACA a significant national leadership role in identifying criminal justice issues, proposing realistic solutions, and developing workable strategies for resolving problems in the field of corrections. The association can and must be on the cutting edge of progressive change. Who else? What other association is better suited than we to fulfill this role (Leeke, 1977)?

The men and women of 1870 dreamed of an ideal correctional system. A correctional system that is driven by professional ideals and policies. One that has adequately funded programs, one that has highly trained correctional staff. They also had a vision of a professional association that brought together correctional professionals to improve conditions in juvenile and adult corrections. This was because . . . whipping, beating, starving, hitching and chaining inmates were commonplace in 1870. Creating and then implementing our vision will take commitment and courage. It will mean examining the principles and policies of the past and present. It means taking positions that may be unpopular. And it will mean striking out into directions where we might not feel comfortable. But I believe the risks we take will be worth it. It has been said, "Do not follow where the path may lead, but go instead where there is no path, and leave a trail (Huskey, 1995)."

One of the wisest men of our times was Mark Twain, who described faith as believing what you know ain't so. I believe we can change things—you can change things. The system can work, but it won't work without each of you nor will this Association. We must be enthusiastic, but more importantly, we must be involved (Cunningham, 1986).

Let me pause here for a moment and make a confession. As you are aware, I thought it was apropos at this Opening Session to pay tribute to ACA's past presidents. It occurred to me that perhaps the most meaningful homage I could pay to those past presidents was to read, absorb, and share with you their problems, passions, and dreams. With that in mind, I decided to craft this address almost entirely from the eloquent words of those predecessors—many of whom are here with us today.

Those of you who know me, know that I have a tremendous respect for the legacy left to us by those who have gone before, especially those whose work and dedication have impacted so strongly on our chosen profession. Indeed, as I prepared for this speech, I thought it was important to share with you, by citing my illustrious predecessors, the age old adage that "the more things change, the more they remain the same."

Each of our philosophies is influenced and shaped by the words and deeds of others in our profession. What greater contribution can one make than to have the opportunity to personally recognize and thank those leaders who blazed the political and social trails of criminal justice success.

Over the last fifteen years, I have had the opportunity to hear, in presidential addresses, lecturettes in the Delegate Assembly, and in other forums, the profound insights of my colleagues here assembled. It also intrigues me to imagine what ACA's first president, Rutherford B. Hayes, who in 1870 was the sitting governor of Ohio, and went on to be the nineteenth president of the United States, would have thought of our progress. It would be my guess that his chest would expand with pride as he reviewed our accomplishments. I also think he would greatly enjoy, talking with our current leaders and members about the failures and successes that got us to where we are today, 127 years after he and his colleagues came together to address penal reform in these United States.

In closing, it is my distinct pleasure to ask you to join me in demonstrating our appreciation to the distinguished group of presidents.

Keynote Speech
by Reginald A. Wilkinson

American Correctional Association/National
Institute of Corrections Technology Conference
Baltimore, Maryland
March 6, 1997

I was one of the thousands of moviegoers who flocked to the newly enhanced Star Wars flick, *The Empire Strikes Back*. It is a graphic demonstration that technology has not only arrived, it has moved on to conquer new frontiers. The entertainment industry is probably the most visible user of technology, but it is important to establish what technology can do for all of us, at home and at work.

By now, nearly all of us have a computer on our desks. Right? I have directed all of my senior staff in Ohio, which includes wardens, deputy directors, department heads to not only have computers in their offices, but to use them. We have created special computer training sessions just for them. The results have been nothing less than phenomenal; I now get e-mail from staff. They are using the internet, and they are crafting some of their own memos.

Those of you familiar with my take on technology know two things about me: one—that I am fascinated and intrigued by technology, and two—that I believe that those who are reluctant to drive on the information superhighway are going to be at a distinct disadvantage—driving a Pinto or a Vega instead of a sporty 4-wheel drive utility vehicle.

Someone once said that if we do not know where we are going, any road will take us there. For computer and technology phobics—that could mean a dead end.

If you think about it, it is incredible how far technology has come in the past ten years or so. After watching an episode of the television program *Wheel of Fortune*, I have come to think of this progress as the "Vanna Factor." Vanna White has been spared the arduous task of actually turning those letters on the clue board, all she has to do now is push a button! She still has to clap about 700 times a program, however.

But seriously, the "Vanna Factor" can be applied to many aspects of our lives. Fifteen years ago there were no PCs on our desks. I did have one of the very first models: a 32K Sinclair 80 with an expandable module that extended the computer's memory to 64K. There were no music CDs or CD ROMs, no laser disks, no Pentium processors. The list goes on.

A decade ago, the internet was a little known vehicle used primarily by the government and libraries to exchange information. I remember when the IBM Selectric III was the best thing going. Hopefully, no one is still using the old mimeograph machines. Most of us still have a manual or, at least, an electric typewriter in the closet somewhere. One of my staff-persons reminded me that ten years ago, we sent maybe two or three press releases out a year. Those were hand typed, reviewed, retyped, put in an envelope, and sent to the post office. Now, we send out press releases at least on a weekly basis, and we broadcast fax them to numbers already entered into the fax machine. Soon we'll be e-mailing them.

I am sure that the dictionary writers are having what my mother called "hissy fits" trying to keep up with just the terminology that we are now encountering: internet, intranet, extranet, ethernet, freenet, and sneakernet; you have bandwiths and backbones, LANs and WANs; there are other acronyms such as PPP, HTML and FTP. When Norbert Wiener in 1948 coined the term "cybernetics," surely he did not anticipate terms such as cyberspace, cyberlingo, cybercast, and cyberwonk. In fact, some refer to this language "dweebonics." I'm sure all of you know what a dweeb is. There is even a Dweebonics Institute. Its mission is to train the dweebonics challenged to better communicate with the dweebabled (or the dweebonics enabled). Learning Latin has never seemed so easy.

So, keeping up with technology can be a laborious task. A well-known general was quoted as saying, "A computer lets you make mistakes faster than any other invention in human history, with the possible exception of handguns and tequila." Computers and technology are to be relished, but we must keep things in perspective. I have determined that we should not work for technology's sake, we want technology to work for us.

From a philosophical perspective, the challenge today should not have a lot to do with technology. The challenge today has more to do with people. With information technology (IT) the change has more to do with information than technology. We really are talking about change, aren't we? How many times have you heard that people are naturally resistant to change? Horse pucky! People are resistant to change if they are not part of the change process. Technology should facilitate the involvement of people rather than exclude them.

Unfortunately, the advent of new technologies creates fear in some persons: it should not. The mission is not to turn people into techno-geeks or cyberwonks, and I use these terms in their most favorable connotations. You and I use technology all day everyday. When you pick up the phone, do you know how your words are sent through space to someone else's ear?

When you tweak the AC knob on your thermostat, do you first require HVAC certification? No, unless you are the manufacturer, you just need to know what those instruments can do for you. In essence, you, as the operator, are the critical element and the recipient of technology.

So, I wholeheartedly endorse and encourage the use of technology. However, I do so with a definite caveat—use technology wisely and effectively.

The Battelle Institute, a well-known think tank and technology lab in Columbus, cautions us that:

- Technology is not the point—achievement of objectives is.

- Technology isn't always "gear," sometimes it's process.

- Technology need not be the latest to be effective.

- Technological solutions are never ultimate.

- Technological solutions may address the problem at hand, but will invariably introduce new problems.

From where I sit, this is sage advice.

I am always in awe, when touring the vendor's booths at various conferences by the myriad applications of technology. Salespersons often latch onto those expressions of interest when we walk by their booths. But if you purchased the product, did you purchase what you really needed? Did you acquire a system that may soon be rendered obsolete by a better version? I am not criticizing the vendor, but more so, I am suggesting that the practitioner should do some introspection regarding our roles. Do we get stuck with software or hardware that was not adequately tested, and is full of bugs? As leaders, consumers, and public servants, we should be very conscious of how tax dollars are spent. The manufacturers and vendors of technology should seek out the advice of practitioners *prior to* stocking warehouse shelves.

Allow me to take you on a tour of the not-so-distant future:

Imagine this: You are a robot on perimeter duty. You are equipped with less-than-lethal weapons like sticky nets and stun-type guns. The facility you are guarding has no fences or towers. Security is maintained by sensors that can detect the static in a human body while ignoring impulses generated by local birds and other creatures.

A microprocessor tracks every person twenty-four hours a day, rendering counts obsolete. Bars and screens have been replaced with hardened, see-through plastic capable of withstanding any type of attempted intrusion or escape.

Picture this: You are an inmate arriving at a prison reception center. Your fingerprints are scanned electronically along with your signature and voice track. Staff take a retina and pupil scan, not only for a medical assessment of current chemicals in your body, but for a "print" of your retina, which will control your access to certain areas. You have a so-called "smart card" or are implanted with a microchip that records classification, movement, medical and mental health information, as well as serving as a debit card to pay for commissary, recreation, and medical copayments out of your prison account.

Imagine this: You and twenty other inmates are watching television. No, that's nothing new—but what is new is that you and your colleagues are taking a course in algebra via distance learning. The lesson is taped or broadcast live from a central location to prison classrooms across the state simultaneously. Teachers and inmate tutors on-site help with your questions.

Down the hall, security staff are keeping their skills sharp and earning recertification by firing laser weapons at electronic targets rather than firing expensive ammo at paper targets on the range.

Picture this: You are a prison physician and today is the day set aside each week for consultations with specialists at the state university hospital. Rather than loading your inmate patients into a bus, under armed escort for the trip across the state, you turn on a video camera, a monitor, and conduct the consultation via video.

Imagine this: You have purposefully flooded your cell to draw attention. Rather than risk staff, the prison administrator sends in a tactical robot team to immobilize and extract you from your cell. A janitor robot cleans up the mess. Later in the day, you participate in a disciplinary hearing via video links from your cell in segregation.

By the way, this technology can be applied to various meetings and conferences, such as parole hearings, disciplinary cases, and classification assessments.

Picture this: You are a prisoner about to be paroled. In the prison's job office, you are given access to a work station that allows you to scan ads for jobs for which you may be qualified. You can request additional information, tailor your resume, or fill out an application. The prospective employer can interview you via a video screen located at the work station.

Computer kiosks throughout the complex allow inmates to request services, visits, special hearings, and the like, replacing the kite system.

As you can see, we can go on and on about the benefits of technology. Many of the advances I have described are not science fiction pie-in-the-sky; they are here—now. Some, such as telemedicine and live scan are in use today. Others are on the horizon. *All* will have a significant and lasting impact on our future as well as the future of corrections.

Technology is all around us. Pick up any newspaper or magazine, some article will address the latest technological advancement. I happen to have brought along some of those articles.

The adage that "the only constant is change" has never been more true. We've got to be prepared for change—more than ever before in history, change is occurring at hyperspace speed. Chewbacca had a hard time fixing the hyperdrive in *The Empire Strikes Back*; I think he has better success in *The Return of the Jedi*.

For most, if not all of you, I'm preaching to the already converted. The fact that you're attending this conference indicates that you have more than a passing interest in technology. But are you leading others? Are you demonstrating confidence in technology? Are you supporting your management information systems? Are you providing resources for staff training?

Our most visible and important role is to provide leadership. Being leaders in the use of technology is no less crucial than providing leadership in critical incident management, offender supervision, professionalism, or any other vital area of our business.

How many of you are familiar with the term "Luddite?" Ned Ludd was an eighteenth-century Englishman who led a group of workmen in destroying labor-saving machines. In the nineteenth century, the Luddites were afraid that the Industrial Revolution would end their way of life—and they were right. The term "Luddite" is now broadly applied to anyone who fears progress, particularly technological innovation. We cannot afford to be Luddites.

Technology, and especially information management, is too important to be left in the hands of only technological staff. It is not their job to set policy for correctional agencies, *it is ours*. It is our *responsibility* to be conversant with the aspects of technology that impact, or can help us achieve, our mission. It is our responsibility to provide leadership in our agencies to facilitate change and to ease the transition.

Developing true partnerships with stakeholders such as the private sector, universities, nonprofit institutes, and sister government agencies is critical. I suggest that we, as corrections professionals and vendors, work together as an entity to explore, examine, distribute information, and act as advocates for technologies that work for all of us.

I want to take this time, on behalf of the American Correctional Association and my fellow members of the National Institute of Justice Technology Advisory Council to thank you for participating in what I know will be an exciting and productive time at this most important technology summit.

Remember—a bend in the road is not the end of the road—unless you fail to make the turn.

Best Practices Yield Best Results
by Reginald A. Wilkinson

Presidential Address
American Correctional Association
127th Congress of Correction
Orlando, Florida
August 10, 1997

Introduction

During my tenure as president, the American Correctional Association has been operating under the theme of "Best Practices." We have searched out the very best in our profession, and shared it with each other. Sharing, networking, and borrowing helps us solve problems, achieve success, and reach new levels of excellence. Some people feel you shouldn't fix something unless it's broken. I say fix it anyway. You just may find a new approach that works better. Today, I'd like to highlight some programs that help us serve our customers in a more effective and efficient manner:

Promising Practices

Paperless Office

I am a record officer in a prison reception center. Many evenings find me staying late, entering data from the dozens of forms filled out by staff on each inmate who enters the system. I often ignore entire sections of the documents, knowing they contain answers to questions asked many times before. The information I enter into the database will not be available for use until tomorrow or the next day. My coworkers and I are under the gun for a rash of early releases due to human error. We blame our mistakes on an overwhelming workload that never seems to diminish.

My warden assigns a multidisciplinary team to find ways to simplify the reception process and make it more accurate. We analyze forms to weed out repetition, and interview staff about the time spent in filling out paperwork. We solicit information from other states on how they run reception, and we hear about the concept of a paperless system. Our recommendation is to employ technology to collect, store, and share information. As a result, reception staff can call up a computer screen containing basic information collected immediately upon the inmates' arrival. They need only ask questions relevant to their area. They enter the information into the electronic "pocket." This gives them more time to formulate treatment plans with the inmates. As record officer, I verify the information and enter it into relevant databases. As the information is entered, it becomes immediately available to others who need it. Morale in the office has risen as we learn the technology and grow confident in our abilities. Errors are rare, and caught right away. The era of the bulky inmate pocket is no more, and I can get home on time.

Choices

I am the director of a shelter for battered women. The victim of a particularly brutal assault comes to me in tears, having heard a rumor that her assailant, a former boyfriend, has been transferred to a minimum-security facility. The victim is afraid her assailant will escape and harm her or her family. In my role as a victim advocate, I have been invited to participate in the development of the prison department's bureau of victims' services, and I am familiar with the program. I call the bureau for information on the case.

The next day I receive a call from the victims' services coordinator at the prison in question. She tells me that the offender is, indeed, at the minimum-security prison. However, as a violent offender, he is not allowed to work outside the fence. He is enrolled in anger management classes and Alcoholics Anonymous. He also is enrolled in a vocational horticulture program.

I meet with the victim and report what I've learned. I also show her a video coproduced with the department, which shows what life is like in prison, and I give her several brochures that delineate her rights as a victim. I tell her that she can contact the bureau of victims' services with any questions or concerns regarding her assailant. The bureau also will notify her of parole or release hearings and accompany her if she wishes to tell the parole board about the assault and its impact on her life. Because of the cooperation that exists between my agency and the department of corrections, this victim has a voice and a measure of control over the situation.

Leadership

I am a warden's assistant and am being groomed for promotion. At the moment, I am dangling from a rope at tree-top level. Sixty-feet down, my leadership course classmates are cheering me on. As I approach a particularly lethal looking contraption dubbed "the birth canal," the full impact of vertigo makes a grab for my gut. Accustomed to making decisions on my own, or unilaterally carrying out the warden's wishes, I find this exercise in teamwork both unfamiliar and daunting. I push down my fear and continue to the final obstacle. The exhilaration I feel when I successfully complete the ropes course and am lowered into the supportive arms of my classmates forms an instant bond among us. Later, when challenged to solve a particularly difficult problem facing the department, we quickly form an effective team, using our combined strengths and diversity to arrive at a unique solution. When and if I become a warden, I will remember this experience, and won't hesitate to use teamwork as a primary change agent in my facility.

Inmates Tutoring Other Inmates

I am an inmate in a state where the legislature has radically reduced college programming in prisons. I ask the prison education coordinator if there is any way I can continue my work toward a degree in elementary education. She tells me about a program that uses college inmates to tutor illiterate inmates. The tutor-training and literacy support system was developed at the prison with a grant from the National Institute of Corrections. In return for tutoring, which is considered part of the prison community-service initiative, I will be able to continue my college courses.

After completing a tutor training program, I am matched with Larry Webster. Inmate Webster is one of fifty inmates housed in a dormitory for inmates who are both school dropouts and in recovery from substance abuse. Webster and I attend classes together. I guide him through computer-assisted learning programs. In the evening, we both work on our homework. Within weeks, Webster, once sullen and uncommunicative, begins to participate in class activities. His successes uncover a natural leadership ability. His communication skills improve. Together we study for his GED test. The day finally arrives when Webster, grinning ear to ear, accepts his diploma from the school administrator. I don't know who is prouder, Webster, or me.

Prison Industries an Interagency Partnership

I am a prison industries sales manager. A major drawback to one of our potentially biggest sellers is the delay incurred in the ordering, manufacturing, and shipping of vanity license plates. The process can take five weeks between the time a customer orders the plate and receives it in the mail. Working in concert with the state bureau of motor vehicles, a rapid shipment program is instituted. Using an electronic data transfer between the bureau of motor vehicles and the prison industries license-tag factory, a customer's order is taken and received on the same day. The vanity plate is manufactured and shipped within a week of the order. The customer, the bureau of motor vehicles, and prison industries all benefit from the interagency partnership and the use of technology.

Telemedicine

I am an inmate in a maximum-security facility located in a rural area of the state. I have been experiencing chest pains, and report to the infirmary. After conducting an examination and tests, the doctor schedules an appointment with a specialist at a major medical center in the state capitol, 130 miles away. I anticipate a long delay and an uncomfortable ride shackled and under full escort in a prison van. To my surprise, I am told to report to the infirmary the very next week. A television and video camera have been installed in the examining room. The prison doctor conducts an examination and consults with the specialist who can be seen on a television monitor. All my test results and X-rays have been sent to the specialist electronically. The specialist asks me about my diet, work, exercise and stress levels. Both doctors agree on a preliminary diagnosis of tachycardia and recommend aerobic exercise, medication, and a "wait and see" approach. We make an appointment for a follow-up visit in a month. I am relived that I'm not having a heart attack, and I feel better having talked with the specialist.

Community Corrections

I am a judge in a large, urban county. I am preparing to sentence Mary Turner who has written bad checks on several occasions to support a drug habit. Ms. Turner has an entry-level job and supports two children. She seems to realize the seriousness of her situation and is anxious to enter drug rehab. A year ago, I would have had no choice but to send her to prison as a repeat offender.

The county recently opened a community-based correctional center, which seems to offer an alternative that fits this situation. I sentence Mary to six months at the center followed by one year of community supervision. She signs a contract agreeing to complete the center's drug rehabilitation program and pursue a GED. She will continue to work every day, support her children, and pay restitution. A court liaison will work with her to try and obtain child support payments from the children's father. Her mother will care for the children while she is at the center. As an officer of the court, I am excited about the possibilities offered by community corrections. In this case, the recipients of the bad checks will receive restitution; Mary will keep her children and get added support; and perhaps most important, she will have the opportunity to turn her life around and become a productive member of the community.

Critical Incident Management

I am the team leader of a special response team. My squad is responsible for responding to prison disturbances in the southern portion of a midwestern state. As an integral part of the state's critical incident management program, we also may be called upon to assist in any other state emergency, such as a tornado or chemical spill. Our state has adopted the National Wildfire Coordinating Group Incident Command System for dealing with emergencies. The Incident Command System provides resources, organization, role expectations, management principles, and other support concepts necessary to effectively resolve and recover from a critical incident. Every employee in the department has received basic critical incident management training, and knows what's expected of them in an emergency.

The department has established letters of understanding with law enforcement and emergency agencies in the areas of the state where we have prisons, so that we can work together smoothly in the event of an incident.

My team has received training from the FBI, the Army Special Forces, the Navy Seals, and the U.S. Marines. We have trained extensively with our hostage negotiation and special tactics and response teams. Team members participate in regular drills, table top exercises, and full-scale interagency scenarios on a regular basis.

The call comes to assemble, suit up, and report to a possible disturbance at the state's maximum-security prison. We're ready.

Community Service

I am a lifer at a large prison for women. Today is a special graduation day. I am standing in the exercise yard. Next to me, in a perfect heeling position, stands Bonnie, a black Labrador retriever. She was given to me after I completed a rigorous training course offered by the Pilot Dog Association. For the past ten months, Bonnie and I have been constant companions. She has attended vocational education classes with me and accompanies me to chow and recreation. At night, she sleeps beside my bunk. On several weekends, Bonnie has gone home with various staff members so she could experience family life, traffic, and shopping malls.

I have trained Bonnie in basic obedience and socialization. She is a quick study and eager to please. When the representative from Pilot Dogs call on us, Bonnie and I demonstrate what she's learned. She sits, heels, stays, and comes to me perfectly. We receive our certificate of course completion. For Bonnie, it's the first step in becoming a life partner to a blind person. I know she'll complete advanced guide dog training with flying colors. For me, it's the end of a very special relationship. As she is led away, I feel pride tinged with sadness. I will miss her. I hope she'll remember me. I think she will. Next week, the new puppies will arrive. I'm already signed up.

Conclusion

Each of these "Best Practices" is in existence today. There are many, many more. Each initiative has required participants to think beyond their traditional parameters. All have asked the "what if?" question. What will happen if we allow victims of crime to participate in our parole process? What will happen if we include other agencies in our emergency plans? What will judges do if they're given a wider range of sanctions? What if we invite line staff to participate in decision making? What is the risk if we invest in this expensive technology? Each time we ask "what if?" we're taking a chance.

It's a risk to step over known boundaries. It's scary to dive into the deep end of the pool. The known is much safer. But, as these and countless other examples illustrate, those who are willing to take chances—even willing to fail—are the ones who eventually come up with the best solutions. They are the leaders of our profession.

As I see it, our opportunities are boundless. It is incumbent upon each of us to continue to pursue wider horizons and creative approaches to our many challenges. We must learn to work with others and accept input from all comers.

The essence of a *good* team is the cooperation exhibited in getting to a common goal. The essence of a *great* team is the commitment to reaching a goal and the collective vision to shoot right past that goal to reach even loftier heights. I see ACA and its membership as a terrific and imposing team. Together we have accomplished great things. It's exciting to imagine the many challenges and solutions we'll see in the future. For now, let's continue to be true to our motto—"Find the best, use the best, share the best, and be the best."

Substance Abuse in America's Prisons: A Case for Detection, Interdiction, and Intervention
by Reginald A. Wilkinson

Testimony to:
The United Nations Office for Drug Control and
Crime Prevention/The NGO Alliance for Crime
Prevention and Criminal Justice
October 27, 1997

Imagine yourself as a twenty-year-old man in a midsized American city. Not only are you a high school dropout, you are, for all intents and purposes, illiterate. You are addicted to crack cocaine. Your only source of income is small-time thievery and drug pushing. Poverty, substance abuse, and failure have followed your family for three generations. You have no concept of a work ethic or of contributing to society. Your plans for the future go as far as this afternoon's score. However, instead of scoring crack, you are arrested for stealing a car phone and are carted off to jail—not an unusual circumstance for you. As a repeat offender, the judge sentences you to eighteen months in state prison.

What I have described is the average prison inmate. Not a grisly murderer. Not a predatory rapist. Just a young man with absolutely nothing going for him. This is the typical inmate received in Ohio's prison system over and over again, day after day, month after month, year after year. If this particular individual does not take advantage of the rehabilitative programs available to him, he'll probably be recommitted to prison soon after release.

The United States' prison population has risen dramatically in the last fifteen years. Individuals under some sort of supervision, according to the U.S. Bureau of Justice Statistics (1996), include over one million prison inmates and 4.3 million offenders on probation or parole. Research, correctional experience, and clinical practice have consistently demonstrated that alcohol and drug problems are among the top-ranked criminogenic factors in need of direct intervention. The Bureau of Justice Statistics (1997) reports that at least 70 percent of incarcerated offenders in the United States evidence substance abuse problems.

Not surprisingly, substance abuse has been tied to a broad range of criminal behaviors and risk for criminal activity, with a link to violence figuring prominently. A national survey of incarcerated Americans conducted by the Bureau of Justice Statistics (1983) found that one-third of all inmates in state prisons had drunk heavily just prior to committing the offenses for which they were convicted. Habitual offenders and individuals convicted of assault, burglary, and rape were more likely to be very heavy drinkers. Approximately one-third were under the influence of an illegal drug at the time they committed the offenses. The survey also revealed that those inmates who committed violent offenses tended to be high-frequency drug users.

According to the National Institute of Justice (1995), substance abuse is also a problem for those offenders under community supervision. Drug-using felons constitute a disproportionate share of offenders committing crimes while under supervision. For example, 60 to 75 percent of untreated parolees who have histories of heroin and/or cocaine use return to using drugs and subsequently become reinvolved in criminal activity within three months of release from prison. The "revolving door" analogy epitomizes the circumstances of drug abusing offenders.

Evidence has been consistent in demonstrating that successful substance abuse treatment not only reduces alcohol and other drug use, but also reduces criminal activity. One can conclude that by lowering crime, the associated social and criminal justice costs also are reduced. Given this information, treatment and other interventions aimed at reducing or eliminating substance abuse are worthy tools for reducing criminal activity and addressing other pervasive societal problems associated with substance abuse.

Nonprison Sanctions

Clearly, prison is not the only answer to America's drug problem. While prisons have a definite role in separating violent and predatory offenders from society, they cannot offer much to the inmate sentenced to only a few short months in prison. The "War on Drugs" and the resultant explosion in prison populations drove an important shift in focus for corrections. Agencies across the country turned to nonprison, community-based punishments to address part of the population boom. To this day, we continue to commit resources to these crucial sanctions, which are less severe than incarceration in a state prison, but more restrictive than simple probation. Many nonprison sanctions are more effective in addressing substance abusing, nonviolent offenders. Examples include:

- Community service

- Restitution

- Intensive probation/parole supervision

- Electronic monitoring

- Day reporting centers

- Halfway houses

- Work release centers

- Boot camps

An Ideal Treatment Continuum

The Center for Substance Abuse Treatment (1994) recommends that correctional agencies consider offenders' needs when developing statewide plans and strategies for improving treatment. Policymakers and others are beginning to understand that neither treatment nor punishment alone is sufficient to deal effectively with substance-abusing offenders. An ideal treatment continuum, as described by the Center for Substance Abuse Treatment (1994) and the National Institute of Corrections (1991), should include:

- *Screening and assessment* at prison reception centers for the purpose of treatment matching. Treatment-matching assesses offenders' needs for supervision, control, and alcohol and other drug service needs. Offenders should be assessed at the earliest possible stage and throughout their involvement with the correctional system. Ideally, assessment data should be collected in electronic files, and be accessible for management, evaluation, and research.

- *A range of quality programs* to meet offenders' control, supervision, and treatment needs in prison. A range of services, from drug education to intensive therapeutic communities should be made available for drug-impacted offenders in prisons, to accommodate individual differences, ensure appropriate treatment-matching, and to maximize the use of resources.

- *Targeted treatment programs* for special needs populations. Correctional populations are made up of diverse groups of individuals, many of whom have distinct cultural heritages and backgrounds. Effective alcohol and other drug programs must consider these unique attributes in designing effective treatment interventions. Examples of specific populations that require specialized alcohol and other drug services include women, especially pregnant women; HIV-positive offenders, sex offenders, the mentally ill, and members of racial and ethnic groups.

- *Alcohol and other drug education* for all offenders. Froehling (1989) notes that estimates of the proportion of offenders with some degree of substance abuse problems related to their criminal activity run as high as 80 percent. Considering the high potential for alcohol and other drug abuse among this population, and the comparatively low cost of education services, the goal of providing programming to all offenders appears reasonable. Introducing alcohol and other drug education during reception also may help to motivate offenders to seek structured treatment by demystifying the treatment and recovery process.

- *Incentives and sanctions* to increase offenders' motivation for treatment. Offenders tend to respond to a reward/punishment approach to initiating and maintaining their commitment to treatment. Good time credits, more desirable environments, increased visitor time, and additional privileges are powerful incentives. Sanctions can include the curtailing of privileges and personal freedom. Incentives and sanctions are most effective when certain, graduated, and immediately applied.

- *Cross training* for all staff involved in working with alcohol and other drug-impacted offenders.

- Comprehensive *drug testing* conducted on offenders throughout their involvement with the criminal justice system. Frequent urinalysis provides a deterrent to relapse of drug-dependent offenders and provides a strong incentive for offenders to maintain abstinence.

- *Self-help groups* as an adjunct to treatment and as an integral part of aftercare. Alcoholics Anonymous and Narcotics Anonymous cannot replace structured treatment. However, self-help groups offer an important adjunct to treatment in prison, and are usually available to an offender after release from prison.

- Education and treatment for *relapse prevention*. Relapse prevention combines elements of lifestyle change and the development of cognitive and behavioral strategies designed to improve self-control. Relapse prevention helps offenders deal with high-risk situations, self-defeating behaviors and attitudes, and drug cravings that can occur well after the completion of formal treatment.

- *Continuing care plans* completed on offenders prior to transitioning between and from correctional agencies. Regardless of which direction the offender is moving within the correctional system, the effectiveness of a program is significantly diminished if a break in treatment occurs. Continuing care requires joint planning involving the offender, the treatment provider, the community supervision officer and other service providers in the community. Continuing care planning eases the transition period and may eliminate gaps in service during a time when the offender is most vulnerable to relapse.

- *Process and outcome evaluations* to ensure program integrity, policy compliance, and program performance. Simply put, evaluations tell us what works. Practitioners and policymakers should use the results of program evaluation to guide them in designing the most effective delivery of alcohol and other drug services.

- A *management information system*, preferably automated, should be established and used within and across the criminal justice and treatment systems to ensure the appropriate delivery of services, the effective utilization of resources, and to collect data for evaluation and research.

Interdiction

The use of illicit drugs by inmates presents a serious threat to the safety and security of correctional institutions. The importing, trafficking and using of drugs threaten the work and program environment for staff and inmates.

Specifically, drug trafficking causes many problems in a prison setting. This includes an increase in assaults, power struggles within the inmate population, establishment of an underground economy, staff corruption, inability to profit from treatment programs, and finally, drug trafficking challenges the credibility of the correctional mission.

If correctional institutions are to have safe, humane, and productive environments, it is imperative that aggressive and positive steps be taken against drugs. *The only possible stance on drugs in prison is one of "zero tolerance."*

Zero tolerance is a multifaceted approach to the problem, and includes heightening security, the dismantling of drug distribution systems, the disrupting of gang activity, and the closing of drug avenues, both externally and internally. In other words; detect, interdict, and intervene. Specific examples of drug interdiction strategies include the following:

- Inmate and staff drug testing

- Enhanced security in visiting areas

- Telephone monitoring

- Drug-sniffing canines

- Drug-tip hotlines

- Targeted drug sweeps

- Increased penalties for conveying contraband

- "Ionscan" drug detection technology

- A continuum of alcohol and drug treatment programs

What Does the Future Hold?

How do we attain maximum results with limited resources? The Center for Substance Abuse Treatment (1995) outlines the various stakeholders and their relationship to the treatment process. They advise the creation of partnerships and collaborative efforts among key stakeholders.

The criminal justice system and substance abuse treatment community can and must work together. The potential contributions of key stakeholders can be immense. The goals of effective collaboration should be to improve treatment for offenders, reduce recidivism, and improve public safety.

According to the Center for Substance Abuse Treatment, stakeholders can be divided into five basic categories:

Community Stakeholders

- The public

- Victims

- Media

- Legislators

- Community organizations

- Businesses

Stakeholders Associated with the Offender

- The offender

- Family members

- Employers

- Social service providers

Stakeholders within the Criminal Justice System

- Police

- Prosecutors

- Defense attorneys

- Judges

- Probation and parole officers

Stakeholders within the Public Health System

- Healthcare organizations

- Mental health service providers

Stakeholders with the Alcohol and Other Drug Treatment System

- Prevention programs

- Correctional institutional treatment programs

- Community treatment programs

The Ohio Experience

Drug abuse and drug-related crimes affect the lives of countless Americans. Efforts to combat crime and violence, and improve the quality of life in neighborhoods scarred by drugs place an enormous burden on the criminal justice system at all levels of government. To successfully address the serious problems associated with alcohol and other drug abuse, Ohio has developed partnerships with state, local, and community stakeholders. The partners have agreed to combine experience and resources in an aggressive fight against drugs and crime. The shared common goals are improving substance abuse treatment for offenders, reducing recidivism, and improving public safety.

One very significant partnership is with Ohio's alcohol and drug agency. In 1989, the Ohio Department of Alcohol and Drug Addiction Services (ODADAS) was created. Ohio is one of only six states to have a cabinet level alcohol and drug agency (California, Maine, New York, South Carolina, and Texas are the other states).

The Department of Rehabilitation and Correction and the Department of Alcohol and Drug Addiction Services have collaborated in many programs, including the development of therapeutic communities within prison walls. Over the past two decades, an increasing body of research documents the effectiveness of substance abuse treatment in correctional settings. Wexler and Lipton (1988) found that programs based on a social learning model were successful. According to this theory, criminal behavior is learned through a process of social interaction with others. Thus, prosocial behaviors must be learned to replace deviant behaviors.

Successful programs encourage relationships between staff and offenders, which are empathic and characterized by open communication and trust. Effective approaches include: therapeutic communities, self-help groups, family therapy, contingency contracting, role playing and modeling, vocational and skills training, training in interpersonal cognitive problem-solving skills, and other programs involving peer monitoring of participants' behavior. Wexler and Lipton furthermore stated that many effective programs use "ex-offender-addict counselors" who serve as credible roles of successful rehabilitation.

The aforementioned treatment modalities can be found in successful programs throughout the country, including "Stay'N Out" in New York, "Cornerstone" in Oregon, "Key" and "Crest" in Delaware, and the Department of Rehabilitation and Correction and the Department of Alcohol and Drug Addiction Services sponsored programs "TAPESTRY" and "OASIS" in Ohio.

The Department of Rehabilitation and Correction and the Department of Alcohol and Drug Addiction Services (1997) also developed the "Ohio Plan," which maps out future initiatives between the two agencies. The plan articulates a vision of interagency collaboration aimed at strengthening alcohol and other drug treatment, education, and support services provided to Ohio offenders. By developing a comprehensive strategy for addressing the needs of this population, the Department of Rehabilitation and Correction and the Department of Alcohol and Drug Addiction Services are positioning Ohio to reduce substance abuse, crime, and recidivism among its inmate population and releasees.

The Ohio Plan, moreover, is the product of a collaboration focused on developing a comprehensive approach to enhancing, expanding, and extending the continuum of substance abuse treatment and care for offenders under Department of Rehabilitation and Correction supervision. More than seventy-five professionals representing diverse interests from around Ohio participated in its development. It is intended to provide strategic direction while remaining flexible to accommodate new challenges and opportunities. Most importantly, implementing the Ohio Plan will result in an improved service delivery system and will serve as a catalyst to enhance the partnerships between the Department of Rehabilitation and Correction and other stakeholders.

The enhanced partnership and improved treatment will result in a higher chance of ex-offender success on the street, and safer communities for us all.

References

Bureau of Justice Statistics. 1993. *A Report to the President, the Attorney General and the Congress.* Winifred Reed, ed. Washington, D.C.: U.S. Department of Justice, Office of Justice Programs.

————. 1996. *Sourcebook of Criminal Justice Statistics—1995.* Kathleen Maguire and Ann L Pastore, eds. Washington, D.C.: U.S. Department of Justice, Office of Justice Programs.

————. 1997. *Sourcebook of Criminal Justice Statistics—1996.* Kathleen Maguire and Ann L. Pastore, eds. Washington, D.C.: U.S. Department of Justice, Office of Justice Programs.

Center for Substance Abuse Treatment. 1994. *Screening and Assessment for Alcohol and Other Drug Abuse Among Adults in the Criminal Justice System, Treatment Improvement Protocol (TIP) Series 7.* Washington, D.C.: U.S. Department of Health and Human Services, Public Health Service, Substance Abuse and Mental Health Services Administration, Publication No. (SMA) 94-2076.

————. 1995. *Alcohol and other Drug Abuse Treatment for Adults in the Criminal Justice System, Treatment Improvement Protocol (TIP) Series 17.* Washington, D.C.: U.S. Department of Health and Human Services, Public Health Service, Substance Abuse and Mental Health Services Administration, Publication No. (SMA) 95-3039.

Froehling, R. 1989. *Promising Approaches to Drug Treatment in Correctional Settings. Criminal Justice Paper No. 7.* Washington, D.C.: National Conference of State Legislatures.

Lipton, D. S., and H. K. Wexler. 1988. *A Criminal Justice Strategy for Treating Cocaine- Heroin Abusing Offenders in Custody.* Washington, D.C.: U.S. Department of Justice, National Institute of Justice.

National Institute of Corrections. 1991. *Report of the National Task Force on Intervening with Substance Abusing Offenders: A Framework for Action.* Boulder, Colorado: National Institute of Corrections.

National Institute of Justice Research Report. 1995. James K. Stewart, ed. Washington, D.C.: U.S. Department of Justice.

Ohio Department of Rehabilitation and Correction, and Ohio Department of Alcohol and Drug Addiction Services. 1997. *Ohio Plan for the Treatment of Alcohol and Other Drug (AOD) Impacted Offenders Under the Supervision of the Ohio Department of Rehabilitation and Correction.* Columbus, Ohio: State of Ohio.

The Future of Adult Corrections
by Reginald A. Wilkinson

Testimony to:
The National Council on Crime and Delinquency's
Conference on "Reducing Crime in America: The
Agenda for the Twenty-first Century"
December 5, 1997

Back in the fifteenth century, Florentine statesman Niccolo Machiavelli said, "It must be considered that there is nothing more difficult to carry out, nor more doubtful of success, nor more dangerous to handle, than to initiate a new order of things." As the criminal justice system approaches the twenty-first century, those words still ring true. The decisions made by justice professionals—the paths we follow, the options we choose—will combine to map the future of corrections.

Outside forces also shape our future. News of crime, especially as portrayed on television, has brought a sense of immediacy and danger into our living rooms. American citizens list the fear of crime as an overriding concern in their lives. Public officials have responded with "get tough on crime" legislation. In many jurisdictions, indefinite sentences and the hope of parole for many have been curtailed or eliminated. As a result, our prison populations will continue to grow, inexorably consuming more and more resources. It is conceivable that a taxpayer backlash will ensue, with a demand for more prudent use of expensive prison beds. Fortunately, a push for community-based sanctions and a greater range of creative punishments for nonviolent offenders is already in effect in various locales.

The influence of the courts on how prisons are managed is also in flux. The pendulum of public opinion and court decisions is swinging away from inmate rights and toward the rights of society and victims. For instance, a 1995 decision by the U.S. Supreme Court, *Sandin v. Conner*, has significantly limited the ability of inmates to claim due process rights in the prison environment. The recently enacted Prison Litigation Reform Act expresses the concern of Congress and imposes substantial limitations on a prisoner's right to bring litigation and on the federal courts' ability to monitor prison management. Many states also are writing legislation to curb frivolous inmate lawsuits.

Currently, prison populations are a mix of short-term offenders and "lifers," definite- and indefinite-sentenced inmates, the young and the old. This diversity is reflected in a wide variety of program offerings. For example, programs which offer a short, strong turnaround—like boot camps and vocational education—primarily benefit younger, short-term inmates. Likewise, higher education, while having intrinsic value, would be less relevant to this population. Barbara Nagle (1996), in an article that appeared in *Corrections Today*, quoted assistant surgeon general and medical director for the Federal Bureau of Prisons Dr. Kenneth Moritsugu. "Flexibility is the best hedge against the future. Within corrections, we do not have the luxury of major errors in planning and operations," asserted Moritsugu. If populations become more long-term, programming must evolve accordingly. Corrections professionals will need to perfect the tenets of managing the long-term offender.

If, indeed, community sanctions are imposed on nonviolent offenders, prisons will increasingly become repositories for the more violent, predatory, and remorseless criminals. A greater concentration of violent offenders may create more tension among inmates and between inmates and staff. Added incidents of violence can be anticipated, resulting in more injuries or worse, and a requirement for more disciplinary cells.

Many of us have determined that removing predatory and other dangerous offenders from the population improves safety and security systemwide. By developing "supermax" prisons, we can isolate problem offenders in one facility. While this concept has come under some criticism, the benefits appear to outweigh perceived problems. Recalcitrant offenders participate in targeted in-cell programming rather than sitting idle in a disciplinary cell. Supermax staff receive specialized training in working with dangerous prisoners, and policies and procedures are specific to problem offenders without restricting the privileges of the general population. Segregation cells in other facilities can be used more effectively when not dogged by repeat offenders, and finally, the "supermax" facility becomes a disincentive for seriously negative behavior. Furthermore, technological advancements have made high security more "user friendly." Ohio's new $65 million supermax prison in Youngstown will feature sophisticated surveillance, security, and fire-control systems. Technology will benefit supermax prisoners by allowing them, even under high-security conditions, to earn academic credits through computer-based educational programming.

Many prison populations are also becoming older. The Ohio Department of Rehabilitation and Correction (1997) projects that inmates age 55 and older will grow from 3,000 in 1997 to almost 4,500 in 2015. Geriatric care and programming are definite necessities for the immediate future. The older offender requires an environment that is more slowly paced as well as specialized programming and medical services. Similarly, more people will be dying in prison, not only due to longer sentences, but also because of scourges such as AIDS and drug-resistant tuberculosis. It may be wise to develop "theme" units for those special needs.

Ameliorating the need for accommodating specialized populations is the concept of prototype prisons. We are no longer bound by the traditional—and costly—high stone walls and guard towers. Agencies are now encouraged to save time and money by designing and building "prototype" prisons. These simplified architectural plans can be utilized over and over again, modified slightly to fit security needs and the terrain. At the same time, high-tech security systems replace and augment human perimeter forces, improving efficiency and allowing us to use valuable manpower resources elsewhere in the facility.

As a society, we also face the dilemma of young offenders who commit unimaginable crimes. Offenders under the age of eighteen incarcerated at adult prisons accounted for one of the fastest-growing inmate groups from 1990 to 1995. Many are in maximum-security settings due to the severity of their crimes. Our adult prisons will have to face mounting numbers of ever-younger inmates serving, in some cases, long, long sentences. An entirely new programming genre will have to be developed including gang member "recovery" programs to help young offenders achieve a productive life outside the counterfeit gang "family." Interdiction, in this case, may not be enough.

Training, also, will become more diverse. Reflecting the prison population, our employees will have to become better versed in supervising and caring for the very young, the very old, the mentally ill, and the infirm. The roles of custody and treatment staff, once sharply delineated must continue to meld.

According to personnel pundits, the work "face" also will change as work "force" diversity continues to evolve. The corrections profession, once the sole purview of white males, has made significant progress in the past decades. The richness, creativity, innovation, and multiple viewpoints generated by a diverse workforce must continue to be encouraged and cultivated.

The next ten years will reveal whether the privatization of prisons will succeed. We recently broke ground on the $30 million, 1,000-bed Lake Erie Correctional Institution. Lake Erie has a legislatively mandated goal of 5 percent savings over state-run institutions. Debate on the pros and cons, right and wrongs, of "punishment for profit" will range back and forth. In the end, the profit margin and public opinion may be the determining factors on how much of the corrections profession will be outsourced to for-profit providers.

Corrections can no longer languish in the backwaters of government. Our ever-growing budgets mandate greater accountability. As communications, information technology and networking make our agencies more and more accessible to the general public, we can expect a greater degree of interest in our profession. Taxpayers and other stakeholders will demand a greater role in how we conduct our affairs.

Technology is having a significant impact on our industry. Computers are replacing hand written files, typewriters, microfiche, offender and staff records, and much more. In *Corrections Today*, deGroot (1997) listed several "hot new technologies under development, including: X-ray body scanners which test for hidden weapons and contraband; noninvasive drug testing using eye scans and skin patches; a smart gun, which is computer coded to be fired only by the registered user; a language translator to communicate with nonnative inmates; and walk-through metal detectors." These and other developments will help us do our jobs better and in a more humane and less intrusive manner.

The phrase "knowledge is power" has been a traditional mainstay of our profession. A fundamental movement toward instilling a cultural change that encourages information sharing is underway to combat that concept. The sharing of data, research, and intelligence will be facilitated. "Surfing the net" will bring us a world of creative ways to address our needs. Networking and benchmarking will enrich all our agencies, as we share what works and what doesn't. The inculcation of teamwork and interagency cooperation will serve to make problem solving and decision making more relevant and more acceptable to our employees. Many correctional agencies have adopted the principles of Wellins, Byham, and Wilson (1991): "The organizations that are implementing teams represent a group of pioneers who truly believe in a new way of looking at work. We believe that self-directed teams will become the standard—not the exception—within the next decade."

And finally, perhaps the most profound change the country may experience in the new millennium is the evolution of the current criminal justice system into a broad-based and balanced justice system. Known variously as restorative, reparative, and community justice, proponents of this concept agree that our current system of dealing with crime, criminals, and victims is not working. According to Ness and Strong (1997), "restorative justice advocates view crime as more than simply lawbreaking . . . crime is understood also to cause multiple injuries to victims, the community, and even to the offender. Proponents argue that the criminal justice process should help repair those injuries."

As president of the American Correctional Association and director of one of the county's largest prison systems, I must agree with both the premise and the wealth of approaches offered by community justice. It is my hope, and the hope of many corrections professionals, that we can link with law enforcement, the courts, our communities, and others to forge a balanced, seamless justice system for this country.

References:

deGroot, G. 1997. Hot New Technologies. *Corrections Today*. July.

Nadel, B. A. 1996. BOP Accommodates Special Needs Offenders. *Corrections Today*. October.

Ness, D. and K. H. Strong. 1997. *Restoring Justice*. Cincinnati, Ohio: Anderson Publishing Co.

Ohio Department of Rehabilitation and Correction. 1997. *Older Offenders: The Ohio Initiative*. August.

Wellins, R. S., W. C. Byham, and J. M. Wilson. 1991. *Empowered Teams*. San Francisco: Jossey-Bass.

"Darkness cannot put out darkness. Only light can do that."
By Reginald A. Wilkinson

A Tribute to
the Reverend Dr. Martin Luther King, Jr.
American Correctional Association
Winter Conference, San Antonio, Texas
January 19, 1998

It is an honor for me to deliver the American Correctional Association's tribute to one of our country's heroes: the Reverend Dr. Martin Luther King, Jr. Today, all across this great nation people are celebrating his life, his memory, and his legacy. Dr. King's legacy was the realization of the American dream for every American.

In pursuing the American dream for those who had not had the opportunity to partake of it, Dr. King was fond of giving life to the famous words, "We hold these truths to be self-evident, that all men are created equal, that they are endowed by their creator with certain unalienable rights. That among these are Life, Liberty and the Pursuit of Happiness."

"We hold these truths to be self-evident." When Dr. King used those powerful words, the words of Thomas Jefferson, as a mantra for granting civil rights to all Americans, even naysayers had to sit up and take notice. It was Dr. King's genius to take the words of a slave owner, and hold our own country's Bill of Rights up as a mirror to our society.

Today, nearly thirty years after his assassination, we can still hear Dr. King's prophetic voice resonating with concern for justice and equality. As we approach a new millennium, political pundits point to the fact [that] the world has never seen such a lengthy period of peace. But is the absence of all-out war really peace? Reverend King reminded us that, "True peace is not merely the absence of tension, it is the presence of justice."

Is there true justice in a society where more young African-American males languish in jail and prison than attend colleges and universities? Is there real peace in a nation experiencing a resurgence of militant hate groups advocating their own brand of justice? Is there justice in a country where money can influence an acquittal and poverty may lead to imprisonment?

What would Dr. King say if he were among us today? I believe he would have a heavy heart about the inequalities that prevail to this very day. I believe he would be saddened by the erosion of the urban family, for example.

Reverend King was the "drum major for justice, and the banner bearer for peace." Would he feel that we as a nation have lost our perspective by pouring our resources into our jails and prison systems rather than into our schools?

Dr. King exclaimed, and I quote: "When an individual is no longer a true participant, when he no longer feels a sense of responsibility to his society, the content of democracy is emptied. When culture is degraded and vulgarity enthroned, when the social system does not build security but induces peril, inexorably the individual is impelled to pull away from a soulless society. This process produces alienation—perhaps the most pervasive and insidious development in contemporary society."

The truth of this statement is painfully clear when we look at the people in our jails and prisons across the country. What would Dr. King have us do to stem this process of alienation?

The answer may be in Dr. King's aforementioned statement that began: "When an individual is no longer a participant . . ." As you know, the criminal element exists at the edges of our civilization. They emerge to raid us, steal from us, frighten us, hurt us, and then retreat back into their counterfeit societies. They are not *participants* in our society.

I believe Dr. King would exhort us to do a better job of nurturing our children and guiding them toward productive lives and away from the path that leads to drugs, crime, gangs, and imprisonment. As corrections professionals, we have the inside track. We have the knowledge and the know-how to lead the way toward a new, truer sense of justice for all—one that encompasses the essence of Dr. King's dream of an America where there is true brotherhood, justice, and harmony.

As a nation, we need to devote our attention, our energy, and our resources to our children. We need to ensure that every child goes to school with a full stomach. We need to ensure that every child has the opportunity to learn and grow. We need to inspire our children to explore their world.

Think about the answers you get when you ask children what they want to be when they grow up. A child who has been exposed to a world of possibilities will enthusiastically answer with a terrifically wide range of answers—from firefighter to astronaut to ballerina.

But what about the child growing up in poverty, in the gang infested ghettoes of our cities? How does he answer the question? If he's lucky enough to attend a good school, he may answer, "I want to be a teacher." If not, the answer will invariably be, "I want to be a gang banger." Why? Because that is the only family he knows. As a society, we need to wrestle that child away from the counterfeit family of gangs, and back into our extended family. We need to make him a *participant* in our culture.

Just last week I read a story in the newspaper about two single mothers in Mississippi. The lead to this story read, "Tammy was out of jail and off drugs. Sandra was away from gangs and her ex-boyfriend's regular beatings. But neither woman had pulled her life together, not yet. Both were losing their welfare benefits, not sure how to find good housing, get a job, or stay away from trouble. Then a local church stepped in, matching each woman with a team of volunteers." The story goes on to describe how several local churches have turned *away* from simply giving charity and *toward* mentoring individuals.

Sandra now has a car and a home for herself and her four children. She is studying for her GED. For the first time in her life, she has hope. She has become a *participant* in our society. The story goes on to describe how Tammy now has an apartment and is enrolled in nursing school. Tammy is now a *participant* in our world.

Reverend Ronald Moore, coordinator of the program that has matched 485 families to mentors, said, "We're asking them to look at the total person, where in the past they were just helping for Thanksgiving or maybe Christmas."

Many of us recognize ourselves in these stories. We are happy to contribute to food baskets for needy families during the holidays. We put money in the church collection plate to feed starving children in Ethiopia. These good deeds, while worthy, lack the hands-on approach that Dr. King preached about.

If we are to turn this country around, and offer the dream of justice and the pursuit of happiness to every American, we are going to have to pitch in and really help. We are going to have to offer long-term solutions that apply to *real* people. And we are going to have to learn how to assist those real people into becoming true participants in our world.

As justice professionals, we are in a unique position to do that. We are the final repositories for society's failures. Society has said to these individuals, "We give up. You cannot live among us. We are separating you from our society for our own safety. You cannot participate in the life of our culture."

The hundreds of thousands of people under our supervision have already failed. They have been labeled as losers. Many see themselves as irredeemable. Others don't care—they see imprisonment as a rite of passage. What can we offer them? Is it enough to separate them and keep society safe from their contamination? Can they be redeemed? If we believe in our mission as corrections professionals, we better hope so.

We can start by doing a self-inventory of where we are and where we need to be. We need to ask ourselves, "What can I do today to make this world a better place?"

Dr. King told us, and I quote, "Everybody can be great. Because anybody can serve. You don't have to have a college degree to serve. You don't have to make your subject and your verb agree to serve. You don't have to know about Plato and Aristotle to serve. You don't have to know Einstein's theory of relativity to serve. You only need a heart full of grace. A soul generated by love."

As corrections professionals we can learn about the programs that really work to turn lives around, and use them. Spread the word and share the possibilities. We've already made a significant impact through our "Best in the Business" concept, and now, with our "Best Practices" initiative.

Many of us field community service programs in which offenders work to improve our schools, parks, and nonprofit agencies. Many of us boast, justifiably, about the thousands of hours our programs devote to the betterment of our communities. But maybe what is most important about those hours is the effect they have on the offenders who are doing the work. I have seen the pride on an inmate's face when he finishes building a reading loft for his prison's Adopt-a-School. As he imagines the learning that will take place in that loft, he is evolving into a *participant* of the world he will some day reenter. He is becoming the person he ought to be.

Let's commit ourselves to even more sharing, more networking, more success, and many more *participants*. In other words, as Dr. King reminded us, "I can never be what I ought to be until you are what you ought to be."

We need to examine our programs. If we have a drug treatment program that just pays lip service to a cure, get rid of it and replace it with one that really helps people turn away from drugs. If we have a sex offender program that looks good on paper but doesn't address the issues of reoffending, throw it out and start over.

If we come across an idea for a program that seems a little far-fetched, let's not ask ourselves why we should invest in it—let's ask, "why not?" Seek out success. Advertise success. Replicate success.

In a commencement speech to Lincoln University students in June of 1961, Dr. King asked the graduates to help America's dream become a reality. "Through our scientific genius we have made of this world a neighborhood; now, through our moral and spiritual development we must make of it a brotherhood. In a real sense, we must all learn to live together as brothers, or we will all perish together as fools. We must come to see that no individual can live alone; no nation can live alone. We must all live together; we must all be concerned about each other."

I believe Dr. King would agree that we are standing at a crossroads today. Our nation is in crisis. There are too many people in prison, and too few people dedicated to changing that. We need to be a force for change. We need to become the recognized experts in this field. We need to make people listen. We need to be leaders.

Dr. King might have been speaking to the people gathered in this room when he advised: "History has thrust upon our generation an indescribably important destiny—to complete a process of democratization which our nation has too long developed too slowly, but which is our most powerful weapon for world respect and emulation. How we deal with this crucial situation will determine our moral health as individuals, our cultural health as a region, our political health as a nation, and our prestige as a leader of the free world. If America is to respond creatively to the present crisis, many groups and agencies must rise above the reiteration of generalities and begin to take an active part in changing the face of their nation."

Welcome and Presidential Remarks by Reginald A. Wilkinson

American Correctional Association
Winter Conference
San Antonio, Texas
January 19, 1998

It is a pleasure for me to welcome you to the Lone Star State, and to San Antonio. If you have been here for any length of time, you will know that this city is a great destination for conference goers, especially this time of year if you are from north of the Mason-Dixon Line. Please, while you are here enjoy the Riverwalk and the other sights that San Antonio has to offer.

As your president, I am pleased to announce to you that the American Correctional Association is meeting the multitude of challenges that affect our profession. I am humbled, yet appreciative, that I can play a small part in helping to address these challenges. I would like to thank the members of the Executive Committee, the Board of Governors, and the Delegate Assembly for their unmatched leadership and commitment to making sure that ACA is a sound and influential entity as it relates to effectuating positive change in our craft.

I would like further to thank the members of the more than forty committees, councils, and task forces that are paying attention to detail and steadily realizing their goals that they set back in 1996. I want to thank ACA Executive Director, James A. Gondles, Jr., and his staff for their professionalism, talent, and uncanny ability to get the job done. I moreover would be remiss not to thank each of you for your support and participation with ACA, but also for your contributions to the justice process back at your respective work sites. I have had the good fortune to visit many of your jurisdictions, so I am familiar with your successes. I realize that you do not hear it often enough, but "thank you" for your efforts.

If I might indulge you for just a few more minutes, I would like to share with you ACA information in the Paul Harvey News format. You need to be aware that ACA is a financially secure association. The leadership and staff of ACA work hard to ensure that our available resources are used for appropriate projects and services designed to enhance the correctional process. The association is not afraid to take on new challenges. Last year, for example, we added *Corrections Compendium* to our family of publications. In several months, we have increased subscriptions by 42 percent. If you have not had the opportunity to see this journal, please stop by the publications booth.

In partnership with the American Bar Association and the American Medical Association, we have joined a consortium of other pertinent organizations to help fight the war against drug addictions. All of you are more than familiar with the need to address issues of substance abuse treatment and interdiction. I am pleased to suggest to you that some very influential associations and agencies are taking seriously this tragedy that affects all of our communities.

Your association will continue to develop partnerships in an attempt to help make a difference whether it is with the National Sheriffs' Association developing educational television or with individual agencies to help augment professional development of correctional staff.

I am pleased that our best practices project is on schedule. Most of you know by now that at the 128th Annual Congress of Correction in Detroit we will give each attendee a copy of our best practices publication [this book]. Outlined in this book will be examples of programs that work in nineteen categorical areas. It is easy in our profession to identify things that go wrong. I think it is time now that we focus on the processes that work well. I appreciate the hard work that the committees with the best practices assignment have given to this effort.

Some of you were participants in a special victims conference that ACA cosponsored at this convention. The mission of this meeting was to share ideas about promising programs that address working with victims and survivors of crime. I believe it is long overdue that correctional agencies put victims on our agendas, not as a sidebar to our business, but victims as significant partners in the justice process.

The lifeblood of our association is our membership. I am pleased to announce that at the Delegate Assembly on Wednesday, we will charter another partner in the ACA dual-membership family: the Hawaii Criminal Justice Association. Congratulations to the members of the Hawaii Criminal Justice Association.

Thanks each of you once again for your attendance, enjoy San Antonio, and have a great conference.

Best Practices: Tools for Correctional Excellence

by Reginald A. Wilkinson

Presidential Address
American Correctional Association
128th Congress of Correction
Detroit, Michigan
August 9, 1998

It is an honor and a privilege for me to deliver this address to this august body. It is also with mixed feelings that I speak to you today. This speech signals that my two-year term as our Association's president is coming to a close. I have immensely enjoyed serving you and this post. Although a two-year term as president is plenty, especially if you have another full-time job, it will be my pleasure to serve on the Executive Committee as the immediate past president for the next two years.

Significant strides have been made during my tenure as president, thanks to contributions of a multitude of ACA corrections professionals. I am very proud of the contribution to correctional knowledge the Best Practices project will have on our vocation. During the General Session tomorrow, I will outline some of the other ACA accomplishments. I have reveled in seeing the Best Practices initiative grow and evolve past the concept stage and into real, three-dimensional, success stories. Those stories can be found in ACA's publication entitled *Best Practices: Excellence in Corrections* [this publication]. Each of you will receive a copy of this publication, compliments of ACA. What you will see is a professionally produced volume of work. What you won't see is the blood, sweat, and tears of its many contributors, writers, and editors.

I want to thank the ACA Best Practices committee chairs and members for soliciting the entries for this undertaking. Without the support of the Executive Committee, the Board of Governors, and the Delegate Assembly, this enterprise may not have been possible. ACA Executive Director James A. Gondles, Jr. and his staff have been consummate professionals. Dr. Edward Rhine, who chairs the Best Practices Coordinating Council, is appreciated for his academic and editorial skills. Last, but assuredly not least, I want to thank the administrators and staff responsible for the programs selected for publication.

Those of us who have been in this profession for any length of time are more than familiar with the academic correctional assertion that "nothing works." That bombshell was dropped back in the 1970s by Professor Robert Martinson following his exhaustive study of 231 prison programs including educational, vocational, treatment, prerelease, and more. Martinson's bleak conclusion was that, in most cases, inmates who were involved in rehabilitative programs were just as likely to recidivate as those who were not involved. Worse, in several instances he found that prisoners in nonparticipating groups seemed to be better off than those who participated in rehabilitative programming. Martinson's findings were so disturbing that his sponsors subsequently declined to publish them and refused him permission to publish them on his own.

Martinson prefaced his study with an introduction that mirrors a predicament not unlike today, and I quote: "The articulate public has entered (into) another one of its sporadic fits of attentiveness to the condition of our prisons and to the perennial questions they pose about the nature of crime and the uses of punishment. The result has been a widespread call for 'prison reform,' in other words, for 'reformed' prisons, which will produce 'reformed' convicts. American prisons, perhaps more than those of any other country, have stood or fallen in public esteem according to their ability to fulfill their promise of rehabilitation."

In today's time of fast-paced change and unending challenges in law enforcement, the courts and in corrections, our feet are once again being held to the fire. We are investing endless tax dollars on offenders, and taxpayers are demanding to know what we have accomplished with the billions of dollars appropriated to correctional agencies. Just as it was during the time of Martinson's study, the bottom line in the minds of most, is recidivism. What are we doing to prevent new crimes from being committed by offenders assigned to our custody? How are we going to prevent further victimization in our communities?

The aggregation of superior correctional programs found in this publication goes a long way in refuting the naysayers by demonstrating, without a doubt, that there is a solid body of successes in our craft. *Best Practices: Excellence in Corrections* is a testament to the individuals and teams who have worked hard and taken "calculated" risks to develop and implement programs that make a measurable difference in the bottom line. This volume not only illustrates that correctional activities can and do work, but it offers blueprints for replication.

During my twenty-five years working in this industry, it has been my privilege to work with strong leaders and true visionaries. My colleagues are a diverse group with a wide range of management and leadership styles. Yet, they all have one thing in common: the ability to inspire correctional employees to produce, to succeed, and to excel. In composing these remarks, I was continually reminded of the many dedicated corrections executives, past and present, who served as role models and sources of inspiration for me. The common denominator with these persons was that they could get the job done. Of course, there is no single magic bullet. Rather, successful leaders and successful programs emanate from environments that are conducive to going one step beyond tradition.

I am reminded of the now famous quotation by former U. S. Attorney General, Bobby Kennedy: "Some men see things as they are and say why? I dream of things that never were and say why not?" In the corrections business, we probably have not asked the "why not" or the "what if" questions as often as we should have. But major impacts on offenders and recidivism are now being made, and the architects of those programs deserve recognition, not necessarily for their own egos, but because we must make a statement about our business, a business that is still very much misunderstood.

Some of you may not know, but I wrote a letter to the HBO producers of the dramatic series entitled: "Oz." I explained that the stereotyping and misrepresentations of the corrections profession in their drama is unacceptable. Of course, the response that I received was that the show was designed to "entertain" and was not meant to depict reality. It is precisely these nonreality depictions that perpetuate the fallacies about our craft. The characterization of corrections on the silver screen and in the mass media serves as a constant reminder that we must be ever vigilant in heralding the positive aspects of our profession. Each of us must accept the additional role of "corrections ambassador" to refute some of the misconceptions of our profession.

Hopefully, this Best Practices' mission will provide substantial evidence that our work is more than a passing notion. The administrators of the documented Best Practices programs have successfully asked and answered the "why not" and the "what if" questions. In addition to the programs ACA has just detailed, there are many more that are worthy of replication.

I have stated on numerous occasions that finding fault with correctional operations is easier than lauding activities that should be highlighted. It is time that we reverse the tide and make it second nature to trumpet our vision for corrections. It is time that we stop making excuses about our work and start putting into action those profound ideas that will certify the contributions we make to our respective communities throughout the United States and internationally. It is time that we stop being adversely driven by dated correctional methodologies and start calling upon our creative juices to inspire positive change. Our correctional toolchest is overflowing with resources and examples by which we can "work harder and smarter," and, as we so often must, "do more with less."

We now have in our toolbox technologies that did not exist five years ago. Of those that did exist, there were many we were reluctant or afraid to use. Most correctional systems are now using computers unlike ever before. We also employ creative MIS networks, interoperability of computer systems, internet and intranet access, satellite technology, telemedicine, distance learning, GPS, e-mail and voice mail, and other types of information technology, and technology transfer applications. Also, there are many agencies, public and private, that can and do provide technical assistance and training opportunities to correctional systems such as the Office of Justice Programs and the National Institute of Corrections. Correctional agencies are depending more heavily on our partners in academic research to guide the decision-making process rather than just depending on tradition or experience.

Employee training is becoming more and more sophisticated in order to keep pace with complex correctional practices. In addition to quality management principles, agencies are depending on teamwork and leadership dynamics to augment operational routines.

The aforementioned are just a few examples of the many more "tools" available to our respective jurisdictions. One vital tool I would like to emphasize is correctional accreditation. In keeping with the need to gain public confidence, I cannot think of a more tried and true process than to comply with hundreds of national accreditation standards. Being awarded accreditation is synonymous with correctional Best Practices. An accredited agency is an agency that has documented proof of public accountability.

Obviously, now *Best Practices: Excellence in Corrections* can be yet another implement in your toolchest, especially if it fosters the intended sense of sharing among correctional jurisdictions.

We have changed in ways that would have been unimaginable to the proponents of the "nothing works" theory. Even though Martinson later recanted his "nothing works" research findings, the damage may have been done already, creating a downward spiral of futility that we still battle today. We have broken down barriers and succeeded despite awesome odds. Now, we can bask in a well-earned reputation as caring, dedicated, and skillful professionals.

Through our tenacity and imagination we have repudiated the negativity of the past and stand bold and proud in the present. As we move forward through a technological revolution and a pending upheaval in the justice system, we only can guess at the future. But one thing we do know, we face that future together with unmitigated confidence in ourselves and in each other. From alcohol and other drug programs to prison industries; from victim awareness to disturbance control; from adult and juvenile justice to jail and field services administration, I applaud the work of the individuals and teams that led to the success stories found in the *Best Practices* publication. To the countless others who have worked and achieved similar success, I encourage you to share your triumph with others. The only way we can face the challenges of the next century is to work together for the continuous improvement of our proud profession.

I once again thank those persons and groups that assisted in the development of the Best Practices project. And, I thank each of you for your correctional contributions and for being a most gracious audience this evening.

Indexes

Subject Index

X

Y

Z

Contact Index